Paris

"All you've got to do is decide to go and the hardest part is over.

So go!"

TONY WHEELER, COFOUNDER – LONELY PLANET

Catherine Le Nevez,
Christopher Pitts, Nicola Williams

Contents

Plan Your Trip 4

Explore Paris 76

Understand Paris 293

Survival Guide 329

Paris Maps 363

CBMETZ19 / BUDGET TRAVEL ©

GURGEN BAKHSHETYAN / SHUTTERSTOCK ©

(left) **Musee du Quai Branly (p84)** This cultural museum sports a thriving *mur végétal* ('vertical garden').

(above) **Eiffel Tower p82** Iconic Paris.

(right) **Pastries p48** Baked treats aplenty.

SAMI SERT / GETTY IMAGES ©

Welcome to Paris

Museums, monument-lined boulevards, boutiques and classical bistros are enhanced by a new wave of multimedia galleries, design shops and tech start-ups.

Iconic Architecture

The cloud-piercing Eiffel Tower; broad Arc de Triomphe guarding the glamorous avenue des Champs-Élysées; gargoyled Notre Dame cathedral; lamplit bridges spanning the Seine; and art nouveau cafes' wicker-chair-lined terraces are enduring Parisian emblems. Despite initial appearances, however, Paris' cityscape isn't static: there are some stunning modern and contemporary icons, too, from the inside-out, industrial-style Centre Pompidou to the *mur végétal* (vertical garden) gracing the Musée du Quai Branly, and the glass sails of the Fondation Louis Vuitton contemporary-art centre.

Glorious Food

France's reputation for its cuisine precedes it, and whether you seek a cosy neighbourhood bistro or a triple-Michelin-starred temple to gastronomy, you'll find that every establishment prides itself on exquisite preparation and presentation of quality produce, invariably served with wine. Enticing patisseries, *boulangeries* (bakeries), *fromageries* (cheese shops) and crowded, colourful street markets are perfect for putting together a picnic to take to the city's beautiful parks and gardens. A host of culinary courses offers instruction for all schedules, abilities and budgets.

Stylish Shopping

'Parisian' is synonymous with style, and fashion shopping is the city's forte. Paris remains at the forefront of international trends, and browsing emerging and established designer boutiques and flagship *haute couture* houses is a quintessential part of any visit. You'll also find hip concept shops, and resplendent art nouveau department stores, along with a trove of vintage shops and flea markets, atmospheric bookshops, adorable children's wear and toy shops, art and antique dealers, venerable establishments selling professional cookware, and, of course, gourmet-food and wine shops galore.

Artistic Treasures

With an illustrious artistic pedigree – Renoir, Rodin, Picasso, Monet, Manet, Dalí and Van Gogh are but a few of the masters who have lived and worked here over the years – Paris is one of the world's great art repositories. In addition to big hitters like the incomparable Louvre, the Musée d'Orsay's exceptional impressionist collection, and the Centre Pompidou's cache of modern and contemporary art, scores of smaller museums showcase every imaginable genre, a diverse range of venues mount major exhibitions through to offbeat installations, plus there's the city's vibrant street art.

DENNIS VAN DE WATER / SHTTERSTOCK ©

Why I Love Paris

By Catherine Le Nevez, Writer

Paris' grandeur is inspiring, but what I love most about the city is its intimacy. Its *quartiers* (quarters) are like a patchwork of villages, and while it's one of the world's major metropolises – with all of the culture and facilities that go with it – there's a real sense of community at the local shops, markets and cafes that hasn't changed since my childhood. Yet because every little 'village' has its own evolving character, I'm constantly discovering and rediscovering hidden corners of the city.

For more about our writers, see p416

Top: View over Pont Alexandre III to Hôtel des Invalides (p231)

Paris' Top 16

Eiffel Tower *(p82)*

1 No one could imagine Paris today without its signature spire. But Gustave Eiffel only constructed this graceful tower – then the world's tallest, at 320m – as a temporary exhibit for the 1889 Exposition Universelle. Luckily, its popularity (and radiotelegraphy antennas) assured its survival beyond the World Fair and its elegant art nouveau webbed-metal design has become the defining fixture of the city's skyline. Head here at dusk for the best day and night views of the glittering city, and toast making it to the top at the sparkling Champagne bar. VIEW TO THE EIFFEL TOWER FROM THE ARC DE TRIOMPHE

Eiffel Tower & Western Paris

Arc de Triomphe *(p94)*

2 If anything rivals the Eiffel Tower as the symbol of Paris, it's this magnificent 1836-built monument to Napoléon's 1805 victory at Austerlitz – Napoléon commissioned the monument the following year. The intricately sculpted triumphal arch stands sentinel in the centre of the Étoile (star) roundabout; use the pedestrian tunnels below ground to reach it safely. Some of the best vistas in Paris radiate from the top, including swooping views along the luxury-shop-lined Champs-Élysées, Paris' most glamorous avenue, now car free on the first Sunday of every month.

Champs-Élysées & Grands Boulevards

FEEL GOOD STUDIO / SHUTTERSTOCK ©

2

GIANCARLO LIGUORI / SHUTTERSTOCK ©

4

Cathédrale Notre Dame de Paris *(p195)*

3 A vision of stained-glass rose windows, flying buttresses and frightening gargoyles, Paris' glorious cathedral, the Cathédrale Notre Dame de Paris, on the larger of the two inner-city islands, is the city's geographic and spiritual heart. This Gothic wonder took nearly 200 years to build, but it would have been demolished following damage during the French Revolution had it not been for the popularity of Victor Hugo's timely novel *The Hunchback of Notre Dame*, which sparked a petition to save it. Climb its 400-odd spiralling steps for magical rooftop views.

The Islands

Louvre *(p108)*

4 The *Mona Lisa* and the *Venus de Milo* are just two of the priceless treasures housed inside the fortress turned royal palace turned France's first national museum, the Musée du Louvre. Stretching along the Seine, this immense museum can seem overwhelming, but there are plenty of ways to experience it even if you don't have the nine months it would take to glance at every artwork and artefact here. One of the best is via its thematic trails, from the 'Art of Eating' to 'Love in the Louvre'.

Louvre & Les Halles

Parisian Dining *(p44)*

5 Whether you're at an unchanged-in-decades neighbourhood haunt, a beautiful art nouveau brasserie, a switched-on, experimental neobistro or a feted *haute cuisine* establishment helmed by a legendary chef – such as Restaurant Guy Savoy, ensconced in the neoclassical former mint, the Monnaie de Paris – the food and the dining experience are considered inseparable. France pioneered what is still the most influential style of cooking in the Western world and Paris is its showcase par excellence. Do as Parisians do and savour every moment.

Eating

Musée Rodin *(p230)*

6 The lovely Musée Rodin is the most romantic of Paris' museums. Auguste Rodin's former workshop and showroom, the 1730-built, beautifully restored Hôtel Biron, is filled with Rodin's own sculptural masterpieces like *The Kiss*, the marble monument to love, as well as creations by his protégée, sculptor Camille Claudel, and by other artists whose works Rodin collected, Monet, Van Gogh and Renoir among them. Its *pièce de résistance* is the mansion's rambling, rose-scented sculpture garden, which provides an entrancing setting for contemplating works like *The Thinker* (pictured below).

St-Germain & Les Invalides

Specialised Shopping *(p65)*

7 Paris, like any major city, offers international chains (including icons that originated here). But what really sets Parisian shopping apart is its incredible array of specialist shops. Candles from the world's oldest candle maker, paints developed with celebrated artists at venerable art-supply shops and edgy fashion designed in the hip Haut Marais are just some of the treats in store. Other unique shopping experiences include *bouquiniste* (secondhand bookshop) stalls lining the banks of the Seine, and grande-dame department stores such as Galeries Lafayette, topped by a century-old stained-glass dome. BOUQUINISTES (P220)

Shopping

6

Musée d'Orsay *(p224)*

8 Richly coloured walls at the Musée d'Orsay make its impressionist and postimpressionist canvases by masters including Renoir, Gauguin, Cézanne, Sisley, Manet, Monet, Degas and Toulouse-Lautrec appear as if they're hung in an intimate home. Completed at the turn of the 20th century, the Gare d'Orsay – the grand former railway station in which the museum is located – is an exemplar of art nouveau architecture, but the star of the show is France's treasured national collection of masterpieces from 1848 to 1914.

St-Germain & Les Invalides

The Seine *(p74)*

9 Paris' most beautiful 'boulevard' of all, the Seine, flows through the city's heart, flanked by Parisian-as-it-gets landmarks like the Eiffel Tower, the Louvre and Notre Dame. Taking to the water on a cruise or Batobus ferry is an idyllic way to acquaint or reacquaint yourself with the city. The river's Unesco World Heritage–listed riverbanks, islands and 37 bridges are perfect for promenading, particularly along the reclaimed car-free stretches on both the left and right banks. Entertainment options abound, including floating bars and summertime beaches.

BATEAUX-MOUCHES RIVER CRUISE (P336)

The Seine

Sacré-Cœur *(p134)*

10 A Paris landmark, Basilique du Sacré-Cœur is a place of pilgrimage in more ways than one. Staircased, ivy-clad streets slink up the hill of the fabled artists' neighbourhood of Montmartre to a funicular gliding up to the church's dove-white domes. The chapel-lined basilica – featuring the shimmering apse mosaic *Christ in Majesty* – crowns the 130m-high Butte de Montmartre (Montmartre Hill). Its lofty position provides dizzying vistas across Paris from the basilica's front steps and, above all, from up inside its main dome.

Montmartre & Northern Paris

Jardin du Luxembourg *(p228)*

11 The city's most popular park, Jardin du Luxembourg offers a snapshot of Parisian life. Couples stroll through the chestnut groves. Children chase wooden sailing boats around the octagonal pond and laugh at the antics of engaging marionettes. Old men play rapid-fire chess with cherished pieces at weathered tables. Students pore over books between lectures. Office workers snatch some sunshine, lounging in iconic sage-green metal chairs. Musicians strike up in the bandstand. Joggers loop past stately statues. And friends meet and make plans to meet again.

St-Germain & Les Invalides

10

Père Lachaise *(p157)*

12 Paris is a collection of villages and this sprawl of cobbled lanes and elaborate tombs, with a population (as it were) of more than one million, qualifies as one in its own right. The world's most visited cemetery was founded in 1804, and initially attracted few funerals because of its distance from the city centre. The authorities responded by exhuming the remains of the famous and resettling them here. Their marketing ploy worked and Cimetière du Père Lachaise has been Paris' most fashionable final address ever since.

Le Marais, Ménilmontant & Belleville

Street Markets *(p184)*

13 Stall after stall of cheeses, punnets of raspberries, stacked baguettes, sun-ripened tomatoes, freshly lopped pigs' trotters, horse-meat sausages, spit-roasted chickens, glass bottles of olives and olive oils, quail eggs, duck eggs, boxes of chanterelle mushrooms and knobbly truffles, long-clawed langoustines and prickly sea urchins on beds of crushed ice – along with belts, boots, wallets, cheap socks, chic hats, colourful scarves, striped T-shirts, wicker baskets, wind-up toys, buckets of flowers... Paris' street markets, such as the wonderful Marché Bastille, are a feast for the senses. MARCHÉ BASTILLE (P184)

Bastille & Eastern Paris

Centre Pompidou *(p116)*

14 The primary-coloured, inside-out Centre Pompidou building houses France's national modern- and contemporary-art museum (Europe's largest), the Musée National d'Art Moderne (MNAM), containing creations from 1905 through to the present day. On display are works from Europeans (Picasso, Matisse, Chagall, Kandinsky and more) and cross-Atlantic artists such as Kahlo, Warhol and Pollock, plus edgy installation pieces, sculpture and videos. The centre's cutting-edge cultural offerings include temporary exhibition spaces, a public library, cinemas and entertainment venues. Topping it off is the spectacular panorama from the roof.

Louvre & Les Halles

Versailles *(p264)*

15 No wonder revolutionaries massacred the Château de Versailles palace guard and ultimately dragged King Louis XVI and his queen, Marie Antoinette, back to Paris to be guillotined: this monumental 700-room palace and sprawling estate – with its fountained gardens, ponds and canals – could not have been in starker contrast to the average taxpayer's living conditions at the time. A Unesco World Heritage–listed wonder, Versailles is easily reached from central Paris; try to time your visit to catch musical fountain displays and equestrian shows. CEILING FRESCO, SALON D'HERCULE

Day Trips From Paris

15

16

Canal St-Martin *(p146)*

16 Bordered by shaded towpaths and traversed by iron footbridges, the charming, 4.5km-long Canal St-Martin was slated to be concreted over when barge transportation declined, until local residents rallied to save it. The quaint setting lured artists, designers and students, who set up artists collectives, vintage and offbeat boutiques, and a bevy of neoretro cafes and bars. Enduring maritime legacies include old swing bridges that still pivot 90 degrees when boats pass through the canal's double locks. A cruise is the best way to experience Paris' lesser-known waterway.

Montmartre & Northern Paris

What's New

Contemporary Art

Spring 2019 sees the high-profile opening of the private Collection Pinault inside Paris' circular former grain market and stock exchange the Bourse de Commerce, with a restaurant by triple-Michelin-starred chef Michel Bras. (p120)

Digital Art

An ex-foundry now provides a blank canvas for the dazzling digital art projections at the city's first museum dedicated to the genre, 2018-opened L'Atelier des Lumières. (p163)

Interactive Architecture

Unveiled in 2018, arts centre EP7 screens digital displays on its gallery-like facade and inside hosts exhibitions, DJs and other happenings. (p258)

Multidisciplinary Space

Experimental art, design and fashion works are explored and exhibited at Lafayette Anticipations, opened in 2018 by the corporate foundation of French retailer Galeries Lafayette in a stunning Rem Koolhaas–designed space. (p161)

Avant-garde Fashion

Yves Saint Laurent's sketches through to his catwalk creations are displayed inside the iconic designer's haute couture studios, which now contain the Musée Yves Saint Laurent Paris. (p85)

Start-up Culture

Opened by tech-savvy president Emmanuel Macron, the world's largest start-up campus Station F is home to some 3000 entrepreneurs and co-working cafes, and runs guided tours. (p254)

Co-working Cafes

Co-working cafes are opening right across the city, with local and visiting creatives plugging in at cool pay-by-the-hour or pay-by-the-day spaces like Le 10h10. (p172)

Cultural Island

Concert venue La Seine Musicale, hosting everything from ballets to rock concerts, is the first of several arts venues to open on the site of a former Renault factory on the Seine island of Île Seguin. (p259)

Nordic Swimming

An art deco treasure, swimming complex Piscine de la Butte aux Cailles has opened Paris' first Nordic pool. (p261)

Department-Store Debuts

Galeries Lafayette will open its Champs-Élysées premises in 2019; the same year sees the long-awaited (re-)opening of Seine-side art nouveau department store La Samaritaine. (p131)

Gourmet Emporiums

Food-hall openings include Le Printemps du Goût, in department store Le Printemps, which is devoted solely to showcasing French specialities. (p105)

Vegan Fare

In a heartbeat Paris has gone from a die-hard meat-centric city to laying on a veritable feast of vegan burger and pizza outlets, fabulous vegan cafes such as Abattoir Végétal and full-blown vegan restaurants. (p140)

For more recommendations and reviews, see **lonelyplanet.com/paris**

Need to Know

For more information, see Survival Guide (p329)

Currency
Euro (€)

Language
French

Visas
Generally no restrictions for EU citizens. Usually not required for most other nationalities for stays of up to 90 days.

Money
ATMs widely available. Visa and MasterCard accepted in most hotels, shops and restaurants; fewer accept American Express.

Mobile Phones
Check with your provider about roaming costs before you leave home, or ensure your phone's unlocked to use a French SIM card (available cheaply in Paris).

Time
Central European Time (GMT/UTC plus one hour)

Tourist Information
Paris Convention & Visitors Bureau (Paris Office de Tourisme; Map p386; ☎01 49 52 42 63; www.parisinfo.com; 29 rue de Rivoli, 4e; ⏲9am-7pm; 📶; Ⓜ Hôtel de Ville) Paris' main tourist office is at the Hôtel de Ville. It sells tickets for tours and several attractions, plus museum and transport passes.

Daily Costs

Budget: Less than €100
➡ Dorm bed: €25–50

➡ Espresso/glass of wine/*demi* (half-pint of beer)/cocktail: from €2/3.50/3.50/9

➡ Metro ticket: €1.90

➡ Baguette sandwich: €4.50–6.50

➡ Frequent free concerts and events

Midrange: €100–250
➡ Double room: €130–250

➡ Two-course meal: €20–40

➡ Admission to museums: free to around €15

➡ Admission to clubs: free to around €20

Top end: More than €250
➡ Double room at historic luxury hotel: from €250

➡ Gastronomic-restaurant *menu*: from €40

➡ Private two-hour city tour: from €150

➡ Premium ticket to opera/ballet performance: from €160

Advance Planning
Two months before Book accommodation, organise opera, ballet or cabaret tickets, check events calendars to find out what festivals will be on, and make reservations for high-end/popular restaurants.

Two weeks before Sign up for a local-led tour and start narrowing down your choice of museums, prepurchasing tickets online where possible to minimise ticket queues.

Two days before Pack your comfiest shoes to walk Paris' streets.

Useful Websites
Lonely Planet (www.lonelyplanet.com/paris) Destination information, hotel bookings, traveller forum and more.

Paris Info (www.parisinfo.com) Comprehensive tourist-authority website.

Sortiraparis (www.sortiraparis.com) Up-to-date calendar listing what's on around town.

Bonjour Paris (www.bonjourparis.com) New openings, old favourites and upcoming events.

Secrets of Paris (www.secretsofparis.com) Loads of resources and reviews.

HiP Paris (www.hipparis.com) Not only vacation rentals ('Haven in Paris') but articles and reviews by expat locals, too.

WHEN TO GO

Spring and autumn are ideal. Summer is the main tourist season, but many places close during August. Sights are quieter and prices lower in winter.

Paris

°C/°F **Temp** — 40/104, 30/86, 20/68, 10/50, 0/32, -10/14

Rainfall Inches/mm — 6/150, 5/125, 4/100, 3/75, 2/50, 1/25, 0

J F M A M J J A S O N D

Arriving in Paris

Charles de Gaulle Airport Trains (RER), buses and night buses to the city centre €6 to €17; taxi €50 to €55, 15% higher evenings and Sundays.

Orly Airport Trains (Orlyval then RER), buses and night buses to the city centre €8.70 to €13.25; T7 tram to Villejuif–Louis Aragon then metro to centre (€3.80); taxi €30 to €35, 15% higher evenings and Sundays.

Beauvais Airport Buses (€17) to Porte Maillot then metro (€1.90); taxi during the day/night around €170/210 (probably more than the cost of your flight!).

Gare du Nord train station Within central Paris; served by metro (€1.90).

For much more on **arrival** see p330

Getting Around

Walking is a pleasure in Paris, and the city has one of the most efficient and inexpensive public-transport systems in the world.

Metro & RER The fastest way to get around. Metros run from about 5.30am and finish around 1.15am (around 2.15am on Friday and Saturday nights), depending on the line. RER commuter trains operate from around 5.30am to 1.20am daily.

Bicycle Virtually free pick-up, drop-off Vélib' bikes have docking stations across the city; electric bikes are also available.

Bus Good for parents with prams and people with limited mobility.

Boat The Batobus is a handy hop-on, hop-off service stopping at nine key destinations along the Seine.

For much more on **getting around** see p332

Sleeping

Paris' wealth of accommodation spans all budgets, but it's often *complet* (full) well in advance. Reservations are recommended year-round and essential during the warmer months (April to October) and all public and school holidays. Although marginally cheaper, accommodation outside central Paris is invariably a false economy given travel time and costs. Choose somewhere within Paris' 20 *arrondissements* (city districts) to experience Parisian life the moment you step out the door.

Resources

Lonely Planet (www.lonelyplanet.com/france/paris/hotels) Reviews of Lonely Planet's top choices.

Paris Attitude (www.parisattitude.com) Thousands of apartment rentals, professional service, reasonable fees.

Haven In (https://havenin.com) Charming Parisian apartments for rent.

For much more on **sleeping** see p278

ARRONDISSEMENTS

Within the *périphérique* (ring road), Paris is divided into 20 *arrondissements* (city districts), which spiral clockwise like a snail shell from the centre. *Arrondissement* numbers (1er, 2e etc) form an integral part of all Parisian addresses. Each *arrondissement* has its own personality, but it's the *quartiers* (quarters, ie neighbourhoods), which often overlap *arrondissement* boundaries, that give Paris its village atmosphere.

First Time Paris

For more information, see Survival Guide (p329)

Checklist

➡ Check passport validity and visa requirements

➡ Arrange travel insurance

➡ Confirm airline baggage restrictions

➡ Book accommodation well ahead

➡ Make reservations for popular and/or high-end restaurants

➡ Buy tickets online for the Louvre, Eiffel Tower etc

➡ Organise international roaming on your phone if needed (and be sure to check roaming charges)

What to Pack

➡ Comfortable shoes – Paris is best explored on foot

➡ Phrasebook – the more French you attempt, the more rewarding your visit will be

➡ Travel plug (adapter)

➡ Corkscrew (corked wine bottles are the norm; screw caps are rare); remember to pack it in your checked baggage for flights

Top Tips for Your Trip

➡ An unforgettable introduction to the city is a river cruise (or hop-on, hop-off Batobus trip) along the Seine, floating past quintessentially Parisian landmarks like the Eiffel Tower, Louvre and Notre Dame.

➡ The metro is inexpensive, efficient and easy to use. Local buses are a scenic alternative.

➡ Prebook attractions online wherever possible to avoid standing in long ticket queues.

➡ Brush up on at least a few basic French phrases. Interacting with locals in French (even if only a little) is not only respectful but will make your time in the city infinitely more rewarding.

➡ Above all, don't try to cram too much into your schedule. Allow time to soak up the atmosphere of Paris' neighbourhoods – lingering over a coffee on a cafe terrace and exploring the backstreets are as much a part of the Parisian experience as visiting major sights.

What to Wear

As the cradle of *haute couture,* Paris is chic: don your smarter threads (and accessories such as scarves). You'll also stand out as a tourist less and therefore be less of a target for pickpockets. Dress up rather than down for the 'nicer' restaurants, clubs and bars – no jeans, shorts or trainers/sneakers.

Bring sturdy shoes whatever the season – cobbled streets aren't kind on high heels or thin soles.

When visiting religious sites such as Notre Dame, be sure to dress respectfully.

Be Forewarned

In general, Paris is a safe and well-lit city. Most areas are well lit and in most areas there's generally no reason not to use the metro late at night, including for women travelling alone. Pickpocketing is typically the biggest concern. Always be alert, ensure you don't carry more money than you need, and keep valuables such as credit cards and passports secure and out of sight.

Money

Visa and MasterCard are the most widely used credit cards; American Express is typically only accepted by upmarket establishments such as international chain hotels, luxury boutiques and department stores. Chip-and-pin is the norm for card transactions. Ask your bank for advice before you leave. ATMs *(points d'argent* or *distributeurs automatiques de billets)* are everywhere. You can change cash at some banks, post offices and money-exchange offices. Many shops don't accept €100 bills or higher.

Taxes & Refunds

Prices displayed in shops etc invariably include France's TVA (*taxe sur la valeur ajoutée;* value-added tax).

Non-EU residents can often claim a refund of TVA paid on goods.

Tipping

Taxis Taxi drivers expect small tips of around 5% of the fare, though the usual procedure is to round up to the nearest €1 regardless of the fare.

Restaurants French law requires that restaurant, cafe and hotel bills include a service charge (usually 15%). Many people leave a few extra euros for good service.

Bars and cafes Not necessary at the bar. If drinks are brought to your table, tip as you would in a restaurant.

Hotels Bellhops usually expect €1 to €2 per bag; it's rarely necessary to tip the concierge, cleaners or front-desk staff.

Language

What are the opening hours?

Quelles sont les heures d'ouverture?

kel son lay zer doo·vair·tewr

French business hours are governed by a maze of regulations, so it's a good idea to check before you make plans.

I'd like the set menu, please.

Je voudrais le menu, s'il vous plait.

zher voo·dray ler mer·new seel voo play

The best-value dining in France is the two- or three-course meal at a fixed price. Most restaurants have one on the chalkboard.

Which wine would you recommend?

Quel vin vous conseillez?

kel vun voo kon·say·yay

Who better to ask for advice on wine than the French?

Can I address you with 'tu'?

Est-ce que je peux vous tutoyer?

es ker zher per voo tew·twa·yay

Before you start addressing someone with the informal 'you' form, it's polite to ask permission first.

Do you have plans for tonight/tomorrow?

Vous avez prévu quelque chose ce soir/demain?

voo za·vay pray·vew kel·ker shoz ser swar/der·mun

To arrange to meet up without sounding pushy, ask friends if they're available rather than inviting them directly.

Etiquette

Overall, communication tends to be formal and reserved, but this shouldn't be mistaken for unfriendliness.

Greetings Always greet/farewell anyone you interact with, such as shopkeepers, with *'Bonjour (bonsoir* at night)/*Au revoir'.*

Shops Particularly in smaller upmarket boutiques, staff may not appreciate your touching the merchandise until you have been invited to do so, nor taking photographs.

Speech Parisians don't speak loudly – modulate your voice to a similarly low pitch.

Terms of address *Tu* and *vous* both mean 'you', but *tu* is only used with people you know very well, children or animals. Use *vous* until you're invited to use *tu*.

Conversation topics Discussing financial affairs (eg salaries or spending outlays) is generally taboo in public.

Waitstaff Never use 'garçon' (literally 'boy') to summon a waiter, rather 'Monsieur' or 'Madame'.

Top Itineraries

Day One

Louvre & Les Halles (p106)

Start with a stroll through the elegant **Jardin des Tuileries**, stopping to view Monet's enormous *Water Lilies* at the **Musée de l'Orangerie** and/or photography exhibits at the **Jeu de Paume**. IM Pei's glass pyramid is your compass point to enter the labyrinthine **Louvre**.

Lunch Nip out for French bistro fare at Chez La Vieille (p123).

Louvre & Les Halles (p106)

Visiting this monumental museum could easily consume a full day, but once you've had your fill, browse the colonnaded arcades of the exquisite **Jardin du Palais Royal**, and visit the beautiful church **Église St-Eustache**. Tap into the soul of the former Les Halles wholesale markets along backstreet legacies like the old oyster market, **rue Montorgueil**. Linger for a drink on **rue Montmartre**, then head to the late-opening **Centre Pompidou** for modern and contemporary art and amazing rooftop views.

Dinner Frenchie (p127) offers walk-in wine-bar dining.

Le Marais, Ménilmontant & Belleville (p154)

There's a wealth to see in Le Marais by day (**Musée National Picasso**, **Musée des Arts et Métiers**...), but the neighbourhood really comes into its own at night, with a cornucopia of hip bars and clubs.

Day Two

Champs-Élysées & Grands Boulevards (p92)

Climb the mighty **Arc de Triomphe** for a pinch-yourself Parisian panorama. Promenade down Paris' most glamorous avenue, the **Champs-Élysées**, and give your credit card a workout in the **Triangle d'Or**, **Galeries Lafayette** or **place de la Madeleine** before going behind the scenes of Paris' opulent opera house, the **Palais Garnier**.

Lunch Café Branly (p91): casual yet classy, with ringside tower views.

Eiffel Tower & Western Paris (p80)

Check out global indigenous art and awesome architecture at the **Musée du Quai Branly**. This cultural neighbourhood is also home to the world's largest Monet collection at the **Musée Marmottan-Monet**, contemporary installations at the **Palais de Tokyo** and Asian treasures at the **Musée Guimet**. Sunset is the best time to ascend the **Eiffel Tower**, to experience both dizzying views during daylight hours, and glittering *la ville lumière* (City of Light) by night.

Dinner Cracking modern French fare at Le CasseNoix (p253).

Montparnasse & Southern Paris (p246)

Detour for a drink at a historic Montparnasse brasserie like **Le Select** or continue straight down the Seine to party at the hip bars within **Les Docks** or aboard floating nightclubs moored near France's national library, the **Bibliothèque Nationale de France**.

Day Three

The Islands (p193)

Starting your day at the city's most visited sight, **Notre Dame**, gives you the best chance of beating the crowds. In addition to admiring its stained-glass interior, allow around an hour to visit the top and another to explore the archaeological **crypt**. For even more beautiful stained glass, don't miss nearby **Sainte-Chapelle**. Cross the **Pont St-Louis** to buy a **Berthillon** ice cream before browsing the Île St-Louis' enchanting boutiques.

Lunch Deliciously Parisian hang-out Café Saint Régis (p202).

St-Germain & Les Invalides (p222)

Swoon over impressionist masterpieces in the magnificent **Musée d'Orsay**, scout out the backstreet boutiques and storied shops of St-Germain, sip coffee on the terrace of literary cafes like **Les Deux Magots** and laze in the lovely **Jardin du Luxembourg**, the city's most popular park.

Dinner French classics in art nouveau jewel Bouillon Racine (p235).

Latin Quarter (p205)

Scour the shelves of late-night bookshops like the legendary **Shakespeare & Company**, then join Parisian students and academics in the Latin Quarter's bars, cafes and pubs on **rue Mouffetard** or hit a jazz club like **Café Universel**.

Day Four

Montmartre & Northern Paris (p132)

Montmartre's slinking streets and steep staircases lined with crooked ivy-clad buildings are enchanting places to meander, especially in the early morning when tourists are few. Head to the hilltop **Sacré-Cœur** basilica, then brush up on the area's fabled history at the **Musée de Montmartre**.

Lunch Local favourite Café Miroir (p148) offers all-day dining.

Montmartre & Northern Paris (p132)

Stroll the shaded towpaths of cafe-lined **Canal St-Martin**, and visit the futuristic **Parc de la Villette**, the kid-friendly **Cité des Sciences** museum and the instrument-filled Musée de la Musique, within the **Cité de la Musique**. Sailing schedules permitting, hop on a **canal cruise** to Bastille.

Dinner Sublime 'small plates' at Le 6 Paul Bert (p186).

Bastille & Eastern Paris (p180)

The Bastille neighbourhood calls for a cafe crawl: classics include the cherry-red **Le Pure Café** and absinthe specialist **La Fée Verte**. Salsa your socks off at the 1936 dance hall **Le Balajo** on nightlife strip **rue de Lappe** or catch electro, funk and hip-hop at **Badaboum**.

If You Like...

Markets

Marché Bastille Arguably the best open-air market in the city. (p184)

Marché d'Aligre Wonderfully chaotic market with all the staples of French cuisine. (p186)

Marché St-Quentin Covered market dating back to 1866. (p144)

Rue Montorgueil Street stalls front the food shops of this pedestrianised strip. (p122)

Marché des Enfants Rouges Glorious maze of food stalls with ready-to-eat dishes from around the globe. (p166)

Marché aux Fleurs Reine Elizabeth II Fragrant flower market. (p203)

Marché Raspail Especially popular for its fabulous Sunday organic market. (p244)

Marché aux Puces de St-Ouen Europe's largest flea market, with over 2500 stalls. (p153)

Marché de Belleville Open-air market in business since 1860, in one of Paris' most multicultural, up-and-coming 'hoods. (p169)

Churches

Cathédrale Notre Dame de Paris Paris' mighty cathedral is without equal; you can also scale its towers. (p195)

Église St-Eustache Architecturally magnificent and musically outstanding, this church has sent souls soaring for centuries. (p119)

Basilique du Sacré-Cœur The city's landmark basilica lords over Montmartre. (p134)

KIEVVICTOR / SHUTTERSTOCK ©

Rue Montorgueil (p122)

Église de la Madeleine Neoclassical landmark with wondrous concerts. (p98)

Sainte-Chapelle Classical concerts provide the perfect opportunity to truly appreciate its beauty. (p200)

Basilique de St-Denis France's first major Gothic structure and still one of its finest. (p142)

Église St-Germain des Prés Built in the 11th century, this is Paris' oldest church. (p233)

Église St-Sulpice Frescoes by Delacroix and a starring role in *The Da Vinci Code*. (p232)

Cathédrale Notre Dame – Chartres Renowned for its brilliant-blue stained glass. (p273)

Romance

Jardin du Palais Royal Elegant urban garden with arcaded galleries and gravel walkways embraced by the neoclassical Palais Royal. (p120)

Le Grand Véfour Savour the romance of 18th-century Paris in one of the world's most beautiful restaurants. (p127)

Square du Vert-Galant Tiny, triangular park at the tip of the Île de la Cité. (p201)

Île aux Cygnes The city's little-known third island has wonderful Eiffel Tower views. (p249)

Eiffel Tower There's a reason the top platform sees up to three marriage proposals an hour. (p82)

Canal St-Martin Stroll the shaded towpaths or sit on the banks and watch the boats float by. (p146)

Place St-Sulpice The *place* (square) in front of Église St-Sulpice is an enchanting spot to linger. (p232)

Musée Rodin Swoon over Rodin's marble monument to love, *The Kiss*, and stroll the museum's rose- and sculpture-filled garden. (p230)

Le Coupe-Chou Dine on timeless French cuisine in an enchanting candlelit room backed by classical music. (p212)

Le Pradey The themed Moulin Rouge room (with heart-shaped door frame) at this design hotel is pure romance. (p282)

Literature

Maison de Victor Hugo Visit the elegant home of novelist Victor Hugo overlooking one of Paris' most sublime city squares. (p160)

Maison de Balzac Honoré de Balzac's residence and writing studio (1840–47) is a charmer. (p86)

Shakespeare & Company Attend a reading or browse the shelves of this magical bookshop and writers' hub. (p218)

Bibliothèque Nationale de France France's national library frequently mounts literary exhibitions. (p250)

L'Hôtel Oscar Wilde died in this historic hotel. (p291)

Bar Hemingway According to legend, Ernest Hemingway helped liberate this bar at the Ritz during WWII. (p127)

Café de Flore Jean-Paul Sartre and Simone de Beauvoir were among the writers who frequented this literary cafe. (p241)

Ernest Hemingway's apartment Snap a photo outside the Latin Quarter apartment where Hemingway lived with his wife Hadley. (p216)

La Closerie des Lilas Hemingway wrote much of *The Sun Also Rises* at this hedge-framed brasserie. (p255)

For more top Paris spots, see the following:

- Museums & Galleries (p40)
- Eating (p44)
- Drinking & Nightlife (p54)
- Entertainment (p60)
- Shopping (p65)
- LGBT Travellers (p70)
- Parks & Activities (p72)

La Belle Hortense Book readings, signings and more take place in this literary wine bar. (p171)

Panoramas

Eiffel Tower Each of this landmark tower's three viewing platforms offers a different perspective of the city. (p82)

Galeries Lafayette Some of the best free views of the city are from the top of this grand department store. (p104)

Cathédrale Notre Dame de Paris Get a gargoyle's-eye view by climbing Notre Dame's bell towers. (p195)

Parc de Belleville The hill in this little-known Belleville park offers some of the best views of the city. (p165)

Arc de Triomphe Swooping views along the Champs-Élysées. (p94)

Centre Pompidou Although only six storeys high, the rooftop views across low-rise Paris are stunning. (p116)

Palais de Chaillot The front-row Eiffel Tower views here are best at night, when the tower sparkles on the hour. (p86)

Basilique du Sacré-Cœur Superb views from Sacré-Cœur's steps; even better views from inside its central dome. (p134)

Art Nouveau

Eiffel Tower The graceful latticed metalwork of Paris' 'iron lady' is art nouveau architecture at its best. (p82)

Abbesses metro entrance Hector Guimard's finest remaining glass-canopied metro entrance, illuminated by twin lamps. (p322)

Musée d'Orsay The 1900-built former railway station housing this monumental museum justifies a visit alone. (p224)

Le Train Bleu Resplendent restaurant inside the Gare de Lyon train station. (p189)

Galeries Lafayette Glorious department store topped by a stunning stained-glass dome. (p104)

Le Carreau du Temple This old covered market in Le Marais is now a cutting-edge cultural and community centre. (p177)

Brasserie Bofinger Dine amid art nouveau brass, glass and mirrors in Paris' oldest brasserie. (p167)

Musée Maxim's Art nouveau artworks, objets d'art and furniture above belle époque bistro Maxim's. (p97)

Grand Palais A 1900-built beauty with an 8.5-ton glass roof. (p96)

Modern & Contemporary Architecture

Centre Pompidou Designed in the 1970s, Paris' premier cultural centre is still cutting-edge today. (p116)

La Défense The only place in the city to see a forest of skyscrapers. (p91)

Musée du Quai Branly Striking Seine-side museum designed by Jean Nouvel. (p84)

Institut du Monde Arabe The building that established Nouvel's reputation blends modern and traditional Arab elements with Western influences. (p209)

Fondation Cartier pour l'Art Contemporain Stunning contemporary-art space courtesy of Nouvel. (p249)

Philharmonie de Paris Futuristic Nouvel-designed symphonic concert hall in the equally futuristic Parc de la Villette. (p138)

Fondation Louis Vuitton Frank Gehry–designed fine-arts centre, topped by a giant glass 'cloud'. (p89)

Louvre glass pyramid Egypt's original pyramid builders couldn't have imagined this. (p108)

Bibliothèque Nationale de France The national library's four towers are shaped like half-open books. (p250)

Cité de l'Architecture et du Patrimoine Inside the 1937-built Palais du Chaillot, the exhibits cover Paris' architectural past, present and future. (p85)

Parks & Gardens

Jardin du Luxembourg Paris' most popular inner-city oasis is filled with activities for kids. (p228)

Jardin des Tuileries View Monet's waterlilies at the Musée de l'Orangerie and admire André Le Nôtre's symmetrical layout. (p118)

Promenade Plantée The world's first elevated park, atop a disused 19th-century railway viaduct. (p182)

Maison et Jardins de Claude Monet Come spring, the flower-filled gardens surrounding Monet's former home take on a palette of hues. (p276)

Parc de la Villette Canal-side 35-hectare pavilion-filled 'park of the future' with state-of-the-art facilities for kids and adults. (p136)

Château de Versailles Gardens & Park Designed by André Le Nôtre, the Château de Versailles' gardens are fit for a king. (p265)

Jardin des Plantes The city's beautiful botanic gardens shelter rare plants and 18th-century glass-and-metal greenhouses. (p208)

Bois de Vincennes Paris' eastern woods were once royal hunting grounds. (p183)

Bois de Boulogne Explore Paris' western woods by rowing boat or bicycle. (p89)

French Revolution–Era History

Place de la Bastille Site of the former prison stormed on 14 July 1789, mobilising the Revolution. (p184)

Château de Versailles The October 1789 march on Versailles forced the royal family to leave the palatial château. (p264)

Conciergerie Louis XVI's queen, Marie Antoinette, was one of the aristocratic prisoners tried and imprisoned here. (p201)

Place de la Concorde Louis XVI and Marie Antoinette were among the thousands guillotined where the obelisk now stands. (p97)

Chapelle Expiatoire Original burial grounds of Louis XVI and Marie Antoinette. (p98)

Basilique de St-Denis Louis XVI and Marie Antoinette's final resting place. (p142)

(Top) Colonne de Juillet (p184), Place de la Bastille
(Bottom) Abbesses metro entrance (p322)

Parc du Champ de Mars This former military training ground was the site of Revolutionary festivals. (p86)

Concorde metro station Ceramic tiles spell out the Declaration of the Rights of Man and of the Citizen. (p97)

Caveau de la Huchette Long a jazz club, this cellar was used as a courtroom and torture chamber during the Revolution. (p218)

Medieval History

Le Marais The Marais' medieval streets largely escaped Baron Haussmann's reformation. (p177)

Notre Dame Constructed between 1163 and the early 14th century. (p195)

Louvre Immense fort turned palace turned museum, constructed 1190–1202. (p108)

Sainte-Chapelle Consecrated in 1248 and famed for its dazzling stained glass. (p200)

Sorbonne University founded in 1253 by Robert de Sorbon, confessor to Louis IX. (p210)

Musée National du Moyen Âge Partly housed in the 15th-century Hôtel de Cluny, Paris' finest civil medieval building. (p207)

Basilique de St-Denis Work on this basilica containing the royal necropolis started around 1136. (p142)

Cathédrale Notre Dame – Chartres France's best-preserved medieval cathedral, built in the 13th century. (p273)

Château de Vincennes The only medieval castle in Paris was originally a 12th-century hunting lodge. (p183)

Month by Month

TOP EVENTS

Paris Plages, July

Bastille Day, July

Paris Cocktail Week, January

French Open, May

Nuit Blanche, October

January

The frosty first month of the year isn't the most festive in Paris, but cocktails – as well as the winter *soldes* (sales) – brighten the mood.

Paris Cocktail Week

Each of the 75-plus cocktail bars all over the city that take part in late January's Paris Cocktail Week (https://pariscocktailweek.fr) creates two signature cocktails for the event. There are also workshops, guest bartenders, masterclasses and food pairings. Sign up for a free pass for cut-price cocktails.

Chinese New Year

Paris' largest lantern-lit festivities and dragon parades take place in the city's main Chinatown in the 13e in late January or early February. Parades are also held in Belleville and Le Marais.

February

Festivities still aren't in full swing in February, but couples descend on France's romantic capital for Valentine's Day, when virtually all restaurants offer special menus.

Salon International de l'Agriculture

At this appetising nine-day international agricultural fair (www.salon-agriculture.com) from late February to early March, produce and animals from all over France are turned into delectable fare at the Parc des Expositions at Porte de Versailles, 15e.

March

Blooms appear in Paris' parks and gardens, leaves start greening the city's avenues and festivities begin to flourish. And days get longer – the last Sunday morning of the month ushers in daylight-saving time.

☆ Printemps du Cinéma

Selected cinemas across Paris offer filmgoers a unique entry fee of €4 per session over three days sometime around the middle of March (www.printempsducinema.com).

☆ Banlieues Bleues

Big-name acts perform jazz, blues and R&B during the Suburban Blues (www.banlieuesbleues.org) festival which runs from mid-March to mid-April at venues in Paris' northern suburbs.

April

Sinatra sang about April in Paris, and the month sees the city's 'charm of spring' in full swing, with chestnuts blossoming and cafe terraces coming into their own.

Foire du Trône

Dating back over a millennium, from 957 AD, this huge funfair is held on the Pelouse de Reuilly of the Bois de Vincennes from around Easter to early June.

Marathon International de Paris

On your marks…the Paris International Marathon (www.schneiderelectric parismarathon.com), usually held on the second Sunday of April, starts on av des Champs-Élysées, 8e, and finishes on av Foch, 16e, attracting 57,000 runners from 144 countries at last count.

May

The temperate month of May has more public holidays than any other in France. Watch out for widespread closures, particularly on May Day (1 May).

La Nuit Européenne des Musées

Key museums across Paris stay open late for the European Museums Night (http://nuitdesmusees.culturecommunication.gouv.fr), on one Saturday in mid-May. Most offer free entry.

Portes Ouvertes des Ateliers d'Artistes de Belleville

More than 200 painters, sculptors and other artists at over 120 Belleville studios open their doors to visitors over four days (Friday to Monday) in late May (http://ateliers-artistes-belleville.fr).

French Open

The glitzy Internationaux de France de Tennis Grand Slam (www.rolandgarros.com) hits up from late May to early June at Stade Roland Garros at the Bois de Boulogne.

June

Paris is positively jumping in June, thanks to warm temperatures, a host of outdoor events and long daylight hours, with twilight lingering until nearly 11pm.

Paris Beer Week

Craft beer's popularity in Paris peaks during Paris Beer Week (www.laparis beerweek.com), held, despite the name, over 10 days in early June, when events take place across the city's bars, pubs, breweries, specialist beer shops and other venues.

Fête de la Musique

This national music festival (http://fetedelamusique.culturecommunication.gouv.fr) welcomes in summer on the solstice (21 June) with fabulous staged and impromptu live performances of jazz, reggae, classical and more all over the city.

Marche des Fiertés (Pride)

Late June's colourful Saturday-afternoon Marche des Fiertés (www.gaypride.fr) celebrates Gay Pride with a march that incorporates over-the-top floats and outrageous costumes, and crosses Paris via Le Marais.

Paris Jazz Festival

Jazz concerts swing every Saturday and Sunday afternoon in the second half of June and throughout July in the Parc Floral de Paris during the Paris Jazz Festival (www.parisjazz festival.fr).

La Goutte d'Or en Fête

Raï, reggae and rap feature at this three-day world-music festival (https://gouttedorenfete.wordpress.com) on square Léon in the 18e's Goutte d'Or neighbourhood in late June/early July.

July

During the Parisian summer, 'beaches' – complete with sunbeds, umbrellas, atomisers, lounge chairs and palm trees – line the banks of the Seine, while shoppers hit the summer *soldes* (sales).

Bastille Day

The capital celebrates France's national day on 14 July with a morning military parade along av des Champs-Élysées and fly-past of fighter aircraft and helicopters. *Feux d'artifice* (fireworks) light up the sky above the Champ de Mars by night.

Paris Plages

From at least mid-July to mid-August, 'Paris Beaches' set up along Paris' riverbanks in two main zones, the Parc Rives de Seine, and the Bassin de la Villette (with swimming pools in the canal).

Tour de France

The last of the 21 stages of this legendary, 3500km-long cycling event (www.letour.com) finishes with a dash up av des Champs-Élysées on the third or fourth Sunday of July.

August

Parisians desert the city in droves during the summer swelter when, despite an influx of tourists, many restaurants and shops shut. It's a prime time to cycle, with far less traffic on the roads.

☆ Rock en Seine

Headlining acts rock the Domaine National de St-Cloud, on the city's southwestern edge, at this popular three-day, late-August music festival (www.rockenseine.com).

September

Tourists leave and Parisians come home: *la rentrée* marks residents' return to work and study after the summer break. Cultural life shifts into top gear and the weather is often at its blue-skied best.

☆ Jazz à la Villette

This two-week jazz festival (www.jazzalavillette.com) in the first half of September has sessions in Parc de la Villette, at the Cité de la Musique and at surrounding venues.

Festival d'Automne

The long-running Autumn Festival of arts (www.festival-automne.com), from mid-September to early January, incorporates painting, music, dance and theatre at venues throughout the city.

(Top) Performers at August's Rock en Seine

(Bottom) June's Marche des Fiertés (Pride; p29)

CHRISTIAN BERTRAND / SHUTTERSTOCK ©

OLGA BESNARD / SHUTTERSTOCK ©

Techno Parade

On one Saturday in mid-September, floats carrying musicians and DJs pump up the volume as they travel through the city's streets during the Techno Parade (www.techno parade.fr).

Journées Européennes du Patrimoine

The third weekend in September sees Paris open the doors of otherwise off-limits buildings – embassies, government ministries and so forth – during European Heritage Days (https://journeesdupatrimoine.culturecommunication.gouv.fr).

October

October heralds an autumnal kaleidoscope in the city's parks and gardens, along with bright, crisp days, cool, clear nights and excellent cultural offerings. Daylight saving ends on the last Sunday morning of the month.

Journée Sans Voiture

Pedestrians and cyclists reclaim Paris' streets from mid-morning to early evening on the first Sunday of October on this annual car-free day.

Nuit Blanche

From sundown until sunrise on the first Saturday and Sunday of October, museums stay open, along with bars and clubs, for one 'White Night' (ie 'All-Nighter').

Fête des Vendanges de Montmartre

This five-day festival (www.fetedesvendangesdemontmartre.com), held over the second weekend in October celebrates Montmartre's grape harvest with costumes, concerts, food events and a parade.

Foire Internationale d'Art Contemporain

Scores of galleries are represented at this contemporary-art fair (www.fiac.com), held over four days in mid-October.

Salon du Chocolat

Chocaholics won't want to miss this five-day chocolate festival's tastings, workshops, demonstrations and more at Paris Expo Porte de Versailles, 15e (www.salonduchocolat.fr), held from late October to early November. There are special activities for kids.

November

Dark, chilly days and long, cold nights see Parisians take refuge indoors: the opera and ballet seasons are going strong and there are plenty of cosy bistros and bars.

Illuminations de Noël

From mid-November to early January, festive lights sparkle along the av des Champs-Élysées, rue du Faubourg Saint-Honoré and av Montaigne, all in the 8e, and others, while window displays enchant kids and adults alike at department stores including Galeries Lafayette and Le Printemps.

Beaujolais Nouveau

At midnight on the third Thursday (ie Wednesday night) in November – as soon as French law permits – the opening of the first bottles of cherry-bright, six-week-old Beaujolais Nouveau is celebrated in Paris wine bars, with more celebrations on the Thursday itself.

December

Twinkling fairy lights, brightly decorated Christmas trees and shop windows, and outdoor ice-skating rinks make December a magical month to be in the City of Light.

Christmas Eve Mass

Mass is celebrated at midnight on Christmas Eve at many Paris churches, including Notre Dame – arrive early to find a place.

Le Festival du Merveilleux

The magical private museum Musée des Arts Forains (www.arts-forains.com), filled with fairground attractions of yesteryear, opens from late December to early January, with enchanting rides, attractions and festive shows.

New Year's Eve

Bd St-Michel, 5e, place de la Bastille, 11e, the Eiffel Tower, 7e, and especially av des Champs-Élysées, 8e, are the Parisian hot spots for welcoming in the New Year.

Travel with Children

Parisians adore les enfants (children) and the city's residential density means you'll find playground equipment in parks and squares throughout. Families will find an overwhelming choice of creative, educational, culinary and 'pure old-fashioned fun' things to see, do and experience.

ELENA DIJOUR / SHUTTERSTOCK ©

Climbing web, Parc Floral de Paris (p183)

Science Museums

Cité des Sciences

If you have time for just one museum, make it this one (p136). Book interactive Cité des Enfants sessions (for children aged two to 12) in advance to avoid disappointment.

Musée des Arts et Métiers

Crammed with instruments and machines, Europe's oldest science and technology museum (p160) is fascinating. Experiment-driven workshops are top notch.

Galerie des Enfants

Natural-history museum (p208) for six- to 12-year-olds within the Jardin des Plantes.

Art Attack

Centre Pompidou

Modern-art hub (p116) with great exhibitions, art workshops (for kids aged three to 12) and teen events in Studio 13/16.

Musée en Herbe

Thoughtful art museum (p120) for children with an excellent bookshop and art workshops for kids aged two to 12.

Palais de Tokyo

Palais de Tokyo (p85) offers interactive installations, art workshops (for kids five to 10 years old) and storytelling sessions (for three- to five-year-olds) as well as family activities for all ages.

Treasure Hunts with THATMuse

All ages will get a burst of art adrenaline with a THATMuse (p337) treasure hunt at the Louvre or the Musée d'Orsay. Play alone or in teams.

Hands-On Activities

Musée du Quai Branly

Mask making, boomerang hurling and experimenting with traditional instruments...the ateliers (for three-year-olds to teenagers) at this museum (p84), devoted to African, Asian and Oceanic art and culture, are diverse and creative.

Music at Philharmonie de Paris

Concerts, shows and instrument workshops are part of the world-music repertoire at the city's cutting-edge philharmonic hall (p138) in Parc de la Villette.

Bag Painting with Kasia Dietz

Design and paint a reversible, hand-printed canvas tote with Paris-based New Yorker **Kasia Dietz** (www.kasiadietzworkshops.com; workshops €115-150) during a half-day bag-painting workshop – ideal for fashion-conscious teens (and parents).

Model Building at Cité de l'Architecture et du Patrimoine

Workshops at Paris' architecture museum (p85) see kids (aged four to 16 years) build art deco houses, châteaux and towers in miniature form.

Animal Mad

Equestrian Shows at Versailles

World-class equestrian shows (p267) at Château de Versailles are mesmerising. Show tickets and training sessions include a stable visit.

Sharks at Aquarium de Paris Cinéaqua

Centrally located Cinéaqua (p88) has a shark tank and 500-plus fish species, and screens ocean-themed films.

Ménagerie du Jardin des Plantes

The collection of animals (p208) in Jardin des Plantes includes snow panthers and pandas; combine with the neighbouring natural-history museum (p208).

Parc Zoologique de Paris

Observe lions, cougars, white rhinos and a whole gaggle of other beasties at this state-of-the-art zoo (p183) in Bois de Vincennes.

Parks & Outdoor Capers

Sailing Boats in Jardin du Luxembourg

Playgrounds, puppet shows, pony rides, chess and an old-fashioned carousel: this legendary park (p228) has pandered to children for generations. The vintage toy sailing boats that are the real heart-stealers.

Jardin des Tuileries

These elegant gardens (p118) stage kids' activities and a summertime amusement park.

Parc Floral de Paris

Easily the best playground (p183) for kids eight years and older: outdoor concerts, puppet shows, giant climbing webs, 30m-high slides and a zip line, among other high-energy-burning attractions.

Jardin d'Acclimatation

At this enormous green area (p89) with cycling paths, forest, lakes and ponds, renting a pedalo or rowing boat is a warm-weather treat (bring a picnic), while 2018 saw a slew of attractions added to its amusement park.

Locks on Canal St-Martin

Watching canal boats navigate the many locks (p146) is fun, fascinating and free. Lunch waterside on fish and chips from the Sunken Chip (p143).

Riverside Play

Giant board games, a climbing wall, a 20m-long blackboard to chalk on, tepees and events 'n' shows galore line this expressway-turned-promenade (p233).

Boat Trips on the Seine

Every kid loves a voyage down the Seine with Bateaux-Mouches (p336) or Bateaux Parisiens (p339). But there is something

NEED TO KNOW

Babysitting *L'Officiel des Spectacles* (www.offi.fr) lists *gardes d'enfants* (babysitters); some hotels organise sitters for guests.

Equipment Rent strollers, scooters, car seats, travel beds and more while in Paris from companies such as Kidelio (www.kidelio.com).

Paris Mômes (www.parismomes.fr) Outstanding bimonthly magazine on Parisian kid culture (up to 12 years); print off playful kids' guides for major art exhibitions before leaving home.

ELENA DIJOUR / SHUTTERSTOCK ©

Riding a quadricycle, Parc Floral de Paris (p183)

extra special about the one-hour 'Paris Mystery' tours designed especially for children by Vedettes de Paris (p336).

Puppet Shows

Parisians have entertained children with outdoor puppet shows for centuries. Head to a city park such as the Jardin du Luxembourg (p228) or Parc Monceau (p137).

Screen Entertainment

Digital Exhibitions at Gaîté Lyrique

Digital-driven exhibitions (p177), video games for older children and teens, laptops to use in the digitally connected cafe and a library with desks shaped like ducks for kids under five to sit at and draw.

Special-Effect Movies at Cité des Sciences

Two special-effect cinemas: Géode with 3D movies, and Cinéma Louis-Lumière screening animation and short films. Top it off with a cinematic trip through the solar system in the planetarium (p136).

Tour at Le Grand Rex

Whiz-bang special effects stun during behind-the-scenes tours at this iconic 1930s cinema (p129). Stand behind the big screen and muck around in a recording studio.

Theme Parks

Disneyland Resort Paris

A magnet for families, this park (p263) 32km east of Paris includes Disneyland and cinema-themed Walt Disney Studios Park.

Parc Astérix

Shuttle buses run from central Paris to this summer-opening **theme park** (☎08 26 46 66 26; www.parcasterix.fr; A1 motorway btwn exit 7 & 8, Plailly; adult/child €47/39; ⊙10am-6pm daily Apr & Jun, 10am-6pm Wed, Sat & Sun May, 10am-7pm daily Jul & Aug, 10am-6pm Sat & Sun Sep & Oct), 35km north of the city. It covers prehistory through to the 19th century with its six 'worlds', adrenaline-pumping attractions and shows for all ages.

Easy Eating

Pink Flamingo Pizza Picnic

Where else are you sent away with a pink balloon when you order? Kids adore takeaway pizza from Pink Flamingo (p144) on Canal St-Martin.

Hand-Pulled Noodles

Watching nimble-fingered chefs pull traditional Chinese noodles by hand at Les Pâtes Vivantes (p101) is spellbinding.

Le Jardin des Pâtes

This Left Bank address (Map p400, E2; ☎01 43 31 50 71; www.restaurant-lejardindespates.fr; 4 rue Lacépède, 5e; pasta €12-15; ⊙noon-2.30pm & 7-11pm; 👶; Ⓜ Place Monge) 🌿, steps from the Jardin des Plantes, cooks up some of Paris' most creative and tasty pasta.

Dip in at Chalet Savoyard

Everyone loves a bubbling pot of cheese, a basket of bread and a fondue fork at **Chalet Savoyard** (Map p394, D4; ☎01 48 05 13 13; www.chalet-savoyard.fr; 58 rue de Charonne,

CITY TRAILS: PARIS

For an insight into Paris aimed directly at kids, pick up a copy of Lonely Planet's *City Trails: Paris*. Perfect for children aged eight and up, it opens up a world of intriguing stories and fascinating facts about Paris' people, places, history and culture.

11e; 3-course menu €33, mains €15-28; ⌚noon-2.30pm & 7-11pm Sun-Thu, to midnight Fri & Sat; Ⓜ Ledru-Rollin).

Vegan fare

Kids' *menus* come with organic fruit juice at Gentle Gourmet Café (p188).

Multicourse Dining

Bustronome

Kids can play 'I spy' spotting Parisian landmarks while dining on delicious multi-course *menus* cooked in the purpose-built galley of this glass-roofed bus (p90).

Le Train Bleu

Train-obsessed kids will also love the multicourse menus at this magnificent railway-station restaurant (p189) inside Gare de Lyon.

Gourmet at Glou

How refreshing to find **Glou** (Map p386, D5; ☎01 42 74 44 32; www.glou-resto.com; 101 rue Vieille du Temple, 3e; 2-/3-course lunch menus €18/22, mains €17-29; ⌚noon-2.30pm & 7.30-11pm Mon-Fri, noon-5pm & 7.30-11.30pm Sat & Sun; 👪; Ⓜ St-Sébastien–Froissart), a hip wine bar in Le Marais that serves excellent food and fine wine, and caters to children with their own gourmet *menu*, colouring pencils and paper.

Ladurée

Kids love nibbling macarons at this historic tearoom (p99) on the Champs-Élysées but can also get their own three-course *menus* here.

Bouillon Racine

A dazzling introduction to French cuisine (p235) and art nouveau architecture.

Rainy-Day Ideas

Cirque d'Hiver Bouglione

Clowns, trapeze artists and acrobats have entertained children of all ages at the city's winter circus (p176) since 1852.

Musée des Arts Forains

Check for seasonal events at this fair-ground museum, such as its Christmas season during **Le Festival du Merveilleux** (www.arts-forains.com; ⌚Dec-Jan; Ⓜ Cour Saint-Émilion).

Les Catacombes

Teens generally get a kick out of Paris' most macabre sight (p248), but be warned: this skull-packed underground cemetery is not for the faint-hearted.

An Afternoon at the Theatre

Paris' diverse theatre scene stages bags of performances for kids, some in English; weekly entertainment mag *L'Officiel des Spectacles* (www.offi.fr) lists what's on.

Musée de la Magie

This museum (Map p386, D8; ☎01 42 72 13 26; www.museedelamagie.com; 11 rue St-Paul, 4e; adult/child €14/9; ⌚2-7pm Wed, Sat & Sun; Ⓜ Sully–Morland, St-Paul) is pure magic!

Playful Le Nid

Older children and teens can kick back with board games over a drink, lunch or tasty weekend brunch at this pioneering **games cafe** (Map p386, B3; ☎07 82 75 23 00; www.lenid-coconludique.com; 227 rue St-Martin, 3e; ⌚5.30pm-1am Mon-Fri, noon-midnight Sat, noon-8.30pm Sun; Ⓜ Arts et Métiers) in Le Marais – as much for adults as big kids.

Like a Local

Paris is among the world's most visited cities, but it's not an urban resort. The city has the highest population density of any European capital, and its parks, cafes and restaurants are its communal backyards, living rooms and dining rooms, while neighbourhood shops and markets are cornerstones of local life.

RIVER THOMPSON/LONELY PLANET ©

Rue Trousseau, Bastille (p180)

Dining Like a Local

Parisians are obsessed with talking about, shopping for, preparing and above all eating food. Quality trumps quantity, which is reflected in the small, specialist gourmet food shops thriving all over the city.

Sunday lunch is traditionally France's main meal of the week, but Sunday (and often Saturday) brunch has become a fixture on the weekend's social calendar from around noon to about 4pm. Be sure to book for popular venues.

Another part of the recent shift towards informal dining is the profusion of casual wine bars where, rather than ordering full *menus* (two- or three-course set menus), locals gather to share small tapas-style plates over *un verre* (a glass).

Drinking Like a Local

Given Paris' high concentration of city dwellers, most bars and cafes close around 2am due to noise restrictions, and nightclubs in the inner city are few. Cocktail bars continue to shake up Paris' drinking scene, though, with a slew of specialists across the city. Craft beer is also staking its claim in this wine-drinking city, with numerous Parisian breweries in fully fledged operation. Paris Cocktail Week (p57) and Paris Beer Week (p57) are now fixtures on the city's calendar.

Although the image of Parisians sipping *un café* on a wicker-chair-lined cafe terrace isn't new, recent years have seen a dramatic improvement in coffee quality. Led by pioneers like Belleville Brûlerie and Coutume, a new wave of Parisian roasteries sees hip Parisians attending cupping sessions and buying beans to brew up at home.

In summer, ephemeral bars, often with pop-up restaurants, food trucks, DJs and live music, open all in unique spaces such as railway-station yards, rooftops, courtyards, parks and along the riverfront. Check www.parisinfo.com for the year's locations.

Conversing Like a Local

Food and drink aside, conversations between locals often revolve around philosophy, art, and sports such as rugby, football (soccer), cycling and tennis. Talking about money (salaries or spending outlays, for example) in public is generally taboo.

Dressing Like a Local

It's nearly impossible to overdress in this fashion-conscious city. Parisians have a finely tuned sense of aesthetics, and take meticulous care in their presentation. Parisians favour style over fashion, mixing basics from chain stores like H&M with designer pieces, vintage and flea-market finds, and statement-making accessories.

Hanging Out Like a Local

Parisians generally work to live rather than the other way round. Thanks to the much-debated 35-hour standard working week, long annual leave and a lot of public holidays, Parisians aren't driven to make and spend money 24/7/365. Instead, leisure activities factor highly in Parisians' *joie de vivre* (spirited enjoyment of life), along with the company of friends and family (children are treated like little adults and welcomed with open arms just about everywhere).

Cinemas, theatres and concert venues as well as art exhibitions, festivals and special events draw huge local crowds.

Sunday is the main day of rest, when most workplaces (including the majority of shops outside the ZTI tourist zones) close and locals head to museums, parks and *jardins partagés* (community gardens); visit www.paris.fr for a list (and map) of gardens that are open to the public.

Year-round, you'll find locals kicking back all along the banks of the Seine but never more so than on warm summer evenings with a picnic and bottle of wine.

Meeting the Locals

The best way to get a feel for local life is to head to areas where Parisians work, live and play away from the busy tourist sights. Great neighbourhoods to start exploring:

- Bastille (p181)
- Belleville (p155)
- Canal St-Martin (p146)
- Les Halles (especially rues Montorgueil and Montmartre; p122)
- Latin Quarter (especially on and around rue Mouffetard; p212)
- Ménilmontant (p155)
- South Pigalle (aka SoPi; p133)
- The 13e (especially the villagey Butte aux Cailles and floating clubs on the Seine; p257)

Local-led tours and activities are also a fantastic way to get an insider's perspective of the city.

Parisien d'un Jour – Paris Greeters (p337) Run by volunteers.

Ça Se Visite (p337) Discover the city's northeastern neighbourhoods.

Localers (p337) Walks and activities such as *pétanque* (similar to lawn bowls).

Meeting the French (p337) Workshops, courses, market tours and more.

NEED TO KNOW

Metro Parisians from all walks of life – from students to celebrity chefs – use the metro. If you're in Paris for a week or more, get a Navigo pass to save money and zip through the turnstiles without queuing for tickets.

Vélib' bikes Virtually free Vélib' bikes are hugely popular – Parisians flit all over the city on two wheels.

Navigation

Street numbers notated *bis* (twice), *ter* (thrice) or *quater* (four times) are similar to the English a, b etc. If you're entering an apartment building, you'll generally need the alphanumeric *digicode* (entry code) to open the door. Once inside, apartments are usually unmarked, without any apartment numbers or even occupants' names. To know which door to knock on, you're likely to be given cryptic directions like *cinquième étage, premier à gauche* (5th floor, first on the left) or *troisième étage, droite droite* (3rd floor, turn right twice). In all buildings, the 1st floor is the floor above the *rez-de-chaussée* (RdC; ground floor).

For Free

Paris might be home to haute couture, haute cuisine and historic luxury hotels, but if you're still waiting for your lottery numbers to come up, don't despair. There are a wealth of ways to soak up the French capital without spending a centime (or scarcely any, at least).

Buskers, Île de la Cité (p194)

FARUK CIFTCI / SHUTTERSTOCK ©

Free Museums

If you can, time your trip to be here on the first Sunday of the month, when you can visit national museums and a handful of monuments for free (some during certain months only).

European citizens under 26 get free entry to national museums and monuments.

At any time you can visit the permanent collections of Paris' *musées municipaux* (www.paris.fr/musees) for free (some only when temporary exhibitions aren't on).

Temporary exhibitions always incur an admission fee. Some museums have reduced entry at various times of the day or week.

Other freebies include Paris' fascinating town-planning and architectural centre, the Pavillon de l'Arsenal (p161), and the Musée du Parfum (p98), which are free all year.

Museums and monuments offering free admission on the first Sunday of the month include the following.

Arc de Triomphe (p94) November to March

Basilique de St-Denis (p142) November to March

Château de Versailles (p264) November to March

Cité de l'Architecture et du Patrimoine (p85)

Conciergerie (p201) November to March

Musée de la Chasse et de la Nature (p162)

Musée de l'Histoire de l'Immigration (p183)

Musée de l'Orangerie (p118)

Musée des Arts et Métiers (p160) Also free every Thursday from 6pm

Musée des Impressionnismes Giverny (p277)

Musée d'Orsay (p224)

Musée du Louvre (p108) October to March

Musée du Quai Branly (p84)

Musée Guimet des Arts Asiatiques (p87)

Musée National d'Art Moderne (p116) Within the Centre Pompidou

Musée National du Moyen Âge (p207) Aka Musée de Cluny

Musée National Eugène Delacroix (p232)

Musée National Gustave Moreau (p98)

Musée National Picasso (p160)

Musée Rodin (p230) October to March

Panthéon (p207) November to March

Sainte-Chapelle (p200) November to March

Tours de Notre Dame (p195) November to March

Free Churches

Some of the city's most magnificent buildings are its churches and other places of worship. Not only exceptional architecturally and historically, they contain exquisite art, artefacts and other priceless treasures. Best of all, entry to general areas within them is, in most cases, free.

Do respect the fact that although many of Paris' places of worship are also major tourist attractions, Parisians come here to pray and celebrate significant events on religious calendars as part of their daily lives. Keep noise to a minimum, obey photography rules (check signs), dress appropriately and try to avoid key times (eg Mass) if you're sightseeing only.

Free Cemeteries

Paris' celebrity-filled cemeteries, including the three largest – Père Lachaise (p157), Cimetière de Montmartre (p139) and Cimetière du Montparnasse (p250) – are free to wander.

Free Entertainment

Music

Concerts, DJ sets and recitals regularly take place for free (or for the cost of a drink) at venues throughout the city.

Busking musicians and performers entertain crowds on Paris' streets and squares and even aboard the metro.

Literary Events

This literary-minded city is an inspired place to catch a reading, author signing or writing workshop. English-language bookshops such as Shakespeare & Company (p218) and Abbey Bookshop (p221) host literary events throughout the year and can point you towards others.

Fashion Shows

Reserve ahead to attend free weekly fashion shows (p104) at Grands Boulevards department store Galeries Lafayette. While you're here, don't miss one of the best free views over the Parisian skyline from Galeries Lafayette's rooftop. Nearby department store Le Printemps (p105) also has amazing – and free – views from the roof.

Festivals

Loads of Paris' festivals and events are free, such as the summertime Paris Plages (p75) riverside beaches.

Getting Around

Walking

Paris is an eminently walkable city, with beautiful parks and gardens, awe-inspiring architecture, and markets and shops (well, window-shopping never goes out of style) to check out along the way.

For a free walking tour (donations encouraged), contact Parisien d'un Jour – Paris Greeters (p337) in advance for a personalised excursion led by a resident volunteer.

Cycling (almost free)

If you'd rather free-wheel around Paris, the Vélib' (p334) system costs next to nothing for a day's subscription, and the first 30 minutes of each bike rental is free.

Buses (cheap as chips)

Instead of taking a bus tour, simply hop on a local bus. Particularly scenic routes include lines 21 and 27 (Opéra–Panthéon), line 29 (Opéra–Gare de Lyon), line 47 (Centre Pompidou–Gobelins), line 63 (Musée d'Orsay–Trocadéro), line 73 (Concorde–Arc de Triomphe) and line 82 (Montparnasse–Eiffel Tower). Time it to avoid peak commuting hours, when buses are packed sardine-can-style.

NEED TO KNOW

- ➡ Paris has hundreds of free wi-fi points at popular locations, including parks, libraries, local town halls and tourist hot spots. Locations are mapped at www.paris.fr.
- ➡ Consider investing in a transport or museum pass.
- ➡ Theatre tickets are sold for half price on the day of performance.
- ➡ Paris' parks are perfect for picnics made from market fare.

MURATART / SHUTTERSTOCK ©

Leonardo da Vinci's *Mona Lisa* (p109), Musée du Louvre

Museums & Galleries

If there's one thing that rivals a Parisian's obsession with food, it's their love of art. Hundreds of museums pepper the city, and whether you prefer classicism, impressionism or detailed exhibits of French military history, you can always be sure to find something new just around the corner.

Paris Museum Pass

If you think you'll be visiting more than two or three museums or monuments while in Paris, the single most important investment you can make is the Paris Museum Pass (http://en.parismuseumpass.com; two/four/six days €48/62/74). The pass is valid for entry to over 50 venues in and around the city, including the Louvre, Centre Pompidou, Musée d'Orsay and Musée Rodin (but not the Eiffel Tower), the châteaux at Versailles and Fontainebleau and the Basilique de St-Denis.

One of the best features of the pass is that you can bypass the long ticket queues at major attractions (though not the security queues). But be warned: the pass is valid for a certain number of days, not hours, so if you activate a two-day pass late Friday afternoon, for instance, you will only be able to use it for a full day on Saturday. Also keep in mind that most museums are closed on either Monday or Tuesday, so think twice before you activate a pass on a Sunday.

The Paris Museum Pass is available online as well as at participating museums, tourist desks at the airports, branches of the Paris Convention & Visitors Bureau, and other locations listed on the website. European citizens under 26 years and children under 18 years get free entry to national museums and monuments, so don't buy this pass if you belong to one of those categories.

For Free

Municipal museums in Paris are free; many other museums have one free day per month (generally the first Sunday of the month, in some cases winter months only). Note that temporary exhibits invariably have a separate admission fee, even at free museums (a few require entry when a temporary exhibition is taking place).

Performances

Many museums host excellent musical concerts and performances, with schedules that generally run from September to early June. Some of the top venues:

Musée du Louvre (p108) Hosts a series of lunchtime and evening classical concerts throughout the week.

Musée d'Orsay (p224) Chamber music every Tuesday at 12.30pm, plus various evening classical performances.

Musée du Quai Branly (p84) Folk performances of theatre, dance and music from around the world.

Centre Pompidou (p116) Film screenings and avant-garde dance and music performances.

Le 104 (p138) A veritable pot-pourri of everything from circus and magic to afternoon breakdancing.

Children's Workshops

If you have kids in tow, make sure you check out the day's *ateliers* (workshops). Although these are usually in French, most activities involve hands-on creation, so children should enjoy themselves despite any language barrier. At major museums (eg the Centre Pompidou), it's best to sign up in advance.

Dining

Although there are plenty of tourist cafeterias to be found in Paris, the dining options in museums are generally pretty good – some are destinations in themselves. Even if you're not out sightseeing, consider a meal at one of the following:

Les Ombres (p90) and **Café Branly** (p91) These two dining options at the Musée du Quai Branly have ringside seats for the Eiffel Tower.

Monsieur Bleu (p85) Hip venue at the Palais du Tokyo.

Le Restaurant (p225) and **Café Campana** (p225) Within the Musée d'Orsay; the former was the art nouveau railway station's showpiece restaurant.

NEED TO KNOW

➡ City museums (eg Petit Palais, Musée Cognacq-Jay) are free.

➡ Temporary exhibits almost always have a separate admission fee, even at free museums.

➡ Ask if you qualify for a reduced-price ticket *(tarif réduit)*: students, seniors and children generally get discounts or free admission.

Musée Jacquemart-André (p138) Lunch or tea in the sumptuous dining room of a 19th-century mansion.

Collection Pinault – Paris (p120) A restaurant by triple-Michelin-starred chef Michel Bras will complement the exhibitions at the Bourse de Commerce when it opens in 2019.

Public Art

Museums and galleries are not the sole repositories of art in Paris. Indeed, art is all around you, including *murs végétaux* (vertical gardens adorning apartment buildings), and street art ranging from small murals to artworks covering entire high-rises to Invader tags (tiled Space Invaders–inspired creations) marking street corners. Enjoying art in Paris is simply a matter of keeping your eyes open.

Big-name installations have become destinations in their own right. Niki de Saint Phalle and Jean Tinguely's playful *Stravinsky Fountain* – a collection of 16 colourful animated sculptures based on the composer's oeuvre – is located next to the Centre Pompidou. Daniel Buren's zebra-striped columns of varying heights at the Palais Royal is another beloved Paris fixture; the installation was originally greeted with derision but has since become an integral part of the historic site. Both the Jardin des Tuileries and the Jardin du Luxembourg are dotted with dozens of sculptures that date from the 19th and early 20th centuries; the Jardin des Tuileries also contains an area with more contemporary works from the likes of Roy Lichtenstein and Magdalena Abakanowicz.

One of the best areas to go hunting for contemporary public art – and architecture – is out in the business district of La Défense, where you'll find dozens of works

TIPS FOR AVOIDING MUSEUM FATIGUE

- Wear comfortable shoes and make use of the cloakrooms.
- Sit down as often as you can; standing still and walking slowly promote tiredness.
- Reflecting on the material and forming associations with it causes information to move from your short- to long-term memory; your experiences will thus amount to more than a series of visual 'bites'. Using an audioguide is a good way to provide context.
- Studies suggest that museum-goers spend no more than 10 seconds viewing an exhibit and another 10 seconds reading the label as they try to take in as much as they can. To avoid this, choose a particular period or section to focus on, or join a guided tour of the highlights.

by well-known artists such as Miró, Calder and Belmondo. Metro stations, too, often contain some iconic or unusual additions, from Hector Guimard's signature art nouveau entrances to the crown-shaped cupolas at the Palais Royal.

Tickets

Consider booking online to avoid queues where possible (eg for the Louvre, Musée d'Orsay, Centre Pompidou); print tickets before you go if necessary. In some cases you can download the tickets onto a smartphone, but check beforehand. Also ensure you can download more than one ticket onto your phone if need be.

If you can't book online, look for automated machines at museum entrances, which generally have shorter queues. Note that credit cards without an embedded smart chip (and some non-European chip-enabled cards) won't work in these machines.

Opening Hours

Most museums are closed on Monday or Tuesday – it's vital that you verify opening days before drawing up your day's schedule.

General opening hours are from 10am to 6pm, though all museums shut their gates between 30 minutes and an hour before their actual closing times. Thus, if a museum is listed as closing at 6pm, make sure you arrive before 5pm.

Major museums are often open one or two nights a week, which is an excellent time to visit as there are fewer visitors.

Museums & Galleries by Neighbourhood

Eiffel Tower & Western Paris (p85) Paris' largest concentration of museums, from the Quai Branly to Musée Marmottan Monet.

Champs-Élysées & Grands Boulevards (p96) Musée des Beaux-Arts de la Ville de Paris, Le Grand Musée du Parfum and more.

Louvre & Les Halles (p120) The Louvre, Centre Pompidou, Musée de l'Orangerie and others.

Montmartre & Northern Paris (p137) Musée Jacquemart-André, Cité des Sciences, Le 104 and others.

Le Marais, Ménilmontant & Belleville (p160) Musée National Picasso, Mémorial de la Shoah, Lafayette Anticipations, L'Atelier des Lumières, among others.

Bastille & Eastern Paris (p182) Cinémathèque Française and others.

Latin Quarter (p207) Musée National du Moyen Âge, Muséum National d'Histoire Naturelle, and Institut du Monde Arabe.

St-Germain & Les Invalides (p232) Musée d'Orsay, Musée Rodin and more.

Montparnasse & Southern Paris (p249) Fondation Cartier and others.

Lonely Planet's Top Choices

Musée du Louvre (p108) The one museum you just can't miss.

Musée d'Orsay (p224) Monet, Van Gogh and company.

Centre Pompidou (p116) One of the top modern-art museums in Europe.

Musée Rodin (p230) Superb collection of Rodin's masterpieces in an intimate setting.

Musée National Picasso (p160) An incomparable overview of Picasso's work and life.

Best Modern Art Museums & Installations

Centre Pompidou (p116) Huge selection of modern art and big-name temporary exhibits.

Palais de Tokyo (p85) Interactive contemporary-art exhibitions and installations against a stark concrete-and-steel backdrop.

Jeu de Paume (p118) Contemporary-photography exhibitions in the Jardin des Tuileries.

L'Atelier des Lumières (p163) A former foundry houses Paris' first digital-art museum.

Fondation Louis Vuitton (p89) Striking glass building staging modern-art exhibitions.

Best Unsung Museums

Cité de l'Architecture et du Patrimoine (p85) Standout museum devoted to French architecture and heritage.

Musée Jacquemart-André (p138) Gorgeous 19th-century home hung with canvases by Rembrandt, Botticelli and Titian.

Musée des Beaux-Arts de la Ville de Paris (p96) Fine arts inside the Petit Palais.

Musée de la Vie Romantique (p139) Dedicated to the work of two Romantic creators.

Musée Nissim de Camondo (p137) Eighteenth-century objets d'art inside a lavish mansion.

Best History Museums

Crypte Archéologique (p197) Layer upon layer of Parisian history beneath the square outside Notre Dame.

Musée de l'Armée (p231) Within the monumental Hôtel des Invalides complex, commemorating French military history.

Musée de Montmartre (p137) Relive the days of Toulouse-Lautrec and Maurice Utrillo.

Mémorial de la Shoah (p156) Moving Holocaust museum and documentation centre.

Best Museums for Non-European Art

Musée du Quai Branly (p84) Overview of indigenous art from around the world, presented in the most striking of manners.

Musée Guimet des Arts Asiatiques (p87) France's foremost Asian art museum.

Musée du Louvre (p108) Mesopotamian, Egyptian and Islamic artefacts.

Institut du Monde Arabe (p209) Art and artisanship from the Middle East and North Africa.

Best Small Museums

Musée de l'Orangerie (p118) For Monet's sublime *Water Lilies* series.

Musée Maillol (p234) Splendid museum focusing on the work of sculptor Aristide Maillol.

Cinémathèque Française (p182) Props, early equipment and short clips bring cinematic history to life.

Musée Marmottan Monet (p86) The world's largest Monet collection.

Best Science Museums

Cité des Sciences (p136) Excellent science-related exhibits and attractions for all ages.

Muséum National d'Histoire Naturelle (p208) Dinosaur skeletons, taxidermic elephants and excellent temporary exhibits.

Musée des Arts et Métiers (p160) Europe's oldest science and technology museum.

Best Residence Museums

Musée National Eugène Delacroix (p232) The Romantic artist's home and studio contains many of his more intimate works.

Musée Cognacq-Jay (p161) Treasure trove of artwork and objets d'art.

Musée Bourdelle (p249) Monumental bronzes displayed in the house and workshop of sculptor Antoine Bourdelle.

Maison de Victor Hugo (p160) Victor Hugo's former quarters, overlooking Paris' most elegant square.

Chicory with clams, Septime (p188)

Eating

The inhabitants of some cities rally around local sports teams, but in Paris they rally around la table – and everything on it. Pistachio macarons, shots of tomato consommé, decadent bœuf bourguignon, a gooey wedge of Camembert running onto the cheese plate...food isn't fuel here; it's the reason you get up in the morning.

Septime (p188)

Paris: A Culinary Renaissance

Home to one of the world's great culinary traditions, France has shaped Western cooking techniques and conceptions of what good food is for centuries – whether it's a multicourse gourmet meal or a crusty baguette. Blessed with a rich and varied landscape, farmers with a strong sense of regional identity and a culture that celebrates life's daily pleasures, it's no surprise that French chefs have long been synonymous with gastronomic genius.

Over the past several decades, though, restaurant culture started to slip. Frozen and industrially prepared ingredients, stultifying business regulations and an over-reliance on formulaic dishes led to a general decline in both quality and innovation. Alarmed by these forbidding trends, a new generation of chefs has emerged in the past several years, reemphasising market-driven cuisine and displaying a willingness to push the boundaries of traditional tastes, while at the same time downplaying the importance of Michelin stars and the formal, chandelier-studded dining rooms of yesteryear.

Even more significantly, the real change that is taking place in Paris today is that more and more of these chefs – and, just as importantly, more and more diners – are open to culinary traditions originating outside France. Some have trained abroad, while others hail from Japan, the US or elsewhere. The latter group has come to Paris specifically because they love French

NEED TO KNOW

Opening Hours

➡ Restaurants generally open from noon to 2pm for lunch and from 7.30pm to 10.30pm for dinner. Peak Parisian dining times are 1pm and 9pm.

➡ Most restaurants shut for at least one full day (usually Sunday). August is the peak holiday month and many places are consequently closed during this time.

Price Ranges

The following price ranges refer to the cost of a two-course meal.

€ less than €20

€€ €20–€40

€€€ more than €40

Reservations

➡ Midrange restaurants will usually have a free table for lunch (arrive by 12.30pm); book a day or two in advance for dinner.

➡ Reservations up to one or two months in advance are crucial for lunch and dinner at popular/high-end restaurants. You may need to reconfirm on the day.

Tipping

A *pourboire* (tip) on top of the bill is not necessary as service is always included. But it is not uncommon to round up the bill if you were pleased with your waiter.

Paying the Bill

Trying to get *l'addition* (the bill) can be maddeningly slow. Do not take this personally. The French consider it rude to bring the bill immediately – you have to be persistent when it comes to getting your server's attention.

Prix-Fixe Menus

➡ Daily *formules* or *menus* (*prix-fixe* menus) typically include two- to four-course meals. In some cases, particularly at market-driven neobistros, there is no *carte* (menu).

➡ Lunch *menus* are often a fantastic deal and allow you to enjoy *haute cuisine* at very affordable prices.

Above: Alfresco dining, Montmartre (p140)
Left: Croissants

THE FIVE BASIC CHEESE TYPES

Charles de Gaulle once famously asked how it was possible to govern a country with 246 types of cheese. A more relevant question for non-Frenchies: how do you come to grips with a shop that sells such a head-spinning variety? The choices on offer at a *fromagerie* (cheese shop) can be overwhelming, but vendors will always allow you to sample before you buy, and they are usually very generous with their guidance and pairing advice.

In shops, cheeses are typically divided into five main groups:

Fromage à pâte demi-dure 'Semi-hard cheese' means uncooked, pressed cheese. Among the finest are Tomme de Savoie, made from either raw or pasteurised cow's milk; Cantal, a cow's-milk cheese from Auvergne that tastes something like cheddar; St-Nectaire, a pressed cheese that has a strong, complex taste; and Ossau-Iraty, a ewe's-milk cheese made in the Basque Country.

Fromage à pâte dure 'Hard cheese' is always cooked and then pressed. Among the most popular are Beaufort, a grainy cow's-milk cheese with a slightly fruity taste from Rhône-Alpes; Comté, a cheese made with raw cow's milk in Franche-Comté; Emmental, a cow's-milk cheese made all over France; and Mimolette, an Edam-like dark-orange cheese from Lille that can be aged for up to 36 months.

Fromage à pâte molle 'Soft cheese' is moulded or rind-washed. Camembert, a classic moulded cheese from Normandy that for many is synonymous with 'French cheese', and Brie de Meaux are both made from raw cow's milk. Munster from Alsace, mild Chaource and strong-smelling Langres from Champagne, and the odorous Époisses de Bourgogne are rind-washed, fine-textured cheeses.

Fromage à pâte persillée 'Marbled' or 'blue cheese' is so called because the veins often resemble *persille* (parsley). Roquefort is a ewe's-milk veined cheese that is to many the king of French cheeses. Fourme d'Ambert is a mild cow's-milk cheese from Rhône-Alpes. Bleu du Haut Jura (also called Bleu de Gex) is a mild, blue-veined mountain cheese.

Fromage de chèvre 'Goat's-milk cheese' is usually creamy and both sweet and slightly salty when fresh, but it hardens and gets much saltier as it matures. Among the best varieties are Ste-Maure de Touraine, a creamy, mild cheese from the Loire region; Crottin de Chavignol, a classic though saltier variety from Burgundy; Cabécou de Rocamadour from Midi-Pyrenées, often served warm with salad or marinated in oil and rosemary; and Chabichou, a soft, slightly aged cheese from Poitou.

cooking, but none are so beholden to its traditions that they are afraid to introduce new concepts or techniques from back home. French cuisine has finally come to the realisation that a global future doesn't necessarily mean a loss of identity – decadent work-of-art pastries and the divine selection of pungent cheeses aren't going anywhere. Instead, there is an opportunity to once again create something new.

How to Eat & Drink Like a Parisian

Eating well is of prime importance to most French people, who spend an inordinate amount of time thinking about, discussing and enjoying food and wine. Yet dining out doesn't have to be a ceremonious occasion or one riddled with pitfalls for the uninitiated. Approach food with even half the enthusiasm *les français* do, and you will be welcomed, encouraged and exceedingly well fed.

WHEN TO EAT

Petit déjeuner (breakfast) The French kick-start the day with a slice of baguette smeared with unsalted butter and jam and *un café* (espresso) or – for kids – hot chocolate. Parisians might grab a coffee and croissant on the way to work, but otherwise croissants (eaten straight, never with butter or jam) are more of a weekend treat or *goûter* (afternoon snack) along with *pains au chocolat* (chocolate-filled croissants) and other *viennoiseries* (sweet pastries).

Déjeuner (lunch) The traditional main meal of the day, lunch incorporates a starter and main course with wine, followed by a short, sharp *café*. During the work week this is less likely to be the case – many busy Parisians now grab a sandwich to go and pop off to run errands – but the standard hour-long lunch break, special *prix-fixe* menus and *tickets restaurant* (company-funded meal vouchers) ensure that many restaurants fill up at lunch.

Apéritif Otherwise known as an *apéro*, the pre-meal drink is sacred. Cafes and bars get packed out from around 5pm onwards as Parisians wrap up work for the day and relax over a glass of wine or beer.

Diner (dinner) Traditionally lighter than lunch, but a meal that is being treated more and more as the main meal of the day. In restaurants the head chef will almost certainly be in the kitchen, which is not always the case during lunch.

Eating a crêpe

WHERE TO EAT

Bistro (or *bistrot*) A small neighbourhood restaurant that serves French standards (duck confit, *steak-frites*). The setting is usually casual; if you're looking for a traditional French meal, a bistro is the place to start. Don't expect *haute cuisine* service; most simply do not have the staff to cater to a diner's every whim.

Brasserie Much like a cafe except it serves full meals, drinks and coffee from morning until 11pm or later. Typical fare includes *choucroute* (sauerkraut) and sausages.

Cafe Many visitors will naturally gravitate towards cafes (which become bars around 5pm) because of the alluring ambience and buzzy sun-kissed terraces. Meals are inexpensive but often consist

DAILY BREAD

Few things in France are as tantalising as the smell of just-baked buttery croissants wafting out of an open bakery door. With roughly 1200 *boulangeries* (bakeries) in Paris – or 11.5 per sq km – you'll likely find yourself inside one at some point during your stay. And, as you'll notice in the extravagant display windows, bakeries bake much more than baguettes: they also sell croissants, chocolate éclairs, quiches, pizzas and an astounding array of pastries and cakes. If you're eating lunch on the cheap, a trip to the closest bakery will do you right.

If it's the bread you're after, try to familiarise yourself with the varieties on sale while you're standing in the queue – not all baguettes are created equal. Most Parisians today will ask for a *baguette tradition* (traditional-style baguette), distinguished by its pointy tips and coarse, handcrafted surface. Other breads you'll see include *boules* (round loaves), *pavés* (flattened rectangular loaves) and *ficelles* (skinny loaves that are half the weight of a baguette).

The shape of a baguette (literally 'stick' or 'wand') evolved when Napoleon Bonaparte ordered army bakers to create loaves for soldiers to stuff down their trouser legs on the march.

Every spring *boulangers* (bakers) battle it out in the official Grand Prix de la Meilleure Baguette de Paris (Best Baguette in Paris). The winner is not only awarded a cash prize but also provides the French president with baguettes for a year.

of industrially prepared food that's simply reheated, so stick to the drinks.

Crêperie A quintessentially Parisian snack is the street crêpe made to order, slathered with Nutella and folded up in a triangular wedge. Crêpes can be so much more than this, however, as a trip to any authentic crêperie will reveal. Savoury crêpes, known as *galettes,* are made with buckwheat flour; dessert crêpes are made with white flour – usually you order one of each accompanied by a bowl of cider.

Gastronomic restaurants Pierre Gagnaire, Guy Savoy, Pascal Barbot… Paris has one of the highest concentrations of culinary magicians in the world. Designed to amaze your every sense, many of these restaurants are once-in-a-lifetime destinations – even for Parisians – so do your homework and reserve well in advance.

Market Fantastic places to wander: here you'll find all the French culinary specialities in the same place, in addition to meals and snacks cooked on site. Scores of food markets set up in the city. Most are open twice weekly from 8.30am to 1pm, though covered markets keep longer hours, reopening around 4pm. For a complete list, visit https://meslieux.paris.fr/marches.

Neobistro Generally small and relatively informal, these are run by young, talented chefs who aren't afraid to experiment. The focus is on market-driven cuisine, hence choices are often limited to one or two dishes per course. Some specialise in small plates designed for sharing.

Wine bar/cave à manger The focus is on sampling wine; the style of cuisine, while often excellent, can be wildly different. Some places serve nothing more than plates of cheese and charcuterie (*saucisson,* pâté); others are full-on gastronomic destinations with a talented chef running the kitchen.

MENU ADVICE

Carte Menu, as in the written list of what's cooking, listed in the order you'd eat it: starter, main course, cheese, then dessert. Note that an entrée is a starter, not the main course (as in the US).

Menu Not at all what it means in English, *le menu* in French is a *prix-fixe* menu: a multicourse meal at a fixed price. It's by far the best-value dining there is and most restaurants chalk one on the board. In some cases, particularly at neobistros, there is no *carte* – only a stripped-down *menu* with one or two choices.

À la carte Order whatever you fancy from the menu (as opposed to opting for a *prix-fixe* menu).

Market bread stall

MARCHÉ INTERNATIONAL DE RUNGIS

Covering an area bigger than Monaco (234 hectares), Paris' **wholesale markets** (☎08 25 05 44 05; www.visiterungis.com; av des Maraîchers, Rungis; tour €85; ⏲by reservation) are sectioned into vast halls for meat, cheese, fish, fruit and vegetables, organic fruit and vegetables, plants and cut flowers. Fascinating behind-the-scenes tours of its operations are conducted in English and French. Prices include a three-hour market tour, a 45-minute breakfast and bus transport to and from central Paris. Pick-up is at 4am from place Denfert-Rochereau, 14e, returning at 10am. Wear warm clothes (and comfortable shoes!). No children under 13 years. The markets are otherwise off-limits to the public.

Formule Similar to a *menu, une formule* is a cheaper lunchtime option comprising a main plus starter or dessert. Wine or coffee is sometimes included.

Plat du jour Dish of the day, invariably good value.

Menu enfant Two- or three-course meal for kids (generally up to the age of 12) at a fixed price; usually includes a drink.

Menu dégustation Fixed-price tasting menu served in many top-end restaurants, consisting of at least five modestly sized courses.

DINING TIPS

Bread Order a meal and within seconds a basket of fresh bread will be brought to the table. Butter is rarely an accompaniment. Except in the most upmarket of places, don't expect a side plate – simply put it on the table.

Water Asking for *une carafe d'eau* (jug of tap water) is perfectly acceptable, although some waiters will presume you don't know this and only offer mineral water, which you have to pay for. Should you prefer bubbles, ask for *de l'eau gazeuze* (fizzy mineral water). Ice *(glaçons)* can be hard to come by.

Service To state the obvious, France is not a service-oriented country. No one is working for tips here, so to get around this, think like a Parisian – acknowledge the expertise of your *serveur* by asking for advice (even if you don't really want

Top: *Fromagerie* (cheese shop), Marché d'Aligre (p186)
Middle: Snails in garlic butter
Bottom: Marché d'Aligre

it) and don't be afraid to flirt. In France flirtation is not the same as picking someone up; it is both a game that makes the mundane more enjoyable and a vital life skill to help you get what you want (such as the bill). Being witty and speaking French with an accent will often help your cause.

Dress Smart casual is best. How you look is very important, and Parisians favour personal style above all else. But if you're going somewhere dressy, don't assume this means suit and tie – that's more business-meal attire. At the other end of the spectrum, running shoes may be too casual, unless, of course, they are more hip than functional, in which case you may fit right in.

Vegetarians & Vegans

Vegetarians and vegans make up a small minority in a country where *viande* (meat) once also meant 'food', but in recent years they have been increasingly well catered for with a slew of new vegetarian and vegan addresses, from casual vegan burger, pizza and hot-dog joints to gourmet vegetarian and vegan restaurants. More and more modern places are also offering vegetarian choices on their set *menus*. Another good bet is non-French cuisine; Middle Eastern cuisine in particular is currently a red-hot trend. See www.happycow.net for a guide to veggie options in Paris.

Gluten-Free

Gluten-free dining options are steadily becoming more prevalent: try Noglu (p124) or Helmut Newcake (p101) for starters, and bakery Chambelland (p169) for bread and cakes. Gluten-free addresses are mapped at www.glutenfreeinparis.com.

Cooking Classes

What better place to discover the secrets of *la cuisine française* than in Paris, the capital of gastronomy? Courses are available at different levels and for various durations.

Cook'n With Class (☎01 42 57 22 84; www.cooknwithclass.com; 6 rue Baudelique, 18e; 2hr classes from €95; Ⓜ Simplon, Jules Joffrin) A bevy of international chefs, small classes and an enchanting Montmartre location are ingredients for success at this informal cooking school, which organises dessert classes for kids, cheese and wine courses, market visits, gourmet food tours and six-course dinners with the chef and sommelier as well as regular cookery classes. Classes are taught in English.

Le Cordon Bleu (Map p414; ☎01 85 65 15 00; www.cordonbleu.edu/paris; 13-15 quai André Citroën, 15e; Ⓜ Javel–André Citroën or RER Javel) One of the world's foremost culinary-arts schools. Prices start at €140 for themed three-hour classes (food and wine pairing, vegetarian cuisine, eclairs, choux pastry etc) and €470 for two-day courses.

La Cuisine Paris (Map p386; ☎01 40 51 78 18; www.lacuisineparis.com; 80 quai de l'Hôtel de Ville, 4e; 2hr cooking class/walking tours from €69/80; Ⓜ Pont Marie, Hôtel de Ville) Classes in English range from how to make bread and croissants to macarons as well as market classes and gourmet 'foodie walks'.

Le Foodist (Map p400; ☎06 71 70 95 22; www.lefoodist.com; 59 rue du Cardinal Lemoine, 5e; Ⓜ Cardinal Lemoine) Classes at this culinary school include classic French cookery and patisserie courses, allowing you to create your own éclairs and choux pastry, macarons or croissants. Market tours, and wine and cheese tastings and pairings are also available. Instruction is in English. Three-hour classes start at €99.

Macarons, La Cuisine Paris

Eating by Neighbourhood

Useful Websites

David Lebovitz (www.davidlebovitz.com) Expat US pastry chef and cookbook author. Good insights and recommendations.

Le Fooding (https://lefooding.com) The French movement that's giving Michelin a run for its money. Le Fooding's mission is to shake up the ossified establishment, so expect a good balance of quirky, under-the-radar reviews and truly fine dining.

La Fourchette (www.thefork.com) Website offering user reviews and great deals of up to 50% off in Paris restaurants.

Paris by Mouth (https://parisbymouth.com) Capital dining and drinking with articles and recommendations searchable by *arrondissement*.

Paris Food Affair (www.parisfoodaffair.com) Keep tabs on Paris' evolving foodie scene.

Lonely Planet's Top Choices

Tomy & Co (p238) Meteorically rising star Tomy Gousset uses organic produce from his own garden.

Restaurant AT (p214) Abstract-art-like masterpieces made from rare ingredients.

Restaurant Guy Savoy (p237) Resplendent triple-Michelin-starred flagship in the neoclassical mint.

Bouillon Racine (p235) Classical French cooking in an art nouveau showpiece.

Berthillon (p202) Arguably the world's most sublime ice cream.

La Maison Plisson (p163) Dazzling gourmet deli with an on-site cafe.

Best by Budget

€

Ladurée Picnic (p252) Gourmet picnics from the famed macaron creator.

La Bête Noire (p210) Mediterranean home cooking sourced from farms and small producers.

Fric-Frac (p142) Wildly creative croques monsieurs by Canal St-Martin.

Au Pied de Fouet (p234) Bistro classics are astonishingly good value at this 150-year-old charmer.

La Butte aux Piafs (p256) Vintage decor and bistro dishes in the villagey Butte aux Cailles neighbourhood.

€€

L'Étable Hugo Desnoyer (p236) Meat-focused dishes from Paris' best butcher at St-Germain's covered market.

Balagan (p123) Creative, ultracontemporary Israeli cuisine.

Maison Maison (p123) Seine-side Mediterranean restaurant hidden by the Pont Neuf.

Au Passage (p166) A springboard for talented chefs.

Anicia (p236) Auvergne produce such as Puy lentils from celebrated chef François Gagnaire.

Le Cassenoix (p253) Terroir specialist footsteps from the Eiffel Tower.

€€€

Restaurant Guy Savoy (p237) A red-carpeted staircase leads to this once-in-a-lifetime destination.

Septime (p188) A beacon of modern cuisine.

L'Astrance (p89) Dazzling gastronomy for a meal to remember.

Frenchie (p127) The bijou bistro that redefined Parisian dining.

Lasserre (p99) Fine dining and flawless service beneath a retractable roof.

Best for Traditional French Cuisine

Bouillon Racine (p235) Traditional fare inspired by age-old recipes.

Chez La Vieille (p123) Homage to the former wholesale markets Les Halles.

Le Bon Georges (p102) For those who thrive on nostalgia.

Le Temps au Temps (p188) Traditional and excellent-value bistro fare on foodie street rue Paul Bert.

Brasserie Bofinger (p167) The city's oldest brasserie.

Best for Seafood

L'Écailler du Bistrot (p186) Extraordinary seafood in a traditional setting.

L'Avant Comptoir de la Mer (p234) Chic St-Germain seafood-tapas bar.

Le Dôme (p255) Magnificent shellfish platters in a timeless art deco brasserie.

Clamato (p188) Seafood-tapas sibling of Michelin-starred Septime.

Huîtrerie Regis (p236) Oyster heaven.

Best for Crêpes

Breizh Café (p164) Among the most authentic Breton crêpes in town.

Crêpe Dentelle (p123) Superb crêpes by Les Halles.

Crêperie Pen-Ty (p140) Northern Paris' best crêperie, with traditional Breton aperitifs.

Little Breizh (p234) Innovative twists such as Breton sardines.

Crêperie Josselin (p256) In the 'Little Brittany' neighbourhood near Gare Montparnasse.

Le Pot O'Lait (p211) Great *galettes* and sweet crêpes in the Latin Quarter.

Best for Vegetarian & Vegan Food

Abattoir Végétal (p140) Plant-filled vegan cafe in Montmartre.

Le Potager de Charlotte (p147) Gourmet vegan restaurant.

Soul Kitchen (p143) Market-driven vegetarian dishes.

Raw Cakes (p252) Not only cakes but yes, it's all raw.

Bob's Juice Bar (p144) Pioneering Parisian veggie address.

Gentle Gourmet Café (p188) All of the dishes are vegan and most are organic at this light-filled cafe.

Les Deux Magots (p239)

Drinking & Nightlife

For the French, drinking and eating go together like wine and cheese, and the line between a cafe, salon de thé (tearoom), bistro, brasserie, bar and even bar à vins (wine bar) is blurred. The line between drinking and clubbing is often nonexistent – a cafe that's quiet midafternoon might have DJ sets in the evening and dancing later on.

Grimbergen beer

Drinking

For most Parisians living in tiny flats, cafes and bars have traditionally served as the *salon* they don't have – a place where they can meet with friends over *un verre* (glass of wine), read for hours over a *café au lait*, debate politics while downing an espresso at a zinc counter, swill cocktails during *apéro* (aperitif; predinner drink) or get the party started aboard a floating club on the Seine.

COFFEE & TEA

Coffee has always been Parisians' drink of choice to kick-start the day. So it's surprising, particularly given France's fixation on quality, that Parisian coffee long lagged behind world standards, with burnt, poor-quality beans and unrefined preparation methods. Recently, however, Paris' coffee revolution has seen local roasteries like Belleville Brûlerie and Coutume priming cafes citywide for outstanding brews made by professional baristas, often using cutting-edge extraction techniques. Caffeine fiends are now spoilt for choice and while there's still plenty of substandard coffee in Paris, you don't have to go far to avoid it.

Surprisingly, too, tea – more strongly associated with France's northwestern neighbours the UK and Ireland – is extremely popular in Paris. Tearooms offer copious varieties; learn about its history at the tea museum within the original Marais branch of Mariage Frères (p178).

WINE

Wine is easily the most popular beverage in Paris and house wine can cost less than bottled water. Of France's dozens of

NEED TO KNOW

Opening Hours

Closing time for cafes and bars tends to be 2am, though some have licences until dawn. Club hours vary depending on the venue, day and event.

Tiered Pricing

Drinking in Paris essentially means paying the rent for the space you take up. So it costs more to sit at a table than to stand at the counter, more for coveted terrace seats, more on a fancy square than a backstreet, more in the 8e than the 18e.

Average Costs

An espresso starts at around €2, a glass of wine from €3.50, a cocktail €9 to €16 and a *demi* (half-pint) of beer €3.50 to €7. In clubs and chic bars, prices can be double. Admission to clubs is free to around €20 and is often cheaper before 1am.

Happy 'Hour'

Most mainstream bars and international-styled pubs have a 'happy hour' – called just that (no French translation) – which ushers in reduced-price drinks for a good two or three hours, usually between around 5pm and 8pm.

Top Tips

- Some wine bars offer free corkage; otherwise it typically costs around €4.50 to €7.
- Although most places serve at least small plates (often full menus), it's normally fine to order a coffee or alcohol if you're not dining.
- The French rarely go drunk-wild and tend to frown upon it.

Coffee Decoded

Un café Single shot of espresso.

Un café allongé Espresso lengthened with hot water (sometimes served separately).

Un café au lait Coffee with milk.

Un café crème Shot of espresso lengthened with steamed milk.

Un double Double shot of espresso.

Une noisette Shot of espresso with a spot of milk.

PARIS CAFE / ALAMY STOCK PHOTO ©

Above: Mariage Frères (p178)
Left: Chez Prune (p146)

Drinking by Neighbourhood

Montmartre & Northern Paris Local gems include canal-side cafes (p148)

Champs-Élysées & Grands Boulevards Swanky hotel bars, glam nightclubs (p103)

Louvre & Les Halles Eclectic mix of bars and clubs (p127)

Le Marais Ménilmontant & Belleville Hip, edgy bars and nightlife venues (p170)

Eiffel Tower & Western Paris Classy bars and cocktail lounges (p90)

St-Germain & Les Invalides Historic literary cafes, stylish bars (p239)

The Islands Quaint tearooms and wine bars (p203)

Latin Quarter Spirited student pubs and bars (p215)

Bastille & Eastern Paris Lively clubs and bars galore (p189)

Montparnasse & Southern Paris Boulevard-facing brasseries and backstreet cafes (p257)

Seine

wine-producing regions, the principal ones are Burgundy, Bordeaux, the Rhône and the Loire valleys, Champagne, Languedoc, Provence and Alsace. Wines are generally named after the location of the vineyard rather than the grape varietal. The best wines are Appellation d'Origine Contrôlée (AOC; currently being relabelled Appellation d'Origine Protégée, AOP), meaning they meet stringent regulations governing where, how and under what conditions they're grown, fermented and bottled.

BEER

Beer hasn't traditionally had a high profile in France and mass-produced varieties such as Kronenbourg 1664 (5.5%), brewed in Strasbourg, dominate. Paris' growing *bière artisanale* (craft beer) scene, however, is going from strength to strength, with an increasing number of city breweries, such as Brasserie BapBap (p174) and Brasserie la Goutte d'Or (p139), microbreweries and cafes offering limited-production brews on tap and by the bottle. The city's artisan-beer festival, **Paris Beer Week** (http://parisbeerweek.fr; ⌚early Jun), takes place in brasseries, bars and specialist beer shops, usually in early June. An excellent resource for hopheads is www.hoppyparis.com.

COCKTAILS

Paris' resurgent cocktail scene spans glitzy hotel bars and neobistros, super-cool backstreet speakeasies and former hostess bars in the hip SoPi ('south Pigalle') neighbourhood. Sample forgotten French liqueurs, fresh fruit, and homemade infusions and syrups at the best of the bunch. Aficionados won't want to miss **Paris Cocktail Week** (https://pariscocktailweek.fr; ⌚Jan), held the last week of January.

NATURAL WINE

Les vins naturels (natural wines) have a fuzzy definition – no one really agrees on the details, but the general idea is that they are produced from organically grown grapes using few or no pesticides or additives. This means natural wines do not contain sulphites, which are added as a preservative in most wines. The good news is that this gives natural wines a much more distinct personality (or *terroir*, as the French say); the bad news is that these wines can also be more unpredictable. For more specifics, see the website www.morethanorganic.com.

Nightlife

Paris' residential make-up means nightclubs aren't ubiquitous. Lacking a mainstream scene, clubbing here tends to be underground and extremely mobile. The best DJs and their followings have short stints in a certain venue before moving on, and the scene's hippest *soirées clubbing* (clubbing events) float between venues – including the many dance-driven bars. In 2017 floating club Concrete (p189) became France's first to have a 24-hour licence. Dedicated clubbers may also want to check out the growing suburban scene – much more alternative and spontaneous in nature but also harder to reach.

Wherever you wind up, the beat is strong. Electronic music is of a particularly high quality in Paris' clubs, with some excellent local house and techno. Funk and groove are also popular, and the Latin scene is huge; salsa-dancing and Latino-music nights pack out plenty of clubs. World music also has a following in Paris, where everything goes at clubs. R&B and hip-hop pickings are decent, if not extensive.

BEFORE, L'AFTER & AFTER D'AFTERS

Seasoned Parisian clubbers, who tend to have a finely tuned sense of the absurd, split their night into three parts. First, *la before* – drinks in a bar that has a DJ playing. Second, they head to a club for *la soirée,* which rarely kicks off before 1am or 2am. When the party continues (or begins) at around 5am and goes until midday, it's *l'after*. Invariably, though, given the lack of any clear-cut distinction between Parisian bars and clubs, the before and after can easily blend into one without any real 'during'. *After d'afters,* meanwhile, kicks off in bars and clubs on Sunday afternoons and evenings, with a mix of strung-out hardcore clubbers pressing on amid those looking for a party that doesn't take place in the middle of the night.

CLUBBING WEBSITES

Track tomorrow's hot 'n' happening soirée with these finger-on-the-pulse Parisian-nightlife links:

Paris DJs (www.parisdjs.com) Free downloads to get you in the groove.

Paris Bouge (www.parisbouge.com) Comprehensive listings site.

Sortir à Paris (www.sortiraparis.com) Click on 'Soirées & Bars', then 'Nuits Parisiennes'.

Tribu de Nuit (www.tribudenuit.com) Parties, club events and concerts galore.

SUBURBAN SCENE

Plug into the indie clubbing scene with the following informal venues and collectives, which organise parties in the northern suburbs.

Otto 10 (www.facebook.com/otto10events)

75021 (www.facebook.com/75021Paris)

Le 6B (www.le6b.fr)

Lonely Planet's Top Choices

Bar Hemingway (p127) Legendary cocktails inside the Ritz.

Pavillon Puebla (p149) Pavilion opening to two terraces in the leafy Parc des Buttes Chaumont.

Le Baron Rouge (p189) Wonderfully convivial barrel-filled wine bar.

Le Perchoir (p172) Hip rooftop bar best visited at sunset.

Les Deux Magots (p239) Watch St-Germain go by from this famous cafe's terrace.

Candelaria (p170) Clandestine cocktail bar hidden behind a taqueria (taco restaurant).

Best for Cocktails

Experimental Cocktail Club (p128) Speakeasy that spawned an international empire.

Le Syndicat (p149) Cocktails incorporate rare French spirits.

Tiger (p241) Gin specialist with 130 varieties.

Cod House (p239) Sake-based cocktails pair with gourmet small plates.

Danico (p128) Cocktails crafted from rare ingredients in a candlelit back room.

Little Bastards (p215) House-creation cocktails in a Latin Quarter backstreet.

Best Wine Bars

Le Garde Robe (p128) Affordable natural wines and unpretentious vibe.

Septime La Cave (p188) Wine and gourmet nibbles just off rue de Charonne.

La Quincave (p241) Bar stools fashioned from wine barrels and over 200 natural wines.

La Cave Paul Bert (p186) Pocket-sized bistro and wine bar.

Au Sauvignon (p239) Original zinc bar and hand-painted ceiling.

Best for Coffee

Belleville Brûlerie (p179) Ground-breaking roastery with Saturday-morning tastings and cuppings.

Beans on Fire (p174) Collaborative roastery and cafe.

La Caféothèque (p171) Coffee house and roastery with an in-house coffee school.

Coutume Café (p242) Artisan roastery with a flagship Left Bank cafe.

Honor (p103) Outdoor coffee bar in an elegant rue du Faubourg St-Honoré courtyard.

Café Lomi (p150) Coffee roastery and cafe in the multi-ethnic La Goutte d'Or neighbourhood.

Best Tearooms

Mariage Frères (p178) Paris' oldest and finest tearoom, founded in 1854.

L'Amaryllis de Gérard Mulot (p235) Wonderful tearoom by patisserie maestro Gérard Mulot.

La Mosquée (p214) Sip sweet mint tea and nibble delicious pastries at Paris' mosque.

Best for Beer

Paname Brewing Company (p149) Craft-brewery taproom in a 19th-century waterside granary with a floating pontoon.

Balthazar (p174) Crowdfunded microbrewery with guest Parisian beers.

Outland (p190) Artisan beer bar serving Outland's own beers.

Le Triangle (p151) Microbrewery with shiny kettles and sharing plates.

Frog & Princess (p241) Long-established microbrewery on a hopping nightlife street.

Best Pavement Terraces

Chez Prune (p146) The boho cafe that put Canal St-Martin on the map.

L'Ebouillanté (p171) A contender for Paris' prettiest cafe terrace (and its best homemade ginger lemonade).

Café des Anges (p190) The terrace of this 11e cafe buzzes night and day.

Shakespeare & Company Café (p215) Live the Parisian Left Bank literary dream.

Best Nightclubs

Le Rex Club (p129) Renowned house and techno club with a phenomenal sound system.

Concrete (p189) Paris' first club with a 24-hour licence is aboard a barge by Gare de Lyon.

Zig Zag Club (p103) Best of the Champs-Élysées venues.

Le Batofar (p258) Iconic tugboat-housed club in the 13e.

Moulin Rouge (p151)

Entertainment

Catching a performance in Paris is a treat. French and international opera, ballet and theatre companies and cabaret dancers take to the stage in fabled venues, while elsewhere a flurry of young, passionate, highly creative musicians, thespians and other artists make the city's fascinating fringe art scene what it is.

Cabarets

Whirling lines of feather-boa-clad, high-kicking dancers at grand-scale cabarets like cancan creator Moulin Rouge (p151) are a quintessential fixture on Paris' entertainment scene – for everyone but Parisians. Still, the dazzling sets, costumes and dancing guarantee an entertaining evening (or matinee).

Tickets to these spectacles start at around €90 (from around €165/190 with lunch/dinner), with the option of Champagne. Reserve ahead.

Live Music

Festivals for just about every musical genre ensure that everyone gets to listen in. Street music is a constant in this busker-filled city, with summer adding stirring open-air concerts along the Seine and in city parks to the year-round serenade of accordions.

JAZZ & BLUES

Paris became Europe's most important jazz centre after WWII and the city's best clubs and cellars still lure international stars Admission generally ranges from free to around €30 depending on artist, time and venue. Download podcasts, tunes, concert information and all that jazz from Paris' jazz radio station, TSF (www.tsfjazz.com).

FRENCH CHANSONS

While *chanson* literally means 'song' in French, it also specifically refers to a style of heartfelt, lyric-driven music typified by Édith Piaf, Maurice Chevalier, Charles Aznavour et al. You'll come across rousing live covers of their most famous songs at traditional venues. Contemporary twists on the genre include the fusion of dance beats with traditional *chanson* melodies. The term also covers intimate cabarets such as Montmartre's Au Lapin Agile (p152).

Admission ranges from free to around €30 depending on artist, time and venue.

ROCK, POP & INDIE

AccorHotels Arena (p191), **Stade de France** (☎01 55 93 00 45; www.stadefrance.com; St-Denis La Plaine; stadium tours adult/child €15/10; Ⓜ St-Denis-Porte de Paris) and Le Zénith (p136) are among the largest venues but also the most impersonal; newer additions include La Seine Musicale (p259) and **U Arena** (www.uarena.com; 99 Jardins de l'Arche, Nanterre; Ⓜ La Défense). Smaller concert halls with real history and charm include La Cigale (p151) and L'Olympia (p104).

NEED TO KNOW

Listings

Paris' top listings guide, *L'Officiel des Spectacles* (www.offi.fr; €1), is published in French but is easy to navigate. It's available from newsstands on Wednesday, and lists everything that's on in the capital.

Useful Websites

LYLO (www.lylo.fr) Short for Les Yeux, Les Oreilles ('eyes and ears'), offering the low-down on concerts, festivals and more.

Le Figaro Scope (http://evene.lefigaro.fr) Music, cinema and theatre listings.

Paris Nightlife (www.parisnightlife.fr) All-encompassing listings site.

Tickets

The most convenient place to purchase concert, theatre and other cultural and sporting-event tickets is from electronics and entertainment megashop **Fnac** (☎08 92 68 36 22; www.fnactickets.com), whether in person at the *billeteries* (ticket offices) or by phone or online. There are branches throughout Paris, including in the Forum des Halles. Tickets generally can't be refunded.

Discount Tickets

On the day of performance, theatre, opera and ballet tickets are sold for half price (plus €3.50 commission) at the central **Kiosque Théâtre Madeleine** (Map p370; www.kiosqueculture.com; opposite 15 place de la Madeleine, 8e; ⏲12.30-7.30pm Tue-Sat, to 3.45pm Sun; Ⓜ Madeleine).

CLASSICAL MUSIC

The city hosts dozens of orchestral, organ and chamber-music concerts each week. In addition to theatres and concert halls, Paris' beautiful, centuries-old stone churches have magnificent acoustics; posters outside advertise upcoming events with ticket information, or visit www.ampconcerts.com, where you can make online reservations. Tickets cost around €23 to €30.

Larger venues include the Jean Nouvel–designed 2400-seat Philharmonie de Paris (p138) concert hall, which opened in the Parc de la Villette in 2015, and the 2017-opened La Seine Musicale (p259).

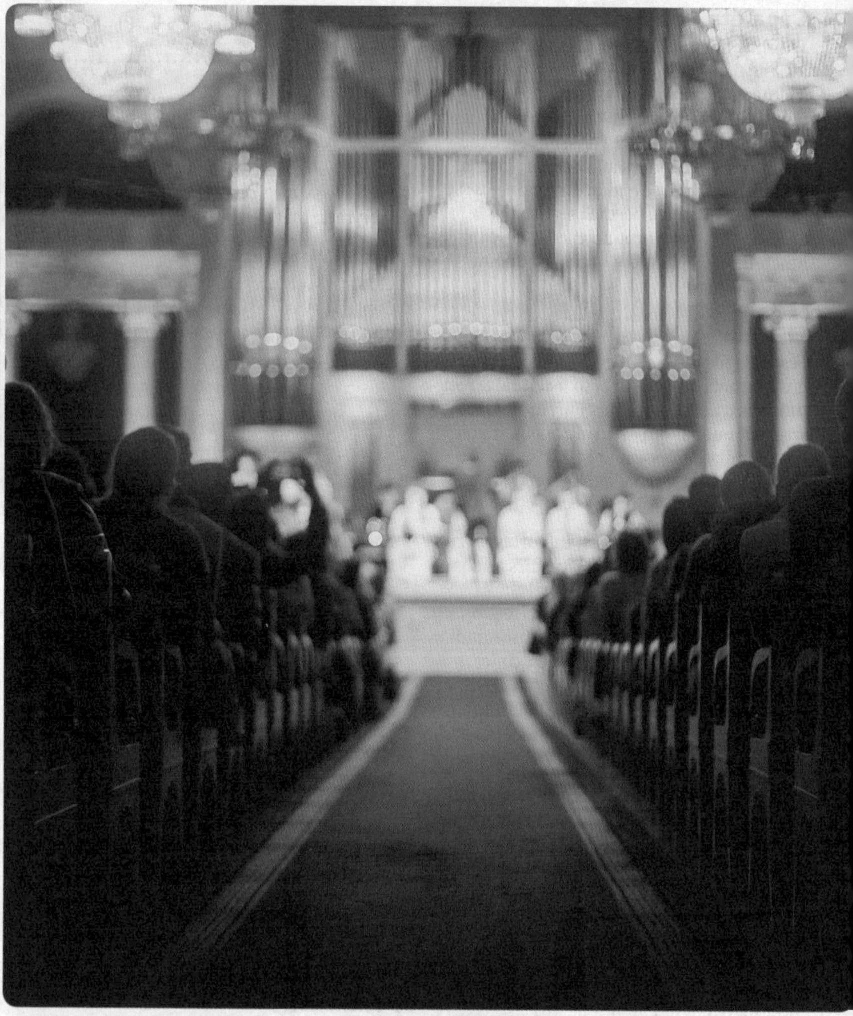

LAPAS77 / SHUTTERSTOCK ©

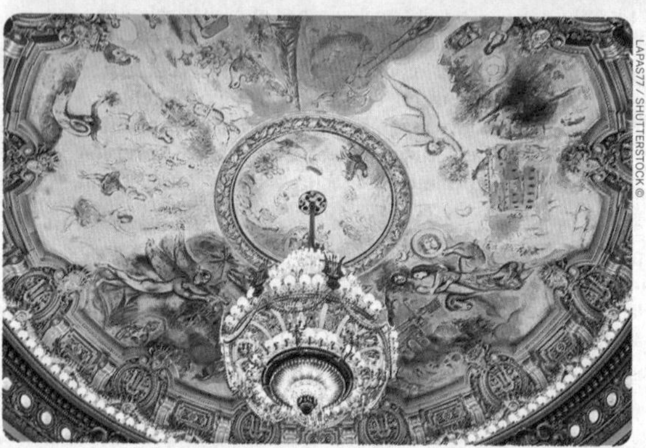

Above: Philharmonie de Paris (p151)
Left: Ceiling of the Palais Garnier (p97), painted by Marc Chagall

WORLD & LATINO

Musiques du monde (world music) has a huge following in Paris, where everything – from Algerian raï and other North African music to Senegalese *mbalax* and West Indian *zouk* – goes at clubs. Many venues have salsa classes.

Cinema

The film-lover's ultimate city, Paris has some wonderful movie houses to catch new flicks, avant-garde cinema and priceless classics.

Foreign films (including English-language films) screened in their original language with French subtitles are labelled 'VO' *(version originale)*. Films labelled 'VF' *(version française)* are dubbed in French. The city's film archive, the Forum des Images (p130), screens films set in Paris.

L'Officiel des Spectacles lists the full crop of Paris' cinematic pickings and screening times; online, check out http://cinema.leparisien.fr.

First-run tickets cost around €11.50 for adults (€13.50 for 3D). Students and over 60s get discounted tickets (usually around €8.50) from 7pm Sunday to 7pm Friday. Discounted tickets for children and teens have no restrictions. Most cinemas have across-the-board discounts before noon.

Opera & Ballet

France's Opéra National de Paris and Ballet de l'Opéra National de Paris perform at Paris' two opera houses, the Palais Garnier (p104) and Opéra Bastille (p191). The season runs between September and July.

Theatre

Theatre productions, including those originally written in other languages, are invariably performed in French. Only occasionally do English-speaking troupes play at smaller venues in and around town. Consult *L'Officiel des Spectacles* (www.offi.fr) for details.

Non-French speakers should check out **Theatre in Paris** (TIP; ☎01 85 08 66 89; www.theatreinparis.com; tickets €20-100; ⊙phone enquiries 10am-7pm Mon-Fri), whose bilingual hosts provide an English-language program and direct you to your seats. Typically there are upwards of 10 shows on offer, from French classics to contemporary comedies and Broadway-style productions with English surtitles. Book via its English online ticketing platform.

Buskers in Paris

Paris' gaggle of clowns, mime artists, living statues, acrobats, in-line skaters, buskers and other street entertainers can be loads of fun and cost substantially less than a theatre ticket (a few coins in the hat is appreciated). Excellent musicians perform in the echo-filled corridors of the metro (artists audition for the privilege). Outside, you can be sure of a good show at the following:

Place Georges Pompidou, 4e The huge square in front of the Centre Pompidou.

Pont St-Louis, 4e The bridge linking Paris' islands.

Pont au Double, 4e The pedestrian bridge linking Notre Dame with the Left Bank.

Place Joachim du Bellay, 1er Musicians and fire-eaters near the Fontaine des Innocents.

Parc de la Villette, 19e African drummers at the weekend.

Place du Tertre, Montmartre, 18e Montmartre's original main square is Paris' busiest busker stage.

Entertainment by Neighbourhood

Champs-Élysées & Grands Boulevards (p103) Famous revues and Paris' palatial 1875-built opera house take top billing here.

Louvre & Les Halles (p130) Swinging jazz clubs, centuries-old theatres and cinemas mix it up with pumping nightclubs.

Montmartre & Northern Paris (p151) Show-stopping cabarets, mythologised concert halls and cutting-edge cultural centres.

Le Marais, Ménilmontant & Belleville (p175) Rockin' live-music venues, old-style *chansons* and arts centres.

Bastille & Eastern Paris (p191) Opera, old-time tea dancing and France's national cinema institute are big drawcards.

Latin Quarter (p217) Swing bands, cinema retrospectives and jam sessions are among the Latin Quarter's offerings.

St-Germain & Les Invalides (p242) Atmospheric cinemas, cultural centres and theatres inhabit this chic, sophisticated neighbourhood.

Montparnasse & Southern Paris (p258) Some of this area's most happening venues are aboard boats moored on the Seine.

Lonely Planet's Top Choices

Palais Garnier (p97) Paris' premier opera house is an artistic inspiration.

Point Éphémère (p151) Ubercool cultural centre on the banks of Canal St-Martin.

Moulin Rouge (p151) The cancan creator razzle-dazzles with spectacular sets, costumes and choreography.

Le 104 (p137) Cultural tour de force in a former funeral parlour.

Café Universel (p217) Brilliant jazz club showcasing a diverse range of styles.

La Seine Musicale (p259) Magnificent 2017-opened concert venue on a Seine island.

Best Cinemas

La Cinémathèque Française (p182) The national cinema institute has a host of cinematic offerings.

Le Louxor (p152) Neo-Egyptian art deco treasure.

Fondation Jérôme Seydoux-Pathé (p259) Black-and-white films accompanied by a live pianist.

Le Champo (p218) Beloved art deco icon screening independent films.

Forum des Images (p130) The Paris film archive.

Le Grand Rex (p129) Art deco landmark with behind-the-scenes tours.

Best Jazz Clubs

Café Universel (p217) Intimate club with unpretentious vibe and no cover.

New Morning (p152) Solid and varied line-up of everything from postbop and Latin to reggae.

Le Baiser Salé (p128) Reputable venue that focuses on Caribbean and Latin sounds.

Sunset & Sunside (p128) Blues, fusion and world sounds, as well as straight-up jazz.

Cave du 38 Riv' (p175) Rue de Rivoli jazz club with concerts and jam sessions.

Best for Rock, Pop & Indie

Le Trianon (p152) Old Montmartre theatre with great acts and an intimate setting.

Le Divan du Monde (p151) Great indie shows in Pigalle.

Cabaret Sauvage (p136) Giant yurt that hosts hip-hop, funk and world concerts.

Bus Palladium (p152) Eclectic rock venue.

La Maroquinerie (p175) Tiny but trendy venue in Ménilmontant with cutting-edge gigs.

Nouveau Casino (p175) Underground and up-to-the-minute acts.

Best for French Chansons

Au Lapin Agile (p152) Legendary Montmartre cabaret.

Chez Louisette (p153) Classic *chansons* at northern Paris' vast flea market.

Le Vieux Belleville (p175) Old-fashioned bistro and *musette* atop Parc de Belleville.

Best for Classical Music

Philharmonie de Paris (p151) Home to the Orchestre de Paris.

La Seine Musicale (p259) Landmark venue with many classical offerings.

Sainte-Chapelle (p200) Unforgettable classical concerts amid jewel-like stained glass.

Maison de la Radio (p91) Top performers recorded live for national radio.

Église St-Eustache (p119) Sunday-afternoon organ concerts.

Église de la Madeleine (p98) Memorable organ recitals.

Best for World & Latino

Favela Chic (p175) Latin, funk and Brazilian pop.

Cabaret Sauvage (p136) From reggae and raï to dance-till-dawn DJ nights.

La Java (p175) Live salsa nights followed by Latin and electro DJs.

La Chapelle des Lombards (p191) Afro jazz, reggae and Latin grooves.

Best for Theatre, Dance & Opera

Palais Garnier (p97) Fabled home of the phantom of the opera, offering an unforgettable experience.

Opéra Bastille (p191) Paris' main, modern opera house, seating an audience of 3400.

Théâtre National de Chaillot (p87) Modern dance.

La Seine Musicale (p259) Ballets, musicals and more.

Galeries Lafayette (p104)

Shopping

Paris has it all: broad boulevards lined with international chains, luxury avenues studded with designer fashion houses, famous grands magasins (department stores) and fabulous markets. But the real charm lies in strolling the city's backstreets, where tiny speciality shops and quirky boutiques selling everything from strawberry-scented wellington boots to heavenly fragranced candles are wedged between cafes, galleries and churches.

NEED TO KNOW

Opening Hours

Generally, shops open 10am to 7pm Monday to Saturday. Smaller shops may shut on Monday and/or close from around noon to 2pm for lunch. Larger stores hold *nocturnes* (late-night shopping), usually on Thursday, until around 10pm. Shops in ZTIs (international tourist zones, eg Le Marais) open late and on Sundays.

Sales

Paris' twice-yearly *soldes* (sales) generally last five to six weeks, starting around mid-January and again around mid-June.

Tax Refunds

Non-EU residents may be eligible for a TVA (*taxe sur la valeur ajoutée*; value-added tax) refund.

Top Shopping Tips

➡ Ring the bell to access ultraexclusive designer boutiques.

➡ Head to a *cabine d'essayage* (fitting room), or check sizes at www.onlineconversion.com/clothing.

➡ Most shops offer free (and very beautiful) gift wrapping – ask for *un paquet cadeau*.

➡ A *ticket de caisse* (receipt) is essential for returning/exchanging an item (within one month of purchase).

Shopping Etiquette

➡ If you're happy browsing, tell sales staff '*Je regarde*' – 'I'm just looking'.

➡ Bargaining is only acceptable at flea markets.

➡ In smaller, exclusive shops, shopkeepers may not appreciate your touching the merchandise until invited to do so.

Parisian Souvenirs

For authentic distinctive and/or nostalgic souvenirs, visit the City of Paris' Paris Rendez-Vous boutique (p176) or online store (http://boutique.paris.fr), which ships worldwide.

At major museums, the Boutiques de Musées (www.boutiquesdemusees.fr) have high-quality replicas and a digital painting-and-frame service: browse masterpieces, choose a frame style and have it mailed to your home.

Fashion

Fashion shopping is Paris' forte. Yet although its well-groomed residents can make the city seem like a giant catwalk, fashion here is foremost about style and quality, rather than status or brand names. A good place to get an overview of Paris fashion is at the famous *grands magasins* such as Le Bon Marché (p244), Galeries Lafayette (p104), Le Printemps (p105) and, from 2019, La Samaritaine (p131).

Tickets for Paris' high-profile *haute couture* and prêt-à-porter fashion shows are like hens' teeth, but you can still see some runway action: reserve ahead to attend free fashion shows (p104) at Galeries Lafayette.

Parisian fashion doesn't have to break the bank: there are fantastic bargains at secondhand and vintage boutiques, along with outlet shops selling previous seasons' collections, and seconds by designers..

Covered Passages

Dating from the 19th century, Paris' glass-roofed *passages couverts* (covered passages) were the precursors to shopping malls and are treasure chests of small, exquisite boutiques. Beautifully preserved arcades include Paris' oldest, **Passage des Panoramas** (Map p372; btwn 10 rue St-Marc & 11 bd Montmartre, 2e; ⏲6am-midnight, shop hrs vary; Ⓜ Grands Boulevards, Richelieu Drouot).

Markets

Not simply places to shop, the city's street markets are social gatherings for the entire neighbourhood, and visiting one will give you a true appreciation of Parisian life.

Nearly every little quarter has its own street market at least once a week (never Monday) where tarpaulin-topped trestle tables bow beneath fresh, cooked and preserved delicacies. *Marchés biologiques* (organic markets) are increasingly sprouting up across the city. Many street markets also sell clothes, accessories, homewares and more. Markets in Paris' more multicultural neighbourhoods are filled with the flavours and aromas of continents beyond Europe.

Bric-a-brac, antiques, retro clothing, jewellery, cheap brand-name clothing, footwear, African carvings, DVDs and electronic items and much more are laid out at the city's flea markets. Watch out for pickpockets!

Above: Passage des Panoramas
Right: Bag from Chanel (p105)

ANDERSPHOTO / SHUTTERSTOCK ©

Shopping by Neighbourhood

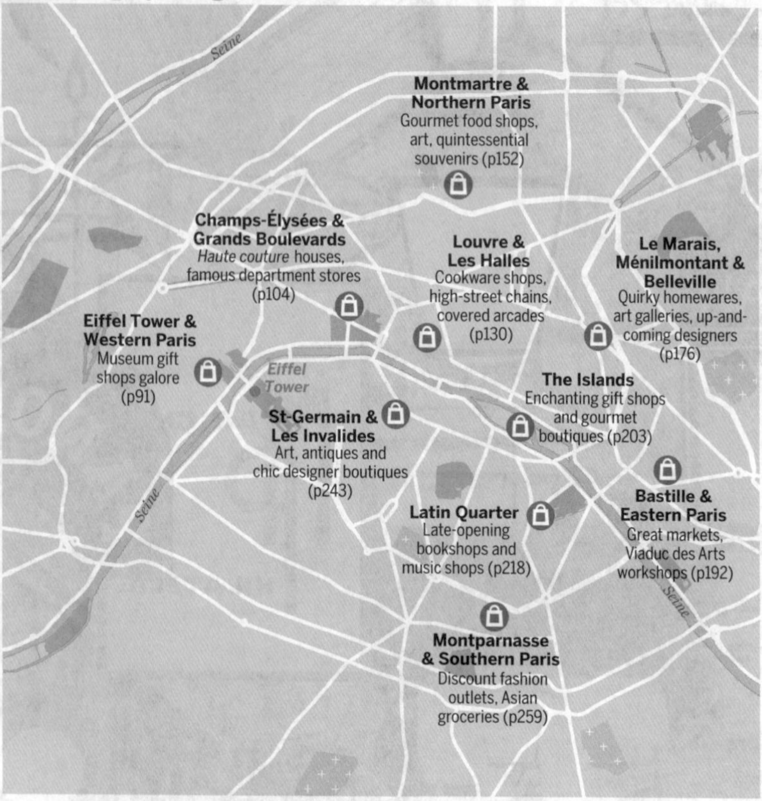

The website https://meslieux.paris.fr/marches lists every market by *arrondissement*, including speciality markets.

Gourmet Goods

Food, wine and tea shops make for mouth-watering shopping. Pastries might not keep, but items you can take home (customs regulations permitting) include light-as-air macarons, chocolates, jams, preserves and, of course, fabulous French cheeses. Many of the best *fromageries* (cheese shops) can provide vacuum packing.

Art, Antiques & Homewares

From venerable antique dealers to edgy art galleries, there's a wealth of places in this artistic city to browse and buy one-off conversation pieces and collectibles.

Paris also has a trove of design shops selling quirky homewares to brighten your living and/or working environment.

Lonely Planet's Top Choices

Bouquinistes (p220) Vintage advertising posters and other treasures along the banks of the Seine.

Le Bonbon au Palais (p219) Artisan sweets from regions throughout France in a geography-classroom-themed boutique.

Didier Ludot (p131) Couture creations of yesteryear.

La Grande Épicerie de Paris (p244) Glorious food emporium.

Magasin Sennelier (p245) Historic art-supply shop with paints, canvases and paraphernalia galore.

Shakespeare & Company (p218) A 'wonderland of books', as Henry Miller described it.

Best Concept Stores

Merci (p176) Fabulously fashionable and unique: all profits go to a children's charity in Madagascar.

Gab & Jo (p243) Stocks only French-made items.

Empreintes (p176) Emporium showcasing some 6000 French artists and designers.

L'Exception (p131) Fashion, homewares, books and more from over 400 French designers.

Hermès (p243) Housed in an art deco ex-swimming pool.

Best for Fashion

Andrea Crews (p176) Bold art and fashion collective.

La Boutique Extraordinaire (p178) Exquisite hand-knitted garments.

Pigalle (p153) Leading Parisian menswear brand.

Mes Demoiselles (p244) Bohemian-influenced women's fashion.

Best Secondhand, Vintage & Discount Boutiques

L'Habilleur (p178) Discount designer wear.

Frivoli (p146) Brand-name cast-offs by the Canal St-Martin.

Kiliwatch (p131) New and used street wear; vintage hats and boots.

Chercheminippes (p245) Several specialist boutiques on one street.

Catherine B (p245) Stocking only Chanel and Hermès vintage pieces.

Best for Kids

Bonton (p178) Vintage-inspired fashion, furnishings and knick-knacks for babies, toddlers and children.

Smallable Concept Store (p244) One-stop shop for babies, children and teens.

Album (p220) Superb collection of *bandes desinées* (graphic novels) and related collectibles.

Finger in the Nose (p244) Streetwise Parisian label for kids.

Les Petits Bla-Blas (p177) *Atelier* (workshop) making children's clothes and offering a personalisation service.

Best Gourmet Shops

La Grande Épicerie de Paris (p244) Now with an outpost on the Right Bank, too.

Place de la Madeleine (p102) Single-item specialist shops and famous emporiums.

La Manufacture de Chocolat (p192) Alain Ducasse's bean-to-bar chocolate factory.

Fromagerie Goncourt (p179) Contemporary *fromagerie* unusually styled like a boutique.

La Dernière Goutte (p243) Wines from small, independent French producers.

Best for Art & Antiques

Marché aux Puces de St-Ouen (p153) One of Europe's largest flea markets, with more than 2500 stalls.

Hôtel Drouot (p104) Famous auction house.

La Maison de Poupée (p244) Adorable antique dolls.

Deyrolle (p242) Historic taxidermist that starred in *Midnight in Paris*.

LGBT Travellers

The city known as 'gay Paree' lives up to its name. Paris is so open that there's less of a defined 'scene' here than in other cities where it's more underground. While Le Marais is the mainstay of gay and lesbian nightlife, you'll find LGBTIQ venues throughout the city attracting a mixed crowd.

Background

Paris was the first European capital to vote in an openly gay mayor when Bertrand Delanoë was elected in 2001. The city itself is very open – same-sex couples commonly display affection in public and checking into a hotel room is unlikely to raise eyebrows. In fact, the only challenge you may have is working out where straight Paris ends and gay Paris starts, as the city is so stylish and sexy.

In 2013 France became the 13th country in the world to legalise same-sex marriage (and adoption by same-sex couples), and polls show that the majority of French citizens support marriage equality. Typically, at least one partner needs to be a resident to get married here. And, of course, there's no end of romantic places to propose.

Drinking & Nightlife

Le Marais, especially the areas around the intersection of rue Ste-Croix de la Bretonnerie and rue des Archives, and eastwards to rue Vieille du Temple, has long been Paris' main centre of gay nightlife and is still the epicentre of gay and lesbian life in Paris. There's also a handful of bars and clubs within walking distance of bd de Sébastopol. The lesbian scene is less prominent than its gay counterpart, and centres on a few cafes and bars, particularly along rue des Écouffes. Bars and clubs are generally all gay- and lesbian-friendly.

Events

By far the biggest event on the gay and lesbian calendar is Gay Pride Day, in late June, when the annual **Marche des Fiertés** (Gay Pride March; www.gaypride.fr; ⏲Jun or Jul) through Paris via Le Marais provides a colourful spectacle, and plenty of parties take place.

Year-round, check gay and lesbian websites or ask at gay bars and other venues to find out about events.

Organisations & Resources

Centre LGBT Paris-Île de France (Map p386; ☎01 43 57 21 47; www.centrelgbtparis.org; 63 rue Beaubourg, 3e; ⏲centre & bar 3.30-8pm Mon-Fri, 1-7pm Sat, library 6-8pm Mon-Wed, 5-7pm Fri & Sat; Ⓜ Rambuteau) is the single best source of information for gay and lesbian travellers in Paris, with a large library of books and periodicals and a sociable bar. It also has details of hotlines, helplines, gay and gay-friendly medical services and politically oriented activist associations.

Guided Tours

For an insider's perspective of gay life in Paris and recommendations on where to eat, drink, sightsee and party, take a tour with the **Gay Locals** (www.thegaylocals.com; 3hr tour from €180, 2½hr gay or lesbian bar crawl €50). English-speaking residents lead tours of Le Marais as well as private tours of other popular neighbourhoods and customised tours based on your interests.

Lonely Planet's Top Choices

Open Café (p173) The wide terrace is prime for talent-watching.

Gibus Club (p173) One of Paris' biggest gay parties.

La Champmeslé (p128) Cabaret nights, fortune-telling and art exhibitions attract an older lesbian crowd.

Best Weekend in Le Marais

Loustic (p172) Among the best coffee (and espresso-bar interior design) in town.

Place des Vosges (p160) Charming city square.

Broken Arm (p165) Fresh juice- and salad-driven cafe adjoining an achingly cool concept store.

Cimetière du Père Lachaise (p157) Oscar Wilde's winged-angel-topped tomb is a highlight.

La Belle Hortense (p171) Creative wine bar with modish mixed crowd and shelves of books.

Derrière (p166) Play ping-pong between courses at this stellar restaurant.

Best Shopping Sprees

Samuel Coraux (p178) Fabulous and occasionally outrageously kitsch creations for guys 'n' gals by one of Paris' funkiest jewellery designers.

État Libre d'Orange (p178) Perfumery that screams Marais hipster, with scents bearing names like Fat Electrician, Jasmin et Cigarette, and Delicious Closet Queen.

L'Éclaireur (p177) Part art space, part lounge and part deconstructionist fashion statement; fashion for men and women.

Best Apéros

L'Étoile Manquante (p173) Trendy, gay-friendly bar with retro interior and fabulous pavement terrace for obligatory after-work drinks.

Open Café (p173) With a four-hour happy hour kicking off daily at 6pm, how can you possibly go wrong?

Le Raidd (p173) Has a laid-back lounge-style ground-floor bar.

Best Gay Hang-Outs

Café Cox (p173) The meeting place for an interesting (and interested) cruisy crowd throughout the evening, from dusk onward.

Le Raidd (p173) Upstairs is a pulsating den of DJs, dancing, themed parties, raunchy shower shows…

Café Voulez-Vous (p173) Sassy New York–styled gay bar and lounge with a mellow vibe.

Best Lesbian Hang-Outs

3w Kafé (p173) Flagship cocktail bar–pub.

La Champmeslé (p128) A fixture on Paris' lesbian scene since the '70s.

Le Tango (p173) Mingle with a mixed and cosmopolitan gay and lesbian crowd.

Best Clubs

Open Café (p173) The only place to be late on a Saturday night.

Le Tango (p173) Set in a historic 1930s dancehall.

Gibus Club (p173) Get ready to party.

Best Party Spots Beyond Le Marais

Ménilmontant (p172) Edgy urban cool.

Pigalle (p148) Montmartre's sexy southern neighbour.

Champs-Élysées (p103) Glam bars and clubs.

Bastille (p189) Lively local vibe.

Canal St-Martin (p148) Arty, indie venues.

Belleville (p172) Increasingly hip, multicultural 'hood.

Parks & Activities

As Paris gears up to host the 2024 Summer Olympics and Summer Paralympics, you'll find increasing opportunities to watch spectator sports or take part yourself. To unwind with the Parisians, check out the city's green spaces, where you can thwack a tennis ball, stroll in style, admire art, or break out some wine and cheese.

Parks

For apartment-dwelling Parisians, the city's parks act as communal backyards. Popular inner-city spaces include the enchanting Jardin du Luxembourg (p228), stately Jardin des Tuileries (p118) and elegant Parc Monceau (p137), as well as the sprawling botanical gardens, greenhouses and museums that make up the Jardin des Plantes (p208). The city's two forests, the western Bois de Boulogne (p89) and eastern Bois de Vincennes (p183), offer easy escapes from the concrete into nature.

Spectator Sports

Paris hosts a great variety of sporting events throughout the year, from the French Open and Paris Masters to local football matches. There's a handful of stadiums in and around the city; for upcoming events, click on Sports & Games (under the Going Out menu) at http://en.parisinfo.com. If you can read French, sports daily *L'Équipe* (www.lequipe.fr) will provide more depth.

PARIS TEAMS

Local teams include football's Paris Saint-Germain (www.psg.fr) and rugby's sky-blue-and-white-dressed Racing 92 (www.racing92.fr) and pink-clad Stade Français Paris (www.stade.fr). Catch France's national football team, Les Bleus (www.fff.fr), at the Stade de France.

HORSE RACING

The city's three horse-racing tracks can make for a thrilling afternoon. The Hippodrome d'Auteuil and the Hippodrome de Longchamp are in the Bois de Boulogne; the Hippodrome de Paris-Vincennes is in the Bois de Vincennes. Every October the Prix de l'Arc de Triomphe (www.prixarcdetriomphe.com), Europe's most prestigious horse race, is held at the Hippodrome de Longchamp.

Cycling

Everyone knows that the Tour de France races up the Champs-Élysées at the end of July every year, but you don't need Chris Froome's leg muscles to enjoy Paris on two wheels. Between the Paris bike-share scheme Vélib' (p334), and the hundreds of kilometres of urban bike paths, cycling around the city has never been easier. Sign up for one of the great city bike tours (p336) or hire a bike yourself (p334). Some streets are closed to vehicle traffic on Sundays – great news for cyclists! Bring your own helmet.

Skating

The next most popular activity after cycling has to be skating, whether on the street or on ice. Rent a pair of in-line skates at Nomadeshop (p179) and join the Friday-evening skate, **Pari Roller** (Map p412; www.pari-roller.com; place Raoul Dautry, 14e; ⏲10pm-1am Fri, arrive 9.30pm; Ⓜ Montparnasse Bienvenüe) FREE, that zooms through the Paris streets, or join the more laid-back Sunday-afternoon skate, Rollers & Coquillages (p179).

During the winter holidays several temporary outdoor rinks are installed around Paris. Venues change from year to year; check www.paris.fr for locations.

Hammams & Spas

Whether you want to hobnob with the stars at a *spa de luxe* or get a *savon noir* (black soap) exfoliation at the neighbourhood *hammam* (Turkish steambath), Paris has spaces to suit every whim.

A *hammam* generally charges an entrance fee, which grants you admission to a steam bath and sauna. Extras – exfoliation scrubs, orange-blossom massages, and mint tea and North African pastries – are tacked onto the initial price (but they're worth it!). Most *hammams* are primarily for women; if men are admitted it's usually only once or twice a week, and only rarely at the same time as women.

Swimming

If you plan to go swimming at either your hotel or in a public pool, you'll need to don a *bonnet de bain* (bathing cap) – even if you don't have any hair. You shouldn't need to buy one ahead of time as they are generally sold at most pools. Men are required to wear skin-tight trunks (Speedos); loose-fitting Bermuda shorts are not allowed.

Boules

You'll often see groups of earnest Parisians playing *boules* (France's most popular traditional game, similar to lawn bowls) in the Jardin du Luxembourg and other parks and squares with suitably flat, shady patches of gravel. The Arènes de Lutèce (p209) *boulodrome* in a 2nd-century Roman amphitheatre in the Latin Quarter is a fabulous spot to absorb the scene. There are usually places to play at Paris Plages (p75).

NEED TO KNOW

Resources

The city-hall website (www.paris.fr/sport) has info on everything from skating and badminton to stadiums and equipment rental. Also useful is http://quefaire.paris.fr/sports, which lists venues for underground football and climbing, and has info on swimming pools open at night and other activities.

Tickets

Tickets for big events can generally be purchased through the venue's website. Reserve well in advance, before you leave for Paris. If you want to try your luck, head to the box office at a Fnac store (www.fnac.com; follow the Magasins link to locate a branch near you).

Parks & Activities by Neighbourhood

Eiffel Tower & Western Paris (p89) Escape to the Bois de Boulogne.

Louvre & Les Halles (p118) Superb vistas unfold from the elegant Jardin des Tuileries.

Montmartre & Northern Paris (p136) Large parks include beautiful Parc Monceau, hilly Parc des Buttes Chaumont and futuristic Parc de la Villette.

Le Marais, Ménilmontant & Belleville (p179) Departure point for in-line skating.

Bastille & Eastern Paris (p183) The expansive Bois de Vincennes, Parc Floral and a host of other great parks.

Latin Quarter (p208) Stroll the Jardin des Plantes.

St-Germain & Les Invalides (p228) Home to the city's most iconic swath of green, the Jardin du Luxembourg.

Montparnasse & Southern Paris (p261) The rails-to-trails Petite Ceinture, Parc Montsouris and unique swimming pools.

The Seine's quays

The Seine

The lifeline of Paris, the Seine sluices through the city, spanned by 37 bridges. Its Unesco World Heritage–listed riverbanks offer picturesque promenades, parks, activities and events, including summertime beaches. After dark, watch the river dance with the watery reflections of city lights and tourist-boat flood lamps.

Riverbank Rejuvenation

The Seine's *berges* (banks) were reborn with the 2013 creation of the completely car-free 2.3km stretch of the Left Bank (p233) from the Pont de l'Alma to the Musée d'Orsay (linked to the water's edge by a grand staircase that doubles as amphitheatre seating). This innovative promenade is dotted with restaurants and bars (some aboard boats), and there are ball-game courts, a skate ramp, a kids' climbing wall, a 100m running track and floating gardens on 1800 sq metres of artificial islands. Temporary events as diverse as film screenings and knitting workshops take place throughout the year.

In 2017 the city of Paris followed up this success by banishing cars on the Right Bank (p160) for 3.3km between the Tuileries and Henry IV tunnels, creating cycle and walking paths, *pétanque* and other sporting facilities, along with kids' play areas, restaurants and bars, and some nifty audiovisual 'timescope' binoculars covering the city's history.

Promenading & Pausing

The Seine's riverbanks are where Parisians come to cycle, jog, in-line skate and stroll; staircases along the banks lead down to the water's edge.

Particularly picturesque spots for a riverside promenade include the areas around Paris' two elegant inner-city islands, the Île de la Cité and Île Saint-Louis. Up at street level, the city's Right and Left Banks are lined with the distinctive green-metal bouquiniste (p220) stalls selling antiquarian books, sheet music and old advertising posters.

A lesser-known island stroll is the artificial Île aux Cygnes (p249) via its tree-shaded walkway, the Allée des Cygnes. Walking from west to east gives you a stunning view of the Eiffel Tower.

The river also acts as a giant backyard for apartment-dwelling Parisians. All along its banks you'll find locals reading, picnicking, canoodling or just basking in the sunshine. Among the best-loved spots is the tiny triangular park Square du Vert-Galant (p201) beneath the Pont Neuf.

Summertime Beaches

Each summer, the **Paris Plages** (Paris Beaches; www.paris.fr; ⏲mid-Jul–mid-Aug) see *pétanque* (a variant on the game of bowls), pop-up bars and cafes, sun lounges, parasols, water fountains and sprays line the river from around mid-July to mid-August (exact dates vary from year to year).

The Paris Plages were established in 2002 for Parisians who couldn't escape to the coast to cool off in the summer months. They now typically cover the square in front of the Hôtel de Ville, 1km along the Right Bank (from the Pont des Arts to the Pont de Sully) and the quays by the Bassin de la Villette in the 19e, featuring clean water-zoned swimming pools from 2017.

Although swimming is otherwise banned in the waterways due to maritime traffic and water quality, it's hoped the Seine will host open-water swimming events during the 2024 Summer Olympics.

NEED TO KNOW

Water's edge There are no fences or barriers. Keep a close eye on children to ensure they don't take an unexpected plunge.

Stair safety Stairs leading to the water can be especially slippery after rain.

Flooding In the event of flooding, heed warning signs and stay well back from the water as currents can be strong.

Seine-Side Entertainment

In addition to riverside park activities, entertainment options include nightclubs aboard boats moored in southern Paris, such as the red-metal tugboat Le Batofar (p259) and France's first club to hold a 24-hour licence, Concrete (p189), and a floating swimming pool, Piscine Joséphine Baker (p261).

On the banks, riverside venues include Les Docks (p251), which incorporates vast outdoor terraces, bars, clubs and restaurants.

River Cruises & Tours

The best way to become acquainted with the Seine is to take a cruise along its waters. A plethora of companies run day- and night-time boat tours (p339), usually lasting around an hour, with commentary in multiple languages. Many cruise companies also offer brunch, lunch and dinner cruises.

An alternative to traditional boat tours is the Batobus (p335), a handy hop-on, hop-off service that stops at quintessentially Parisian attractions: the Eiffel Tower, Champs-Élysées, Musée d'Orsay, Musée du Louvre, St-Germain des Prés, Hôtel de Ville, Notre Dame and Jardin des Plantes. Single- and multiday tickets allow you to spend as long as you like sightseeing between stops.

Explore Paris

PARIS' TOP SIGHTS

Left: Arc de Triomphe

Neighbourhoods at a Glance

❶ Eiffel Tower & Western Paris p80

Home to very well-heeled Parisians, this grande dame of a neighbourhood is where you can get up close and personal with the city's symbolic tower as well as more contemporary architecture in the high-rise business district of La Défense just outside the *périphérique* (ring road) encircling central Paris.

❷ Champs-Élysées & Grands Boulevards p92

Baron Haussmann famously reshaped the Parisian cityscape around the Arc de Triomphe, from which 12 avenues radiate like the spokes of a wheel, including the glamorous Champs-Élysées. To its east are gourmet shops garlanding the Église de la Madeleine and the Grands Boulevards' art nouveau department stores.

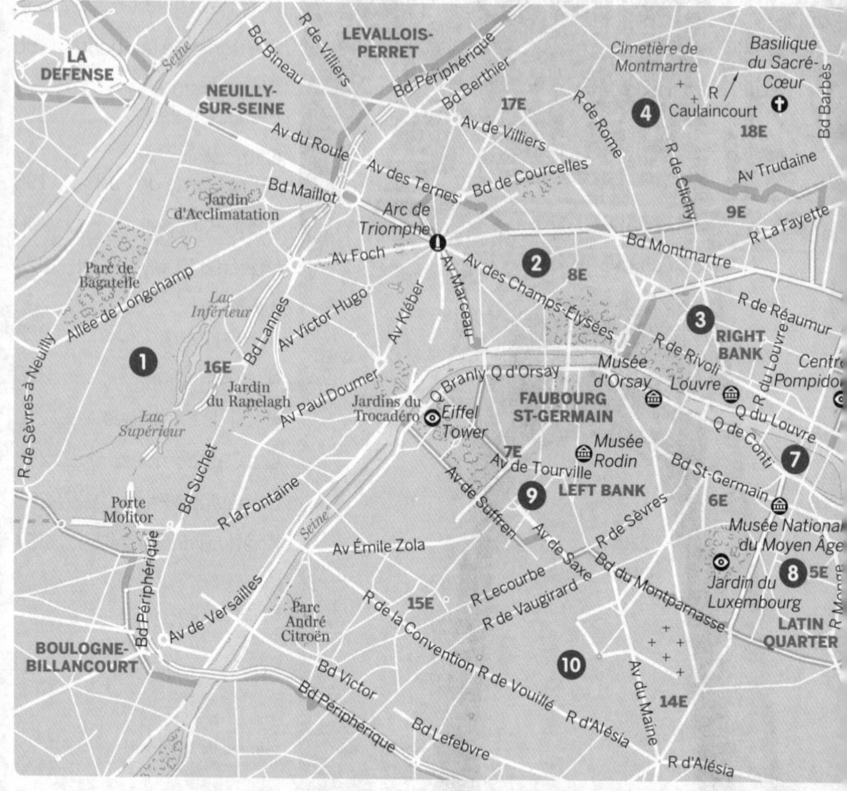

❸ Louvre & Les Halles p106

Paris' splendid line of monuments, the *axe historique* (historic axis; also called the grand axis), passes through the Tuileries gardens before reaching IM Pei's glass pyramid at the entrance to the world's most visited museum, the Louvre. Nearby, the Forum des Halles shopping mall and park has recently emerged from a much-needed makeover.

❹ Montmartre & Northern Paris p132

Montmartre's lofty views, wine-producing vines and hidden village squares have lured painters since the 19th century. Crowned by the Sacré-Cœur basilica, Montmartre is the city's steepest quarter, and its slinking streets lined with crooked ivy-clad buildings retain a fairy-tale charm. The grittier neighbourhoods of Pigalle and Canal St-Martin are hotbeds of creativity with a trove of hip drinking, dining and shopping addresses.

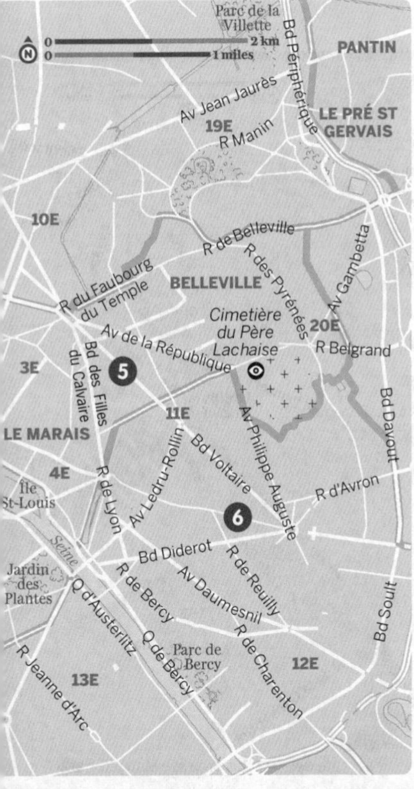

❺ Le Marais, Ménilmontant & Belleville p154

Fashionable bars and restaurants, emerging designers' boutiques, and thriving gay and Jewish communities all squeeze into Le Marais' narrow medieval lanes. Neighbouring Ménilmontant has some of the city's most happening nightlife, while hilly Belleville is vibrant and multicultural.

❻ Bastille & Eastern Paris p180

Fabulous markets, intimate bistros and cutting-edge drinking and dancing venues make this neighbourhood one of the best places to discover the Parisians' Paris.

❼ The Islands p193

Paris' geographic and spiritual heart is here in the Seine. The larger of the two inner-city islands, the Île de la Cité, is dominated by the magnificent Notre Dame cathedral. Serene little Île St-Louis is graced with charming eateries and boutiques.

❽ Latin Quarter p205

So named because international students communicated in Latin here until the French Revolution, it remains Paris' hub of academic life. This lively area is also home to museums and churches, plus a beautiful art deco mosque and botanic gardens.

❾ St-Germain & Les Invalides p222

Literary buffs, antique collectors and fashionistas flock to this legendary part of Paris, where the presence of writers such as Sartre, de Beauvoir and Hemingway still lingers in historic cafes.

❿ Montparnasse & Southern Paris p246

Fabled Montparnasse has brasseries from its mid-20th-century heyday and re-energised backstreets buzz with local life. It is the premium *arrondissement* for edgy street art.

Eiffel Tower & Western Paris

Neighbourhood Top Five

❶ **Eiffel Tower** (p82) Ascending the icon at dusk to watch its sparkling lights blink across Paris.

❷ **Musée du Quai Branly** (p84) Finding inspiration in traditional art and craftmanship from around the world.

❸ **Cité de l'Architecture et du Patrimoine** (p85) Wandering past cathedral portals, gargoyles and intricate scale models in this standout museum dedicated to French architecture.

❹ **Bois de Boulogne** (p89) Exploring western Paris' oasis of greenery: from bike rides, rowing boats and horse races to an amusement park kids will adore!

❺ **Musée Marmottan Monet** (p86) Taking a trip to see the world's largest collection of Monet canvases, alongside other impressionist and postimpressionist painters.

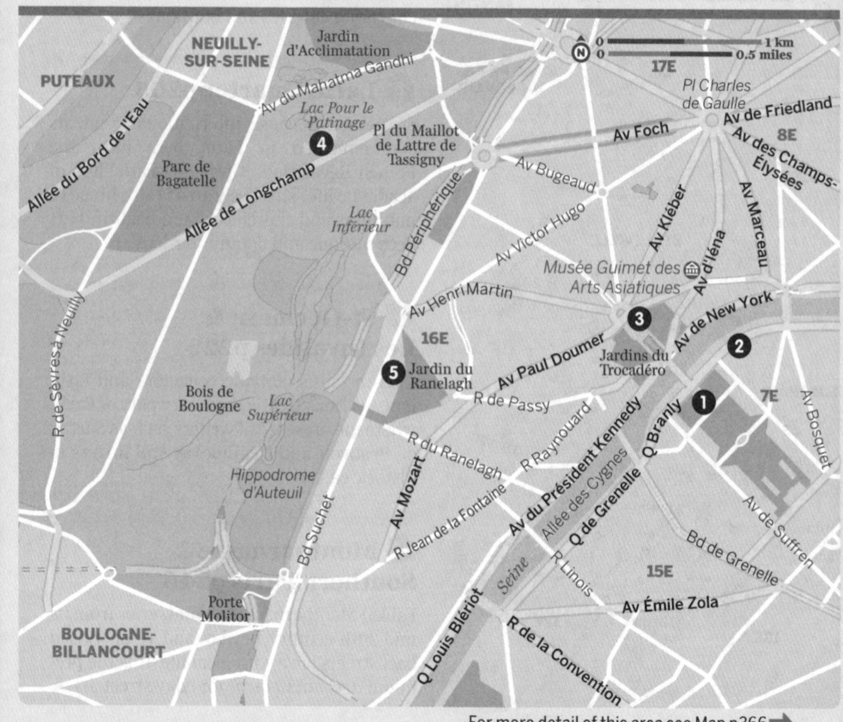

For more detail of this area see Map p366

Explore Paris

With its hourly sparkles that illuminate the evening skyline, the Eiffel Tower (p82) needs no introduction. Ascending to its viewing platforms will offer you a panorama over the whole of Paris, with the prestigious neighbourhood of Passy (the 16e *arrondissement*) stretching along the far banks of the Seine to the west. In the 18th and 19th centuries, Passy was home to luminaries such as Benjamin Franklin and Balzac. Defined by its sober, elegant buildings from the Haussmann era, it was only annexed to the city in 1860.

While the Eiffel Tower is the area's highlight, Passy is also home to some fabulous museums, and culture fans will be busy. There's the Musée Marmottan Monet (p86); the hip Palais de Tokyo (p85), with modern art installations; the Musée Guimet des Arts Asiatiques (p87); the underrated Cité de l'Architecture et du Patrimoine (p85), with captivating sculptures and murals; and a host of smaller collections devoted to fashion, anthropology and even wine. On the Left Bank is the prominent Musée du Quai Branly (p84), with art and culture from outside Europe, while at the city's western edge is the leafy refuge of the Bois de Boulogne (p89). Beyond this lies the business district of La Défense.

Local Life

➡ **Museum hopping** Parisians flock to this part of town for its fine museums.

➡ **Green space** Leafy Bois de Boulogne is where locals escape for cycling, skating or *footing* (jogging).

➡ **Morning commute** More than 150,000 people squeeze onto trains to La Défense, the city's business district, where skyscrapers rub shoulders with modern art.

Getting There & Away

➡ **Metro** Line 6 runs south from Charles de Gaulle–Étoile past the Eiffel Tower (views are superb from the elevated section); line 9 runs southwest from the Champs-Élysées. Line 1 terminates at La Défense.

➡ **RER** RER A runs west past La Défense; RER C runs east–west along the Left Bank, with a stop at the Eiffel Tower.

➡ **Bus** Scenic bus 69 runs from the Champ de Mars (Eiffel Tower) along the Left Bank, crosses the Seine at the Louvre, and continues east to Père Lachaise.

➡ **Bicycle** Handy Vélib' stations include 2 av Octave Creard (for the Eiffel Tower) and 3 av Bosquet (for Musée du Quai Branly).

➡ **Boat** Batobus (p336) has an Eiffel Tower stop.

Lonely Planet's Top Tip

There are excellent top-end restaurants in the 16e, but it is substantially more affordable – and fun in nice weather – to follow the local flock and picnic. Build your own feast with sweet and savoury goodies from *boulangeries* (bakeries), markets, speciality food shops or takeaway delis.

Best Places to Eat

➡ L'Astrance (p89)

➡ Arnaud Nicolas (p88)

➡ Le Jules Verne (p83)

➡ Atelier Vivanda (p88)

➡ Bustronome (p90)

For reviews, see p88 ➡

Best Places to Drink

➡ St James Paris (p90)

➡ Bô Zinc Café (p90)

➡ Frog XVI (p90)

For reviews, see p90 ➡

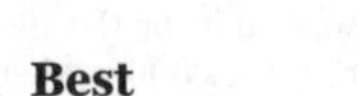

Best Museums

➡ Musée du Quai Branly (p84)

➡ Cité de l'Architecture et du Patrimoine (p85)

➡ Musée Marmottan Monet (p86)

➡ Musée Guimet des Arts Asiatiques (p87)

➡ Palais de Tokyo (p85)

➡ Musée Yves Saint Laurent (p85)

For reviews, see p84 

TRAVELMAMA / BUDGET TRAVEL ©

TOP SIGHT
EIFFEL TOWER

There are different ways to experience the Eiffel Tower, from an evening ascent amid twinkling lights to a meal in one of its two restaurants. And even though some 6.2 million people come annually, few would dispute that each visit is unique – and something that simply has to be done when in Paris.

Metal Asparagus

Named after its designer, Gustave Eiffel, the Tour Eiffel was built for the 1889 Exposition Universelle (World's Fair). It took 300 workers, 2.5 million rivets and two years of nonstop labour to assemble. Upon completion the tower became the tallest human-made structure in the world (324m or 1063ft) – a record held until the completion of the Chrysler Building in New York (1930). A symbol of the modern age, it faced massive opposition from Paris' artistic and literary elite, and the 'metal asparagus', as some Parisians snidely called it, was originally slated to be torn down in 1909. It was spared only because it proved an ideal platform for the transmitting antennas needed for the newfangled science of radiotelegraphy.

1st Floor

Of the tower's three floors, the 1st (57m) has the most space but the least impressive views. The glass-enclosed **Pavillon Ferrié** – open since summer 2014 – houses an immersion film along with a small cafe and souvenir shop, while the outer walkway features a discovery circuit to help visitors learn more about the tower's ingenious design. Check out the sections of glass flooring that proffer a dizzying view of the antlike people walking on the ground far below.

DON'T MISS

- 2nd-floor panorama
- Top-floor Champagne bar

PRACTICALITIES

- Map p366, F5
- ☎08 92 70 12 39
- www.toureiffel.paris
- Champ de Mars, 5 av Anatole France, 7e
- adult/child lift to top €25/6.30, lift to 2nd fl €16/4, stairs to 2nd fl €10/2.50
- ⏰lifts & stairs 9am-12.45am mid-Jun–Aug, lifts 9.30am-11.45pm, stairs 9.30am-6.30pm Sep–mid-Jun
- Ⓜ Bir Hakeim or RER Champ de Mars–Tour Eiffel

This level also hosts the restaurant **58 Tour Eiffel** (Map p366; ☎01 76 70 04 86; www.restaurants-toureiffel.com; menus lunch €37.20, dinner €93.70-113.70; ⊙11.30am-4.30pm & 6.30-11pm; ⓥ ⓗ).

Not all lifts stop at the 1st floor (check before ascending), but it's an easy walk down from the 2nd floor should you accidentally end up one floor too high.

2nd Floor

Views from the 2nd floor (115m) are the best – impressively high but still close enough to see the details of the city below. Telescopes and panoramic maps placed around the tower pinpoint locations in Paris and beyond. Story windows give an overview of the lifts' mechanics, and the vision well allows you to gaze through glass panels to the ground. Also up here are toilets, a souvenir shop and the Michelin-starred restaurant **Jules Verne** (Map p366; ☎01 45 55 61 44; www.lejulesverne-paris.com; 5-/6-course menus €190/230, 3-course lunch menu €105; ⊙noon-1.30pm & 7-9.30pm).

Top Floor

Views from the wind-buffeted top floor (276m) stretch up to 60km on a clear day, though at this height the panoramas are more sweeping than detailed. Celebrate your ascent with a glass of bubbly (€13 to €22) from the Champagne bar (open noon to 5.15pm and 6.15pm to 10.45pm). Afterwards peep into Gustave Eiffel's restored top-level office where lifelike wax models of Eiffel and his daughter Claire greet Thomas Edison.

To access the top floor, take a separate lift on the 2nd floor (closed during heavy winds).

Ticket Purchases & Queueing Strategies

Ascend as far as the 2nd floor (either on foot or by lift), from where it is lift-only to the top floor. Pushchairs must be folded in lifts and you are not allowed to take bags or backpacks larger than aeroplane-cabin size.

Buying tickets in advance online usually means you avoid the monumental queues at the ticket offices. Print your ticket or show it on a smartphone screen. If you can't reserve your tickets ahead of time, expect waits of well over an hour in high season.

Stair tickets can't be reserved online. They are sold at the south pillar, where the staircase can also be accessed: the climb consists of 360 steps to the 1st floor and another 360 steps to the 2nd floor.

If you have reservations for either restaurant, you are granted direct access to the lifts.

MAN ON WIRE

In 1989 tightrope artist Philippe Petit walked up an inclined 700m cable across the Seine, from Palais Chaillot to the Eiffel Tower's 2nd floor. The act, performed before an audience of 250,000 people, was held to commemorate the French Republic's bicentennial.

Every hour on the hour, the entire tower sparkles for five minutes with 20,000 6-watt lights. They were first installed for Paris' millennium celebration in 2000 – it took 25 mountain climbers five months to install the current bulbs and 40km of electrical cords. For the best view of the light show, head across the Seine to the Jardins du Trocadéro.

PAINT

Slapping a fresh coat of paint on the tower is no easy feat. It takes a 25-person team 18 months to complete the 60-tonnes-of-paint task, redone every seven years. Painted red and bronze since 1968, it's had six different colours throughout its lifetime, including yellow.

VENIAMIN KRASKOV / SHUTTERSTOCK ©

TOP SIGHT
MUSÉE DU QUAI BRANLY

No other museum in Paris provides such inspiration for travellers, armchair anthropologists and those who simply appreciate the beauty of traditional craftwork. A tribute to the incredible diversity of human culture, the Musée du Quai Branly presents an overview of indigenous and folk art from around the world.

Divided into four main sections (Oceania, Asia, Africa and the Americas) the museum showcases an impressive array of masks, carvings, weapons, jewellery and more, all displayed in a refreshingly unique interior without rooms or high walls. Although its sheer vastness can be intimidating, there are numerous aids on hand to help you navigate the collection and delve deeper into particular sections. Strategically placed multimedia touch screens provide more context for certain pieces, while tailored walks (available online and upon request at the entrance) focus on specific themes, from masks and funerary objects to jewellery and musical instruments.

Highlights to look out for include remarkable carvings from Papua New Guinea (Oceania); clothing, jewellery and textiles from ethnic groups from India to Vietnam (Asia); an impressively diverse collection of masks (Africa); and artefacts from the great American civilisations – the Mayas, Aztecs and Incas.

Must-sees include temporary exhibits and performances, which are generally excellent.

DON'T MISS

- The Papua New Guinea collection, Oceania
- The Evenk shaman cloak, Asia (Siberia)
- West African masks, Africa
- The grizzly totem pole, Americas

PRACTICALITIES

- Map p366, G4
- 01 56 61 70 00
- www.quaibranly.fr
- 37 quai Branly, 7e
- adult/child €10/free
- 11am-7pm Tue, Wed & Sun, 11am-9pm Thu-Sat
- Alma Marceau or RER Pont de l'Alma

SIGHTS

The Eiffel Tower may get top billing here, but it's the incredible assortment of museums that ensures you'll be a repeat visitor. Most destinations are found on the Right Bank of the Seine, with stars such as the Musée Guimet, Cité de l'Architecture and Palais de Tokyo mixed in with smaller attractions, such as the Musée Yves Saint Laurent. Further west is the Musée Marmottan Monet and the leafy expanse of the Bois de Boulogne. Paris' business district is also located in the western suburbs. Begun in the 1950s, La Défense is the only place in Paris where you'll see skyscrapers.

EIFFEL TOWER LANDMARK

See p82.

MUSÉE DU QUAI BRANLY MUSEUM

See p84.

MUSÉE YVES SAINT LAURENT PARIS MUSEUM

Map p366 (01 44 31 64 00; www.museeyslparis.com; 5 av Marceau, 16e; adult/child €10/7; 11am-6pm Tue-Thu, Sat & Sun, to 9pm Fri; M Alma-Marceau) Housed in the legendary designer's studios (1974–2002), this museum holds retrospectives of YSL's avant-garde designs, from early sketches to finished pieces. Temporary exhibitions give an insight into the creative process of designing a *haute couture* collection and the history of fashion throughout the 20th century. The building can only accommodate a small number of visitors at a time, so buy tickets online or expect to queue outside.

MUSÉE D'ART MODERNE DE LA VILLE DE PARIS GALLERY

Map p366 (01 53 67 40 00; www.mam.paris.fr; 11 av du Président Wilson, 16e; 10am-6pm Tue, Wed, Fri-Sun, 10am-10pm Thu; M Iéna) FREE The permanent collection at Paris' modern-art museum displays works representative of just about every major artistic movement of the 20th and (nascent) 21st centuries, with works by Modigliani, Matisse, Braque and Soutine. The real jewel, though, is the room hung with canvases by Dufy and Bonnard. Look out for cutting-edge temporary exhibitions (not free).

PALAIS DE TOKYO GALLERY

Map p366 (01 81 97 35 88; www.palaisdetokyo.com; 13 av du Président Wilson, 16e; adult/child €12/free; noon-midnight Wed-Mon; M Iéna) The Tokyo Palace, created for the 1937 Exposition Internationale des Arts et

TOP SIGHT
CITÉ DE L'ARCHITECTURE ET DU PATRIMOINE

In the eastern wing of the Palais de Chaillot, directly across from the Eiffel Tower, is this standout museum devoted to French architecture and heritage. The burgundy walls and skylit rooms showcase 350 plaster casts taken from the country's greatest monuments, a collection whose seeds were sown following the desecration of many buildings during the French Revolution.

Some of the original details from which the casts were made, such as sculptures from the Reims Cathedral, were later destroyed in the wars that followed. Although they're not in situ, wandering through such a magnificent collection of church portals, gargoyles, and saints and sinners from around France is an incomparable experience for anyone interested in the elemental stories that craftspeople chose to preserve in stone.

On display on the upper floors are reproduced murals and stained-glass windows from some of France's most important monuments, which are arranged in an intriguing labyrinthine layout. One of the most beautiful reproductions in this section is the Cathédrale of St-Etienne cupola.

DON'T MISS

- Casts Gallery
- Murals and Stained-Glass Galleries
- Cathédrale of St-Étienne cupola

PRACTICALITIES

- Map p366, E4
- www.citechaillot.fr
- 1 place du Trocadéro et du 11 Novembre, 16e
- adult/child €8/free
- 11am-7pm Wed & Fri-Sun, to 9pm Thu
- M Trocadéro

Techniques dans la Vie Moderne (International Exposition of Art and Technology in Modern Life), has no permanent collection. Instead, its shell-like interior of concrete and steel is a stark backdrop to interactive contemporary-art exhibitions and installations. Its bookshop is fabulous for art and design magazines, and its eating and drinking options are magic.

PARC DU CHAMP DE MARS PARK

Map p366 (Champ de Mars, 7e; MÉcole Militaire or RER Champ de Mars–Tour Eiffel) Running southeast from the Eiffel Tower, the grassy Champ de Mars – an ideal summer picnic spot – was originally used as a parade ground for the cadets of the 18th-century **École Militaire**, the vast French-classical building at the southeastern end of the park, which counts Napoléon Bonaparte among its graduates. The steel-and-etched-glass **Wall for Peace Memorial** (Map p366; http://wallforpeace.org; MÉcole Militaire or RER Champ de Mars–Tour Eiffel), erected in 2000, is by Clara Halter.

PALAIS GALLIERA MUSEUM

Map p366 (☎01 56 52 86 00; www.palaisgalliera.paris.fr; 10 av Pierre 1er de Serbie, 16e; adult/child €10/free; ⏲10am-6pm Tue-Sun, to 9pm Thu; MIéna) Paris' Fashion Museum warehouses some 100,000 outfits and accessories – from canes and umbrellas to fans and gloves – from the 18th century to the present day. The permanent collection will go on display beginning in 2019; until then only temporary exhibits will be shown. The sumptuous Italianate palace and gardens dating from the mid-19th century are worth a visit in themselves.

MAISON DE BALZAC MUSEUM

Map p366 (47 rue Raynouard, 16e; adult/child €6/free; ⏲10am-6pm Tue-Sun; MPassy or RER Avenue Président Kennedy) FREE This pretty, three-storey spa house is where realist novelist Honoré de Balzac (1799–1850) lived and worked from 1840 to 1847, editing the entire *Comédie Humaine*. There's a lot of memorabilia, letters, prints and portraits – perfect for die-hard Balzac fans.

PALAIS DE CHAILLOT HISTORIC BUILDING

Map p366 (place du Trocadéro et du 11 Novembre, 16e; MTrocadéro) The two curved, colonnaded wings of this building (built for the 1937 International Expo) and central terrace afford an exceptional panorama of the **Jardins du Trocadéro**, Seine and Eiffel Tower.

TOP SIGHT
MUSÉE MARMOTTAN MONET

Housed in the duc de Valmy's former hunting lodge (well, let's call it a mansion), this intimate museum houses the world's largest collection of Monet paintings and sketches. It provides an interesting if patchy cross-section of his work, beginning with paintings such as the seminal *Impression Soleil Levant* (1873) and *Promenade près d'Argenteuil* (1875), passing through numerous water-lily studies, before moving on to the rest of the collection, which is considerably more abstract and dates to the early 1900s. Some of the masterpieces to look out for include *La Barque* (1887), *Cathédrale de Rouen* (1892), *Londres, le Parlement* (1901) and the various *Nymphéas* – many of these were smaller studies for the works now on display in the Musée de l'Orangerie (p118).

Temporary exhibitions, included in the admission price and always excellent, are generally shown either in the basement or on the 1st floor. Also on display are a handful of canvases by Renoir, Pissaro, Gauguin and Morisot, and a collection of 13th- to 16th-century illuminations, which are quite lovely if somewhat out of place.

DON'T MISS

- *Impression Soleil Levant*
- *Promenade près d'Argenteuil*
- *Londres, le Parlement*

PRACTICALITIES

- Map p366, C5
- ☎01 44 96 50 33
- www.marmottan.fr
- 2 rue Louis Boilly, 16e
- adult/child €11/7.50
- ⏲10am-6pm Tue, Wed & Fri-Sun, to 9pm Thu
- MLa Muette

TOP SIGHT
MUSÉE GUIMET DES ARTS ASIATIQUES

France's foremost Asian arts museum, the Musée Guimet has a superb collection of sculptures, paintings and religious articles that originated in the vast stretch of land between Afghanistan and Japan. In fact, it's possible to observe the gradual transmission of both Buddhism and artistic styles along the Silk Road in some of the museum's pieces, from the 1st-century Gandhara Buddhas from Afghanistan and Pakistan to the later Central Asian, Chinese and Japanese Buddhist sculptures and art.

Other strong points of the museum include the Southeast Asian statuary on the ground floor (which has the world's largest collection of Khmer artefacts outside Cambodia), the Nepalese and Tibetan bronzes and mandalas, and the vast China collection, which encompasses everything from ink paintings and calligraphy to funerary statuary and early bronzes.

Part of the collection, comprised of Chinese furniture, teaware and temporary exhibits, is housed in the nearby **Hôtel d'Heidelbach** (Map p366; 19 av d'Iéna, 16e; incl in Musée Guimet admission; ⏲10am-5.30pm Wed-Mon, garden to 5pm; Ⓜléna). Don't miss the wonderful Japanese garden here.

DON'T MISS

- Afghan collection
- Southeast Asian statuary
- China collection
- Himalayan mandalas and thangkas

PRACTICALITIES

- Map p366, F4
- ☎01 56 52 53 00
- www.guimet.fr
- 6 place d'Iéna, 16e
- adult/child €8.50/free
- ⏲10am-6pm Wed-Mon
- ⓂIéna

The eastern wing houses the standout Cité de l'Architecture et du Patrimoine (p85), devoted to French architecture and heritage, as well as the **Théâtre National de Chaillot** (Map p366; ☎01 53 65 30 00; http://theatre-chaillot.fr), staging dance and theatre. The western wing houses the **Musée de la Marine** (Maritime Museum; Map p366; ☎01 53 65 69 69; www.musee-marine.fr), closed for renovations until 2021, and the Musée de l'Homme.

MUSÉE DE L'HOMME — MUSEUM

Map p366 (Museum of Humankind; ☎01 44 05 72 72; www.museedelhomme.fr; 17 place Trocadéro et du 11 Novembre, 16e; adult/child €10/free; ⏲10am-6pm Wed-Mon; ⓂPassy, Iéna) Originally opened in 1882 and completely renovated in 2015, this museum traces the evolution of humankind through artefacts gathered from around the world. There are few English labels, and the transitions between exhibits sometimes lack coherency, but there are nevertheless some fascinating pieces on display, including a Cro-Magnon shell necklace, delicately carved mammoth tusks and reindeer jawbones, a variety of Paleolithic stone tools and a Peruvian mummy. Eiffel Tower views extend from the ground-floor restaurant and 2nd-floor cafe.

MUSÉE DU VIN — MUSEUM

Map p366 (☎01 45 25 63 26; www.museeduvinparis.com; 5 sq Charles Dickens, 16e; adult/child €13.90/free; ⏲10am-6pm Tue-Sun; ⓂPassy) The Wine Museum, headquarters of the prestigious International Federation of Wine Brotherhoods, introduces visitors to the fine art of viticulture with mock-ups and tool displays. End museum visits with a glass of AOP wine (€5) or a 20-minute wine tasting (€25). If you lunch in the attached restaurant (noon to 3pm Tuesday to Saturday), museum admission is free.

FLAME OF LIBERTY MEMORIAL — MONUMENT

Map p366 (place de l'Alma, 8e; ⓂAlma Marceau) This bronze sculpture, a replica of the one topping the Statue of Liberty, was placed here in 1987 as a symbol of friendship between France and the USA. More famous is its location, above the place d'Alma tunnel where, on 31 August 1997, Diana, Princess of Wales, was killed in a car accident.

GALERIE-MUSÉE BACCARAT — MUSEUM

Map p366 (11 place des États-Unis, 16e; adult/child €10/free; ⏲10am-6pm Tue-Sat; ⓂBoissière, Kléber) Showcasing 1000 stunning pieces of crystal, many of them custom-made for

…d dictators of former colonies, …museum is at home in its striking …oco-style premises designed by …e Starck in the ritzy 16e. It is also …me to an upmarket restaurant called – what else? – Le Cristal Room.

AQUARIUM DE PARIS CINÉAQUA AQUARIUM
Map p366 (☎01 40 69 23 23; www.cineaqua.com; av des Nations Unies, 16e; adult/child €20.50/13; ⏲10am-7pm; Ⓜ Trocadéro) Paris' aquarium, on the eastern side of the Jardins du Trocadéro, has a shark tank and 500-odd fish species to entertain families on rainy days. Three cinemas screen ocean-related and other films (dubbed in French, with subtitles). Budget tip: show your ticket from the nearby Musée Guimet to get reduced aquarium admission (adult/child €16.40/10.40).

EATING

In addition to the pickings of the 16e *arrondissement*, the many restaurants of Les Invalides and the buzzing market street of rue Cler (7e) are a short walk from the Eiffel Tower. For a memorable experience, dine in the icon itself.

MALITOURNE PASTRIES €
Map p366 (☎01 47 20 52 26; www.patisserie-malitourne.com; 30 rue de Chaillot, 16e; ⏲7.30am-7.30pm Mon-Fri; Ⓜ Alma-Marceau) Indulge in something sweet at this great little patisserie, chocolate-maker and *traiteur* (caterer). It has the added bonus of street entertainment: watch chocolate-makers at work in their streetside kitchen with a huge window designed to show it all off.

MARCHÉ PRÉSIDENT WILSON MARKET €
Map p366 (av du Président Wilson, 16e; ⏲7am-2.30pm Wed & Sat; Ⓜ Iéna, Alma-Marceau) This open-air market across from Palais de Tokyo is the most convenient in the neighbourhood. Organic wines, heirloom vegetables and artisanal charcuterie are some of the many temptations.

ARNAUD NICOLAS FRENCH €€
Map p366 (☎01 45 55 59 59; http://arnaudnicolas.paris/en; 46 ave de la Bourdonnais, 7e; 2-/3-course lunch menu €28/32, tasting menu €62; ⏲2-9.45pm Mon, noon-1.45pm & 2-9.45pm Tue-Sat; Ⓜ École Militaire) The upmarket hybrid restaurant and boutique of chef Arnaud Nicolas combines two natural French loves: gastronomy and charcuterie. Be it a posh pork pie (flavoured with herbs, or foie gras and quail pie with pear and pistachio perhaps), fancy terrine or a simple plate of cold cuts, this sleek address serves it to astonishing effect.

LE PETIT RÉTRO BISTRO €€
Map p366 (☎01 44 05 06 05; http://petitretro.fr; 5 rue Mesnil, 16e; 2-/3-course menus lunch €26/31, dinner €31/36; ⏲noon-2.30pm & 7-10.30pm Mon-Sat; Ⓜ Victor Hugo) From the gorgeous 'Petit Rétro' emblazoned on the zinc bar to the ceramic, floral art nouveau tiles on the wall, this 1904-opened old-style bistro is now a historic monument. Fare prepared using seasonal ingredients is classic French: for example, blood sausage and *oreilles de cochon* (pig's ears). Delicious.

WAKNINE FRENCH €€
Map p366 (☎01 47 23 48 18; www.waknine.fr; 9 av Pierre 1er de Serbie, 16e; mains €23.50-31.50; ⏲noon-10.30pm; Ⓜ Iéna) It may look unremarkable from the outside, but this cosy hideaway is a local secret. The cuisine and service are both excellent without being overbearing; think steak with a parmesan and truffle emulsion or roast chicken in a delicate wholegrain mustard sauce, followed by Roquefort with confit prunes. Meals bookend tea and pastries in the early afternoon and tapas for *apéro* (premeal drinks).

ATELIER VIVANDA FRENCH €€
Map p366 (☎01 40 67 10 00; www.ateliervivanda.com; 18 rue Lauriston, 16e; 2-/3-course meal €32/38, mains €28; ⏲noon-2.30pm & 7.30-10.30pm Mon-Fri; Ⓜ Charles de Gaulle–Étoile) A micro outpost of carnivore heaven, tucked away down an inconspicuous side street 10 minutes from the Arc de Triomphe. The Atelier focuses uniquely on high-quality meat and poultry; the three-course meal is a deal in this neighbourhood. Reserve.

LES GRANDS VERRES MEDITERRANEAN €€
Map p366 (☎01 85 53 03 61; www.quixotic-projects.com; 13 av du Président Wilson; lunch menu €23, mains €27-31; ⏲noon-2.30pm & 7-10.30pm, bar to 2am; Ⓜ Alma-Marceau) American chef Preston Miller helms the kitchen at the Palais de Tokyo's sustainably themed hangout, where you'll find an inspired menu that stretches from trout with olives, fennel, burnt orange and candied linseed to crispy confit pork belly with za'atar flatbread. Just here for the

WORTH A DETOUR

BOIS DE BOULOGNE

The 845-hectare **Bois de Boulogne** (Map p366; bd Maillot, 16e; MPorte Maillot) owes its informal layout to Baron Haussmann, who, inspired by London's Hyde Park, planted 400,000 trees here in the 19th century. Along with various gardens and other sights, the park has 15km of cycle paths and 28km of bridle paths in 125 hectares of forested land.

Be warned that the area becomes a distinctly adult playground after dark, especially along the Allée de Longchamp running northeast from the Étang des Réservoirs (Reservoirs Pond), where all kinds of prostitutes cruise for clients.

The Bois de Boulogne is served by metro lines 1 (Porte Maillot, Les Sablons), 2 (Porte Dauphine), 9 (Michel-Ange-Auteuil) and 10 (Michel-Ange-Auteuil, Porte d'Auteuil), and the RER C (Avenue Foch, Avenue Henri Martin). Vélib' stations are found near most of the park entrances, but not within the park itself.

Jardin d'Acclimatation (Map p366; 01 40 67 90 85; http://jardindacclimatation.fr; av du Mahatma Gandhi; admission €3.50, per attraction €2.90; 11am-6pm Mon-Fri, 10am-6pm Sat & Sun; MLes Sablons) Families adore this green, flowery amusement park on the Bois de Boulogne's northern fringe.

Lac Inférieur (Map p366; 06 95 14 00 01; Carrefour du Bout des Lacs; 1hr €10, plus deposit €50; noon-5pm Mon-Fri, 10am-6pm Sat & Sun mid-Feb–Oct; MAvenue Henri Martin) Rent an old-fashioned rowing boat to explore Lac Inférieur, the largest of Bois de Boulogne's lakes – romance guaranteed.

Parc de Bagatelle (Map p366; rte de Sèvres à Neuilly, 16e; adult/child Jun-Oct €6/3, Nov-May free; 9.30am-8pm Apr-Sep, shorter hours rest of year; MPorte Maillot) Few Parisian parks are as romantic as this, created as the result of a wager between Marie-Antoinette and the Count of Artois. Irises bloom in May, roses between June and October, and water lilies in August.

Pré Catelan (Catelan Meadow; Map p366; rte de Suresnes, 16e; 9.30am-8pm Apr-Oct, Jardin Shakespeare 2-4pm, shorter hours Nov-Mar; MRanelagh) FREE This area within Parc de Bagatelle has a wonderful Jardin Shakespeare where plants and trees mentioned in Shakespeare's plays are cultivated. Watch summer performances in the open-air theatre.

Jardin des Serres d'Auteuil (Map p366; 01 40 72 16 16; av de la Porte d'Auteuil, 16é; 8am-8.30pm summer, shorter hours rest of year; MPorte d'Auteuil) FREE At the southeastern end of the Bois de Boulogne is this garden with impressive conservatories, which opened in 1898 and are home to a large collection of tropical plants.

Stade Roland Garros-Musée de la Fédération Française de Tennis (Map p366; www.fft.fr; 2 av Gordon Bennett, 16e; MPorte d'Auteuil) The home of the French Open tennis tournament also shelters the world's most extravagant tennis museum, which traces the sport's 500-year history through paintings, sculptures and posters.

Fondation Louis Vuitton (Map p366; 01 40 69 96 00; www.fondationlouisvuitton.fr; 8 av du Mahatma Gandhi, 16e; adult/child €16/5; hours vary with exhibit; MLes Sablons) Hosts temporary shows such as the MOMA in Paris, the Sergei Shchukin collection and Art/Africa.

cocktails? Take a seat at the 13m-long bar made of compacted earth.

★L'ASTRANCE GASTRONOMY €€€

Map p366 (01 40 50 84 40; www.astrancerestaurant.com; 4 rue Beethoven, 16e; 3-/5-course lunch menus €75/170, 7-course dinner menu €250; 12.15-1.15pm & 8.15-9.15pm Tue-Fri, closed Aug; MPassy) It's almost two decades since Pascal Barbot's dazzling cuisine at the triple-Michelin-starred L'Astrance made its debut, but it's shown no signs of losing its cutting edge. Look beyond the complicated descriptions on the menu and expect exquisite elements making up intricate plates. Reserve one to two months in advance.

FIRMIN LE BARBIER FRENCH €€€

Map p366 (01 45 51 21 55; www.firminlebarbier.fr; 20 rue de Monttessuy, 7e; 3-/6-course menu €39/64, mains €27; noon-2pm & 7-10.30pm Sun-Mon & Wed-Fri, 7-10.30pm Sat; MÉcole Militaire or RER Pont de l'Alma) A five-minute walk from the Eiffel Tower, this bistro was opened by a retired surgeon turned gourmet whose passion is apparent in everything from the personable service to the wine list. The market-driven menu is traditional French (sirloin steak with polenta, bœuf bourguignon), while the interior has an open kitchen. There are just eight tables, so reserve ahead.

LES OMBRES FRENCH €€€
Map p366 (☎01 47 53 68 00; www.lesombres-restaurant.com; 27 quai Branly, 7e; 2-/3-course weekday lunch menu €32/42, dinner menu €71; ⏱noon-2.15pm & 7-10.30pm; Ⓜléna or RER Pont de l'Alma) This glass-enclosed rooftop restaurant on the 5th floor of the Musée du Quai Branly is named the 'Shadows' after the patterns cast by the Eiffel Tower's webbed ironwork. Dramatic Eiffel views are complemented by creations such as confit lamb shoulder with smoked aubergine caviar and yellow courgettes, or roast cod in watercress sauce. Book ahead.

DRINKING & NIGHTLIFE

Ogling the illuminated Eiffel Tower aside, being in the wealthy and predominantly residential 16e after dark doesn't translate to much when it comes to buzzing bars and clubs. The pace picks up around Palais de Tokyo, and the lively bars and cafes of St-Germain are a short metro ride away.

★ST JAMES PARIS BAR
Map p366 (www.saint-james-paris.com; 43 av Bugeaud, 16e; ⏱7pm-1am; 📶; ⓂPorte Dauphine) Hidden behind a stone wall, this historic mansion-turned-hotel opens its bar nightly to nonguests – and the setting redefines extraordinary. Winter drinks are in the wood-panelled library, in summer they're on the impossibly romantic 300-sq-metre garden terrace with giant balloon-shaped gazebos (the first hot-air balloons took flight here). There are over 70 cocktails and an adjoining Michelin-starred restaurant.

BÔ ZINC CAFÉ BAR
Map p366 (☎01 42 24 69 05; 59 av Mozart, 16e; ⏱7am-2am; ⓂRanelagh) With its soft sage-green façade and buzzing pavement terrace, Bô Zinc is one of those great hybrid addresses – perfect for hanging with locals over coffee, tea or after-work cocktails. Seating is a mix of wooden bistro chairs and 'flop-in' armchairs, while potted palm trees – inside and out – add a touch of chic. Top-notch nosh too, served until 11pm.

UPPER CRÈMERIE BAR
Map p366 (☎01 40 70 93 23; 71 av Marceau, 16e; ⏱9am-midnight Mon-Fri; 📶; ⓂKléber, George V) The sun-flooded tables at this hybrid cafe-cocktail bar in a quintessential Parisian pavement terrace heave at lunchtime and after work with a well-dressed crowd from surrounding offices, while inside, vivid colours and neon lighting reassure trendsetters that the place is anything but traditional. Cocktails and food (€11 to €13) hit the spot.

FROG XVI PUB
Map p366 (☎01 47 27 88 88; www.frogpubs.com; 110 av Kléber, 16e; ⏱8am-1am Sun-Wed, 8am-2am Thu-Sat; 📶; ⓂTrocadéro) This popular Parisian pub and brewery has several locations, but for beer drinkers this one is the saving grace, as there simply isn't much else in the way of craft brews in the posh 16e. IPA on tap, a family-friendly menu and live sports on the big screen. On weekdays, pints are €5 during happy hour (5pm to 8pm).

YOYO CLUB
Map p366 (http://yoyo-paris.com; 13 av du Président Wilson, 16e; ⏱hours vary; Ⓜléna) Deep in the basement of the Palais de Tokyo, Yoyo has an edgy, raw-concrete Berlin-style vibe and a capacity of 800. Techno and house dominate, with diversions into hip-hop,

MOVEABLE FEAST

A true moveable feast, **Bustronome** (Map p366; ☎09 54 44 45 55; www.bustronome.com; 2 av Kléber, 16e; 4-course lunch €65, 6-course dinner €100; ⏱by reservation 12.15pm, 12.45pm, 7.45pm & 8.45pm; 🌿👶; ⓂKléber, Charles de Gaulle–Étoile) is a voyage into French gastronomy aboard a glass-roofed bus. Paris' famous monuments – the Arc de Triomphe, Grand Palais, Palais Garnier, Notre Dame and Eiffel Tower – glide by as you dine on seasonal creations prepared in the vehicle's lower-deck galley. Children's menus for lunch/dinner cost €40/50; vegetarian, vegan and gluten-free menus are available.

WORTH A DETOUR

LA DÉFENSE

More than just office space, La Défense is an engaging, open-air art gallery. Calder, Miró, Agam, César and Torricini are among the international artists behind the often-surprising sculptures and murals that pepper the central 1km-long promenade. Pick up a map and excellent booklets in English outlining walks to discover its art and surprising green spaces at **Info Défense** (☎01 46 93 19 00; www.ladefense.fr; place de la Défense; ⏲9am-6pm Mon-Fri, 10am-5pm Sat & Sun; ⓂLa Défense), located at the heart of the promenade.

La Défense's landmark edifice is the marble **Grande Arche** (☎01 40 90 52 20; www.lagrandearche.fr; 1 Parvis de la Défense; adult/child €15/7; ⏲10am-7pm), a cube-like arch built in the 1980s to house government and business offices. The arch marks the western end of the *axe historique* (historic axis), though Danish architect Johan-Otto von Sprekelsen deliberately placed the Grande Arche fractionally out of alignment. After several years of renovations, it reopened in 2017, with spectacular views from the rooftop. Temporary photojournalism exhibits are held in the museum (adult/child €19/11).

electro, funk, disco, R&B and soul. Hours can vary; check the website to see what's on.

CAFÉ BRANLY — CAFE

Map p366 (☎01 47 53 68 01; 27 quai Branly, 7e; ⏲10am-6pm Sun, Tue & Wed, to 7pm Thu-Sat; ⓂIéna or RER Pont de l'Alma) This casual spot at the Musée du Quai Branly has ringside views of the Eiffel Tower and cafe fare (cauliflower soup, cod in green curry; dishes €14 to €18) to tuck into before a cup of coffee. The peaceful setting, within the museum's modernist garden, is superb.

ENTERTAINMENT

MAISON DE LA RADIO — LIVE MUSIC

Map p366 (☎01 56 40 15 16; http://maisondelaradio.fr; 116 av du Président Kennedy, 16e; concerts from €10; ⓂPassy or RER Avenue du Président Kennedy) Catch a classical concert at Radio France's concert space, which opened in 2014. With some 200 annual performances, expect a wide variety of music, from organ and chamber music to appearances by the national orchestra. To browse performance times on the website, click on 'Agenda'.

LES MARIONNETTES DU CHAMP DE MARS — PUPPET THEATRE

Map p366 (☎01 48 56 01 44; www.guignolduchampdemars.fr; allée du Général Margueritte, 7e; €4.50; ⓂÉcole Militaire or RER Champ de Mars–Tour Eiffel) For time-honoured French entertainment, take the kids to a show in this Napoleon III–style puppet theatre. Shows are in French, but performances still amuse. Check the website for performance times, usually Wednesday, weekends and school holidays.

SHOPPING

The best and most varied options for shopping in western Paris will be in the many museum gift shops. Apart from this, the area is largely residential.

LORETTE & JASMIN — VINTAGE

Map p366 (☎06 14 08 06 22; www.lorettejasmin.com; 6 rue François Millet, 16e; ⏲10.30am-12.45pm & 2.15-7pm Tue-Sat; ⓂJasmin, Mirabeau) One of the most well-known consignment stores in Paris, Lorette & Jasmin carries a diverse range of gently used luxury brands (Louis Vuitton, Dior, Chanel) yet remains small and personable enough to make browsing pleasant. Lorette's bag bar will let you rent that designer handbag you've always coveted for up to several days.

ARLETTIE — FASHION & ACCESSORIES

Map p366 (☎01 84 16 12 12; www.arlettie.fr; 17 ave Raymond Poincaré; ⏲hours vary; ⓂTrocadéro) Arlettie specialises in four-day sales of overstock from contemporary designers: think Lancel, Claudie Pierlot, Tara Jarmon, Vanessa Bruno. Here's the catch – you need to be a member (€50 annual fee) to get in on most days. Fridays are usually open to the public, however; register online for access.

LA GRANDE ÉPICERIE RIVE DROITE — FOOD & DRINKS

Map p366 (☎01 44 14 38 00; www.lagrandeepicerie.com; 80 rue de Passy, 16e; ⏲8.30am-9pm Mon-Sat; ⓂLa Muette or RER Boulainvilliers) Branch of the beloved gourmet grocery (p244) on the Left Bank, with four floors of French goodies and a handful of eat-in options.

Champs-Élysées & Grands Boulevards

Neighbourhood Top Five

❶ **Arc de Triomphe** (p94) Climbing Napoleon's arch to survey the *axe historique,* extending from the Louvre to La Défense, and paying tribute to the Tomb of the Unknown Soldier.

❷ **Palais Garnier** (p97) Taking in a performance or touring the mythic 19th-century opera house, where Chagall's ceiling mural is on display.

❸ **Galeries Lafayette** (p104) Catching a free fashion show showcasing seasonal trends at the magnificent art nouveau department store and admiring the rooftop panorama.

❹ **Grand Palais** (p96) Viewing exceptional art exhibitions beneath the 8.5-tonne art nouveau glass roof.

❺ **Champs-Élysées** (p96) Strolling the over-the-top avenue – you can't leave Paris without doing it once.

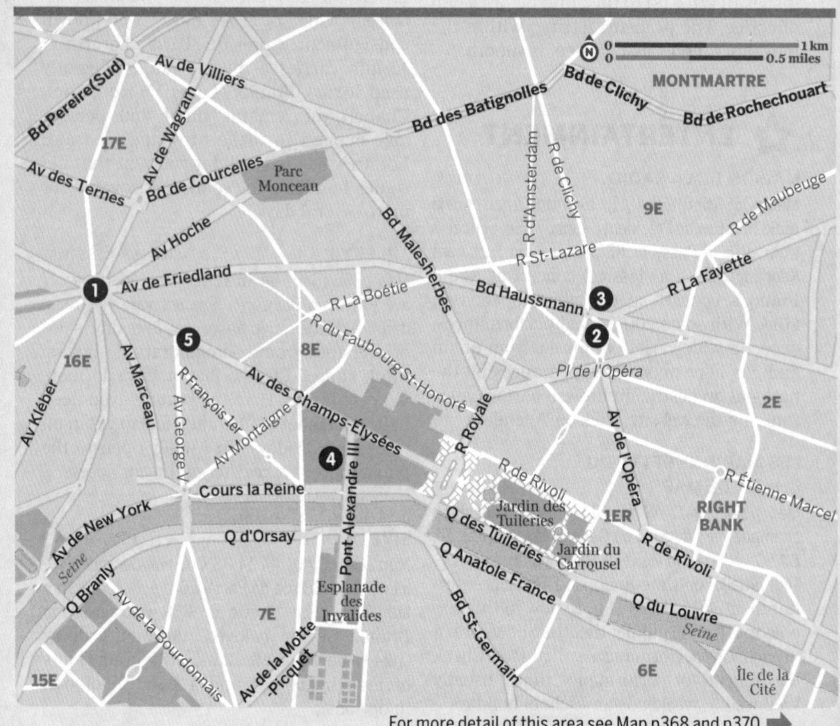

For more detail of this area see Map p368 and p370

Explore Champs-Élysées & Grands Boulevards

The Champs-Élysées and Grands Boulevards area is grandiose in layout. The main landmarks – the Arc de Triomphe (p94), place de la Concorde (p97), place de la Madeleine (p102) and the Palais Garnier (p97) – are joined by majestic boulevards, each lined with harmonious rows of Haussmann-era buildings.

Monumental vistas will keep your eyes occupied, but high-end shops and elegant department stores are this district's *raison d'être* and you will soon find your gaze slipping to the luxury display windows. Dior, Chanel, Louis Vuitton…fans of *haute couture* will find themselves pulled into the famed Triangle d'Or (Golden Triangle), south from the Champs-Élysées (p96). Further east along the Grands Boulevards are the historic *grands magasins* (department stores) like Le Printemps (p105) and Galeries Lafayette (p104), which will appeal to shoppers interested in a broader overview of French fashion.

But there's much more to this area than fashion overload. The vestiges of the 1900 World's Fair – the Grand Palais (p96) and Petit Palais (p96), along with the bridge Pont Alexandre III – play host to a variety of excellent exhibits.

Entertainment, too, has a strong tradition in this area, the most notable venue being the famed 19th-century opera house, the Palais Garnier (p97). While non-French speakers will skip the theatres along the Grands Boulevards, there are plenty of music venues – from classical to rock – that require no language skills to appreciate.

Local Life

- **Epicurean life** Shop for luxury gourmet goods around Place de la Madeleine (p102).
- **Art life** Parisians' thirst for art is unquenchable – join locals viewing exhibitions in museums like the Petit Palais (p96).
- **Park life** Seek serenity in the tiny, secreted Jardin de la Nouvelle France (p96).

Getting There & Away

- **Metro & RER** Metro line 1 follows the Champs-Élysées below ground, while lines 8 and 9 serve the Grands Boulevards. RER A stops at Auber (Opéra) and Charles de Gaulle–Étoile.
- **Bicycle** You'll find Vélib' stations on side streets off the Champs-Élysées.
- **Boat** The hop-on, hop-off Batobus' Champs-Élysées stop is just east of Pont Alexandre III.

Lonely Planet's Top Tip

Haute cuisine – and *haute* prices – are the rule in the 8e, but if you eat at one of the finer restaurants for lunch on a weekday, you'll save a bundle and still get to treat your tastebuds to an extraordinary meal. Make sure to reserve.

Best Places to Eat

- Richer (p101)
- Le Hide (p99)
- Mamou (p102)
- Lasserre (p99)
- Détour (p101)

For reviews, see p98

Best Places to Drink

- PanPan (p103)
- Blaine (p103)
- Zig Zag Club (p103)
- Honor (p103)

For reviews, see p103

Best Shopping

- Galeries Lafayette (p104)
- Le Printemps (p105)
- Triangle d'Or (p105)
- À la Mère de Famille (p104)
- Place de la Madeleine (p102)

For reviews, see p104 

PIGPROX / SHUTTERSTOCK ©

TOP SIGHT
ARC DE TRIOMPHE

Napoléon's armies never did march through the Arc de Triomphe showered in honour, but the monument has nonetheless come to stand as the very symbol of French patriotism. It's not for nationalistic sentiments, however, that so many visitors huff up the narrow, spiralling staircase. Rather it's the sublime panoramas from the top that make the arch such a notable attraction.

History

The arch was first commissioned in 1806 in the style of a Roman triumphal arch, following Napoléon's victory at Austerlitz the year before. At the time, the victory seemed like a watershed moment that confirmed the tactical supremacy of the French army, but a mere decade later, Napoléon had already fallen from power and his empire had crumbled. The Arc de Triomphe was never fully abandoned – simply laying the foundations, after all, had taken an entire two years – and in 1836, after a series of starts and stops under the restored monarchy, the project was finally completed. In 1840 Napoléon's remains were returned to France and passed under the arch before being interred at Invalides.

DON'T MISS

- Tomb of the Unknown Soldier
- Multimedia exhibit
- Viewing platform

PRACTICALITIES

- Map p368, A2
- www.paris-arc-de-triomphe.fr
- place Charles de Gaulle, 8e
- viewing platform adult/child €12/free
- 10am-11pm Apr-Sep, to 10.30pm Oct-Mar
- M Charles de Gaulle–Étoile

Beneath the Arch

Beneath the arch at ground level lies the **Tomb of the Unknown Soldier**. Honouring the 1.3 million French soldiers who lost their lives in WWI, the Unknown Soldier was laid to rest in 1921, beneath an eternal flame that is rekindled daily at 6.30pm.

Also here are a number of bronze plaques laid into the ground. Take the time to try and decipher some: these mark significant moments in modern French history, such as the proclamation of the Third French Republic (4 September 1870) and the return of Alsace and Lorraine to French rule (11 November 1918). The most notable plaque is the text from Charles de Gaulle's famous London broadcast on 18 June 1940, which sparked the French Resistance to life: 'Believe me, I who am speaking to you with full knowledge of the facts, and who tell you that nothing is lost for France. The same means that overcame us can bring us victory one day. For France is not alone! She is not alone!'

The Sculptures

The arch is adorned with four main sculptures, six panels in relief, and a frieze running beneath the top. Each was designed by a different artist; the most famous sculpture is the one to the right as you approach from the Champs-Élysées: *La Marseillaise* (Departure of the Volunteers of 1792). Sculpted by François Rude, it depicts soldiers of all ages gathering beneath the wings of victory, en route to drive back the invading armies of Prussia and Austria. The higher panels depict a series of important victories for the Revolutionary and imperial French armies, from Egypt to Austerlitz, while the detailed frieze is divided into two sections: the *Departure of the Armies* and the *Return of the Armies*. Don't miss the **multimedia section** beneath the viewing platform, which provides more detail and historical background for each of the sculptures.

Viewing Platform

Climb the 284 steps to the viewing platform at the top of the 50m-high arch and you'll be suitably rewarded with magnificent panoramas over western Paris. From here, a dozen broad avenues – many of them named after Napoléonic victories and illustrious generals – radiate towards every compass point. The Arc de Triomphe is the highest point in the line of monuments known as the *axe historique* (historic axis, also called the grand axis); it offers views that swoop east down the Champs-Élysées to the gold-tipped obelisk at place de la Concorde (and beyond to the Louvre's glass pyramid), and west to the skyscraper district of La Défense, where the colossal Grande Arche marks the axis' western terminus.

ARCH ACROBATICS

On 7 August 1919, three weeks after the WWI victory parade, Charles Godefroy flew a biplane through the arch (14.5m wide) to honour the French pilots who had fought in the war. It was no easy feat: Jean Navarre, the pilot originally chosen to perform the flight, crashed his plane while practising and died.

Don't cross the traffic-choked roundabout above ground if you value your life! Stairs lead from the northern side of the Champs-Élysées to pedestrian tunnels (not linked to metro tunnels) that bring you out safely beneath the arch. Tickets to the viewing platform are sold in the tunnel.

BASTILLE DAY CELEBRATION

The military parade commemorating Bastille Day (14 July) kicks off from the arch, which is adorned by a billowing tricolour.

SIGHTS

Strolling down the Champs-Élysées from the Arc de Triomphe will leave you in the museum-rich neighbourhood surrounding the unparalleled vistas of place de la Concorde. Just west of the square are three architectural beauties from fin-de-siècle Paris: the Grand Palais, Petit Palais and the Palais de la Découverte. North of Concorde is place de la Madeleine, with its neoclassical Église de la Madeleine. Further east towards the Grands Boulevards is the legendary Palais Garnier, the city's 19th-century opera house.

Champs-Élysées

ARC DE TRIOMPHE — LANDMARK

See p94.

AVENUE DES CHAMPS-ÉLYSÉES — STREET

Map p368 (8e; MCharles de Gaulle–Étoile, George V, Franklin D Roosevelt, Champs-Élysées–Clemenceau) No trip to Paris is complete without strolling this broad, tree-shaded avenue lined with luxury shops. Named for the Elysian Fields ('heaven' in Greek mythology), the Champs-Élysées was laid out in the 17th century and is part of the *axe historique,* linking place de la Concorde with the Arc de Triomphe (p94). It's where presidents and soldiers parade on Bastille Day, where the Tour de France holds its final sprint, and where Paris turns out for organised and impromptu celebrations.

Cars are banished on the first Sunday of the month.

GRAND PALAIS — GALLERY

Map p368 (☎01 44 13 17 17; www.grandpalais.fr; 3 av du Général Eisenhower, 8e; adult/child €14/free; ⏲10am-8pm Thu-Mon, to 10pm Wed; MChamps-Élysées–Clemenceau) Erected for the 1900 Exposition Universelle (World's Fair), the Grand Palais today houses several exhibition spaces beneath its huge 8.5-tonne art nouveau glass roof. Some of Paris' biggest shows (Renoir, Chagall, Turner) are held in the **Galeries Nationales**, lasting three to four months. Hours, prices and exhibition dates vary significantly for all galleries. Reserving a ticket online for any show is strongly advised. Note that the Grand Palais will close for renovations from late 2020 to mid-2024.

Other exhibit spaces include the imaginative **Nef** – which plays host to concerts, art installations, a seasonal amusement park and horse shows – and several other minor galleries, entered from av Winston Churchill. There's also an **MK2 cinema** and fabulous restaurant, Mini Palais (p99).

PETIT PALAIS — GALLERY

Map p368 (Musée des Beaux-Arts de la Ville de Paris; ☎01 53 43 40 00; www.petitpalais.paris.fr; av Winston Churchill, 8e; suggested donation €2; ⏲10am-6pm Tue-Sun, to 9pm Fri; MChamps-Élysées–Clemenceau) FREE This architectural stunner was built for the 1900 Exposition Universelle, and is home to the **Musée des Beaux-Arts de la Ville de Paris** (City of Paris Museum of Fine Arts). It specialises in medieval and Renaissance objets d'art, such as porcelain and clocks, tapestries, drawings, and 19th-century French paintings and sculpture; there are also paintings by such artists as Rembrandt, Colbert, Cézanne, Monet, Gauguin and Delacroix. The cafe here has lovely garden seating.

PALAIS DE LA DÉCOUVERTE — MUSEUM

Map p368 (☎01 56 43 20 20; www.palais-decouverte.fr; av Franklin D Roosevelt, 8e; adult/child €9/7; ⏲9.30am-6pm Tue-Sat, 10am-7pm Sun; MChamps-Élysées–Clemenceau) Attached to the Grand Palais, this children's science museum has excellent temporary exhibits (eg moving lifelike dinosaurs) as well as an interactive permanent collection focusing on astronomy, biology, physics and the like. Some of the older exhibits have French-only explanations, but overall this is a dependable family outing. The museum will close for renovations from late 2020 to mid-2024.

JARDIN DE LA NOUVELLE FRANCE — PARK

Map p368 (cnr av Franklin D Roosevelt & cours la Reine, 8e; ⏲24hr; MFranklin D Roosevelt) Descending rustic, uneven staircases (by the white-marble Alfred de Musset sculpture on av Franklin D Roosevelt, or the upper garden off cours la Reine) brings you to the tiny 0.7-hectare Jardin de la Nouvelle France, an unexpected wonderland of lilacs, and lemon, orange, maple and weeping beech trees. There's also a wildlife-filled pond, waterfall, wooden footbridge and benches to soak up the serenity.

LE GRAND MUSÉE DU PARFUM — MUSEUM

Map p368 (☎01 42 65 25 44; www.grandmuseeduparfum.fr; 73 rue du Faubourg St-Honoré, 8e;

TOP SIGHT
PALAIS GARNIER

Few other Paris monuments have provided artistic inspiration in the way that the Palais Garnier has. From Degas' ballerinas to Gaston Leroux' Phantom and Chagall's ceiling, the layers of myth painted on gradually over the decades have bestowed a particular air of mystery and drama to its ornate interior. Designed in 1860 by Charles Garnier (then an unknown 35-year-old architect), the opera house was part of Baron Haussmann's massive urban renovation project.

The opera house is open to visitors during the day, and the building is a fascinating place to explore even if you're not taking in a show. Highlights include the opulent Grand Staircase, the library-museum (1st floor) and the horseshoe-shaped auditorium (2nd floor), with its extravagant gilded interior and red velvet seats. Above the massive chandelier is Chagall's gorgeous ceiling mural (1964), which depicts scenes from 14 operas.

Visits are either unguided (audioguides available; €5; 10am-5pm), or you can reserve a spot online for an English-language guided tour (11am & 2.30pm). Check the website for updated schedules.

DON'T MISS

- Grand Staircase
- Library-Museum
- Chagall's ceiling

PRACTICALITIES

- Map p370, C4
- ☎08 92 89 90 90
- www.operadeparis.fr
- cnr rues Scribe & Auber, 9e
- self-guided tours adult/child €12/8, guided tours adult/child €15.50/8.50
- Ⓜ Opéra

adult/child €14.50/5; ⏲10.30am-7pm Tue-Sun; Ⓜ Miromesnil) There are several perfume museums in Paris, but this is the only one that's not run by a major brand. Opened in 2016, it starts with history exhibits (ancient perfume bottles, interpretive French/English panels) in the basement, but the most engaging sections are upstairs. The 1st floor is a heady sensory guide, revealing the chemical processes while you identify scents. The 2nd floor showcases the art of fragrance creation and the 'instruments' with which professional perfumers work.

Afterwards, you'll exit through the ground-floor gift shop where you can see perfume being distilled and bottles hand-painted – and, of course, you can stock up too. It's inside a beautiful 17th-century *hôtel particulier* (private mansion) once occupied by Christian Lacroix' fashion house.

MUSÉE MAXIM'S MUSEUM

Map p368 (☎01 42 65 30 47; http://maxims-de-paris.com; 3 rue Royale, 8e; adult/child €25/free; ⏲English tours 2pm Tue & Wed; Ⓜ Concorde) During the belle époque, Maxim's bistro was the most glamorous place to be in Paris. The restaurant has lost much of its cachet (though the food is actually excellent), but for art nouveau buffs, the real treasure is the upstairs museum. Opened by Maxim's owner, fashion designer Pierre Cardin, its 12 rooms are filled with some 550 pieces of art nouveau artworks, objets d'art and furniture detailed during one-hour guided tours.

French-language tours depart at 3.15pm on Tuesday and Wednesday.

PLACE DE LA CONCORDE SQUARE

Map p368 (8e; Ⓜ Concorde) Paris spreads around you, with views of the Eiffel Tower (p82), the Seine and along the Champs-Élysées, when you stand in the city's largest square. Its 3300-year-old pink granite obelisk was a gift from Egypt in 1831. The square was first laid out in 1755 and originally named after King Louis XV, but its royal associations meant that it took centre stage during the Revolution – Louis XVI was the first to be guillotined here in 1793.

During the next two years, 1343 more people, including Marie Antoinette, Danton and Robespierre, also lost their heads here. The square was given its present name after the Reign of Terror in the hope that it would become a place of peace and harmony. The corners of the square are marked by eight statues representing what were once the largest cities in France.

Grands Boulevards

MUSÉE NATIONAL GUSTAVE MOREAU GALLERY

Map p370 (01 48 74 38 50; www.musee-moreau.fr; 14 rue de la Rochefoucauld, 9e; adult/child €6/free; 10am-12.45pm & 2-5.15pm Mon, Wed & Thu, 10am-5.15pm Fri-Sun; M Trinité) Symbolist painter Gustave Moreau's former studio is crammed with 4800 of his paintings, drawings and sketches – although symbolism received more attention as a literary movement in France (Baudelaire, Verlaine, Rimbaud). A particular highlight is *La Licorne* (The Unicorn), inspired by *La Dame à la Licorne* (The Lady with the Unicorn) cycle of tapestries in the Musée National du Moyen Âge.

ÉGLISE DE LA MADELEINE CHURCH

Map p370 (Church of St Mary Magdalene; www.eglise-lamadeleine.com; place de la Madeleine, 8e; 9.30am-7pm; M Madeleine) Place de la Madeleine is named after the 19th-century neoclassical church at its centre, the Église de la Madeleine. Constructed in the style of a massive Greek temple, 'La Madeleine' was consecrated in 1842 after almost a century of design changes and construction delays.

The church is a popular venue for classical-music concerts (some free); check the posters outside or the website for dates.

On the south side, the monumental staircase affords one of the city's most quintessential Parisian panoramas. From here, you can see down rue Royale to place de la Concorde and its obelisk and across the Seine to the Assemblée Nationale. The Invalides' gold dome appears in the background.

NOUVEAU MUSÉE DU PARFUM MUSEUM

Map p370 (01 40 06 10 09; https://musee-parfum-paris.fragonard.com; 3-5 square de l'Opéra Louis Jouvet, 9e; 9am-6pm Mon-Sat; M Opéra or RER Auber) FREE If the art of perfume-making entices, stop by Fragonard's Perfume Museum. One of a trio of Paris locations, it has 30-minute guided tours (in multiple languages) that walk visitors through the history of perfume making, the different layers of perfume composition and the ingenious processes of distilling a flower's fragrance. Tours finish in the shop, where you can test your nose on different scents.

Two other wings can be found at **rue Scribe** (Map p370; 01 47 42 04 56; 9 rue Scribe, 9e; 9am-6pm Mon-Sat, to 5pm Sun; M Opéra or RER Auber) FREE, an old townhouse with a collection of copper distillery vats and antique flacons, and the **Théâtre-Musée des Capucines** (Map p370; 01 42 60 37 14; 39 blvd des Capucines, 2e; 9am-6pm Mon-Sat; M Opéra or RER Auber) FREE, which concentrates on the bottling and packaging side of perfume production.

CHAPELLE EXPIATOIRE CHAPEL

Map p370 (www.chapelle-expiatoire-paris.fr; square Louis XVI, 8e; adult/child €6/free; 10am-12.30pm & 1.30-6pm Tue-Sat Apr-Sep, shorter hours Oct-Mar; M St-Augustin) The austere, neoclassical Atonement Chapel, opposite 36 rue Pasquier, sits atop the section of a cemetery where Louis XVI, Marie Antoinette and many other victims of the Reign of Terror were buried after their executions in 1793. It was erected by Louis' brother, the restored Bourbon king Louis XVIII, in 1815. Two years later the royal bones were removed to the Basilique de St-Denis.

EATING

The Champs-Élysées area is known for its big-name chefs (Alain Ducasse, Pierre Gagnaire) and culinary icons (Taillevent), but there are a few under-the-radar restaurants too, where Parisians who live and work in the area dine on a regular basis. Rue de Ponthieu, running parallel to the Champs-Élysées, is a good spot to hunt for casual eateries, bakeries and cafes. Head to the Grands Boulevards for a more diverse dining selection – everything from hole-in-the-wall wine bars to organic cafes.

Champs-Élysées

FRAMBOISE CRÊPES €

Map p368 (01 74 64 02 79; www.creperieframboise.fr; 7 rue de Ponthieu, 8e; 2-course lunch €13.90, crêpes from €8.70; noon-2.30pm & 7-10pm; M Franklin D Roosevelt) Tucked in among a string of Asian takeaways is this delightful, contemporary crêperie. With an emphasis on quality (eg organic buckwheat flour), this is a top pick for an inexpensive meal off the Champs-Élysées.

★LADURÉE PASTRIES €€

Map p368 (☎01 40 75 08 75; www.laduree.com; 75 av des Champs-Élysées, 8e; pastries from €2.60, mains €18-47, 2-/3-course menu €35/42; ⏲7.30am-11pm Sun-Thu, 7.30am-midnight Fri & Sat; 👪; Ⓜ George V) One of Paris' oldest patisseries, Ladurée has been around since 1862 and first created the lighter-than-air, ganache-filled macaron in the 1930s. Its tearoom is the classiest spot to indulge on the Champs. Alternatively, pick up some pastries to go – from croissants to its trademark macarons, it's all quite heavenly. A three-course children's menu costs €19.

LE HIDE FRENCH €€

Map p368 (☎01 45 74 15 81; www.lehide.fr; 10 rue du Général Lanrezac, 17e; 2-/3-course menus €36/48; ⏲6-10.30pm Mon-Sat; Ⓜ Charles de Gaulle–Étoile) A perpetual favourite, Le Hide is a tiny neighbourhood bistro serving scrumptious traditional French fare: snails, seared duck breast with celery puree and truffle oil, baked shoulder of lamb, and monkfish with *beurre blanc* (white sauce). Unsurprisingly, this place fills up faster than you can scamper down the steps of the nearby Arc de Triomphe (p94) – reserve well in advance.

86 CHAMPS PASTRIES €€

Map p368 (☎01 70 38 77 38; www.86champs.com; 86 av Champs-Élysées, 8e; ⏲8.30am-11.30pm Sun-Thu, to 12.30am Fri & Sat; Ⓜ George V) A swirling fantasy of floral aromas – verveine, rose, lavender – lures visitors into this opulent shrine to French pastries. It's half Pierre Hermé (of macaron fame), half Occitane (Provençe-themed beauty products); after you're done browsing the boutique, head to the horseshoe-shaped dessert bar in the back, where you can dine on whimsical creations prepared in front of you.

MINI PALAIS FRENCH €€

Map p368 (☎01 42 56 42 42; www.minipalais.com; av Winston Churchill, 8e; mains €17-39; ⏲kitchen 10am-midnight, bar to 2am; Ⓜ Champs-Élysées–Clemenceau, Invalides) Set inside the fabulous Grand Palais (p96), the Mini Palais resembles an artist's studio on a colossal scale, with unvarnished hardwood floors, industrial lights suspended from ceiling beams and a handful of plaster casts on display. Its sizzling success means that the crowd is anything but bohemian; dress to impress for a taste of the lauded modern cuisine.

LASSERRE GASTRONOMY €€€

Map p368 (☎01 43 59 02 13; www.restaurant-lasserre.com; 17 av Franklin D Roosevelt, 8e; 3-course lunch menu €60, tasting menu €190, mains €85-130; ⏲noon-2pm Thu & Fri, 7-10pm Tue-Sat; Ⓜ Franklin D Roosevelt) Since 1942, this exceedingly elegant restaurant in the Triangle d'Or has hosted style icons, including Audrey Hepburn, and is still a superlative choice for a Michelin-starred meal to remember. A bellhop-attended lift (elevator), white-and-gold chandeliered decor, extraordinary retractable roof and flawless service set the stage for inspired creations like roast blue lobster *à la Parisienne* with tarragon sauce. Observe the dress code.

MAKOTO AOKI FRENCH €€€

Map p368 (☎01 43 59 29 24; 19 rue Jean Mermoz, 8e; 3-course/tasting menu €38/68; ⏲noon-2pm Mon-Fri, 7.30-9.30pm Tue-Sat; Ⓜ Franklin D Roosevelt) In an *arrondissement* known for grandiose interiors and superstar chefs who are often elsewhere, this intimate neighbourhood restaurant is a real find. The Japanese chef is a French-trained *haute cuisine* perfectionist; lunch might include an extravagant bacon-morel brioche; dinner a divine risotto with John Dory or truffles.

PHILIPPE & JEAN-PIERRE FRENCH €€€

Map p368 (☎01 47 23 57 80; 7 rue du Boccador, 8e; 4-/5-course menu €44/54, mains €26-43; ⏲noon-2.15pm Mon-Fri, 7.15-10.45pm Mon-Sat; Ⓜ Alma Marceau) Philippe graciously oversees the elegant, white-tableclothed dining room, while co-owner Jean-Pierre helms the kitchen. Seasonal menus incorporate dishes like cauliflower cream soup with mushrooms and truffles, sautéed scallops with leek and Granny Smith sauce, and melt-in-the-middle *moelleux au chocolat* cake. Given the service, quality and gilt-edged Triangle d'Or location, prices are almost a bargain.

Grands Boulevards

★RICHER BISTRO €

Map p370 (www.lericher.com; 2 rue Richer, 9e; mains €17-21; ⏲noon-2.30pm & 7.30-10.30pm; Ⓜ Poissonière, Bonne Nouvelle) Run by the same team as across-the-street neighbour L'Office (p102), Richer's pared-back, exposed-brick decor is a smart setting for genius creations like smoked duck breast

Neighbourhood Walk
Arc de Triomphe to Palais Garnier

START ARC DE TRIOMPHE
END PALAIS GARNIER
LENGTH 3.5KM; TWO HOURS

Paris is at its most glamorous along this walk, which takes you from the Arc de Triomphe along the famed av des Champs-Élysées to the opulent Palais Garnier opera house.

The city's sense of grandeur peaks beneath the mighty 1 **Arc de Triomphe** (p94). Access is via the pedestrian tunnels beneath the roundabout.

A dozen avenues radiate from the Étoile, including the incomparable 2 **av des Champs-Élysées** (p96). Take your time strolling this broad, tree-shaded avenue past car showrooms and luxury shops.

Parkland unfolds at the Champs-Élysées Marcel Dassault roundabout; turn right on av Franklin D Roosevelt then left on av du Général Eisenhower: on your right is the gorgeous 3 **Grand Palais** (p96), built for the 1900 World's Fair.

Heading south across av Winston Churchill, you'll arrive at the smaller but equally striking art nouveau 4 **Petit Palais** (p96), also built for the 1900 World's Fair.

Beyond the Petit Palais, turn left on av Dutuit onto the Champs-Élysées, continuing east to 5 **place de la Concorde** (p97), the vast square between the Champs-Élysées and the Jardin des Tuileries, with 360-degree views taking in the Eiffel Tower and Seine. The pink granite obelisk marks the site of a French Revolution guillotine.

Turn left on rue Royale to place de la Madeleine. The Greek-temple-style 6 **Église de la Madeleine** (p98) dominates the centre, while the place itself is home to some of the city's finest gourmet shops, as well as the colourful Marché aux Fleurs Madeleine flower market, trading since 1832.

Continue north along rue Tronchet and right onto bd Haussmann. On your left you'll see the *grands magasins* (department stores) Le Printemps then 7 **Galeries Lafayette** (p104) – be sure to head inside and up to the rooftop for a fabulous, free panorama.

Turn right on rue Halévy to reach the resplendent 8 **Palais Garnier** (p97).

ravioli in miso broth, and quince and lime cheesecake for dessert. It doesn't take reservations, but it serves snacks and Chinese tea, and has a full bar (open until midnight). Fantastic value.

HELMUT NEWCAKE BAKERY €

Map p370 (☎09 81 31 28 31; www.helmutnewcake.com; 28 rue Vignon, 9e; plats du jour €6.80-11.50; ⏰11am-7pm Tue-Sat; Ⓜ Madeleine) Combining the French genius for pastries with a 100% gluten-free kitchen, Helmut Newcake is one of those Parisian addresses that some will simply have to hang on to. Eclairs, fondants, cheesecake and tarts are some of the dessert options, while you can count on lunch (salads, quiches, soups, pizzas) to be scrumptious and market driven. Takeaway only.

SUPERNATURE CANTINE HEALTH FOOD €

Map p370 (☎01 47 70 21 03; www.super-nature.fr; 12 rue de Trévise, 9e; mains from €15.50; ⏰noon-2.30pm Mon-Fri, 11.30am-3.30pm Sun; Ⓜ Cadet, Grands Boulevards) Clever veggie creations at this funky organic cafe and **restaurant** (Map p370; ☎01 42 46 58 04; 15 rue de Trévise, 9e; mains €17-18; ⏰noon-2.30pm & 7.30-10pm Mon-Sat) include curried split-pea soup, and cantaloupe, pumpkin seed and feta salad but, being France, it's not all legumes – you can still order a healthy cheeseburger with sprouts.

A takeaway **branch** (Map p370; 8 rue de Trévise, 9e; sandwiches & soups from €4.90; ⏰11.30am-2pm Mon-Fri) two doors down serves salads and thick slices of sweet potato and gorgonzola quiche.

CHEZ PLUME ROTISSERIE €

Map p370 (☎01 48 78 65 43; www.chezplume.fr; 6 rue des Martyrs, 9e; dishes €8.40-8.90; ⏰10.15am-2.30pm & 5-8.30pm Mon-Fri, 9.30am-9pm Sat, 9.30am-3pm Sun; Ⓜ Notre Dame de Lorette) This rotisserie specialises in free-range chicken from southwest France, prepared in a variety of fashions: simply roasted, as a crumble, or even in a quiche or sandwich. It's wonderfully casual: add a side or two (potatoes, polenta, seasonal veggies) and pull up a counter seat.

CHÉRI CHARLOT SANDWICHES €

Map p370 (☎09 80 41 78 27; www.chericharlot.com; 33 rue Richer, 9e; sandwiches €8-13; ⏰noon-3pm Mon-Fri, 6.30-10pm Tue-Fri; Ⓜ Cadet) If every French cheese had a charcuterie soulmate, who would be paired up with whom? This tiny deli seeks to answer this question with its excellent choice of sandwiches: Le Serra (Saint Nectaire, Serrano ham), Le Rai (Comté, Speck) and Le Chon (Reblochon, smoked bacon) are just some of its delicious creations. A glass of wine and sandwich will set you back a mere €9.50.

LE VALENTIN CAFE €

Map p370 (☎01 47 70 88 50; http://restaurantparis9.fr; 30-32 passage Jouffroy, 9e; dishes €8-14.50; ⏰8.30am-7.30pm Mon-Sat, 10am-7pm Sun; Ⓜ Grands Boulevards) Inside beautiful covered arcade passage Jouffroy, this enchanting, two-storeyed *salon de thé* (tea house) slash patisserie slash *chocolaterie* is an equally lovely spot for breakfast, light lunches like quiches, salads, *feuilletés* (savoury-filled puff pastries) and brochettes (skewers), and dozens of varieties of tea, accompanied by exquisite *tartelettes* and delectable cakes.

LES PÂTES VIVANTES CHINESE €

Map p370 (☎01 45 23 10 21; www.lespatesvivantes.net; 46 du Faubourg Montmartre, 9e; noodles €9.80-12; ⏰noon-3pm & 7-11pm; Ⓜ Le Peletier) This is one of the only spots in Paris for *là miàn* (hand-pulled noodles) made to order in the age-old northern Chinese tradition. It packs in a crowd, so arrive early to stake out a table on the ground floor and watch the nimble noodle-maker work his magic.

DÉTOUR FRENCH €€

Map p370 (☎01 45 26 21 48; www.facebook.com/DetourRestaurant; 15 rue de la Tour des Dames, 9e; lunch menu €28, dinner menu €35-50; ⏰noon-1.30pm Wed-Sat, 7.30-10.30pm Tue-Sat; Ⓜ Trinité) As the name suggests, Adrien Cachot's 16-seat neobistro is off the beaten path, both literally and figuratively. Diners choose between just two options (meat or fish), leaving the rest in the hands of the highly original chef. Expect dishes like sweet carrots puréed with miso and topped with shaved Mimolette, or veal tartare with coffee vinaigrette and truffled egg cream.

ABRI SOBA JAPANESE €€

Map p370 (☎01 45 23 51 68; 10 rue Saulnier, 9e; lunch €9-18, shared plates €9-20; ⏰noon-2pm Tue-Sat, 7-10.30pm Tue-Sun; Ⓜ Cadet) A team of Japanese chefs in blue aprons calls out orders from Katsuaki Okiyama's open kitchen, while diners feast on delectable small plates in the natural wood interior. Sample the delightfully chewy soba noodles in one

LOCAL KNOWLEDGE

GOURMET FOOD SHOPS: PLACE DE LA MADELEINE

Ultragourmet food shops garland **place de la Madeleine** (Map p370; place de la Madeleine, 8e; MMadeleine); many have in-house dining options. Notable names include: **La Maison de la Truffe** (Map p370; 01 42 65 53 22; www.maison-de-la-truffe.com; 19 place de la Madeleine, 8e; 10am-10pm Mon-Sat; MMadeleine) Truffle dealers.

Hédiard (Map p370; 01 43 12 88 88; www.hediard.fr; 21 place de la Madeleine, 8e; MMadeleine) Luxury food shop ; reopening in 2019 after head-to-toe renovations.

Boutique Maille (Map p370; www.maille.com; 6 place de la Madeleine, 8e; 10am-7pm Mon-Sat; MMadeleine) Mustard specialist.

Fauchon (Map p370; 01 70 39 38 00; www.fauchon.fr; 26 & 30 place de la Madeleine, 8e; 10am-8.30pm Mon-Sat; MMadeleine) Paris' most famous caterer, with mouthwatering delicacies from foie gras to jams, chocolates and pastries.

Patrick Roger (Map p370; 09 67 08 24 47; www.patrickroger.com; 3 place de la Madeleine, 8e; 10.30am-7.30pm; MMadeleine) Extravagant chocolate sculptures.

of 15 ways – our favourite was cold with sesame sauce – alongside lightly battered, crisp tempura vegetables or an assortment of sashimi.

MAMOU — BISTRO €€

Map p370 (01 44 63 09 25; 42 rue Taitbout, 9e; 2-/3-course lunch menu €19/22, mains €21-26; noon-2.30pm Mon-Fri, 7.30-10.30pm Wed-Fri; MChaussée d'Antin) Fans of *haute cuisine* sans *haute* attitude should seek out this casual bistro by the Palais Garnier (p97). Chef Romain Lalu, who previously worked at Michelin-starred icons, runs the kitchen, and diners can expect all the playful flavour combos of a chef free to follow his whims, such as salmon gravlax with beetroot. There's an excellent natural wine selection. Reserve ahead.

LE BON GEORGES — BISTRO €€

Map p370 (01 48 78 40 30; http://lebongeorges.com; 45 rue St-Georges, 9e; 2-course lunch menu €21, mains €24-32; 12.15-2.30pm Mon-Fri, 7.15-10.45pm Sun-Fri; MSt-Georges) For a classic French meal, look no further. Le Bon Georges thrives on nostalgia, focusing on personable service (the proprietor works the room himself) and a hearty bistro menu consisting of standards like cheesy onion soup, shoulder of lamb and a delicious steak tartare. Beef from the Polmard butchers (who raise their own cattle) and seasonal produce are guaranteed.

L'OFFICE — FRENCH €€

Map p370 (01 47 70 67 31; www.office-resto.com; 3 rue Richer, 9e; 2-/3-course lunch menus €22/27, mains €23-29; noon-2pm & 7.30-10.30pm Mon-Fri; MPoissonière, Bonne Nouvelle) Don't judge this one by the simple chalkboard descriptions ('beef/polenta'), which belie the rich and complex flavours emerging from the kitchen. The market-inspired menu is mercifully short – as in there are only two choices for lunch – but outstanding. Alternatively, cross the street to its sleek sibling, Richer (p101).

LE J'GO — FRENCH €€

Map p370 (01 40 22 09 09; www.lejgo.com; 4 rue Drouot, 9e; 2-/3-course lunch menus €18/22, mains €24-29; noon-3pm & 6-11.30pm Tue-Sat; MRichelieu Drouot) With sunflower-coloured walls decorated with bullfighting posters, this contemporary bistro magics you away to southwestern France – perfect on a grey Parisian day. Flavourful regional cooking is based around the rotisserie and other Gascogne standards like *cassoulet* and foie gras.

The roasting takes a minimum 20 minutes, giving you the opportunity to sample a choice selection of sunny southern wines.

BIEN ÉLEVÉ — FRENCH €€

Map p370 (01 45 81 44 35; www.bieneleve.fr; 47 rue Richer, 9e; lunch/dinner menus €19/36; noon-2.30pm & 7.30-10pm Tue-Sat; MLe Peletier) For those days when all you need is a simple grilled steak or roast chicken, there's Bien Élevé. It's all about sourcing at this convivial bistro (as indicated by the tongue-in-cheek name, meaning 'well raised', but generally used to describe children), and each type of meat or fish comes from one specific producer. Good wine list too.

DRINKING & NIGHTLIFE

The Champs-Élysées is home to a mix of exclusive nightspots, tourist haunts and a handful of large dance clubs that party all night. As a rule, you'll want to look as chic as possible to get in the door.

Champs-Élysées

HONOR COFFEE

Map p368 (www.honor-cafe.com; 54 rue du Faubourg St-Honoré, 8e; ⌚9am-6pm Mon-Sat; Ⓜ Madeleine) Hidden off ritzy rue du Faubourg St-Honoré in a courtyard adjoining fashion house Comme des Garçons is Paris' 'first and only outdoor independent coffee shop', an opaque-plastic-sheltered black-and-white timber kiosk brewing coffee from small-scale producers around the globe. It also serves luscious cakes, filled-to-bursting lunchtime sandwiches, quiches and salads (dishes €5 to €10.50), along with fresh juices, wine and beer.

BLAINE COCKTAIL BAR

Map p368 (☎06 60 97 01 35; www.blainebar.com; 65 rue Pierre Charron, 8e; ⌚7pm-2am Tue-Thu, 9pm-4am Fri & Sat; Ⓜ Franklin D Roosevelt) Hidden in plain sight is this underground speakeasy: enter through an unmarked black door, relay the password (hint: contact them on social media) and enter into a re-created Prohibition-era bar. Elaborate cocktails start at €15; there's occasional live jazz and DJ sets.

ZIG ZAG CLUB CLUB

Map p368 (http://zigzagclub.fr; 32 rue Marbeuf, 8e; ⌚11.30pm-7am Fri & Sat; Ⓜ Franklin D Roosevelt) With star DJs, a great sound and light system, and a spacious dance floor, Zig Zag has some of the hippest electro beats in western Paris. It can be pricey, but it still fills up quickly, so don't start the party too late.

BUGSY'S PUB

Map p368 (☎01 42 68 18 44; http://bugsys.fr; 15 rue Montalivet, 8e; ⌚noon-1am Mon-Sat; Ⓜ Miromesnil) There aren't many bars in western Paris that come attitude-free, so if you're in search of a friendly welcome to pair with a beer and burger, Bugsy's is for you. It gets crowded, though.

Grands Boulevards

PANPAN BAR

Map p370 (☎01 42 46 36 06; 32 rue Drouot, 9e; ⌚10am-2am Mon-Fri, 6pm-2am Sat; Ⓜ Le Peletier) This unassuming locals' hangout doesn't even bother with a sign, but it keeps things interesting with activities, like blind taste tests, throughout the week. Happy hour from 6pm to 8pm.

AU GÉNÉRAL LA FAYETTE BAR

Map p370 (☎01 47 70 59 08; http://augenerallafayette.fr; 52 rue la Fayette, 9e; ⌚8am-1am; 📶; Ⓜ Le Peletier) With its archetypal belle époque decor (brass fittings, polished wood, large murals) and excellent wines by the glass, this old-style brasserie is an atmospheric spot for an afternoon coffee or evening drink.

IBRIK CAFE

Map p370 (☎01 73 71 84 60; www.ibrik.fr; 43 rue Laffitte, 9e; ⌚8.30am-5pm Mon-Fri, 11.30am-5.30pm Sat; Ⓜ Notre-Dame-de-Lorette) Nothing will warm your heart more on a rainy day than popping into this two-floor coffee shop for a shot of cortado or rich hot chocolate. Bare concrete floors and a single coat of primer on the walls only adds to the quirky appeal. Mezze and pita sandwiches served at lunch.

ENTERTAINMENT

Entertainment in the Champs-Élysées and Grands Boulevards neighbourhoods revolves around the landmark Palais Garnier, which stages opera and ballet performances. A handful of smaller music venues are located further east, where you can catch lesser-known acts passing through Paris.

PALAIS GARNIER OPERA, BALLET

Map p370 (place de l'Opéra, 9e; Ⓜ Opéra) The city's original opera house (p97) is smaller than its Bastille counterpart, but has perfect acoustics. Due to its odd shape, some seats have limited or no visibility – book carefully. Ticket prices and conditions (including last-minute discounts) are available from the **box office** (Map p370; ☎international calls 01 71 25 24 23, within France 08 92 89 90 90; www.operadeparis.fr; cnr rues Scribe & Auber; ⌚10am-6.30pm Mon-Sat; Ⓜ Opéra). Online flash sales are held from noon on Wednesdays.

L'OLYMPIA LIVE MUSIC

Map p370 (08 92 68 33 68; www.olympiahall.com; 28 bd des Capucines, 9e; MMadeleine, Opéra) Opened by the founder of the Moulin Rouge in 1888, the Olympia has hosted all the big names over the years, from Édith Piaf to Jimi Hendrix, Jeff Buckley and the Arctic Monkeys, though it's small enough to put on a fairly intimate show.

SALLE PLEYEL LIVE MUSIC

Map p368 (01 76 49 43 13; www.sallepleyel.com; 252 rue du Faubourg St-Honoré, 8e; ; MTernes) Having mostly moved on from classical music following the opening of the Philharmonie de Paris (p138), this concert hall now hosts performers such as Patricia Kaas, the Pretenders, Status Quo and Jamiroquai, as well as acts like the Ballet Nacional de Cuba.

FOLIES-BERGÈRE LIVE MUSIC

Map p370 (08 92 68 16 50; www.foliesbergere.com; 32 rue Richer, 9e; MCadet) This is the legendary club where Charlie Chaplin, WC Fields and Stan Laurel appeared on stage together one night in 1911, and where Josephine Baker – accompanied by her diamond-collared pet cheetah and wearing only stilettos and a skirt made from bananas – bewitched audience members including Hemingway. Today shows span everything from solo acts such as Ben Harper and Damien Rice to musicals.

SHOPPING

Global chains line the Champs-Élysées, but it's the luxury fashion houses in the Triangle d'Or and on rue du Faubourg St-Honoré that have made Paris famous. The area around Opéra and the Grands Boulevards is where you'll find flagship *grands magasins* (department stores).

★GALERIES LAFAYETTE DEPARTMENT STORE

Map p370 (01 42 82 34 56; http://haussmann.galerieslafayette.com; 40 bd Haussmann, 9e; 9.30am-8.30pm Mon-Sat, 11am-7pm Sun; ; MChaussée d'Antin or RER Auber) Grande-dame department store Galeries Lafayette is spread across the main store (whose magnificent stained-glass dome is over a century old), men's store, and homewares store with a gourmet emporium.

Catch modern art in the 1st-floor **gallery** (Map p370; 01 42 82 81 98; www.galeriedesgaleries.com; 11am-7pm Tue-Sun) FREE, take in a **fashion show** (Map p370; bookings 01 42 82 81 98; 3pm Fri Mar-Jun & Sep-Dec by reservation), ascend to a free, windswept rooftop panorama, or take a break at one of its 24 restaurants and cafes.

The main store will stay open during renovations by architect Amanda Levete's studio AL_A. On the av des Champs-Élysées, a new Galeries Lafayette **store** (Map p368; www.galerieslafayette.com; 52 av Champs-Élysées; MFranklin D Roosevelt) is under construction and is expected to open in 2019.

LANCEL FASHION & ACCESSORIES

Map p368 (01 42 25 18 35; www.lancel.com; 4 Rond Point des Champs-Élysées, 8e; 10am-8pm Mon-Sat, to 7pm Sun; MFranklin D Roosevelt) Open racks of luscious totes fill this handbag designer's gleaming premises.

À LA MÈRE DE FAMILLE FOOD & DRINKS

Map p370 (01 47 70 83 69; www.lameredefamille.com; 35 rue du Faubourg Montmartre, 9e; 9.30am-8pm Mon-Sat, 10am-7.30pm Sun; MLe Peletier) Founded in 1761, this is the original location of Paris' oldest chocolatier. Its beautiful belle époque façade is as enchanting as the rainbow of sweets, caramels and chocolates inside.

HÔTEL DROUOT ART, ANTIQUES

Map p370 (01 48 00 20 20; www.drouot.com; 7-9 rue Drouot, 9e; 11am-6pm Mon-Fri, to 11pm Thu; MRichelieu Drouot) Selling everything from antiques and jewellery to rare books and art, Paris' most established auction house has been in business for more than a century. Viewings are from 11am to 6pm the day before and from 11am to noon the morning of the auction. Pick up the catalogue *Gazette de l'Hôtel Drouot,* published Fridays, in-house or at newsstands.

LES CAVES AUGÉ WINE

Map p368 (01 45 22 16 97; www.cavesauge.com; 116 bd Haussmann, 8e; 10am-7.30pm Mon-Sat; MSt-Augustin) Founded in 1850, this fantastic wine shop, with bottles stacked in every conceivable nook and cranny, should be your first choice if you trust the taste of Marcel Proust, who was a regular customer. The shop organises tastings every other Saturday (see website), where you can meet local winemakers from different regions.

HISTORIC HAUTE COUTURE

A stroll around the legendary Triangle d'Or (bordered by avs George V, Champs-Élysées and Montaigne, 8e) or on rue du Faubourg St-Honoré constitutes the walk of fame of exclusive French fashion. Rubbing shoulders with the world's top international designers are Paris' most influential French fashion houses:

Chanel (Map p368; ☎01 44 50 73 00; www.chanel.com; 42 av Montaigne, 8e; ⏰10am-7pm; Ⓜ George V)

Chloé (Map p368; ☎01 47 23 00 08; www.chloe.com; 50 av Montaigne, 8e; ⏰10.30am-7pm Mon-Sat; Ⓜ Franklin D Roosevelt)

Dior (Map p368; ☎01 45 63 12 51; www.dior.com; 30 av Montaigne, 8e; ⏰10am-7pm Mon-Sat, 1-9pm Sun; Ⓜ George V)

Givenchy (Map p368; ☎01 44 43 99 90; www.givenchy.com; 36 av Montaigne, 8e; ⏰10am-7pm Mon-Sat, 1-7pm Sun; Ⓜ George V)

Hermès (Map p368; ☎01 40 17 46 00; www.hermes.com; 24 rue du Faubourg St-Honoré, 8e; ⏰10.30am-6.30pm Mon-Sat; Ⓜ Concorde)

Lanvin (Map p368; ☎01 44 71 31 73; www.lanvin.com; 22 rue du Faubourg St-Honoré, 8e; ⏰10.30am-7pm Mon-Sat; Ⓜ Concorde)

Louis Vuitton (Map p368; ☎01 53 57 52 00; www.louisvuitton.com; 101 av des Champs-Élysées, 8e; ⏰10am-8pm Mon-Sat, 11am-7pm Sun; Ⓜ George V)

Saint Laurent (Map p368; ☎01 42 65 74 59; www.ysl.com; 38 rue du Faubourg St-Honoré, 8e; ⏰10.30am-7.30pm Mon-Sat; Ⓜ Concorde)

ERES — FASHION & ACCESSORIES

Map p370 (☎01 47 42 28 82; www.eresparis.com; 2 rue Tronchet, 8e; ⏰10am-7pm Mon-Sat; Ⓜ Madeleine) Women who have despaired of buying a swimsuit in the past will understand why those designed by Eres have become a must-have item. The stunning suits are cut to flatter all shapes and sizes, with bikini tops and bottoms sold separately. It also stocks magnificent lingerie.

LA MAISON DU MIEL — FOOD & DRINKS

Map p370 (☎01 47 42 26 70; www.maisondumiel.com; 24 rue Vignon, 9e; ⏰9.30am-7pm Mon-Sat; Ⓜ Madeleine) In this sticky, very sweet business since 1898, 'the Honey House' stocks more than 50 kinds of honey, with such flavours as Corsican chestnut flower, Turkish pine and Tasmanian leatherwood.

LE PRINTEMPS — DEPARTMENT STORE

Map p370 (☎01 42 82 50 00; www.printemps.com; 64 bd Haussmann, 9e; ⏰9.35am-8pm Mon-Sat, to 8.45pm Thu, 11am-7pm Sun; 📶; Ⓜ Havre Caumartin) Famous department store Le Printemps encompasses Le Printemps de la Mode, for women's fashion, and **Le Printemps de l'Homme** (Map p370; rue de Provence, 9e; Ⓜ Havre Caumartin), for men's fashion, both with established and up-and-coming designer wear. Le Printemps de la Beauté et Maison, for beauty and homewares, offers a staggering display of perfume, cosmetics and accessories. There's a free panoramic rooftop terrace and luxury eateries, including Ladurée.

GUERLAIN — PERFUME

Map p368 (☎spa 01 45 62 11 21; www.guerlain.com; 68 av des Champs-Élysées, 8e; ⏰10.30am-8pm Mon-Sat, noon-8pm Sun; Ⓜ Franklin D Roosevelt) Guerlain is Paris' most famous parfumerie, and its shop (dating from 1912) is one of the most beautiful in the city. With its shimmering mirror and marble art deco interior, it's a reminder of the former glory of the Champs-Élysées. For total indulgence, make an appointment at its heavenly spa.

BARBARA BUI — FASHION & ACCESSORIES

Map p368 (☎01 42 66 05 87; www.barbarabui.com; 62 rue du Faubourg Saint-Honoré, 8e; ⏰10am-7pm Mon-Sat; Ⓜ Étienne Marcel) Paris-born designer Barbara Bui opened Kabuki in 1983 and currently has three boutiques in the capital, selling prêt-à-porter, shoes, handbags and accessories.

MARCHÉ AUX FLEURS MADELEINE — MARKET

Map p370 (place de la Madeleine, 8e; ⏰8am-7.30pm Mon-Sat; Ⓜ Madeleine) This colourful flower market has been trading since 1832.

Louvre & Les Halles

Neighbourhood Top Five

❶ **Musée du Louvre** (p108) Getting lost in the mother of all museums, with timeless masterpieces every which way you turn.

❷ **Centre Pompidou** (p116) Contemplating Europe's largest collection of modern art and admiring the view from the top of one of the city's most whimsical buildings.

❸ **Jardin des Tuileries** (p118) Meeting Monet's waterlilies, having a picnic in the park and revelling in Paris at its symmetrical best.

❹ **Église St-Eustache** (p119) Feasting on exquisite sacred art and soulful music in this Gothic landmark.

❺ **Jardin du Palais Royal** (p120) Browsing designer boutiques beneath the arcaded galleries and letting the kids run free amid Daniel Buren's zebra-striped columns.

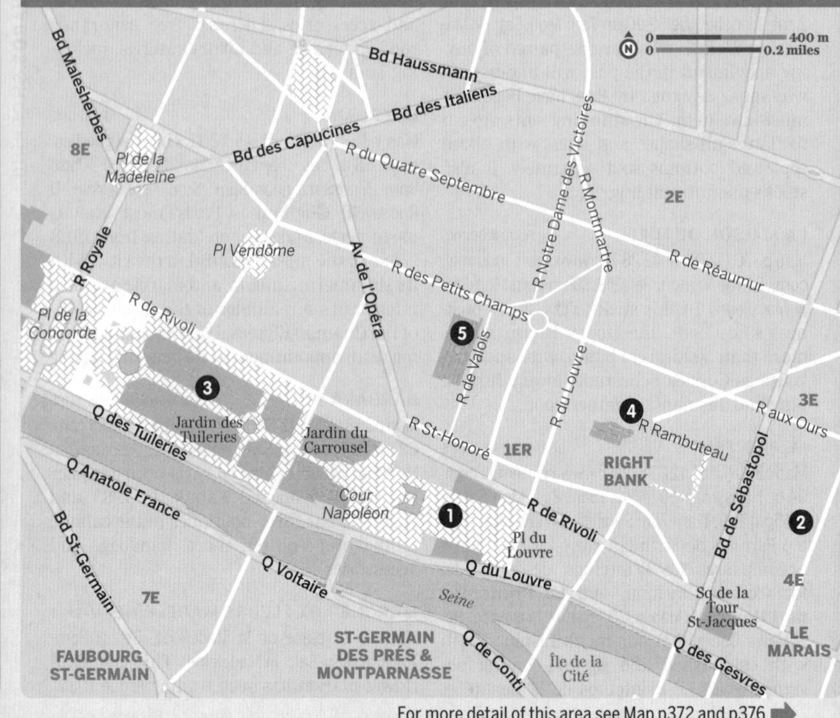

For more detail of this area see Map p372 and p376

Explore Louvre & Les Halles

The banks of the Seine make an enchanting starting point. A wonderful exploratory loop snakes westwards along quai des Tuileries, past the sculptures and green lawns of Jardin des Tuileries (p118), to the Musée de l'Orangerie (p118) and Jeu de Paume (p118). Continue north to ritzy place Vendôme (p120), then loop back along shop-chic rue St-Honoré to the Palais Royal (p120).

Set aside at least half a day for the Musée du Louvre (p108). Avoid museum fatigue by combining the often-intimidating gallery with a long lunch or a picnic and invigorating mooch around the gardens of Jardin du Palais Royal. Serious art lovers will likewise want to set aside a half-day minimum for the Centre Pompidou (p116).

Once you cross rue du Louvre into Les Halles, the timeless sophistication of the Louvre area is replaced with the bright lights, jostling crowds and swinging jazz clubs of rue des Lombards. The mainly pedestrian zone between the Centre Pompidou and Forum des Halles (p121; with rue Étienne Marcel to the north and rue de Rivoli to the south) is packed with people, just as it was for the 850-odd years when Paris' main *halles* (marketplace) was here.

Local Life

➡ **After-Work Drinks** Rue Montorgueil has a good selection of cafe-bars, but it is rue St-Saveur's cocktail clubs (p128) and the hip bars on rue Montmartre that steal the late-night show.

➡ **Museums** Visit during late-night openings (less crowded) or one-off cultural events and happenings.

➡ **Japantown** Busy rue St-Anne, just west of Jardin du Palais Royal, is loaded with Asian eateries, though the best choices are found in the side streets.

Getting There & Away

➡ **Metro & RER** The Louvre has two metro stations: Palais Royal–Musée du Louvre (lines 1 and 7) and Louvre Rivoli (line 1). Numerous metro and RER lines converge at Paris' main hub, Châtelet–Les Halles.

➡ **Bus** Major bus lines include the 27 from rue de Rivoli (for bd St-Michel and place d'Italie) and the 69 near the Louvre Rivoli metro (for Invalides and Eiffel Tower).

➡ **Bicycle** Stations at 1 place Ste-Marguerite de Navarre and 2 rue de Turbigo are best placed for the Châtelet–Les Halles metro/RER hub; for the Louvre pedal to/from 165 rue St-Honoré.

➡ **Boat** The hop-on, hop-off Batobus (p335) stops outside the Louvre.

Lonely Planet's Top Tip

Some of Paris' top tables are here, but you need to book in advance: plan at least a month ahead for a table at Frenchie (p127), Yam'Tcha (p127) or Verjus (p126). Frenchie has a neighbouring wine bar where you simply rock up and wait for a stool so you can feast on lighter creations from the same talented chefs.

Best Places to Eat

➡ Frenchie (p127)

➡ Verjus (p126)

➡ Uma (p123)

➡ Balagan (p123)

➡ Maison Maison (p123)

➡ Chez La Vieille (p123)

For reviews, see p121 ➡

Best Places to Drink

➡ Experimental Cocktail Club (p128)

➡ Bar Hemingway (p127)

➡ Le Garde Robe (p128)

➡ Danico (p128)

➡ L'Ivress (p129)

For reviews, see p127 

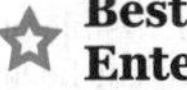

Best Entertainment

➡ Le Grand Rex (p129)

➡ La Place (p130)

➡ Comédie Française (p130)

➡ Louvre Auditorium (p130)

➡ Le Baiser Salé (p128)

For reviews, see p130 ➡

SAILORR / SHUTTERSTOCK ©

TOP SIGHT
MUSÉE DU LOUVRE

Few art galleries are as prized or as daunting as the Louvre, Paris' pièce de résistance that no first-time visitor to the city can resist. This is, after all, one of the world's largest and most diverse museums, showcasing 35,000 works of art. It would take nine months to glance at every piece, rendering advance planning essential.

Palais du Louvre

The Louvre today rambles over four floors and through three wings: the Sully Wing creates the four sides of the Cour Carrée (literally 'Square Courtyard') at the eastern end of the complex; the Denon Wing stretches 800m along the Seine to the south; and the northern Richelieu Wing skirts rue de Rivoli. The building started life as a fortress built by Philippe-Auguste in the 12th century – medieval remnants are still visible on the lower ground floor (Sully). In the 16th century it became a royal residence and after the Revolution, in 1793, it was turned it into a national museum. Its booty was no more than 2500 paintings and objets d'art.

Over the centuries French governments amassed the paintings, sculptures and artefacts displayed today. The 'Grand Louvre' project inaugurated by the late President Mitterrand in 1989 doubled the museum's exhibition space, and both new and renovated galleries have since opened, including the state-of-the-art Islamic art galleries (lower ground floor, Denon) in the stunningly restored Cour Visconti.

DON'T MISS

- Mesopotamian and Egyptian collections
- 1st floor, Denon Wing
- *Mona Lisa*

PRACTICALITIES

- Map p372, F7
- ☎01 40 20 53 17
- www.louvre.fr
- rue de Rivoli & quai des Tuileries, 1er
- adult/child €15/free
- 9am-6pm Mon, Thu, Sat & Sun, to 9.45pm Wed & Fri
- Ⓜ Palais Royal–Musée du Louvre

Mona Lisa

Easily the Louvre's most admired work (and world's most famous painting) is Leonardo da Vinci's *La Joconde* (in French; *La Gioconda* in Italian), the lady with that enigmatic smile known as *Mona Lisa* (Room 6, 1st floor, Denon). For centuries admirers speculated on everything about the painting, from the possibility that the subject was mourning the death of a loved one to the possibility that she might have been in love or in bed with her portraitist.

Mona (*monna* in Italian) is a contraction of *madonna,* and Gioconda is the feminine form of the surname Giocondo. Canadian scientists used infrared technology to peer through paint layers and confirm the identity of the *Mona Lisa* as Lisa Gherardini (1479–1542?), wife of Florentine merchant Francesco de Giocondo. Scientists also discovered that her dress was covered in a transparent gauze veil typically worn in early-16th-century Italy by pregnant women or new mothers; it's surmised that the work was painted to commemorate the birth of her second son around 1503, when she was aged about 24.

Priceless Antiquities

Whatever your plans are, don't rush by the Louvre's astonishing cache of treasures from antiquity: both Mesopotamia (ground floor, Richelieu) and Egypt (ground and 1st floors, Sully) are well represented, as seen in the *Code of Hammurabi* (Room 3, ground floor, Richelieu) and *The Seated Scribe* (Room 22, 1st floor, Sully). Room 12 (ground floor, Sully Wing) holds impressive friezes and an enormous **two-headed-bull column** from the Darius Palace in ancient Iran, while an enormous seated **statue of Pharaoh Ramesses II** highlights the temple room (Room 12, Sully).

Also worth a look are the mosaics and figurines from the Byzantine empire (lower ground floor, Denon), and the Greek statuary collection, culminating with the world's most famous armless duo, the **Venus de Milo** (Room 16, ground floor, Sully) and the **Winged Victory of Samothrace** (top of Daru staircase, 1st floor, Denon).

French & Italian Masterpieces

The 1st floor of the Denon Wing, where the *Mona Lisa* is found, is easily the most popular part of the Louvre - and with good reason. Rooms 75 through 77 are hung with monumental French paintings, many iconic: look for the *Consecration of the Emperor Napoléon I* (David), *The Raft of the Medusa* (Géricault) and *Grande Odalisque* (Ingres).

Rooms 1, 3, 5 and 8 are also must-visits. Filled with classic works by Renaissance masters (Raphael,

LOUIS XV'S CROWN

French kings wore their crowns only once – at their coronation. Lined with embroidered satin and topped with openwork arches and a fleur-de-lis, and crafted in 1722, Louis XV's crown (Room 66, 1st floor, Denon) was originally adorned with pearls, sapphires, rubies, topazes, emeralds and diamonds.

RENOVATING THE LOUVRE

In late 2014 the Louvre embarked on a 30-year renovation plan, with the aim of modernising the museum to make it more accessible. Phase 1 increased the number of main entrances to reduce security wait times (even still, buy tickets online or use the Paris Museum Pass; lines at the underground Carrousel du Louvre entrance are often shorter). It also revamped the central Hall Napoléon to vastly improve what was previously bewildering chaos. Important changes to come include increasing the number of English-language signs and artwork texts to aid navigation.

LOUVRE

Napoleon III Apartments
Richelieu Wing
The Seated Scribe
Sully Wing
Consecration of the Emperor Napoléon I
Denon Wing
The Raft of the Medusa
Mona Lisa
Winged Victory of Samothrace
Crown of Louis XV

First Floor

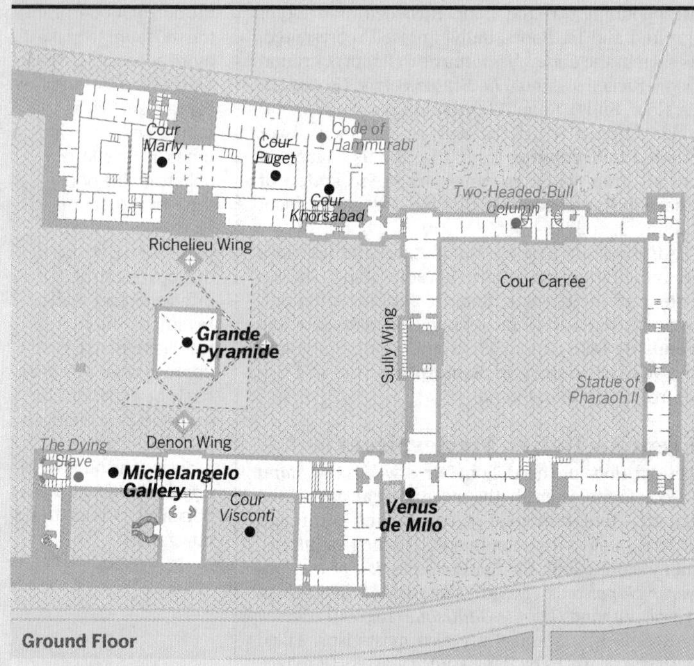

Ground Floor

Hall Napoléon

Titian, Uccello, Botticini), this area culminates in the crowds around the *Mona Lisa*. But you'll find plenty else to contemplate, from Botticelli's graceful frescoes (Room 1) to the superbly detailed *Wedding Feast at Cana* (Room 6). On the ground floor of the Denon Wing, take time for the Italian sculptures, including Michelangelo's *The Dying Slave* and Canova's *Psyche and Cupid* (Room 4).

Northern European Painting

The 2nd floor of the Richelieu Wing, directly above the gilt and crystal of the Napoleon III Apartments (1st floor), allows for a quieter meander through the Louvre's inspirational collection of Flemish and Dutch paintings spearheaded by works by Peter Paul Rubens and Pieter Bruegel the Elder. Vermeer's *The Lacemaker* can be found in Room 38, while Room 31 is devoted chiefly to works by Rembrandt.

Trails & Tours

Self-guided thematic trails range from Louvre masterpieces and the art of eating to family-friendly topics. Download trail brochures in advance from the website. Another good option is to rent a Nintendo 3DS multimedia guide (€5; ID required). More formal, English-language **guided tours** (Map p372; ☎01 40 20 52 63; adult/child €12/9; ⏲11am & 2pm except 1st Sun of month; Ⓜ Palais Royal–Musée du Louvre) depart from the Hall Napoléon. Reserve a spot by telephone up to 14 days in advance or sign up on arrival at the museum.

THE PYRAMID INSIDE & OUT

Almost as stunning as the masterpieces inside is the 21m-high glass pyramid designed by Chinese-born American architect IM Pei that bedecks the main entrance to the Louvre in a dazzling crown. Beneath Pei's Grande Pyramide is the Hall Napoléon, the museum's main entrance area. To revel in another Pei pyramid of equally dramatic dimensions, head towards the **Carrousel du Louvre** (Map p372; http://carrouseldulouvre.com; 99 rue de Rivoli, 1er; ⏲8.30am-11pm, shops 10am-8pm; 📶; Ⓜ Palais Royal–Musée du Louvre), a busy shopping mall that loops underground from the Grande Pyramide to the **Arc de Triomphe du Carrousel** (Map p376; place du Carrousel, 1er; Ⓜ Palais Royal–Musée du Louvre) – its centrepiece is Pei's Pyramide Inversée (inverted glass pyramid).

NEW ROOMS

In 2018, two new rooms were opened to the public on the 2nd floor of the Richelieu Wing, displaying a handful of artworks stolen during the Nazi occupation of France. Many objects were recovered by the French government after the war, though some of them went unclaimed by their original owners.

1

ARTEFACT / ALAMY STOCK PHOTO ©

2

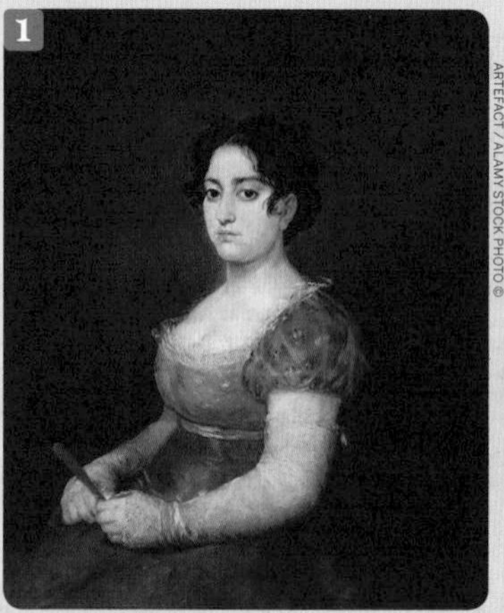

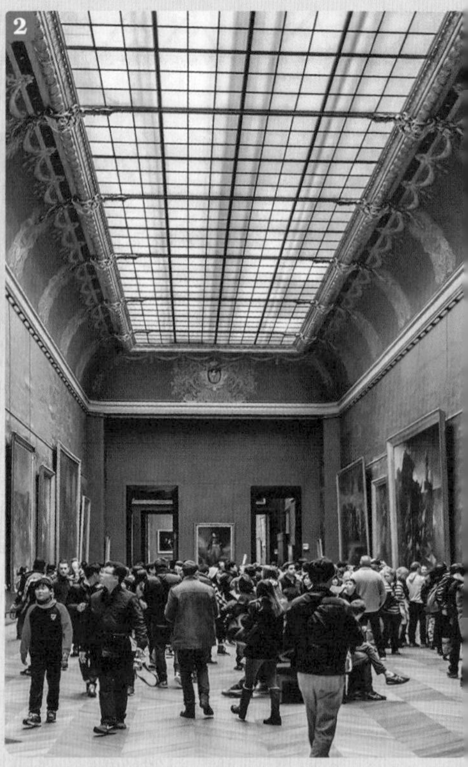

1. A portrait by Francisco Goya
This Spanish artist was an important figure in the romantic period.

2. Glass-ceilinged hall
The Palais du Louvre itself is a building of historic and architectural importance.

3. Winged Victory of Samothrace
Despite having long-since lost its head and arms, this statue of the goddess Nike remains impressive.

4. *Death of Sardanapalus* by Eugène Delacroix
The legend of decadent Assyrian king Sardanapalus and his outrageous demise also inspired a play by Byron.

4

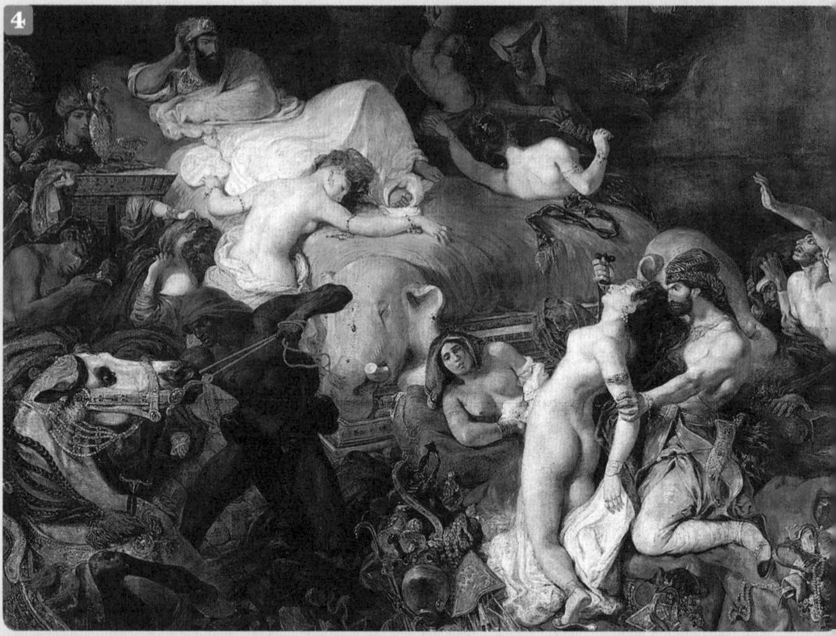

MURATART / ALAMY STOCK PHOTO ©

The Louvre

A HALF-DAY TOUR

Successfully visiting the Louvre is a fine art. Its complex labyrinth of galleries and staircases spiralling three wings and four floors renders discovery a snakes-and-ladders experience. Initiate yourself with this three-hour itinerary – a playful mix of *Mona Lisa*–obvious and up-to-the-minute unexpected.

Arriving in the newly renovated **1 Hall Napoléon** beneath IM Pei's glass pyramid, pick up colour-coded floor plans at an information stand, then ride the escalator up to the Sully Wing and swap passport or credit card for a multimedia guide (there are limited descriptions in the galleries) at the wing entrance.

The Louvre is as much about spectacular architecture as masterful art. To appreciate this, zip up and down Sully's Escalier Henri II to admire **2 Venus de Milo**, then up parallel Escalier Henri IV to the palatial displays in **3 Cour Khorsabad**. Cross Room 1 to find the escalator up to the 1st floor and the opulent **4 Napoleon III apartments**. Next traverse 25 consecutive galleries (thank you, floor plan!) to flip conventional contemplation on its head with Cy Twombly's **5 The Ceiling**, and the hypnotic **6 Winged Victory of Samothrace sculpture**, which brazenly insists on being admired from all angles. End with the impossibly famous **7 The Raft of the Medusa**, **8 Mona Lisa** and **9 Virgin & Child**.

TOP TIPS

➡ Don't even consider entering the Louvre's maze of galleries without a floor plan, free from the information desk in the Hall Napoléon.

➡ The Denon Wing is always packed; visit on late nights (Wednesday or Friday) or trade Denon in for the notably quieter Richelieu Wing.

➡ Tickets to the Louvre are valid for the whole day, meaning that you can nip out for lunch.

Napoleon III Apartments
1st Floor, Richelieu
Napoleon III's gorgeous gilt apartments were built from 1854 to 1861, featuring an over-the-top decor of gold leaf, stucco and crystal chandeliers that reaches a dizzying climax in the Grand Salon and State Dining Room.

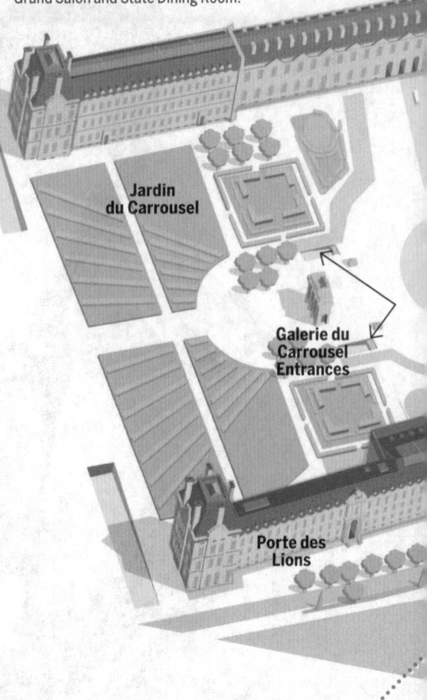

LOUVRE AUDITORIUM

Classical-music concerts are staged several times a week at the Louvre Auditorium (off the main entrance hall). Don't miss the Thursday lunchtime concerts featuring emerging composers and musicians. The season runs from September to April or May, depending on the concert series.

Mona Lisa
Room 6, 1st Floor, Denon
No smile is as enigmatic or bewitching as hers. Da Vinci's diminutive *La Joconde* hangs opposite the largest painting in the Louvre – sumptuous, fellow Italian Renaissance artwork *The Wedding at Cana*.

The Raft of the Medusa

Room 77, 1st Floor, Denon

Decipher the politics behind French romanticism in Théodore Géricault's *Raft of the Medusa.*

Cour Khorsabad

Ground Floor, Richelieu

Time travel with a pair of winged human-headed bulls to view some of the world's oldest Mesopotamian art. **DETOUR»** Night-lit statues in Cour Puget.

The Ceiling

Room 32, 1st Floor, Sully

Admire the blue shock of Cy Twombly's 400-sq-metre contemporary ceiling fresco – the Louvre's latest, daring commission. **DETOUR»** *The Braque Ceiling*, Room 33.

Rue de Rivoli Entrance

Cour Khorsabad

Cour Puget

Cour Marly

SULLY WING

Cour Carrée

RICHELIEU WING

Cour Napoléon

Pyramid Main Entrance

Inverted Pyramid

Cour Visconti

Pont des Arts

DENON WING

Pont du Carrousel

Venus de Milo

Room 16, Ground Floor, Sully

No one knows who sculpted this seductively realistic goddess from Greek antiquity. Naked to the hips, she is a Hellenistic masterpiece.

Winged Victory of Samothrace

Escalier Daru, 1st Floor, Sully

Draw breath at the aggressive dynamism of this headless, handless Hellenistic goddess. **DETOUR»** The razzle-dazzle of the Apollo Gallery's crown jewels.

Virgin & Child

Grande Galerie, 1st Floor, Denon

In the spirit of artistic devotion save the Louvre's most famous gallery for last: a feast of Virgin-and-child paintings by Da Vinci, Raphael, Domenico Ghirlandaio, Giovanni Bellini and Francesco Botticini.

TOP SIGHT
CENTRE POMPIDOU

CENTRE POMPIDOU, STUDIO PIANO + ROGERS, ARCHITECT. SCOTT NORSWORTHY / SHUTTERSTOCK ©

The Centre Pompidou has amazed and delighted visitors ever since it opened in 1977, not just for its outstanding collection of modern art but also for its radical architectural statement. The dynamic and vibrant arts centre delights and enthrals with its irresistible cocktail of galleries and exhibitions, hands-on workshops, dance performances, bookshop, design boutique, cinemas, a research library and other entertainment venues.

Musée National d'Art Moderne

Europe's largest collection of modern art fills the bright and airy, well-lit galleries of the National Museum of Modern Art, covering two complete floors of the Pompidou. For art lovers, this is one of the jewels of Paris. On a par with the permanent collection are the two temporary exhibition halls (on the ground floor/basement and the top floor), which showcase some memorable blockbuster exhibits. Also of note is the fabulous children's gallery on the 1st floor.

The permanent collection changes every two years, but the basic layout generally stays the same. The 5th floor showcases artists active between 1905 and 1970 (give or take a decade); the 4th floor focuses on more contemporary creations, roughly from the 1990s onward.

The dynamic presentation of the 5th floor mixes up works by Picasso, Matisse, Chagall and Kandinsky with lesser-known contemporaries from as far afield as Argentina and Japan, as well as more famous cross-Atlantic names such as Arbus, Warhol, Pollock and Rothko.

DON'T MISS

- The Musée National d'Art Moderne
- Cutting-edge temporary exhibitions
- The 6th floor and its sweeping panorama of Paris

PRACTICALITIES

- Map p376, F7
- ☎01 44 78 12 33
- www.centrepompidou.fr
- place Georges Pompidou, 4e
- museum, exhibitions & panorama adult/child €14/free, panorama only ticket €5/free
- 11am-9pm Wed-Mon, temporary exhibits to 11pm Thu
- M Rambuteau

One floor down on the 4th, you'll find monumental paintings, installation pieces, sculpture and video take centre stage. The focus here is on contemporary art, architecture and design.

Architecture & Views

Former French President Georges Pompidou wanted an ultracontemporary artistic hub and he got it: competition-winning architects Renzo Piano and Richard Rogers designed the building inside out, with utilitarian features like plumbing, pipes, air vents and electrical cables forming part of the external façade.

Viewed from a distance (such as from Sacré-Cœur), the Centre Pompidou's primary-coloured, boxlike form amid a sea of muted grey Parisian rooftops makes it look like a child's Meccano set abandoned on someone's elegant living-room rug. Although the Centre Pompidou is just six storeys high, the city's low-rise cityscape means stupendous views extend from its roof (reached by external escalators enclosed in tubes). Rooftop admission is included in museum and exhibition admission – or buy a panorama ticket (€5) just for the roof.

Atelier Brancusi

West of the Centre Pompidou main building, this reconstruction of the **studio** (Map p376; www.centrepompidou.fr; 55 rue de Rambuteau, 4e; incl in admission to Centre Pompidou €14/free; ⏲2-6pm Wed-Mon; Ⓜ Rambuteau) of Romanian-born sculptor Constantin Brancusi (1876–1957) – known for works such as *The Kiss* and *Bird in Space* – contains over 100 sculptures in stone and wood. You'll also find drawings, pedestals and photographic plates from his original Paris studio.

Tours & Guides

Guided tours in English take place at 2pm on Saturday and sometimes Sunday (€4.50; reserve online). The museum no longer provides audioguides; instead, visitors are encouraged to download the Centre Pompidou app (which unfortunately receives only so-so reviews) and bring headphones.

STREET FUN

The full-monty Pompidou experience is as much about hanging out in the busy streets and squares around it, packed with souvenir shops and people, as absorbing the centre's contents. West of the Centre Pompidou, fun-packed place Georges Pompidou and its nearby pedestrian streets attract bags of buskers, musicians, jugglers and mime artists. Don't miss place Igor Stravinsky with its fanciful mechanical fountains of skeletons, hearts, treble clefs, and a big pair of ruby-red lips by Jean Tinguely and Niki de St-Phalle.

LUIS COURTOT / 500PX ©

TOP SIGHT
JARDIN DES TUILERIES

Filled with fountains, classical sculptures and magnificent panoramas every way you turn, this quintessentially Parisian park was laid out in 1664 by André Le Nôtre, who also created the gardens at Vaux-le-Vicomte and Versailles.

The 16th-century Palais des Tuileries (home to Napoléon, among others) stood at the garden's western end until 1871, when it was razed during the upheaval of the Paris Commune. All that remains of the palace today are two buildings, both museums. The ensemble now forms part of the Banks of the Seine Unesco World Heritage site.

The **Musée de l'Orangerie** (Map p372; ☎01 44 77 80 07; www.musee-orangerie.fr; place de la Concorde, 1er; adult/child €9/free; ⊙9am-6pm Wed-Mon; MConcorde), set in a 19th-century edifice built to shelter the garden's orange trees in winter, is a treat. The two oval rooms of the purpose-built top floor are the show-stealer; here you'll find eight of Monet's enormous, ethereal *Water Lilies* canvases bathed in natural light.

Downstairs is the private collection of art dealer Paul Guillaume (1891–1934), with works by all the big names of early modern art: Cézanne, Matisse, Picasso, Renoir, Modigliani, Soutine and Utrillo.

There's always a queue, so arrive early. A combination ticket covering admission to the Musée d'Orsay costs €16.

The other museum is the wonderfully airy **Jeu de Paume** (Map p372; ☎01 47 03 12 50; www.jeudepaume.org; 1 place de la Concorde, 1er; adult/child €10/free; ⊙11am-9pm Tue, to 7pm Wed-Sun; MConcorde), set in the palace's erstwhile royal tennis court. It stages innovative photography exhibitions.

DON'T MISS

- Monet's *Water Lilies*
- Paul Guillaume collection
- Jeu de Paume
- Picnic or stroll in the park

PRACTICALITIES

- Map p372, C5
- rue de Rivoli, 1er
- ⊙7am-9pm Apr-late Sep, 7.30am-7.30pm late Sep-Mar
- MTuileries, Concorde

SYLVAIN KERDREUX/500PX ©

TOP SIGHT
ÉGLISE ST-EUSTACHE

Just north of the gardens snuggling up to the city's old marketplace, now the Forum des Halles, is one of the most beautiful churches in Paris. Majestic, architecturally magnificent and musically outstanding, St-Eustache has made spirits soar for centuries.

Tales of spiritual pomp and circumstance are plentiful. It was here that Richelieu and Molière were baptised, Louis XIV celebrated his first Holy Communion and Colbert was buried. Mozart chose St-Eustache for the funeral Mass of his mother and in 1855 Berlioz's *Te Deum* premiered here – the church's acoustics are extraordinary.

Built between 1532 and 1637, the church is primarily Gothic, though a neoclassical façade was added on the western side in the mid-18th century. Artistic highlights include a work by Rubens, Raymond Mason's colourful bas-relief of market vendors (1969) and Keith Haring's bronze triptych (1990) in the side chapels. Outside is a gigantic sculpture of a head and hand entitled *L'Écoute* (Listen; 1986) by Henri de Miller. Audioguides are available for €3.

One of France's largest organs is above the church's western entrance; it has 101 stops and 8000 pipes dating from 1854. Free organ recitals at 5.30pm on Sunday are a must for music lovers, as is June's Festival des 36 Heures de St-Eustache – 36 hours of nonstop music embracing a symphony of genres.

DON'T MISS

- *L'Écoute*
- Free Sunday-afternoon organ recitals
- Artwork in the side chapels

PRACTICALITIES

- Map p376, C5
- www.st-eustache.org
- 2 impasse St-Eustache, 1er
- 9.30am-7pm Mon-Fri, 9am-7.15pm Sat & Sun
- M Les Halles or RER Châtelet–Les Halles

SIGHTS

History and culture meet head on along the banks of the Seine in the 1er *arrondissement*, home to some of the most important sights for visitors to Paris, including the world-renowned Louvre and Centre Pompidou. It was in this same neighbourhood that Louis VI created *halles* (markets) in 1137 for the merchants who converged on the city centre to sell their wares, and for more than 800 years they were, in the words of Émile Zola, the 'belly of Paris'. The wholesalers were moved lox, stock and cabbage out to the suburbs in 1971.

MUSÉE DU LOUVRE — MUSEUM

See p108.

CENTRE POMPIDOU — MUSEUM

See p116.

JARDIN DES TUILERIES — PARK

See p118.

ÉGLISE ST-EUSTACHE — CHURCH

See p119.

MUSÉE DES ARTS DÉCORATIFS — GALLERY

Map p372 (☎01 44 55 57 50; www.lesartsdecoratifs.fr; 107 rue de Rivoli, 1er; adult/child €11/free; ⏲11am-6pm Tue-Sun, to 9pm Thu; Ⓜ Palais Royal–Musée du Louvre) A trio of privately administered collections – Applied Arts & Design, Advertising & Graphic Design, and Fashion & Textiles – sit in the Rohan Wing of the vast Palais du Louvre. They are collectively known as the Musée des Arts Décoratifs; admission includes entry to all three. For an extra €2, you can scoop up a combo ticket that also includes the Musée Nissim de Camondo (p137) in the 8e.

COLLECTION PINAULT PARIS

Paris' newest art museum is housed in the eye-catching **Bourse de Commerce** (Map p376; www.collectionpinaultparis.com; 2 rue de Viarmes, 1er; Ⓜ Les Halles or RER Châtelet–Les Halles) – an 18th-century rotunda that once held the city's grain market and stock exchange. Japanese architect Tadao Ando designed the ambitious new interior, where three floors of galleries will display contemporary art from the $1.4 billion collection of François Pinault, who previously teamed up with Ando to open the Palazzo Grassi and Punta della Dogana in Venice. It's slated to open in early 2019.

JARDIN DU PALAIS ROYAL — GARDENS

Map p372 (www.domaine-palais-royal.fr; 2 place Colette, 1er; ⏲8am-10.30pm Apr-Sep, to 8.30pm Oct-Mar; Ⓜ Palais Royal–Musée du Louvre) The Jardin du Palais Royal is a perfect spot to sit, contemplate and picnic between boxed hedges, or shop in the trio of beautiful arcades that frame the garden: the **Galerie de Valois** (east), **Galerie de Montpensier** (west) and **Galerie Beaujolais** (north). However, it's the southern end of the complex, polka-dotted with sculptor Daniel Buren's 260 black-and-white striped columns, that has become the garden's signature feature.

This elegant urban space is fronted by the neoclassical **Palais Royal** (closed to the public), constructed in 1633 by Cardinal Richelieu but mostly dating to the late 18th century. Louis XIV hung out here in the 1640s; today it is home to the **Conseil d'État** (Council of State; Map p372; 1 place du Palais Royal, 1er; Ⓜ Palais Royal–Musée du Louvre).

The Galerie de Valois is the most upmarket arcade with designer boutiques like Stella McCartney and Pierre Hardy. Across the garden, in the Galerie de Montpensier, the Revolution broke out on a warm mid-July day, just three years after the galleries opened, in the Café du Foy. The third arcade, tiny Galerie Beaujolais, is crossed by **Passage du Perron**, a passageway above which the writer Colette (1873–1954) lived out the last dozen years of her life.

MUSÉE EN HERBE — GALLERY

Map p376 (☎01 40 67 97 66; www.musee-en-herbe.com; 23 rue de l'Arbre-Sec, 1er; €6; ⏲10am-7pm; 👪; Ⓜ Louvre Rivoli, Pont Neuf) One of the city's great backstreet secrets, this children's museum is a surprise gem for art lovers of every age. Its permanent exhibition changes throughout the year and focuses on the work of one artist or theme through a series of interactive displays.

PLACE VENDÔME — SQUARE

Map p372 (Ⓜ Tuileries, Opéra) Octagonal place Vendôme and the arcaded and colonnaded buildings around it were constructed between 1687 and 1721. In March 1796 Napoléon married Josephine, Viscountess Beauharnais, in the building at No 3. Today the buildings surrounding the square house the posh Hôtel Ritz Paris and some of the city's most fashionable boutiques.

The 43.5m-tall **Colonne Vendôme** (Vendôme Column; Map p372) in the centre of the square consists of a stone core wrapped in a 160m-long bronze spiral made from hundreds of Austrian and Russian cannons captured by Napoléon at the Battle of Austerlitz in 1805.

TOUR JEAN SANS PEUR — TOWER

Map p376 (Tower of John the Fearless; ☎01 40 26 20 28; www.tourjeansanspeur.com; 20 rue Étienne Marcel, 2e; adult/child €6/3.50; ⏲1.30-6pm Wed-Sun; Ⓜ Étienne Marcel) This 29m-high Gothic tower was built during the Hundred Years' War by the Duke of Bourgogne so that he could take refuge from his enemies – such as the supporters of the Duke of Orléans, whom he had assassinated. Part of a splendid mansion in the early 15th century, it is one of the few examples of feudal military architecture extant in Paris. Climb 140 steps up the spiral staircase to the top turret (no views).

TOUR ST-JACQUES — TOWER

Map p376 (☎01 83 96 15 05; https://en.parisinfo.com; 39 rue de Rivoli, 4e; adult/child €10/8; ⏲by reservation 10am-5pm Fri-Sun Jul-Oct, Sat & Sun Nov; Ⓜ Châtelet) Just north of place du Châtelet, the Flamboyant Gothic, 54m-high St James Tower is all that remains of the Église St-Jacques la Boucherie, built by the powerful butchers guild in 1523 as a starting point for pilgrims setting out for the shrine of St James at Santiago de Compostela in Spain. The tower has recently been restored, and guided 50-minute tours (in French; book online at www.desmotset-desarts.com) take visitors up 300 stairs to an expansive panorama. Children must be 10 years or older.

FORUM DES HALLES — NOTABLE BUILDING

Map p376 (www.forumdeshalles.com; 1 rue Pierre Lescot, 1er; ⏲shops 10am-8pm Mon-Sat, 11am-7pm Sun; Ⓜ Les Halles or RER Châtelet–Les Halles) Paris' main wholesale food market stood here for nearly 800 years before being replaced by this underground shopping mall in 1971. Long considered an eyesore by many Parisians, the mall's exterior was finally demolished in 2011 to make way for its golden-hued translucent canopy, unveiled in 2016. Below, four floors of stores (more than 100), some 20 eateries and entertainment venues including cinemas and a swimming pool extend down to the city's busiest metro hub.

Spilling out from the canopied centre, new gardens will have *pétanque* (a variant on the game of bowls) courts and chess tables, a central patio and pedestrian walkways – it's expected to be completed by mid- to late 2018. The project has also opened up the shopping centre, allowing for more natural light.

LOCAL KNOWLEDGE

ART IN THE MAKING: 59 RIVOLI

In such a classical part of Paris filled with elegant historic architecture, **59 Rivoli** (Map p376; www.59rivoli.org; 59 rue de Rivoli, 1er; ⏲1-8pm Tue-Sun; Ⓜ Châtelet, Pont Neuf) FREE is a bohemian breath of fresh air. Take time out to watch artists at work in the 30 ateliers (studios) strung on six floors of the long-abandoned bank building, now a legalised squat where some of Paris' most creative talent works (but doesn't live). The ground-floor gallery hosts a new exhibition every fortnight and free gigs, concerts and shows pack the place out at weekends.

EATING

The dining scene in central Paris is excellent, and there is no shortage of choices, from eat-on-the-go bakeries to casual foodie favourites to Michelin-starred cuisine. By all means reserve a table at a big-name restaurant, but also try wandering market streets like rue Montorgueil or, for something different, sample ramen or udon at one of the innumerable Japanese noodle shops along rue St-Anne.

SALATIM — ISRAELI €

Map p376 (☎01 42 36 30 03; www.facebook.com/SalatimParis; 15 rue des Jeûneurs, 2e; mains €8-16; ⏲8.30am-4pm Sun, Mon & Fri, 8.30am-11pm Tue-Thu; Ⓜ Sentier) Chipped plates and organised chaos reign at Yariv Berreby's overflowing sardine-tin-sized eatery. It takes its name from the Hebrew word for salad, and you'd be remiss not to try the eponymous mixed plate (eggplant caviar, pickled red cabbage, hummus etc). But don't overlook

LOCAL KNOWLEDGE

RUE MONTORGUEIL

A splinter of the historic Les Halles, rue Montorgueil was once the oyster market and the final stop for seafood merchants hailing from the coast. Immortalised by Balzac in *La Comédie humaine*, this compelling strip still draws Parisians to eat and shop – it's lined with *fromageries* (cheese shops), cafes, and street stalls selling fruit, veg and other foodstuffs.

Aux Tonneaux des Halles (Map p376; ☎01 42 33 36 19; 28 Rue Montorgueil, 1er; mains €15-20; ⊙noon-2.30pm & 5-9pm Mon-Fri, noon-9pm Sat & Sun; Ⓜ Les Halles or RER Châtelet–Les Halles) Originally a hotel, Aux Tonneaux only became a cafe in the 1920s – a relatively recent addition compared to some of the other addresses here. It features a fine outdoor terrace, as well as classic bistro fare such as *steak-frites*.

Charles Chocolatier (Map p376; 15 rue Montorgueil, 1er; ⊙10am-7.45pm Tue-Sat; Ⓜ Les Halles or RER Châtelet–Les Halles) Delectable artisan chocolates made with 100% cocoa butter (no milk, butter or cream).

Fou de Pâtisserie (Map p376; 45 rue Montorgueil, 2e; ⊙11am-8pm Mon-Fri, 10am-8pm Sat, 10am-6pm Sun; Ⓜ Les Halles, Sentier, or RER Châtelet–Les Halles) Single-name patisseries scatter across the city, but for a greatest-hits range from its finest pastry chefs – Cyril Lignac, Christophe Adam (L'Éclair de Génie), Jacques Genin, Pierre Hermé and Philippe Conticini included – head to this one-stop concept shop. A Paris first, it's the brainchild of the publishers of pastry magazine *Fou de Pâtisserie* (also sold here).

Stohrer (Map p376; www.stohrer.fr; 51 rue Montorgueil, 2e; ⊙7.30am-8.30pm; Ⓜ Étienne Marcel, Sentier) Opened in 1730 by Nicolas Stohrer, the Polish pastry chef of queen consort Marie Leszczyńska (wife of Louis XV), Stohrer's house-made specialities include its own inventions, the *baba au rhum* (rum-soaked sponge cake) and *puits d'amour* (caramel-topped, vanilla-cream-filled puff pasty). The beautiful pastel murals were added in 1864 by Paul-Jacques-Aimé Baudry, who also decorated the Palais Garnier's Grand Foyer.

Le Compas (Map p376; ☎01 42 33 94 73; www.lecompas-restaurant.com; 62 rue Montorgueil, 2e; mains €12.50-26; ⊙kitchen noon-1am, bar 7am-1am; Ⓜ Les Halles or RER Châtelet–Les Halles) Although a newcomer on ancient market street rue Montorgueil, this relaxed corner brasserie feels like it's been here forever. Filled with regulars from the time it opens for early-morning coffee until late into the night, its wraparound terrace offers fantastic people-watching. Brasserie classics (French onion soup, Burgundy snails, bavette steak with Béarnaise sauce, beef tartare with quail eggs) are spot-on.

Au Rocher de Cancale (Map p376; ☎01 42 33 50 29; 78 rue Montorgueil, 2e; dozen oysters €20, seafood platter €30; ⊙8am-2am; Ⓜ Sentier, Les Halles, or RER Châtelet–Les Halles) This 19th-century timber-lined restaurant (first opened in 1804 at No 59) is the last remaining legacy of the old oyster market. You can feast on oysters and seafood from Cancale (in Brittany) as well as other *plats du jour*.

À la Mère de Famille (Map p376; ☎01 47 70 83 69; www.lameredefamille.com; 82 rue Montorgueil, 2e; ⊙9.30am-8pm Mon-Sat, 10am-7.30pm Sun; Ⓜ Sentier, Les Halles, or RER Châtelet–Les Halles) The oldest confectionery house in Paris, with over 250 years of experience creating chocolates, *bonbons* and other sweet temptations.

La Fermette (Map p376; 86 rue Montorgueil, 2e; ⊙4-8pm Mon, 8.30am-8pm Tue-Sat, 8.30am-2pm Sun; Ⓜ Sentier, Les Halles, or RER Châtelet–Les Halles) Not the most stylish *fromagerie* in town, but it always has great deals out the front, where you can pick up a preselected assortment of cheese for less than €10.

Nysa (Map p376; ☎01 40 26 17 80; www.nysa.fr; 94 rue de Montorgueil, 2e; ⊙10.30am-2pm & 2.30-9pm Sun & Mon, 10.30am-9pm Tue-Sat; Ⓜ Sentier) This unpretentious wine store supports independent vineyards and has an interesting selection of bottles for less than €15.

the sandwiches, *limonana* (iced mint lemonade) or Wednesday's chicken schnitzel. If you can't get a seat, the takeaway window beckons.

BONESHAKER DOUGHNUTS FAST FOOD €

Map p376 (☎01 45 08 84 02; www.boneshakerparis.com; 77 rue d'Aboukir, 2e; doughnuts €3-4.20; ⊙10am-5pm Tue-Fri, to 6pm Sat; MSentier) Beginning life as a pop-up enterprise and now in a hip hole-in-the-wall, Boneshaker creates dazzling small-batch, homemade doughnuts in fun flavour combinations: maple and bacon; chocolate, marshmallow and spicy Dutch *speculaas*; coconut and lime; summer berry crumble; and peach and basil. Wash them down with freshly squeezed lemonade. Come early: they usually sell out by 4.30pm.

MAISIE CAFÉ HEALTH FOOD €

Map p372 (☎01 40 39 99 16; www.maisiecafe.com; 32 rue du Mont Thabor, 1er; breakfast €7-10, lunch €10; ⊙9am-6pm Mon-Fri, 11am-3pm Sat; MConcorde) Banana-leaf prints line the walls of this organic, gluten-free cafe, where in addition to salads and açaí bowls, you can detox with fresh juices, avocado shakes and raw energy balls (cocoa, dates, cashews and raw veggies).

CRÊPE DENTELLE CRÊPES €

Map p376 (☎01 40 41 04 23; 10 rue Léopold Bellan, 2e; crêpes €8.20-15, lunch menu €12; ⊙noon-3pm & 7.30-11pm Mon-Fri; MSentier) Named after a style of crêpe that's as delicate as fine lace *(dentelle)*, this is probably not the place to go if you're starving. However, it is an excellent choice for a light and inexpensive lunch, and is certainly the best bet for crêpes near Les Halles. Arrive by 12.15pm or you may not get a seat.

DAME TARTINE CAFE €

Map p376 (☎01 42 77 32 22; 2 rue Brisemiche, 4e; tartines €9.90-14; ⊙9am-11.30pm; ; MHôtel de Ville) One of the few reasonable dining options near the Centre Pompidou, Dame Tartine makes the most of its lively location across from the whimsical Stravinsky Fountain. Don't expect miracles on the culinary front, but its speciality – the tartine (open-face sandwich) – will hit the spot after a morning in the museum.

★MAISON MAISON MEDITERRANEAN €€

Map p376 (☎09 67 82 07 32; www.facebook.com/maisonmaisonparis; opposite 16 quai du Louvre, 1er; 2-/3-course lunch menu €20/25, small plates €7-16; ⊙10am-2am Wed-Sun, 6pm-2am Tue; MPont Neuf) Halfway down the stairs by Pont Neuf is this wonderfully secret space beneath the *bouquinistes*, where you can watch the bateaux-mouches float by as you dine on artful creations like beetroot and pink-grapefruit-cured bonito or gnocchi with white asparagus and broccoli pesto. In nice weather, cocktails at the glorious riverside terrace are not to be missed.

★UMA FUSION €€

Map p372 (☎01 40 15 08 15; www.uma-restaurant.fr; 7 rue du 29 Juillet, 1er; 2-/3-course lunch €25/29, 7-/9-course dinner €67/82; ⊙12.30-2.30pm & 7.30-10.30pm Mon-Sat; MTuileries) Embark on a culinary voyage at Uma, where chef Lucas Felzine infuses contemporary French sensibilities with Nikkei: Peruvian-Japanese fusion food. The lunch menu comes with two exquisitely prepared starters (think ceviche with daikon radish or smoked duck with lychees); grab a table upstairs to spy on the open kitchen. Mezcal, pisco and vodka cocktails served until 1.30am. Reserve.

★BALAGAN ISRAELI €€

Map p372 (☎01 40 20 72 14; www.balagan-paris.com; 9 rue d'Alger, 1er; lunch menus from €24, mains €23-28; ⊙noon-2pm Mon-Sat, 7-10pm daily; MTuileries) Cool navy blues and creamy diamond tiling contrast with the chic vibe at this Israeli hot spot. Come here to sample delectable small plates: deconstructed kebabs, crispy halloumi cheese with dates, onion confit Ashkenazi chicken liver, or, our favourite, a spicy, succulent tuna tartare with fennel, cilantro, capers and pistachios. Mains, such as the seabream black pasta, are just as praiseworthy.

CHEZ LA VIEILLE FRENCH €€

Map p376 (☎01 42 60 15 78; www.chezlavieille.fr; 1 rue Bailleul, 1er; mains €24-26; ⊙noon-2.30pm Fri & Sat, 6-10.30pm Tue-Sat; MLouvre–Rivoli) In salvaging this history-steeped eatery within a 16th-century building, star chef Daniel Rose pays homage to the former wholesale markets, the erstwhile legendary owner Adrienne Biasin (many of her timeless dishes have been updated, from terrines and rillettes to veal blanquette), and the soul of Parisian bistro cooking itself. Dine at the street-level bar or upstairs in the peacock-blue dining room.

LOCAL KNOWLEDGE

LIVING WALL

On the corner of rue des Petits Carreaux (the northern extension of foodie street rue Montorgueil; p122), an extraordinary *mur végétal* ('vertical garden') was installed on a 25m-high blank building façade by the modern innovator of the genre, French botanist Patrick Blanc, in 2013. **L'Oasis d'Aboukir** (Map p376; 83 rue d'Aboukir, 2e; MSentier) has since flourished to cover a total surface area of 250 sq metre in greenery. Subtitled Hymne à la Biodiversité (Ode to Biodiversity), the 'living wall' incorporates some 7600 different plants from 237 different species.

TRADI — BISTRO €€

Map p376 (01 44 82 07 83; www.tradi.paris; 4 rue du Mail, 2e; mains €20-26; noon-2.30pm & 7-11pm Tue-Sat; MSentier) This traditional bistro has been reborn and now only uses sustainable French produce, which can be traced from farm to plate. Everything is made on site, including the pâtés, smoked salmon and baked bread. Menus change daily but might feature roast duck with honey and pistachios, or line-caught dorade with tarragon leaves and white beans.

CHAMPEAUX — BRASSERIE €€

Map p376 (01 53 45 84 50; www.restaurant-champeaux.com; La Canopée, Forum des Halles, Porte Rambuteau, 1er; mains €18-34; noon-midnight Sun-Wed, to 1am Thu-Sat; MLes Halles or RER Châtelet–Les Halles) This landmark brasserie by superstar chef Alain Ducasse sits beneath the golden-hued canopy topping the Forum des Halles (p121), the one-time wholesale market-turned-shopping mall and transport hub. A train-station-like information board dominates the contemporary space and updates diners on its house-speciality soufflés (such as lobster bisque or pistachio and salted caramel). Unlike most Ducasse establishments, there's no dress code.

A NOSTE — TAPAS €€

Map p372 (01 47 03 91 91; www.a-noste.com; 6bis rue du Quatre Septembre, 2e; tapas €10-22, menus lunch/dinner from €29/49; noon-11pm; MBourse) Pull up a stool at one of A Noste's communal tables and feast on original Gascon- and Basque-style tapas: from the airy cornmeal *fougasse* with smoked duck and goat's cheese to the deep-fried *panisse* (chickpea flour) and chorizo nuggets. The more refined restaurant upstairs ensures that a return trip is in order.

FRENCH PARADOX — FRENCH €€

Map p372 (09 81 83 95 69; http://french-paradox.paris; 57 passage des Panoramas, 2e; lunch €10-21, dinner €28-64; noon-2.30pm & 7-10.30pm; MGrands Boulevards) Presided over by a wall-sized photo of Louis de Funès' *Grand Restaurant*, the French Paradox is a fun, unabashed celebration of two particularly Gallic loves: duck and Champagne. Menus pair the bird (*confit* or *magret*) with a glass or three of bubbly, or you can keep it simple with a French Paradox duck burger and allumette fries, followed by chocolate mousse.

LOULOU — ITALIAN €€

Map p372 (01 42 60 41 96; https://loulou-paris.com; 107 rue de Rivoli, 1er; €20-39; noon-2am; MPalais Royal–Musée du Louvre) Hidden inside the Musée des Arts Decoratifs (p120), Loulou is naturally stylish: vintage banquettes and velvet curtains create a cosy salon-like dining space. However, the real treat here is the crisp-white summer terrace, overlooking the emerald green manicured Jardin du Carrousel and the inimitable majesty of the Louvre.

LE COCHON À L'OREILLE — FRENCH €€

Map p376 (01 40 15 98 24; 15 rue Montmartre, 1er; lunch/dinner menus from €16/19.50; 10am-2am Tue-Sat; MLes Halles or RER Châtelet–Les Halles) A Parisian jewel and listed monument, the hole-in-the-wall Le Cochon à l'Oreille retains 1890-laid tiles depicting vibrant market scenes of the old *halles*, while an iron staircase leads to a second dining room upstairs. Bistro-style dishes are traditional French (the steak tartare is excellent), and are accompanied by well-chosen wines. Hours can vary. Cash only.

NOGLU — FRENCH €€

Map p372 (01 40 26 41 24; www.noglu.fr; 16 passage des Panoramas, 2e; mains €17-21; noon-3pm Mon-Fri, 11am-4pm Sat, 7.30-10.30pm Tue-Sat; ; MRichelieu-Drouot, Grands Boulevards) Gluten-free kitchens are hard to find in France, but that's only one of the reasons that Noglu is such a jewel – this chic address builds on French tradition (bœuf bourguignon) while simultaneously

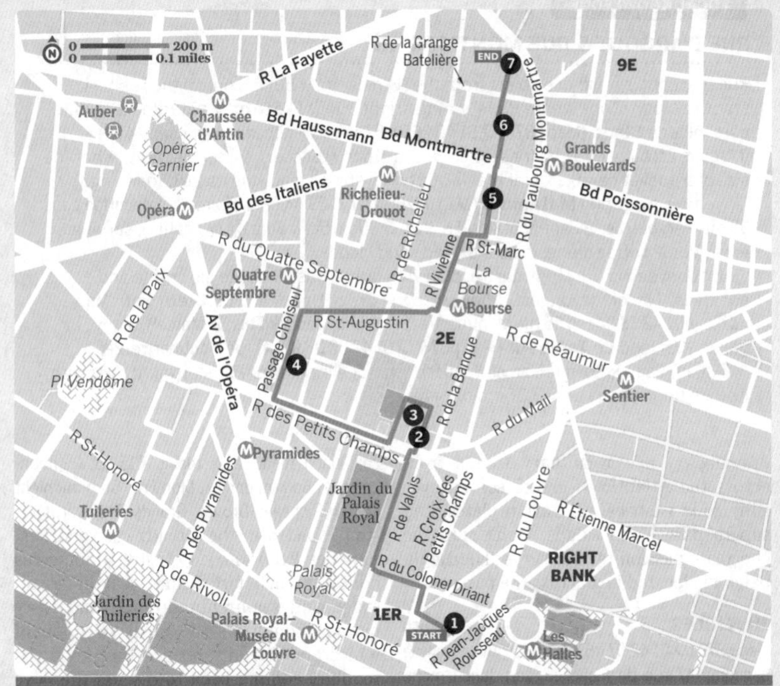

Neighbourhood Walk
Right Bank Covered Passages

START GALERIE VÉRO DODAT
END PASSAGE VERDEAU
LENGTH 3KM; TWO HOURS

The Right Bank's sumptuously decorated *passages couverts* (covered arcades) offer a walk through early-19th-century Paris. Avoid Sundays, when some are shut.

At 19 rue Jean-Jacques Rousseau, the 1823 1 **Galerie Véro Dodat** retains its 19th-century skylights, ceiling murals, Corinthian columns, tiled floor, gas globe fittings (now electric) and bijou shopfronts. Continue to the Jardin du Palais Royal, and follow the arcades to Passage des Deux Pavillons and up the stairs to rue des Petits Champs. Turn right and duck into 2 **Galerie Vivienne** (1826), decorated with floor mosaics and bas-reliefs on the walls. Don't miss wine shop Legrand Filles & Fils, Wolff et Descourtis, selling silk scarves, and the Emilio Robba flower shop.

Exit on rue Vivienne and peek in at 3 **Galerie Colbert**, featuring a huge glass dome and rotunda. West along rue des Petits Champs is 4 **Passage Choiseul** (1824), a 45m-long covered arcade, now filled with cheap eateries. Paul Verlaine (1844–96) drank absinthe here and Céline (1894–1961) grew up in his mother's lace shop at No 62.

Passing La Bourse will take you to 5 **Passage des Panoramas** (p66), Paris' oldest covered arcade (1800) and the first to be lit by gas (1817). It was expanded in 1834 with four interconnecting passages – Feydeau, Montmartre, St-Marc and Variétés – and is full of excellent eateries and unusual shops.

Enter at 10-12 bd Montmartre into 6 **Passage Jouffroy**, Paris' last major passage (1847). There's a wax museum, the Musée Grévin, and wonderful boutiques, including bookshops, silversmiths and M&G Segas, where Toulouse-Lautrec bought his walking sticks.

Cross the road to 7 **Passage Verdeau**. There's lots to explore: vintage comic books, antiques, old postcards and more. The northern exit is at 31bis rue du Faubourg Montmartre.

LOCAL KNOWLEDGE

RUE D'ARGOUT & RUE MONTMARTRE

Rue d'Argout is a slip of a street from the 13th century, but it's one of those short, stumble-upon strips where Paris' young bright things like to be. Favourite hang-outs here include **Blend** (Map p376; ☎01 40 26 84 57; www.blendhamburger.com; 44 rue d'Argout, 2e; burger €10-14, fries €4-5; ⊙noon-11pm; Ⓜ Sentier), a gourmet burger bar the size of a pocket handkerchief that is still going strong following its 2012 opening.

Nearby is buzzing **Matamata** (Map p376; ☎01 71 39 44 58; www.matamatacoffee.com; 58 rue d'Argout, 2e; ⊙8am-5pm Mon-Fri, 9am-5.30pm Sat & Sun; 📶; Ⓜ Sentier), serving exceptional coffee alongside cakes and sandwiches.

Just beyond is rue Montmartre, clad with numerous places to sip coffee and cocktails. Two of the longest running are the Crazy Heart, aka **Le Cœur Fou** (Map p376; ☎01 42 33 04 98; 55 rue Montmartre, 2e; ⊙5pm-2am; Ⓜ Étienne Marcel), a tiny gallery-bar, and **Le Tambour** (Map p376; ☎01 42 33 06 90; 41 rue Montmartre, 2e; ⊙8.30am-6am; Ⓜ Étienne Marcel, Sentier), a vintage mecca for Parisian night owls with its long hours (food until 3.30am or 4am).

drawing on newer culinary trends from across the Atlantic to create some devilishly good pastries, vegetarian plates, and superb pizzas and salads. Don't skip the chocolate-passion tart. Reserve. The Noglu bakery is located just across the passage.

JUVENILES — BISTRO €€

Map p372 (☎01 42 97 46 49; http://juvenileswinebar.com; 47 rue de Richelieu, 1er; lunch menu €16.50, mains €19-23; ⊙noon-11pm Tue-Sat; Ⓜ Pyramides) Likely the only place in Paris where you'll find haggis 2.0, this low-key wine bar is a hallowed retreat by the Palais Royal. Don't be deterred if sheep innards aren't your thing, as hostess Margaux and chef Romain offer a variety of other, more accessible dishes, such as butternut-squash gnocchi or *magret de canard* (duck breast) and sweet potatoes. Unusual wine list.

LA TOUR DE MONTLHÉRY – CHEZ DENISE — FRENCH €€

Map p376 (☎01 42 36 21 82; 5 rue des Prouvaires, 1er; mains €23-28; ⊙noon-3pm & 7.30pm-5am Mon-Fri mid-Aug–mid-Jun; Ⓜ Les Halles or RER Châtelet–Les Halles) The most traditional eatery near the former Les Halles marketplace, this boisterous old half-timbered bistro with red-chequered tablecloths stays open until dawn and has been run by the same family since 1966. If you're ready to feast on all the French classics – snails in garlic sauce, veal liver, steak tartare, braised beef cheeks and house-made pâté – reservations are in order.

COINSTOT VINO — FRENCH €€

Map p372 (☎01 44 82 08 54; https://lecoinstotvino.com; 26bis passage des Panoramas, 2e; lunch menu €18, mains €15-25; ⊙noon-2pm & 6pm-midnight Mon-Fri, 6pm-midnight Sat; Ⓜ Richelieu-Drouot, Grands Boulevards) A simple bistro in the already crowded Passage des Panoramas, Coinstot Vino serves honest French fare (think veal in cream sauce and sea-urchin tarama) and tasty pizzas, though it's the great selection of wines and friendly service that keep the regulars coming back to discuss life, love and the lack of affordable real estate deep into the night.

★VERJUS — MODERN AMERICAN €€€

Map p372 (☎01 42 97 54 40; http://verjusparis.com; 52 rue de Richelieu, 1er; menu €78, with wine €133; ⊙7-11pm Mon-Fri; Ⓜ Bourse, Pyramides) Opened by American duo Braden Perkins and Laura Adrian, Verjus was born out of their former clandestine supper club, the Hidden Kitchen. The restaurant builds on that tradition, offering a chance to sample some excellent, creative cuisine in a casual space. The tasting menu is a series of small plates, using ingredients sourced straight from producers. Reserve well in advance.

If you're just after an aperitif or a prelude to dinner, the downstairs **Verjus Bar à Vins** (Map p372; 47 rue de Montpensier, 1er; ⊙6-11pm Mon-Fri) serves a handful of charcuterie and cheese plates. For lunch or a more casual dinner, don't miss nearby **Ellsworth** (Map p372; ☎01 42 60 59 66; www.ellsworthparis.com; 34 rue de Richelieu, 1er; 2-/3-course lunch menu €22/28, mains €12-30; ⊙12.15-2.15pm & 7-10.30pm Mon-Sat, 11.30am-3pm Sun; Ⓜ Pyramides), Verjus' sister restaurant.

★**FRENCHIE** BISTRO €€€

Map p376 (☎01 40 39 96 19; www.frenchie-restaurant.com; 5 rue du Nil, 2e; 4-course lunch menu €45, 5-course dinner menu €74, with wine €175; ⏲6.30-11pm Mon-Fri, noon-2.30pm Thu & Fri in summer; Ⓜ Sentier) Tucked down an inconspicuous alley, this tiny bistro with wooden tables and old stone walls is always packed and for good reason: excellent-value dishes are modern, market-driven and prepared with unpretentious flair by French chef Gregory Marchand. Reserve well in advance or arrive early and pray for a cancellation (it does happen). Alternatively, head to neighbouring **Frenchie Bar à Vins** (Map p376; www.frenchie-restaurant.com; 6 rue du Nil, 2e; dishes €9-23; ⏲6.30-11pm; Ⓜ Sentier).

No reservations at Frenchie Bar à Vins – write your name on the sheet of paper strung outside and wait for your name to be called.

During the day, swing by its adjacent deli-style takeaway outlet **Frenchie to Go** (Map p376; ☎01 40 26 23 43; www.frenchietogo.com; 9 rue du Nil, 2e; dishes €8-18; ⏲8.30am-4.30pm Mon-Fri, 9.30am-5.30pm Sat & Sun; 📶; Ⓜ Sentier).

LE GRAND VÉFOUR GASTRONOMY €€€

Map p372 (☎01 42 96 56 27; www.grand-vefour.com; 17 rue de Beaujolais, 1er; lunch/dinner menu €115/315, mains €99-126; ⏲noon-2.30pm & 7.30-10.30pm Mon-Fri; Ⓜ Pyramides) Holding two Michelin stars, this 18th-century jewel on the northern edge of the Jardin du Palais Royal has been a dining favourite since 1784; the names ascribed to each table span Napoléon and Victor Hugo to Colette (who lived next door). Expect a voyage of discovery from chef Guy Martin in one of the most beautiful restaurants in the world.

YAM'TCHA FUSION €€€

Map p376 (☎01 40 26 08 07; www.yamtcha.com; 121 rue St-Honoré, 1er; lunch/7-course dinner €70/150, tea/wine pairing €55/70; ⏲noon-1.30pm Wed-Fri, 8-9.30pm Wed-Sat; Ⓜ Louvre Rivoli) Adeline Grattard's ingeniously fused French and Cantonese flavours (fried squid with sweet-potato noodles) have earned her no shortage of critical praise along with a Michelin star. Pair dishes on the frequently changing menu with wine or tea, or indulge in the famous steamed buns *(bāozi)* over a pot of oolong at the **Boutique Yam'Tcha** (Map p376; ☎01 40 26 06 06; 4 rue Sauval, 1er; steamed buns from €4, dishes €8-16; ⏲noon-6pm Wed-Fri, to 8pm Sat; Ⓜ Louvre Rivoli). Reserve minimum one month ahead.

CLOVER GRILL GRILL €€€

Map p376 (☎01 40 41 59 59; www.jeanfrancoispiege.com; 6 Rue Bailleul, 1er; mains €20-76; ⏲noon-2.15pm & 7-10.30pm; Ⓜ Louvre Rivoli) Don't let the power lunch crowd or €72 Angus ribeye steaks deter you from snagging a seat at Jean-François Piège's fantastic grill – even simple burgers (€23) and steak-frites (au poivre or Béarnaise) are a treat. Another cult favourite on the menu is the calamari à la carbonara, where the squid is cut into strips to resemble spaghetti. Superb.

ACCENTS GASTRONOMY €€€

Map p372 (☎01 40 39 92 88; https://accents-restaurant.com; 24 rue Feydeau, 2e; lunch menus €34-52, 6-course dinner menu €75; ⏲noon-2pm & 7-9.30pm Tue-Sat; Ⓜ Bourse) Teal and exposed brick walls give way to the intimate dining room at Accents. Spy on pastry chef Ayumi Sugiyama preparing artwork-quality desserts and sample Jean-Christophe Rizet's marvelously creative flavor combinations, including wild cod with oranges, radishes and shimeji mushrooms, or cream of red kuri squash with chestnut raviolis.

DRINKING & NIGHTLIFE

The area north of Les Halles is a prime destination for night owls. Cocktails predominate, but you'll also find wine and Champagne bars, studenty hang-outs, open-till-dawn dives and a smattering of fun nightclubs. Rue St-Sauveur, rue Tiquetonne and rue Montmartre are the best streets to explore.

★**BAR HEMINGWAY** COCKTAIL BAR

Map p372 (www.ritzparis.com; Hôtel Ritz Paris, 15 place Vendôme, 1er; ⏲6pm-2am; 📶; Ⓜ Opéra) Black-and-white photos and memorabilia (hunting trophies, old typewriters and framed handwritten letters by the great writer) fill this snug bar inside the Ritz (p282). Head bartender Colin Field mixes monumental cocktails, including three different Bloody Marys made with juice from freshly squeezed seasonal tomatoes. Legend has it that Hemingway himself, wielding a machine gun, helped liberate the bar during WWII.

★EXPERIMENTAL COCKTAIL CLUB
COCKTAIL BAR

Map p376 (ECC; www.experimentalevents.com; 37 rue St-Sauveur, 2e; ⏲7pm-2am; ⓂRéaumur Sébastopol) With a black curtain façade, this retro-chic speakeasy – with sister bars in London, Ibiza, New York and, *bien sûr,* Paris – is a sophisticated flashback to those *années folles* (crazy years) of Prohibition New York. Cocktails (€13 to €15) are individual and fabulous, and DJs keep the party going until dawn at weekends. It's not a large space, however, and fills to capacity quickly.

★LE GARDE ROBE
WINE BAR

Map p376 (☎01 49 26 90 60; 41 rue de l'Arbre Sec, 1er; ⏲12.30-2.30pm & 6.30pm-midnight Tue-Fri, 4.30pm-midnight Mon-Sat; ⓂLouvre Rivoli) Le Garde Robe is possibly the world's only bar to serve alcohol alongside a detox menu. While you probably shouldn't come here for the full-on cleansing experience, you can definitely expect excellent, affordable natural wines, a casual atmosphere and a good selection of food, ranging from cheese and charcuterie plates to adventurous options (tuna gravlax with black quinoa and guacamole).

★DANICO
COCKTAIL BAR

Map p372 (www.facebook.com/danicoparis; 6 rue Vivienne, 2e; ⏲6pm-2am; ⓂBourse) While not exactly a secret, Danico still feels like one – first you'll need to find the hidden, candlelit backroom in **Daroco** (Map p372; ☎01 42 21 93 71; www.daroco.fr; 6 rue Vivienne, 2e; mains €14-40; ⏲noon-2.30pm & 7-11.30pm; 🖉; ⓂBourse) before you get to treat yourself to one of Nico de Soto's extravagant cocktails. Chia seeds, kombucha tea, ghost peppers and pomegranate Champagne are some of the more unusual ingredients you'll find on the drink list.

> **JAZZ DUO**
>
> Rue des Lombards is the street to swing by for live jazz.
>
> **Le Baiser Salé** (Map p376; ☎01 42 33 37 71; www.lebaisersale.com; 58 rue des Lombards, 1er; ⏲daily, hours vary; ⓂChâtelet) Known for its Afro and Latin jazz, and jazz fusion concerts, the Salty Kiss combines big names and unknown artists. The place has a relaxed vibe, with sets usually starting at 7.30pm or 9.30pm.
>
> **Sunset & Sunside** (Map p376; ☎01 40 26 46 60; www.sunset-sunside.com; 60 rue des Lombards, 1er; ⏲daily, hours vary; ⓂChâtelet) There are two venues in one at this well-respected club, which hosts electric jazz, fusion and occasional salsa at Sunset, in the vaulted cellar, and acoustics and concerts on the ground floor at Sunside.

HARRY'S NEW YORK BAR
COCKTAIL BAR

Map p372 (☎01 42 61 71 14; http://harrysbar.fr; 5 rue Daunou, 2e; ⏲noon-2am Mon-Sat, 4pm-1am Sun; ⓂOpéra) One of the most popular American-style bars in the prewar years, Harry's once welcomed writers including F Scott Fitzgerald and Ernest Hemingway, who no doubt sampled the bar's unique cocktail and creation: the Bloody Mary. The Cuban mahogany interior dates from the mid-19th century and was brought over from a Manhattan bar in 1911.

HOPPY CORNER
CRAFT BEER

Map p376 (☎09 83 06 90 39; www.facebook.com/hoppycorner; 34 rue des Petits Carreaux, 2e; ⏲5pm-2am Mon-Fri, 2pm-2am Sat; ⓂSentier) Mainly French beers rotate on the 15 taps of this convivial craft beer specialist, such as Indigo IPA from Deck & Donohue, made in Montreuil just east of central Paris. A handful of European (and occasionally American) brews also make the blackboard listing the day's offerings; super-knowledgable staff can help you decide. Dried hops are served as bar snacks.

LA CHAMPMESLÉ
BAR

Map p372 (4 rue Chabanais, 2e; ⏲4pm-dawn Mon-Sat; ⓂPyramides) The grande dame of Parisian dyke bars, around since 1979, is a cosy, relaxed spot that attracts an older crowd (about 75% are lesbians, the rest mostly gay men). Cabaret nights, tarot-card reading and fortune-telling sessions, and art exhibitions.

CAFÉ LA FUSÉE
BAR

Map p376 (☎01 42 76 93 99; 168 rue St-Martin, 3e; ⏲9am-2am Mon-Fri, 10am-2am Sat & Sun; ⓂRambuteau, Étienne Marcel) A short walk from the Centre Pompidou (p116), the Rocket is a lively, laid-back indie hang-out with a red-and-white-striped awning strung with fairy lights outside, and tobacco-coloured walls indoors. You can grab simple meals here (€8 to €13), and it's got a decent wine selection by the glass.

L'IVRESS WINE BAR

Map p376 (☎06 61 40 27 97; http://livress.fr; 5 rue Poissonnière, 2e; ⊙6pm-1am Mon-Sat; MSentier) Make sure to reserve an armchair or oak barrel (for those who prefer to stand) at this cosy bar and wine shop, otherwise your chances of getting a table may be slim. Expect a choice selection of wines from independent vineyards and enough quality nibbles to keep the after-work crowd lingering long past happy hour. Book by text message.

MABEL COCKTAIL BAR

Map p376 (☎01 42 33 24 33; www.mabelparis.com; 58 rue d'Aboukir, 2e; ⊙7pm-midnight Mon-Wed, to 2am Thu-Sat; MSentier) Find your inner corsair in one of the countless varieties of rum here (the selection spans 35 countries) or perhaps the gooey goodness of an accompanying grilled cheese sandwich – a favourite of plunderers everywhere. Great cocktails and low-slung leather sofas extend the easy-going vibe late into the night.

MARCELLE CAFE

Map p376 (☎01 40 13 04 04; www.restaurantmarcelle.fr; 22 rue Montmartre, 1er; ⊙8am-6pm Mon-Fri, 9am-7pm Sat & Sun; 📶; MLes Halles or RER Châtelet–Les Halles) Add some zest to your day at this bright two-level cafe, where you can power up with a freshly squeezed juice, gluten-free museli and homemade chestnut bread in the morning, and soups and salads at lunch.

MA CAVE FLEURY WINE BAR

Map p376 (☎01 40 28 03 39; https://macavefleury.wordpress.com; 177 rue St-Denis, 2e; ⊙5-9pm Mon, 11am-1pm & 5-10pm Tue-Fri, noon-9pm Sat; MRéamur Sébastopol) Morgane Fleury opened this welcoming little place in 2009 to promote organic and biodynamic wines. The emphasis is on Champagne – her family has been producing biodynamic Champagne for 20 years now – but you can also sample a decent selection of organic wines from around France, with a strong emphasis on the Loire region.

Ô CHATEAU WINE BAR

Map p376 (☎01 44 73 97 80; http://o-chateau.com; 68 rue Jean-Jacques Rousseau, 1er; ⊙4pm-midnight Mon-Sat; 📶; MLes Halles or RER Châtelet–Les Halles) Wine aficionados can thank this young, fun, cosmopolitan wine bar for bringing affordable tasting to Paris. Choose from 50 *grands vins* served by the glass (or 1000-plus by the bottle!). Or sign up in advance for a 'tour de France' of French wines (€59) or a guided cellar tasting in English over lunch (€75) or dinner (€99).

Other options include Champagne cruises along the Seine (€55) and a day trip to Champagne (€245).

ANGELINA TEAHOUSE

Map p372 (☎01 42 60 82 00; www.angelina-paris.fr; 226 rue de Rivoli, 1er; ⊙7.30am-7pm Mon-Fri, 8.30am-7.30pm Sat & Sun; MTuileries) Clink china with lunching ladies, their posturing poodles and half the students from Tokyo University at Angelina, a grande-dame tearoom dating from 1903. Decadent pastries are served here, but it's the super-thick 'African' hot chocolate (€8.20), which comes with a pot of whipped cream and a carafe of water, that prompts the constant queue for a table.

LE REX CLUB CLUB

Map p376 (☎01 42 36 10 96; www.rexclub.com; 5 bd Poissonnière, 2e; ⊙midnight-7am Wed-Sat; MBonne Nouvelle) Attached to the art deco Grand Rex cinema, this is Paris' premier house and techno venue where some of the world's hottest DJs strut their stuff on a 70-speaker, multidiffusion sound system.

BACKSTAGE AT THE FLICKS

A trip to 1932 art deco cinematic icon **Le Grand Rex** (Map p376; ☎01 45 08 93 89; www.legrandrex.com; 1 bd Poissonnière, 2e; tours adult/child €11/9, cinema tickets adult/child €11/4.50; ⊙tours 10am-6pm Wed, Sat & Sun, extended hours during school holidays; MBonne Nouvelle) is like no other trip to the flicks. Screenings aside, the cinema runs 50-minute behind-the-scenes tours (English soundtracks available) during which visitors – tracked by a sensor slung around their neck – are whisked right up (via a lift) behind the giant screen, tour a soundstage and get to have fun in a recording studio. Whizz-bang special effects along the way will stun adults and kids alike.

LA CORDONNERIE BAR

Map p376 (☎01 40 28 95 35; 28 rue Greneta, 2e; ⌚9am-2am; MRéamur Sébastopol) If you're counting the centimes in your pocket, this is your spot for cheap drinks and a good time. The €3 pints during happy hour (5pm to 8.30pm) turn into crowds spilling out onto the pavement late into the night.

CAFÉ MARLY CAFE

Map p372 (☎01 49 26 06 60; http://cafe-marly.com; 93 rue de Rivoli, 1er; ⌚8am-2am; MPalais Royal–Musée du Louvre) This chic venue facing the Louvre's inner courtyard is an unparalleled spot for a drink with some serious wow factor. Food is also served throughout the day, though it's painfully expensive for what you get – unless you consider the view of the glass pyramid, which is, of course, priceless.

ENTERTAINMENT

Les Halles has a handful of good entertainment options, starting with the two underground cinemas in the shopping centre, one of which is the city's film archive. Further north, near the Grands Boulevards, is the mythic Grand Rex, a must visit for cinephiles. Live jazz, classical, opera and dance performances are on almost nightly at the various venues scattered throughout the neighbourhood.

LA PLACE CULTURAL CENTRE

Map p376 (☎01 70 22 45 48; http://laplace.paris; 10 passage de la Canopée, Forum des Halles, 1er; ⌚bar 1-7pm Tue-Sat, concert hrs vary; MLes Halles or RER Châtelet–Les Halles) The overhaul of the vast shopping mall Forum des Halles (p121) saw the launch of Paris' inaugural hip-hop cultural centre under its custard-yellow glass canopy, with a 400-capacity concert hall, a 100-capacity broadcast studio, several recording studios and street-art graffiti workrooms, along with a relaxed bar. Some concerts are free, while ticket prices vary for others – check the program online.

LOUVRE AUDITORIUM CLASSICAL MUSIC

Map p372 (☎01 40 20 55 00; www.louvre.fr/musiques; Hall Napoléon, Musée du Louvre, rue de Rivoli & quai des Tuileries, 1er; MPalais Royal–Musée du Louvre) Excellent classical-music concerts are staged several times a week at the Louvre Auditorium (off the main entrance hall). Don't miss the Thursday lunchtime concerts featuring emerging composers and musicians, which cost a mere €15/6 per adult/child. The season runs from September to April or May, depending on the concert series.

COMÉDIE FRANÇAISE THEATRE

Map p372 (☎01 44 58 15 15; www.comedie-francaise.fr; place Colette, 1er; MPalais Royal–Musée du Louvre) Founded in 1680 under Louis XIV, this state-run theatre bases its repertoire on the works of classic French playwrights. The theatre has its roots in an earlier company directed by Molière at the Palais Royal.

The French playwright and actor was seized by a convulsion on stage during the fourth performance of the *Imaginary Invalid* in 1673 and died later at his home on nearby rue de Richelieu.

FORUM DES IMAGES CINEMA

Map p376 (☎01 44 76 63 00; www.forumdesimages.fr; Forum des Halles, 2 rue du Cinéma, Porte St-Eustache, 1er; cinema tickets adult/child €6/4; ⌚12.30-9pm Tue-Fri, 2-9pm Sat & Sun; MLes Halles or RER Châtelet–Les Halles) A five-screen cinema showing films set in Paris is the centrepiece of the city's film archive. Created in 1988 to establish an audiovisual archive of the city, and renovated in shades of pink, grey and black, the complex has a library and research centre with newsreels, documentaries and advertising. Its online program lists thematic series, festivals and events.

SHOPPING

The 1er and 2e *arrondissements* are mostly about fashion. Indeed the Sentier district is something of a garment heaven, while rue Étienne Marcel, place des Victoires and rue du Jour flaunt prominent labels and shoe shops. Nearby rue Montmartre and rue Tiquetonne are the streets to shop for streetwear and avant-garde designs; the easternmost part of the 1er around Palais Royal, for fancy period and conservative label fashion.

L'EXCEPTION DESIGN

Map p376 (☎01 40 39 92 34; www.lexception.com; 24 rue Berger, 1er; ⌚10am-8pm Mon-Sat, 11am-7pm Sun; MLes Halles or RER Châtelet–Les Halles) Over 400 different French designers come together under one roof at this light-filled concept store, which showcases rotating collections of men's and women's fashion along with accessories including lingerie and swimwear, shoes, eyewear, gloves, hats, scarves, belts, bags, watches and jewellery. It also sells design books, cosmetics, candles, vases and other gorgeous homewares, and has a small in-house coffee bar.

LEGRAND FILLES & FILS FOOD & DRINKS

Map p372 (☎01 42 60 07 12; www.caves-legrand.com; 1 rue de la Banque, 2e; ⏰11am-7pm Mon, 10am-7.30pm Tue-Sat; Ⓜ Bourse) Tucked inside Galerie Vivienne since 1880, Legrand sells fine wine and all the accoutrements: corkscrews, tasting glasses, decanters etc. It also has a fancy wine bar, *école du vin* (wine school; courses from €60 for two hours) and *éspace dégustation* with several tastings a month, including ones accompanied by live concerts; check its website for details.

DIDIER LUDOT FASHION & ACCESSORIES

Map p372 (☎01 42 96 06 56; www.didierludot.fr; 24 Galerie de Montpensier, 1er; ⏰10.30am-7pm Mon-Sat; Ⓜ Palais Royal–Musée du Louvre) In the rag trade since 1975, collector Didier Ludot sells the city's finest couture creations of yesteryear, hosts exhibitions and has published a book portraying the evolution of the little black dress.

E DEHILLERIN HOMEWARES

Map p376 (☎01 42 36 53 13; www.edehillerin.fr; 18-20 rue Coquillière, 1er; ⏰9am-12.30pm & 2-6pm Mon, 9am-6pm Tue-Sat; Ⓜ Les Halles) Founded in 1820, this extraordinary two-level store (more like an old-fashioned warehouse than a shiny, chic boutique) carries an incredible selection of professional-quality *matériel de cuisine* (kitchenware). Poultry scissors, turbot poacher, copper cookware or an Eiffel Tower–shaped cake tin – it's all here.

ROOM SERVICE FASHION & ACCESSORIES

Map p376 (☎01 77 11 27 24; 52 rue d'Argout, 2e; ⏰11am-7.30pm Mon-Sat; Ⓜ Sentier) *'Atelier Vintage'* (Vintage Workshop) is the thrust of this chic boutique that reinvents vintage pieces. Scarves, headpieces, sequins, bangles and beads casually strung up to be admired...the place oozes the femininity and refinement of an old-fashioned Parisian boudoir.

NOSE PERFUME

Map p376 (☎01 40 26 46 03; http://nose.fr; 20 rue Bachaumont, 2e; ⏰10.30am-7.30pm Mon-Sat; Ⓜ Sentier) Come to this concept shop for a personal perfume diagnosis, after which the knowledgable staff (English spoken) will be able to narrow down a selection of fragrances that suit you best. You could easily spend over an hour here, so come with time to spare. Perfumes and cosmetics available for both men and women.

LA SAMARITAINE REDUX

One of Paris' four big department stores, the 10-storey **La Samaritaine** (Map p376; ☎01 56 81 28 40; www.lasamaritaine.com; 19 rue de la Monnaie, 1er; Ⓜ Pont Neuf) is finally emerging from its much contested and drawn-out 14-year overhaul. Pritzker Prize–winning Japanese firm Sanaa has preserved much of the gorgeous art nouveau and art deco exterior, in addition to the glass ceiling topping the central Hall Jourdain. It's slated to open in 2019.

SEPT CINQ FASHION & ACCESSORIES

Map p376 (☎09 83 00 44 01; www.sept-cinq.com; 26 rue Berger, 1er; ⏰11am-7:30pm; 📶; Ⓜ Les Halles or RER Châtelet–Les Halles) Scarves, designer T-shirts, Paris-themed stationery and locally made jewellery make this boutique worth a peek. The in-house tearoom also serves light lunches and sweet nibbles.

KILIWATCH FASHION & ACCESSORIES

Map p376 (☎01 42 21 17 37; http://kiliwatch.paris; 64 rue Tiquetonne, 2e; ⏰10.30am-7pm Mon, to 7.30pm Tue-Sat; Ⓜ Étienne Marcel) A Parisian institution, Kiliwatch gets jam-packed with hip guys and gals rummaging through racks of new and used streetwear, along with vintage hats and boots plus art and photography books, eyewear and the latest sneakers.

BOÎTES À MUSIQUE ANNA JOLIET GIFTS & SOUVENIRS

Map p372 (Palais Royal, 9 rue de Beaujolais, 1er; ⏰noon-7pm Tue-Sat, closed Jan; Ⓜ Bourse) This wonderful shop at the northern end of the Jardin du Palais Royal specialises in music boxes, new and old, from Switzerland.

ANTOINE FASHION & ACCESSORIES

Map p372 (☎01 42 96 01 80; www.antoine1745.com; 10 av de l'Opéra, 1er; ⏰10.30am-1pm & 2-6.30pm Mon-Sat; Ⓜ Pyramides, Palais Royal–Musée du Louvre) Antoine has been the Parisian master of bespoke canes, umbrellas, fans and gloves since 1745.

Montmartre & Northern Paris

Neighbourhood Top Five

❶ **Basilique du Sacré-Cœur** (p134) Hiking up the steps for panoramic city views and some of the city's finest street entertainers outside, and a glittering mosaic within.

❷ **Parc de la Villette** (p136) Enjoying a performance or exhibit at the city's largest cultural playground or taking the kids to its world-class science museum.

❸ **Musée Jacquemart-André** (p138) Stepping into opulent surrounds at this elegant art museum, a rare snapshot of 19th-century Parisian high society.

❹ **Basilique de St-Denis** (p142) Discovering the tombs of French royalty at this popular pilgrimage site in St-Denis.

❺ **Le Mur des je t'aime** (p141) Learning how to say 'I love you' in every language under the sun in a pretty city park in Montmartre.

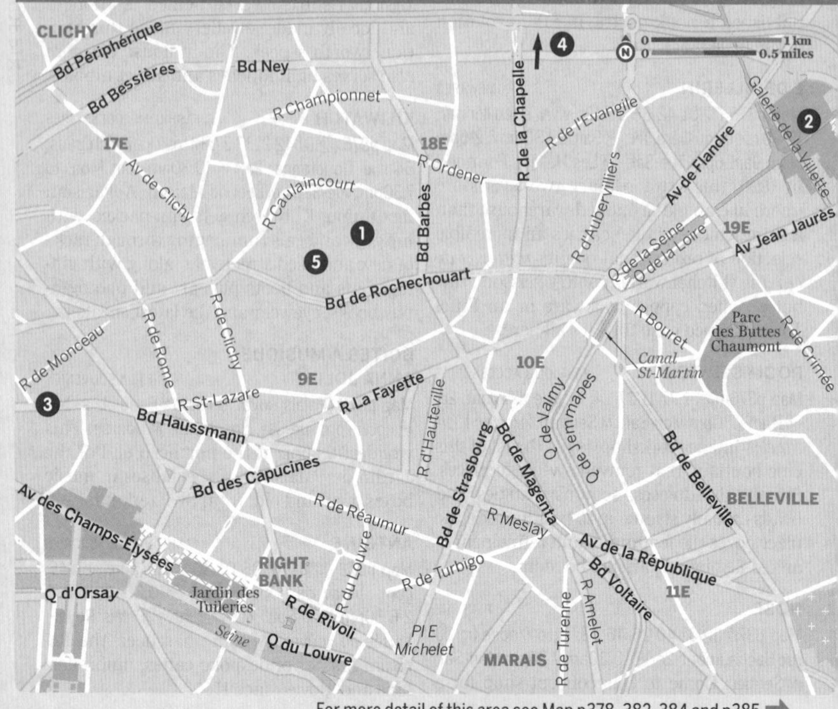

For more detail of this area see Map p378, 382, 384 and p385

Explore Montmartre & Northern Paris

One of the wellsprings of Parisian myth, Montmartre has always stood apart. Bohemians, revolutionaries, artists, cancan dancers and headless martyrs have all played a role in its story, and while it belongs to Paris today, vestiges of the original village – ivy-clad buildings, steep narrow streets – remain. Crowned by the white-domed Sacré-Cœur, dragged back to earth by red-light Pigalle, it has long encompassed contrast and conflict.

An ideal base, Montmartre is rich in sights, cuisine, shopping and entertainment. Most visitors spend half a day or more exploring the side streets that tumble from the summit in all directions, with stunning vistas out over the city. When the crowds get too much, there are the rarely visited streets on the backside of the Butte (as the hill is known) to explore or some excellent lesser-known museums to the southwest, beyond place de Clichy.

Night owls will enjoy drinking and dining in style in south Pigalle (aka 'SoPi'). This edgy but increasingly hip area bustles with local life in its sensational cocktail bars. Head east into the 10e *arrondissement*, another traditional working-class area that is slowly gentrifying, with gourmet cafes, bars and barista-run coffee shops. For a taste of fully fledged *bobo* (bourgeois bohemian) lifestyle, head east again to Canal St-Martin, a vibrant 'hood with everything from all-day brunches and late-night drinks to offbeat shopping and romantic waterside strolls.

Local Life

➡ **Food shopping** Join locals shopping for gourmet treats at Pain Pain (p143) along foodie street rue des Martyrs.

➡ **Urban farm** Cultural centre/urban farm La REcyclerie (p137) is a hub for eco-conscious locals.

➡ **Canal lounging** On spring and summer weekends, join the cyclists, picnickers or cafe goers along the picturesque quays of Canal St-Martin (p146).

➡ **Little Africa** Locals love the colourful, predominantly North African *quartier* of La Goutte d'Or, not least for its artisan coffee-bean roastery Café Lomi (p150).

Getting There & Away

➡ **Metro** Lines 2, 4 and 12 serve Montmartre; lines 5 and 7 serve northeastern Paris (Canal St-Martin and La Villette). To the west, the museums in Clichy are accessed via lines 2 and 13. Lines 4 and 5 serve Gare du Nord.

➡ **RER** RER B and D link Gare du Nord with central Paris.

➡ **Bicycle** Vélib' stations along Canal St-Martin, include place République and place Jacques Bonsergent.

Lonely Planet's Top Tip

Although not quite as pretty or pristine as Seine-side Paris, the neighbourhoods in the north and northeast of Paris are still fairly safe as far as big cities go, providing you use your common sense. Stay on your guard, however, at the foot of the hill that leads up to Sacré-Cœur and also on Montmartre's place du Tertre. It's not unusual for pickpockets and con artists to work the crowds here.

Best Places to Eat

➡ Marrow (p144)

➡ Le Verre Volé (p140)

➡ Du Pain et des Idées (p140)

➡ Abattoir Végétal (p140)

➡ Holybelly 5 (p143)

For reviews, see p140 ➡

Best Places to Drink

➡ Le Très Particulier (p149)

➡ Le Syndicat (p149)

➡ Gravity Bar (p149)

➡ Pavillon Puebla (p149)

For reviews, see p148 ➡

Best Entertainment

➡ Philharmonie de Paris (p151)

➡ Point Éphémère (p151)

➡ La Cigale (p151)

➡ Le Divan du Monde (p151)

➡ Moulin Rouge (p151)

For reviews, see p151 ➡

MANJIK PHOTOGRAPHY/ GETTY IMAGES ©

TOP SIGHT
BASILIQUE DU SACRÉ-CŒUR

More than just a place of worship, the distinctive dove-white domed Basilique du Sacré-Cœur (Sacred Heart Basilica) is a veritable experience. Reached by 270 steps, the parvis (forecourt) in front of the basilica provides a postcard-perfect city panorama. Buskers and street artists perform on the steps, while picnickers spread out on the hillside park.

History

It may appear to be a place of peacefulness and quiet contemplation today, but Sacré-Cœur's foundations were laid amid bloodshed and controversy. Its construction began in 1875, in the wake of France's humiliating defeat by Prussia and the subsequent chaos of the Paris Commune. Following Napoléon III's surrender to von Bismarck in September 1870, angry Parisians, with the help of the National Guard, continued to hold out against Prussian forces – a harrowing siege that lasted four long winter months. By the time a ceasefire was negotiated in early 1871, the split between the radical working-class Parisians (supported by the National Guard) and the conservative national government (supported by the French army) had become insurmountable.

Over the next several months, the rebels, known as Communards, managed to overthrow the reactionary government and take over the city. It was a particularly chaotic and bloody moment in Parisian history, with mass executions on both sides and a wave of rampant destruction that spread throughout Paris. Montmartre was a key Communard stronghold. It was on the future site of Sacré-Cœur that the rebels won their first victory and it was consequently the first neighbourhood to

DON'T MISS

- The views from the parvis
- The apse mosaic *Christ in Majesty*
- The dome

PRACTICALITIES

- Map p378, F3
- 01 53 41 89 00
- www.sacre-coeur-montmartre.com
- Parvis du Sacré-Cœur
- basilica free, dome adult/child €6/4, cash only
- basilica 6am-10.30pm, dome 8.30am-8pm May-Sep, 9am-5pm Oct-Apr
- Ⓜ Anvers, Abbesses

be targeted when the French army returned in full force in May 1871. Ultimately, many Communards were buried alive in the gypsum mines beneath the Butte.

The Basilica

Within the historical context, the construction of an enormous basilica to expiate the city's sins seemed like a gesture of peace and forgiveness – indeed, the seven million French francs needed to construct the church's foundations came solely from the contributions of local Catholics. However, the Montmartre location was certainly no coincidence: the conservative old guard desperately wanted to assert its power in what was then a hotbed of revolution. The battle between the two camps – Catholic versus secular, royalist versus republican – raged on and in 1882 the construction of the basilica was even voted down by the city council on the grounds that it would continue to fan the flames of civil war. It was overturned in the end by a technicality.

The Romano-Byzantine–style basilica's travertine stone exudes calcite, ensuring it remains white despite weathering and pollution. Six successive architects oversaw construction of the basilica, and it wasn't until 1919 that Sacré-Cœur was finally consecrated, contrasting the surrounding area's bohemian lifestyle.

While criticism of its design and white travertine stone has continued throughout the decades (one poet called it a giant baby's bottle for angels), the interior is enlivened by the glittering apse mosaic *Christ in Majesty*, designed by Luc-Olivier Merson in 1922 and one of the largest in the world.

On Sundays, you can catch the organ being played during Mass and Vespers.

The Dome & Crypt

Outside, to the west of the main entrance, 300 spiralling steps lead you to the basilica's dome, which affords one of Paris' most spectacular panoramas; it's said you can see for 30km on a clear day. Weighing in at 19 tonnes, the bell in the tower above, called La Savoyarde, is the largest in France.

The huge chapel-lined crypt is closed indefinitely to the public.

A PLACE OF PILGRIMAGE

In a sense, atonement here has never stopped: a prayer 'cycle' that began in 1885 before the basilica's completion still continues around the clock, with perpetual adoration of the Blessed Sacrament continually on display above the high altar.

DIVINE INTERVENTION?

In 1944, 13 Allied bombs were dropped on Montmartre, falling just next to Sacré-Cœur. Although the stained-glass windows all shattered from the force of the explosions, miraculously no one died and the basilica sustained no other damage.

TOP SIGHT
PARC DE LA VILLETTE

The vast green Parc de la Villette is a cultural centre, kids playground and landscaped urban space rolled into one. The French love of geometric forms defines the layout – the colossal mirror-like sphere of the Géode cinema, an undulating strip of corrugated steel stretching for hundreds of metres, the bright-red cubical pavilions known as *folies* – but the intersection of two canals, the Ourcq and the St-Denis, brings the most natural and popular element: water.

Although it's a fair hike from central Paris, consider the trip here to attend one of the many events (world, rock and classical music concerts; art exhibits; outdoor cinema; circuses; modern dance). Throughout the year, events are staged in the wonderful old Grande Halle, **Le Zénith** (Map p384; www.le-zenith.com; 211 av Jean Jaurès, 19e; Ⓜ Porte de Pantin), the **Cabaret Sauvage** (Map p384; ☎01 42 09 03 09; www.cabaretsauvage.com; 211 av Jean Jaurès, 19e; Ⓜ Porte de la Villette) and Paris' stunning, cutting-edge Cité de la Musique – Philharmonie de Paris complex (p138).

It's also a winner with families. In fine weather, children (and adults) will enjoy exploring the numerous themed gardens, the best of which double as playgrounds. For kids, however, the star attraction is **Cité des Sciences** (Map p384; ☎01 40 05 80 00; www.cite-sciences.fr; 30 av Corentin Cariou, Parc de la Villette, 19e; per attraction adult/child €12/9; ⏲10am-6pm Tue-Sat, to 7pm Sun, La Géode 10.30am-8.30pm Tue-Sun; Ⓜ Porte de la Villette) and its attached cinemas. The brilliant Cité des Enfants is the most popular section, with a construction site, a TV studio, robots and water-based physics experiments, all designed for children.

DON'T MISS

- ➡ Evening performances
- ➡ The themed gardens
- ➡ Cité des Sciences

PRACTICALITIES

- ➡ Map p384, C1
- ➡ www.lavillette.com
- ➡ 211 av Jean Jaurès, 19e
- ➡ ⏲6am-1am
- ➡ Ⓜ Porte de la Villette, Porte de Pantin

SIGHTS

The hilltop neighbourhood of Montmartre safeguards some of Paris' most iconic sights, including the white domed Sacré-Cœur basilica and a Parisian vineyard. The *quartier's* museums evoke its fabled artistic heritage and it's easy to stroll between them. West, past place de Clichy and beyond to Parc Monceau, there are a couple of excellent lesser-known art museums at home in historic mansions. Canal St-Martin, a sight in itself with its vintage bridges and canal boats, flows to the east.

BASILIQUE DU SACRÉ-CŒUR — BASILICA

See p134.

PARC DE LA VILLETTE — PARK

See p136.

MUSÉE DE MONTMARTRE — MUSEUM

Map p378 (☎01 49 25 89 39; www.museedemontmartre.fr; 12 rue Cortot, 18e; adult/child €9.50/5.50, garden only €4; ⊙10am-7pm Apr-Sep, to 6pm Oct-Mar; Ⓜ Lamarck–Caulaincourt) This delightful 'village' museum showcases paintings, lithographs and documents illustrating Montmartre's bohemian, artistic and hedonistic past – one room is dedicated entirely to the French cancan. It's housed in a 17th-century manor where several artists, including Renoir and Raoul Dufy, had their studios in the 19th century. You can also visit the studio of painter Suzanne Valadon, who lived and worked here with her son Maurice Utrillo and partner André Utter between 1912 and 1926.

Allow ample time to stroll the museum gardens, named after Renoir, who painted his masterpieces *Bal du Moulin de la Galette* and *Jardin de la rue Cortot* while working in his studio here from 1875 to 1877. Find the tree strung with a swing to evoke the impressionist painter's famous work *La Balançoire,* also painted here. Follow the path to the end of the garden for a stunning 'secret' view of the Clos Montmartre vineyards. Museum admission includes an audioguide.

LA RECYCLERIE — CULTURAL CENTRE

(www.larecyclerie.com; 83 bd Ornano, 18e; ⊙8am-midnight Mon-Thu, to 2am Fri & Sat, to 10pm Sun early Jan–mid-Dec; Ⓜ Porte de Clignancourt) An abandoned Petite Ceinture train station has been repurposed as an eco-hub with an urban farm along the old railway line, featuring community vegetable and herb gardens and chickens. They provide ingredients for the mostly vegetarian cafe-canteen (tables stretch trackside in summer and the station houses a cavernous dining space). In turn, food scraps replenish the chickens and gardens. Beehives on the roof produce honey. Look out for regular upcycling and repair workshops, flea markets and various other events.

PARC MONCEAU — PARK

Map p385 (35 bd de Courcelles, 8e; ⊙7am-10pm May-Aug, to 9pm Sep, to 8pm Oct-Apr; Ⓜ Monceau) Marked by a neoclassical rotunda at its main bd Courcelles entrance, beautiful Parc Monceau sprawls over 8.2 lush hectares. It was laid out by Louis Carrogis Carmontelle in 1778–79 in English style with winding paths, ponds, and flower beds. An Egyptian-style pyramid is the only original folly remaining today, but other distinctive features include a bridge modelled after Venice's Rialto, a Renaissance arch and a Corinthian colonnade. There are play areas, a carousel and scheduled puppet shows for kids.

Throughout the park, look out for statues including those depicting composers Frédéric Chopin and Charles-François Gounod (known for 'Ave Maria'), and writer Guy de Maupassant.

MUSÉE NISSIM DE CAMONDO — GALLERY

Map p385 (☎01 44 55 57 50; www.lesartsdecoratifs.fr; 63 rue de Monceau, 8e; adult/child €9/free; ⊙10am-5.30pm Wed-Sun; Ⓜ Monceau, Villiers) Housed in a sumptuous mansion modelled on the Petit Trianon at Versailles, this museum displays 18th-century furniture, wood panelling, tapestries, porcelain and other objets d'art collected by Count Moïse de Camondo, a Sephardic Jewish banker who moved from Constantinople to Paris in the late 19th century.

He bequeathed the mansion and his collection to the state on the proviso that it would be turned into a museum named in memory of his son Nissim (1892–1917), a pilot killed in action during WWI.

LE 104 — GALLERY

Map p382 (☎01 53 35 50 00; www.104.fr; 5 rue Curial, 19e; ⊙noon-7pm Tue-Fri, from 11am Sat & Sun; Ⓜ Riquet) A former funeral parlour turned city-funded alternative art space, Le 104 is a hive of activity. It essentially supports and encourages young artists, and a

TOP SIGHT
MUSÉE JACQUEMART-ANDRÉ

If you belonged to the cream of Parisian society in the late 19th century, chances are you would have been invited to one of the dazzling soirées held at this mansion. The home of prolific art collectors Nélie Jacquemart and Édouard André, this opulent residence was designed in the then-fashionable eclectic style, which combined elements from various eras – seen here in the presence of Greek and Roman antiquities, Egyptian artefacts, period furnishings and portraits by Dutch masters.

A wander through the mansion's 16 rambling rooms offers an absorbing glimpse of the lifestyle and tastes of Parisian high society: from the library, hung with canvases by Rembrandt and Van Dyck, to the marvellous Jardin d'Hiver – a glass-paned garden room backed by a magnificent double-helix staircase. Upstairs is an impressive collection of Italian Renaissance works by Botticelli, Donatello and Titian, among others.

The mansion's architect, Henri Parent, was nearly hired to work on the even more prestigious Paris opera house, the Palais Garnier – he was eclipsed only by the then-unknown Charles Garnier.

DON'T MISS

- The library
- The Jardin d'Hiver
- The tearoom

PRACTICALITIES

- Map p385, C4
- 01 45 62 11 59
- www.musee-jacquemart-andre.com
- 158 bd Haussmann, 8e
- adult/child €13.50/10.50
- 10am-6pm, to 8.30pm Mon during temporary exhibitions
- M Miromesnil

random wander through its public areas uncovers breakdancers, wacky art installations and rehearsing actors. Check the schedule for events, such as theatre, circus, concerts, balls and magic shows, to make the most of it. There is also a pizza truck, a retro 1950s-styled cafe and an industrial loft-like restaurant-bar on site.

PLACE DU TERTRE SQUARE

Map p378 (18e; M Abbesses) Today filled with visitors, buskers and portrait artists, place du Tertre was originally the main square of the village of Montmartre before it was incorporated into the city proper. One of the more popular claims of Montmartre mythology is staked to La Mère Catherine at No 6: in 1814, so it's said, Cossack soldiers first introduced the term *bistro* (Russian for 'quickly') into the French lexicon. Another big moment came on Christmas Eve 1898, when Louis Renault's first car was driven up the Butte to the place du Tertre, igniting the start of the French auto industry.

PARC DES BUTTES CHAUMONT PARK

Map p384 (rue Manin & rue Botzaris, 19e; 7am-10pm May-Sep, to 8pm Oct-Apr; M Buttes Chaumont, Botzaris) One of the city's largest green spaces, Buttes Chaumont's landscaped slopes hide grottoes, waterfalls, a lake and even an island topped with a temple to Sibylle. Once a gypsum quarry and rubbish dump, it was given its present form by Baron Haussmann in time for the opening of the 1867 Exposition Universelle. The tracks of the abandoned 19th-century Petite Ceinture railway line, which once circled Paris, run through the park.

It's a favourite with Parisians, who come here to practise t'ai chi, take the kids to a puppet show or simply to relax with a bottle of wine and a sundown picnic.

MUSÉE DE LA MUSIQUE MUSEUM

Map p384 (www.philharmoniedeparis.fr; 221 av Jean Jaurès, 19e; adult/child €8/free; noon-6pm Tue-Fri, from 10am Sat & Sun; M Porte de Pantin) Inside the Cité de la Musique building within the Cité de la Musique – Philharmonie de Paris complex that also includes the Philharmonie de Paris, this music museum's collection spans 7000 rare musical instruments, of which 1000-plus are on display; you can hear many of them being played on the audioguide (included in admission). Live musicians play from 2pm to 5pm. Temporary exhibitions incur an additional entrance fee. Highlights include a piano owned by Chopin and a guitar owned by Georges Brassens.

MUSÉE DE LA VIE ROMANTIQUE MUSEUM

Map p378 (☎01 55 31 95 67; www.vie-romantique.paris.fr; 16 rue Chaptal, 9e; ⊙10am-6pm Tue-Sun; MBlanche, St-Georges) Framed by green shutters, this mansion where George Sand (Amantine Lucile Aurore Dupin) and painter Ary Scheffer once lived sits in a cobbled courtyard at the end of a tree-shaded alley. The objects exhibited create a wonderful flashback to Romantic-era Paris when Chopin (Sand's lover), Delacroix et al attended salons here. Admission is free except when there's a temporary exhibition. End your visit with tea and cake in the museum's cafe, open spring to autumn, in the enchanting garden.

CIMETIÈRE DE MONTMARTRE CEMETERY

Map p378 (20 av Rachel, 18e; ⊙8am-6pm Mon-Sat, from 9am Sun May-Sep, 8am-5.30pm Mon-Sat, 9am-5pm Sun Oct-Apr; MPlace de Clichy) This 11-hectare cemetery opened in 1825. It contains the graves of writers Émile Zola (whose ashes are now in the Panthéon), Alexandre Dumas *fils* and Stendhal, composers Jacques Offenbach and Hector Berlioz, artists Edgar Degas and Gustave Moreau, film director François Truffaut and dancer Vaslav Nijinsky, among others. Steps from the rue Caulaincourt road bridge, built in 1888, lead down to the entrance on av Rachel, just off bd de Clichy.

ESPACE DALÍ GALLERY

Map p378 (☎01 42 64 40 21; www.daliparis.com; 11 rue Poulbot, 18e; adult/child €12/9; ⊙10am-6pm Sep-Jun, to 8pm Jul & Aug; MAbbesses) More than 300 works by Salvador Dalí (1904–89), the flamboyant Catalan surrealist printmaker, painter, sculptor and self-promoter, are on display at this basement museum located just west of place du Tertre. The collection includes Dalí's strange sculptures, lithographs, and many of his illustrations and furniture, including the famous *Mae West Lips Sofa*.

MUSÉE CERNUSCHI GALLERY

Map p385 (☎01 53 96 21 50; www.cernuschi.paris.fr; 7 av Vélasquez, 8e; ⊙10am-6pm Tue-Sun; MVilliers) FREE The Cernuschi Museum comprises an excellent and rare collection of ancient Chinese art (funerary statues, bronzes, ceramics), much of which predates the Tang dynasty (618–907), in addition to diverse pieces from Japan. Milan banker and philanthropist Henri Cernuschi (1821–96), who settled in Paris before the unification of Italy, assembled the collection during an 1871–73 world tour.

HALLE ST-PIERRE GALLERY

Map p378 (☎01 42 58 72 89; www.hallesaint-pierre.org; 2 rue Ronsard, 18e; adult/child €9/6; ⊙11am-6pm Mon-Fri, to 7pm Sat, noon-6pm Sun; MAnvers) Founded in 1986, this museum and gallery is in a lovely former covered market. It focuses on the primitive and Art Brut schools; there is no permanent collection, but the museum stages several temporary exhibitions a year. It also has an auditorium, a cafe and a bookshop.

BRASSERIE LA GOUTTE D'OR BREWERY

Map p382 (☎09 80 64 23 51; www.brasserielagouttedor.com; 28 rue de la Goutte d'Or, 18e; ⊙5-7pm Thu & Fri, from 2pm Sat; MChâteau Rouge, Barbès-Rochechouart) FREE An earthy reflection of the gutsy, multiethnic *quartier* of La Goutte d'Or, this craft brewery (established 2012) is the brainchild of brewmaster Thierry Roche, who turns to the local 'hood for inspiration: spicy red beer Château Rouge is named after the local metro station; fruity India pale ale Ernestine evokes the street where La Goutte d'Or's early beers were brewed in the early 1900s; and aromatic, bitter La Môme was created for a local restaurant. Free guided tours include tastings.

INSTITUT DES CULTURES D'ISLAM-LÉON CULTURAL CENTRE

Map p382 (ICIC; www.institut-cultures-islam.org; 19-23 rue Léon, 18e; ⊙1-8pm Tue-Thu, from 4pm Fri, from 10am Sat & Sun; MChâteau Rouge) FREE The Islam Cultural Institute hosts concerts, poetry readings, film screenings, temporary exhibitions, art workshops and cooking classes, all generally related to North Africa or the Middle East. There's a North African cafe with a mosaic-tiled terrace. Ask about fascinating walking tours of the surrounding Goutte d'Or neighbourhood (prices vary), with themes such as street art or flavours of Africa. The ICIC has a **second building** (Map p382; ☎01 53 09 99 84; www.institut-cultures-islam.org; 56 rue Stéphenson, 18e; ⊙1-8pm Tue-Thu, from 4pm Fri, from 10am Sat & Sun; MMarx Dormoy) FREE nearby with more exhibition space and a *hammam*.

PLAYGROUND DUPERRÉ SPORTS GROUND

Map p378 (22 rue Duperré, 9e; ⏲10am-8pm May-Sep, shorter hours Oct-Apr; Ⓜ Pigalle) Looking more like a dramatic street-art installation, Paris' 'most beautiful basketball court' was redone in 2017 by Parisian design studio Ill-Studio in eye-popping shades of yellow, blue, indigo and fuchsia-pink. Incongruously wedged between classical Haussmannian buildings, the rubber court was originally renovated by Ill-Studio for streetwear brand Pigalle's founder Stephane Ashpool and Nike in 2015. Blue mesh fencing lets you check out the sporting action inside.

EATING

Western Paris' culinary scene evolves slowly, but once you cross over that invisible border somewhere in the middle of the 9th *arrondissement*, it's a different world, with a constant flurry of new openings in south Pigalle, along Canal St-Martin and in the cosmopolitan 10e west of place de la République: young chefs here head up some of the most exciting dining venues in Paris today. *Rues commerçantes* (shopping streets) where food stalls set up on the pavement outside shops include rue des Martyrs and, in the 17e, rue Poncelet.

★DU PAIN ET DES IDÉES BAKERY €

Map p382 (www.dupainetdesidees.com; 34 rue Yves Toudic, 10e; breads €1.20-7, pastries €2.50-6.50; ⏲6.45am-8pm Mon-Fri; Ⓜ Jacques Bonsergent) This traditional bakery with an exquisite interior from 1889 is famed for its naturally leavened bread, orange-blossom brioche and *escargots* (scroll-like 'snails') in four sweet flavours. Its mini savoury *pavés* (breads) flavoured with reblochon cheese and fig, or goat's cheese, sesame and honey are perfect for lunch on the run. A wooden picnic table sits on the pavement outside.

★ABATTOIR VÉGÉTAL VEGAN €

Map p378 (61 rue Ramey, 18e; 3-course lunch menu €18, mains €13-16, Sunday brunch adult/child €25/5; ⏲9am-6pm Tue & Wed, 9am-11.45pm Thu & Fri, 10am-11.45pm Sat, 10.30am-4.30pm Sun; 📶✍; Ⓜ Jules Joffrin) Mint-green wrought-iron chairs and tables line the pavement outside the 'plant slaughterhouse' (it occupies a former butcher shop), while the light, bright interior has bare-bulb downlights, distempered walls and greenery-filled hanging baskets. Each day there's a choice of three raw and cooked organic dishes per course, cold-pressed juices and craft beers from Parisian brewery BapBap.

★LE VERRE VOLÉ BISTRO €

Map p382 (☎01 48 03 17 34; www.leverrevole.fr; 67 rue de Lancry, 10e; mains €11-22, sandwiches €7.90; ⏲bistro 12.30-2.30pm & 7.30-11.30pm, wine bar 10am-2am; 📶; Ⓜ Jacques Bonsergent) The tiny 'Stolen Glass' – a wine shop with a few tables – is one of Paris' most popular wine bar–restaurants, with outstanding natural and unfiltered wines and expert advice. Unpretentious, hearty *plats du jour* are excellent. Reserve in advance for meals, or stop by to pick up a gourmet sandwich (such as mustard-smoked burrata with garlic-pork sausage) and a bottle.

LE PETIT CHÂTEAU D'EAU FRENCH €

Map p382 (☎01 42 08 72 81; 34 rue du Château d'Eau, 10e; mains €13.50-17.50; ⏲kitchen noon-3pm Mon, noon-3pm & 7-11.30pm Tue-Sat, bar 8am-3.30pm Mon, to 2am Tue-Fri, 9am-2am Sat; Ⓜ Jacques Bonsergent) Scarcely changed in a century, with lemon- and lime-tiled walls, horseshoe-shaped zinc bar and burgundy banquettes, this neighbourhood treasure endures in defiance of the post-industrial co-working cafes that have sprung up around it. Classical cooking ranges from duck with honey sauce to beef entrecôte with roast garlic potatoes. You can also just stop by for a morning coffee or afternoon kir.

LE GRENIER À PAIN BAKERY €

Map p378 (www.legrenierapain.com; 38 rue des Abbesses, 18e; ⏲7.30am-8pm Thu-Mon; Ⓜ Abbesses) A past winner of Paris' annual 'best baguette' prize, this enchanting bakery with a semi-open kitchen is an ideal place to pick up picnic fare. Join the queue for a crusty baguette sandwich, Provence-style *fougasse* bread and alluring mini breads topped with fig and goat's cheese or bacon and olives. End on a sweet high with a fruit-bejewelled loaf cake.

CRÊPERIE PEN-TY CRÊPES €

Map p378 (☎01 48 74 18 49; 65 rue de Douai, 9e; galettes €4-15, crêpes €4.90-10.40; ⏲noon-2.30pm & 7.30-11.15pm Mon-Fri, 12.30-4pm & 6.30-11.30pm Sat, to 10.30pm Sun; Ⓜ Place de Clichy) Hailed as the best crêperie in northern Paris, Pen-Ty is well worth the detour. Book ahead, and don't miss the selection of

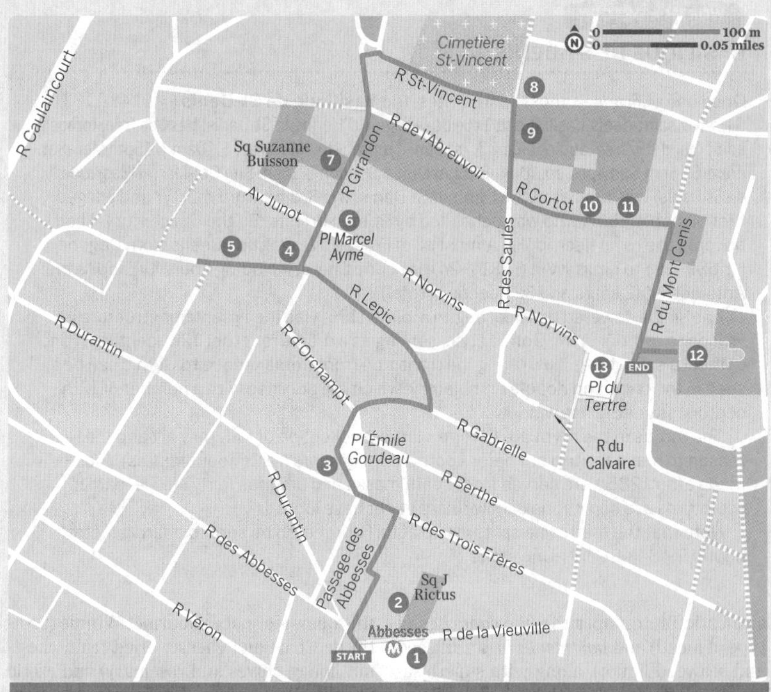

Neighbourhood Walk
Mythic Montmartre

START ABBESSES METRO STATION
END PLACE DU TERTRE
LENGTH 1KM; ONE HOUR

Begin on 1 **place des Abbesses**, where Hector Guimard's iconic art-nouveau metro entrance (p322) still stands. Learn how to say 'I love you!' in another language or 10 with 2 **Le Mur des je t'aime**, hidden in a park, Sq Jehan Rictus, on place des Abbesses.

Head up passage des Abbesses to place Émile Goudeau. At No 11bis you'll find 3 **Le Bateau Lavoir**, where Max Jacob, Amedeo Modigliani and Pablo Picasso once had art studios.

Continue the climb up rue Lepic to Montmartre's two surviving windmills: 4 **Moulin Radet** and, 50m west, 5 **Moulin Blute Fin**. In the 19th century, the latter became an open-air dance hall, immortalised by Renoir's *Bal du Moulin de la Galette*.

Just north, on place Marcel Aymé, you'll see a man pop out of a stone wall. This 6 **Passe-Muraille sculpture** portrays Dutilleul, the hero of Marcel Aymé's short story 'Le Passe-Muraille' (The Walker Through Walls). Aymé lived in the adjacent building. Continue along rue Girardon to Sq Suzanne Buisson, home to a 7 **statue of St-Denis**, the 3rd-century martyr and patron saint of France beheaded by Roman priests.

After passing by Cimetière St-Vincent you'll come upon celebrated cabaret 8 **Au Lapin Agile** (p152), with a mural of a rabbit jumping out of a cooking pot by caricaturist André Gill. Opposite is 9 **Clos Montmartre**, a vineyard dating from 1933, whose 2000 vines produce an average of 800 bottles of wine each October.

Uphill is Montmartre's oldest building, a 17th-century manor house. One-time home to painters Renoir, Utrillo and Raoul Dufy, it's now the 10 **Musée de Montmartre** (p137). Continue past composer 11 **Eric Satie's former residence** (No 6) and turn right onto rue du Mont Cenis; you'll come to historic 12 **Église St-Pierre de Montmartre**. End on busy 13 **place du Tertre** (p138), once the main village square.

WORTH A DETOUR

BASILIQUE DE ST-DENIS

Once one of France's most sacred sites, the **Basilique de St-Denis** (☎01 48 09 83 54; www.saint-denis-basilique.fr; 1 rue de la Légion d'Honneur, St-Denis; basilica free, tombs adult/child €9/free, audioguide €3, 1st Sun of month Nov-Mar free; ⏱10am-6.15pm Mon-Sat, noon-6.15pm Sun Apr-Sep, 10am-5.15pm Mon-Sat, noon-5.15pm Sun Oct-Mar; MBasilique de St-Denis) was built atop the tomb of St Denis, the 3rd-century martyr and alleged first bishop of Paris who was beheaded by Roman priests. By the 6th century it had become the royal necropolis. Almost all of France's kings and queens from Dagobert I (r 629–39) to Louis XVIII (r 1814–24) are buried here, including Louis XVI and Marie Antoinette (42 kings and 32 queens in total).

The single-towered basilica, begun around 1136, was the first major structure in France to be built in the Gothic style, serving as a model for other 12th-century French cathedrals. Features illustrating the transition from Romanesque to Gothic can be seen in the choir and double ambulatory, which are adorned with a number of 12th-century stained-glass windows.

The tombs in the crypt are Europe's largest collection of funerary art and the real reason to make the trip out here. Adorned with *gisants* (recumbent figures), those made after 1285 were carved from death masks and are thus fairly lifelike; earlier sculptures are depictions of how rulers might have looked.

Note that the metro line splits in two at La Fourche, so be sure to board a metro bound for Saint-Denis-Université.

authentic Breton aperitifs like *chouchen* (a type of mead) and *pastis marin* (an aniseed and seaweed liquor), along with superb savoury *galettes* (made with buckwheat flour) and sweet crêpes. There is a takeaway window too.

MESDEMOISELLES MADELEINES — PASTRIES €

Map p378 (www.mllesmadeleines.com; 37 rue des Martyrs, 9e; madeleines small €0.70, large €2.50-4.50; ⏱10.30am-7pm Tue-Sat, 10.30am-2pm & 3.30-6.30pm Sun; MSt-Georges) Shell-shaped French madeleine cakes, immortalised by Marcel Proust, are the sole product of this ingenious spot, in a dazzling array of flavours: 'simple' (Tahitian vanilla; Ethiopian coffee), 'savoury' (red onion, chives and crème fraîche; basil, feta and pine nuts), and 'gourmet' (Rhône valley raspberries with raspberry coulis; caramelised hazelnuts, salted caramel mousse and a caramel shell), along with bite-sized mini-madeleines. Even a single madeleine is beautifully packaged in a white box with gold lettering.

FRIC-FRAC — SANDWICHES €

Map p382 (☎01 42 85 87 34; www.fricfrac.fr; 79 quai de Valmy, 10e; sandwiches €11.50-15; ⏱noon-3pm & 7.30-11pm Tue-Fri, noon-11pm Sat & Sun; MJacques Bonsergent) Traditional snack croque monsieur (a toasted cheese and ham sandwich) gets a contemporary makeover at this quayside space. Gourmet Winnie (Crottin de Chavignol cheese, dried fruit, chestnut honey, chives and rosemary) and exotic Shaolin (king prawns, lemongrass paste, shitake mushrooms and Thai basil) are among the creative combos served with salad and fries. Eat in or head to the canal.

L'AFFINEUR AFFINÉ — CHEESE €

Map p378 (☎09 66 94 22 15; www.laffineuraffine.com; 51 rue Notre Dame de Lorette, 9e; cheese platters €6.50-39, weekend brunch €20; ⏱kitchen noon-2.30pm Mon, noon-2.30pm & 5.30-9pm Wed-Sat, 11.30am-2pm & 5.30-7pm Sun, shop 10.30am-2.30pm Mon, to 9pm Wed-Sat, to 7pm Sun; MSt-Georges) With 120 French cheeses, this *fromagerie* (cheese shop) is a fabulous place to stock up and taste them at its on-site *bar à fromages* (cheese bar). Let the staff know your preferences and they'll prepare platters of two to 15 varieties, with charcuterie available as well as paired wines. Weekend brunch is a multicourse feast.

52 FAUBOURG ST-DENIS — CAFE, BISTRO €

Map p382 (www.faubourgstdenis.com; 52 rue du Faubourg St-Denis, 10e; mains €17-20; ⏱kitchen noon-2.30pm & 7-11pm, bar 8am-midnight, closed Aug; 📶; MChâteau d'Eau) With its polished concrete floors, stone walls and exposed ducting, this contemporary neighbourhood cafe-restaurant is a brilliant space to hang out in, from breakfast through to lunch, dinner and drinks. Creative cuisine might include tuna sashimi salad with beetroot jelly, egg-yolk ravioli with ham and mushrooms or lamb-shoulder pie with cinnamon fig jus. No reservations.

SUNKEN CHIP FAST FOOD €

Map p382 (☎01 53 26 74 46; www.thesunkenchip.com; 39 rue des Vinaigriers, 10e; fish & chips €12-14; ⊙noon-2.30pm & 7-10pm Mon-Fri, noon-3.30pm & 7-10pm Sat & Sun; MJacques Bonsergent) It's hard to argue with the battered, fried goodness at this ideally located fish-and-chip shop near Canal St-Martin. Nothing is frozen here: it's all line-caught fish fresh from Brittany (three varieties per day), accompanied by thick-cut chips (peeled and chopped *sur place*), brown malt vinegar and minty mushy peas. Pickled eggs and onions are optional. Takeaway is available.

BRASSERIE BARBÈS CAFE €

Map p382 (☎01 42 64 52 23; www.brasseriebarbes.com; 2 bd Barbès, 18e; mains €11-33, weekend brunch €18; ⊙kitchen 8am-10.30pm, bar to 2am; 📶; MBarbès-Rochechouart) With vintage ceiling fans, potted plants, a wonderful glass rotunda and spectacular rooftop terrace, this bright brasserie-style cafe provides a welcome retreat from the hustle and bustle of the raucous Marché Barbès that brings chaos to the 'hood Wednesday and Saturday mornings. Indulge in an egg-and-bacon breakfast, pastrami and sautéed-apple sandwich lunch, or a green detox juice.

HOLYBELLY 5 CAFE €

Map p382 (www.holybellycafe.com; 5 rue Lucien Sampaix, 10e; dishes €6.50-16.50; ⊙9am-5pm; 📶✍; MJacques Bonsergent) Light-filled Holybelly's regulars never tire of its outstanding coffee, cuisine and service. Sarah Mouchot's breakfast pancakes (with eggs, bacon, bourbon butter and maple syrup) and chia-seed porridge are legendary, while her lunch menu features everything from beetroot gnocchi to slow-cooked pork belly with sweet potato purée. Wash them down with a Bloody Mary or Deck & Donahue beer. No reservations.

SOUL KITCHEN VEGETARIAN €

Map p378 (☎01 71 37 99 95; 33 rue Lamarck, 18e; 3-course lunch menus €14, snacks €3-4.50; ⊙8.30am-6pm Tue-Fri, 10am-6.30pm Sat & Sun; 📶✍👪; MLamarck–Caulaincourt) This vegetarian eatery with a shabby-chic vintage interior and tiny open kitchen serves market-driven dishes including creative salads, homemade soups, savoury tarts, burritos and wraps – all gargantuan in size and packed with seasonal veggies. Round off lunch or snack between meals with muffins, cakes and mint-laced *citronnade maison* (homemade lemonade). Families should check out the sage-green 'games' cupboard.

TEN BELLES CAFE €

Map p382 (www.tenbelles.com; 10 rue de la Grange aux Belles, 10e; dishes €3-7; ⊙8am-5pm Mon-Fri, 9am-6pm Sat & Sun; 📶; MJacques Bonsergent) A stone's skim from the canal, this lively cafe with mezzanine seating and pavement tables overflows with regulars drinking Parisian-roasted Belleville Brûlerie coffee and dining on homemade soups, salads, filled focaccia, toasted sandwiches and *tartines* as well as home-baked scones, cookies and cakes.

PAIN PAIN BAKERY €

Map p378 (www.pain-pain.fr; 88 rue des Martyrs, 18e; sandwiches & pastries €2.20-5.25; ⊙7am-8pm Tue-Sat, 7.30am-7.30pm Sun; MAbbesses) Sébastien Mauvieux is famed for his baguettes (his accolades include Paris' 'best baguette' prize) and bakes delicious corn bread, rye and chestnut loaves and other varieties of *pain*. Pick up a sandwich to take away, along with exquisite pastries, such as a layered Opéra cake with yuzu and raspberries or signature Zéphyr tart with white chocolate and sweetened Chantilly cream.

SCARAMOUCHE ICE CREAM €

Map p378 (www.glaces-scaramouche.com; 22 rue la Vieuville, 18e; ice cream 1/2/3/4 scoops €3/5/6.50/8; ⊙noon-midnight Apr-Dec; MAbbesses) Raw Jersey milk, organic eggs and fresh fruit, and wild herbs from Provence's Luberon region go into Scaramouche's sublime ice creams. Some 40 flavours are available each day, such as lavender, geranium and pistachio, saffron, honey and thyme, black truffle, fennel seed, and olive oil, pine nut and rosemary. Expect lengthy queues (they're worth it).

YAFO MIDDLE EASTERN €

Map p382 (www.yafo-restaurant.com; 96 rue d'Hauteville, 10e; dishes €8-11.50; ⊙noon-2.30pm Mon & Wed-Fri, noon-2.30pm & 7-10pm Tue; 📶✍; MPoissonnière) Middle Eastern cuisine is having a moment in Paris and YAFO is among those leading the charge. Creamy hummus – made with tahini from

Nazareth and chickpeas from the south of France – is served warm by itself or with veggies or meat, with fluffy charred pita to scoop it up. Drinks include a homemade pink lemonade and cardamom coffee.

BOB'S JUICE BAR VEGETARIAN, CAFE €

Map p382 (☎09 50 06 36 18; www.bobsjuicebar.com; 15 rue Lucien Sampaix, 10e; dishes €3.50-6, pastries €1.75-3; ⌚8am-3pm Mon-Fri, 8.30am-4pm Sat; ✍; Ⓜ Jacques Bonsergent) Craving a protein shake or green smoothie? This pocket-sized space with bags of rice flour and flaxseed above the kitchen is the original hot spot in Paris for smoothies and cold-pressed organic juices, but it's also great for vegan breakfasts, gluten-free muffins or buckwheat pancakes with raspberry coulis, and generously filled bagels such as cream cheese and alfalfa sprouts.

L'ÉTÉ EN PENTE DOUCE CAFE €

Map p378 (☎01 42 64 02 67; http://lete-en-pente-douce.business.site; 8 rue Paul Albert, 18e; mains €10.50-17; ⌚noon-midnight; Ⓜ Château Rouge) Parisian terraces don't get much better than 'Summer on a Gentle Slope' (named after the 1987 French film): a hidden square wedged between two flights of steep staircases on the back side of Montmartre, in an untouristy, residential neighbourhood. Quiches, giant salads and dishes such as potato and leek soup or veal stew with mushrooms make up the menu.

MARCHÉ ST-QUENTIN MARKET €

Map p382 (85bis bd de Magenta, 10e; ⌚8am-8pm Tue-Sat, to 1.30pm Sun; Ⓜ Gare de l'Est) Dating from 1866, this iron-and-glass covered market has an enticing range of French specialities and produce, as well as affordable lunches at a variety of stalls (including African and Lebanese).

MARCHÉ BIOLOGIQUE DES BATIGNOLLES MARKET €

Map p385 (34 bd des Batignolles, 17e; ⌚9am-3pm Sat; Ⓜ Place de Clichy, Rome) 🍃 Abuzz with market stalls, this busy boulevard in northern Paris is renowned for its organic produce. Many of the stalls offer tastings and everything is super fresh.

PINK FLAMINGO PIZZA €

Map p382 (☎01 42 02 31 70; www.pinkflamingopizza.com; 67 rue Bichat, 10e; pizzas €11.50-17.50; ⌚7-11.30pm Mon-Thu, noon-2.30pm & 7-11.30pm Fri & Sat, noon-11.30pm Sun; Ⓜ Jacques Bonsergent) Once the weather warms up, the Flamingo unveils its secret weapon – pink helium balloons that delivery staff use to locate you and your perfect canal-side picnic spot (GPS not needed). Order a Poulidor (duck, apple and chèvre) or a Basquiat (Gorgonzola, figs and cured ham), and pop into Le Verre Volé (p140) across the canal for the perfect bottle of vino.

MARCHÉ ST-MARTIN MARKET €

Map p382 (31-33 rue du Château d'Eau, 10e; ⌚9am-8pm Tue-Sat, to 2pm Sun; Ⓜ Château d'Eau, Jacques Bonsergent) This lovely covered market, built in 1859 and revamped in 1880, is a delightful spot to mooch around stalls selling high-quality food produce. Join locals afterwards for breakfast, brunch or a burger lunch at Allen's Market, a cafe in the market with a pavement terrace.

BOUILLON PIGALLE BRASSERIE €

Map p378 (www.bouillonpigalle.com; 22 bd de Clichy, 18e; mains €8.50-11.50; ⌚noon-midnight; Ⓜ Pigalle) Brilliant prices, all-day service and quality ingredients used in unapologetically traditional dishes – snails with garlic and parsley butter, welks with sorrel l'aïoli, *pot-au-feu* (hotpot) and *tête de veau* (boiled calf's head) – are the keys to the success of this new-generation *bouillon* (workers' canteen-style 'soup kitchen'). It doesn't take reservations, so arrive outside peak times or expect to queue.

ROBERTA ITALIAN €

Map p378 (www.roberta.fr; 5 rue la Vieuville, 18e; antipasti €7-16, pasta €13-22; ⌚noon-3pm & 7-10.45pm Mon-Fri, noon-5pm & 7-10.45pm Sat & Sun; 📶✍; Ⓜ Abbesses) Salamis, hams and cheeses are displayed in glass-fronted cupboards at contemporary deli-restaurant Roberta. Start off with antipasti plates loaded with Italian delicacies (creamy burrata, prosciutto di Parma or ricotta-stuffed courgettes) but save room for house-made pastas like spaghetti with *botargo* (salted fish roe), squid-ink linguine with truffle cream, or triangular *pansotti* filled with spinach and walnuts. No reservations.

★MARROW BISTRO €€

Map p382 (☎09 81 34 57 00; 128 rue du Faubourg St-Martin, 10e; mains €11-19; ⌚6-10pm Tue-Sat, bar to 2am, closed Aug; Ⓜ Gare de l'Est) Hay-smoked quail with peat vinaigrette, grilled octopus and fennel confit, and breaded roast bone marrow are among the adven-

LOCAL KNOWLEDGE

STREET ART MUSEUMS

Art 42 (www.art42.fr; 96 bd Bessières, 17e; ⏲tours in English 7pm Tue, 4pm 1st Sun of month; Ⓜ Porte de Clichy) Street art and post-graffiti now have their own dedicated space at this 'anti-museum', with works by Banksy, Bom.K, Miss Van, Swoon, and Invader (who's behind the Space Invader motifs on buildings all over Paris), among other boundary-pushing urban artists. Compulsory guided tours, generally lasting 1½ to two hours, lead you through 4000 sq metres of subterranean rooms sheltering some 150 works. Entry's free but you need to reserve tours online (ideally several weeks in advance, although last-minute cancellations can arise). Tours in French depart from 6.30pm to 8.30pm on Tuesdays and from 2.30pm to 5.30pm on the first Sunday of the month.

L'Aerosol (www.laerosol.fr; 54 rue de l'Évangile, 18e; adult/child €5/3; ⏲11am-9pm Wed-Sun; Ⓜ Marx Dormoy) Street art is showcased at this cavernous museum inside a former SNCF freight railway station. French and international artists here include Mr Chat, Speedy Graphito, Invader and Banksy. You can test out your own tagging skills on the walls outside (BYO aerosols) or ask about taking a street-art course. Festivals, food trucks and a summer roller nightclub also set up here.

turous flavour combinations from Hugo Blanchet, who partnered with mixologist Arthur Combe to open this neobistro that's taking Paris' foodie scene by storm. Rough stone walls, blonde wood tables and a small pavement terrace create a relaxed backdrop.

Don't miss the house cocktail Vieux Rectangle, with cognac, Aperol, vermouth, bitters and absinthe.

LE BISTROT DE LA GALETTE — BISTRO €€

Map p378 (☎01 46 06 19 65; www.bistrotdelagalette.fr; 102ter rue Lepic, 18e; mains €14-17; ⏲11am-10pm Tue-Sun; Ⓜ Abbesses, Lamarck–Caulaincourt) In the shadow of Montmartre windmill Moulin de la Galette, this vintage-fitted bistro is the creation of pastry chef Gilles Marchal, who uses locally hand-milled flour in *feuilletés* (delicately laminated pastry puffs) that accompany most dishes, such as *galette parisienne* (roast ham, sautéed mushrooms and Comté) and *galette provençale* (shredded roast lamb, aubergine, garlic and sun-dried tomatoes).

Traditional bistro staples are also available daily, alongside all-natural wines and craft beers. Tables cover the cobbled street in warm weather.

LE BEL ORDINAIRE — MEDITERRANEAN €€

Map p382 (☎01 46 27 46 67; www.lebelordinaire.com; 54 rue de Paradis, 10e; 2-/3-course midweek lunch menus €18/22, dishes €5-15; ⏲kitchen noon-2.30pm & 7-10.30pm, bar 11am-11.30pm; 📶; Ⓜ Poissonnière) Floor-to-ceiling, wall-to-wall open shelves lined with bottles and gourmet products (hams, cheeses, shellfish, preserves, straw baskets of farm eggs and fresh fruit and vegetables) fire up your appetite for tapas-style small plates, such as tuna gravlax with grated apple, smoked burrata with sesame pesto, cuttlefish-ink risotto with blue cheese, at this contemporary wine bar. Over 300 winemakers are represented. Seating is at a long communal oak table, high counters and, in fine weather, out on the terrace.

BONHOMIE — TAPAS €€

Map p382 (☎09 83 88 82 51; www.bonhomie.paris; 22 rue d'Enghien, 10e; tapas €9-23; ⏲kitchen 8.30am-10pm Mon-Fri, from 10.30am Sat & Sun, bar to 2am daily; Ⓜ Bonne Nouvelle) Good-time Bonhomie serves home-brewed beer and creative cocktails (Pina Sage, with sage-infused mezcal, almond liqueur and sherry; Bon Americano, with dry vermouth, bitters and rhubarb soda), but the biggest draw is the food. Small plates whipped up in its open kitchen might include mussels with gin sauce, beetroot tartare or scallops with trout roe and artichoke crème.

BELLE MAISON — SEAFOOD €€

Map p378 (☎01 42 81 11 00; 4 rue de Navarin, 9e; mains lunch €11-14, dinner €22-26; ⏲12.30-2pm & 7.30-10pm Tue-Sat; Ⓜ St-Georges) With a hip blue-and-white-tiled decor and happening SoPi (south Pigalle) location, Belle Maison is named after a small beach on Île d'Yeu, off France's Atlantic coast, where its owners holiday. Breton scallops with parsnip purée, line-caught whiting with Cévennes onion brûlée, Earl Grey–marinated mullet, and grilled mackerel with crispy wasabi root and miso caramel are among its specialities.

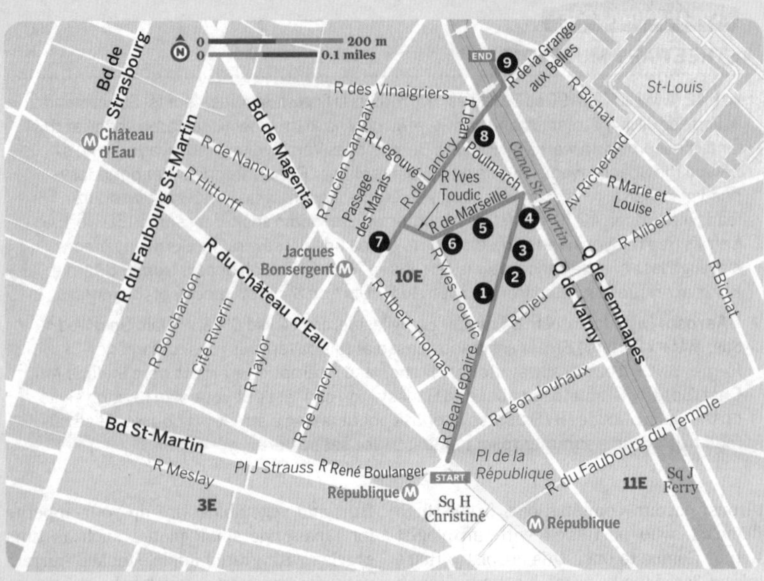

Local Life
Exploring the Canal St-Martin

Bordered by shaded towpaths and criss-crossed with iron footbridges, Canal St-Martin wends through the city's northern neighbourhoods. You can float by on a canal cruise, but strolling among this rejuvenated *quartier*'s cool cafes, one-off boutiques and hip bars lets you see why it's beloved by Parisians of all ages, especially young creatives.

❶ Rock 'n' Roll Fashion
Kick off on the boutique-lined rue Beaurepaire. One of the first designers to open up a store here was **Liza Korn** (Map p382; www.liza-korn.com; 19 rue Beaurepaire, 10e; ⌚11am-7.30pm Mon-Sat; Ⓜ République, Jacques Bonsergent), whose collections range from rock 'n' roll fashion to a children's line.

❷ Go Retro
Across the street, flip through colour-coded racks of brand-name cast-offs at vintage boutique **Frivoli** (Map p382; 26 rue Beaurepaire, 10e; ⌚1-7pm Mon, from 11am Tue-Sat, from 2pm Sun; Ⓜ République, Jacques Bonsergent).

❸ Culture Vulture
Local artwork is often on display at **Espace Beaurepaire** (Map p382; ☎01 42 45 59 64; www.espacebeaurepaire.com; 28 rue Beaurepaire, 10e; Ⓜ Jacques Bonsergent) FREE, a gallery and cultural centre that also hosts events such as book signings and pop-up stores.

❹ Canalside Cafes
Watch the passing boats from **Chez Prune** (Map p382; 36 rue Beaurepaire, 10e, cnr quai de Valmy; ⌚8am-2am Mon-Sat, 10am-2am Sun; Ⓜ Jacques Bonsergent, République), the vibrant cafe that put Canal St-Martin on the map.

❺ Alternative Médecine
On rue de Marseille you'll find a clutch of famous Parisian brands but don't overlook **Medecine Douce** (Map p382; www.bijouxmedecinedouce.com; 10 rue de Marseille, 10e; ⌚11am-7pm Mon-Sat; Ⓜ Jacques Bonsergent), a studio-showroom displaying gorgeous jewellery handmade on site.

❻ L'Heure du Gôuter
Kids from the neighbouring school pour into the belle époque bakery Du Pain et Des Ideés (p140) at snack time, seeking out the lemon and blackberry *escargots* ('snails', so called because of the shape of the pastry) and croissants.

Canal St-Martin

7 Say Cheese

If you're in need of supplies for a picnic on the canal quays, pop into local deli **La Crèmerie** (Map p382; 41 rue de Lancry, 10e; ⊙9.30am-1.30pm & 4-8pm Tue-Fri, 10am-8pm Sat; Ⓜ Jacques Bonsergeant) for heavenly cheeses, cured hams, *saucisson* (dried cured sausage) and housemade jams.

8 Designer Books & Looks

Artazart (Map p382; www.artazart.com; 83 quai de Valmy, 10e; ⊙10.30am-7.30pm Mon-Fri, from 11am Sat, from 1pm Sun; Ⓜ Jacques Bonsergent) is the leading design bookshop in Paris and, along with a fabulous collection of design and photography books in French and English, it stocks quirky collector's items such as pinhole cameras and sleek kitchen utensils.

9 Historic Hotel & Cafe

Hôtel du Nord (Map p382; www.hotel dunord.org; 102 quai de Jemmapes, 10e; ⊙9am-1.30am; 📶; Ⓜ Jacques Bonsergent) is the setting for Marcel Carné's 1938 film of the same name, which depicted the intersecting lives of the hotel's residents. The film was based on the stories of author Eugène Dabit, who once lived here. Today it's a cafe.

ABRI BISTRO €€

Map p382 (☎01 83 97 00 00; 92 rue du Faubourg Poissonnière, 9e; lunch/dinner menus €26/49; ⊙12.30-2pm Mon, 12.30-2pm & 7.30-10pm Tue-Fri, 12.30-3pm & 7.30-10pm Sat; Ⓜ Poissonnière) It's no bigger than a shoebox and the decor is borderline nonexistent, but that's all part of the charm. Katsuaki Okiyama is a seriously talented chef with an artistic flair, and his surprise tasting menus (three courses at lunch, six at dinner) are exceptional. On Saturdays, a giant gourmet sandwich is all that's served for lunch. Reserve months in advance.

MATIÈRE À. MODERN FRENCH €€

Map p382 (☎09 70 38 61 48; www.matiere-a.com; 15 rue Marie et Louise, 10e; 2-/3-course lunch menus €21/25, 4-course dinner menus €46; ⊙noon-2pm & 7.30-11pm Mon-Fri, 7.30-11pm Sat; Ⓜ Goncourt, Jacques Bonsergent) The short but stunning seasonal menu changes daily at this unique space. *Table d'hôte*–style dining for up to 14 is around a shared oak table lit by dozens of naked light bulbs. In the kitchen is young chef Anthony Courteille, who prides himself on doing everything *fait maison* (homemade), including bread and butter to die for. Reservations essential.

RESTAURANT BOUILLON BISTRO €€

Map p378 (☎09 51 18 66 59; www.restaurant bouillon.fr; 47 rue de Rochechouart, 9e; 2-/3-course midweek lunch menus €21/28, mains €16-29; ⊙noon-2.30pm & 7-11pm Tue-Sat; Ⓜ Cadet, Anvers) It seats just 18 people inside and (weather permitting) four more out on the pavement, so it's worth making a reservation to dine at this excellent bistro. A meal might start with seared scallops with watercress sauce, followed by smoked duck with poached pears or beef braised in red wine with salt-roasted beetroot and finish with aromatic cheeses and fig confit.

LE POTAGER DE CHARLOTTE VEGAN €€

Map p378 (☎01 44 65 09 63; www.lepotager decharlotte.fr; 12 rue de la Tour d'Auvergne, 9e; mains €14.50-16, Sunday brunch €29; ⊙7-10.30pm Wed & Thu, noon-2.30pm & 7-10.30pm Fri & Sat, 11am-3pm Sun; 🌶; Ⓜ Cadet) Vegan brothers David and Adrien are dedicated to gourmet plant-based cuisine. Farmers-market-sourced ingredients come together in dishes like chickpea and rice pancakes with cashew cream, and quinoa with pomegranate, marinated tofu and roasted hazelnuts. Sunday brunch is an all-in feast of granola, pancakes, avocado, hummus and more, but is also available à la carte.

CAFÉ MIROIR BISTRO €€

Map p378 (☎01 46 06 50 73; www.cafemiroir.com; 94 rue des Martyrs, 18e; 3-course midweek lunch menu €19.50, mains €23-37; ⊗8am-10pm Tue-Sat; MAbbesses) Smack in the middle of the Montmartre tourist trail, this local favourite offers continuous all-day dining. Delightful pâtés and *rillettes* – guinea hen with dates, duck with mushrooms, haddock and lemon – are followed by its signature stuffed veal shoulder or daily changing specials like shellfish soup, salmon *mille-feuille* (layered pastry) or filet mignon with foie gras.

LA MASCOTTE SEAFOOD €€

Map p378 (☎01 46 06 28 15; www.la-mascotte-montmartre.com; 52 rue des Abbesses, 18e; 2-course lunch menus €32, 3-course dinner menus €49, mains €26-36; ⊗noon-11.30pm; ; MAbbesses) Founded in 1889, this cavernous bar with green-and-white-striped awnings, gleaming timber and tiles is as authentic as it gets in Montmartre. It specialises in quality seafood (lobster, langoustine, scallops and more); you can just pull up a seat at the bar for a glass of wine and plate of oysters in season. The children's *menu* is €22. Alternatively, pick up seafood to go from its fishmonger next door.

LE PANTRUCHE FRENCH €€

Map p378 (☎01 48 78 55 60; 3 rue Victor Massé, 9e; 2-/3-course lunch menus €19/36, mains €22; ⊗12.30-2.30pm & 7.30-10.30pm Mon-Fri; MPigalle) Oak-furnished Pantruche woos foodies in the dining hot spot of south Pigalle with its intimate setting, reasonable prices and seasonal neobistro fare. Daring creations might include oysters with green lettuce foam, lamb ravioli with mimolette and mint, wild hare with beetroot jus, or red mullet and bacon-wrapped polenta. Some mains incur a supplement. Reserve well in advance.

CHEZ TOINETTE FRENCH €€

Map p378 (☎01 42 54 44 36; 20 rue Germain Pilon, 18e; mains €19-28; ⊗7-10.30pm Mon-Sat, closed Aug; MAbbesses) The atmosphere of this convivial restaurant is rivalled only by its fine cuisine (seared duck with honey, veal with chanterelles, sole meunière, poached pear with salted caramel). In the heart of one of the capital's most touristy neighbourhoods, Chez Toinette has kept alive the tradition of old Montmartre with its simplicity and culinary expertise.

POJO BISTRO €€

Map p378 (☎06 82 58 57 92; www.pojopojo.fr; 38 rue de Douai, 9e; mains lunch €11-19, dinner €17-20; ⊗noon-3pm & 7-11pm Mon-Sat, noon-4pm & 7-11pm Sun, bar to 2am; ; MBlanche) An old corner cafe has been stripped back to reveal its honeycomb-coloured Parisian stone walls, while its timber beams have been whitewashed to brighten the space. Roast figs with goats cheese and honey, or pan-fried cod with sweet potato and chorizo mash are among the neobistro dishes you might find chalked on the blackboard.

ASPIC BISTRO €€€

Map p378 (☎09 82 49 30 98; 24 rue de la Tour d'Auvergne, 9e; 7-course tasting menu €65, with wine €100; ⊗7.30-9.30pm Tue-Sat; MAnvers) Chef Quentin Giroud ditched the high-flying world of finance for the stoves, and this small vintage-style space with a semi-open kitchen is testament to his conviction. Weekly changing, no-choice tasting menus feature inspired creations like peppercorn pancetta with kaffir lime butter, warm octopus with cashew purée, skin-on plaice with popcorn capers, and celeriac with mustard shoots and grated raw cauliflower.

DRINKING & NIGHTLIFE

Crowded around place Pigalle at the foot of Montmartre you'll find an eclectic selection of nightlife options, from local cafes and hipster dives to dance clubs and hostess bars. In contrast, the trend around the Canal St-Martin is more barista-run cafes, though wonderful summer nights (and days) see everyone decamp to the canal-side quays with blankets, baguettes and bottles of wine. In the 10e, parallel rue du Faubourg St-Martin and rue du Faubourg St-Denis and surrounding streets are speckled with cocktail bars, hybrid bistro-bars and hip cafes.

★LE TRÈS PARTICULIER COCKTAIL BAR

Map p378 (☎01 53 41 81 40; www.hotel-particulier-montmartre.com; Pavillon D, 23 av Junot, 18e; ⊗6pm-2am; MLamarck–Caulaincourt) The clandestine cocktail bar of boutique Hôtel Particulier Montmartre (p285) is an entrancing spot for a summertime alfresco cocktail. Ring the buzzer at the unmarked black gated entrance and make a beeline for the 1871 mansion's flowery walled garden (or, if it's raining, the adjacent conservatory-style interior). DJs spin tunes from 9.30pm Wednesday to Saturday and from 7pm on Sunday.

★LE SYNDICAT COCKTAIL BAR
Map p382 (www.syndicatcocktailclub.com; 51 rue du Faubourg St-Denis, 10e; ⌚6pm-2am Mon-Sat, from 7pm Sun; Ⓜ Château d'Eau) Plastered top to bottom in peeling posters, an otherwise unmarked façade conceals one of Paris' hottest cocktail bars, but it's no fly-by-night. Le Syndicat's subtitle, Organisation de Défense des Spiritueux Français, reflects its impassioned commitment to French spirits. Ingeniously crafted (and named) cocktails include Saix en Provence (Armagnac, chilli syrup, lime and lavender).

★PAVILLON PUEBLA BEER GARDEN
(www.leperchoir.tv; Parc des Buttes Chaumont, 39 av Simon Bolivar, 19e; ⌚6pm-2am Wed-Fri, from noon Sat, noon-10pm Sun; 📶; Ⓜ Buttes Chaumont) Strung with fairy lights, this rustic ivy-draped cottage's two rambling terraces in the Parc des Buttes Chaumont evoke a *guinguette* (old-fashioned outdoor tavern/dance venue), with a 21st-century vibe provided by its Moroccan decor, contemporary furniture, and DJ beats from Thursdays to Saturdays. Alongside mostly French wines and craft beers, cocktails include its signature Spritz du Pavillon (Aperol, Prosecco and soda).

Its restaurant serves dinner from Wednesday to Saturday and lunch on Saturday and Sunday. Kids are catered for with activities (workshops, games, colouring and shared pizzas) on Sundays.

★GRAVITY BAR COCKTAIL BAR
Map p382 (44 rue des Vinaigriers, 10e; ⌚6pm-2am Tue-Sat; Ⓜ Jacques Bonsergent) Gravity's stunning wave-like interior, crafted from slats of plywood descending to the curved concrete bar, threatens to distract from the business at hand – serious cocktails, such as Back to My Roots (Provence herb-infused vodka, vermouth, raspberry purée and lemon juice), best partaken in the company of excellent and inventive tapas-style small plates such as clam gnocchi.

LOCAL KNOWLEDGE

RUE DES MARTYRS

Stretching 960m from Montmartre in the 18e (metro Abbesses) to the 9e (metro Notre Dame de Lorette) in the Grands Boulevards neighbourhood, sloping rue des Martyrs is a foodie's fantasyland, lined with gourmet shops (cheese, tea, wine, jam and more), award-winning *boulangeries* (bakeries) and patisseries (pastry shops). Interspersed between them are Parisian bistros and regional and international eateries (Corsican, Portuguese, Spanish, Greek...). Down the southern end, grocers, fishmongers and butchers set up pavement stalls.

PANAME BREWING COMPANY BREWERY
Map p384 (www.panamebrewingcompany.com; 41bis quai de la Loire, 19e; ⌚11am-2am; 📶; Ⓜ Crimée, Laumiere) Spectacularly situated in an industrial 1850s former granary on Bassin de la Villette, Paname's tap room has floor-to-ceiling windows and opens on to a terrace shaded by an ancient cherry tree and a floating table-strewn pontoon. Its five seasonal beers typically include a pilsner, session, märzen, Berliner Weisse, pale ale or IPA (look out for them around Paris too). The pick of its gastropub menu is the All Black lamb burger with barbecue beer sauce on a black sesame seed bun.

LA FONTAINE DE BELLEVILLE COFFEE
Map p382 (www.lafontaine.cafesbelleville.com; 31-33 rue Juliette Dodu, 10e; ⌚8am-10pm; Ⓜ Colonel Fabien) Beans roasted by Belleville Brûlerie are the toast of Paris and the roastery has since opened its own cafe near Canal St-Martin, updating a long-standing local corner spot with gold lettering, woven sky-blue-and-cream bistro chairs and matching tables, and retaining its vintage fittings. Spectacular coffee is complemented by sandwiches, salads and small sharing plates.

LULU WHITE COCKTAIL BAR
Map p378 (www.luluwhite.bar; 12 rue Frochot, 9e; ⌚7pm-2am Mon, Wed, Thu & Sun, to 4am Fri & Sat; Ⓜ Pigalle) Sip absinthe-based cocktails in Prohibition-era New Orleans surrounds at this elegant, serious and supremely busy cocktail bar named for an infamous early-20th-century brothel owner. It hosts regular live jazz and folk music.

CANAL CRUISES

Seine boat rides are well known, but for something different, take a canal cruise. Two companies run seasonal 2½-hour trips along the Canal St-Martin between central Paris and Parc de la Villette. Boats pass through four double locks, two swing bridges and an underground section with an art installation.

Canauxrama (Map p382; ☎01 42 39 15 00; www.canauxrama.com; 13 quai de la Loire, 19e; adult/child €18/9; ⊙hours vary; MJaurès) Cruises depart from the Bassin de la Villette near Parc de la Villette and from the Port de l'Arsenal (Map p394; ☎01 42 39 15 00; www.canauxrama.com; opposite 50 bd de la Bastille, Port de l'Arsenal, 12e; adult/child €18/9; ⊙vary; MBastille); summertime evening weekend cruises are particularly enchanting. Gourmand and thematic cruises too.

Paris Canal Croisières (Map p384; ☎01 42 40 96 97; www.pariscanal.com; Parc de la Villette, 19e; adult/child €22/14; ⊙mid-Mar–mid-Nov; MPorte de Pantin) Cruises depart from Parc de la Villette and from quai Anatole France (Map p406; ☎01 42 40 96 97; www.pariscanal.com; quai Anatole France, 7e; adult/child €22/14; ⊙Mar–mid-Nov; MSolférino, RER Musée d'Orsay) near the Musée d'Orsay.

CAFÉ LOMI COFFEE

Map p382 (☎09 80 39 56 24; www.lomi.paris; 3ter rue Marcadet, 18e; ⊙8am-6pm Mon-Fri, 10am-7pm Sat & Sun; MMarcadet–Poissonniers) Lomi's internationally sourced beans are roasted here on site in the multiethnic La Goutte d'Or neighbourhood adjacent to its cafe. Brews include filter coffee (mug, Aeropress or Chemex) and wacky creations like Bleu d'Auvergne cheese dipped in espresso or tonic water with espresso. Three-hour coffee workshops in French or English (filter techniques, world coffee tours, latte art) start from €72. Breakfast, lunch and weekend brunch too.

LIPSTICK COCKTAIL BAR

Map p378 (www.lipstickparis.com; 5 rue Frochot, 9e; ⊙6pm-5am Tue-Sat; MPigalle) If the name isn't a clue, the decor certainly is: its bordello-like leopard-print lounges, red velour drapes and a pole in the centre of the bar reflect its former incarnation as a brothel in this gentrifying red-light district. Stupendous cocktails include Queen P (rose syrup, gin, Aperol, ginger ale and grapefruit juice) Happy hour, from 6pm to 10pm, gets the party started; DJs play on Fridays and Saturdays from 11pm.

HARDWARE SOCIÉTÉ COFFEE

Map p378 (☎01 42 51 69 03; 10 rue Lamarck, 18e; ⊙9am-4pm Mon-Fri, 9.30am-4.30pm Sat & Sun; 📶; MChâteau Rouge) With its black-and-white floor, Christian Lacroix butterflies fluttering across one wall and perfect love-heart-embossed cappuccinos, this is a fine spot around the Sacré-Cœur to linger over superb barista-crafted coffee (yes, that is a Slayer espresso machine). It's the Paris outpost of Melbourne's Hardware Société, with bountiful breakfasts and brunches served at marble-topped tables.

CHEZ BOUBOULE SPORTS BAR

Map p378 (www.chezbouboule.fr; 79 rue de Dunkerque, 9e; ⊙5pm-2am Tue-Sat; 📶; MAnvers) *Pétanque* game washed out? Head to Chez Bouboule, which has a packed-sand indoor *boulodrome* (pitch for playing the bowls-like sport) right inside the buzzing bar (equipment is free). Craft beers, wines and ciders are available alongside cocktails such as its signature Bouboule, with gin, mint, cinnamon, pepper and juniper berries. It also has table football and shows big-screen sporting fixtures.

LA MACHINE DU MOULIN ROUGE CLUB

Map p378 (www.lamachinedumoulinrouge.com; 90 bd de Clichy, 18e; admission €9-16; ⊙midnight-6am Fri & Sat, variable Sun-Thu; MBlanche) Part of the original Moulin Rouge (well, the boiler room, anyway), this club packs 'em in on weekends with a dance floor, a concert hall, a Champagne bar and an outdoor terrace. Check the agenda online for weekday soirées and happenings.

LA FOURMI BAR

Map p378 (74 rue des Martyrs, 18e; ⊙8am-2am Mon-Thu, to 4am Fri 9am-4am Sat, 10am-2am Sun; MPigalle) A Pigalle institution, sociable La Fourmi hits the mark with its high ceilings, long zinc bar, timber-panelled walls and unpretentious vibe. It's a great place to find out about live music and club nights or grab a drink before heading out to a show. Bonus: table football.

DIRTY DICK COCKTAIL BAR

Map p378 (10 rue Frochot, 9e; ⏲6pm-2am; Ⓜ Pigalle) A former girly bar (as if you couldn't guess) has been bought out and is now the city's favourite tiki bar. Punch bowls serve up to four people; tropical cocktails include Monkey Seed (pineapple-infused whisky, banana and salted caramel).

LE TRIANGLE MICROBREWERY

Map p382 (www.triangleparis.com; 13 rue Jacques Louvel-Tessier, 10e; ⏲6-10.30pm Tue-Sat; Ⓜ Goncourt) Kettles gleam behind the bar at this microbrewery, whose eight taps have four of its own brews – pale ale, porter, IPA and smoked beer – alongside international guest beers. Beer aside, there are craft whiskies from as far afield as Taiwan, and a small natural wine list. Small and large tasting plates are also served in the cosy terracotta-tiled space.

GLASS COCKTAIL BAR

Map p378 (www.quixotic-projects.com/venue/glass; 7 rue Frochot, 9e; ⏲7pm-4am Sun-Thu, to 5am Fri & Sat; Ⓜ Pigalle) Pop into this bar for Parisian-brewed Paname beers, spectacular cocktails such as Ticket de Metro (tequila, campari, thyme-infused honey, mint, lemon and blonde beer), whisky, and punk rock on the stereo.

ENTERTAINMENT

Diverse venues in this vast neighbourhood range from iconic cabarets and hallowed concert halls to intimate jazz clubs, edgy arts centres and a host of stages at Parc de la Villette.

★PHILHARMONIE DE PARIS CONCERT VENUE

Map p384 (☎01 44 84 44 84; www.philharmoniedeparis.fr; 221 av Jean Jaurès, 19e; ⏲box office noon-6pm Tue-Fri, 10am-6pm Sat & Sun; Ⓜ Porte de Pantin) Major complex the Cité de la Musique – Philharmonie de Paris hosts an eclectic range of concerts, from classical to North African and Japanese, in the Philharmonie building's Grande Salle Pierre Boulez, with an audience capacity of 2400 to 3600. The adjacent Cité de la Musique's Salle des Concerts has a capacity of 900 to 1600.

Equally entertaining are its atmospheric *ciné* concerts, when a symphonic orchestra, jazz ensemble or organist accompanies a classic film or new box-office film screening.

POINT ÉPHÉMÈRE LIVE MUSIC

Map p382 (☎01 40 34 02 48; www.pointephemere.org; 200 quai de Valmy, 10e; ⏲12.30pm-2am Mon-Sat, to 11pm Sun; 📶; Ⓜ Jaurès, Louis Blanc) On the banks of Canal St-Martin in a former fire station and later squat, this arts and music venue attracts an underground crowd for concerts, dance nights and art exhibitions. Its rockin' restaurant, Animal Kitchen, fuses gourmet cuisine with music from Animal Records (Sunday brunch from 1pm is a highlight). The rooftop bar, Le Top, opens in fine weather.

LE DIVAN DU MONDE LIVE MUSIC

Map p378 (☎01 40 05 08 10; www.divandumonde.com; 75 rue des Martyrs, 18e; Ⓜ Pigalle) Take some cinematographic events and *nouvelles chansons françaises* (new French songs). Add in soul/funk fiestas, air-guitar face-offs and rock parties of the Arctic Monkeys/Killers/Libertines persuasion... You may now be getting some idea of the inventive, open-minded approach at this excellent cross-cultural venue in Pigalle.

MOULIN ROUGE CABARET

Map p378 (☎01 53 09 82 82; www.moulinrouge.fr; 82 bd de Clichy, 18e; show only from €87, lunch & show from €165, dinner & show from €190; ⏲show only 2.45pm, 9pm & 11pm, lunch & show 1.45pm, dinner & show 7pm; Ⓜ Blanche) Immortalised in Toulouse-Lautrec's posters and later in Baz Luhrmann's film, Paris' legendary cabaret twinkles beneath a 1925 replica of its original red windmill. Yes, it's packed with bus-tour crowds. But from the opening bars of music to the last high cancan kick, it's a whirl of fantastical costumes, sets, choreography and Champagne. Book in advance and dress smartly (no trainers or sneakers). No entry for children under six years.

LA CIGALE LIVE MUSIC

Map p378 (☎01 49 25 89 99; www.lacigale.fr; 120 bd de Rochechouart, 18e; Ⓜ Pigalle) Now classed as a historical monument, this music hall dates from 1887 but was redecorated a century later by Philippe Starck. Artists who have performed here include Ryan Adams, Ibrahim Maalouf and the Dandy Warhols.

LE LOUXOR CINEMA

Map p382 (☎01 44 63 96 98; www.cinemalouxor.fr; 170 bd de Magenta, 10e; tickets adult/child €9.70/5; ⓂBarbès-Rochechouart) Built in neo-Egyptian art-deco style in 1921 and saved from demolition by a neighbourhood association seven decades later, this historical monument is a palatial place to catch a new release, classic, piano-accompanied 'ciné-concert', short-film festival, special workshop (such as singalongs) or live-music performance. The bar opens onto an elevated terrace overlooking Sacré-Cœur.

BUS PALLADIUM LIVE MUSIC

Map p378 (☎01 45 26 80 35; www.buspalladium.com; 6 rue Pierre Fontaine, 9e; ⏲Tue-Sat; ⓂPigalle, Blanche) The place to be in the 1960s (Dalí, Hallyday and Jagger all hung out here), the Bus is back in business half-a-century later, with performances by DJs and indie and pop groups. The upstairs restaurant makes a good place to dine before a show.

NEW MORNING JAZZ, BLUES

Map p382 (☎01 45 23 51 41; www.newmorning.com; 7-9 rue des Petites Écuries, 10e; ⓂChâteau d'Eau) This highly regarded auditorium with excellent acoustics hosts big-name jazz concerts (Ravi Coltrane, Lake Street Dive) as well as a variety of blues, rock, funk, salsa, Afro-Cuban and Brazilian music.

AU LAPIN AGILE CABARET

Map p378 (☎01 46 06 85 87; www.au-lapin-agile.com; 22 rue des Saules, 18e; adult €28, student except Sat €20; ⏲9pm-1am Tue-Sun; ⓂLamarck–Caulaincourt) Named after *Le Lapin à Gill*, a mural of a rabbit jumping out of a cooking pot by caricaturist André Gill, which can still be seen on the western exterior wall, this rustic cabaret venue was favoured by artists and intellectuals in the early 20th century and traditional *chansons* are still performed here. The evening-long show includes singing and poetry.

LE TRIANON LIVE MUSIC

Map p378 (☎01 44 92 78 00; www.letrianon.fr; 80 bd de Rochechouart, 18e; ⓂAnvers) Opened in 1902, this music hall features two levels of balconies as well as a main floor area. An intimate spot to catch a quality show: think Macy Gray, John Butler, Rihanna and Ke$ha. Its cafe, **Le Petit Trianon** (Map p378; ☎01 44 92 78 08; 80 bd de Rochechouart, 18e; ⏲8am-2am; ⓂAnvers), is an atmospheric place for a drink or a meal.

SHOPPING

There's a growing number of boutiques in Pigalle but the finest strips for fashion shoppers are rue Beaurepaire and rue de Marseille by Canal St-Martin. While Montmartre has its fair share of keyring-filled souvenir shops, there are some exquisite specialist boutiques selling everything from handcrafted jewellery to antique perfume bottles, vinyl and vintage fashion. The enormous Marché aux Puces de St-Ouen flea market sprawls to the neighbourhood's north, while gourmet shops line rue des Martyrs.

★BELLE DU JOUR FASHION & ACCESSORIES

Map p378 (www.belle-de-jour.fr; 7 rue Tardieu, 18e; ⏲11am-1pm & 2-7pm Tue-Fri, 11am-1pm & 2-6pm Sat; ⓂAnvers, Abbesses) Be whisked back in time to the elegance of belle époque Paris at this Montmartre shop specialising in perfume bottles. Gorgeous 19th-century atomisers, smelling salts and powder boxes in engraved or enamelled Bohemian, Baccarat and Saint-Louis crystal share shelf space with more contemporary designs. Whether you're after art deco or art nouveau, pink-frosted or painted glass, it's here.

★FROMAGERIE ALLÉOSSE CHEESE

Map p385 (www.fromage-alleosse.com; 13 rue Poncelet, 17e; ⏲9am-1pm & 3.30-7pm Tue-Sat, 9am-1pm Sun; ⓂTernes) On stall-filled foodie street rue Poncelet, heady *fromagerie* Alléosse has its own cheese-ripening *caves* (cellars) spanning 300 sq metres with four separate environments. Its 250-plus cheeses are grouped into five main categories: *fromage de chèvre* (goat's milk), *fromage à pâte persillée* (veined or blue), *fromage à pâte molle* (soft), *fromage à pâte demi-dure* (semihard) and *fromage à pâte dure* (hard).

BALADES SONORES MUSIC

Map p378 (www.baladessonores.com; 1-3 av Trudaine, 9e; ⏲noon-8pm Mon-Sat; ⓂAnvers) One of Paris' best vinyl shops, Balades Sonores sprawls over two adjacent buildings. The ground floor of 1 av Trudaine stocks contemporary pop, rock metal, garage and all genres of French music. Its basement holds secondhand blues, country, new wave and punk from the '60s to '90s. Next door, No 3 has soul, jazz, funk, hip-hop, electronica and world music.

O/HP/E DESIGN

Map p382 (27 rue du Château d'Eau, 10e; ⌚2-7.30pm Tue, 8.30am-7.30pm Wed-Fri, 9.30am-7.30pm Sat, to 6.30pm Sun; Ⓜ Jacques Bonsergent) White-on-white concept store O/HP/E stocks chic homewares – ceramics, textiles, light fittings, candles and kitchenware (rolling pins, mats, chopping boards, chopsticks et al) – along with cosmetics, stationery and gifts. Also here is an *épicerie* (specialist grocer) with gourmet delicacies (preserves, nougats, sugar-coated olives and chocolates) and a cafe with baked treats such as hazelnut praline tarts.

PIGALLE FASHION & ACCESSORIES

Map p378 (www.pigalle-paris.com; 7 rue Henry Monnier, 9e; ⌚noon-8pm Mon-Sat, from 2pm Sun; Ⓜ St-Georges) Pick up a hoodie emblazoned with the black-and-white Pigalle logo from this leading Parisian menswear brand, created by designer and basketball player Stéphane Ashpool, who grew up in the 'hood.

SPREE FASHION & ACCESSORIES

Map p378 (☎01 42 23 41 40; www.spree.fr; 16 rue de la Vieuville, 18e; ⌚11am-7.30pm Tue-Sat, 3-7pm Sun & Mon; Ⓜ Abbesses) Allow plenty of time to browse this super-stylish boutique-gallery, with a carefully selected collection of designer fashion put together by stylist Roberta Oprandi and artist Bruni Hadjadj. What makes shopping here fun is that all the furniture – vintage 1950s to 1980s pieces by Eames and other midcentury designers – is also for sale, as is the contemporary artwork on the walls.

DESIGNERS OUTLET L'EXCEPTION DESIGN

Map p382 (www.lexception.com; 28 rue Bichat, 10e; ⌚11am-2pm & 3-7pm Thu-Sat, 1-6pm Sun; Ⓜ Goncourt) At any one time, the discount outlet shop of design showcase L'Exception (p130) has 3000 pieces at up to 70% off from more than 400 French fashion and homewares labels.

JEREMIE BARTHOD JEWELLERY

Map p378 (www.jeremiebarthod.com; 7 rue des Trois Frères, 18e; ⌚11.30am-7pm; Ⓜ Abbesses) Fantasy-inspired necklaces, bracelets and other jewellery pieces are crafted from metal springs dipped in antique silver, bronze or copper at this hybrid boutique-*atelier* (workshop) in Montmartre.

WORTH A DETOUR

FLEA MARKET

Spanning 9 hectares, vast **Marché aux Puces de St-Ouen** (www.marcheauxpuces-saintouen.com; rue des Rosiers, St-Ouen; ⌚Sat-Mon; Ⓜ Porte de Clignancourt) was founded in 1870 and is said to be Europe's largest flea market. More than 2000 stalls are grouped into 15 *marchés* (markets) selling everything from 17th-century furniture to 21st-century clothing. Each market has different opening hours – check the website for details. There are miles upon miles of 'freelance' stalls; come prepared to spend some time.

Dining options here include the legendary **Chez Louisette** (☎01 40 12 10 14; Marché Vernaison, 130 av Michelet, St-Ouen, Marché aux Puces de St-Ouen; mains €14-17; ⌚11am-7pm Sat-Mon; Ⓜ Porte de Clignancourt), where singers perform rousing *chansons*.

CENTRE COMMERCIAL FASHION & ACCESSORIES

Map p382 (www.centrecommercial.cc; 2 rue de Marseille, 10e; ⌚1-7.30pm Mon, 11am-8pm Tue-Sat, 2-7pm Sun; Ⓜ Jacques Bonsergent) Just off Canal St-Martin, this concept store is first choice for sustainable French-made fashion for men and women, and lifestyle objects for the home. Its peppermint- and pine-perfumed mug candles, handmade in Paris, make beautiful gifts to take home.

Its store catering to **kids** (Map p382; www.centrecommercial.cc; 22 rue Yves Toudic, 10e; ⌚1-7pm Mon, 10.30am-7.30pm Tue-Fri, to 8pm Sat, 2-7pm Sun; Ⓜ Jacques Bonsergent) is located nearby.

ANTOINE ET LILI CLOTHING, HOMEWARES

Map p382 (www.antoineetlili.com; 95 quai de Valmy, 10e; ⌚11am-8pm Mon-Fri, from 10am Sat, 11am-7pm Sun; Ⓜ Jacques Bonsergent, Gare de l'Est) All the colours of the rainbow and all the patterns in the world congregate in this Parisian institution, with designer clothing for women (pink store) and children (green store), and eclectic homewares (yellow store), from ceramics to retro telephones.

Le Marais, Ménilmontant & Belleville

Neighbourhood Top Five

1 Cimetière du Père Lachaise (p157) Admiring incredible sculptures and tomb art while paying your respects to the rich, famous and infamous buried in the world's most visited cemetery.

2 Maison de Victor Hugo (p160) Visiting the renowned author's former home overlooking beautiful place des Vosges.

3 Musée National Picasso (p160) Immersing yourself in the life and artworks of one of the world's most eccentric modern artists, Pablo Picasso, and admiring the museum's exquisitely grand 17th-century mansion.

4 Hôtel de Ville (p161) Taking in a world-class art exhibition for free at Paris' neo-Renaissance city hall.

5 Mémorial de la Shoah (p156) Gaining a poignant insight into German-occupied Paris and Holocaust horrors.

For more detail of this area see Map p386 and p390

Explore Le Marais, Ménilmontant & Belleville

Sublime place des Vosges is a perfect starting point – this elegant city square is a triumph of architectural symmetry, and is also where you'll find the Maison de Victor Hugo. Meander west along busy rue de Rivoli or backstreet rue du Roi de Sicile, with shops, cafes and bars. Essential for history buffs is the Mémorial de la Shoah.

Bearing north towards the fashionable Haut Marais, strips laden with hip drinking and dining options include rue Vieille du Temple, rue du Bourg Tibourg, and rue des Rosiers in the heart of the historic Jewish quarter Pletzl.

From the Haut Marais, bar-busy rue Oberkampf and rue Jean-Pierre Timbaud duck east into the grittier district of Ménilmontant. Further on, leave the crowds behind in the vibrant, multicultural 'village' of Belleville. Pencil in at least half a day for the Cimetière du Père Lachaise. In fine weather, make a point of heading to the river for a stroll along the banks – host to summer's Paris Plages (Paris Beaches).

Local Life

- **River life** Stroll along riverside Parc Rives de Seine (p160), play a game of *pétanque* or stop for a drink at this former expressway turned promenade.
- **Alfresco hangouts** Hang out at lofty Parc de Belleville (p165), charming Square Maurice Gardette (p163), or cafe-ringed place du Marché Ste-Catherine (p171).
- **Serious coffee** Join discerning coffee lovers for a cupping session at Belleville Brûlerie (p179) or drop into collaborative roastery Beans on Fire (p174).
- **Market lunch** Lunch with locals around communal tables in Paris' oldest covered market (p166).

Getting There & Away

- **Metro** Stops for the lower Marais include Hôtel de Ville (line 1 and line 11), St-Paul (line 1) and Rambuteau (line 11); for the Haut Marais, use Filles du Calvaire and St-Sébastien-Froissart (line 8) and Temple (line 3). To reach Ménilmontant, hop off at Ménilmontant (line 2), Parmentier (line 3) and Oberkampf (lines 5 and 9). For Belleville, use Belleville (lines 2 and 11) or Couronnes (line 2).
- **Bus** Bus 76 runs from rue de Rivoli to the 20e and Porte de Bagnolet.
- **Bicycle** Handy Vélib' stations include place de l'Hôtel de Ville, Filles du Calvaire metro station, bd de Ménilmontant and bd de Belleville.
- **Boat** The Batobus stops at the Hôtel de Ville.

Lonely Planet's Top Tip

Le Marais is flat, but Ménilmontant becomes hilly and Belleville is (for Paris) super-steep. Save your calf muscles by catching the metro to your easternmost destination to walk or cycle west downhill.

Best Places to Eat

- Breizh Café (p164)
- La Maison Plisson (p163)
- Au Passage (p166)
- Jacques Genin (p163)

For reviews, see p163

Best Places to Drink

- Candelaria (p170)
- Le Perchoir (p172)
- Café Charbon (p174)
- PasDeLoup (p171)
- La Caféothèque (p171)
- Le Mary Céleste (p171)

For reviews, see p170

Best Shopping

- Merci (p176)
- Empreintes (p176)
- Fromagerie Goncourt (p179)
- Kerzon (p176)
- Paris Rendez-Vous (p176)

For reviews, see p176

ALIZADA STUDIOS / SHUTTERSTOCK ©

TOP SIGHT
MÉMORIAL DE LA SHOAH

Founded in 1956 as a memorial to the unknown Jewish martyr, the Mémorial de la Shoah is now one of Europe's most important Holocaust museums and documentation centres. A vast permanent collection and well-thought-out temporary exhibits all pertain to the Holocaust and the German occupation of parts of France and Paris during WWII.

The entrance to the Mémorial de la Shoah remembers the victims of the Shoah – a Hebrew word meaning 'catastrophe' that's synonymous in France with the Holocaust – with the **Mur des Noms** (Wall of Names; 2006), a wall inscribed with the names of 76,000 Jews, including 11,000 children, deported from France to Nazi extermination camps during WWII. Most died in Auschwitz and other camps between 1942 and 1944; only 2500 survived deportation.

Deep in the appropriately sombre, bunker-like building lies the **crypt** and **tomb to the unknown Jewish martyr** – all six million Jews with no grave of their own. Ashes from some Jews who died in death camps and also the Warsaw ghetto are entombed in the star of David, sculpted from black marble and pierced in its centre with an eternal flame.

DON'T MISS

- Mur des Noms
- Crypt
- Guided tours in English, 3pm second Sunday of month

PRACTICALITIES

- Map p386, B7
- www.memorialdelashoah.org
- 17 rue Geoffroy l'Asnier, 4e
- admission free
- 10am-6pm Sun-Wed & Fri, to 10pm Thu
- M Pont Marie, St-Paul

TOP SIGHT
CIMETIÈRE DU PÈRE LACHAISE

The world's most visited cemetery opened in 1804. A stroll among its more than 70,000 ornate tombs is akin to exploring a verdant sculpture garden. Père Lachaise was a response to local neighbourhood graveyards being full – at the time, it was ground-breaking for Parisians to be buried outside the *quartier* in which they'd lived.

Paris residency was the only criterion needed to be buried here, hence the cemetery's cosmopolitan population. Among the 800,000-odd buried here are composer Chopin; playwright Molière; poet Apollinaire; writers Proust, Gertrude Stein and Colette; actors Simone Signoret, Sarah Bernhardt and Yves Montand; painters Pissarro, Modigliani and Delacroix; *chanteuse* Édith Piaf; and dancer Isadora Duncan.

The grave of Irish playwright and humorist **Oscar Wilde** (1854–1900), division 89, is among the most visited (as the glass barrier erected around his sculpted tomb, designed to prevent fans impregnating the stone with red lipstick imprints, attests). The other big hitter, likewise barricaded from overzealous fans, is 1960s rock star **Jim Morrison** (1943–71), division 6. He died in a Le Marais **apartment** (Map p386; 17 rue Beautreillis, 4e; Ⓜ St-Paul).

Up in division 92, protests saw the removal of a fence around the grave of **Monsieur Noir**, aka journalist Yvan Salman (1848–70), shot aged 22 by Pierre Bonaparte, great-nephew of Napoléon. Legend says women who stroke the amply filled crotch of Monsieur Noir's prostrate bronze effigy will enjoy increased fertility.

Commemorative memorials to victims of almost every war in modern history form a poignant alley alongside the **Mur des Fédérés**, an unmemorable plain brick wall against which Communard insurgents were lined up, shot and buried in a mass grave in 1871.

DON'T MISS

- Jim Morrison
- Édith Piaf
- Oscar Wilde
- Monsieur Noir
- Mur des Fédérés and commemorative war memorials

PRACTICALITIES

- Map p390, G8
- ☎ 01 55 25 82 10
- www.pere-lachaise.com
- 16 rue du Repos & 8 bd de Ménilmontant, 20e
- 8am-6pm Mon-Fri, from 8.30am Sat, from 9am Sun mid-Mar–Oct, shorter hours Nov–mid-Mar
- Ⓜ Père Lachaise, Gambetta

Cimetière du Père Lachaise

A HALF-DAY TOUR

There is a certain romance to getting lost in Cimetière du Père Lachaise, a jungle of graves spun from centuries of tales. But to search for one grave among one million in this 44-hectare land of the dead is no joke – narrow the search with this itinerary.

From the main bd de Ménilmontant entrance (metro Père Lachaise or Philippe Auguste), head up av Principale, turn right onto av du Puits and collect a map from ❶ **the Bureaux de la Conservation**.

Backtrack along av du Puits, turn right onto av Latérale du Sud, scale the stairs and bear right along chemin Denon to New Realist artist ❷ **Arman**, film director ❸ **Claude Chabrol** and ❹ **Chopin**.

Follow chemin Méhul downhill, cross av Casimir Périer and bear right onto chemin Serré. Take the second left (chemin Lebrun – unsigned), head uphill and near the top leave the footpath to weave through graves on your right to rock star ❺ **Jim Morrison**. Back on chemin Lauriston, continue uphill to roundabout ❻ **Rond-Point Casimir Périer**.

Admire the funerary art of contemporary photographer ❼ **André Chabot**, av de la Chapelle. Continue uphill for energising city views from the ❽ **chapel** steps, then zig-zag to ❾ **Molière & La Fontaine**, on chemin Molière.

Cut between graves onto av Tranversale No 1 – spot potatoes atop ❿ **Parmentier's** headstone. Continue straight onto av Greffülhe and left onto av Tranversale No 2 to rub ⓫ **Monsieur Noir's** shiny crotch.

Navigation to ⓬ **Édith Piaf** and the ⓭ **Mur des Fédérés** is straightforward. End with angel-topped ⓮ **Oscar Wilde** near the Porte Gambetta entrance.

TOP TIPS

➡ Père Lachaise is a photographer's paradise any time of the day or year, but best are sunny autumn mornings after the rain.

➡ Cemetery-lovers will appreciate themed guided tours (two hours) led by entertaining cemetery historian Thierry Le Roi (www.necro-romantiques.com).

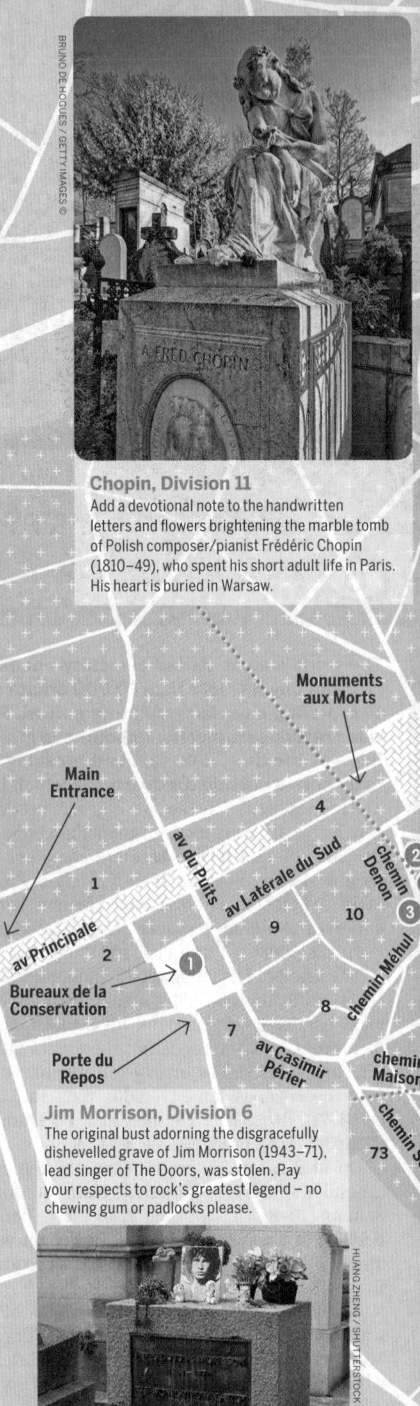

Chopin, Division 11
Add a devotional note to the handwritten letters and flowers brightening the marble tomb of Polish composer/pianist Frédéric Chopin (1810–49), who spent his short adult life in Paris. His heart is buried in Warsaw.

Jim Morrison, Division 6
The original bust adorning the disgracefully dishevelled grave of Jim Morrison (1943–71), lead singer of The Doors, was stolen. Pay your respects to rock's greatest legend – no chewing gum or padlocks please.

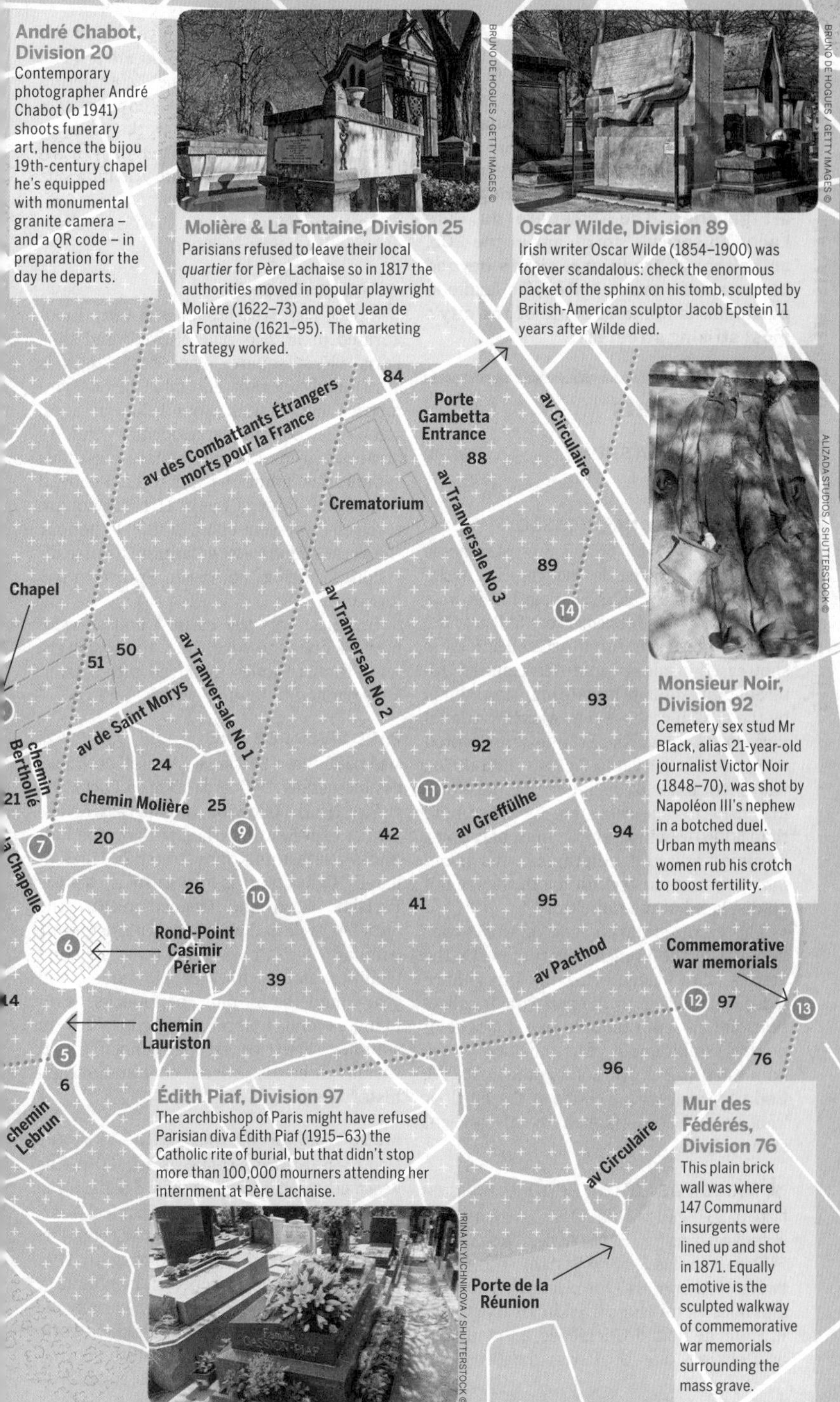
André Chabot, Division 20
Contemporary photographer André Chabot (b 1941) shoots funerary art, hence the bijou 19th-century chapel he's equipped with monumental granite camera – and a QR code – in preparation for the day he departs.
BRUNO DE HOGUES / GETTY IMAGES ©
Molière & La Fontaine, Division 25
Parisians refused to leave their local *quartier* for Père Lachaise so in 1817 the authorities moved in popular playwright Molière (1622–73) and poet Jean de la Fontaine (1621–95). The marketing strategy worked.
BRUNO DE HOGUES / GETTY IMAGES ©
Oscar Wilde, Division 89
Irish writer Oscar Wilde (1854–1900) was forever scandalous: check the enormous packet of the sphinx on his tomb, sculpted by British-American sculptor Jacob Epstein 11 years after Wilde died.
ALIZADA STUDIOS / SHUTTERSTOCK ©
Monsieur Noir, Division 92
Cemetery sex stud Mr Black, alias 21-year-old journalist Victor Noir (1848–70), was shot by Napoléon III's nephew in a botched duel. Urban myth means women rub his crotch to boost fertility.
Édith Piaf, Division 97
The archbishop of Paris might have refused Parisian diva Édith Piaf (1915–63) the Catholic rite of burial, but that didn't stop more than 100,000 mourners attending her internment at Père Lachaise.
IRINA KLYUCHNIKOVA / SHUTTERSTOCK ©
Mur des Fédérés, Division 76
This plain brick wall was where 147 Communard insurgents were lined up and shot in 1871. Equally emotive is the sculpted walkway of commemorative war memorials surrounding the mass grave.
84
Porte Gambetta Entrance
av des Combattants Étrangers morts pour la France
av Circulaire
88
Crematorium
av Tranversale No 3
89
Chapel
14
51
50
av Tranversale No 2
av Tranversale No 1
av de Saint Morys
93
92
chemin Bertholle
24
21
chemin Molière
25
11
av Greffülhe
20
7
9
42
94
la Chapelle
26
10
41
95
Rond-Point Casimir Périer
6
Commemorative war memorials
av Pachod
39
12
97
13
14
chemin Lauriston
5
76
96
6
chemin Lebrun
av Circulaire
Porte de la Réunion

SIGHTS

The majority of sights in this neighbourhood concentrate in the narrow, medieval streets and sheltered squares of Le Marais, which are easily accessed on foot. Museums here include an increasing number of cutting-edge art galleries. The Cimetière du Père Lachaise sprawls northeast in the 20e, and although traditional sights beyond Le Marais are more limited, Belleville in particular is home to some of the city's most striking street art.

Le Marais

MÉMORIAL DE LA SHOAH MUSEUM
See p156.

★MUSÉE NATIONAL PICASSO MUSEUM
Map p386 (☎01 85 56 00 36; www.museepicassoparis.fr; 5 rue de Thorigny, 3e; adult/child €12.50/free; ⊙10.30am-6pm Tue-Fri, from 9.30am Sat & Sun; Ⓜ Chemin Vert, St-Paul) One of Paris' most treasured art collections is showcased inside the mid-17th-century Hôtel Salé, an exquisite private mansion owned by the city since 1964. The Musée National Picasso is a staggering art museum devoted to Spanish artist Pablo Picasso (1881–1973), who spent much of his life living and working in Paris. The collection includes more than 5000 drawings, engravings, paintings, ceramic works and sculptures by the *grand maître* (great master), although they're not all displayed at the same time.

The extraordinary cache of works was donated to the French government by the artist's heirs in lieu of paying inheritance taxes. In addition to the permanent collection, the museum mounts two major temporary exhibitions a year (included in the admission price). An audioguide costs €5. End your visit with a coffee at the 1st-floor 'rooftop cafe', overlooked by an ancient stone sphinx.

★MAISON DE VICTOR HUGO MUSEUM
Map p386 (☎01 42 72 10 16; www.maisonsvictorhugo.paris.fr; 6 place des Vosges, 4e; ⊙10am-6pm Tue-Sun; Ⓜ Bastille) FREE Between 1832 and 1848 the celebrated novelist and poet Victor Hugo lived in an apartment in Hôtel de Rohan-Guéménée, a townhouse overlooking one of Paris' most elegant squares. Hugo moved here a year after the publication of *Notre Dame de Paris* (The Hunchback of Notre Dame), completing *Ruy Blas* during his stay. It's now a museum devoted to his life and works, with an impressive collection of his personal drawings and portraits. Temporary exhibitions command an admission fee.

An audioguide costs €5. A cafe is scheduled to open on site in 2020.

PLACE DES VOSGES SQUARE
Map p386 (4e; Ⓜ Bastille, Chemin Vert) Inaugurated in 1612 as place Royale and thus Paris' oldest square, place des Vosges is a strikingly elegant ensemble of 36 symmetrical houses with ground-floor arcades, steep slate roofs and large dormer windows arranged around a leafy square with four symmetrical fountains and an 1829 copy of a mounted statue of Louis XIII. The square received its present name in 1800 to honour the Vosges *département* (administrative division) for being the first in France to pay its taxes.

In Paris, only the earliest houses were built of brick; to save time, the rest were given timber frames and faced with plaster, later painted to resemble brick.

PARC RIVES DE SEINE PARK
Map p386 (btwn Bassin de l'Arsenal, 4e & quai des Tuileries, 1er; Ⓜ Quai de la Rapée, Pont Marie or Pont Neuf) Following the success of the former expressway turned park on the Left Bank (p233), this 3.3km stretch of Unesco-listed Right Bank is now also a car-free Parisian playground. Opened in 2017, the park has cycle and walking paths, *pétanque* (similar to lawn bowls) and other sporting facilities, along with kids' play areas, and year-round bars, plus hammocks, sun-loungers and umbrella-shaded tables in summer. Free 'timescope' binoculars at various intervals provide cool audiovisual history lessons.

MUSÉE DES ARTS ET MÉTIERS MUSEUM
Map p386 (www.arts-et-metiers.net; 60 rue de Réaumur, 3e; adult/child €8/free, 6-9.30pm Thu & 1st Sun of month free; ⊙10am-6pm Tue, Wed & Fri-Sun, to 9.30pm Thu; Ⓜ Arts et Métiers) The Arts and Crafts Museum, dating to 1794 and Europe's oldest science and technology museum, is a must for families – or anyone with an interest in how things tick or work. Housed inside the sublime 18th-century priory of St-Martin des Champs, some 2400

instruments, machines and working models from the 18th to 20th centuries are displayed across three floors. In the priory's attached church is Foucault's original pendulum, introduced to the world at the Universal Exhibition in Paris in 1855.

Louis Blériot's monoplane from 1909 is also here. Guided tours are in French only but the excellent English audioguides (€5) – one for adults and another aimed at children aged seven to 12 years – more than compensates.

LAFAYETTE ANTICIPATIONS MUSEUM

Map p386 (Fondation d'entreprise Galeries Lafayette; ☎01 57 40 64 17; www.lafayetteanticipations.com; 9 rue du Plâtre, 4e; adult/child €8/free; ⊙11am-8pm Mon, Wed & Sun, to 10pm Thu-Sat; MRambuteau) In 2018 the corporate foundation of French retailer Galeries Lafayette opened this unique multidisciplinary space for producing, experimenting with and exhibiting new works of contemporary art, design and fashion. Transformed by Dutch architect Rem Koolhaas, the 1891 building now has 2500 sq metres of exhibition space and a striking 18m-high glass tower. Three to four exhibitions take place annually alongside performances and workshops.

HÔTEL DE VILLE ARCHITECTURE

Map p386 (www.paris.fr; place de l'Hôtel de Ville, 4e; MHôtel de Ville) FREE Paris' beautiful town hall was gutted during the Paris Commune of 1871 and rebuilt in luxurious neo-Renaissance style between 1874 and 1882. The ornate façade is decorated with 108 statues of illustrious Parisians, and the outstanding temporary exhibitions (admission free; enter at 29 rue de Rivoli, 4e) have a Parisian theme.

PAVILLON DE L'ARSENAL MUSEUM

(www.pavillon-arsenal.com; 21 bd Morland, 4e; ⊙11am-7pm Tue-Sun; MSully–Morland) FREE Built in 1879 as a museum, this magnificent glass-roofed building with arched wrought-iron girders wasn't actually used as one until over a century later, when it opened as a centre for Parisian urbanism and architecture. Exhibitions (30 per year) showcase the city's past, present and future. Interpretative information is in French but it's fascinating for anyone with an interest in the evolution of Paris. There's a small but excellent architectural bookshop on the ground floor.

HÔTEL DE SULLY HISTORIC BUILDING

Map p386 (www.hotel-de-sully.fr; 62 rue St-Antoine, 4e; ⊙courtyards 9am-7pm; MSt-Paul, Bastille) In the southwestern corner of place des Vosges, duck beneath the arch to find two beautifully decorated, late-Renaissance courtyards festooned with allegorical reliefs of the seasons and the elements. It's the back entrance to the aristocratic mansion Hôtel de Sully, built between 1624 and 1630. Since 1967 it has housed the headquarters of the Centre des Monuments Nationaux, responsible for many of France's historical monuments, and is normally closed to the public, but check the website for occasional guided tours.

MUSÉE COGNACQ-JAY MUSEUM

Map p386 (www.cognacq-jay.paris.fr; 8 rue Elzévir, 3e; ⊙10am-6pm Tue-Sun; MSt-Paul, Chemin Vert) FREE This museum inside the Hôtel de Donon displays oil paintings, pastels, sculpture, objets d'art, jewellery, porcelain and furniture from the 18th century assembled by Ernest Cognacq (1839–1928), founder of La Samaritaine department store, and his wife Louise Jay.

Although Cognacq appreciated little of his collection, boasting that he had never visited the Louvre and was only acquiring collections for the status, the artwork and objets d'art give a good idea of upper-class tastes during the Age of Enlightenment.

Temporary exhibitions incur an admission fee.

FROM MARSH TO FASHIONABLE ADDRESS

The Marais (meaning 'marsh' or 'swamp' in French) was exactly what its name implies until the 13th century, when it was converted to farmland. In the early 17th century Henri IV built place Royale (today's place des Vosges), turning the area into Paris' most fashionable residential address. When the aristocracy moved out of Paris to Versailles and Faubourg St-Germain in the 18th century, Le Marais' townhouses passed into the hands of ordinary Parisians. The 110-hectare area was given a major facelift in the late 1960s and early '70s, and today it is one of the city's most coveted addresses.

MUSÉE D'ART ET D'HISTOIRE DU JUDAÏSME MUSEUM

Map p386 (☎01 53 01 86 62; www.mahj.org; 71 rue du Temple, 3e; adult/child €9/free; ⏱11am-6pm Tue-Fri, from 10am Sat & Sun; Ⓜ Rambuteau) Inside the Hôtel de St-Aignan, dating from 1650, this museum traces the evolution of Jewish communities from the Middle Ages to the present, including French Jewish history. Highlights include documents relating to the Dreyfus Affair, and artworks by Chagall, Modigliani and Soutine. Creative workshops (adult/child from €9/7) for children, adults and families complement excellent temporary exhibitions (from €8.50/5.50). To learn more about Le Marais' Jewish history, take a guided walking tour of the neighbourhood (including museum entrance €12/9; English available).

MAISON EUROPÉENNE DE LA PHOTOGRAPHIE MUSEUM

Map p386 (www.mep-fr.org; 5-7 rue de Fourcy, 4e; adult/child €9/5; ⏱11am-7.45pm Wed-Sun; Ⓜ St-Paul) The European House of Photography, housed in the overly renovated Hôtel Hénault de Cantobre (dating – believe it or not – from the early 18th century), has cutting-edge temporary exhibits (usually retrospectives on single photographers), as well as an enormous permanent collection on the history of photography and its connections with France. There are frequent showings of short films and documentaries on weekend afternoons.

JEWISH PLETZL

Cacher (kosher) grocery shops, butchers, restaurants, delis and takeaway felafel joints cram the narrow streets of Pletzl (from the Yiddish for 'little square'), home to Le Marais' long-established Jewish community. It starts in rue des Rosiers and continues along rue Ste-Croix de la Bretonnerie to rue du Temple. Don't miss the **art nouveau synagogue** (Agoudas Hakehilos Synagogue; Map p386; 10 rue Pavée, 4e; Ⓜ St-Paul) designed in 1913 by Hector Guimard, who was also responsible for the city's famous metro entrances.

For an in-depth look at Jewish history, visit the Musée d'Art et d'Histoire du Judaïsme, housed in Pletzl's sumptuous Hôtel de St-Aignan, dating from 1650.

MUSÉE DE LA CHASSE ET DE LA NATURE MUSEUM

Map p386 (☎01 53 01 92 40; www.chassenature.org; 62 rue des Archives, 3e; adult/child €8/free; ⏱11am-6pm Tue & Thu-Sun, to 9.30pm Wed; Ⓜ Rambuteau) The Hunting and Nature Museum, inside the delightful Hôtel de Guénégaud (1651), is positively crammed with weapons, paintings, sculptures and objets d'art related to hunting and, of course, lots and lots of trophies (horns, antlers, heads). Particularly appealing are its nature-themed workshops for children (€15; English available).

MUSÉE DES ARCHIVES NATIONALES MUSEUM

Map p386 (☎01 40 27 60 96; www.archives-nationales.culture.gouv.fr; 60 rue des Francs Bourgeois, 3e; adult/child €5/free; ⏱10am-5.30pm Mon & Wed-Fri, from 2pm Sat & Sun; Ⓜ Rambuteau) France's National Archives and small museum are set in a stunning pair of *hôtels particuliers* (mansions) amid beautiful gardens. Dating from the early 18th century, Hôtel de Rohan and Hôtel de Soubise are extravagantly painted and gilded in the rococo style inside, with antique furniture and 18th-century paintings alongside a fascinating collection of documents on display, such as the Edict of Nantes and Marie-Antoinette's final letter. The audiovisual room screens films and has multimedia exhibits. Admission is more expensive during temporary exhibitions.

FONDATION HENRI CARTIER-BRESSON MUSEUM

Map p412 (☎01 56 80 27 00; www.henricartierbresson.org; 70 rue des Archives, 3e; adult/child €8/5, 6.30-8.30pm Wed free; ⏱1-6.30pm Tue, Thu, Fri & Sun, 1-8.30pm Wed, 11am-6.45pm Sat; Ⓜ Temple) Founded by renowned French humanist photographer Henri Cartier-Bresson (1908–2004) and his portrait-photographer wife Martine Franck (1938–2012), this gallery displays their works and also mounts rotating exhibitions by French and international photographers, including the winner of the Henri Cartier-Bresson Award every two years. Cartier-Bresson pioneered artistic photojournalism, set up a photography department for the Resistance and co-founded the collective agency Magnum. In 2018 it relocated to a former garage in Le Marais; check the website for hours and prices.

Ménilmontant & Belleville

CIMETIÈRE DU PÈRE LACHAISE CEMETERY

See p157.

L'ATELIER DES LUMIÈRES MUSEUM

Map p390 (www.atelier-lumieres.com; 38-40 rue St-Maur, 11e; adult/child €14.50/9.50; 10am-6pm Sun-Thu, to 10pm Fri & Sat; M Voltaire) A former foundry dating from 1835 that supplied iron for the French navy and railroads now, since opening in 2018, houses Paris' first digital art museum. The 1500-sq-metre La Halle mounts dazzling light projections that take over the bare walls. Long programs lasting around 30 minutes are based on historic artists' works; there's also a shorter contemporary program. Screenings are continuous. In the separate Le Studio space, you can discover emerging and established digital artists.

ÉGLISE ST-AMBROISE CHURCH

Map p390 (www.paris.catholique.fr/-saint-ambroise; 71bis bd Voltaire, 11e; 7.30am-12.30pm & 3-7.30pm Tue-Fri, 8.30am-noon & 3-7.30pm Sat, 8.30am-12.30pm & 3-7.30pm Sun & Mon; M St-Ambroise) Built between 1863 and 1868 on the site of a former church, Notre-Dame de la Procession, this distinctive church with twin towers rising 68m was designed by architect Théodore Ballu and consecrated in 1910. It's linked to bd Richard-Lenoir by the Jardin Truillot, a 5600-sq-metre *coulée verte* ('green belt') walkway that opened in 2018.

SQUARE MAURICE GARDETTE PARK

Map p390 (rue du Général Blaise, 11e; 8am-9.30pm Mon-Fri, 9am-9.30pm Sat & Sun May-Aug, to 8.30pm Apr & Sep, shorter hours Oct-Mar; M St-Ambroise, Rue St-Maur) In the heart of the vibrant 11e, this square was first laid out in 1872 on the former site of the Ménilmontant slaughterhouses, and in 1979 was transformed into the charming little park you see today. Filled with elms, chestnuts, silver birches and magnolias, with hollyhocks, irises and asters blooming in spring and summer, Square Maurice Gardette is a favourite with locals and makes an idyllic spot for a picnic. Dating from 1899, the wrought-iron bandstand at the centre of the park hosts occasional concerts.

MUSÉE ÉDITH PIAF MUSEUM

Map p390 (01 43 55 52 72; 5 rue Crespin du Gast, 11e; by reservation 1-6pm Mon-Wed, 10am-noon Thu; M Ménilmontant) FREE This private museum in Ménilmontant, some 1.5km from the birthplace of the iconic singer Édith Piaf and closer to her final resting place in Père Lachaise, follows the life and career of the 'urchin sparrow' through memorabilia, recordings, personal objects, letters and other documentation. Admission is by reservation only at least several days in advance; you'll receive the door codes upon booking. Donations are welcome. Be aware that there are several flights of stairs, and that only French is spoken.

EATING

Packed with eateries of every imaginable type, Le Marais is one of Paris' premier dining neighbourhoods with many restaurants and bistros requiring a reservation. Despite the huge concentration of eating addresses, new openings pop up seemingly every week. Multi-ethnic Belleville is tops for Asian fare. Some of the Bastille and Eastern Paris neighbourhood's best neobistros are within easy walking distance of Cimetière du Père Lachaise.

Le Marais

★JACQUES GENIN PASTRIES €

Map p386 (01 45 77 29 01; www.jacquesgenin.fr; 133 rue de Turenne, 3e; pastries €9; 11am-7pm Tue-Fri & Sun, to 7.30pm Sat; M Oberkampf, Filles du Calvaire) Wildly creative *chocolatier* Jacques Genin is famed for his flavoured caramels, *pâtes de fruits* (fruit jellies) and exquisitely embossed *bonbons de chocolat* (chocolate sweets). But what completely steals the show at his elegant chocolate showroom is the *salon de dégustation* (aka tearoom), where you can order a pot of outrageously thick hot chocolate and legendary Genin *mille-feuille*, assembled to order.

★LA MAISON PLISSON CAFE, DELI €

Map p386 (www.lamaisonplisson.com; 93 bd Beaumarchais, 3e; mains €8-15; 9.30am-9pm Mon, from 8.30am Tue-Sat, 9.30am-8pm

LOCAL KNOWLEDGE

STREET ART SIGHTS

Rue Dénoyez (Map p390; 20e; Ⓜ Belleville) One block east of bd de Belleville, narrow rue Dénoyez has some of Paris' most dazzling street art. Everything on the small cobbled street, from litter bins and flower pots to lamp posts and window shutters, is covered in colourful graffiti. Artists' workshops pepper the paved street where local kids kick footballs around and street art 'happenings' break out on summer nights.

Le MUR (Map p390; www.lemur.fr; rue Oberkampf, 11e; Ⓜ Parmentier) Meaning 'the wall' but also standing for Modulable Urbain Réactif (Modular Urban Reactive), street-art canvas Le MUR, on the southern side of the building housing **Café Charbon** (p174), is overseen by an arts collective, with hundreds of murals painted on it to date.

Sun; Ⓜ St-Sébastien–Froissart) Framed by glass-canopied wrought-iron girders, this gourmand's dream incorporates a covered-market-style, terrazzo-floored food hall filled with exquisite, mostly French produce: meat, vegetables, cheese, wine, chocolate, jams, freshly baked breads and much more. If your appetite's whet, its cafe, opening to twin terraces, serves charcuterie, foie gras and cheese planks, bountiful salads and delicacies such as olive-oil-marinated, Noilly Prat–flambéed sardines.

★BREIZH CAFÉ — CRÊPES €

Map p386 (☎01 42 72 13 77; www.breizhcafe.com; 109 rue Vieille du Temple, 3e; crêpes & galettes €6.80-18.80; ⊙11.30am-11pm Mon-Sat, to 10pm Sun; Ⓜ St-Sébastien–Froissart) Everything at the Breizh ('Breton' in Breton) is 100% authentic, including its organic-flour crêpes and *galettes* that top many Parisians' lists for the best in the city. Other specialities include Cancale oysters and 20 types of cider. Tables are limited and there's often a wait; book ahead or try its deli, **L'Épicerie** (Map p386; ☎01 42 71 39 44; 111 rue Vieille du Temple, 3e; crêpes & galettes €6.80-18.80; ⊙11.30am-10pm; Ⓜ St-Sébastien–Froissart), next door.

L'AS DU FALLAFEL — FELAFEL €

Map p386 (34 rue des Rosiers, 4e; takeaway €5.50-8.50, mains €12-18; ⊙noon-midnight Sun-Thu, to 4pm Fri; 🌶; Ⓜ St-Paul) The lunchtime queue stretching halfway down the street from this place says it all. This Parisian favourite, 100% worth the inevitable wait, is the address for kosher, perfectly deep-fried falafel (chickpea balls) and turkey or lamb shawarma sandwiches. Do as every Parisian does and get them to take away.

Testament to its popularity, a second takeaway window has opened at 44 rue des Rosiers to cope with demand.

CAFÉ PINSON — CAFE, VEGETARIAN €

Map p386 (☎09 83 82 53 53; www.cafepinson.fr; 6 rue du Forez, 3e; 2-course lunch menus €17.50, mains €13.50-14.50, Sunday brunch €27; ⊙9am-10pm Mon-Fri, from 10am Sat, noon-6pm Sun; 📶🌶; Ⓜ Filles du Calvaire) 🍃 Tucked down a narrow Haut Marais side street, this stylish cafe with an interior by celebrity designer Dorothée Meilichzon sees a fashionable lunchtime crowd flock for its organic vegetarian and vegan dishes such as beetroot-stuffed squash with vegetable crumble and chia pudding with cranberry sauce. Freshly squeezed juices are excellent, as is Sunday brunch (noon and 2.30pm).

BONTEMPS PÂTISSERIE — PASTRIES €

Map p386 (☎01 42 74 10 68; 57 rue de Bretagne, 3e; pastries from €4; ⊙11am-2pm & 3-7.30pm Wed-Fri, 10am-2pm & 2.30-7.30pm Sat, 10am-2pm & 3-6pm Sun; Ⓜ Temple) Buttery *sablés* (shortbread biscuits), rich chocolate fondant and light-as-air *tarte au citron* (lemon tart) are among the exquisite treats at this jewel-box-like patisserie (cake shop) on foodie rue de Bretagne. If you can't wait to tuck in, there's a handful of aqua-painted metallic tables and chairs outside the stone shopfront.

MIZNON — ISRAELI €

Map p386 (☎01 42 74 83 58; 22 rue des Écouffes, 4e; pita sandwiches €6-12.50; ⊙noon-11pm Sun-Thu, to 4pm Fri; 🌶; Ⓜ St-Paul, Hôtel de Ville) Parisians can't get enough of this hip outpost of celebrity chef Eyal Shani's famed Tel Aviv restaurant. Head past the grocery crates to the bar to order a warm, fluffy pita (such as lamb, fish or roasted cauliflower) and phenomenal house-made hummus. Don't miss the sweet *banane au chocolat* pita to finish. Takeaway is available if you can't get a seat.

PASTELLI GELATO €

Map p386 (Mary; 60 rue du Temple, 3e; gelato 1/2/3/4 scoops €3.50/5/6.50/7.50; ⌚11am-10pm; ⓂRambuteau) The youngest winner of Milan's prestigious Cone d'Oro (Golden Cone), artisan gelato maker Mary Quarta has more than 100 different flavours in her all-natural repertoire, and serves around a dozen different freshly made small batches each day at her light, white-painted Haut Marais shop. Standouts include avocado, black sesame, peach Champagne bellini and coffee-laced tiramisu.

CAUSSES DELI, CAFE €

Map p386 (☎01 42 71 33 33; www.causses.org; 222 rue St-Martin, 3e; 2-course midweek lunch menus €15, dishes €5-8, Saturday brunch €21; ⌚10am-9pm Mon-Sat; ; ⓂArts et Métiers) Shelves at this upmarket grocer are laden with fruit, veggies, cheeses, yoghurt, sardines, smoked salmon, olive oil and wines. Hidden down the back, its cafe serves soups, sandwiches, salads and quiches made from fresh produce delivered daily to the shop at a handful of tables.

BROKEN ARM CAFE €

Map p386 (☎01 44 61 53 60; www.the-brokenarm.com; 12 rue Perrée, 3e; mains €11-14; ⌚cafe 9am-6pm Tue-Sat, shop 11am-7pm; ; ⓂTemple, Arts et Métiers) Small but stylish, this cafe opens directly onto the street and from its adjacent concept store stocking men's and women's fashion, shoes and bags along with books and homewares. Kick off with a fresh apple, kiwi and mint juice. The daily menu is limited but packed with goodness, particularly its imaginative salads such as blood orange, fennel and fresh herbs.

POZZETTO GELATO €

Map p386 (www.pozzetto.biz; 16 rue Vieille du Temple, 4e; gelato per cone or cup €4-7, dishes €7-14.50; ⌚noon-11.30pm Mon-Thu, to 12.45am Fri & Sat, to midnight Sun; ⓂHôtel de Ville, St-Paul) This gelato maker opened when friends from northern Italy couldn't find their favourite ice cream in Paris so they imported the ingredients to make it themselves. The 12 flavours – spatula'd, not scooped – include *gianduia* (hazelnut chocolate) and *zabaione*, made from egg yolks, sugar and sweet Marsala wine. It also serves antipasti platters of imported Italian produce and great *caffè* too. You can also get gelato at its original outlet, located just around the corner at 39 rue du Roi de Sicile, 4e.

HANKBURGER VEGAN, BURGERS €

Map p386 (☎09 72 44 03 99; www.hankrestaurant.com; 55 rue des Archives, 3e; burgers €8.50; ⌚noon-10pm; ; ⓂRambuteau) No animal products are involved in the burgers at Hank, an acronym for 'Have A Nice Karma'. Soy-based burgers include La Catcheuse (alfalfa and sweet mustard sauce) and Tata Monique (minced black olives and basil sauce). The stylish space is a pleasure to linger in and the kitchen works strictly with fresh, organic and often local produce.

Its vegan pizza restaurant, **Hankpizza** (Map p386; www.hankrestaurant.com/pizza; 18 rue des Gravilliers, 3e; pizza per slice €5; ⌚noon-10pm; ; ⓂArts et Métiers), is a 400m walk north.

SAUCETTE FRENCH €

Map p386 (☎09 67 89 32 73; www.saucette.fr; 30 rue Beaubourg, 3e; dishes €8.50-16; ⌚noon-3pm & 6.30-10.30pm Tue-Sat; ; ⓂRambuteau) At this *bar à saucisses* (sausage bar), sausages from across France are the star of the show. Regional varieties include *boudin noir* from Mortagne-au-Perche in Normandy, *andouillette* from Lyon, and frankfurter-style *strasbourg saucisse* from Alsace. Four-sausage tasting plates are a great way to sample several kinds. Sides include sauerkraut, fries, salad or mash.

LOCAL KNOWLEDGE

SCENIC PICNIC

A few blocks east of bd de Belleville, the lovely but little-known **Parc de Belleville** (Map p390; rue des Couronnes & rue Piat, 20e; ⌚8am-9.30pm Jul & Aug, shorter hours Sep-Jun; ⓂCouronnes, Pyrénées) unfolds across a hill 128m above sea level amid 4.5 hectares of greenery. Climb to the top for some of the best views of the city armed with a bread-and-cheese picnic bought in Belleville from two of the finest in their field: *boulangerie* (bakery) **Au 140** (Map p390; www.au140.com; 140 rue de Belleville, 20e; sandwiches €3-5.50; ⌚7am-8pm Tue-Fri, from 7.30am Sat, 7am-7pm Sun; ⓂJourdain) and **Fromagerie Beaufils** (Map p390; www.fromagerie-beaufils.com; 118 rue de Belleville, 20e; ⌚8.30am-8pm Tue-Sat, to 1pm Sun; ⓂJourdain).

★AU PASSAGE
BISTRO €€

Map p386 (☎01 43 55 07 52; www.restaurant-aupassage.fr; 1bis passage St-Sébastien, 11e; small plates €9-18, meats to share €25-70; ⏰7-10.30pm Tue-Sat; Ⓜ St-Sébastien-Froissart) Rising-star chefs continue to make their name at this *petit bar de quartier* (little neighbourhood bar). Choose from a good-value, uncomplicated selection *of petites assiettes* (small tapas-style plates) of cold meats, raw or cooked fish, vegetables and so on, and larger meat dishes such as slow-roasted lamb shoulder or *côte de bœuf* (rib steak) to share. Reservations are essential.

DERRIÈRE
FRENCH €€

Map p386 (☎01 44 61 91 95; www.derriere-resto.com; 69 rue des Gravilliers, 3e; 2-/3-course lunch menus €25/30, mains €22-38, Sunday brunch €38, with Champagne €56; ⏰noon-2.30pm & 7.30-11.30pm Mon-Sat, noon-4pm & 7.30-11.30pm Sun; Ⓜ Arts et Métiers) Play table tennis, sit on the side of the bed, glass of Champers in hand, or lounge between bookcases at this apartment-style restaurant in a beautiful courtyard (idyllic for lunch in the sunshine). Chilled vibe aside, Derrière ('behind') is deadly serious in the kitchen. Classic French bistro dishes and more inventive creations are excellent, as is Sunday's buffet brunch.

BIGLOVE CAFFÈ
ITALIAN, CAFE €€

Map p386 (www.bigmammagroup.com; 30 rue Debelleyme, 3e; pizza & pasta €13-18, weekend brunch €7-14; ⏰noon-2.30pm & 7-10.30pm Mon-Fri, 9am-4.30pm & 7-10.30pm Sat & Sun; Ⓜ Filles du Calvaire) Weekend brunch is the big event at this Italian-run cafe: expect blackberry pancakes with ricotta and maple syrup; avocado toast with prosciutto and lemon; eggs Benedict with homemade brioche and feta. Throughout the week, drop by for wood-fired, gluten-free pizzas (black truffle and mushroom or burrata, pesto and potato) and regularly changing pastas. No reservations.

CAM
ASIAN €€

Map p386 (☎06 26 41 10 66; www.cam-paris.fr; 55 rue au Maire, 3e; mains €12.50-24; ⏰7pm-11pm Wed-Sat; Ⓜ Arts et Métiers) Don't be fooled by the façade reading 'CAM Import Export' – this former miniature Eiffel Tower wholesaler has been stripped back to create a hip space for small pan-Asian plates that fire up the spice (bonito head with spring onion relish; smoked cuttlefish with ginger dressing; fermented soy-marinated steak with lettuce, mint and cilantro) accompanied by well-priced natural wines. No reservations.

ROBERT ET LOUISE
FRENCH €€

Map p386 (☎01 42 78 55 89; www.robertetlouise.com; 64 rue Vieille du Temple, 4e; 2-course lunch menus €14, mains €13-26; ⏰7-11pm Tue & Wed, noon-3pm & 7-11pm Thu & Fri, noon-11pm Sat & Sun; Ⓜ Rambuteau) Going strong since 1958, this wonderfully convivial 'country inn' with red gingham curtains and rustic timber beams offers simple and inexpensive French food, including *côte de bœuf* (side of beef for two or three people) cooked on an open fire. Arrive early to snag the farmhouse table next to the fireplace – the makings of a real jolly Rabelaisian evening.

LE CLOWN BAR
FRENCH €€

Map p386 (☎01 43 55 87 35; www.clown-bar-paris.com; 114 rue Amelot, 11e; mains €28-34; ⏰kitchen noon-2.30pm & 7-10.30pm Wed-Sun, bar 8am-2am; Ⓜ Filles du Calvaire) The former staff dining room of the city's winter circus, the 1852-built Cirque d'Hiver, is a historic monument with colourful clown-themed ceramics and mosaics, painted glass ceilings and its original zinc bar. Modern French cuisine spans line-caught whiting with whelks to Mesquer pigeon stuffed with anchovies. The pavement terrace gets packed out on sunny days.

LOCAL KNOWLEDGE

MARCHÉ DES ENFANTS ROUGES

Built in 1615, Paris' oldest covered market, **Marché des Enfants Rouges** (Map p386; 39 rue de Bretagne & 33bis rue Charlot, 3e; ⏰8.30am-1pm & 4-7.30pm Tue-Sat, 8.30am-2pm Sun, individual stall hours vary; Ⓜ Filles du Calvaire), is secreted behind an inconspicuous green-metal gate. A glorious maze of 20-odd food stalls selling ready-to-eat dishes from around the globe (Moroccan couscous, Japanese bento boxes, and more), as well as produce, cheese and flower stalls, it's a great place to meander and to dine with locals at communal tables.

BRASSERIE BOFINGER BRASSERIE €€

Map p386 (☎01 42 72 87 82; www.bofinger-paris.com; 5-7 rue de la Bastille, 4e; 2-/3-course menus €26/32, mains €19.50-29.50; ⊙noon-3pm & 6.30pm-midnight Mon-Fri, noon-3.30pm & 6.30pm-midnight Sat, noon-11pm Sun; 📶👶; Ⓜ Bastille) Founded in 1864, Bofinger is reputedly Paris' oldest brasserie, though its polished art-nouveau brass, glass and mirrors indicate redecoration a few decades later. Alsatian-inspired specialities include six kinds of *choucroute* (sauerkraut), along with oysters (€11 to €35 per half-dozen) and magnificent seafood platters (€30 to €140). Ask for a seat downstairs beneath the *coupole* (stained-glass dome).

Kids are catered for with a two-course children's menu (€14.50).

LE TAGINE MOROCCAN €€

Map p386 (☎01 47 00 28 67; www.letagine.fr; 13 rue de Crussol, 11e; mains €17-25; ⊙7-11pm Tue, noon-2.15pm & 7-11pm Wed-Sun; Ⓜ Oberkampf) Moroccan wines, including a fruity Amazigh Beni M'Tir red and dry Guerrouane Gris rosé, accompany delicious tagines (such as chicken and duck with honey and raisins or lamb with lemon and olives), nine types of couscous and spicy merguez sausages dipped in Mont d'Or cheese at this homey, cushion-strewn restaurant. Look for the vivid blue façade.

RAINETTES FRENCH €€

Map p386 (☎09 70 38 61 61; www.rainettes.com; 5 rue Caron, 4e; 2-/3-course lunch menus €16/20, mains €17-25; ⊙7-11.45pm Tue & Wed, from 6pm Thu, from noon Fri-Sun; Ⓜ St-Paul) *Bar à grenouilles* (frog legs bar) Rainettes serves five types of frog legs platters, including Normandes (with apples, calvados and crème fraîche), Alsaciennes (Riesling, shallots and parsley), and Provençales (aubergine and garlic), as well as a daily vegetarian and meat dish. The street-level dining room has a *mur végétal* (vertical garden); there are another 30 tables in the cellar.

Cocktails, all named for frog species, include Okipipi (gin, blue curaçao, St-Germain liqueur and lime) and Dalmatina (spiced rum, ginger beer and bitters).

VINS DES PYRÉNÉES BISTRO €€

Map p386 (☎01 42 72 64 94; www.vinsdespyrenees.com; 25 rue Beautreillis, 4e; mains €16-29; ⊙kitchen noon-2.30pm & 7.30-10pm, bar to 2am; Ⓜ Bastille) Originally opened in 1905, this beautifully restored bistro has a reinvigorated menu (beef tartare with anchovies and smoked egg yolk; slow-cooked lamb croquettes). A spiralling metal staircase leads upstairs to its cocktail bar and a heated terrace with a retractable roof. Its tequila-fuelled Les Gens Sont Étranges (People Are Strange) is named for former regular Jim Morrison, who lived nearby.

LOCAL KNOWLEDGE

ASIAN EAT STREETS

Paris' largest Chinatown is on the Left Bank in the 13e but on the Right Bank, Belleville is home to a small but thriving Chinatown around the Belleville metro station, at the nexus of the 10e, 11e, 19e and 20e arrondissements, with hole-in-the-wall eateries through to large restaurants and Asian supermarkets. In the 3e, rue au Maire, 3e (metro Arts et Métiers) is a small restaurant- and shop-lined street with authentic Chinese food.

CARBÓN BISTRO €€

Map p386 (☎01 42 72 49 12; www.carbonparis.com; 14 rue Charlot, 3e; lunch mains €20-22, dinner sharing plates small €7-12, large €36-60; ⊙kitchen noon-2.30pm & 7-10.30pm Tue-Sat, noon-2.30pm Sun, bar 7pm-2am Tue-Sat; Ⓜ Filles du Calvaire) Exposed stone walls, leather seating, marble-topped tables and indoor plants (plus a cocktail bar in the vaulted cellar) give Carbón a rustic appeal. Many dishes, such as mezcal-marinated tuna, guinea fowl with quince and hay-infused duck with pontoise cabbage, are smoked over beech wood. Of an evening, choose from tapas-size small plates or large plates for two to four people.

ISTR SEAFOOD, BRETON €€

Map p386 (☎01 43 56 81 25; 41 rue Notre Dame de Nazareth, 3e; half-dozen oysters €12-20, mains €13-25, 2-/3-course lunch menus €19/24; ⊙kitchen noon-2.30pm & 6-10pm Tue-Fri, 6-11pm Sat, bar to 2am Tue-Sat; Ⓜ Temple) Fabulously patterned wallpaper and a gleaming zinc bar set the stage for innovative Breton-inspired cuisine. The region's famed *istr* ('oyster' in Breton) is the star of the show here, served plain, as a Bloody Mary–style shot, or with sauces such as soy and ginger. Other creations include buckwheat chips with smoked haddock fishcakes. It doubles as a rocking bar.

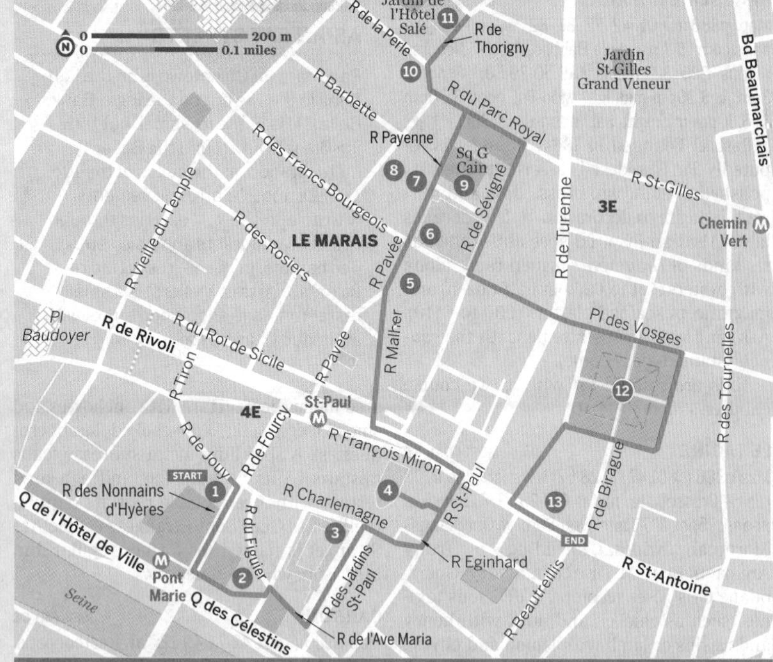

Neighbourhood Walk
Medieval Marais Meanderings

START HÔTEL D'AUMONT
END HÔTEL DE SULLY
LENGTH 2.6KM; TWO HOURS

While Henri IV was busy building place Royale (today's place des Vosges), aristocrats were commissioning gold-brick *hôtels particuliers* (private mansions) – the city's most beautiful Renaissance structures that lend the Marais a particular architectural harmony.

At 7 rue de Jouy stands majestic 1 **Hôtel d'Aumont**, built in 1648 for a councillor of the king. Continue south along rue des Nonnains d'Hyères and turn left onto rue de l'Hôtel de Ville; at 1 rue du Figuier is 2 **Hôtel de Sens**, the oldest Marais mansion, with geometric gardens and a neo-Gothic turret. It was begun around 1475 for the archbishops of Sens and restored in 1930 (look for the cannonball lodged above the main gate during the 1830 Trois Glorieuses).

Head northeast along rue des Jardins de St-Paul. To the left, two truncated towers are all that remain of the 77 that once guarded Philippe-Auguste's 3 **enceinte**, a fortified wall built between 1190 and 1209. Cross rue Charlemagne, duck into rue Eginhard and follow it to rue St-Paul and 4 **Église St-Paul St-Louis** (1641). At the end of rue St-Paul, turn left, then walk north up rue Malher and rue Pavée, the city's first cobbled road. At No 24 is the 5 **Hôtel Lamoignon** (1538–1619) built for the legitimised daughter of Henri II.

North along rue Payenne is the back of the 6 **Musée Carnavalet** (closed for renovations until 2020); the Revolutionary-era 'Temple of Reason' 7 **Chapelle de l'Humanité** at No 5; and the rear of the 8 **Musée Cognacq-Jay** (p161). From grassy 9 **Sq George Cain** opposite 11 rue Payenne, walk northwest to more spectacular 17th-century *hôtels particuliers:* 10 **Hôtel de Libéral Bruant** at 1 rue de la Perle, and 11 **Hôtel Salé**, housing the Musée National Picasso (p160).

Retrace your steps to rue du Parc Royal, walk south down rue de Sévigné and follow rue des Francs Bourgeois eastwards to end with sublime 12 **place des Vosges** (p160) and 13 **Hôtel de Sully** (p161).

CHEZ JULIEN BRASSERIE €€€

Map p386 (☎01 42 78 31 64; www.chezjulien.paris; 1 rue du Pont Louis-Philippe, 4e; 2-course lunch menus €26, mains lunch €16-24, dinner €28-38; ⊙noon-4pm & 7-11pm Mon, noon-11pm Tue-Fri, 12.30-11.30pm Sat & Sun; MPont Marie) A listed historical monument, this belle époque showpiece overlooking the Seine has one of Paris' most photographed façades. Its vine-draped terrace and gorgeous art-nouveau interior with painted-glass ceilings create an impossibly romantic backdrop for classical French cooking (scallop tartare; chateaubriand with béarnaise and frites).

Ménilmontant & Belleville

CHAMBELLAND BAKERY €

Map p390 (☎01 43 55 07 30; www.chambelland.com; 14 rue Ternaux, 11e; lunch menus €10-12, pastries €2.50-5.50; ⊙9am-8pm Tue-Sat, to 6pm Sun; MParmentier) Using rice and buckwheat flour from its own mill in southern France, this pioneering 100% gluten-free bakery creates exquisite cakes and pastries as well as sourdough loaves and brioches peppered with nuts, seeds, chocolate and fruit. Stop for lunch at one of the handful of formica tables in this relaxed space, strewn with sacks of flour and books.

LA CANTINE BELLEVILLE FRENCH €

Map p390 (☎01 43 15 99 29; www.lacantinebelleville.fr; 108 bd de Belleville, 20e; 2-/3-course lunch menus €12/14, dinner menus €15/18, mains €10-17.50; ⊙kitchen 10am-9.30pm, bar to 2am; 📶; MBelleville) Belleville's local 'canteen' is a vibrant one-stop shop for dining, drinking and dancing after dark. Old-school chairs, vintage lighting and red brick and graffitied concrete give the place an appealing garage vibe. Cuisine is classic French; excellent steaks include a *côte de boeuf* for two. Happy hour runs from 5pm to 8.30pm. Regular concerts take place in the vaulted cellar.

MARCHÉ DE BELLEVILLE MARKET €

Map p390 (bd de Belleville, 11e & 20e; ⊙7am-2.30pm Tue & Fri; MBelleville) Belleville Market has filled busy thoroughfare bd de Belleville with open-air fruit, veg and other fresh-produce stalls since 1860. Food shopping aside, it provides a fascinating insight into the large, vibrant community of this eastern neighbourhood, home to artists, students and immigrants from Africa, Asia and the Middle East.

TAI YIEN CANTONESE €

Map p390 (☎01 42 41 44 16; 5 rue de Belleville, 20e; dumplings €4-7.50, mains €8-16; ⊙10am-2am; MBelleville) Crispy-skinned ducks and roast pork hang in the windows of this wholly authentic Hong Kong–style 'steam restaurant' in Belleville's Chinatown. *Har gow* (prawn dumplings) and *sui mai* (minced pork dumplings) are served alongside specialities such as hen's feet and turnip cakes. Arrive early or late to beat the lunchtime crush.

ZOÉ BOUILLON CAFE €

Map p390 (☎01 42 02 02 83; www.zoebouillon.fr; 66 rue Rébeval, 19e; 2-/3-course menu €12.50/13.50, mains €8; ⊙11.30am-3.30pm Mon, Tue & Sat, 11.30am-3.30pm & 6.30-10pm Wed-Fri; 📶✎; MPyrénées) Delicious homemade soups, quiches, savoury cakes and tarts are the stock-in-trade of this pastel-blue-fronted cafe on a Belleville backstreet. Pile in with locals, order at the bar, grab some cutlery and enjoy the mellow vibe.

PIERRE SANG FRENCH €€

Map p390 (☎09 67 31 96 80; www.pierresang.com; 55 rue Oberkampf, 11e; 2-/3-/5-course lunch menus €20/25/35, 5-course dinner menus €39; ⊙noon, 7pm & 9.30pm; 👪; MParmentier, Oberkampf) At *Top Chef* finalist Pierre Sang's flagship, modern French cuisine has a strong fusion lilt thanks to his French and Korean background, and the vibe is casual and fun. He also has a neighbouring French–Korean 'atelier' annex at 6 rue Gambey, and experimental 'signature' restaurant at 8 rue Gambey. Kids under eight years eat free here and at the atelier.

LE BARATIN BISTRO €€

Map p390 (☎01 43 49 39 70; 3 rue Jouye-Rouve, 20e; lunch menus €19, mains €22-34; ⊙noon-2.30pm Tue-Fri, plus 7.30-11.15pm Tue-Sat; MPyrénées, Belleville) *Baratin* (chatter) rhymes with *bar à vins* (wine bar) in French and this animated venue located just steps from the lively Belleville quarter does both brilliantly. In addition it offers some of the best (and very affordable) French food in the 20e with its ever-changing blackboard options. The selection of wines (some organic) by the glass or carafe is excellent.

LA CAVE DE L'INSOLITE BISTRO €€

Map p390 (☎01 53 36 08 33; www.lacavedelinsolite.fr; 30 rue de la Folie Méricourt, 11e; 2-/3-course midweek lunch menus €18/20, mains €18-21; ⊙noon-2.30pm & 7.30-10.30pm Tue-Sat, to 10pm Sun; 📶; Ⓜ St-Ambroise, Parmentier) Brothers Axel and Arnaud, who have worked at some of Paris' top addresses, run this rustic-chic wine bar with barrels, timber tables and a wood-burning stove. Duck pâté with cider jelly, haddock rillettes with lime and endive confit, and beef with mushroom and sweetbread sauce are among the seasonal dishes; its 100-plus hand-harvested wines come from small-scale French vineyards.

BØTI BISTRO €€

Map p390 (☎06 65 49 12 29; 74 bd de Ménilmontant, 20e; 2-/3-course menus lunch €13/16, dinner €22/25; ⊙noon-3pm & 7-11pm Tue-Sat; Ⓜ Père Lachaise) There's always at least one vegetarian option (such as roast beetroot and purple-carrot crumble) on the small but superb weekly menu at this welcoming little stone-walled bistro footsteps from Père Lachaise, alongside meat and poultry dishes like confit spiced lamb shoulder or duck terrine with pickled lotus root. Wines are excellent; artisanal beers include a quinoa-based gluten-free brew. Cash only.

LE CADORET BISTRO €€

Map p390 (☎01 53 21 92 13; 1 rue Pradier, 19e; 2-/3-course lunch menus €16.50/19.50, mains €19-23; ⊙noon-2pm & 7-10pm Tue-Sat; Ⓜ Pyrénées) Neighbourhood bistro Le Cadoret, with terrazzo floors, mirrored walls and a sunny corner terrace shaded by a teal awning, is run by siblings Louis and Léa Fleuriot. Louis orchestrates the service, while in the kitchen, Léa composes dishes such as eggs mimosa, chestnut and sumac soup, and *boudin blanc* (white blood sausage) with celeriac purée and hazelnut butter.

LE CHATEAUBRIAND BISTRO €€€

Map p390 (☎01 43 57 45 95; www.lechateaubriand.net; 129 av Parmentier, 11e; tasting menus €75; ⊙7-11pm Tue-Sat; Ⓜ Goncourt) Michelin-starred Le Chateaubriand is an elegantly tiled, art-deco dining room with strikingly imaginative cuisine. Basque chef Iñaki Aizpitarte is well travelled and his dishes display global exposure again and again in their unexpected combinations (watermelon and mackerel, milk-fed veal with langoustines and truffles). Reservations open 21 days in advance and are essential.

DRINKING & NIGHTLIFE

Le Marais is a spot par excellence when it comes to a good night out – the lively scene embraces everything from gay-friendly and gay-only venues to arty cafes, eclectic bars and raucous pubs. Rue Oberkampf and parallel rue Jean-Pierre Timbaud are hubs of the Ménilmontant bar crawl, a scene that is edging out steadily through cosmopolitan Belleville.

Le Marais

★CANDELARIA COCKTAIL BAR

Map p386 (www.quixotic-projects.com; 52 rue de Saintonge, 3e; ⊙bar 6pm-2am, taqueria noon-10.30pm Sun-Wed, to 11.30pm Thu-Sat; Ⓜ Filles du Calvaire) A lime-green *taqueria* serving homemade tacos, quesadillas and tostadas conceals one of Paris' coolest cocktail bars through an unmarked internal door. Phenomenal cocktails made from agave spirits, including mezcal, are inspired by Central and South America, such as a Guatemalan El Sombrerón (tequila, vermouth, bitters, hibiscus syrup, pink-pepper-infused tonic and lime). Weekend evenings kick off with DJ sets.

LITTLE RED DOOR COCKTAIL BAR

Map p386 (☎01 42 71 19 32; www.lrdparis.com; 60 rue Charlot, 3e; ⊙6pm-2am Sun-Thu, to 3am Fri & Sat; Ⓜ Filles du Calvaires) Behind an inconspicuous timber façade, a tiny crimson doorway is the illusionary portal to this low-lit, bare-brick drinking den filled with flickering candles. Ranked among the World's 50 Best Bars, it's a must for serious mixology fans. Its annual collection of 11 cocktails, in themes from 'art' to 'architecture', are intricately crafted from ingredients like glacier ice and paper syrup.

LA CAFÉOTHÈQUE COFFEE

Map p386 (☎01 53 01 83 84; www.lacafeotheque.com; 52 rue de l'Hôtel de Ville, 4e; ⊙8.30am-7.30pm Mon-Fri, from noon Sat & Sun; 📶; Ⓜ Pont Marie, St-Paul) From the industrial grinder to elaborate tasting notes, this coffee house and roastery is serious. Grab a seat, and pick your bean, filtration method (Aeropress, V60 filter, piston or drip) and preparation style. The in-house coffee school has tastings of different *crus* and various courses including two-hour Saturday-morning tasting initiations (five *terroirs*, five extraction methods) for €60 (English available).

LA BELLE HORTENSE BAR

Map p386 (www.cafeine.com/belle-hortense; 31 rue Vieille du Temple, 4e; ⏲5pm-2am; Ⓜ Hôtel de Ville) Behind its charming chambray-blue façade, this creative wine bar named after a Jacques Roubaud novel fuses shelf after shelf of literary novels with an excellent wine list, rare varieties of armagnac, cognac, calvados and pastis, and an enriching weekly agenda of book readings, signings and art events.

LE MARY CÉLESTE COCKTAIL BAR

Map p386 (www.quixotic-projects.com/venue/mary-celeste; 1 rue Commines, 3e; ⏲6pm-2am, kitchen 7-11.30pm; Ⓜ Filles du Calvaire) Snag a stool at the central circular bar at this uber-popular brick-and-timber-floored cocktail bar or reserve one of a handful of tables online. Innovative cocktails such as Ahha Kapehna (grappa, absinthe, beetroot, fennel and Champagne) are the perfect partner to tapas-style 'small plates' (grilled duck hearts, devilled eggs) to share.

BOOT CAFÉ COFFEE

Map p386 (19 rue du Pont aux Choux, 3e; ⏲10am-6pm; 📶; Ⓜ St-Sébastien–Froissart) The charm of this three-table cafe is its façade. An old cobbler's shop, its original washed-blue exterior, 'Cordonnerie' lettering and fantastic red-boot sign above are beautifully preserved. Excellent coffee is roasted in Paris, to boot.

SHERRY BUTT COCKTAIL BAR

Map p386 (www.sherrybuttparis.com; 20 rue Beautreillis, 4e; ⏲6pm-2am Tue-Sat, from 8pm Sun & Mon; Ⓜ Bastille) Named for the sherry-seasoned oak casks used to age whisky, this dimly lit, stone-walled bar is one for serious cocktail connoisseurs. Seasonal menus might include Sherring is Caring (sweet and dry sherries, tonka bean syrup, lemon and soda) or Nux Aeterna (cognac, sweet sherry, red-wine-based Byrrh, dry vermouth and chocolate liqueur). It's standing room only on weekends when DJs play.

PASDELOUP COCKTAIL BAR

Map p386 (☎09 54 74 16 36; www.pasdeloupparis.com; 108 rue Amelot, 11e; ⏲6pm-1am Mon-Wed, to 2am Thu-Sat, to midnight Sun; Ⓜ Filles du Calvaire) Next to the Cirque d'Hiver Bouglione (Winter Circus), a small front bar with timber shelving gives way to a larger space out back where epicureans head for stunning cocktails such as Gardenia (absinthe, St-Germain elderflower liqueur, freshly squeezed OJ and lime) accompanied by superbly gourmet small plates and a loungey retro soundtrack. Happy hour runs from 6pm to 8pm.

LOCAL KNOWLEDGE

APÉRO HOUR

Clad with benches and shaded by trees, pretty pedestrian square **Place du Marché Ste-Catherine** (Map p386; 4e; Ⓜ St-Paul) is framed on three sides by atmospheric cafe pavement terraces that are perfect for that all-essential early-evening *apéro* (predinner drink) beneath the fairy lights at dusk.

AUX DEUX AMIS CAFE, BAR

Map p390 (☎01 58 30 38 13; 45 rue Oberkampf, 11e; ⏲9.30am-2am Tue-Fri, from noon Sat; Ⓜ Oberkampf, Parmentier) From the well-worn, tiled floor to the day's menu scrawled in marker on the vintage mirror, quintessential neighbourhood cafe Aux Deux Amis is perfect for a coffee, a glass of natural wine or tapas-style dishes including the house speciality – *tartare de cheval* (hand-chopped, herb-seasoned horse meat). Its adjacent crate-filled grocery store has deli-style dishes to eat in or take away.

L'EBOUILLANTÉ CAFE

Map p386 (www.ebouillante.fr; 6 rue des Barres, 4e; ⏲noon-10pm Tue-Sun Jun-Aug, to 7pm Tue-Sun Sep-May; 📶; Ⓜ Pont Marie, Hôtel de Ville) Set on a pedestrian, stone-flagged street just footsteps from the Seine, with one of the city's prettiest terraces, cornflower-blue-painted L'Ebouillanté buzzes with Parisians sipping refreshing glasses of homemade *citronnade* (ginger lemonade), hibiscus-flower cordial and over two dozen varieties of tea. Delicious cakes, jumbo salads and savoury crêpes complement the long drinks menu.

LE BALLON ROUGE WINE BAR

Map p386 (☎09 86 29 13 01; www.leballonrouge.fi; 51 rue Notre Dame de Nazareth, 3e; ⏲kitchen 7pm-12.30am Mon-Fri, noon-4pm & 7pm-12.30am Sat, bar from 3pm Mon-Fri, from noon Sat; Ⓜ Strasbourg–St-Denis) Sleek new-generation wine bar Le Ballon Rouge has 150 natural-wine references covering every major French region, and hosts regular tastings with winemakers. Wines by the glass and bottle pair with small plates such as confit vegetables with parmesan crumble, baked St-Marcellin cheese with rosemary honey, and mini croque-monsieurs with black truffles.

LE PICK-CLOPS BAR

Map p386 (16 rue Vieille du Temple, 4e; 7am-2am Mon-Sat, from 8am Sun; ; MHôtel de Ville) This spirited 1950s-styled bar-cafe – all shades of yellow and lit by neon – has a mosaic-tiled façade, formica tables, red-vinyl lounges, framed concert posters and plenty of mirrors. Attracting a friendly flow of locals and passers-by, it's a great place for morning or afternoon coffee, occasional live gigs, or that last drink alone or with friends.

LE LOIR DANS LA THÉIÈRE CAFE

Map p386 (www.leloirdanslatheiere.com; 3 rue des Rosiers, 4e; 9am-7.30pm; ; MSt-Paul) The *Alice in Wonderland*-inspired Dormouse in the Teapot is a wonderful old space filled with retro toys, wooden tables, mismatched chairs and comfy couches. Its dozen different teas, poured in the company of excellent savoury tarts and desserts including its signature lemon meringue pie, ensure a constant queue on the street outside, especially for weekend brunch.

FLUCTUAT NEC MERGITUR CAFE

Map p386 (01 42 06 42 81; www.fluctuat-cafe.paris; 18 place de la République, 10e; 8am-1am Mon-Fri, from 9am Sat & Sun; ; MRépublique) On pedestrianised place de la République, this glass-box cafe-bar and sprawling terrace overlook the square's 9.4m-high bronze statue of Marianne, symbol of the French Republic. Parisian beers include Demory and Gallia; locally inspired cocktails range from the namesake République (chartreuse, gin, cucumber syrup and Perrier) to the vodka-laced Rive Droite (Right Bank; with lemon) and Rive Gauche (Left Bank; with lime).

WILD & THE MOON JUICE BAR

Map p386 (www.wildandthemoon.com; 55 rue Charlot, 3e; 8am-8pm Mon-Fri, from 9am Sat & Sun; MFilles du Calvaire) Nut milks, vitality shots, smoothies, cold-pressed juices and raw food are the specialities of this sleek juice bar. All-vegan, ethically sourced ingredients are fresh, seasonal and organic; dishes such as avocado slices on almond and rosemary crackers are served all day.

Other Parisian branches include one at 25 rue des Gravilliers, 3e, and another at Lafayette Anticipations (p161).

LE 10H10 CAFE

Map p386 (www.le10h10.com; 210 rue St-Martin, 3e; 9am-8pm Mon-Fri, from 10.10am Sat, from 1pm Sun; ; MRambuteau, Réaumur-Sébastopol) Lightning-fast wi-fi, the use of a scanner, colour printer, lockers and an on-site kitchen, and coffee, soft drinks and snacks are included in the rate at this co-working cafe, which charges €4.50/20 per hour/day and a flat fee of €24 for the weekend. Wallpapered in groovy '70s-style prints and strewn with retro sofas and lava lamps, it accommodates 100 people.

LOUSTIC COFFEE

Map p386 (www.cafeloustic.com; 40 rue Chapon, 3e; 8.30am-6pm Mon-Fri, from 9.30am Sat, from 10am Sun; ; MArts et Métiers) Hermès wallpaper, geometric prints, exposed brick and 1950s and '60s French films screened on the back wall make Loustic (old Breton for 'smart Alec') a stylish space for lounging over excellent coffee (roasted in Antwerp and ground in situ on a Florentine Marzocco machine), or a revitalising chai-tea latte with a cinnamon scroll or wedge of carrot cake.

Ménilmontant & Belleville

★LE PERCHOIR ROOFTOP BAR

Map p390 (01 48 06 18 48; www.leperchoir.tv; 14 rue Crespin du Gast, 11e; 6pm-2am Tue-Fri, from 4pm Sat; ; MMénilmontant) Sunset is the best time to head up to this 7th-floor bar for a drink overlooking Paris' rooftops, where DJs spin on Saturday nights. Greenery provides shade in summer; in winter, it's covered by a sail-like canopy and warmed by fires burning in metal drums. It's accessed off an inner courtyard via a lift (or a spiralling staircase).

Great cocktails include Beale Street (JD, San Pellegrino Limonata and cherry juice) and Suzebucker (gin, absinthe, lemon juice

GAY & LESBIAN MARAIS

Open Café (Map p386; www.opencafe.fr; 17 rue des Archives, 4e; ⏰11am-2am Sun-Thu, to 3am Fri & Sat; Ⓜ Hôtel de Ville) A gay venue for all types at all hours, this spacious bar-cafe, with twinkling disco balls strung from the starry ceiling, has bags of appeal – including a big, awning-shaded pavement terrace that's always busy, an all-day kitchen, and a four-hour happy 'hour' kicking in daily at 6pm.

Le Tango (Map p386; www.boite-a-frissons.fr; 13 rue au Maire, 3e; admission Fri & Sat €9, Sun €6; ⏰10pm-5am Fri & Sat, 6-11pm Sun; Ⓜ Arts et Métiers) Billing itself as a *boîte à frissons* (club of thrills), Le Tango hosts a mixed and cosmopolitan, gay and lesbian crowd in a historic 1930s dancehall. Its atmosphere and style is retro and festive, with waltzing, salsa and tango from the moment it opens. From about 12.30am onwards DJs play. Sunday's gay tea dance is legendary.

3w Kafé (Map p386; www.facebook.com/3wkafe; 8 rue des Écouffes, 4e; ⏰7pm-3am Wed & Sun, to 4am Thu, to 6.30am Fri & Sat; Ⓜ St-Paul) The name of this flagship cocktail-bar-pub means 'women with women'. It's relaxed and there's no ban on men (but they must be accompanied by a woman). On weekends there's dancing downstairs with a DJ. Themed evenings take place regularly; check its Facebook page for events.

Gibus Club (Map p386; ☎01 77 15 73 09; www.gibusclub.fr; 18 rue du Faubourg du Temple, 11e; admission €12-25; ⏰11pm-7am Thu-Sat; Ⓜ République) What started out as a summer party thrown by Scream Club has since morphed into a permanent fixture on the city's gay scene, rebranded as Gibus Club and still working hard to stay top dog as one of Paris' biggest gay parties.

Café Voulez-Vous (Map p386; ☎01 83 62 22 20; www.facebook.com/cafevoulezvous; 18 rue du Temple, 4e; ⏰11am-2am Sun-Thu, to 3am Fri, to 4am Sat; Ⓜ Hôtel de Ville) This New York–styled gay bar and lounge is a mellow place in which to hang out over a coffee or brilliant house cocktail like Second Boyfriend (whisky, peach liqueur, lime and cream) or numerous Champagne varieties. Happy hour runs from 6pm to 10pm daily and, to see you on your way, from 2am to 4am on Saturday nights.

Le Raidd (Map p386; 23 rue du Temple, 4e; ⏰6pm-4am, to 5am Fri & Sat; Ⓜ Hôtel de Ville) Don't be deceived by the laid-back lounge atmosphere of the ground-floor bar, one of the busiest gay hang-outs in Le Marais. Upstairs, it is a pulsating den of DJs and electro dance music, themed parties, disco nights, Brazilian soirées, raunchy shower shows and all sorts.

Quetzal (Map p386; 10 rue de la Verrerie, 4e; ⏰5pm-4am; Ⓜ Hôtel de Ville) This perennial favourite gay bar is opposite rue des Mauvais Garçons (Bad Boys' Street), named after the brigands who congregated here in 1540. It's always busy, with house and dance music playing at night ('80s and '90s tunes on Thursdays), and cruisy at all hours. Plate-glass windows allow you to check out the talent before it arrives. Happy hours run from 5pm to 6pm and from 11pm to midnight.

L'Étoile Manquante (Map p386; www.cafeine.com/etoile-manquante; 34 rue Vieille du Temple, 4e; ⏰9am-2am; 📶; Ⓜ Hôtel de Ville, St-Paul) With its fabulous pavement terrace spilling onto rue Ste-Croix de la Bretonnerie, the Missing Star is a trendy, gay-friendly bar with a retro interior of cherry-red banquettes and 38 different wines by the glass.

Café Cox (Map p386; www.coxbar.fr; 15 rue des Archives, 4e; ⏰5pm-2am; Ⓜ Hôtel de Ville) This small gay bar with decor that changes every quarter is the meeting place for an interesting (and interested) crowd throughout the evening from dusk onwards. Happy hour runs from 6pm to 10pm (until 2am Sunday).

and ginger ale). One floor down, its restaurant serves modern French fish, meat and vegetarian multicourse *menus* from 7.30pm (reservations recommended).

BEANS ON FIRE COFFEE

Map p390 (www.thebeansonfire.com; 7 rue du Général Blaise, 11e; ⏰8.30am-5pm Mon-Fri, 9.30am-6pm Sat & Sun; 📶; Ⓜ St-Ambroise) Outstanding coffee is guaranteed at this innovative space. Not only a welcoming local cafe, it's also a collaborative roastery, where movers and shakers on Paris' reignited coffee scene come to roast their beans (ask about two-hour roasting workshops, available in English, if you're keen to roast your own). Overlooking a park, the terrace is a neighbourhood hot spot on sunny days.

CAFÉ CHARBON BAR

Map p390 (www.lecafecharbon.fr; 109 rue Oberkampf, 11e; ⏲8am-2am Mon-Wed, to 5am Thu, to 6am Fri & Sat; 📶; Ⓜ Parmentier) Canopied by a gold-stencilled navy-blue awning, Charbon was the first of the hip bars to catch on in Ménilmontant and it remains one of the best. It's always crowded and worth heading to for the belle époque decor (high ceilings, chandeliers and leather booths) and sociable atmosphere. Happy hour is 5pm to 8pm; DJs and musicians play Friday and Saturday.

THE HOOD CAFE

Map p390 (www.thehoodparis.com; 80 rue Jean-Pierre Timbaud, 11e; ⏲9.30am-5.30pm Mon & Wed-Fri, 10am-6pm Sat & Sun; 📶; Ⓜ Parmentier) First and foremost this light-filled local hangout is about the coffee (Parisian-roasted Belleville Brûlerie beans are brewed to absolute perfection here), but it takes its music just as seriously with a great vinyl collection, spontaneous jam sessions and acoustic Sunday-afternoon 'folkoff' gigs. Fantastic lunches might include cinnamon-roasted chicken with red cabbage and soba noodles. Ask about English-language coffee-brewing workshops.

LA CARAVANE BAR

Map p390 (www.lacaravane.eu; 35 rue de la Fontaine au Roi, 11e; ⏲11am-2am Mon-Sat, from 5pm Sun; 📶; Ⓜ Goncourt) Tucked between République and Oberkampf, this kitsch bar and restaurant is a colourful little jewel; look for the tiny campervan above the window. Lunch with a relaxed local crowd on international burgers (including Thai, French, Mexican and American, plus a veggie burger), or join the after-work party for drinks, DJs and concerts.

LOCAL BREWS

Brasserie BapBap (Map p390; ☎01 77 17 52 97; www.bapbap.paris; 79 rue St-Maur, 11e; guided tours €15; ⏲guided tours 11am Sat, shop 6-8pm Tue-Fri, from 3pm Sat; Ⓜ Rue St-Maur) BapBap, whose name means 'Brassée à Paris, Bue à Paris' (Brewed in Paris, Beloved in Paris; the latter a twist on 'drunk in Paris', as in 'consumed in Paris'), brews craft beer in an iron-girdered 20th-century warehouse turned garage. Saturday brewery visits (one hour, English available; book online) include a peek at the filtering, boiling, whirlpool and fermentation tanks, plus five tastings. Its street-front shop sells its brews and merchandise (T-shirts, beer glasses, bottle openers etc), and has a tasting area. Alternatively, nip into neighbouring Hop Malt Market (Map p390; ☎01 55 28 77 24; 79 rue St-Maur, 11e; ⏲10am-12.30pm & 3pm-midnight; Ⓜ Rue St-Maur) to buy some bottles. Blue-labelled BapBap Originale is a fruity pale ale mixing wheat and barley malts with hops; yellow-labelled Blanc Bec is like an American wheat beer; while red Vertigo is a dry India pale ale (IPA) with lots of fabulous hoppy body.

Balthazar (Map p390; 20 bd Ménilmontant, 20e; ⏲5pm-1.30am Thu-Sat; Ⓜ Père Lachaise) Balthazar's house brews, such as La Vibe (fruity pale ale), La Badas (black IPA), La Pickpocket (a double IPA), L'Ibu Profane (session IPA) and La Tiramistout (milk stout with aromas of coffee and chocolate) rotate on the taps at this crowd-funded microbrewery, along with guest beers from other French breweries including Paris' Outland (p190) and Brasserie la Goutte d'Or (p139). Tasting flights per five/nine beers cost €11/19. There are tables inside the industrial space and out on the pavement beneath a string of multicoloured lights.

La Beer Fabrique (Map p390; ☎01 71 27 71 02; www.labeerfabrique.com; 6 rue Guillaume Bertrand, 11e; 2/4hr brewing course €60/160; ⏲by reservation; Ⓜ Rue St-Maur) During a two-hour course at this brewing school, you'll brew your own beer (and take it away with you, along with three of La Beer Fabrique's own beers), and enjoy six tastings accompanied by charcuterie. Four-hour courses will see you brew 15L of beer that you also get to take with you. Instruction is in English and French. All 24 of its own beers are available for sale. Look out for events such as 'meet the brewers'.

ENTERTAINMENT

Repurposed art-nouveau markets, 19th-century concert halls, jazz cellars and the city's winter circus are all on the bill in this buzzing neighbourhood.

LE BATACLAN LIVE MUSIC

Map p386 (☎01 43 14 00 30; www.bataclan.fr; 50 bd Voltaire, 11e; Ⓜ Oberkampf, Filles du Calvaire) Built in 1864, intimate concert, theatre and dance hall Le Bataclan was Maurice Chevalier's debut venue in 1910. The 1497-capacity venue reopened with a concert by Sting on 12 November 2016, almost a year to the day following the tragic 13 November 2015 terrorist attacks that took place here, and once again hosts French and international rock and pop legends.

L'ALIMENTATION GÉNÉRALE LIVE MUSIC

Map p390 (☎01 43 55 42 50; www.alimentation-generale.net; 64 rue Jean-Pierre Timbaud, 11e; admission Wed, Thu & Sun free, Fri & Sat €10; ⏲7pm-2am Wed, Thu & Sun, to 5am Fri & Sat; Ⓜ Parmentier) This true hybrid, known as the Grocery Store to Anglophones, is a massive space, fronted at street level by its in-house Italianate canteen-bar with big glass windows and retro 1960s Belgian furniture. But music is the big deal here, with an impressive line-up of live gigs and DJs spinning pop, rock, electro, soul and funk to a packed dance floor.

LA MAROQUINERIE LIVE MUSIC

(☎01 40 33 35 05; www.lamaroquinerie.fr; 23 rue Boyer, 20e; ⏲6pm-2am; Ⓜ Gambetta) This tiny but trendy venue in Ménilmontant entices a local crowd with cutting-edge gigs – many bands kick off their European tours here. Past acts have included PJ Harvey, Bruno Mars, Pete Doherty and Coldplay. Also here are an alfresco courtyard and a restaurant with a short but excellent menu.

FAVELA CHIC WORLD MUSIC

Map p386 (☎01 40 21 38 14; www.favelachic.com; 18 rue du Faubourg du Temple, 11e; ⏲7.30pm-2am Tue-Thu, to 5am Fri & Sat; Ⓜ République) Favela Chic starts as a convivial restaurant and then gives way to caipirinha- and mojito-fuelled flirting and dancing (mostly on the long tables). The music is typically bossa nova, samba, *baile* (dance), funk and Brazilian pop, and it can get very crowded and hot.

POP IN LIVE MUSIC

Map p386 (www.popin.fr; 105 rue Amelot, 4e; ⏲6.30pm-1.30am; Ⓜ St-Sébastien–Froissart) Free concerts by local and international artists (mainly rock and indie) kick off from 9pm Monday to Saturday at this laid-back space, while Sundays see open-mic nights from 8.30pm – check the online agenda for upcoming gigs.

LA JAVA WORLD MUSIC

Map p390 (☎01 42 02 20 52; www.la-java.fr; 105 rue du Faubourg du Temple, 11e; concerts free-€10; ⏲8pm-dawn Mon-Sat; Ⓜ Goncourt) Built in 1922, this is the dance hall where Édith Piaf got her first break, and it now reverberates to the sound of live salsa, rock and world music. Live concerts usually take place at 8pm or 9pm during the week. Afterwards a festive crowd gets dancing to electro, house, disco and Latino DJs.

LE VIEUX BELLEVILLE LIVE MUSIC

Map p390 (☎01 44 62 92 66; www.le-vieux-belleville.com; 12 rue des Envierges, 20e; ⏲concerts 8pm-2am Tue & Thu-Sat; Ⓜ Pyrénées) This old-fashioned bistro and *musette* at the top of Parc de Belleville is an atmospheric venue for performances of *chansons* featuring accordions and an organ grinder three times a week. It's a lively favourite with locals, so booking ahead is advised.

NOUVEAU CASINO LIVE MUSIC

Map p390 (☎01 43 57 57 40; www.nouveaucasino.net; 109 rue Oberkampf, 11e; Ⓜ Parmentier) This club-concert annexe of Café Charbon (p174) is revered for its live-music concerts (usually Tuesday, Thursday and Friday) and lively club nights on weekends. Electro, pop, deep house, rock – the program is eclectic, underground and always up to the minute.

CAVE DU 38 RIV' JAZZ

Map p386 (☎01 48 87 56 30; www.38riv.com; 38 rue de Rivoli, 4e; concerts €15-30; ⏲concerts from 8.30pm Mon-Sat, from 5pm Sun; Ⓜ Hôtel de Ville) In the heart of Le Marais on busy rue de Rivoli, a tiny street frontage gives way to a fantastically atmospheric vaulted stone cellar with jazz concerts most nights; check the agenda online. Jam sessions with free admission typically take place on Mondays, Thursdays and Fridays.

CIRQUE D'HIVER BOUGLIONE CIRCUS

Map p386 (☎01 47 00 28 81; www.cirquedhiver.com; 110 rue Amelot, 11e; tickets from €15;

Oct-Mar; Filles du Calvaire) Clowns, trapeze artists and acrobats have entertained children of all ages since 1852 at the city's winter circus on the edge of Le Marais. Performances last around 2½ hours.

The distinctive 20-sided oval polygon building with Corinthian columns was designed by architect Jacques Ignace Hittorff.

SHOPPING

Le Marais has an ever-expanding fashion presence, with tiny ateliers (workshops) and boutiques with rising and just-established designers at work. In the Haut Marais, young designers have colonised the upper reaches of the 3e on and around rue Charlot and rue de Turenne. To the south, in the 4e, rue des Francs Bourgeois and rue François Miron have well-established boutique shopping for clothing, hats, home furnishings and stationery. Place des Vosges is lined with very high-end art and antique galleries. Both areas form one of Paris' ZTIs (international tourist zones) with late-night and Sunday trading.

Le Marais

★MERCI — GIFTS & SOUVENIRS

Map p386 (01 42 77 00 33; www.merci-merci.com; 111 bd Beaumarchais, 3e; 10am-7.30pm; St-Sébastien–Froissart) A Fiat Cinquecento marks the entrance to this unique concept store, which donates all its profits to a children's charity in Madagascar. Shop for fashion, accessories, linens, lamps and nifty designs for the home. Complete the experience with a coffee in its hybrid used-bookshop-cafe, a juice at its **Cinéma Café** (Map p386; 11am-2pm Mon-Sat) or lunch in its stylish **La Cantine de Merci** (Map p386; mains €16-21; 10am-7.30pm).

★EMPREINTES — DESIGN

Map p386 (www.empreintes-paris.com; 5 rue de Picardie, 3e; 11am-7pm Mon-Sat; Temple) Spanning more than 600 sq metres over four floors, this design emporium has over 1000 items for sale at any one time from more than 6000 emerging and established French artists and designers. Handcrafted jewellery, fashion and art are displayed alongside striking homewares (ceramics, cushions, furniture, lighting and more). Upstairs there's a cafe and a reference library. The basement houses a projection room.

★KERZON — HOMEWARES, COSMETICS

Map p386 (www.kerzon.paris; 68 rue de Turenne, 3e; 11.30am-8pm Tue-Sat; St-Sébastien–Froissart) Candles made from natural, biodegradable wax in Parisian scents such as Jardin du Luxembourg (with lilac and honey), Place des Vosges (rose and jasmine) and Parc des Buttes-Chaumont (cedar and sandalwood) make aromatic souvenirs of the city. The pretty white and sage-green boutique also stocks room fragrances, scented laundry liquids, and perfumes, soaps, bath oils and other toiletries.

ANDREA CREWS — FASHION & ACCESSORIES

Map p386 (www.andreacrews.com; 83 rue de Turenne, 3e; 1-7.30pm Wed-Fri, to 7pm Sat; St-Sébastien–Froissart) Using everything from discarded clothing to electrical fittings and household bric-a-brac, this bold art and fashion collective sews, recycles and reinvents to create the most extraordinary pieces. Watch out for 'happenings' in its Marais boutique.

PARIS RENDEZ-VOUS — GIFTS & SOUVENIRS

Map p386 (www.rendezvous.paris.fr; 29 rue de Rivoli, 4e; 10am-7pm Mon-Sat; Hôtel de Ville) This chic city has its own designer line of souvenirs, sold in its own ubercool concept store inside the Hôtel de Ville (town hall). Shop here for everything from clothing and homewares to Paris-themed books, wooden toy sailing boats and signature Jardin du Luxembourg Fermob chairs. *Quel style!*

CANDORA — PERFUME

Map p386 (01 43 48 76 05; www.candora.fr; 1 rue du Pont Louis-Philippe, 4e; 2-7pm Tue-Sat; Pont Marie) At this brother-and-sister-run *parfumerie* near the Seine, you can have bespoke scents made up in just 10 minutes. Or learn how to create fragrances yourself during a perfume-making workshop for adults and children. Workshops in English take place at 2.30pm on Tuesday and Friday and last 90 minutes (€79/54 per adult/child), and include a 15mL bottle.

Private 90-minute courses for two people cost €360.

L'ÉCLAIREUR FASHION & ACCESSORIES

Map p386 (☎01 48 87 10 22; www.leclaireur.com; 40 rue de Sévigné, 3e; ⊙11am-7pm Mon-Sat, from 2pm Sun; ⓂSt-Paul) Part art space, part lounge and part deconstructionist fashion statement, this shop is known for having the next big thing first. Two tons of wooden planks, 147 TV screens and walls that move to reveal the men's and women's collection all form part of the stunning interior design by Belgian artist Arne Quinze.

LES PETITS BLA-BLAS CHILDREN'S CLOTHING

Map p386 (Atelier Pascaline Delcourt; www.facebook.com/atelierpascalinedelcourt; 7 rue de Crussol, 11e; ⊙11am-7pm Mon-Fri; ⓂFilles du Calvaire) At her 11e *atelier* (workshop), Pascaline Delcourt makes children's clothing (up to six years), bibs, bags and onesies, and also stocks children's jewellery, toys, paper animal lanterns and soft cuddly toys. A personalisation service lets you add a name, date of birth or message to individual items.

EDWART CHOCOLATE

Map p386 (www.edwart.fr; 17 rue Vielle du Temple, 4e; ⊙11am-noon & 1-8pm Mon-Wed, 11am-8pm Thu-Sun; ⓂHôtel de Ville) Wunderkind chocolatiers Edwin Yansané and Arthur Heinze (collectively 'Edwart') take their inspiration from Paris (and – as a global melting pot – by extension, the world). Feisty chocolates using unique ingredients such as Indian curry, Iranian saffron and Japanese whisky are sparingly displayed in their sleek Marais boutique.

SUPERFLY RECORDS MUSIC

Map p386 (www.superflyrecords.com; 53 rue Notre Dame de Nazareth, 3e; ⊙noon-8pm Tue-Sat; ⓂStrasbourg–St-Denis) Rare Japanese jazz, Nigerian funk, Kenyan rock, Ivory Coast reggae, West African folk and some truly obscure film soundtracks are among the diverse genres that turn up in this small space, thanks to Superfly's rotating stock and its own reissues label. Vinyl is decently priced (with bargain crates) and DJs often play.

BHV DEPARTMENT STORE

Map p386 (www.bhv.fr; 52 rue de Rivoli, 4e; ⊙9.30am-8pm Mon-Sat, 11am-7.30pm Sun; ⓂHôtel de Ville) BHV (pronounced bay-ash-vay) is a vast, straightforward department store in Le Marais where you can buy everything from guidebooks on Paris to men's, women's and kids' clothing and accessories, stationery, luggage and every imaginable type of hammer, power tool, nail, plug and hinge.

Drinking and dining options include a rooftop cocktail bar, and a covered courtyard with street-food stalls.

LOCAL KNOWLEDGE

CULTURAL CENTRES

Look out for exhibitions, concerts, workshops and a diverse range of other events at the following cultural centres:

Le Carreau du Temple (Map p386; ☎01 83 81 93 30; www.carreaudutemple.eu; 2 rue Perrée, 3e; ⊙box office 10am-9pm Mon-Fri, to 7pm Sat; ⓂTemple) In an art nouveau former covered market.

Gaîté Lyrique (Map p386; ☎01 53 01 51 51; www.gaite-lyrique.net; 3bis rue Papin, 3e; exhibitions from €6, concerts vary; ⊙2-9pm Tue-Sat, noon-6pm Sun; ⓂRéaumur–Sébastopol) Has art installations and a video-game room.

La Bellevilloise (☎01 46 36 07 07; www.labellevilloise.com; 19-21 rue Boyer, 20e; ⊙7pm-1am Wed & Thu, to 2am Fri, 11am-2am Sat, 11.30am-midnight Sun; ⓂGambetta) Vibrant centre in Ménilmontant.

VILLAGE ST-PAUL ANTIQUES, DESIGN

Map p386 (www.levillagesaintpaul.com; rue St-Paul, rue des Jardins St-Paul & rue Charlemagne, 4e; ⊙individual shop hours vary; ⓂSt-Paul) It's quiet on weekdays, but come the weekend these five cobbled courtyards, refashioned in the 1970s from the 14th-century walled gardens of King Charles V, are filled with shoppers. Meander away an afternoon on a stroll of the courtyards' 80-plus artisan boutiques, galleries and antique shops.

LA BOUTIQUE EXTRAORDINAIRE FASHION & ACCESSORIES

Map p386 (www.laboutiqueextraordinaire.com; 67 rue Charlot, 3e; ⊙11am-8pm Tue-Sat, 3-7pm Sun; ⓂFilles du Calvaire) Mohair, silk, llama, camel, yak and other natural, organic and ethical materials are hand-knitted into exquisite garments, almost too precious to wear, at this unusual and captivating Haut Marais boutique.

BONTON CHILDREN, FASHION

Map p386 (www.bonton.fr; 5 bd des Filles du Calvaire, 3e; ⏲10am-7pm Mon-Sat; Ⓜ St-Sébastien–Froissart) Chic concept store Bonton stocks vintage-inspired fashion, furnishings and knick-knacks for babies, toddlers and children. Don't leave without donning an old-fashioned, floppy sunhat or pair of oversized sunglasses and getting your photo snapped in its retro photo booth. Parents will find a bathroom with a changing mat in the basement.

MÉLODIES GRAPHIQUES STATIONERY

Map p386 (10 rue du Pont Louis-Philippe, 4e; ⏲2-7pm Mon, from 11am Tue-Sat; Ⓜ Pont Marie) On a street renowned for its fine paper and stationery boutiques, Mélodies Graphiques' soundtrack of classical music makes it an especially charming spot to browse its exquisite range of paper, notebooks, greeting cards, bookmarks, sealing wax, ink and calligraphy pens. Owner-calligraphist Eric de Tugny is also an entomologist and sells his intricate insect illustrations in store.

ODETTA VINTAGE VINTAGE

Map p386 (www.odettavintage.com; 76 rue des Tournelles, 3e; ⏲2-7.30pm Tue-Sat; Ⓜ Chemin Vert) Behind its bright white façade, this boutique specialises in luxury vintage from the 1960s to 1980s: women's shoes, accessories and clothing fashion, as well as the odd piece of remarkable vintage furniture. If you're going to find a runway sample, it's here.

L'HABILLEUR FASHION & ACCESSORIES

Map p386 (www.habilleur.fr; 44 rue de Poitou, 3e; ⏲noon-7pm Mon-Sat; Ⓜ St-Sébastien–Froissart) Discount men's and women's designer wear – 50% to 70% off original prices – is the draw of this veteran boutique. It generally stocks last season's collections.

MARIAGE FRÈRES DRINKS

Map p386 (www.mariagefreres.com; 30, 32 & 35 rue du Bourg Tibourg, 4e; ⏲10am-8pm; Ⓜ Hôtel de Ville) Founded in 1854, Paris' first and arguably finest tea shop has more than 500 varieties of tea sourced from some 35 countries. On the same street there's a **tearoom** (kitchen noon to 7pm), where you can sample its teas along with light dishes, and a tiny **tea museum** (admission free, 10.30am to noon and 3pm to 5pm Thursday to Saturday).

SAMUEL CORAUX JEWELLERY

Map p386 (www.samuelcoraux.paris; 18 rue Ste-Anastase, 3e; ⏲10am-5.30pm Mon-Fri, 11am-7pm Sat & Sun; Ⓜ St-Sébastien–Froissart) The stark black façade at this hybrid boutique-workshop provides a dramatic contrast to the brilliantly coloured, contemporary creations crafted inside by film producer-director-turned-jewellery designer Samuel Coraux using materials such as Murano glass and shiny plastic.

ÉTAT LIBRE D'ORANGE PERFUME

Map p386 (www.etatlibredorange.com; 69 rue des Archives, 3e; ⏲noon-7.30pm Mon-Sat; Ⓜ Arts et Métiers) With scents bearing names such as Fat Electrician, Jasmin et Cigarette, Malaise of the 1970s and Delicious Closet Queen, there really is something for everyone at this Marais perfumery.

BRING FRANCE HOME GIFTS & SOUVENIRS

Map p386 (☎09 81 64 91 09; www.bringfrancehome.com; 3 rue de Birague, 4e; ⏲11am-7pm; Ⓜ Bastille) All of the quality items in this terrific little shop are made in France: jewellery, perfume, cards, tea towels, plates, posters, board games, *pétanque* sets, speciality foodstuffs such as foie gras, tinned sardines, Parisian honey, beer and absinthe kits, and much more. If you don't want to be laden down with shopping bags, purchases can be delivered to your hotel.

JAMIN PUECH FASHION & ACCESSORIES

Map p386 (www.jamin-puech.com; 68 rue Vieille du Temple, 4e; ⏲10am-7.30pm Mon-Sat, 1-7pm Sun; Ⓜ Chemin Vert) Established by former theatre and opera costume designers Isabelle Puech and Benoît Jamin, who trained together in Paris, this design house creates beautiful handbags in all manner of bold colours, textures and textiles. For vintage pieces from the 1990s, head to the couple's first boutique at 61 rue d'Hauteville, 10e.

CHEZ HÉLÈNE FOOD

Map p386 (www.chezhelene-paris.com; 28 rue St-Gilles, 3e; ⏲11am-2pm & 3-7.30pm Mon-Fri, 11am-2pm & 2.30-7.30pm Sat; Ⓜ Chemin Vert) This irresistible *bonbon* (sweet) boutique is filled with old-fashioned toffees and caramels, fudge, liquorice, Eiffel Tower sugar cubes, designer lollipops, artisanal marshmallows and Provençal *calissons*. The choice of quality *bonbons* and *gourmandises* (sweet treats) is outstanding.

Ménilmontant & Belleville

★FROMAGERIE GONCOURT — CHEESE

Map p390 (01 43 57 91 28; 1 rue Abel Rabaud, 11e; 9am-1pm & 4-8.30pm Tue-Fri, 9am-8pm Sat; Goncourt) Styled like a boutique, this contemporary *fromagerie* is a must-discover. Clément Brossault ditched a career in banking to become a *fromager* and his cheese selection – 70-plus types – is superb. Cheeses flagged with a bicycle symbol are varieties he discovered in situ during a two-month French cheese tour he embarked on as part of his training.

LA CAVE LE VERRE VOLÉ — WINE

Map p390 (www.leverrevole.fr; 38 rue Oberkampf, 11e; 4-8.30pm Mon, 10am-1pm & 4-8.30pm Tue-Sat; Oberkampf) One of Paris' largest collections of natural wines is stocked at this wondrous wine shop. Its famous bistro (p140) is located by Canal St-Martin, and its **épicerie** (Map p390; 01 48 05 36 55; www.leverrevole.fr; 54 rue de la Folie Méricourt, 11e; 2-course lunch menus €9.90, sandwiches €4.90-6.90; 11am-2.30pm & 4.30-8pm Mon & Fri, 11am-8pm Tue-Thu & Sat; ; Oberkampf), where for €7 corkage you can drink bottles purchased here while dining on deli platters and gourmet sandwiches, is just around the corner.

KOCHÉ — FASHION & ACCESSORIES

Map p390 (01 71 27 66 10; www.koche.fr; 8 Cité du Labyrinthe, 20e; by appointment; Ménilmontant) Koché, with an atelier far from the madding fashion crowd in edgy Ménilmontant and rapidly rising designer Christelle Kocher at the helm, continues to rock Paris Fashion Week. Contemporary street art and traditional French craftsmanship heavily influence the funky, ready-to-wear street gear that mixes denim, jersey and other easy fabrics with elaborately crocheted feathers, chiffon, beads and sequins.

BELLEVILLE BRÛLERIE — COFFEE

Map p390 (09 83 75 60 80; http://cafesbelleville.com; 10 rue Pradier, 19e; 11.30am-6.30pm Sat; Pyrénées) With its understated steel-grey façade, this ground-breaking roastery in Belleville is easy to miss. Don't! Belleville Brûlerie brought good coffee to Paris and its beans go into some of the best espressos in town. Taste the week's selection, compare tasting notes, and buy a bag to take home.

MADE BY MOI — FASHION, HOMEWARES

Map p390 (01 58 30 95 78; www.madebymoi.fr; 86 rue Oberkampf, 11e; 2.30-8pm Mon, from 10am Tue-Sat, 2.30-7pm Sun; Parmentier) 'Made by Me', aka handmade, is the driver of this appealing boutique on trendy rue Oberkampf – a perfect address to buy unusual gifts, from women's fashion to homewares such as 'Bobo brunch' scented candles by Bougies La Française and other beautiful objects such as coloured glass carafes, feathered headdresses, funky contact-lens boxes and retro dial telephones.

SPORTS & ACTIVITIES

NOMADESHOP — SKATING

Map p386 (01 44 54 07 44; www.nomadeshop.com; 37 bd Bourdon, 4e; half-/full-day skate rental from €5/8; 11am-1.30pm & 2.30-7.30pm Tue-Fri, 10am-7pm Sat, noon-6pm Sun Apr-Oct, closed Sun Nov-Mar; Bastille) Nomadeshop rents and sells inline equipment and accessories, including wheels, helmets, elbow and knee guards; a rental deposit of €150 is required. One-hour group/private skating lessons cost €18/40; 48 hours' notice is required.

ROLLERS & COQUILLAGES — SKATING

(www.rollers-coquillages.org; place de la Bastille; 2.30pm Sun; Bastille) This inline skating club organises a weekly three-hour 'Randonnée en Rollers' (a 17km to 23km skate around town), departing from place de la Bastille. Rent skates from the adjacent Nomadeshop.

Bastille & Eastern Paris

Neighbourhood Top Five

❶ **Opéra Bastille** (p191) Taking in a backstage tour and opera, ballet or concert recital at this modern monolith, on the landmark square where revolutionaries stormed the Bastille in 1789.

❷ **Promenade Plantée** (p182) Joining Parisians for a jog or stroll along the foliage-laced path of this elevated city park, uniquely at home atop a 19th-century railway viaduct.

❸ **Château de Vincennes** (p183) Exploring Paris' only medieval castle, complete with a prerequisite keep and a sublime 16th-century royal chapel.

❹ **Parc Zoologique de Paris** (p183) Spotting lions, white rhinos, giraffes and wolverines through camouflaged spy towers at the city's state-of-the-art zoo in Bois de Vincennes.

❺ **Cinémathèque Française** (p182) Catching timeless cinematic classics at this little-known cinema museum and complex.

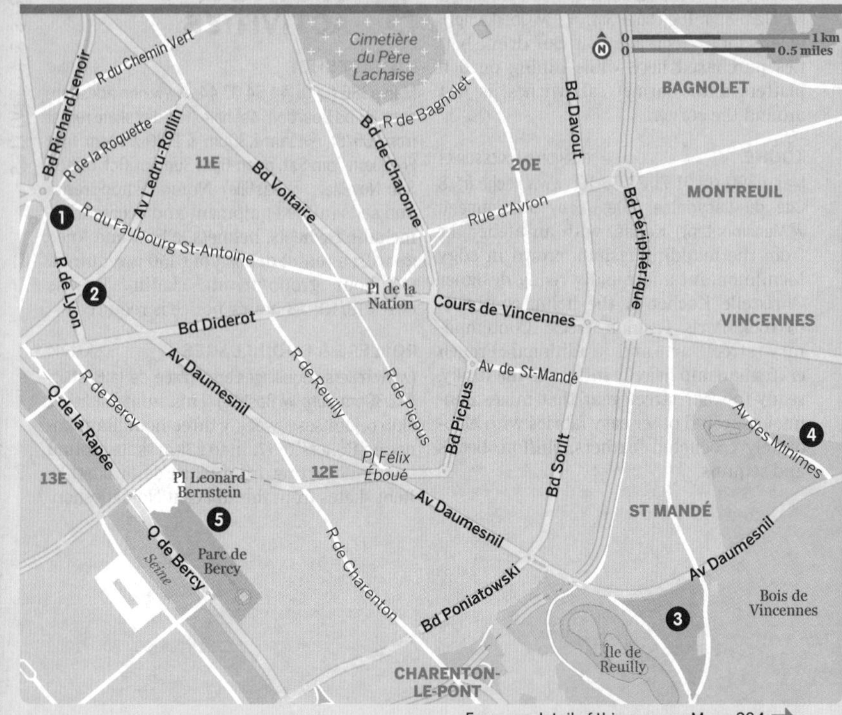

For more detail of this area see Map p394

Explore Bastille & Eastern Paris

Bastille isn't known for its sights, but it's nonetheless a fascinating area to explore on foot. As it's still residential in most parts, a wander will give you a taste of everyday life in one of Paris' most dynamic neighbourhoods. For a bird's eye perspective, ascend to elevated park Promenade Plantée, which looks down on the surrounding streets.

A dramatic facelift to place de la Bastille will see it linked to the boat-filled Port de l'Arsenal marina by a 1.1-hectare 'pedestrian peninsula' and reduce vehicle traffic by 40% by mid-2019. Yet Bastille's main attraction is not aimless *flâneurie* (urban strolling): the area's real appeal is dipping your toes into a vibrant restaurant scene dominated by young, creative chefs; its scores of popular, inexpensive bars and cafes; and the profusion of evening entertainment, from avant-garde opera to indie rock.

You may be reluctant to leave the city behind with so much to explore, but an easy trip to the Bois de Vincennes, the city's largest park, never disappoints. It's one of the most-loved spots in the capital to unwind alfresco.

Local Life

➡ **Bistros** The 11e and 12e have an unusually high number of old-school bistros that have preserved much of their original decor, such as the venerable Chez Paul (p187) and vaunted Le Chardenoux (p189).

➡ **Markets** Fabulous markets include classic Parisian street markets like the Marché Bastille (p184) and Marché d'Aligre (p186).

➡ **Cultural hub** An urban garden, workshops, studios, food trucks, buses and trains, and a bevy of bars sprawl over industrial site Ground Control (p182).

➡ **Green spaces** The Promenade Plantée (p182) and Parc de Bercy (p184) are easy escapes; on weekends many Parisians decamp to the much larger Bois de Vincennes (p183), with the beautifully landscaped family favourite Parc Floral de Paris (p183) at its heart.

Getting There & Away

➡ **Metro** Lines 1, 5 and 8 serve Bastille; lines 1 and 8 are major east–west arteries, while line 5 heads south across the Seine and north to the Gare du Nord. Line 14 links Bercy with St-Lazare in the northwest and the 13e in southeastern Paris.

➡ **RER** The east–west RER A stops at Nation and Gare de Lyon en route to central and western Paris, while RER D links Gare de Lyon with Gare du Nord.

➡ **Bicycle** Find Vélib' stations around place de la Bastille on bd Richard Lenoir, bd Bourdon and rue de Lyon.

Lonely Planet's Top Tip

While the area immediately surrounding the Bastille has spawned a clutch of faceless bars and restaurant chains, walking east along rue de Charonne or rue du Faubourg St-Antoine to Ledru-Rollin and Faidherbe-Chaligny brings you to a much more interesting neighbourhood, filled with all the exciting dining addresses, atmospheric cafes and quirky, unusual shops that make a city great.

Best Places to Eat

➡ Septime (p188)
➡ Le Servan (p186)
➡ Le Chardenoux (p189)
➡ Buffet (p187)
➡ CheZaline (p185)

For reviews, see p184 ➡

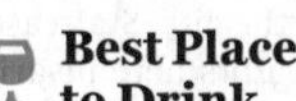

Best Places to Drink

➡ Le Baron Rouge (p189)
➡ Concrete (p189)
➡ Septime La Cave (p188)
➡ Bluebird (p190)
➡ Outland (p190)

For reviews, see p189 ➡

Best Shopping

➡ La Manufacture de Chocolat (p192)
➡ Marché aux Puces d'Aligre (p186)
➡ Viaduc des Arts (p192)
➡ La Cocotte (p192)
➡ So We Are (p192)

For reviews, see p192 

SIGHTS

Historic place de la Bastille – at the intersection of the 4e, 11e and 12e *arrondissements,* and being transformed from a busy roundabout into a much more pedestrian-friendly zone by mid-2019 – is the obvious place to start exploring. Take a waterside stroll south along the city's only pleasure port, Port de l'Arsenal. Southeast of here is the busy Gare de Lyon station area, with the unusual Promenade Plantée, which can be followed on foot for 4.5km to Bois de Vincennes on the far eastern fringe of this neighbourhood. Several key sights are clustered in and around the green urban woodland.

PROMENADE PLANTÉE — PARK

Map p394 (La Coulée Verte René-Dumont; cnr rue de Lyon & av Daumesnil, 12e; ⌚8am-9.30pm Mon-Fri, from 9am Sat & Sun Mar-Oct, 8am-5.30pm Mon-Fri, from 9am Sat & Sun Nov-Feb; Ⓜ Bastille, Gare de Lyon, Daumesnil) The disused 19th-century Vincennes railway viaduct was reborn as the world's first elevated park, planted with a fragrant profusion of cherry trees, maples, rose trellises, bamboo corridors and lavender. Three storeys above ground, it provides a unique aerial vantage point on the city. Staircases provide access (lifts/elevators here invariably don't work). Along the first, northwestern section, above av Daumesnil, art-gallery workshops beneath the arches form the Viaduc des Arts (p192).

Waking southeast, look out for the spectacular art-deco-style police station at the start of rue de Rambouillet, which was built in 1991 and is topped with a dozen huge, identical telamones (male figures used as pillars) based on Michelangelo's *Dying Slave.*

The viaduct later drops back to street level at Jardin de Reuilly (1.5km); it's possible to follow it all the way (4.5km) to the Bois de Vincennes (p183). This latter section can also be done on a bike or in-line skates. A small section of the former **Petite Ceinture** (PC 12; 21 rue Rottembourg, 12e; ⌚8am-sunset Mar-Oct, from 9am Nov-Feb; Ⓜ Michel Bizot) railway line is accessible from here, and a larger section is due to open by 2020.

GROUND CONTROL — ARTS CENTRE

Map p394 (www.groundcontrolparis.com; 81 rue du Charolais, 12e; ⌚noon-midnight Wed-Fri, 11am-midnight Sat, 11am-10pm Sun; Ⓜ Gare de Lyon) An industrial area that once housed a postal sorting centre was transformed into a pop-up cultural space and will now operate year-round until at least 2020. Spread across a 4500-sq-metre hall and 1500-sq-metre terrace are an urban kitchen garden with gardening workshops, a plant shop and veggie stand, yoga, reiki and meditation classes, 19 bars, cafes and restaurants (some inside old buses and trains), 13 shops and galleries, DJ sets, live-music gigs and kids' play areas.

Globe-spanning food options include a Danish salmon smokery, a crêperie, a burger bar, a fish and chips shack, a bakery, an empanada truck and Mexican, African, Italian and Chinese eateries; bars include a speakeasy, a wine bar and a craft-beer bar. A bookshop, curiosity bric-a-brac shop and photography studio can also be found here.

CINÉMATHÈQUE FRANÇAISE — MUSEUM

(☎01 71 19 33 33; www.cinematheque.fr; 51 rue de Bercy, 12e; adult/child €5/2.50, with film €8; ⌚noon-7pm Wed-Mon; Ⓜ Bercy) A little-known gem near Parc de Bercy, the Cinémathèque Française was originally created in 1936 by film archivist Henri Langlois. Devoted to the history of cinema, the permanent collection contains costumes, props (including some from Méliès' classic *A Trip to the Moon,* featured in *Hugo*), early equipment, old advertising posters and short clips of a few classics. Temporary exhibitions usually take a behind-the-scenes look at a particular film. Enter via place Léonard-Bernstein by the park. Its cinema (p191) screens up to 10 films daily.

OPÉRA BASTILLE — NOTABLE BUILDING

Map p394 (☎within France 08 92 89 90 90; www.operadeparis.fr; 2-6 place de la Bastille, 12e; Ⓜ Bastille) Designed by architect Carlos Ott, this concrete, glass and steel opera house (p191) is Paris' largest, with a 2745-seat main auditorium. During his presidency, François Mitterrand instigated its creation as one of his *grands projets* (great projects), and inaugurated it on 13 July 1989, the eve of the 200th anniversary of the storming of the Bastille prison. The date was symbolic as the new opera house was intended to strip opera of its elitist airs.

Guided tours lasting 1½ hours (in French; September to mid-July) take you behind the scenes. Tour schedules are online; the box office sells tickets (guided tours adult/child €15/11) 10 minutes beforehand.

WORTH A DETOUR

BOIS DE VINCENNES

Originally royal hunting grounds, Paris' eastern woodlands, **Bois de Vincennes** (bd Poniatowski, 12e; MPorte de Charenton, Porte Dorée), were annexed by the army following the Revolution and then donated to the city in 1860 by Napoléon III. A fabulous place to escape the endless stretches of Parisian concrete, the woods also contain a handful of notable sights, and are close to the **Musée de l'Histoire de l'Immigration** (www.histoire-immigration.fr; 293 av Daumesnil, 12e; adult/child €4.50/free, 1st Sun of month free, with Aquarium Tropical €8; 10am-5.30pm Tue-Fri, to 7pm Sat & Sun; MPorte Dorée) and **Aquarium Tropical** (www.aquarium-portedoree.fr; 293 av Daumesnil, 12e; adult/child €5/3.50, with Musée de l'Histoire de l'Immigration €8; 10am-5.30pm Tue-Fri, to 7pm Sat & Sun; MPorte Dorée).

Metro lines 1 (St-Mandé, Château de Vincennes) and 8 (Porte Dorée, Porte de Charenton) will get you to the edges of the park. Pick up picnic supplies on rue de Midi, Vincennes' main shopping street.

Château de Vincennes (01 48 08 31 20; www.chateau-de-vincennes.fr; 1 av de Paris, Vincennes; adult/child €9/free; 10am-6pm mid-May–mid-Sep, to 5pm mid-Sep–mid-May; MChâteau de Vincennes) This fortified royal residence on Paris' fringe, originally a 12th-century hunting lodge, was expanded several times throughout the centuries until it reached its present size under Louis XIV. Notable features of the striking medieval château include the beautiful 52m-high keep (1370) and royal chapel (1552). Note that the chapel is only open between 10.30am and 1pm, and 2pm and 5.30pm mid-May to mid-September (until 4.30pm mid-September to mid-May).

Parc Zoologique de Paris (Zoo de Vincennes; 08 11 22 41 22; www.parczoologiquedeparis.fr; cnr av Daumesnil & rte de Ceinture du Lac Daumesnil, 12e; adult/child €22/16.50; 9.30am-8.30pm May-Aug, shorter hours Sep-Apr; MPorte Dorée) Paris' largest, state-of-the-art zoo focuses on the conservation of species and habitats, with camouflaged vantage points (no peering through fences). Its biozones include Patagonia (sea lions, pumas); the Sahel-Sudan savannah (lions, white rhinos, giraffes); forested Europe (wolves, lynxes, wolverines); rainforested Amazon-Guyana (jaguars, monkeys, anacondas); and Madagascar (lemurs). Tickets are slightly cheaper online.

Parc Floral de Paris (01 49 57 24 81; www.parcfloraldeparisjeux.com; Esplanade du Chateau de Vincennes or rte de la Pyramide; adult/child €2.50/1.50; 9.30am-8pm Apr-Sep, to 6.30pm Oct, to 5pm Nov-Feb, to 6.30pm Mar; MChâteau de Vincennes) This magnificent botanical park is a highlight of the Bois de Vincennes. Natural landscaping, a Japanese bonsai pavilion, an azalea garden and several ponds with water lilies and lotuses impress garden lovers, while Paris' largest play area (slides, jungle gyms, sandboxes) thrills families with young children. For bigger kids, there are plenty of paid-for activities too, including minigolf, a ropes course and table tennis (equipment rental available). Free open-air concerts staged throughout summer make it a first-rate picnic destination. Not all facilities open outside the warmer months.

Lac Daumesnil (01 43 28 19 20; rte de Ceinture du Lac Daumesnil, 20e, Bois de Vincennes; hourly boat hire for 2-/4-person boat €12.80/13.80; boat hire 10am-1hr before dark mid-Feb–mid-Nov; MPorte Dorée) Like something out of a Renoir painting, the largest lake in Bois de Vincennes is a popular destination for walks and rowboat excursions in warmer months (cash only; €20 deposit required). A Buddhist temple is nearby.

Hippodrome de Vincennes (01 49 77 17 17; www.vincennes-hippodrome.com; 2 rte de la Ferme, 12e; adult/child €3/free; ; MChâteau de Vincennes or RER Joinville-le-Pont) First opened in 1863 and rebuilt in 1879 following the Franco-Prussian War, this hippodrome hosts horse races and trotting races. Binoculars are available for rent. Free shuttle buses run from the metro and RER stations.

PARC DE BERCY PARK

(rues Paul Belmondo, de l'Ambriosie & François Truffaut, 12e; ⌚8am-sunset Mar-Oct, from 9am Nov-Feb; Ⓜ Cour St-Émilion, Bercy) Built on the site of a former wine depot, this large, landscaped park is a great place to break for a picnic and let the kids run free. Vestiges of its former incarnation are spread across the park and the Cour St-Émilion, where the warehouses were located. In some spots you'll see the old railroad tracks; in others you'll find grape vines.

Bercy reached its height as the 'world's wine cellar' in the 19th century: it was right on the Seine, close to Paris yet outside the city walls, meaning that shipping was convenient and commerce tax-free.

RUE CRÉMIEUX STREET

Map p394 (12e; Ⓜ Quai de la Rapée, Gare de Lyon) Like something out of a fairy tale, this photogenic pedestrian cobbled street stretching just 158m from rue de Bercy to rue de Lyon is lined with shutter-framed houses painted in a rainbow of pastel hues – pink, tangerine, lemon, lime, pale blue and lilac – and trompe l'œil effects such as vines clambering up the façades. It's often used as a backdrop for fashion and advertising shoots, but be respectful of its residents when taking photos.

PLACE DE LA BASTILLE SQUARE

Map p394 (12e; Ⓜ Bastille) A 14th-century fortress built to protect the city gates, the Bastille became a prison under Cardinal Richelieu, which was mobbed on 14 July 1789, igniting the French Revolution. At the centre of the square is the 52m-high **Colonne de Juillet** (Map p394; www.colonne-de-juillet.fr) a green-bronze column topped by a gilded, winged Liberty. Revolutionaries from the uprising of 1830 are buried beneath; the crypt will open to the public as part of a major redevelopment that will link the square to Bassin de l'Arsenal.

As part of the works, which are due for completion in 2019, the location of the old fortress prison of the Bastille will be marked on the ground (currently you can see a triple row of paving stones that traces the building's outline on the ground between bd Henri IV and rue St-Antoine). The foundations are also marked below ground in the Bastille metro station, on the platform of line 5. When complete, the square's overhaul will reduce traffic by 40%, making it pedestrian- and cyclist-friendly.

EATING

Bastille dining tends to swing between a highly lauded group of up-and-coming chefs, who run the hip new neobistros that have reinspired Parisian cooking, and the die-hard traditionalists, who rarely venture beyond the much-loved standards of French cuisine. The neighbourhood caters to all budgets, tastes and time constraints – along with the area's sensational markets, speciality food shops and *boulangeries* (bakeries), you'll find gourmet burger, sandwich and pizza addresses in the mix too.

MARCHÉ BASTILLE MARKET €

Map p394 (bd Richard Lenoir, 11e; ⌚7am-2.30pm Thu, to 3pm Sun; Ⓜ Bastille, Bréguet–Sabin) If you only get to one open-air street market in Paris, this one – stretching between the Bastille and Richard Lenoir metro stations – is among the very best. Its 150-plus stalls are piled high with fruit and vegetables, meats, fish, shellfish, cheeses and seasonal specialities such as truffles. You'll also find clothing, leather handbags and wallets, and a smattering of antiques.

MOKONUTS CAFE €

Map p394 (☎09 80 81 82 85; 5 rue St-Bernard, 11e; dishes €2-3.50, mains €7-18; ⌚8.45am-6pm Mon-Fri, closed Aug; 📶🌱; Ⓜ Faidherbe-Chaligny) Much-loved hole-in-the-wall Mokonuts, with a beautiful mosaic-tiled floor, makes a cosy refuge for snacks like flourless chocolate layer cake, clementine almond cake and pecan pie. Other treats include white-chocolate and roasted-almond cookies, while sea bream with chickpeas and capers, and lamb shoulder with hummus are among the all-organic lunchtime mains. Natural wines and craft beers feature on the drinks list.

CAFÉ MIRABELLE CAFE €

Map p394 (https://cafemirabelleparis.wixsite.com; 16 rue la Vacquerie, 11e; dishes €2-7.50; ⌚8am-6pm Wed-Fri, from 9am Sat & Sun; 📶; Ⓜ Philippe Auguste, Voltaire) A black-and-white stencilled outline of Paris' skyline stretches across one wall of this charming cafe, whose home-baked treats include custard- and banana-filled croissants, Grand Marnier gateau and lemon meringue pie. Its *gianduja* (choc-hazelnut) hot chocolate is a winter warmer; in summer, cool down with a freshly squeezed juice. Granola with seasonal berries makes a great start to the day.

NANINA CHEESE €

Map p394 (☎06 12 67 04 76; 24bis rue Basfroi, 11e; 3-course lunch menu €11.50, dishes €2.50-9; ⏰10am-8.30pm Mon-Thu, to 10pm Fri & Sat; Ⓜ Voltaire) Nanina's creamy mozzarella and ricotta, made from Auvergne-sourced buffalo milk and handmade here on the premises, supply some of Paris' most prestigious restaurants. You can taste the cheeses here on their own, on focaccia bread, or as part of a lunch *menu* that might include lasagne or pasta. Staff are happy to show you around and explain the cheese-making process.

CHEZALINE SANDWICHES €

Map p394 (85 rue de la Roquette, 11e; sandwiches €5.50-8.50; ⏰11am-5.30pm Mon-Fri; Ⓜ Voltaire) A former horse-meat butcher's shop (*chevaline,* hence the spin on the name; look for the gold horse head above the door) is now a fabulous deli for baguettes filled with ingredients such as Prince de Paris ham and house-made garlic pesto, salads and home-made terrines. There's a handful of seats (and plenty of parks nearby). Prepare to queue at lunchtime.

LE BAR À SOUPES SOUP €

Map p394 (www.lebarasoupes.com; 33 rue de Charonne, 11e; soups €4.80-6.40, 2-course lunch menu €13.50; ⏰noon-3pm & 6.30-10.30pm Mon-Sat; ✎; Ⓜ Ledru-Rollin) With six different soups served daily, chances are you'll find something here to warm you up. Choices might include leek, potato and chorizo, pumpkin-chestnut borscht, cauliflower and Bleu d'Auvergne cheese, and the vodka-laced Bloody Mary. There's a handful of tables; otherwise pick up a steaming cup to take away.

LE GRAND BRÉGUET CAFE €

Map p394 (☎09 70 75 54 59; 14 rue Bréguet, 11e; 2-course menus €9-11; ⏰8am-2am Mon-Sat, 9am-midnight Sun; 📶✎; Ⓜ Bréguet–Sabin) Adjoining a courtyard terrace, this vast, contemporary canteen-style space centres on an island kitchen. Many of its all-organic dishes are vegetarian or vegan, with plenty of gluten-free options. Rotating art on the walls is for sale, as is all of the furniture and lighting. Look out for regular live music and DJs.

Its on-site grocery sells local organic produce; yoga classes take place on weekends.

LES DOMAINES QUI MONTENT FRENCH €

Map p394 (☎01 43 56 89 15; www.lesdomainesquimontent.com; 136 bd Voltaire, 11e; 2-course lunch menu €16.60; ⏰kitchen noon-3pm Mon-Sat, shop 10.30am-7.30pm Mon, 10am-8pm Tue-Thu, 10am-8.30pm Fri & Sat; Ⓜ Voltaire) Les Domaines Qui Montent was around before the *cave à manger* trend began, and while it's not as trendy as most newcomers, it is very much the real thing. Above all a wine shop, it offers simple two-course lunch *menus* made from premium ingredients like smoked black Bigorre pork sausage that you can pair with any of its available bottles.

L'ENCRIER BISTRO €

Map p394 (☎01 44 68 08 16; www.lencrierrestaurant.com; 55 rue Traversière, 12e; 2-/3-course lunch menus €13.50/15.50, dinner menus €17.50/21.50; ⏰noon-2.15pm & 7.30-11pm Mon-Fri, 7.30-11pm Sat; Ⓜ Ledru-Rollin) Especially at lunch, the 'Inkwell' draws in the crowds with its open kitchen, large picture window and great-value prices. Generously sized traditional French dishes range from steak with Roquefort sauce or delicate pig's cheeks with spices to honey-marinated duck.

CRÊPERIE BRETONNE FLEURIE DE L'EPOUSE DU MARIN CRÊPES €

Map p394 (☎01 43 55 62 29; 67 rue de Charonne, 11e; crêpes €4.50-11.20, 2-course weekday lunch menu €13; ⏰noon-2.15pm & 7-11.15pm Mon-Fri, 7-11.15pm Sat; Ⓜ Charonne) Authentic down to its savoury buckwheat *galettes* and sweet crêpes smothered with fillings such as chestnut puree and caramelised hazelnut, this delightful Breton crêperie with a sky-blue façade, half-timbered walls and lace curtains is filled with emotive black-and-white photos of Brittany. Joy of joys, it even serves dry Val de Rance cider. *Yec'hed mat* (cheers)!

LES GALOPINS BISTRO €

Map p394 (☎01 47 00 45 35; 24 rue des Taillandiers, 11e; 2-/3-course lunch menus €13/16.50, mains €15.50-19.50; ⏰noon-2.30pm & 7.30-11pm Mon-Fri, 7.30-11.30pm Sat & Sun; Ⓜ Bastille) Vintage posters on the walls give a retro ambience to this warm and buzzing bistro filled with locals feasting on huge platefuls of traditional French country fare. Hearty appetites should order the *côté de bœuf* (rib steak) served with Béarnaise sauce or *épaule d'agneau* (lamb shoulder) for two. Staff go out of their way to please.

LOCAL KNOWLEDGE

MARCHÉ D'ALIGRE

A favourite with chefs and locals, the stalls of chaotic **Marché d'Aligre** (Map p394; rue d'Aligre, 12e; ⌚8am-1pm Tue-Sun; Ⓜ Ledru-Rollin) are piled with fruit, vegetables and seasonal delicacies such as truffles. Behind them, specialist shops stock cheeses, coffee, chocolates, meat, seafood and wine. More are located in the adjoining covered market hall, **Marché Beauvau** (Map p394; place d'Aligre, 12e; ⌚9am-2pm & 4-7.30pm Tue-Sat, 9am-2pm Sun; Ⓜ Ledru-Rollin). The small but bargain-filled flea market **Marché aux Puces d'Aligre** (Map p394; place d'Aligre, 12e; ⌚8am-1pm Tue-Sun; Ⓜ Ledru-Rollin) takes place on the square.

BLÉ SUCRÉ — BAKERY €

Map p394 (7 rue Antoine Vollon, 12e; pastries €1-5.50; ⌚7am-7.30pm Tue-Sat, to 1.30pm Sun; Ⓜ Ledru-Rollin) Fabulously flaky, ultra-buttery croissants are baked at this *boulangerie* near the foodie nexus of Marché d'Aligre. It also turns out sourdoughs, focaccia with sea salt and rosemary, crunchy baguettes, and a slew of sweet treats including madeleine cakes. On weekends especially, queues stretch well out the door. There's a handful of pavement tables and a leafy park opposite.

★LE SERVAN — BISTRO €€

Map p394 (☎01 55 28 51 82; http://leservan.com; 32 rue St-Maur, 11e; 3-course lunch menu €27, mains €25-38; ⌚7.30-10.30pm Mon, noon-2.30pm & 7.30-10.30pm Tue-Fri; Ⓜ Voltaire, Rue St-Maur, Père Lachaise) Ornate cream-coloured ceilings with moulded cornices and pastel murals, huge windows and wooden floors give this neighbourhood neobistro near Père Lachaise a light, airy feel on even the greyest Parisian day. Sweetbread wontons, cockles with chilli and sweet basil, and roast pigeon with tamarind *jus* are among the inventive creations on the daily changing menu. Reserve to avoid missing out.

LE BISTROT PAUL BERT — BISTRO €€

Map p394 (☎01 43 72 24 01; 18 rue Paul Bert, 11e; 2-/3-course lunch/dinner menu €19/41; ⌚noon-2pm & 7.30-11pm Tue-Sat, closed Aug; Ⓜ Faidherbe-Chaligny) When food writers list Paris' best bistros, Paul Bert's name consistently pops up. The timeless vintage decor and classic dishes like *steak-frites* and hazelnut-cream Paris-Brest pastry reward those booking ahead. Look for its siblings in the same street: **L'Écailler du Bistrot** (Map p394; ☎01 43 72 76 77; 22 rue Paul Bert, 11e; oysters per half-dozen €9-20, mains €32-46, seafood platters per person from €40; ⌚noon-2.30pm & 7.30-11pm Tue-Sat) for seafood; **La Cave Paul Bert** (Map p394; ☎01 58 53 50 92; 16 rue Paul Bert, 11e; ⌚noon-midnight, kitchen noon-2pm & 7.30-11.30pm), a wine bar with small plates; and **Le 6 Paul Bert** (Map p394; ☎01 43 79 14 32; www.le6paulbert.com; 6 rue Paul Bert, 12e; 6-course menu €60, mains €24-35; ⌚noon-2pm & 7.30-11pm Tue-Sat) for modern cuisine. Produce for all three restaurants is grown on its farm in Normandy.

PASSERINI — ITALIAN €€

Map p394 (☎01 43 42 27 56; www.passerini.paris; 65 rue Traversière, 12e; lunch menus €24-48, dinner mains €18-42; ⌚6-10pm Tue, noon-2.30pm & 6-10pm Wed-Sat, closed early May & Aug; Ⓜ Ledru-Rollin) Rome native Giovanni Passerini is one of the finest Italian chefs cooking in Europe today. Delectable specialities include roast pigeon with smoked ricotta, and tagliolini with red Sicilian shrimp, and are complemented by natural wines sourced from small vineyards. Pastas are made fresh and are also sold at its adjoining deli, Pastificio Passerini.

LES DÉSERTEURS — FRENCH €€

Map p394 (☎01 48 06 95 85; 46 rue Trousseau, 11e; menus €30-49; ⌚7.30-9.45pm Tue, 12.30-2pm & 7.30-9.45pm Wed-Sat; Ⓜ Ledru-Rollin) Deserting their previous workplace, Les Déserteurs' chef Daniel Baratier and sommelier Alexandre Céret have combined their talents here at their own premises. In a contemporary space with high blonde oak tables, grey-painted walls and open kitchen, they serve exquisitely presented multicourse *menus* (no à la carte) with an emphasis on market-sourced vegetables, complemented by small-scale, pan-European wines.

Dishes change daily but might include smoked asparagus with a soft egg yolk in wild garlic sauce or roasted snails with a plankton reduction, followed by maple syrup-filled choux pastry with caramelised almonds.

BUFFET BISTRO €€

Map p394 (☎01 83 89 63 82; www.restaurantbuffet.fr; 8 rue de la Main d'Or, 11e; 2-/3-course lunch menu €16.50/19, small plates €5-15; ⏲7.30-11pm Tue, noon-2.30pm & 7.30-11pm Wed-Sat; Ⓜ Ledru-Rollin) Tucked away on a charming Bastille backstreet behind a mulberry-coloured façade, Buffet has burgundy leather seating, wooden tables, mirrors and terrazzo floors. Despite its name, there's no smorgasbord but a short daily changing blackboard menu of bistro dishes like lemon sole with hand-cut chips, lamb shoulder with prunes, and chestnut and chocolate mousse that belies the complexity of the cooking.

CHEZ PAUL BISTRO €€

Map p394 (☎01 47 00 34 57; www.chezpaul.com; 13 rue de Charonne, 11e; 2-/3-course weekday lunch menu €18/21, mains €17-27; ⏲noon-12.30am; Ⓜ Ledru-Rollin) This is Paris as your grandmother knew it: chequered red-and-white napkins, faded photographs on the walls, old red banquettes and traditional French dishes such as pig trotters, *andouillette* (a feisty tripe sausage) and *tête de veau et cervelle* (calf head and brains). If offal isn't for you, alternatives include a steaming bowl of *pot au feu* (beef stew).

LA ROBE DE LA GIRAFE BISTRO €€

Map p394 (☎09 82 37 18 52; www.la-robe-de-la-girafe.com; 5 rue Froment, 11e; 2-/3-course lunch menu €16/21, 3-course dinner menu €25, mains €13.50-19.50, platters €8-19.50; ⏲kitchen noon-11pm Mon-Sat, wine bar 6pm-midnight Tue-Sat; 📶; Ⓜ Bréguet–Sabin) Named for the first giraffe in France – an 1820s gift from the Vice Consul of Egypt to Charles X, which sparked a mania for giraffe-patterned items – this corner bistro is a charming spot for classic French dishes such as eggs poached in red wine or bavette steak with grilled shallots and tarte tatin. Its next-door wine bar serves charcuterie platters.

À LA BICHE AU BOIS FRENCH €€

Map p394 (☎01 43 43 34 38; 45 av Ledru-Rollin, 12e; 3-course lunch menu €32.80, mains €17.50-23.50; ⏲noon-2.30pm & 7-10.45pm Tue-Fri, 7-10.45pm Mon & Sat; Ⓜ Gare de Lyon) Game, especially *la biche* (venison), is the speciality of convivial 'doe in the woods', but dishes like foie gras and coq au vin add to the countryside ambience, as do the green awning and potted plants. The cheeses and wines are excellent, but game aside, top honours have to go to the sensational *frites* (fries).

COUP D'ŒIL FRENCH €€

Map p394 (☎01 43 57 59 68; www.coupdoeil.paris; 80 rue Sedaine, 11e; 3-course weekday lunch menu €18, mains €12-26; ⏲noon-3pm & 6-10pm, bar to 2am; 📶; Ⓜ Voltaire) Traditional decor (exposed brick, patterned tiles) meets contemporary design (wave-form timber ceiling panels) at this striking wine bar. Lobster consommé, fennel-marinated grilled octopus, and potato and cheese soufflé with crab sauce are among the dishes that accompany all-natural wines; small plates and charcuterie platters are served until the bar closes. Live jazz, blues and soul often plays on Saturday nights.

JOUVENCE BISTRO €€

Map p394 (☎01 56 58 04 73; www.jouvence.paris; 172bis rue du Faubourg St-Antoine, 12e; mains €19-26, 2-/3-course lunch menu €19/24; ⏲noon-2pm & 7-10pm Tue-Sat; Ⓜ Faidherbe-Chaligny) Retaining exquisite timber cabinetry and floor tiles from its early 1900s incarnation as an apothecary, this mirror-lined space is now a locally loved neobistro serving inventive modern French cuisine. Owner-chef Romain Thibault creates daily changing, market-inspired dishes such as salt-crusted line-caught Oléron whiting, blackberry- and honey-marinated duck fillet, roast langoustine with citrus-braised endives and clementine meringue pie for dessert.

L'ÉBAUCHOIR BISTRO €€

Map p394 (☎01 43 42 49 31; www.lebauchoir.com; 43-45 rue de Cîteaux, 12e; lunch menus €14-29, mains €18-27; ⏲8-11pm Mon, noon-2.30pm & 8-11pm Tue-Thu, noon-2.30pm & 7.30-11pm Fri & Sat; Ⓜ Faidherbe-Chaligny) Drop in to this convivial gourmet bistro for inventive creations from chef Thomas Dufour. French classics form the base of his dishes, such as seared scallops with toasted wild almonds or whole roasted veal kidneys with citrus compote and *dolce forte* (chocolate, vinegar and raisin) sauce. In the evening, there's usually at least one vegetarian main on the à la carte menu.

Across the street, the same team offers walk-in wine-bar dining at **Le Siffleur de Ballons** (Map p394; www.lesiffleurdeballons.fr; 34 rue de Citeaux, 12e; 2-course lunch menu €14, dishes €5-17; ⏲5.30-10.30pm Tue, 10.30am-3pm & 5.30-11.30pm Wed-Fri, 10.30am-11pm Sat).

LE SQUARE TROUSSEAU FRENCH €€

Map p394 (☎01 43 43 06 00; www.squaretrousseau.com; 1 rue Antoine Vollon, 12e; mains €18-27;

⌚8am-2am, kitchen noon-2.30pm & 7-10pm; 📶👪; Ⓜ Ledru-Rollin) With etched glass, a zinc bar and polished wood panelling, this belle époque cafe-restaurant dating from 1907 is a local landmark. A real all-rounder, this is a place where Parisians flock for a coffee-and-croissant breakfast, a classic French meal like frogs' legs or hare stew, or an after-work drink on the delightful terrace overlooking a lovely leafy square.

Chalk is provided for kids to get creative on the pavement out front.

À LA BANANE IVOIRIENNE — AFRICAN €€

Map p394 (☎01 43 70 49 90; www.facebook.com/ALaBananeIvoirienne; 10 rue de la Forge Royale, 11e; menu €29.50, mains €11-16.50; ⌚kitchen 7-11pm Tue-Sat, bar to 1am Fri & Sat; 🖉; Ⓜ Faidherbe-Chaligny) An institution in Paris since 1989, À la Banane Ivoirienne dishes up the best Ivorian food in Paris along with fabulous live music and dancing on Friday nights. West African specialities – including stuffed crab, braised *attiéké* (fermented cassava pulp), *alloco* (fried plaintain) and plenty of fiery meats and fish – are dished up in a colourful interior bristling with gewgaws.

LE TEMPS AU TEMPS — BISTRO €€

Map p394 (☎01 43 79 63 40; 13 rue Paul Bert, 11e; 2-/3-course menu lunch €20/22, dinner €28/32, mains €24-27; ⌚7.30-11.30pm Tue, 11.45am-1.30pm & 7.30-11.30pm Wed-Sat; Ⓜ Faidherbe-Chaligny) Foodie street rue Paul Bert is the perfect spot for this delightfully traditional and excellent-value bistro with a quaint ginger façade and menu chalked on a blackboard outside. Lunch *menus* include a glass of wine – just the job for washing down a deliciously garlicky snail fricassee, roast leg of lamb, or scallops with braised endives and spicy chorizo.

À LA RENAISSANCE — CAFE €€

Map p394 (☎01 43 79 83 09; 87 rue de la Roquette, 11e; mains €20-30, platters €6-15.50; ⌚kitchen 8am-10pm, bar to 2am; Ⓜ Voltaire) This vintage neighbourhood cafe with a curvaceous zinc bar, a ceramic tile floor and an enclosed terrace is a great place to dine on quintessential Paris cafe fare. Along with cheese and charcuterie platters, it serves wild boar terrine, steak tartare and duck-heat *cassoulet* (slow-cooked casserole). Natural wines dominate its excellent wine list.

GENTLE GOURMET CAFÉ — VEGAN €€

Map p394 (☎01 43 43 48 49; https://gentlegourmet.fr; 24 bd de la Bastille, 12e; 2-/3-course lunch menu €23/30, mains €21-25; ⌚noon-2.30pm & 6.30-10pm Tue-Sun; 📶🖉👪; Ⓜ Quai de la Rapée, Bastille) 🍃 Large windows and lots of natural light create an elegant setting to dine on 100% vegan dishes such as almond-encrusted tofu, tarragon-laced beetroot ravioli or a portobello-mushroom burger in sesame brioche bun, washed down with a lovely choice of fruit juices and teas. Many ingredients come from its own garden in Normandy. For young appetites, the €12 kids' menu comes with organic fruit juice.

CITEAUX SPHERE — FRENCH €€

Map p394 (☎06 11 76 65 89; 45 rue de Citeaux, 12e; mains €12-18; ⌚11am-3pm & 5.30-10.30pm Tue-Sat; 📶; Ⓜ Faidherbe-Chaligny) On one of Paris' *rues végétales* (green-focused, low-traffic streets) lined with planter boxes, this hybrid space combines a vinyl record shop stocked with treasures, a wine bar and a laid-back restaurant under one roof. Written on vinyl discs, its menu lists *tartines* (open-faced sandwiches such as St-Marcellin and smoked ham), salads and specials sourced from the nearby Marché Aligre.

★SEPTIME — GASTRONOMY €€€

Map p394 (☎01 43 67 38 29; www.septime-charonne.fr; 80 rue de Charonne, 11e; 4-course lunch menu €42, with wine €70, 7-course dinner menu €80, with wine €135; ⌚7.30-10pm Mon, 12.15-2pm & 7.30-10pm Tue-Fri; Ⓜ Charonne) The alchemists in Bertrand Grébaut's Michelin-starred kitchen produce truly beautiful creations, served by blue-aproned waitstaff. The menu reads like an obscure shopping list: each dish is a mere listing of three ingredients, while the mystery *carte blanche* dinner *menu* puts you in the hands of the innovative chef. Reservations require planning and perseverance – book at least three weeks in advance.

Its nearby wine bar **Septime La Cave** (Map p394; 3 rue Basfroi, 11e; ⌚4-11pm) is ideal for a pre- or post-meal drink. For stunning seafood tapas, its sister restaurant **Clamato** (Map p394; http://clamato-charonne.fr; 80 rue de Charonne, 11e; tapas €8-16, dozen oysters €18-48; ⌚7-11pm Wed-Fri, from noon Sat & Sun) is right next door.

LE CHARDENOUX — BISTRO €€€

Map p394 (☎01 43 71 49 52; www.restaurantlechardenoux.com; 1 rue Jules Vallès, 11e;

2-/3-course lunch menus €25/30, 3-course dinner menu €41; ⌚noon-2.30pm & 7-11pm; Ⓜ Charonne) Dating from 1908, this picture-perfect Parisian bistro with a polished-timber façade, patterned tiled floors, marble-topped tables, mirrored walls, bevelled frosted-glass screens and a centrepiece zinc bar is a listed historic monument. Star chef Cyril Lignac recreates classical French dishes: Aubrac beef tartare and *frites*, chicken in white wine, and brioche toast with poached pears and hazelnut caramel.

It's across the road from Lignac's combined chocolate boutique and tearoom **La Chocolaterie Cyril Lignac** (Map p394; www.cyrillignac.com; 25 rue Chanzy, 11e; pastries €1.40-4; ⌚8am-7pm) to the east, and from his bakery/pastry shop **La Pâtisserie** (Map p394; www.gourmand-croquant.com; 24 rue Paul Bert, 11e; pastries €3-6.50; ⌚7am-7pm Mon, to 8pm Tue-Sun) to the south.

DERSOU BISTRO €€€

Map p394 (☎09 70 38 52 86; www.dersouparis.com; 21 rue St-Nicolas, 12e; 5-/6-/7-course tasting menu with paired cocktails €95/115/135, mains €15-30, Sunday brunch dishes €8-19; ⌚7.30-11pm Tue-Fri, noon-3pm & 7.30-11-pm Sat, noon-3pm Sun; Ⓜ Ledru-Rollin) Much of the seating at this hot spot, which turns out creative fusion cuisine, is at the counter, where you get first-class views of chef Taku Sekine at work. Intricately constructed tasting menus are a highlight, with each course exquisitely paired with a bespoke cocktail. Reservations are essential.

TABLE FRENCH €€€

Map p394 (☎01 43 43 12 26; www.tablerestaurant.fr; 3 rue de Prague, 12e; 2-/3-course lunch menu €25/29, mains €39-69; ⌚noon-3pm & 7.45-10.30pm Mon-Fri, 7.30-10pm Sat; Ⓜ Ledru-Rollin) Unusual and rare artisan products sourced from all over France decide the day's menu at Michelin-starred Table, styled like a contemporary *table d'hôte*, with diners seated at the curvaceous zinc bar while talented food writer and chef Bruno Verjus performs in his open kitchen. Delicious meats are spit-roasted on the rotisserie and Verjus delights in talking food with diners. To enter, press the button and wait for the glass door to slide open.

LE TRAIN BLEU FRENCH €€€

Map p394 (☎01 43 43 09 06; www.le-train-bleu.com; 1st fl, Gare de Lyon, 26 place Louis Armand, 12e; 2-/3-/6-course menus €49/65/110, mains €29-48; ⌚restaurant 11.30am-2.45pm & 7-10.45pm, bar 7.30am-10.30pm Mon-Sat, 9am-10pm Sun; 📶👶; Ⓜ Gare de Lyon) This spectacular belle époque train-station restaurant has been an elegant port of call since 1901. Cuisine is traditional French – Salers beef tartare is prepared at your table – and even if you can't dine here, indulging in a silver pot of tea or a cocktail in its comfortable lounge-bar is well worth the top-end prices. A two-course children's menu costs €20.

DRINKING & NIGHTLIFE

Bastille invariably draws a crowd, particularly along rue de Lappe, 11e, which is awash with raucous bars. Continue further east and the options become much more stylish and appealing, with wine bars, intimate clubs and backstreet cocktail dens.

★LE BARON ROUGE WINE BAR

Map p394 (☎01 43 43 14 32; www.lebaronrouge.net; 1 rue Théophile Roussel, 12e; ⌚5-10pm Mon, 10am-2pm & 5-10pm Tue-Fri, 10am-10pm Sat, 10am-4pm Sun; Ⓜ Ledru-Rollin) Just about the ultimate Parisian wine-bar experience, this wonderfully unpretentious local meeting place, where everyone is welcome, has barrels stacked against the bottle-lined walls and serves cheese, charcuterie and oysters in season. It's especially busy on Sunday after the Marché d'Aligre wraps up. For a small deposit, you can fill up 1L bottles straight from the barrel for less than €5.

★CONCRETE CLUB

Map p394 (www.concreteparis.fr; 69 Port de la Rapée, 12e; ⌚Thu-Sun; Ⓜ Gare de Lyon) Moored by Gare de Lyon on a barge on the Seine, this wild-child club with two dance floors is famed for introducing an 'after-hours' element to Paris' somewhat staid clubbing scene, with the country's first 24-hour licence. Watch for world-class electro DJ appearances and all-weekend events on social media.

LA FÉE VERTE BAR

Map p394 (☎01 43 72 31 24; 108 rue de la Roquette, 11e; ⌚7am-2am Mon-Sat, from 8am Sun; 📶; Ⓜ Voltaire) Absinthe is the speciality of the Green Fairy, a thronging neighbourhood bar with dark-wood furniture, huge

RUE DE LAPPE

Although at night it's one of the rowdiest bar-hopping streets in Paris, rue de Lappe is actually quite peaceful during the day. Like most streets in the area, it dates back to the 17th century and was originally home to cabinetmakers, who first moved into the area to escape the taxes and restrictions imposed by guilds operating within the city limits.

In the centuries that followed, the street was gradually taken over by metalworkers, who equipped the city with its zinc bars, copper piping and the like: one of the busiest bars on the street, **Bar des Ferrailleurs** (Map p394; ☎01 48 07 89 12; 18 rue de Lappe, 11e; ⊙6pm-2am Sat-Thu, from 5pm Fri; MBastille), is a hip homage to these workers. At the same time, immigrants from the central French region of Auvergne also moved in, opening up *cafés-charbons*, places where you could go for a drink and buy coal at the same time. In this way the street eventually became a popular drinking strip, and its accordion-driven dance halls, which hosted *bals-musettes*, were to become famous throughout Paris. The dance hall Le Balajo (p192) dates back to 1936 and continues to host weekly *bals musettes*.

You can still find an Auvergne speciality shop here, **Chez Teil** (Map p394; 6 rue de Lappe, 11e; ⊙10am-1pm & 4-8pm Tue-Sat; MBastille), at No 6, as well as a beautiful old cafe-bar and bistro, **Les Sans-Culottes** (Map p394; ☎01 48 05 42 92; www.bistrotlessansculottes.fr; 27 rue de Lappe, 11e; ⊙8am-2am Mon-Sat; MBastille), at No 27.

mirrors and a zinc bar. It serves over 20 different types of the devilish drink (served traditionally, with slotted spoons and sugar cubes) as well as good food, including house-speciality burgers. Happy hour runs from 5pm to 8m.

BLUEBIRD COCKTAIL BAR

Map p394 (12 rue St-Bernard, 11e; ⊙6pm-2am; MFaidherbe-Chaligny) The ultimate neighbourhood hang-out, Bluebird is styled like a 1950s apartment with retro decor, a giant fish tank along one wall, and a soundtrack of smooth lounge music. Cocktail recipes date from the 1800s and early 1900s and change seasonally, but the menu always features six gin-based creations, six with other spirits, and three low-alcohol wine- and Champagne-based drinks.

Guest bartenders often drop by for a stint; ask about cocktail masterclasses.

CAFÉ DES ANGES CAFE

Map p394 (☎01 47 00 00 63; www.cafedesanges-paris.com; 66 rue de la Roquette, 11e; ⊙7.30am-2am; 📶; MBastille) With its pastel-shaded paintwork and locals sipping coffee beneath the terracotta-coloured awning on its busy pavement terrace, Angels Cafe lives up to the 'quintessential Paris cafe' dream. In winter wrap up beneath a blanket outside, or squeeze through the crowds at the zinc bar to snag a coveted table inside. Happy hour runs from 5pm to 9pm.

From 8am to 11.30am it serves breakfast (granola, pancakes, avocado toast), followed by burgers (including a vegan option), steak and other bistro dishes until 1am.

OUTLAND CRAFT BEER

Map p394 (https://outland-beer.com; 6 rue Emile Lepeu, 11e; ⊙6pm-2am Mon-Sat, to midnight Sun; MCharonne) Of the 12 beers on tap at this artisanal beer bar, eight are Outland's own, brewed just east of central Paris in Fontenay-sous-Bois near the Bois de Vincennes. Among them are a double IPA, a session pale ale, a porter and a fabulously fermented plum göse. Soak them up with tapas like duck liver pâté, organic burrata and stuffed calamari.

Guest beers come from as close as other breweries in the greater Paris area such as Montreuil's Deck & Donohue to as far afield as Canada. It also serves natural wines.

LOUVE WINE BAR

Map p394 (☎01 43 38 90 80; www.louve.vin; 17 rue Bréguet, 11e; ⊙11am-11pm Tue-Fri, 4pm-midnight Mon & Sat; 📶; MBréguet–Sabin) More than 400 wines from 200 different winemakers across France can be paired with charcuterie and/or cheese platters at this spiffing glass-and-steel wine bar with floor-to-ceiling windows and timber-topped tables. It's also a great place to pick up a bottle to take away, along with picnic ingredients from its on-site deli. Check ahead as hours can fluctuate seasonally.

LE BISTROT DU PEINTRE BAR

Map p394 (www.bistrotdupeintre.com; 116 av Ledru-Rollin, 11e; ⏲7am-2am; 📶; Ⓜ Ledru-Rollin) The 1902 art-nouveau bar, elegant terrace, Auvergne-inspired bistro dishes and creative *grignotage* ('nibbles') menu make this belle-époque treasure an atmospheric stop day or night.

LE PURE CAFÉ CAFE

Map p394 (www.lepurecafe.fr; 14 rue Jean Macé, 11e; ⏲7am-1am Mon-Fri, 8am-1am Sat, 9am-midnight Sun; Ⓜ Charonne) A classic Parisian corner cafe, Le Pure is a charming spot to drop into for a morning coffee, aperitif, contemporary bistro meal or Sunday brunch. Its selection of natural and organic wines by the glass is particularly good. Film buffs might recognise its cherry-red façade and vintage-wood and zinc bar from the Richard Linklater film *Before Sunset*.

TWENTY ONE SOUND BAR CLUB

Map p394 (☎01 43 70 78 01; http://twentyonesoundbar.com; 20 rue de la Forge Royale, 11e; ⏲9pm-2am Tue, Wed, Fri & Sat, from 8pm Thu; Ⓜ Faidherbe-Chaligny) Stark steel and concrete amp up the acoustics at this hip-hop haven, with regular drinks specials and big-name DJs mixing on the decks.

ENTERTAINMENT

Paris' east is home to major venues such as the AccorHotels Arena (www.accorhotelsarena.com) and Opéra Bastille, as well as a host of smaller spaces staging intimate gigs. Other highlights include screenings at the national film institute La Cinémathèque Française.

OPÉRA BASTILLE OPERA

Map p394 (☎international calls 01 71 25 24 23, within France 08 92 89 90 90; www.operadeparis.fr; 2-6 place de la Bastille, 12e; ⏲box office 11.30am-6.30pm Mon-Sat, 1hr prior to performances Sun; Ⓜ Bastille) Paris' premier opera hall, Opéra Bastille's 2745-seat main auditorium also stages ballet and classical concerts. Online tickets go on sale up to three weeks before telephone or box-office sales (from noon on Wednesdays; online flash sales offer significant discounts). Standing-only tickets (*places débouts;* €5) are available 90 minutes before performances. French-language 90-minute guided tours (p182) take you backstage. Significant discounts are available for those aged under 28.

BADABOUM LIVE MUSIC

Map p394 (☎01 48 06 50 70; http://badaboum.paris; 2bis rue des Taillandiers, 11e; ⏲bar 7pm-2am Wed & Thu, to 6am Sat, club & concerts vary; Ⓜ Ledru-Rollin) The onomatopoeically named Badaboum hosts a mixed bag of concerts on its up-close-and-personal stage, but focuses on electro, funk and hip hop. Great atmosphere, super cocktails and a chill-out room upstairs.

LA CINÉMATHÈQUE FRANÇAISE CINEMA

(☎01 71 19 33 33; www.cinematheque.fr; 51 rue de Bercy, 12e; tickets adult/child €6.50/4; ⏲2.30-9pm or later Wed-Sun; Ⓜ Bercy) This national institution (p182) is a temple to the 'seventh art' and always screens its foreign offerings in their original versions. Up to 10 films a day are shown, usually retrospectives (eg Spielberg, Altman, Eastwood) mixed in with related but more obscure films.

LE RÉSERVOIR LIVE MUSIC

Map p394 (☎01 43 56 39 60; www.reservoirclub.com; 16 rue de la Forge Royale, 11e; mains €19-27, weekend brunch €27; ⏲8pm-2am Tue-Thu, to 5am Fri, 11.30am-4.30pm & 8pm-5am Sat, 11.30am-4.30pm Sun; Ⓜ Faidherbe-Chaligny) Dimmed lighting, baroque decor and cabaret-style tables facing the raised stage set the scene for intimate gigs at this atmospheric former royal forge (after which the street is named). There's no entry fee, but you're expected to dine (or at least drink). Acts range from emerging to established artists across genres as diverse as jazz, hip-hop, rock, metal and disco.

LE MOTEL LIVE MUSIC

Map p394 (www.lemotel.fr; 8 passage Josset, 11e; ⏲6pm-2am Tue-Sun; Ⓜ Ledru-Rollin) This hole-in-the-wall venue in the hot-to-boiling-point 11e has become the go-to indie bar around Bastille. It's especially well loved for its comfy sofas, inexpensive but quality drinks (craft beers on tap and indie cocktails; happy hour is from 6pm to 9pm) and excellent music, with live bands and DJs Tuesday to Saturday (plus quiz nights or karaoke on Sunday).

LA CHAPELLE DES LOMBARDS LIVE MUSIC

Map p394 (☎01 43 57 24 24; www.la-chapelle-des-lombards.com; 19 rue de Lappe, 11e; ⏲11pm-5am Wed, Thu & Sun, to 6am Fri & Sat; Ⓜ Bastille)

World music dominates this perennially popular Bastille dance club, with happening Latino DJs and live reggae, funk and Afro jazz concerts. Prices vary from night to night; when admission is free, you're expected to buy a drink.

LE BALAJO LIVE MUSIC

Map p394 (☎01 47 00 07 87; www.balajo.fr; 9 rue de Lappe, 11e; ⏲hours vary; Ⓜ Bastille) A mainstay of Parisian nightlife since 1936, this ancient ballroom is devoted to evening salsa classes and Latino music during the week, with an R&B slant on weekends when the dance floor rocks until *aube* (dawn). But the best time to visit is for its old-fashioned *musette* (accordion music) gigs, on from 2pm to 7pm Sundays and Mondays.

SHOPPING

Superb markets aside, Bastille and eastern Paris are not really known for shopping, but there's a select choice of unique boutiques and specialist shops. Key fashion brands have stores on the western end of trendy rue de Charonne, between av Ledru-Rollin and rue du Faubourg St-Antoine, and arts and crafts studio-showrooms are tucked under the viaduct arches beneath the Promenade Plantée.

LA MANUFACTURE DE CHOCOLAT FOOD

Map p394 (www.lechocolat-alainducasse.com; 40 rue de la Roquette, 11e; ⏲9.30am-6pm Mon-Fri; Ⓜ Bastille) If you dine at superstar chef Alain Ducasse's restaurants, the chocolate will have been made here at Ducasse's own chocolate factory (the first in Paris to produce 'bean-to-bar' chocolate), which he set up with his former executive pastry chef Nicolas Berger. Deliberate over ganaches, pralines and truffles and no fewer than 44 flavours of chocolate bar.

You can also buy Ducasse's chocolates at other outlets including his Left Bank boutique, **Le Chocolat Alain Ducasse** (Map p402; ☎01 45 48 87 89; 26 rue St-Benoît, 6e; ⏲1.30-7.30pm Mon, 10.30am-7.30pm Tue-Sat; Ⓜ St-Germain des Prés).

LA COCOTTE HOMEWARES

Map p394 (www.lacocotteparis.com; 5 rue Paul Bert, 11e; ⏲noon-7pm Tue-Sat; Ⓜ Faidherbe-Chaligny) If the gourmet restaurants along rue Paul Bert have inspired you to get into the kitchen, stop by the boutique of designers Andrea Wainer and Laetitia Bertrand for stylish, often Paris- and/or French-themed accoutrements such as tea towels, oven mitts, aprons, mugs, shopping bags and more, many incorporating La Cocotte's signature hen motif.

VIADUC DES ARTS ARTS & CRAFTS

Map p394 (www.leviaducdesarts.com; 1-129 av Daumesnil, 12e; ⏲hours vary; Ⓜ Bastille, Gare de Lyon) Located beneath the red-brick arches of the Promenade Plantée (p182) elevated park, the Viaduc des Arts's line-up of traditional artisans and contemporary designers – including furniture and tapestry restorers, interior designers, cabinetmakers, violin- and flute-makers, embroiderers and jewellers – carry out antique renovations and create new items using time-honoured methods.

SO WE ARE FASHION & ACCESSORIES

Map p394 (www.soweare-shop.fr; 40 rue de Charonne, 11e; ⏲11.30am-7.30pm Mon-Sat; Ⓜ Ledru-Rollin) Founded by friends Hélène and Magali, So We Are specialises in hard-to-find French and European women's fashion labels. Look out for embroidered T-shirts by Keur Paris, art deco-inspired geometric jewellery from Paris-based Aurélie Joliff, dresses and jackets by La Petite Française, knitwear from Belgian-based Roos Vandekerckhove, and trousers, shirts and shoes from Danish designers Samsøe & Samsøe.

SOUFFLE CONTINU MUSIC

Map p394 (www.soufflecontinu.com; 20-22 rue Gerbier, 11e; ⏲noon-8pm Mon-Sat; Ⓜ Philippe Auguste) Owners Bernard Ducayron and Théo Jarrier have their own record label, and their spacious, terrazzo-tiled shop specialises in vinyl, discs, books and DVDs spanning genres as diverse as electronic, jazz, rock, experimental, avant-garde garage, industrial poetry and medieval metal.

BERCY VILLAGE MALL

(www.bercyvillage.com; Cour St-Émilion, 12e; ⏲shops 11am-9pm, restaurants & bars to 2am; Ⓜ Cour St-Émilion) Set in the former Bercy wine warehouses, this popular outdoor mall has an 18-screen cinema, restaurants, bars and a string of stores catering to the needs of Parisian families: home design, clever kitchen supplies, quality toy stores and more.

The Islands

Neighbourhood Top Five

❶ **Cathédrale Notre Dame de Paris** (p195) Revelling in the crowning glory of medieval Gothic architecture before ascending the cathedral's towers to take in awe-inspiring panoramas over Paris.

❷ **Sainte-Chapelle** (p200) Reading richly coloured biblical tales, exquisitely told through stained-glass imagery with a grace and beauty impossible to find elsewhere.

❸ **Conciergerie** (p201) Learning how Marie-Antoinette and thousands of others lived out their final days at this 14th-century palace-turned-prison before being beheaded.

❹ **Crypte Archéologique** (p197) Delving underground to discover fascinating Gallo-Roman, medieval and Haussmanian archaeological remains.

❺ **Berthillon** (p202) Savouring the sweetness of this famous Parisian ice cream during a stroll along the riverbanks.

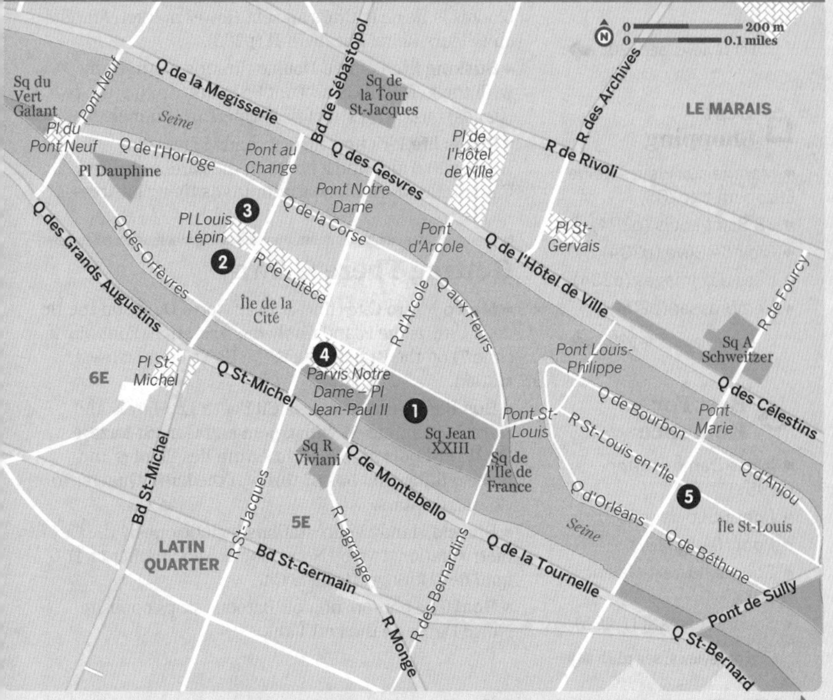

For more detail of this area see Map p396

Lonely Planet's Top Tip

Queues to see the sunlight stream through spectacular stained glass at Sainte-Chapelle can be staggeringly long. To speed things up, first visit the Conciergerie and buy a combination ticket covering admission to both the old prison and the chapel. With this *billet jumelé* you can skip Sainte-Chapelle's ticket queue and enter via the line for museum-pass holders and combination tickets. You'll still need to go through a security check.

Best Places to Eat

- Berthillon (p202)
- Café Saint Régis (p202)
- Sequana (p203)
- Huré (p202)
- Le Caveau du Palais (p202)

For reviews, see p202

Best Shopping

- Marché aux Fleurs Reine Elizabeth II (p203)
- 38 Saint Louis (p204)
- Clair de Rêve (p204)
- L'Îles aux Images (p204)
- L'embrasser (p204)

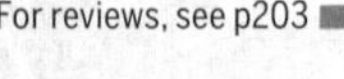

For reviews, see p203

Best For Romance

- Notre Dame rooftop (p195)
- Pont St-Louis (p202)
- Pont Neuf (p201)
- Square du Vert-Galant (p201)
- Square Jean XXIII (p195)

For reviews, see p195

Explore The Islands

Where better to start your explorations than Notre Dame? Heading here first also means you'll beat the crowds. In addition to viewing its stained-glass interior, allow around an hour to climb the spiralling stairs to the top of the towers, and another to explore the archaeological crypt.

For even more beautiful stained glass, don't miss the exquisite Sainte-Chapelle (p200), a few footsteps from intriguing Revolution prison the Conciergerie (p201).

Cross Pont St-Louis (p202) to the enchanting little Île St-Louis. After brunch or lunch at the deliciously Parisian hang-out Café Saint Régis (p202), browse the island's boutiques and buy an iconic Berthillon (p202) ice cream from its flagship premises to take to the river's edge.

Come late afternoon, stroll back over Pont St-Louis – where you're likely to catch buskers – for a pre-dinner drink at Le Bar du Caveau (p203); allow ample time to lap up the quaint, old-world vibe of car-free place Dauphine. Afterwards, dine at gastronomic Sequana (p203).

Local Life

- **Art life** Europe's largest surviving medieval hall, the Conciergerie (p201), hosts cutting-edge art exhibitions.
- **Market life** The most atmospheric place to buy blooms is Île de la Cité's ancient flower market, Marché aux Fleurs Reine Elizabeth II (p203).
- **Busking life** Pont au Double (linking Notre Dame with the Left Bank) and Pont St-Louis (linking the two islands) buzz with street performers in summer.
- **Picnic life** Pick up gourmet sandwiches from Huré (p202) and find a bench in the gardens behind Cathédrale Notre Dame to admire its flying buttresses.

Getting There & Away

- **Metro** Metro Cité (line 4), near Notre Dame on the Île de la Cité, is the islands' only metro station. Pont Marie (line 7) on the Right Bank is the Île St-Louis' closest station.
- **Bus** Bus 47 links Île de la Cité with Le Marais and Gare de l'Est; bus 21 with Opéra and Gare St-Lazare. On Île St-Louis it's bus 67 to Jardin des Plantes and place d'Italie, and bus 87 through the Latin Quarter to Champ de Mars.
- **Bicycle** Handy Vélib' stations include one by the Cité metro station, two by Notre Dame, and another at 41 quai de l'Horloge, Île de la Cité.
- **Boat** The hop-on, hop-off Batobus stops opposite Notre Dame on the Left Bank.

TOP SIGHT
CATHÉDRALE NOTRE DAME DE PARIS

ELI_ASENOVA / GETTY IMAGES ©

Majestic and monumental in equal measure, Paris' iconic French Gothic cathedral is the capital's most visited unticketed site: more than 14 million cross its threshold a year. Views of the city laid out at your feet from the top of its gargoyle-encrusted northern bell tower are among the best there are.

Architecture

Built on a site occupied by earlier churches and, a millennium prior, a Gallo-Roman temple, Notre Dame was begun in 1163 and largely completed by the early 14th century. The cathedral was badly damaged during the Revolution, prompting architect Eugène Emmanuel Viollet-le-Duc to oversee extensive renovations between 1845 and 1864. Enter the magnificent forest of ornate **flying buttresses** that encircle the cathedral chancel and support its walls and roof.

Notre Dame is known for its sublime balance, though if you look closely you'll see all sorts of minor asymmetrical elements introduced to avoid monotony, in accordance with standard Gothic practice. These include the slightly different shapes of each of the three main **portals**, whose statues were once brightly coloured to make them more effective as a *Biblia pauperum* – a 'Bible of the poor' to help the illiterate faithful understand Old Testament stories, the Passion of the Christ and the lives of the saints.

Rose Windows

A cathedral highlight, the three rose windows colouring its vast 127m-long, 48m-wide interior are its most spectacular feature. Admire a 10m-wide window over the western

DON'T MISS

- Rose windows
- Treasury
- Bell towers
- Flying buttresses

PRACTICALITIES

- Map p396, D4
- ☎01 42 34 56 10, towers 01 53 10 07 00
- www.notredamedeparis.fr
- 6 Parvis Notre Dame – place Jean-Paul-II, 4e
- cathedral free, adult/child towers €10/free, treasury €5/3
- ⏱cathedral 7.45am-6.45pm Mon-Fri, to 7.15pm Sat & Sun, towers 10am-6.30pm Sun-Thu, 10am-11pm Fri & Sat Jul & Aug, 10am-6.30pm Apr-Jun & Sep, 10am-5.30pm Oct-Mar, treasury 9.45am-5.30pm
- Ⓜ Cité

CATHÉDRALE NOTRE DAME DE PARIS

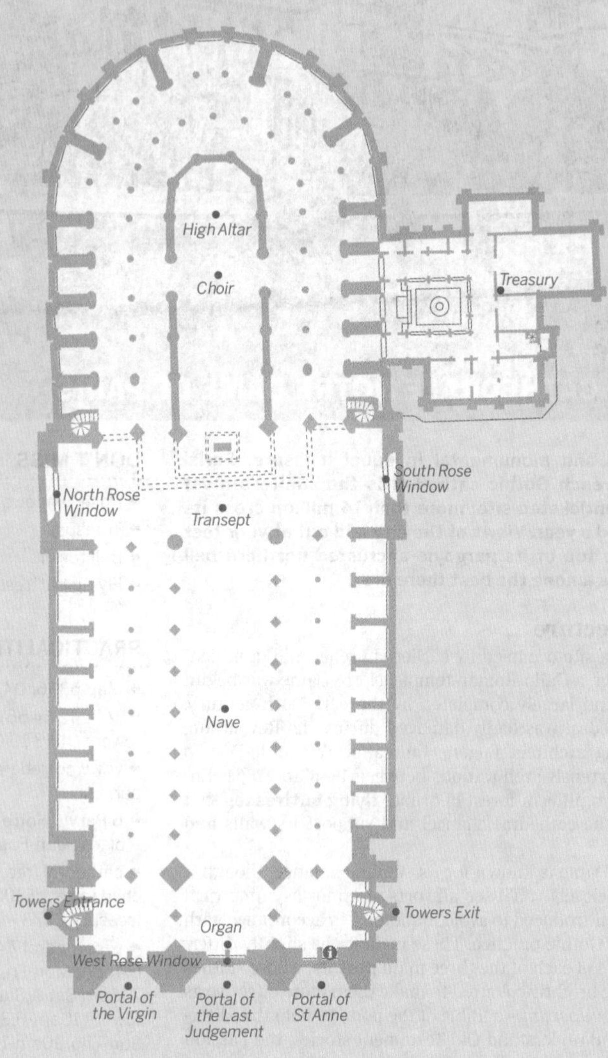

façade above the organ – one of the largest in the world, with 7800 pipes (900 of which have historical classification), 111 stops, five 56-key manuals and a 32-key pedalboard – and the window on the northern side of the transept (virtually unchanged since the 13th century).

Towers

A constant queue marks the entrance to the **Tours de Notre Dame** (www.tours-notre-dame-de-paris.fr), the cathedral's bell towers. Climb the 400-odd spiralling steps to the top of the western façade of the North Tower, where gargoyles grimace and grin on the rooftop **Galerie des Chimères** (Gargoyles Gallery). These grotesque statues divert rainwater from the roof to prevent masonry damage, with the water exiting through the elongated, open mouth; they also, purportedly, ward off evil spirits. Although they appear medieval, they were installed by Eugène Viollet-le-Duc in the 19th century. From the rooftop there's a spectacular view over Paris.

In the South Tower hangs Emmanuel, the cathedral's original 13-tonne bourdon bell (all of the bells are named). During the night of 24 August 1944, when the Île de la Cité was retaken by French, Allied and Resistance troops, the tolling of the Emmanuel announced Paris' approaching liberation. Emmanuel's peal purity comes from the precious gems and jewels Parisian women threw into the pot when it was recast from copper and bronze in 1631.

Treasury

Pay a small fee to enter the *trésor* (treasury), dazzling treasure chest of sacred jewels and gems squirrelled away in the cathedral's southeastern transept. The **Ste-Couronne** (Holy Crown), purportedly the wreath of thorns placed on Jesus' head before he was crucified, is only exhibited between 3pm and 4pm on the first Friday of each month, 3pm to 4pm every Friday during Lent, and 10am to 5pm on Good Friday.

Crypt

Under the square in front of Notre Dame lies the **Crypte Archéologique** (Archaeological Crypt; Map p396; ☎01 55 42 50 10; www.crypte.paris.fr; 7 Parvis Notre Dame – place Jean-Paul II, 4e; adult/child €8/free; ⏲10am-6pm Tue-Sun; Ⓜ Cité), a 117m-long and 28m-wide area displaying the remains of structures built on this site during the Gallo-Roman period, a 4th-century enclosure wall, the foundations of the medieval foundlings hospice and a few of the original sewers sunk by Haussmann. To better explore, rent a highly worthwhile 30-minute audioguide (€5).

NOTRE DAME MUSIC

Music has been a sacred part of Notre Dame's soul since birth. The best day to appreciate its musical heritage is on Sunday at a Gregorian or polyphonic Mass (10am and 6.30pm respectively) or a free organ recital (4.30pm).

October to June the cathedral stages evening concerts (tickets €15 and €25); find the program online at www.musique-sacree-notredamedeparis.fr.

If you can't make it in person, tune into Sunday's 6.30pm Mass on Radio Notre Dame 1 (100.7 FM), or streamed on the cathedral's website.

THE HEART OF PARIS

Notre Dame is very much the heart of Paris – so much so that distances from Paris to every part of metropolitan France are measured from Parvis Notre Dame – place Jean-Paul II, the vast square in front of the Cathedral of Our Lady of Paris, where crowds gather in the afternoon sun to admire the cathedral's façade. A bronze star across the street from the cathedral's main entrance marks the exact location of **Point Zéro des Routes de France** (Map p396).

Notre Dame

TIMELINE

1160 Maurice de Sully becomes bishop of Paris. Mission: to grace growing Paris with a lofty new cathedral.

1182–90 The ① **choir with double ambulatory** is finished and work starts on the nave and side chapels.

1200–50 The ② **west façade**, with rose window, three portals and two soaring towers, goes up. Everyone is stunned.

1345 Some 180 years after the foundation stone was laid, the Cathédrale de Notre Dame is complete. It is dedicated to notre dame (our lady), the Virgin Mary.

1789 Revolutionaries smash the original ③ **Gallery of Kings**, pillage the cathedral and melt all its bells except the great bell Emmanuel. The cathedral becomes a Temple of Reason then a warehouse.

1831 Victor Hugo's novel *The Hunchback of Notre Dame* inspires new interest in the half-ruined Gothic cathedral.

1845–64 Architect Viollet-le-Duc undertakes its restoration. Twenty-eight new kings are sculpted for the west façade. The heavily decorated ④ **portals** and ⑤ **spire** are reconstructed. The neo-Gothic ⑥ **treasury** is built.

1860 The area in front of Notre Dame is cleared to create the parvis, an al fresco classroom where Parisians can learn a catechism illustrated on sculpted stone portals.

1935 A rooster bearing part of the relics of the Crown of Thorns, St Denis and Ste Geneviève is put on top of the cathedral spire to protect those who pray inside.

1991 The architectural masterpiece of Notre Dame and its Seine-side riverbanks become a Unesco World Heritage Site.

2013 Notre Dame celebrates 850 years since construction began with a bevy of new bells and restoration works.

PAL TERAVAGIMOV PHOTOGRAPHY / GETTY IMAGES ©

North Rose Window
See prophets, judges, kings and priests venerate Mary in vivid blue and violet glass, one of three beautiful rose blooms (1225–70), each almost 10m in diameter.

Virgin & Child
Spot all 37 artworks representing the Virgin Mary. Pilgrims have revered the pearly cream sculpture of her in the sanctuary since the 14th century. Light a devotional candle and write some words to the *Livre de Vie* (Book of Life).

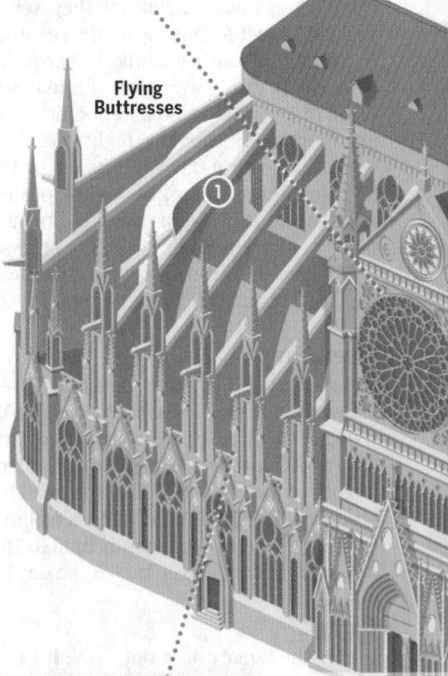

DIGITALIMAGINATION / GETTY IMAGES ©

Choir Screen
No part of the cathedral weaves biblical tales more evocatively than these ornate wooden panels, carved in the 14th century after the Black Death killed half the country's population. The faintly gaudy colours were restored in the 1960s.

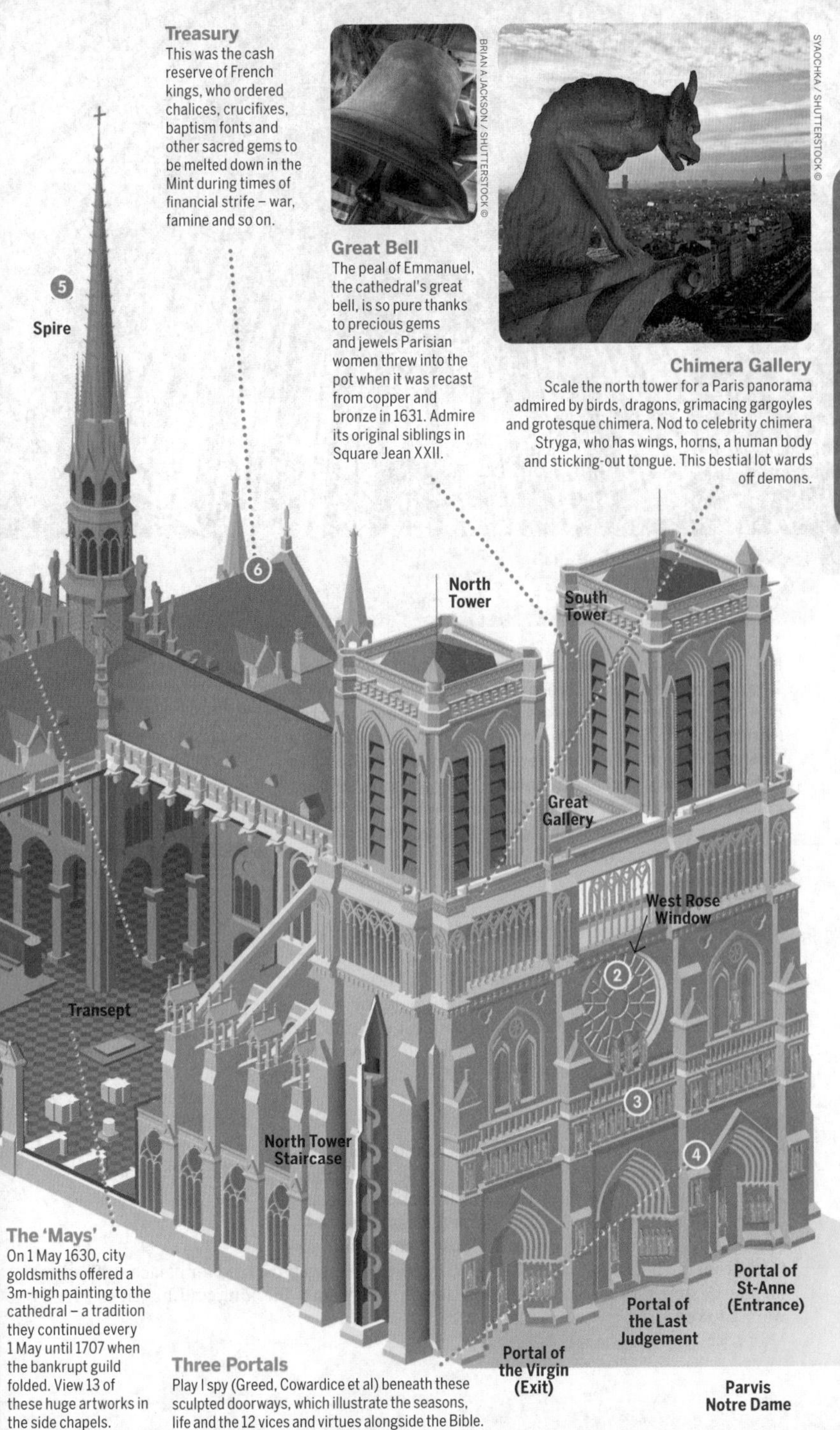
Treasury
This was the cash reserve of French kings, who ordered chalices, crucifixes, baptism fonts and other sacred gems to be melted down in the Mint during times of financial strife – war, famine and so on.
BRIAN A JACKSON / SHUTTERSTOCK ©
SYAOCHKA / SHUTTERSTOCK ©
Great Bell
The peal of Emmanuel, the cathedral's great bell, is so pure thanks to precious gems and jewels Parisian women threw into the pot when it was recast from copper and bronze in 1631. Admire its original siblings in Square Jean XXII.
Chimera Gallery
Scale the north tower for a Paris panorama admired by birds, dragons, grimacing gargoyles and grotesque chimera. Nod to celebrity chimera Stryga, who has wings, horns, a human body and sticking-out tongue. This bestial lot wards off demons.
5
Spire
6
North Tower
South Tower
Great Gallery
West Rose Window
2
3
4
Transept
North Tower Staircase
The 'Mays'
On 1 May 1630, city goldsmiths offered a 3m-high painting to the cathedral – a tradition they continued every 1 May until 1707 when the bankrupt guild folded. View 13 of these huge artworks in the side chapels.
Three Portals
Play I spy (Greed, Cowardice et al) beneath these sculpted doorways, which illustrate the seasons, life and the 12 vices and virtues alongside the Bible.
Portal of the Virgin (Exit)
Portal of the Last Judgement
Portal of St-Anne (Entrance)
Parvis Notre Dame

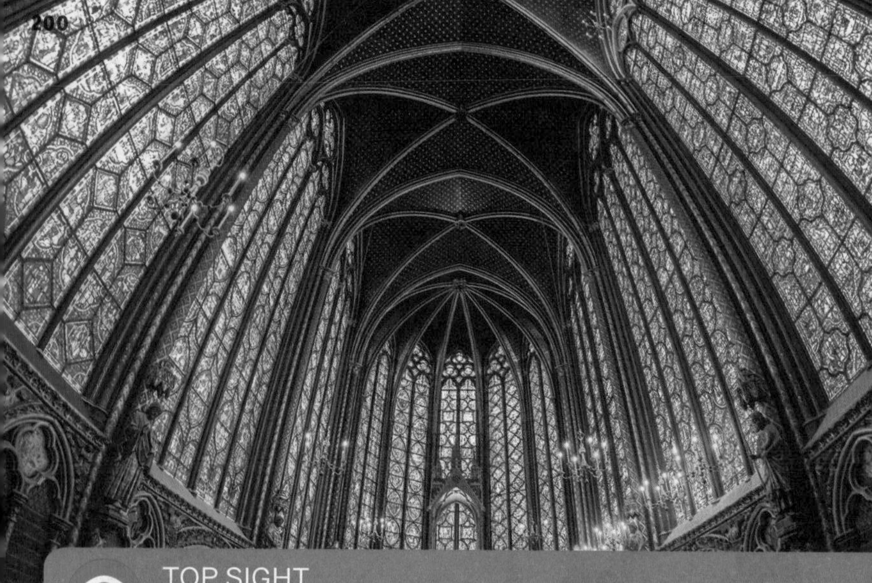

TOP SIGHT
SAINTE-CHAPELLE

No single sight is as dazzling as this bijou Holy Chapel, hidden away like a precious gem – which it is – within the city's Palais de Justice (Law Courts). Paris' oldest, finest stained glass laces its exquisite Gothic interior – best viewed on sunny days when the light floods in to create a mesmerising rainbow of bold colour. throughout. Sainte-Chapelle was built in just six years (compared with nearly 200 years for Notre Dame) and consecrated in 1248.

History

The chapel was conceived by Louis IX to house his personal collection of holy relics, including the famous Ste-Couronne (Holy Crown), acquired by the French king in 1239 from the emperors of Constantinople for a sum of money easily exceeding the amount it cost to build the chapel. The wreath of thorns is safeguarded today in the treasury at Cathédrale Notre Dame de Paris.

Stained Glass

Statues, foliage-decorated capitals, angels and so on decorate this sumptuous, bijou chapel. But it is the 1113 biblical scenes, from Genesis through to the resurrection of Christ, depicted in its 15 floor-to-ceiling stained-glass windows – 15.5m high in the nave, 13.5m in the apse – that stun visitors. From the bookshop in the former ground-floor chapel reserved for palace staff, spiral up the 15-step staircase to the upper chapel, where only the king and his close friends were allowed.

DON'T MISS

- Stained glass
- Classical- and sacred-music concerts
- Guided tours

PRACTICALITIES

- Map p396, C2
- ☎01 53 40 60 80, concerts 01 42 77 65 65
- www.sainte-chapelle.fr
- 8 bd du Palais, 1er
- adult/child €10/free, joint ticket with Conciergerie €15
- 9am-7pm Apr-Sep, to 5pm Oct-Mar
- M Cité

SIGHTS

Île de la Cité was the site of the first settlement in Paris (c 3rd century BC) and later the centre of Roman Lutetia. The island remained the hub of royal and ecclesiastical power, even after the city spread to both banks of the Seine in the Middle Ages. Smaller Île St-Louis was actually two uninhabited islets called Île Notre Dame (Our Lady Isle) and Île aux Vaches (Cows Island) in the early 17th century – until a building contractor and two financiers worked out a deal with Louis XIII to create one island and build two stone bridges to the mainland.

CATHÉDRALE NOTRE DAME DE PARIS — CATHEDRAL

See p195.

SAINTE-CHAPELLE — CHAPEL

See p200.

CONCIERGERIE — MONUMENT

Map p396 (☎01 53 40 60 80; www.paris-conciergerie.fr; 2 bd du Palais, 1er; adult/child €9/free, joint ticket with Sainte-Chapelle €15; ⌚9.30am-6pm; Ⓜ Cité) A royal palace in the 14th century, the Conciergerie later became a prison. During the Reign of Terror (1793–94) alleged enemies of the Revolution were incarcerated here before being brought before the Revolutionary Tribunal next door in the **Palais de Justice**. Top-billing exhibitions take place in the beautiful, Rayonnant Gothic **Salle des Gens d'Armes**, Europe's largest surviving medieval hall.

Of the almost 2800 prisoners held in the dungeons during the Reign of Terror (in various 'classes' of cells, no less) before being sent in tumbrels to the guillotine, star prisoner was Queen Marie-Antoinette – see a reproduction of her cell. As the Revolution began to turn on its own, radicals Danton and Robespierre made an appearance at the Conciergerie and, finally, the judges of the tribunal themselves.

To get the most out of your visit, rent a HistoPad (a tablet-device guide €6.50) to explore the Conciergerie in augmented reality and take part in an interactive, 3D treasure hunt.

SQUARE DU VERT-GALANT — PARK

Map p396 (place du Pont Neuf, 1er; ⌚24hr; Ⓜ Pont Neuf) Chestnut, yew, black walnut and weeping willow trees grace this picturesque park at the westernmost tip of the Île de la Cité, along with migratory birds including mute swans, pochard and tufted ducks, black-headed gulls and wagtails. Sitting at the islands' original level, 7m below their current height, the waterside park is reached by stairs leading down from the Pont Neuf. It's romantic at any time of day, but especially so in the evening as the sun sets over the river.

PONT NEUF — BRIDGE

Map p396 (Ⓜ Pont Neuf) Paris' oldest bridge, misguidingly named 'New Bridge', has linked the western end of Île de la Cité with both riverbanks since 1607, when the king, Henri IV, inaugurated it by crossing the bridge on a white stallion.

View the bridge's arches (seven on the northern stretch and five on the southern span), decorated with 381 *mascarons* (grotesque figures) depicting barbers, dentists, pickpockets, loiterers etc, from a spot along the river or afloat.

The inaugural crossing is commemorated by an equestrian **statue of Henri IV**, known to his subjects as the Vert Galant ('jolly rogue' or 'dirty old man', perspective depending).

Pont Neuf and nearby place Dauphine were used for public exhibitions in the 18th century. In the last century the bridge became an *objet d'art* in 1963, when School of Paris artist Nonda built, exhibited and lived in a huge Trojan horse of steel and wood on the bridge; in 1985 when Bulgarian-born 'environmental sculptor' Christo famously wrapped the bridge in beige fabric; and in 1994 when Japanese designer Kenzo covered it with flowers.

MÉMORIAL DES MARTYRS DE LA DÉPORTATION — MONUMENT

Map p396 (☎01 46 33 87 56; square de l'Île de France, 1er; ⌚10am-7pm Apr-Sep, to 5pm Tue-Sun Oct-Mar; Ⓜ Cité, RER St-Michel–Notre Dame) FREE The Memorial to the Victims of the Deportation, erected in 1962, remembers the 200,000 French residents (including 76,000 Jews, of whom 11,000 were children) who were deported to and murdered in Nazi concentration camps during WWII. A single barred 'window' separates the bleak, rough-concrete courtyard from the waters of the Seine. Inside lies the **Tomb of the Unknown Deportee**.

PONT ST-LOUIS BRIDGE

Map p396 (Ⓜ Pont Marie) The Île de la Cité and Île St-Louis are connected by the postcard-perfect Pont St-Louis.

ÉGLISE ST-LOUIS EN L'ÎLE CHURCH

Map p396 (☎01 46 24 11 69; www.saintlouisenlile.catholique.fr; 19 rue St-Louis en l'Île, 4e; ⏲9.30am-1pm & 2-7.30pm Mon-Sat, 9am-1pm & 2-7pm Sun; Ⓜ Pont Marie) French baroque Église St-Louis en l'Île was built between 1664 and 1726. It hosts classical music and organ concerts some Sundays; check the agenda online.

EATING

Île St-Louis is a pleasant if pricey and often touristy place to dine. Otherwise barren of decent eating places, Île de la Cité has a handful of lovely addresses on its western tip. Self-caterers will find a couple of *fromageries* (cheese shops), chocolate shops and a small grocery store on rue St-Louis en l'Île, 4e.

★BERTHILLON ICE CREAM €

Map p396 (www.berthillon.fr; 29-31 rue St-Louis en l'Île, 4e; 1/2/3/4 scoops take away €3/4.50/6/7.50; ⏲10am-8pm Wed-Sun, closed mid-Feb–early Mar & Aug; Ⓜ Pont Marie) Founded here in 1954, this esteemed *glacier* (ice-cream maker) is still run by the same family today. Its 70-plus all-natural, chemical-free flavours include fruit sorbets (pink grapefruit, raspberry and rose) and richer ice creams made from fresh milk and eggs (salted caramel, candied Ardèche chestnuts, Armagnac and prunes, gingerbread, liquorice, praline and pine kernels). Watch for tempting new seasonal flavours.

Breakfast (€11), afternoon tea and cake, not to mention the most sumptuous ice-cream sundaes topped with lashings of chantilly (sweetened whipped cream) and homemade fruit coulis are served in its adjoining, timber-fronted tearoom.

★CAFÉ SAINT RÉGIS CAFE €

Map p396 (☎01 43 54 59 41; www.cafesaintregisparis.com; 6 rue Jean du Bellay, 4e; breakfast & snacks €3.50-15.50, mains €18-32; ⏲6.30am-2am, kitchen 8am-midnight; 📶; Ⓜ Pont Marie) Waiters in long white aprons, a ceramic-tiled interior and retro vintage decor make hip Le Saint Régis a deliciously Parisian hang-out any time of day – for eating or drinking. From breakfast pastries, organic eggs and bowls of fruit-peppered granola to mid-morning pancakes or waffles, lunch-time salads, burgers, dusk-time oysters and late-night cocktails, it is the hobnobbing hot spot on the islands.

All-day Sunday brunch and happy hour (7pm to 9pm daily) pack in the crowds.

HURÉ BAKERY €

Map p396 (www.facebook.com/HureCreateurDePlaisir/; 1 rue d'Arcole, 4e; sandwiches €4.40; ⏲6.30am-8pm Mon-Sat; Ⓜ St-Michel Notre Dame, Châtelet) *'Createur de plaisir'* (creator of pleasure) is the titillating strapline of this contemporary, street-smart *boulangerie* (bakery) where glass cabinets burst with feisty savoury tarts and quiches, jumbo salads, giant cookies and a rainbow of cakes. For a light, alfresco lunch to eat in a park, you'll be hard-pushed to find a better-value spot near Notre Dame.

There are two other branches in Paris, **one** (Map p386; ☎01 42 72 32 18; www.hurecreateur.fr; 18 rue Rambuteau, 3e; pastries €1.50-5, sandwiches €5.50-9.50; ⏲6.30am-8.30pm Tue-Sat; Ⓜ Rambuteau) handily by the Centre Pompidou and **another** (Map p410; ☎01 43 31 33 93; 10 place d'Italie, 31e; sandwiches from €3.50; ⏲7am-8pm Mon-Sat; Ⓜ Place d'Italie) on place d'Italie in the 13e.

LE CAVEAU DU PALAIS MODERN FRENCH €€

Map p396 (☎01 43 26 04 28; www.caveaudupalais.fr; 19 place Dauphine, 1er; mains €20-27; ⏲noon-2.30pm & 7-10pm; Ⓜ Pont Neuf) Even when the western Île de la Cité shows few other signs of life, the Caveau's half-timbered dining areas and (weather permitting) alfresco terrace are packed with diners tucking into bountiful fresh fare: pan-seared scallops with artichokes, grilled codfish with smoked haddock cream and coriander-spiced cauliflower, or vegetable risotto.

More informal dishes are served at its adjacent wine bar, Le Bar du Caveau.

MA SALLE À MANGER BISTRO €€

Map p396 (☎01 43 29 52 34; 26 place Dauphine, 1er; mains €20; ⏲9am-10.30pm; 👪; Ⓜ Pont Neuf) Framed by a pretty blue-and-white striped awning and colourful pavement tables, bistro-wine bar 'My Dining Room' chalks its daily menu on the blackboard. No-fuss dishes include French onion soup, wine-baked Camembert, duck confit with baked apple, crayfish risotto and a featherlight crème brûlée. Its terrace overlooking enchanting place Dauphine, with purple-and-cream rugs to cuddle up in on friskier days, is idyllic in summer.

L'ÎLOT VACHE FRENCH €€

Map p396 (☎01 46 33 55 16; www.lilotvache.fr; 35 rue St-Louis en l'Île, 4e; menu €39, mains €24.50-35; ⊙7-11pm; 📶; MPont Marie) Named for one of the Île St-Louis' previous two islands and decorated with cow statuettes, this former butcher shop flickers with candles that give its exposed stone walls and dark wood beams a romantic glow. Traditional French classics range from Burgundy snails in parsley butter to bœuf bourguignon grandma-style, duck breast with raspberry *jus,* and roast seasonal fruits with black-currant sorbet.

LES FOUS DE L'ÎLE FRENCH €€

Map p396 (☎01 43 25 76 67; www.lesfousdelile.com; 33 rue des Deux Ponts, 4e; 2-/3-course menus lunch €21/26, dinner €27/33, mains €17-20; ⊙noon-11pm; 📶; MPont Marie) Families flock to this island brasserie with a rustic cockerel theme celebrating the French national symbol and female chef Anaïs Dutilleul in the kitchen. Comforting French fare includes *parmentier de boeuf confit* (French 'shepherd's pie'), smoked haddock with creamy leeks, and fried snails with goat's cheese foam and blinis. Vegetarians are catered for with a daily *belle assiette vegetarienne du moment* (seasonal veggie dish). Handily, service is continuous from noon to 11pm.

SEQUANA MODERN FRENCH €€€

(☎01 43 29 78 81; http://sequana.paris; 72 quai des Orfèvres, 1er; 2-/3-/4-course lunch menu €24/32/50, 4-/6-course dinner menu €50/70; ⊙noon-2.30pm & 7.30-11pm Tue-Fri, 7.30-11pm Sat; MPont Neuf) At home in a chic steel-grey dining room with 1950s-style banquet-seating on Île de la Cité's southwestern tip, sleek Sequana evokes the Gallo-Roman goddess of the River Seine. In the kitchen are well-travelled Philippe and Eugénie, whose childhood in Senegal finds its way into colourful combos such as wild turbot with spinach, mallard and butternut pumpkin, parsnip and China black tea.

Vegetarian menus are available; half-portions are available for children under 12 years.

DRINKING & NIGHTLIFE

Drinking venues on the islands are in short supply. They do exist, but use them as a starting point as very few places stay open late.

LE BAR DU CAVEAU WINE BAR

Map p396 (www.barducaveau.fr; 17 place Dauphine, 1er; ⊙bar 8am-6.30pm Mon-Fri, kitchen noon-4pm Mon-Fri; MPont Neuf) The wine bar of neighbouring restaurant Le Caveau du Palais is not only a good spot for a glass of wine from France's flagship regions, but also small, inexpensive dishes such as salads, *tartines* (open-faced sandwiches), and croques madame and monsieur (toasted ham and cheese sandwiches, the former with a fried egg on top).

LE FLORE EN L'ÎLE CAFE

Map p396 (☎01 43 29 88 27; www.lefloreenlile.fr; 42 quai d'Orléans, 4e; ⊙8am-2am; MPont Marie) A tourist crowd piles into this green-and-gold awning-shaded, old-world people-watching spot with prime views of the buskers on Pont St-Louis. There's an extensive menu of brasserie-style fare ranging from salads to steaks; if you're looking to linger over a Berthillon ice cream, note it's pricier here than other spots around the island, including Berthillon's own nearby premises.

LA CHARLOTTE DE L'ISLE TEAHOUSE

(☎01 43 54 25 83; www.lacharlottedelisle.fr; 24 rue St-Louis en l'Île, 4e; ⊙2-7pm Wed-Fri, 11am-7pm Sat & Sun; MPont Marie) This tiny *salon de thé* (tearoom) has a tempting array of hot chocolate, chocolate sculptures, cakes and pastries as well as a fine collection of tea to taste while you're here, or buy to sip at home.

SHOPPING

Île St-Louis is a shopper's delight for craft-filled boutiques and tiny, charming specialist stores. Head to Île de la Cité for souvenirs and tourist kitsch.

★MARCHÉ AUX FLEURS REINE ELIZABETH II MARKET

Map p396 (place Louis Lépin, 4e; ⊙8am-7.30pm Mon-Sat; MCité) Blooms have been sold at this flower market since 1808, making it the oldest market of any kind in Paris. On Sunday, it transforms into a cacophonous bird market, the **Marché aux Oiseaux** (Map p396; place Louis Lépin, 4e; 8am-7pm Sun; Cité).

★38 SAINT LOUIS FOOD & DRINKS

Map p396 (38 rue St-Louis en l'Île, 4e; 8.30am-10pm Tue-Sat, 9.30am-4pm Sun; Pont Marie) Not only does this contemporary, creamy white-fronted *fromagerie* (cheese shop) run by young, dynamic, food-driven duo Didier Grosjean and Thibault Lhirondelle have an absolutely superb selection of first-class French cheese; it also offers Saturday wine tastings, artisan fruit juices and prepared dishes to go such as sheep's-cheese salad with truffle oil, and wooden boxes filled with vacuum-packed cheese to take home.

L'EMBRASSER ART

(01 42 38 87 95; 24 rue St-Louise, 4e; 11am-7pm Wed-Sun) A glass and steel facade opens onto a minimalist interior at this stylish art gallery dedicated to Japanese art: think prints, paintings, pottery and ceramics.

L'ÎLES AUX IMAGES ART

Map p396 (01 56 24 15 22; www.vintage-photos-lithos-paris.com; 51 rue Saint-Louis en l'Île, 4e; 2-7pm Mon-Sat & by appointment; Pont Marie) Original and rare vintage posters, photographs and lithographs dating from 1850 onwards from artists including Man Ray, Salvador Dalí, Paul Gauguin and Picasso are stocked at this gallery-boutique. Many depict Parisian scenes and make evocative home decorations. Framing can be arranged.

CLAIR DE RÊVE TOYS

Map p396 (01 43 29 81 06; www.clairdereve.com; 35 rue St-Louis en l'Île, 4e; 11am-1pm & 1.30-7.15pm Mon-Sat; Pont Marie) Stringed marionettes made of papier mâché, leather and porcelain bob from the ceiling of this endearing little shop. It also sells wind-up toys and music boxes.

LIBRAIRIE ULYSSE BOOKS

Map p396 (01 43 25 17 35; www.ulysse.fr; 26 rue St-Louis en l'Île, 4e; 2-8pm Tue-Fri, mornings & Sat by appointment; Pont Marie) Stuffed to the rafters with antiquarian and new travel guides, *National Geographic* back editions and maps, this bijou boutique was the world's first travel bookshop when it was opened in 1971 by the intrepid Catherine Domaine. Hours vary, but ring the bell and Catherine will open up if she's around.

IL CAMPIELLO ARTS & CRAFTS

Map p396 (01 44 27 00 22; www.ilcampiello.com; 88 rue St-Louis en l'Île, 4e; noon-7pm; Pont Marie) Venetian carnival masks – intricately crafted from papier mâché, ceramics and leather – are the speciality of this exquisite shop, which also sells jewellery made from Murano glass beads. It was established by a native of Venice, to which the Île St-Louis bears more than a passing resemblance.

Latin Quarter

Neighbourhood Top Five

❶ **Panthéon** (p207) Paying homage to France's greatest thinkers buried beneath this domed neoclassical mausoleum.

❷ **Shakespeare & Company** (p218) Browsing the shelves of Paris' most magical bookshop and refuelling at its inspirational, literary-themed cafe.

❸ **Institut du Monde Arabe** (p209) Visiting the fascinating exhibits inside the stunning Jean Nouvel–designed building before heading to the roof to admire the panorama.

❹ **Jardin des Plantes** (p208) Strolling around Paris' sprawling botanical gardens and visiting its historic greenhouses, zoo and the many branches of the Natural History Museum located here.

❺ **Caveau de la Huchette** (p218) Lapping up the Latin Quarter vibe and dancing after dark at a jazz gig in a mythical medieval cellar much loved by many a jazz great.

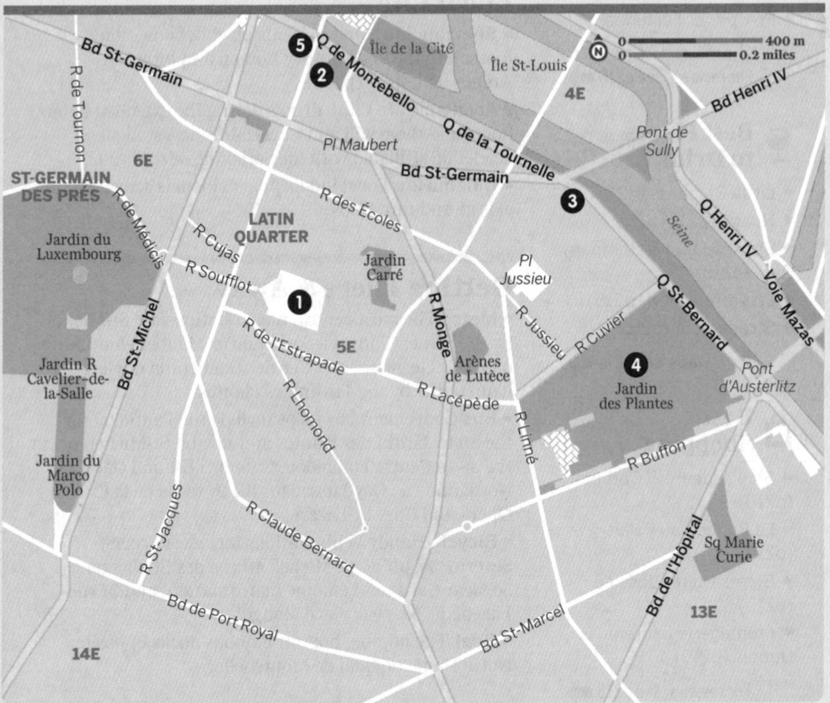

For more detail of this area see Map p398 and p400

Lonely Planet's Top Tip

While hungry first-time visitors are often drawn into the maze of tiny streets between the Seine, rue St-Jacques and bd St-Germain, you'd be wise to simply avoid this overpriced area altogether. Instead, grab some bread, cheese, charcuterie and wine from local speciality shops and enjoy some multimillion-dollar views with lunch or dinner – try the quays along the Seine, place du Panthéon (a fave with students) or the leafy Jardin des Plantes.

Best Places to Eat

- Restaurant AT (p214)
- La Bête Noire (p210)
- Café de la Nouvelle Mairie (p210)
- OnoPoké (p210)
- Prosper et Fortunée (p213)

For reviews, see p210

Best Places to Drink

- Little Bastards (p215)
- Nuage (p215)
- Shakespeare & Company Café (p215)
- Le Verre à Pied (p215)
- Strada Café (p216)

For reviews, see p215

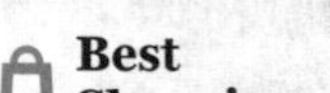

Best Shopping

- Shakespeare & Company (p218)
- Le Bonbon au Palais (p219)
- Bières Cultes Jussieu (p219)
- Fromagerie Laurent Dubois (p219)

For reviews, see p218

Explore Latin Quarter

The Latin Quarter has been student central for Parisian higher education since the Middle Ages. Rub shoulders with some of France's greatest literati at the neoclassical Panthéon (p207), followed by *un café* at Café de la Nouvelle Mairie (p210) (if hungers strikes early, this is a top spot for lunch too).

Meander south to thriving market street rue Mouffetard (p221). Flit from food stall to tantalising food shop, stopping for lunch at a restaurant here. (Skip on Mondays, when the market stalls are shut.) End with an espresso at *nouvelle génération* coffee shop Dose (p217).

Parisian men gather to play boules, as they have done so for centuries, at Roman amphitheatre Arènes de Lutèce (p209). Catch a game, then mooch east to while away a serene afternoon exploring Jardin des Plantes. Don't miss the magnificent 18th-century greenhouses, the Natural History Museum's Grande Galerie de l'Évolution (p208) and a sweet mint tea in the Mosquée de Paris (p214).

Kick off the evening with a guided tasting of six French wines and Champagne at Wine Tasting in Paris (p221). Dine in a local bistro, then duck down into a medieval cellar for a jazz and jam session or into one of the quarter's lively pubs to hobnob with local students.

Local Life

- **Sporting life** Join the locals playing boules and football in the 2nd-century Roman amphitheatre Arènes de Lutèce (p209).
- **Academic life** Clink drinks during the extended happy hours and there will almost certainly be a student or academic affiliated with the Sorbonne next to you.
- **Cinema life** Local independent cinemas screen cult, classic and rare films.

Getting There & Away

- **Metro** The most central metro stations are St-Michel by the Seine; Cluny–La Sorbonne or Maubert-Mutualité on bd St-Germain; and Censier Daubenton or Gare d'Austerlitz by the Jardin des Plantes.
- **Bus** Convenient bus stops include the Panthéon for the 89 to Jardin des Plantes and 13e; bd St-Michel for the 38 to Centre Pompidou, Gare de l'Est and Gare du Nord; and rue Gay Lussac for the 27 to Île de la Cité, Opéra and Gare St-Lazare.
- **Bicycle** Handy Vélib' stations include 42 rue St-Severin, 5e, off bd St-Michel; 40 rue des Boulangers, 5e, near Cardinal Lemoine metro station; and 27 rue Lacépède, 5e, near place Monge.
- **Boat** The hop-on, hop-off Batobus docks opposite Notre Dame on quai de Montebello.

SIGHTS

The Latin Quarter's Roman and medieval roots can be seen throughout the neighbourhood. Natural history buffs won't want to miss the museums making up the Muséum National d'Histoire Naturelle in the beautifully green Jardin des Plantes. Watch for the partial reopening after extensive renovation of the neighbourhood's premier museum and France's finest medieval-history museum, the Musée National du Moyen Âge.

MUSÉE NATIONAL DU MOYEN ÂGE
MUSEUM

Map p398 (01 53 73 78 16; www.musee-moyenage.fr; 6 place Paul Painlevé, 5e; adult/child €8/free; 9.15am-5.45pm Wed-Mon; M Cluny–La Sorbonne) Undergoing renovation until late 2020, the National Museum of the Middle Ages is considered one of Paris' top small museums. It showcases a series of sublime treasures, from medieval statuary, stained glass and objets d'art to its celebrated series of tapestries, *The Lady with the Unicorn* (1500). Other highlights include ornate 15th-century mansion Hôtel de Cluny and the *frigidarium* (cold room) of an enormous Roman-era bathhouse.

On Hôtel de Cluny's 1st floor is the late-Gothic chapel, **La Chapelle de l'Hôtel de Cluny**, with rich carvings of Christ on the cross, 13 angels, and floral and foliage ornaments. Outside, the museum's beautiful medieval gardens – today in a dangerous state of disrepair – are closed to the public.

When the museum partially reopens in July 2018, a new contemporary building, designed by architect Bernard Desmoulin, will house the ticket office, bookshop, souvenir boutique and visitors' cloakroom. By 2020, when renovation works are complete, the museum will boast a state-of-the-art layout with enhanced explanatory panels and interactive displays.

MOSQUÉE DE PARIS
MOSQUE

Map p400 (01 45 35 97 33; www.mosqueedeparis.net; 2bis place du Puits de l'Ermite, 5e; adult/child €3/2; 9am-noon & 2-7pm Sat-Thu Apr-Sep, 9am-noon & 2-6pm Sat-Thu Oct-Mar; M Place Monge) Paris' central mosque, with a

TOP SIGHT PANTHÉON

Elegant and regal in equal measure, the massive neoclassical **dome** of the Left Bank's iconic Panthéon is an icon of the Parisian skyline. Louis XV originally commissioned the vast architectural masterpiece around 1750 as an abbey dedicated to Ste Geneviève in thanksgiving for his recovery from an illness. Due to financial and structural problems, it wasn't completed until 1789.

The Panthéon reverted to religious duties twice after the Revolution but has played a secular role ever since 1885. Its **crypt** serves as the resting place of some of France's greatest thinkers, including Voltaire, Rousseau, Braille and Hugo. In 1995 the first woman was interred in the Panthéon: in recognition of her extraordinary achievements, two-time Nobel Prize–winner, Polish-born Marie Curie (1867–1934) was reburied here, along with husband, Pierre. The pair previously lay in the small-town cemetery of Sceaux, south of Paris.

The last to be interred here (2015) were Resistance fighters Germaine Tillion, Genèvieve de Gaulle-Anthonioz, Pierre Brossolette and Jean Zay. They joined Resistance leader Jean Moulin, at rest in the Panthéon since 1964.

A copy of **Foucault's pendulum**, first hung from the dome in 1851 to demonstrate the rotation of the earth, takes pride of place.

DON'T MISS

- The architecture
- Foucault's Pendulum
- Crypt

PRACTICALITIES

- Map p400, C1
- 01 44 32 18 00
- www.paris-pantheon.fr
- place du Panthéon, 5e
- adult/child €9/free
- 10am-6.30pm Apr-Sep, to 6pm Oct-Mar
- M Maubert-Mutualité or RER Luxembourg

striking 26m-high minaret, was completed in 1926 in an ornate art deco Moorish style. You can visit the interior to admire the intricate tile work and calligraphy. A separate entrance leads to the wonderful North African-style hammam (p214), restaurant (p214) and tearoom (p214), and a small *souk* (actually more of a gift shop). Visitors must be modestly dressed.

JARDIN DES PLANTES PARK

Map p400 (www.jardindesplantes.net; place Valhubert & 36 rue Geoffroy-St-Hilaire, 5e; ⌚7.30am-8pm early Apr–mid-Sep, shorter hours rest of year; Ⓜ Gare d'Austerlitz, Censier Daubenton, Jussieu) Founded in 1626 as a medicinal herb garden for Louis XIII, Paris' 24-hectare botanic gardens – visually defined by the double alley of plane trees that run the length of the park – are an idyllic spot to stroll around, break for a picnic (watch out for the automatic sprinklers!) and escape the city concrete for a spell. Upping its appeal are three museums from the Muséum National d'Histoire Naturelle and a small zoo, La Ménagerie.

Other attractions include peony and rose gardens, an alpine garden, and the gardens of the École de Botanique, used by students of the school and green-fingered Parisians. The beautiful glass-and-metal **Grandes Serres** (Map p400; adult/child €7/5; ⌚10am-6pm Apr-Sep, to 5pm Oct-Mar), a series of four greenhouses, have been in use since 1714; several of Henri Rousseau's jungle paintings, sometimes on display in the Musée d'Orsay (p224), were inspired by his frequent visits here.

LA MÉNAGERIE ZOO

Map p400 (Le Zoo du Jardin des Plantes; www.zoodujardindesplantes.fr; 57 rue Cuvier, 5e; adult/child €13/10; ⌚9am-6pm Mon-Sat, to 6.30pm Sun Mar-Oct, to 5pm or 5.30pm Nov-Feb; Ⓜ Gare d'Austerlitz) Like the Jardin des Plantes in which it's located, this 170-species zoo is more than a tourist attraction; it also doubles as a research centre for the reproduction of rare and endangered species. During the Prussian siege of 1870, the animals of the day were themselves endangered, when almost all were eaten by starving Parisians.

MUSÉUM NATIONAL D'HISTOIRE NATURELLE MUSEUM

Map p400 (www.mnhn.fr; place Valhubert & 36 rue Geoffroy-St-Hilaire, 5e; Ⓜ Gare d'Austerlitz, Censier Daubenton, Jussieu) Despite the name, the National Museum of Natural History is not a single building, but a collection of sites throughout France. Its historic home is in the Jardin des Plantes, and it's here you'll find the greatest number of branches: taxidermied animals in the excellent **Grande Galerie de l'Évolution** (Map p400; ☎01 40 79 54 79; www.grandegaleriedelevolution.fr; adult/child €9/free, with Galeries des Enfants €11/9; ⌚10am-6pm Wed-Mon); fossils and dinosaur skeletons in the **Galeries d'Anatomie Comparée et de Paléontologie** (Map p400; ☎01 40 79 56 01; 2 rue Buffon, 5e; adult/child €7/free; ⌚10am-6pm Wed-Mon Apr-Sep, to 5pm Wed-Mon Oct-Mar); and meteorites and crystals in the **Galerie de Minéralogie et de Géologie** (Map p400; ☎01 40 79 56 01; www.galeriedemineralogieetgeologie.fr; adult/child €7/5; ⌚10am-6pm Wed-Mon Apr-Sep, to 5pm Wed-Mon Oct-Mar).

Created in 1793, the National Museum of Natural History became a site of significant scientific research in the 19th century. Of the three museums here, the four-floor Grande Galerie de l'Évolution is a particular winner if you're travelling with kids: life-sized elephants, tigers and rhinos play safari, and imaginative exhibits on evolution, extinction and global warming fill 6000 sq metres. The temporary exhibits are generally excellent. Within this building is a separate attraction, the **Galerie des Enfants** (Map p400; www.galeriedesenfants.fr; adult/child €11/9; ⌚10am-6pm Wed-Mon) – a hands-on science museum tailored to children aged from six to 12 years.

MUSÉE DE LA SCULPTURE EN PLEIN AIR MUSEUM

Map p398 (quai St-Bernard, 5e; Ⓜ Gare d'Austerlitz) FREE Along quai St-Bernard, this open-air sculpture museum (also known as the Jardin Tino Rossi) has more than 50 late-20th-century unfenced sculptures, and makes a great picnic spot. A salad beneath a César or a baguette beside a Brancusi is a pretty classy way to see the Seine up close.

ABBAYE ROYALE DU VAL-DE-GRÂCE CHURCH

Map p400 (☎01 40 51 51 92; www.ecole-valdegrace.sante.defense.gouv.fr; 1 place Alphonse Laveran; adult/child €5/2.50; ⌚noon-6pm Tue-Thu, Sat & Sun Sep-Jul; Ⓜ RER Port Royal) One of the city's grandest remnants of pre-Revolution Paris, Chapelle de la Val-de-Grâce was built in 1645 to celebrate the

TOP SIGHT
INSTITUT DU MONDE ARABE

Be it Arabic art and culture, history, music, religion or the evolution of writing and language in the Arab world, Paris' groundbreaking Institut du Monte Arabe is a one-stop shop for learning about the Arab world, both today and a millennia ago. It was created in 1980, in partnership with 18 Middle Eastern and North African nations, to foster cross-cultural dialogue.

Its museum on the 4th to 7th floors of the vast building introduces elements from disparate time periods and cultures, focusing on art, artisanship and science. You'll find everything from pre-Islamic ceramics to ancient astronomical instruments, and from regional music displays to Arabic calligraphy. Temporary exhibitions compliment the permanent collections.

You certainly can't miss the building: this is one of the city's many architectural landmarks, with French architect Jean Nouvel using traditional Arabic latticed-wood windows *(mashrabiya)* as his inspiration for the eye-catching glass façade. Dazzling when the sun shines, the imposing façade incorporates thousands of photo-electrically sensitive apertures that allow those inside the building to peer out without being seen. Electric motors open and close the apertures to regulate the amount of light and heat that reach the institute's interior.

DON'T MISS

- Museum
- Observation terrace
- Le Zyriab

PRACTICALITIES

- Arab World Institute
- Map p398, F3
- ☎01 40 51 38 38
- www.imarabe.org
- 1 place Mohammed V, 5e
- adult/child €8/4
- ⏲10am-6pm Tue-Fri, to 7pm Sat & Sun
- Ⓜ Jussieu

birth of Anne of Austria and King Louis XIII's first son after 23 years of childless marriage. Its beautiful, baroque dome is a joy to behold. After the revolution, in 1795, the 17th-century chapel and its surrounding royal abbey became a military hospital. A small museum in the original abbey cloister, the **Musée du Service de Santé des Armées**, explores its work.

Once a month music concerts are held in the chapel; check the website for schedules.

ÉGLISE ST-ÉTIENNE DU MONT CHURCH

Map p400 (☎01 43 54 11 79; www.saintetiennedumont.fr; 1 place Ste-Geneviève, 5e; ⏲8.45am-7.30pm Tue-Fri, 8.45am-noon & 2-7.45pm Sat, 8.45am-12.15pm & 2.30-7.45pm Sun; Ⓜ Cardinal Lemoine) FREE The Church of Mount St Stephen, built between 1492 and 1655, contains Paris' only surviving rood screen (1521–45), separating the chancel from the nave; the others were removed during the late Renaissance because they prevented the faithful in the nave from seeing the priest celebrate Mass.

In the nave's southeastern corner, the tomb of Ste Geneviève lies in a chapel. The patron of Paris, Ste Geneviève was born at Nanterre in AD 422 and turned away Attila the Hun from Paris in AD 451. A highly decorated reliquary near her tomb contains her finger bone.

Fans of the Woody Allen film *Midnight in Paris* will recognise the stone steps on the northwestern corner as the place where Owen Wilson's character is collected by vintage car and transported back to the 1920s.

ARÈNES DE LUTÈCE RUINS

Map p400 (49 rue Monge, 5e; ⏲8am-9.30pm May-Aug, to 8.30pm Apr & Sep, shorter hours rest year; Ⓜ Place Monge) FREE The 2nd-century Roman amphitheatre Lutetia Arena once seated 10,000 people for gladiatorial combats and other events. Found by accident in 1869 when rue Monge was under construction, it's now used by locals playing football and, especially, boules (similar to lawn bowls). Hours can vary.

SQUARE RENÉ VIVIANI PARK

Map p398 (quai de Montebello, 5e; ⏲24hr; Ⓜ St-Michel) Opened in 1928 on the site of the former graveyard of adjoining church Église

St-Julien le Pauvre (p218), this picturesque little park is home to the oldest tree in Paris. The black locust *(Robinia pseudoacacia)* was planted here in 1602 by Henri III, Henri IV and Louis XII's gardener, Jean Robin, and is now supported by concrete pillars disguised as branches and trunks.

A 1995-installed fountain by Georges Jeanclos depicts the legend of St Julien. Roses bloom in spring and summer.

ÉGLISE ST-SÉVERIN CHURCH

Map p398 (☎01 42 34 93 5; www.saint-severin.com; 1 rue des Prêtres St-Séverin, 5e; ⊙11am-7.30pm Mon-Sat, 9am-8.30pm Sun; MCluny–La Sorbonne) FREE Extensively renovated in the 15th century, this Gothic church contains one of the oldest bells in Paris, cast in 1412. Also of note are the seven modern stained-glass windows depicting the seven sacraments, designed by Jean René Bazaine in 1970.

SORBONNE UNIVERSITY

Map p398 (www.sorbonne.fr; 12 rue de la Sorbonne, 5e; MCluny–La Sorbonne or RER Luxembourg) The crème de la crème of academia flock to this distinguished university, one of the world's most famous. Today 'La Sorbonne' embraces most of the 13 autonomous universities – some 45,215 students in all – created when the University of Paris was reorganised after the student protests of 1968. Visitors are not permitted to enter.

CHAPELLE DE LA SORBONNE CHURCH

Map p398 (www.sorbonne.fr; place de la Sorbonne, 5e; MCluny–La Sorbonne) The Sorbonne university's distinctive domed church was built between 1635 and 1642. The remains of Cardinal Richelieu (1585–1642) lie in a tomb with an effigy of a cardinal's hat suspended above. Its interior is only visitable by a 1½-hour guided tour (in French; €9) by online reservation.

COLLÈGE DES BERNARDINS HISTORIC BUILDING

Map p398 (☎01 53 10 74 44; www.collegedesbernardins.fr; 18-24 rue de Poissy, 5e; ⊙10am-6pm Mon-Sat, 2-6pm Sun; MCardinal Lemoine) FREE Dating back to 1248, this former Cistercian college originally served as living quarters and place of study for novice monks. It's now an art gallery and centre for Christian culture with events ranging from lectures to film screenings and music performances; check schedules online.

EATING

From chandelier-lit palaces loaded with history to cheap-eat student haunts, the 5e *arrondissement* caters to every budget and culinary taste. Rue Mouffetard is famed for its food market and food shops, though you'll have to trek down side streets for the neighbourhood's best meals. Other busy eat streets lined with cafes, restaurants and takeaway joints include rue St-Séverin, rue de la Harpe and delightfully car-free rue du Pot de Fer.

★CAFÉ DE LA NOUVELLE MAIRIE CAFE €

Map p400 (☎01 44 07 04 41; 19 rue des Fossés St-Jacques, 5e; mains €10-20; ⊙8am-midnight Mon-Fri, kitchen noon-2.30pm & 8-10.30pm Mon-Thu, 8-10pm Fri; MCardinal Lemoine) Shhhh… just around the corner from the Panthéon (p207) but hidden away on a small, fountained square, this hybrid cafe-restaurant and wine bar is a tip-top neighbourhood secret, serving natural wines by the glass and delicious seasonal bistro fare from oysters and ribs *(à la française)* to grilled lamb sausage over lentils. It takes reservations for dinner but not lunch – arrive early.

★LA BÊTE NOIRE MEDITERRANEAN €

Map p400 (☎06 15 22 73 61; www.facebook.com/labetenoireparis; 58 rue Henri Barbusse, 5e; mains lunch €12-15, dinner €20, brunch €25; ⊙8am-5pm Tue, 8am-11pm Wed-Fri, 9.30am-5.30pm Sat & Sun; 🛜; MRER Port Royal) Funky music and a small, fashionably minimalist interior with open kitchen ensure bags of soul at this off-the-radar *'cantine gastronomique'*, showcase for the sensational home cooking of passionate chef-owner Maria. Inspired by her Russian-Maltese heritage, she cooks just one meat and one vegetarian dish daily using seasonal products sourced from local farmers and small producers, washed down with Italian wine.

★ONOPOKÉ HAWAIIAN €

Map p400 (☎09 82 29 81 87; www.onopoke.fr; 167 rue St-Jacques, 5e; mains €9.50-15; ⊙noon-5pm Mon & Tue, noon-5pm & 7.30-9.30pm Wed, noon-9.30pm Thu & Fri, 12.30-9.30pm Sat; MCardinal Lemoine) Head here for creative beans, grains, pulses and veg topped with raw or smoked fish (tuna, salmon, white fish) and your chosen sprinkling of fried onions, chilli, sunflower seeds or wasabi-laced sesame seeds. Always rammed with cent-smart students from the neighbouring Sorbonne, OnoPoké cooks turbo-sized salad bowls inspired by traditional Hawaiian poke (raw diced fish with sushi rice) in a hip, laid-back space.

Order at the counter, grab a seat at a shared table and await your made-to-measure bowl. Meat lovers will appreciate the French duck or *viande séchée* (air-dried meat) bowl, and there is tofu-peppered poke for vegetarians. Takeaway too.

CROQ' FAC SANDWICHES €

Map p398 (160 rue St-Jacques, 5e; sandwich menu €5.50; ⊙8am-7pm Mon-Sat; Ⓜ Cardinal Lemoine) Latin Quarter students pack out this *sandwicherie* (sandwich bar) at lunchtime and for good reason. Delicious, made-to-measure sandwiches embrace dozens of bread types (wraps, ciabatta, panini, bagels, *pan bagnat* etc) and fillings (the world's your oyster). Arrive before noon to ensure a table – inside or on the people-watching pavement terrace – or takeaway.

LES BAUX DE PARIS FRENCH €

Map p400 (☎01 47 07 91 58; 71 rue Mouffetard, 5e; 2-/3-course lunch menu €13/16; ⊙11.30am-2am; Ⓜ Censier Daubenton) Centuries-old wooden beams and exposed stone add instant charm to this busy restaurant-bar on rue Mouffetard, a market street. Be it a dozen freshly shucked oysters, deep-fried squid, tuna tartare or traditional *magret de canard* (duck breast) with figs and pecan nuts, there is a dish or small plate to suit every taste.

LE POT O'LAIT CRÊPES €

Map p400 (41 rue Censier, 5e; lunch menus €11.50-14-90, crêpes €5-12; ⊙11am-2.30pm & 7-10.30pm Tue-Sat; 👪; Ⓜ Censier Daubenton) A bright, contemporary spot, the Milk Can is the business when it comes to *galettes* (savoury buckwheat crêpes) – try smoked salmon or goat's cheese and bacon – and sweet crêpes (pistachio ice cream, zesty orange, hot chocolate and whipped cream). Salads are spectacular; kids will love the ice-cream sundaes.

LA SALLE À MANGER FRENCH €

Map p400 (☎01 55 43 91 99; 138 rue Mouffetard, 5e; mains €10-18, weekend brunch €18-34; ⊙9am-5pm Wed-Sun; 📶; Ⓜ Censier Daubenton) With a sunny pavement terrace beneath trees enviably placed at the foot of foodie street rue Mouffetard, the 'Dining Room' is prime real estate. Its 360-degree outlook – market stalls, fountain, church and garden with a playground for tots – couldn't be prettier, and its salads, *tartines* (open sandwiches), tarts and pastries ensure packed tables at breakfast, lunch and weekend brunch.

LE COMPTOIR DU PANTHÉON CAFE €

Map p400 (☎01 43 54 75 36; 5 rue Soufflot, 5e; salads €12.10-13.90, mains €15-18; ⊙kitchen 7am-11pm Mon-Sat, 8am-11pm Sun; 📶; Ⓜ Cardinal Lemoine or RER Luxembourg) Enormous, creative meal-size salads are the reason to choose this as a dining spot. Magnificently placed across from the domed Panthéon (p207) on the shady side of the street, its pavement terrace is big, busy and quintessentially Parisian – turn your head away from Voltaire's burial place and the Eiffel Tower pops into view. The bar closes daily at 1.45am.

BOULANGERIE ERIC KAYSER BAKERY €

Map p398 (www.maison-kayser.com; 8 rue Monge, 5e; ⊙6.45am-8.30pm Mon & Wed-Fri, 6.30am-8.30pm Sat & Sun; Ⓜ Maubert–Mutualité) This original branch of Eric Kayser – now a household name in Paris with 16 addresses across the city and several more worldwide – is one of the best bakeries that's reasonably close to the Seine and the islands. A few doors down is a second **shop** (Map p398; ☎01 44 07 17 81; www.maison-kayser.com; 14 rue Monge, 5e; ⊙7am-8.15pm Mon, 7.30am-8.15pm Wed-Sun; Ⓜ Maubert–Mutualité), with seating, coffee and light, flaky pastries.

PETITS PLATS DE MARC CAFE €

Map p400 (☎01 43 36 60 79; www.facebook.com/LesPetitsPlatsDeMarc; 6 rue de l'Arbalète, 5e; mains €18-31, weekend brunch €18-23; ⊙9am-3.30pm Tue & Wed, to 7pm Thu-Sat, to 5pm Sun; 📶; Ⓜ Censier Daubenton) This tiny pit stop off rue Mouffetard is wonderfully cosy and a change from the usual humdrum tourist spots; the homemade soups, quiches, pastries and salads are delicious and easy on the wallet. Tea and coffee are served throughout the day, and its weekend brunch is among Paris' finest. To brunch on the cheap (€15.50 to €19), dine and leave before noon.

ODETTE PATISSERIE €

Map p398 (☎01 43 26 13 06; www.odette-paris.com; 77 rue Galande, 5e; 1/6/12 pastry puffs €1.90/10.90/19.80; ⊙noon-8pm Mon-Fri,

LOCAL KNOWLEDGE

RUE MOUFFETARD

Originally a Roman road, the sloping, cobbled rue Mouffetard acquired its name in the 18th century, when the now underground River Bièvre became the communal waste disposal for local tanners and wood pulpers. The odours gave rise to the name Mouffette ('skunk'), which evolved into Mouffetard. The street's now filled with market stalls (bar Mondays), cheap eateries and lively bars.

10am-8pm Sat & Sun; MSt-Michel) Odette's ground-floor space sells *choux* (pastry puffs) with seasonal flavoured cream fillings (nine at any one time), such as coffee, lemon, green tea, salted caramel, pistachio and forest berries. Upstairs, its art deco tearoom plays 1920s music and serves *choux* along with tea, coffee and Champagne. The black-painted timber façade, fronted by tables, and a geranium-filled 1st-floor window box are charming.

BONJOUR VIETNAM VIETNAMESE €

Map p400 (01 43 54 78 04; 6 rue Thouin, 5e; mains €10-14; noon-2.30pm & 7-11pm Wed-Mon; MCardinal Lemoine) Stop by this lauded Vietnamese spot for a bowl of pho (noodle soup with thin slices of rare beef, mint, anise and lime) or *bobun* (cold rice-noodle salad with marinated beef). There's only a handful of tables; reserve.

CHEZ NICOS CRÊPES €

Map p400 (01 45 87 28 13; www.facebook.com/ChezNicos; 44 rue Mouffetard, 5e; crêpes €1.50-5.50; 10am-2am; ; MPlace Monge) The signboard outside crêpe artist Nicos' unassuming little shop lists dozens of fillings but ask by name for his masterpiece, 'La Crêpe du Chef', stuffed with aubergines, feta, mozzarella, lettuce, tomatoes and onions. There's a handful of tables inside; otherwise get it wrapped up in foil and head to a nearby park.

LE PUITS DE LÉGUMES VEGETARIAN, ORGANIC €

Map p398 (01 43 25 50 95; www.lepuitsdelegumesbio.fr; 18 rue du Cardinal Lemoine, 5e; lunch menus €12-18, mains €12-20; noon-4pm & 7-10pm Mon-Sat; ; MCardinal Lemoine) Homemade tarts, quiches, omelettes, fish and rice dishes loaded with fresh seasonal vegetables are the draw of the 'Vegetable Well', an all-organic vegetarian (plus fish) student favourite with cheery apple-green façade. From the tiny kitchen a comforting waft of homemade cooking pervades the simple dining room, filled with a handful of condiment-laden tables. Specials are chalked on the board outside.

LES PAPILLES BISTRO €€

Map p400 (01 43 25 20 79; www.lespapillesparis.fr; 30 rue Gay Lussac, 5e; 2-/4-course menus €28/35; noon-2pm & 7-10.30pm Tue-Sat; MRaspail or RER Luxembourg) This hybrid bistro, wine cellar and *épicerie* (specialist grocer) with a sunflower-yellow façade is one of those fabulous Parisian dining experiences. Meals are served at simply dressed tables wedged beneath bottle-lined walls, and fare is market driven: each weekday cooks up a different *marmite du marché* (market casserole). But what really sets it apart is its exceptional wine list.

It only seats around 15 people; reserve a few days in advance to guarantee a table. After your meal, stock your own *cave* (wine cellar) at Les Papilles' *cave à vins*.

LE COUPE-CHOU FRENCH €€

Map p398 (01 46 33 68 69; www.lecoupechou.com; 9 & 11 rue de Lanneau, 5e; menu lunch €15, 2-/3-course dinner €27/33, mains €17.50-29.50; noon-1.30pm & 7-10.30pm Mon-Sat, 7-10.30pm Sun Sep-Jun, 7-10.30pm Jul & Aug; MMaubert-Mutualité) This maze of candlelit rooms inside a vine-clad 17th-century townhouse is overwhelmingly romantic. Ceilings are beamed, furnishings are antique, open fireplaces crackle and background classical music mingles with the intimate chatter of diners. As in the days when Marlene Dietrich dined here, reservations are essential. Timeless French dishes include Burgundy snails, steak tartare and bœuf bourguignon.

LE PRÉ VERRE BISTRO €€

Map p398 (01 43 54 59 47; www.lepreverre.com; 8 rue Thénard, 5e; lunch menu €16.50, mains €18-21; noon-2pm & 7.30-10.30pm Tue-Sat; ; MMaubert-Mutualité) Noisy, busy and buzzing, this jovial bistro plunges diners into the heart of a Parisian's Paris. Long the stronghold of the legendary Delacourcelle brothers, current owner Jean-François Paris continues to woo foodies with a predominantly organic kitchen and buzzing pavement terrace. At lunchtime join the flock for the fabulous-value *formule dejéuner* (lunch menu), which spices up French classics with the odd 'exotic' ingredient.

PROSPER ET FORTUNÉE MODERN FRENCH €€

Map p400 (01 43 37 70 39; 50 rue Broca, 5e; menus €55; from 8.30pm Tue-Sat, closed Aug; Les Gobelins) Eric Lévy's 15-seat premises is effectively a clandestine supper club where you can watch the chef prepare daily changing dishes (raw mackerel with yuzu and lemon confit; prime fillet with black radish) using mostly organic premium produce in his open kitchen. Dinner kicks off at a fixed time (8.30pm Tuesday to Thursday, 6.30pm and 9pm Friday and Saturday); reservations essential weekends.

A sensational meal of several courses climaxes with dessert – always two of them, one fruity and the other creamy. Expect less courses at the shorter, 6.30pm sitting (€35).

L'AGRUME BISTRO €€

Map p400 (01 43 31 86 48; http://restaurant-lagrume.fr; 15 rue des Fossés St-Marcel, 5e; 2-/3-course lunch menu €23/26, dinner menu €48; 12.15-2.30pm & 7.30-10.30pm Tue-Sat; Censier Daubenton) Reserve a table in advance (online or by telephone) at this chic bistro where you can watch chefs work with seasonal products in the open kitchen while you dine at a table or the *comptoir* (counter). Lunch is magnificent value and a real gourmet experience. Evening dining is an exquisite, daily changing no-choice *dégustation* (tasting) medley of five courses.

ANAHUACALLI MEXICAN €€

Map p398 (01 43 26 10 20; 30 rue des Bernardins, 5e; mains €18-22; 7-10.30pm Mon-Thu, 7-11pm Fri & Sat, noon-2.30pm & 7-10.30pm Sun; ; Maubert-Mutualité) This upmarket restaurant behind a discreet rosemary-coloured façade cooks up some of the best Mexican cuisine in Paris. Enjoy authentic, elegantly presented enchiladas, tamales and mole poblano in a sparingly decorated interior lined with mirrors and statuettes. Fish lovers, you'll adore the *pescado à la veracruzana* (fish of the day flambéed with tequila).

DANS LES LANDES BASQUE, TAPAS €€

Map p400 (01 45 87 06 00; http://dansleslandes.fr; 119bis rue Monge, 5e; tapas €9-17; noon-2.30pm & 7-11pm Mon-Fri, noon-11pm Sat & Sun; Censier Daubenton) Treat yourself to a trip to the Basque Country: Gascogne chef Julien Duboué presents his artful, tapas-size take on southwestern cuisine, with whimsical shared plates that range from duck hearts with parsley and chilli-smothered *xistoria* (Basque sausages) to fried camembert with green apple, duck-neck confit and jars of foie gras. It's one of the best places in Paris for Basque wines.

LE ZYRIAB BY NOURA LEBANESE €€

Map p398 (01 55 42 55 42; www.noura.com; Institut du Monde Arabe, 1 rue des Fossés, 5e; menus €39-65; noon-3pm & 7.30pm midnight Tue-Sat, noon-3pm Sun, salon de thé 3-6pm Tue-Sat; Jussieu, Cardinal Lemoine) Savour Lebanese gastronomy and a sensational view of Paris at this elegant restaurant on the 9th floor of the Institut du Monde Arabe. Be it fragrant vine leaves stuffed with tomato- and parsley-laced rice, traditional *moussakaa* (eggplant) or spicy *sojok* (lamb sausages), the menu tempts. Or nip in for afternoon tea and a sweet platter of syrupy *baklawa* or pistachio-stuffed *karabige* (shortbread biscuits).

DESVOUGES FRENCH €€

Map p400 (01 47 07 91 25; http://restaurant-desvouges.fr; 6 rue des Fosses St-Marcel, 5e; mains €19-25; 11.30am-3.30pm Mon & Tue, 11.30am-3.30pm & 7-11pm Wed, 11.30am-3.30pm & 7pm-midnight Thu, 11.30am-3.30pm & 7pm-1am Fri; St-Marcel, Les Gobelins) Expect a healthy dose of humour as well as top-notch bistro cuisine and *'fromages qui puent un peu'* ('cheeses that pong a bit') at this neighbourhood bistro, the passion of Jérôme Desvouges, who ditched a 17-year career in IT journalism to open his own restaurant. Sea bass roasted in honey and *confit de canard* cannelloni are among the treats on the creative menu.

LE BUISSON ARDENT MODERN FRENCH €€

Map p400 (01 43 54 93 02; www.lebuissonardent.fr; 25 rue Jussieu, 5e; 2-/3-course lunch menus €19/24, mains €22-38; noon-2.30pm & 7.30-10.30pm; Jussieu) Housed in a former coach house, this time-worn bistro (front-room murals date to the 1920s) serves classy, exciting French fare. The menu changes every week and includes varied dishes such as grilled tuna with capers and black olives, veal cutlets with candied ginger sauce and beef in porto. End on a sweet high with homemade vanilla, pistachio and chocolate profiteroles.

LES PIPOS FRENCH €€

Map p398 (☎01 43 54 11 40; www.facebook.com/lespiposbaravins; 2 rue de l'École Polytechnique, 5e; 2-course weekday menu €14.50, mains €11.90-19.90; ⏰9am-midnight Mon-Sat, kitchen 11.30am-11pm; Ⓜ Maubert-Mutualité) Natural wines are the speciality of this *bar à vins,* which it keeps in its vaulted stone cellar. First-rate food – served all day – includes a fish of the day and oysters from Brittany, along with standards like confit of duck and a mouthwatering cheese board, which includes all the French classics (Comté, Bleu d'Auvergne, Brie de Meaux, Rocamadour and St-Marcellin).

LE PETIT PONTOISE BISTRO €€

Map p398 (☎01 43 29 25 20; www.lepetitpontoise.fr; 9 rue de Pontoise, 5e; 2-/3-course weekday lunch menu €23/29, 3-course weekend lunch menu €34, mains €21-30; ⏰noon-2.30pm & 6.30-10.30pm; Ⓜ Maubert-Mutualité) Entering this tiny bistro with traditional lace curtains and simple wooden tables is like stepping into old-world Paris. And the kitchen lives up to expectation with fantastic old-fashioned classics like calf kidneys, veal liver cooked in raspberry vinegar, roast quail, *cassoulette d'escargots* (snail stew) and honey- and almond-baked camembert (out of this world). Everything is deliciously *fait maison* (homemade).

MOSQUÉE DE PARIS NORTH AFRICAN €€

Map p400 (☎01 43 31 14 32; www.restaurantauxportesdelorient.com; 39 rue Geoffroy-St-Hilaire, 5e; mains €10-28; ⏰kitchen noon-midnight; Ⓜ Censier Daubenton, Place Monge) Dig into one of 10 types of couscous, or choose a heaping tajine or meaty grill at this richly decorated, authentic-as-it-gets North African restaurant tucked within the walls of the city's art deco–Moorish mosque (p207), or enjoy sweet mint tea and a *pâtisserie orientale* beneath the trees in the courtyard of the **tearoom** (Map p400; ☎01 43 31 38 20; www.restaurantauxportesdelorient.com; ⏰noon-midnight).

Feeling decadent? Book a *formule orientale* (€63), which includes a body scrub, 10-minute massage and a lounge in the women-only **hammam** (Map p400; www.la-mosquee.com; admission €18, spa package from €43; ⏰10am-9pm Wed-Mon) – bring a swimsuit – as well as lunch, mint tea and a sweet pastry.

LA RÔTISSERIE D'ARGENT ROTISSERIE €€

Map p398 (☎01 43 54 17 47; www.rotisseriedargent.com; 19 quai de la Tournelle, 5e; mains €19-34; ⏰noon-2.15pm & 7-10.30pm; Ⓜ Cardinal Lemoine) Spit-roasted suckling pigs, chickens, ducks, shoulder of lamb, pigeons and more turn on rotating skewers over an open flame within view of your table at this relaxed quayside bistro run by its Michelin-starred neighbour La Tour d'Argent. Order off the daily chalkboard and save room for classic desserts like crème brûlée or lavish seasonal fruit tarts. The wine list is extensive and excellent.

BISTRO LE MAUZAC BISTRO €€

Map p400 (☎01 46 33 75 22; www.bistro-mauzac.com; 7 rue de l'Abbé de l'Epée, 5e; 2-course lunch menu €15, mains €14.50-26.90; ⏰7am-11pm Mon-Sat, 10am-6pm Sun Mar-Oct, 7am-11pm Mon-Sat Nov-Feb; 📶; Ⓜ Place Monge or RER Luxembourg) With a moon-shaped zinc bar and traditional furnishings, Le Mauzac is a quintessential old-school Parisian bistro. Drinks and food are served nonstop, kicking off with egg-fuelled breakfasts (€2 to €10), followed by lunchtime steaks, hearty bowls of *soupe à l'oignon* (onion soup) and croques monsieurs (cheese and ham toasties) made with Poilâne bread. Sweet crêpes, pastries and ice-creams too.

★ **RESTAURANT AT** GASTRONOMY €€€

Map p398 (☎01 56 81 94 08; www.atsushitanaka.com; 4 rue du Cardinal Lemoine, 5e; 6-course lunch menu €55, 12-course dinner tasting menu €105; ⏰12.15-2pm & 8-9.30pm Mon-Sat; Ⓜ Cardinal Lemoine) Trained by some of the biggest names in gastronomy (Pierre Gagnaire included), chef Atsushi Tanaka showcases abstract artlike masterpieces incorporating rare ingredients (charred bamboo, kohlrabi turnip cabbage, juniper berry powder, wild purple fennel, Nepalese Timut pepper) in a blank-canvas-style dining space on stunning outsized plates. Ingeniously, dinner menus can be paired with wine (€70) or juice (€45). Reservations essential.

LA TOUR D'ARGENT GASTRONOMY €€€

Map p398 (☎01 43 54 23 31; www.latourdargent.com; 15 quai de la Tournelle, 5e; lunch menu €105, dinner menus €280-350, mains €78-146; ⏰12.30-2pm & 7-10pm Tue-Sat, closed Aug; Ⓜ Cardinal Lemoine) The venerable Michelin-starred 'Silver Tower' is famous for its *caneton* (duckling), rooftop garden with glimmering

Notre Dame (p195) views and fabulous history harking back to 1582 – from Henry III's inauguration of the first fork in France to inspiration for the winsome animated film *Ratatouille*. Its wine cellar is one of Paris' best; dining is dressy and exceedingly fine.

Reserve eight to 10 days ahead for lunch, three weeks ahead for dinner. Various set *menu* options include a duckling *menu*, Îles Chausey lobster *menu* and a truffle *menu* in season.

Buy fine food, accessories and Champagnes from its own vineyard in La Tour d'Argent's **boutique** (Map p398; ☎01 46 33 45 58; 2 rue du Cardinal Lemoine, 5e; ⊙noon-8pm Tue-Sat; Ⓜ Cardinal Lemoine) on the same street and dine for a snip of the price at its casual bistro La Rôtisserie.

LA TRUFFIÈRE GASTRONOMY €€€

Map p400 (☎01 46 33 29 82; www.latruffiere.fr; 4 rue Blainville, 5e; 2-/3-course lunch menu €32/40, dinner menus €68-180; ⊙noon-2pm & 7-10.30pm Tue-Sat; Ⓜ Place Monge) As its name implies, truffles are the centrepiece of this Michelin-starred restaurant's menu, featuring in most (albeit not all) of its weekly changing dishes, from classic Italian gnocchi to miso and sake-marinated tuna with samphire, roast venison with juniper berries and smoked Jerusalem artichokes, and oxtail stew with mash. To go all-out, order the six-course black truffle tasting menu (€180).

DRINKING & NIGHTLIFE

Rive Gauche romantics, well-heeled cafe-society types and students by the gallon drink in the 5e *arrondissement*, where nostalgic haunts, swish bars and new-generation coffee shops ensure a deluge of early-evening happy hours and a quintessential Parisian *soirée*.

★SHAKESPEARE & COMPANY CAFÉ CAFE

Map p398 (☎01 43 25 95 95; www.shakespeareandcompany.com; 2 rue St-Julien le Pauvre, 5e; ⊙9.30am-7pm Mon-Fri, to 8pm Sat & Sun; 📶; Ⓜ St-Michel) Instant history was made when this literary-inspired cafe opened in 2015 adjacent to magical bookshop Shakespeare & Company (p218), designed from long-lost sketches to fulfil a dream of late bookshop founder George Whitman from the 1960s. Organic chai tea, turbo-power juices and specialist coffee by Parisian roaster Café Lomi (p150) marry with soups, salads, bagels and pastries by Bob's Bake Shop (of Bob's Juice Bar; p144).

Not to be missed: a Golden Latte (€5.50), aka milky coffee spiced with turmeric, cinnamon, ginger, nutmeg, black pepper and coconut oil. Before leaving, buy a 250g bag of 'Assemblage Shakespeare' coffee beans (€13) to take home as a Parisian souvenir.

★LITTLE BASTARDS COCKTAIL BAR

Map p400 (☎01 43 54 28 33; www.facebook.com/lilbastards; 5 rue Blainville, 5e; ⊙6pm-2am Mon-Thu, 6pm-4am Fri & Sat; Ⓜ Place Monge) Only house-creation cocktails (€12) are listed on the menu at uberhip Little Bastards – among them Balance Ton Cochon (bacon-infused rum, egg white, lime juice, oak wood–smoked syrup and bitters) and Deep Throat (Absolut vodka, watermelon syrup and Pernod). The barmen will mix up classics too if you ask.

★NUAGE CAFE

Map p398 (☎09 82 39 80 69; www.nuagecafe.fr; 14 rue des Carmes, 5e; per hr/day €5/25; ⊙8.30am-7pm Mon-Fri, 11am-8pm Sat & Sun; 📶; Ⓜ Maubert-Mutualité) One of a crop of co-working cafes to mushroom in Paris, Nuage (Cloud) lures a loyal following of nomadic digital creatives with its cosy, home-like spaces in an old church (and subsequent school where Cyrano de Bergerac apparently studied). Payment is by the hour or day, craft coffee is by Parisian roaster Coutume (p242) and gourmet snacks stave off hunger pangs. Super-fast wi-fi, books to browse, games to play, music and a silent zone only add to the appeal.

LE VERRE À PIED CAFE

Map p400 (☎01 43 31 15 72; 118bis rue Mouffetard, 5e; ⊙9am-9pm Tue-Sat, 9.30am-4pm Sun; Ⓜ Censier Daubenton) This *café-tabac* is a pearl of a place where little has changed since 1870. Its nicotine-hued mirrored wall, moulded cornices and original bar make it part of a dying breed, but it epitomises the charm, glamour and romance of an old Paris everyone loves, including stallholders from the rue Mouffetard market who yo-yo in and out.

Contemporary photography and art adorns one wall. Lunch (two-course *formule* €16.50, *plat du jour* €13) is a busy, lively affair thanks to the kitchen's wholesome homemade cuisine. Live music quickens the pulse a couple of evenings a week.

LATIN QUARTER LITERARY ADDRESSES

Like its Left Bank neighbours, the Latin Quarter is steeped in literary history.

James Joyce's flat (Map p400; 71 rue du Cardinal Lemoine, 5e; Ⓜ Cardinal Lemoine) Somewhat fittingly, squint through the wrought-iron gates of 71 rue du Cardinal Lemoine to see the courtyard flat where a near-blind James Joyce finished editing *Ulysses*. The Irish writer and his wife, Nora, were put up rent-free by French novelist Valery Larbaud who owned the apartment marked with an 'E'. It's not open to the public, but Joyce is said to have scribbled away at the manuscript with his head laid almost sideways as it was the only way he was able to see what he had written.

Ernest Hemingway's apartment (Map p400; 74 rue du Cardinal Lemoine, 5e; Ⓜ Cardinal Lemoine) A few doors down from chez Joyce, at 74 rue du Cardinal Lemoine, is the townhouse where Ernest Hemingway (1899–1961) and his first wife, Hadley, lived it up between January 1922 and August 1923. Conveniently for the party-loving novelist, his 3rd-floor apartment was right above one of the hottest dance halls in town, the Bal au Printemps: Hemingway was one of the most loyal regulars at the parties and literary soirées thrown many Friday nights here by English writer and editor Ford Madox.

Paul Verlaine's garret (Map p400; 39 rue Descartes, 5e; Ⓜ Cardinal Lemoine) Hemingway might have lived on rue du Cardinal Lemoine in the 1920s but his writing desk was around the corner, in a top-floor garret of a hotel at 39 rue Descartes – today a traditional French restaurant with vintage decor and plenty of time-faded old photographs on the wall. A popular stopover for impoverished writers, French poet Paul Verlaine (1844–96) lived for a while – and died – in the same hotel.

Place de la Contrescarpe Rue Descartes runs south into place de la Contrescarpe (place Monge), now a well-scrubbed square with four Judas trees and a fountain, but once a 'cesspool' (said Hemingway), especially Café des Amateurs at 2 to 4 place de la Contrescarpe, now Café Delmas.

George Orwell's boarding house (Map p400; 6 rue du Pot de Fer, 5e; Ⓜ Place Monge) George Orwell (1903–50) arrived in Paris in spring 1928 and checked into a cheap boarding house above 6 rue du Pot de Fer, where he stayed until he moved to London in December 1929. Despite its slumminess, the boarding house – or 'Hotel X' as he called it in *Down and Out in Paris and London* (1933) – seemed 'like a holiday' after a day slaving away washing dishes at a restaurant on nearby rue du Commerce.

STRADA CAFÉ — COFFEE

Map p398 (www.stradacafe.fr; 24 rue Monge, 5e; ⌚8am-6.30pm Mon-Fri, 10am-6.30pm Sat & Sun; 📶; Ⓜ Cardinal Lemoine) Beans from Parisian roastery L'Arbre à Café and Lyon's Mokxa roastery underpin the success of this sunlit corner cafe, strewn with an eclectic mix of armchairs and wooden-chair seating. Electrical sockets are plentiful (no laptops at weekends) and international baristas are passionate about their brews. Breakfast, salad-and-soup lunch (€11.50 to €13.50), weekend brunch (€22) and gluten-free cakes.

CAFÉ DELMAS — CAFE

Map p400 (☎01 43 26 51 26; www.cafedelmas.com; 2 place de la Contrescarpe, 5e; ⌚7.30am-2am Sun-Thu, to 4am Fri & Sat; 📶; Ⓜ Place Monge) Enviably situated on tree-studded place de la Contrescarpe, Delmas is perfect for *un café*, all-day breakfast or St-Germain Spritz (St-Germain liqueur, Prosecco and peach coulis) at sunset. Get cosy beneath overhead heaters outside and soak up the street atmosphere or snuggle between books in the library-style interior – awash with students from the nearby universities.

LE VIOLON DINGUE — PUB

Map p398 (☎01 43 25 79 93; www.facebook.com/TheViolonDingue; 46 rue de la Montagne Ste-Geneviève, 5e; ⌚7pm-5am Tue-Sat; Ⓜ Maubert-Mutualité) Students pack out the loud, lively 'Crazy Violin', with big-screen sports upstairs and the flirty 'Dingue Lounge' downstairs. Its name is a pun on the expression *le violon d'Ingres,* meaning 'hobby' in French because the celebrated painter Jean-Auguste-Dominique Ingres played fiddle in his spare time. Happy hour is 7pm to 10pm Tuesday to Saturday. Expect beer pong and other anglophone pub antics.

CAVE LA BOURGOGNE BAR

Map p400 (☎01 47 07 82 80; 144 rue Mouffetard, 5e; ⏱7am-2am Mon-Sat, to 11pm Sun; Ⓜ Censier Daubenton) A prime spot for soaking up rue Mouffetard's contagious 'saunter-all-day' spirit, this neighbourhood hangout sits on square St-Médard, one of the Latin Quarter's loveliest, with flower-bedecked fountain, centuries-old church and market stalls spilling across one side. Inside, locals and their pet dogs meet for coffee around dark wood tables alongside a local wine-sipping set. In summer everything spills outside.

PUB ST-HILAIRE PUB

Map p398 (☎01 46 33 52 42; www.facebook.com/pubsthilaire; 2 rue Valette, 5e; ⏱4pm-2am Mon-Thu, to 5am Fri & Sat; Ⓜ Maubert-Mutualité) 'Buzzing' fails to do justice to the pulsating vibe inside this student-loved pub. Generous happy hours last from 5pm to 9pm and the place is kept packed with a trio of pool tables, board games, music on two floors, hearty bar food and various gimmicks to rev up the party crowd (a metre of cocktails, 'be your own barman' etc).

L'ACADÉMIE DE LA BIÈRE PUB

Map p400 (☎01 43 54 66 65; www.academie-biere.com; 88bis bd de Port Royal, 5e; ⏱10am-2am; Ⓜ Vavin or RER Port Royal) Serious students of Belgian beer should head to this 'beer academy' to try its 12 on tap or choose from more than 150 bottled varieties, including Trappist (Monk-made) beers like prized Westmalle, abbey beers including Grimbergen and Leffe, fruit beers, and Cantillon gueuze (double-fermented Lambic beer made in Brussels). Happy hour is an early starter, from 3.30pm to 7.30pm.

In true Belgian tradition, it also serves *moules* (mussels), delivered and cleaned each morning, cooked in creative ways including with mustard, curry or Roquefort, and served continuously.

DOSE COFFEE

Map p400 (www.dosedealerdecafe.fr; 73 rue Mouffetard, 5e; ⏱8am-6pm Mon-Fri, 9am-7pm Sat & Sun; 📶; Ⓜ Place Monge) Artisan Breton roastery Caffè Cataldi supplies the beans for a potent dose of caffeine at this hip coffee shop and organic juice bar. Plump for a lovely cushioned bench seat in the heated alley outside or join the line-up of digital creatives hooked up to various devices, browsing bookshelves or reading newspapers in the inside galley space.

Great choice of milks (including almond), tea, beer and light bites (cookies, cakes, open sandwiches, avocado toasts).

LA BRÛLERIE DES GOBELINS COFFEE

Map p400 (☎01 43 31 90 13; www.comptoirsrichard.fr/magasin-brulerie-des-gobelins; 2 ave des Gobelins, 5e; ⏱9.30am-7.30pm Tue-Sat; Ⓜ Gobelins) It might be part of Comptoirs Richard today, but this historic Parisian roastery has been the place in the 5e *arrondissement* to savour serious coffee made from beans roasted in situ for the last five decades or so. Post-espresso with aromatic notes of cinnamon, honey, cocoa and vanilla, purchase a bag of coffee to take home – beans are ground to order

TEA CADDY TEAHOUSE

Map p398 (☎01 43 54 15 56; www.the-tea-caddy.com; 14 rue St-Julien le Pauvre, 5e; ⏱11am-7pm; 📶; Ⓜ St-Michel) Arguably the most English of the 'English' tearooms in Paris, this institution, founded by a certain Miss Klinklin in 1928, is a fine spot to break for light meals like omelettes or a genteel cream tea with a Devon scone after visiting nearby Notre Dame, Sainte-Chapelle or the Conciergerie. Weekend brunch (€28.80) is served until 4pm.

LE PIANO VACHE BAR

Map p398 (☎01 46 33 75 03; 8 rue Laplace, 5e; ⏱6pm-2am Mon-Sat; Ⓜ Maubert-Mutualité) Down the hill from the Panthéon, this shabby backstreet bar is covered in old posters above old couches and drenched in 1970s and '80s rock ambience. A real student fave, it has bands and DJs playing mainly rock, plus some Goth, reggae and pop. Happy hour runs from 6pm to 9pm. Check its Facebook page for events.

☆ ENTERTAINMENT

Jazz and independent cinema are the twin strengths of the Latin Quarter's entertainment scene, with a host of venues for both.

★CAFÉ UNIVERSEL JAZZ, BLUES

Map p400 (☎01 43 25 74 20; www.facebook.com/cafeuniverseljazzbar; 267 rue St-Jacques, 5e; ⏱8.30pm-1.30am Tue-Sat; 📶; Ⓜ Censier Daubenton or RER Port Royal) Café Universel hosts a brilliant array of live concerts with everything from bebop and Latin sounds to vocal jazz sessions. Plenty of freedom is given to young producers and artists, and its convivial relaxed atmosphere attracts a mix of students and jazz lovers. Concerts are free, but you should tip the artists when they pass the hat around.

CAVEAU DE LA HUCHETTE JAZZ, BLUES

Map p398 (☎01 43 26 65 05; www.caveaudelahuchette.fr; 5 rue de la Huchette, 5e; admission €13-15; ⌚9pm-2.30am Sun-Thu, to 4am Fri & Sat; Ⓜ St-Michel) Housed in a medieval *caveau* (cellar) used as a courtroom and torture chamber during the Revolution, this club is where virtually all the jazz greats (Georges Brassens, Thibault...) have played since the end of WWII. It attracts its fair share of tourists, but the atmosphere can be more electric than at the more serious jazz clubs. Sessions start at 10pm.

ÉGLISE ST-JULIEN LE PAUVRE CLASSICAL MUSIC

Map p398 (☎01 42 26 00 00; www.concertinparis.com; 1 rue St-Julien le Pauvre, 5e; hours vary; Ⓜ St-Michel) Piano recitals (Chopin, Liszt) are staged at least two evenings a week in one of the oldest churches in Paris. Higher-priced tickets directly face the stage. Payment is by cash only at the door.

L'EPÉE DE BOIS CINEMA

Map p400 (☎08 92 68 75 35; www.cine-epeedebois.fr; 100 rue Mouffetard, 5e; adult/child €7.90/5; Ⓜ Censier Daubenton) Even locals find it easy to miss the small doorway leading to rue Mouffetard's little two-screen cinema, which shows art-house flicks such as Julie Delpy–directed films, as well as major new releases. Show times are posted online.

LE PETIT JOURNAL ST-MICHEL JAZZ, BLUES

Map p400 (☎01 43 26 28 59; http://petitjournalsaintmichel.fr; 71 bd St-Michel, 5e; admission incl 1 drink €20-25, with dinner €49-59; ⌚7.30pm-1am Mon-Sat; Ⓜ Cluny–La Sorbonne or RER Luxembourg) Classic jazz concerts kick off at 9.15pm in the atmospheric downstairs cellar of this sophisticated jazz venue across from the Jardin du Luxembourg (p228). Everything ranging from Dixieland and vocals to big band and swing sets patrons' toes tapping. Dinner is served at 8pm (but it's the music that's the real draw).

LE CHAMPO CINEMA

Map p398 (www.cinema-lechampo.com; 51 rue des Écoles, 5e; tickets adult/child €9/4; Ⓜ Cluny–La Sorbonne) This is one of the most popular of the many Latin Quarter cinemas, featuring classics and retrospectives looking at the films of such actors and directors as Alfred Hitchcock, Jacques Tati, Alain Resnais, Frank Capra, Tim Burton and Woody Allen. One of the two *salles* (cinemas) has wheelchair access.

LE GRAND ACTION CINEMA

Map p398 (www.legrandaction.com; 5 rue des Écoles, 5e; tickets adult/child €9.50/6; Ⓜ Cardinal Lemoine) Cult films screen in their original languages at this cinephiles' favourite.

SHOPPING

Bookworms will love this part of the Left Bank, home to some wonderful bookshops. Other student-frequented shops include camping stores, comic shops, old-school vinyl shops where collectors browse for hours and cheap, colourful homewares stores, interspersed with the occasional *droguerie-quincaillerie* (hardware store; easily spotted by the jumble of laundry baskets, buckets etc piled on the pavement out the front).

★SHAKESPEARE & COMPANY BOOKS

Map p398 (☎01 43 25 40 93; www.shakespeareandcompany.com; 37 rue de la Bûcherie, 5e; ⌚10am-10pm; Ⓜ St-Michel) Shakespeare's enchanting nooks and crannies overflow with new and secondhand English-language books. The original shop (12 rue l'Odéon, 6e; closed by the Nazis in 1941) was run by Sylvia Beach and became the meeting point for Hemingway's 'Lost Generation'. Readings by emerging and illustrious authors take place at 7pm most Mondays and there's a wonderful cafe (p215) next door.

The bookshop is fabled for nurturing writers, and at night its couches turn into beds where 'Tumbleweeds' (aspiring writers and book-mad students) overnight in exchange for stacking shelves.

American-born George Whitman opened the present incarnation in 1951, attracting a beat-poet clientele, and scores of authors have since passed through its doors. In 2006

Whitman was awarded the Officier des Arts et Lettres by the French Minister of Culture, recognising his significant contribution to the enrichment of the French cultural inheritance. Whitman died in 2011, aged 98; he is buried in division 73 of Cimetière du Père Lachaise (p157). Today his daughter, Sylvia Beach Whitman, maintains Shakespeare & Company's serendipitous magic.

★LE BONBON AU PALAIS FOOD

Map p398 (☎01 78 56 15 72; www.bonbonsaupalais.fr; 19 rue Monge, 5e; ⊙10.30am-7.30pm Tue-Sat; Ⓜ Cardinal Lemoine) Kids and kids-at-heart will adore this sugar-fuelled *tour de France*. The school-geography-themed boutique stocks rainbows of artisan sweets from around the country. Old-fashioned glass jars brim with treats like *calissons* (diamond-shaped, icing-sugar-topped ground fruit and almonds from Aix-en-Provence), *rigolettes* (fruit-filled pillows from Nantes), *berlingots* (striped, triangular boiled sweets from Carpentras and elsewhere) and *papalines* (herbal liqueur-filled pink-chocolate balls from Avignon).

FROMAGERIE LAURENT DUBOIS CHEESE

Map p398 (☎01 43 54 50 93; www.fromageslaurentdubois.fr; 47ter bd St-Germain, 5e; ⊙8.30am-7.30pm Tue-Sat, 8.30am-1pm Sun; Ⓜ Maubert-Mutualité) One of the best *fromageries* in Paris, this cheese-lover's nirvana is filled with to-die-for delicacies, such as St-Félicien with Périgord truffles. Rare, limited-production cheeses include blue Termignon and Tarentaise goat's cheese. All are appropriately cellared in warm, humid or cold environments. There's also a 15e **branch** (Map p414; ☎01 45 78 70 58; 2 rue de Lourmel, 15e; ⊙9am-1pm & 4-7.45pm Tue-Fri, 8.30am-7.45pm Sat, 9am-1pm Sun; Ⓜ Dupleix).

BIÈRES CULTES JUSSIEU DRINKS

Map p400 (☎09 51 27 04 84; http://bierescultes.fr; 44 rue des Boulangers, 5e; ⊙noon-2pm & 3-9pm Tue, Wed & Fri, to 11pm Thu & Fri; Ⓜ Cardinal Lemoine) At any one time this beer-lovers' fantasyland stocks around 500 different craft and/or international brews, along with two on tap to taste on the spot. Just some of its wares when you visit might include US-brewed Alaskan Smoked Porter, German smoked Aecht Schlenkerla Rauchbier from Bamberg and New Zealand Monteith's. Check its website and Facebook page for events and seasonal releases.

FROMAGERIE MAURY CHEESE

Map p400 (☎09 52 81 84 98; 1 rue des Feuillantines, 5e; ⊙2-9pm Tue-Thu, 10.30am-1.30pm & 3-8.30pm Fri & Sat; Ⓜ Censier Daubenton or RER Port Royal) This wonderful little *fromagerie* feels more like a farm shop you'd find in the countryside than an inner-city Parisian boutique. Organic eggs sit in straw baskets (cartons are available) and owner Christophe Maury insists that you try his amazing range of carefully selected cheeses from small-scale producers in southwestern France, the Jura mountains, Corsica, Italy and Spain before you buy.

MOCOCHA CHOCOLATE

Map p400 (☎01 47 07 13 66; www.chocolatsmococha.com; 89 rue Mouffetard, 5e; ⊙11am-8pm Tue-Sun; Ⓜ Censier Daubenton) Light, luscious macarons in flavours such as jasmine, raspberry and blackcurrant, and a mouth-watering range of chocolates by several *maîtres chocolatiers* (master chocolate-makers) are laid out like jewels at this chocolate shop.

ANDROUET CHEESE

Map p400 (☎01 45 87 85 05; www.androuet.com; 134 rue Mouffetard, 5e; ⊙9.30am-1pm & 4-7.30pm Tue-Thu, 9.30am-7.30pm Fri & Sat, 9.30am-1.30pm Sun; Ⓜ Censier Daubenton) All of the cheeses at this great *fromagerie* can be vacuum-packed for free to take home – look up to admire the beautiful murals on the building's cherry-red façade. Androuet is one of three tantalising cheese shops on rue Mouffetard.

DELIZIUS FOOD & DRINKS

Map p400 (☎01 42 17 00 23; 134 rue Mouffetard, 5e; ⊙9.30am-8pm Tue-Sat, 9am-2pm Sun; Ⓜ Censier Daubenton) Stuffed olives and capsicums and marinated aubergine are among the picnic goodies at this gourmet Italian deli, which also sells ready-to-eat hot meals and fresh and dried pasta.

BOULANGERIE BRUNO SOLQUES FOOD

Map p400 (☎01 43 54 62 33; 243 rue St-Jacques, 5e; ⊙6.45am-8pm Mon-Fri; Ⓜ Place Monge or RER Luxembourg) Inventive *pâtissier* Bruno Solques crafts wonderfully rustic breads (sold by weight measured on old-fashioned scales) using only organic flours. The small, bare-boards shop is also filled with Solques' creatively shaped flat tarts with mashed fruit, fruit-filled brioches and subtly spiced gingerbread. It's on the pricey side but worth it – kids from the school across the way can't get enough.

AU VIEUX CAMPEUR SPORTS & OUTDOORS

Map p398 (☎01 53 10 48 48; www.auvieuxcampeur.fr; 48 rue des Écoles, 5e; ⏲11am-7.30pm Mon-Wed & Fri, 11am-9pm Thu, 10am-7.30pm Sat; Ⓜ Maubert-Mutualité) This outdoor store has colonised the Latin Quarter, with 30-odd different boutiques scattered around its original shop that opened on rue St-Jacques in 1941 (actually a few doors down at No 38). Each space is devoted to a different sport: climbing, skiing, diving, camping, biking, water sports and so on.

The **branch** (Map p398; ☎01 53 10 48 21; www.auvieuxcampeur.fr; 40 rue St-Jacques, 5e; ⏲11am-7.30pm Mon-Wed & Fri, 11am-9pm Thu, 10am-7.30pm Sat; Ⓜ Maubert-Mutualité) a couple of doors down sells everything imaginable for running and walking. Join Parisian runners every Thursday at 7.30pm for a free trail-running training session, departing from in front of the shop.

MAYETTE LA BOUTIQUE DE LA MAGIE GAMES, HOBBIES

Map p398 (☎01 43 54 13 63; www.mayette.com; 8 rue des Carmes, 5e; ⏲2-7.30pm Tue-Sat; Ⓜ Maubert-Mutualité) One of a kind, this 1808-established magic shop is said to be the world's oldest. Since 1991 it's been in the hands of world-famous magic pro Dominique Duvivier. Professional and hobbyist magicians flock here to discuss king sandwiches, reverse assemblies, false cuts and other card tricks with him and his daughter, Alexandra.

Should you want to learn the tricks of the trade, Duvivier has magic courses up his sleeve.

ALBUM COMICS

Map p398 (☎01 53 10 00 60; www.albumcomics.com; 67 bd St-Germain, 5e; ⏲10am-6pm Mon-Sat, noon-7pm Sun; Ⓜ Cluny–La Sorbonne) Album specialises in *bandes dessinées* (comics and graphic novels), which have an enormous following in France, with everything from Tintin and Babar to erotic comics and the latest Japanese manga. Serious comic collectors – and anyone excited by Harry Potter wands, *Star Wars, Superman* and other superhero figurines and T-shirts (you know who you are!) – shouldn't miss it.

LIBRAIRIE EYROLLES BOOKS

Map p398 (☎01 44 41 11 74; www.eyrolles.com; 55-61 bd St-Germain, 5e; ⏲10am-8pm Mon-Sat; Ⓜ Maubert-Mutualité) One of Paris' largest bookshops sells titles in English, has stacks of browsing space, and stocks an exceptional range of maps, guides and travel lit.

MARCHÉ MAUBERT MARKET

Map p398 (place Maubert, 5e; ⏲7am-2.30pm Tue & Thu, 7am-3pm Sat; Ⓜ Maubert-Mutualité) Shop for fruit and veg (some organic), cheese, bread and so on at this welcoming, village-like food market that spills across place Maubert thrice weekly.

BOUQUINISTES

With some 3km of forest-green boxes lining the Seine – containing over 300,000 secondhand (and often out-of-print) books, rare magazines, postcards and old advertising posters – Paris' **bouquinistes** (quai Voltaire, 7e, to quai de la Tournelle, 5e, & Pont Marie, 4e, to quai du Louvre, 1er; ⏲11.30am-dusk) are as integral to the cityscape as Notre Dame. Many open only from spring to autumn (and many shut in August), but year-round you'll still find some to browse.

These used-books sellers have been in business since the 16th century, when they were itinerant peddlers selling their wares on Parisian bridges; back then their sometimes subversive (eg Protestant) materials could get them into trouble with the authorities. By 1859 the city had finally wised up: official licences were issued, space (10m of railing) was rented and eventually the permanent green boxes were installed.

Today, *bouquinistes* (the official count ranges from 200 to 240) are allowed to have four boxes, only one of which can be used to sell souvenirs. Look hard enough and you just might find some real treasures: old comic books, forgotten 1st editions, maps, stamps, erotica and prewar newspapers – as in centuries past, it's all there, waiting to be rediscovered.

MARCHÉ MONGE
MARKET

Map p400 (place Monge, 5e; ⏲7am-2pm Wed, Fri & Sun; Ⓜ Place Monge) Open-air Marché Monge is laden with wonderful cheeses, baked goods and a host of other temptations.

ABBEY BOOKSHOP
BOOKS

Map p398 (☎01 46 33 16 24; https://abbeybookshop.wordpress.com; 29 rue de la Parcheminerie, 5e; ⏲10am-7pm Mon-Sat; Ⓜ Cluny–La Sorbonne) Inside 18th-century Hôtel Dubuisson, this chaotic but welcoming Canadian-run bookshop serves free coffee (sweetened with maple syrup) to sip while you browse thousands upon thousands of new and used books. Watch for occasional literary events.

AUX MERVEILLEUX DE FRED
FOOD

Map p398 (☎01 43 54 63 72; www.auxmerveilleux.com; 2 rue Monge, 5e; ⏲7.30am-8pm Tue-Sat, to 7pm Sun; Ⓜ Maubert-Mutualité) This chandeliered boutique – one of several in Paris – concentrates on one dessert, the marvellous *merveilleux:* meringue layered with whipped cream and rolled in one of six seasonal flavours, such as chocolate flakes, *speculoos* (spiced biscuit) powder, almond slivers, caramel dust or rose sugar crystals. Watch staff hand-making the delicacy while you queue.

NICOLAÏ
PERFUME

Map p400 (☎01 44 55 02 00; www.pnicolai.com; 240 rue St-Jacques, 5e; ⏲10.30am-2pm & 3-6.30pm Mon-Sat; Ⓜ Place Monge) Established in Paris in 1986 by esteemed *parfumeuse* Patricia de Nicolaï, whose great-grandfather Pierre-François Pascal Guerlain founded Guerlain 150 years earlier, Nicolaï remains a family-run business today. Recent fragrances include Cococabana (with notes of ylang-ylang, palm, vanilla and tonka flower), Kiss Me Tender (orange blossom, almond, jasmine and cloves) and Musc Monoï (lemon, magnolia, coconut and sandalwood).

CROCODISC
MUSIC

Map p398 (www.crocodisc.com; 40 & 42 rue des Écoles, 5e; ⏲11am-7pm Tue-Sat, closed late Jul–mid-Aug; Ⓜ Maubert-Mutualité) Music might be more accessible than ever before in the digital age, but for many, digital recordings will never replace rummaging through racks for treasures. New and secondhand CDs and vinyl discs at 40 rue des Écoles span world music, rap, reggae, salsa, soul and disco, while No 42 has pop, rock, punk, new wave, electro and soundtracks.

Its nearby sister shop **Crocojazz** (Map p398; ☎01 43 54 47 95; 64 rue de la Montagne Ste-Geneviève, 5e; ⏲11am-1pm & 2-7pm Tue-Sat, closed late Jul–mid-Aug; Ⓜ Maubert-Mutualité) specialises in jazz, blues, gospel and timeless crooners, with books and DVDs as well as recordings.

MARCHÉ MOUFFETARD
MARKET

Map p400 (rue Mouffetard, 5e; ⏲8am-7.30pm Tue-Sat, to noon Sun; Ⓜ Censier Daubenton) Grocers, butchers, fishmongers and other food purveyors set their goods out on street stalls during this almost-daily market. Many stalls close from lunchtime onwards.

SPORTS & ACTIVITIES

WINE TASTING IN PARIS
WINE

Map p400 (☎06 76 93 32 88; www.wine-tasting-in-paris.com; 14 rue des Boulangers, 5e; tastings from €46; ⏲tastings 5-7.30pm Tue, Thu & Sat; Ⓜ Jussieu) Find this wine-tasting school on a winding cobblestone backstreet. With the knowledgeable Thierry from wine-rich Burgundy at the helm, themed tastings and tours do not disappoint. The comprehensive French Wine Tour (€62, 2½ hours, six wines) covers tasting methodology, wine vocabulary and French wine-growing regions. Foodies will adore the tasty, lunchtime cheese-wine pairing (€46, 1½ hours, four wines). All classes are in English.

PISCINE PONTOISE
SWIMMING

Map p398 (☎01 55 42 77 88; http://equipement.paris.fr/piscine-pontoise-2918; 19 rue de Pontoise, 5e; adult/child €4.80/2.90; ⏲hours vary; Ⓜ Maubert-Mutualité) A beautiful art-deco-style indoor pool in the heart of the Latin Quarter. An €11.10 evening ticket (from 8pm) covers entry to the pool, gym and sauna. It has shorter hours during term time – check schedules online.

St-Germain & Les Invalides

Neighbourhood Top Five

❶ **Musée d'Orsay** (p224) Revelling in a wealth of world-famous impressionist masterpieces and art nouveau architecture at this glorious national museum.

❷ **Jardin du Luxembourg** (p228) Strolling through the chestnut groves and orchards, past ponds and statues, at the city's most popular park.

❸ **Musée Rodin** (p230) Indulging in an exquisitely Parisian moment in the sculpture-filled gardens of the magnificently renovated Hôtel Biron.

❹ **La Grande Épicerie de Paris** (p244) Feasting your eyes on the fantastical food displays at this food emporium attached to Paris' first department store, Le Bon Marché, designed by Gustave Eiffel.

❺ **Hôtel des Invalides** (p231) Visiting Napoléon's elaborate tomb within the monumental complex housing France's largest military museum.

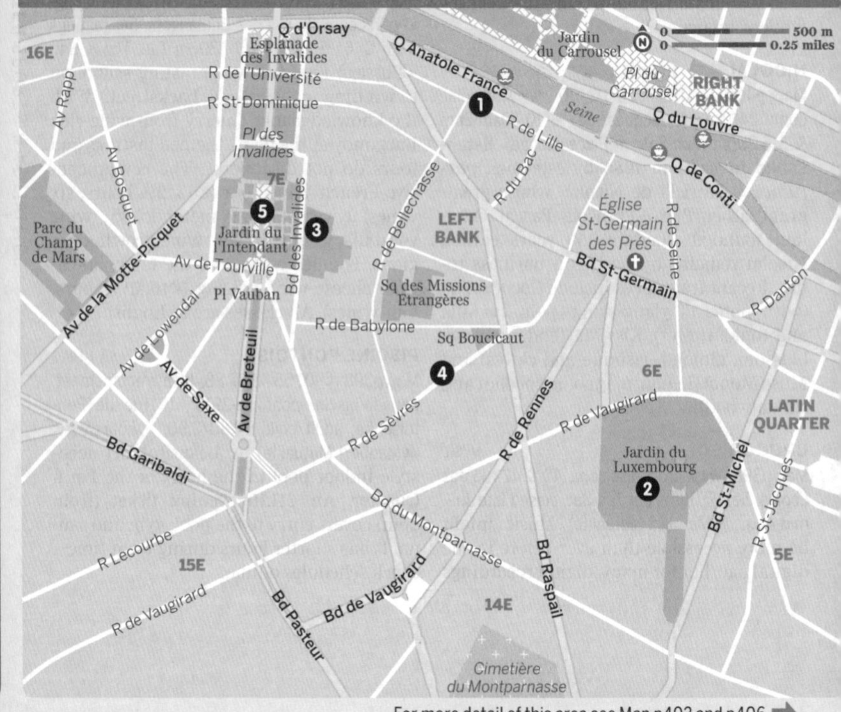

For more detail of this area see Map p402 and p406 ➡

Explore St-Germain & Les Invalides

Despite gentrification since its early-20th-century bohemian days, there remains a startling cinematic quality to this soulful part of the Left Bank where artists, writers, actors and musicians cross paths.

This is one of those neighbourhoods whose very atmosphere is an attraction in itself, so allow plenty of time to stroll its side streets and stop at its fabled literary cafes, prêt-à-porter stores, gourmet shops, covered market and grand department store Le Bon Marché (p244) with its vast white spaces showcasing interior design. Nearby, admire the exquisite art nouveau façade of Hôtel Lutetia (1910), a glittering stunning pearly cream after recent renovation: built to accommodate wealthy customers from Le Bon Marché, the luxurious palace hotel was one of the capital's first 'modern' luxury hotels. View Delacroix's works at the Église St-Sulpice (p232) and his former studio, the Musée National Eugène Delacroix (p232); linger in the masterpiece-filled sculpture garden of the Musée Rodin.

Entry to the exceptional Musée d'Orsay (p224) is cheaper in the late afternoon, so it's an ideal time to check out its breathtaking collections, before dining at the area's stylish restaurants and swizzling cocktails at its bars.

Local Life

➡ **River life** Join locals jogging, skating, cycling, bar-hopping or just Zenning out along the riverside promenade Les Berges de Seine (p233).

➡ **Market life** Street markets where St-Germain denizens stock up on bountiful fresh produce include Marché Raspail (p244) and rue Cler.

➡ **Fashion life** Scour the racks for designer cast-offs at St-Germain's secondhand boutiques.

Getting There & Away

➡ **Metro** This area is especially well served by metro and RER. Get off at metro stations St-Germain des Prés, Mabillon or Odéon for its busy bd St-Germain heart. RER line C shadows the Seine along the Left Bank and is a fast way to get from St-Michel–Notre Dame to the Musée d'Orsay.

➡ **Bicycle** Convenient Vélib' stations include 141 bd St-Germain, 6e; opposite 2 bd Raspail, 6e; and 62 rue de Lille, 7e.

➡ **Boat** Batobus boats dock by quai Malaquais for St-Germain des Prés and quai de Solférino for the Musée d'Orsay.

Lonely Planet's Top Tip

The St-Germain and Les Invalides neighbourhood's two biggest-hitting museums – the impressionist-filled Musée d'Orsay and magnificently renovated Musée Rodin – offer a discounted combination ticket costing €18. But you don't need to cram both into one day; the joint ticket is valid for a single visit to each museum within three months.

Best Places to Eat

➡ Bouillon Racine (p235)
➡ Tomy & Co (p238)
➡ Clover (p236)
➡ Anicia (p236)
➡ Epoca (p238)
➡ L'Étable Hugo Desnoyer (p236)

For reviews, see p234 ➡

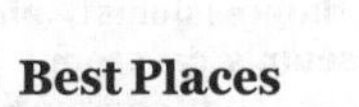

Best Places to Drink

➡ Coutume Café (p242)
➡ Le Bar des Prés (p241)
➡ Prescription Cocktail Club (p241)
➡ Les Deux Magots (p239)
➡ Au Sauvignon (p239)
➡ Cod House (p239)

For reviews, see p239 ➡

Best Shopping

➡ Le Bon Marché (p244)
➡ La Grande Épicerie de Paris (p244)
➡ Cantin (p245)
➡ Magasin Sennelier (p245)
➡ Cire Trudon (p243)

For reviews, see p243 

SOKOLOVSKI / SHUTTERSTOCK ©

TOP SIGHT
MUSÉE D'ORSAY

After the Louvre, this eye-catching art gallery, at home in a former railway station overlooking the River Seine, is a one-stop shop for some of the world's most celebrated paintings by impressionist, postimpressionist and art nouveau artists. The museum's cavernous interiors, vintage monumental clocks and contemporary styled galleries are as dazzling as the art itself.

History

The Gare d'Orsay railway station was designed by competition-winning architect Victor Laloux. Even on its completion, just in time for the 1900 Exposition Universelle, painter Edouard Detaille declared that the new station looked like a Palais des Beaux Arts. It had its own hotel and all the mod-cons of the day – including luggage lifts and passenger elevators – but by 1939 the increasing electrification of the rail network meant the platforms were too short for mainline trains, and within a few years rail services ceased.

The station was used as a mailing centre during WWII, and in 1962 Orson Welles filmed Kafka's *The Trial* in the then-abandoned building. Fortunately, it was saved from being demolished and replaced with a hotel complex by a Historical Monument listing in 1973, before the government set about establishing the palatial museum.

Transforming the languishing building into the country's premier showcase for art from 1848 to 1914 was the grand project of President Valéry Giscard d'Estaing, who signed off on it in 1977. The museum opened its doors in 1986.

Far from resting on its laurels, major renovations at the Musée d'Orsay between 2008 and 2011 incorporated a re-energised layout and increased exhibition space. World-renowned

DON'T MISS

- The building
- Painting collections
- Decorative-arts collections
- Sculptures
- Graphic-arts collections

PRACTICALITIES

- Map p406, G2
- ☎01 40 49 48 14
- www.musee-orsay.fr
- 1 rue de la Légion d'Honneur, 7e
- adult/child €12/free
- 9.30am-6pm Tue, Wed & Fri-Sun, to 9.45pm Thu
- Ⓜ Assemblée Nationale, RER Musée d'Orsay

paintings now gleam from richly coloured walls that create an intimate, stately-home-like atmosphere, with high-tech illumination literally casting the masterpieces in a new light.

Paintings

Most visitors make a beeline for the world's largest collection of impressionist and postimpressionist art, the highlights of which include Manet's *On the Beach* and *Woman with Fans;* Monet's gardens at Giverny and *Rue Montorgueil, Paris, Celebration of June 30, 1878;* Cézanne's card players, *Green Apples* and *Blue Vase;* Renoir's *Ball at the Moulin de la Galette* and *Young Girls at the Piano;* Degas' ballerinas; Toulouse-Lautrec's cabaret dancers; Pissarro's *The Seine and the Louvre;* Sisley's *View of the Canal St-Martin;* and Van Gogh's self-portraits, *Bedroom in Arles* and *Starry Night over the Rhône.* Less high-profile but classified a National Treasure is James Tissot's 1868 painting *The Circle of the Rue Royale.*

Decorative & Graphic Arts

Household items such as hat and coat stands, candlesticks, desks, chairs, bookcases, vases, pot-plant holders, freestanding screens, wall mirrors, water pitchers, plates, goblets and bowls become works of art in the hands of their creators, who incorporated exquisite design elements from the era.

Drawings, pastels and sketches from major artists are another of the d'Orsay's lesser-known highlights. Look for Georges Seurat's *The Black Bow* (c 1882), which uses crayon on paper to define forms by contrasting between black and white, and Paul Gaugin's poignant self-portrait (c 1902–03), drawn near the end of his life.

Sculptures

The cavernous former station is a magnificent setting for sculptures, including works by Degas, Gaugin, Camille Claudel, Renoir and Rodin.

Dining

Grab a snack or light bite at the ground-floor Café de l'Ours, overlooking Francois Pompon's sculpted *Polar Bear* (1923–33).

On the 5th floor, one of the Orsay's two monumental clocks keeps watch in the shimmering, orange-and-turquoise **Café Campana** (Map p406; dishes €9-19; ⌚10.30am-5pm Tue, Wed & Fri-Sun, 11am-9pm Thu). Think salads, tasting platters and international fare.

Furniture and menu aside, time has scarcely changed at the Orsay's original **Le Restaurant** (Map p406; ☎01 45 49 47 03; 2-/3-course lunch menu €22.50, mains €18-27; ⌚11.45am-5.30pm Tue, Wed & Fri-Sun, 11.45am-2.45pm & 7-9.30pm Thu; 👪).

GUIDED TOURS

For a thorough introduction to the museum, 90-minute 'Masterpieces of the Musée d'Orsay' guided tours (€6) in English run at 11.30am and 2.30pm on Tuesday and 11.30am from Wednesday to Saturday.

Kids under 13 years aren't permitted on adult tours; look out for family tours (six to 12 years; €4.50) and themed children's workshops (six to eight years; €7) instead.

An audioguide costs €5.

VIEWS

Look down on Paris (spot Montmartre's Sacré-Cœur) through the former railway station's two giant glass clock faces – one in Café Campana (p225), with adjacent roof terrace (closed in winter) and another immediately after the impressionist galleries.

1. ***Woman with Fans* by Édouard Manet**
Manet often depicted middle-class Parisians.

2. ***On the Beach* by Édouard Manet**
Manet's works are among the Musée d'Orsay's extensive collection of impressionist paintings.

3. ***The Garden at Giverny* by Claude Monet**
A leading figure in the impressionist movement, Monet was inspired by his garden.

4. ***Ball at the Moulin de la Galette* by Pierre-Auguste Renoir**
Take a stroll through Montmartre to see the Moulin Blute Fin (p141), the inspiration for this painting.

3

SUPERSTOCK / GETTY IMAGES ©

TOP SIGHT
JARDIN DU LUXEMBOURG

NEIRFY / SHUTTERSTOCK ©

Playing the quintessential French *flâneur* (indulgent stroller or meanderer) in this romantic city park is a classic 'I'm in Paris!' moment. Elegant and timeless in equal measure, the 23 hectare large garden squirrels away a lush medley of pea-green lawns and crunchy gravel paths, formal terraces and chestnut groves, ornamental ponds and orchards – with their own charm in every season.

History

The Jardin du Luxembourg's history stretches further back than Napoléon's dedication. The gardens are a backdrop to the Palais du Luxembourg, built in the 1620s for Marie de Médici, Henri IV's consort, to assuage her longing for the Pitti Palace in Florence. The Palais is now home to the French Senate, which, in addition to parliamentary-assembly activities like voting on legislation, is charged with promoting the palace and its gardens.

Numerous overhauls over the centuries have given the Jardin du Luxembourg a blend of traditional French- and English-style gardens that is unique in Paris.

All of the gardens' nostalgic childhood activities are still here today, as well as modern play equipment, tennis and other sporting and games venues.

DON'T MISS

- Grand Bassin
- Puppet shows
- Orchards
- Palais du Luxembourg
- Musée du Luxembourg

PRACTICALITIES

- Map p402, E6
- www.senat.fr/visite/jardin
- hours vary
- Mabillon, St-Sulpice, Rennes, Notre Dame des Champs, RER Luxembourg

Grand Bassin

It is for good reason that the Luxembourg Gardens hold a place in the heart of every Parisian: for centuries, this is where children (and grown-up 'children') have come to witter away a weekend afternoon chasing **toy sailboats** (Map p402; sailboat rental per 30min €4; 11am-6pm Apr-Oct) on the octagonal **Grand Bassin** (Map p402), a serene ornamental pond. Nearby, younger children tots can take **pony rides** (Map p402; 06 07 32 53 95; www.

animaponey.com; 600m/900m pony ride €6/8.50; ⏲3-6pm Wed, Sat, Sun & school holidays) or romp around the **playgrounds** (Map p402; adult/child €1.50/2.50; ⏲hours vary) – the green half is for kids aged seven to 12 years, the blue half for under-sevens.

Puppet Shows

Puppetry is an ancient tradition in France and alfresco puppet shows at the Jardin du Luxembourg's bijou **Théâtre du Luxembourg** (Map p402; ☎01 43 29 50 97; www.marionnettesduluxembourg.fr; tickets €6.40; ⏲Wed, Sat & Sun, daily during school holidays) are as entertaining as marionette shows come – regardless of whether you speak French or are a child. Show times vary; check the program online and arrive 30 minutes before.

Orchards

Dozens of apple varieties grow in the **orchards** (Map p402) in the gardens' south. Bees have produced honey in the nearby apiary, the **Rucher du Luxembourg** (Map p402), since the 19th century. The annual Fête du Miel (Honey Festival) offers two days of tasting and buying its sweet harvest around late September in the ornate **Pavillon Davioud** (Map p402; 55bis rue d'Assas, 6e).

Palais du Luxembourg

The **Palais du Luxembourg** (Map p402; www.senat.fr; rue de Vaugirard, 6e) was built in the 1620s and has been home to the Sénat (French Senate) since 1958. It's occasionally visitable by guided tour.

East of the palace is the ornate, Italianate **Fontaine des Médici** (Map p402), built in 1630. During Baron Haussmann's 19th-century reshaping of the roads, the fountain was moved 30m and the pond and dramatic statues of the giant bronze Polyphemus discovering the white-marble lovers Acis and Galatea were added.

Musée du Luxembourg

Top-billing temporary art exhibitions, such as 'Cézanne et Paris', are invariably held in the beautiful **Musée du Luxembourg** (Map p402; ☎01 40 13 62 00; http://museeduluxembourg.fr; 19 rue de Vaugirard, 6e; most exhibitions €13; ⏲10.30am-7pm Sat-Thu, to 10pm Fri).

Around the back of the museum, lemon and orange trees, palms, grenadiers and oleanders shelter from the cold in the palace's **orangery** (Map p402). Nearby, the heavily guarded **Hôtel du Petit Luxembourg** was where Marie de Médici lived while the Palais du Luxembourg was being built. The president of the Senate has called it home since 1825.

CHAIRS

If you fancy taking home a classic Jardin du Luxembourg chair, pick one up from Fermob (p243).

The Jardin du Luxembourg plays a pivotal role in Victor Hugo's Les Misérables: the novel's lovers Marius and Cosette meet here for the first time.

SCULPTURES

The gardens are studded with over 100 sculptures. Look out for statues of Stendhal, Chopin, Baudelaire and Delacroix.

TOP SIGHT
MUSÉE RODIN

Even if you're not an art lover, it is worth visiting this high-profile art museum to lose yourself in its romantic gardens. One of the most peaceful green oases in Paris, the formal flowerbeds and boxed-hedge arrangements framing 18th-century mansion Hôtel Biron house original sculptures by sculptor, painter, sketcher, engraver and collector Auguste Rodin. This is where he lived and worked while in Paris.

Sculptures

The first large-scale cast of Rodin's famous sculpture **The Thinker** (*Le Penseur*), made in 1902, resides in the garden – the perfect place to contemplate this heroic naked figure conceived by Rodin to represent intellect and poetry (it was originally titled *The Poet*).

The Gates of Hell (*La Porte de l'Enfer*) was commissioned in 1880 as the entrance for a never-built museum, and Rodin worked on his sculptural masterpiece up until his death in 1917. Standing 6m high by 4m wide, its 180 figures comprise an intricate scene from Dante's *Inferno*.

Marble monument to love **The Kiss** (*Le Baiser*) was originally part of *The Gates of Hell*. The sculpture's entwined lovers caused controversy on its completion due to Rodin's then-radical approach of depicting women as equal partners in ardour.

The museum also features many sculptures by Camille Claudel, Rodin's protégé and muse.

Collections

In 1908 Rodin donated his entire art collection to the French state on the proviso that they dedicate his former workshop and showroom, the 18th-century mansion Hôtel Biron (1730), to displaying his works. In addition to his own paintings and sketches, don't miss his prized collection of works by artists including Van Gogh and Monet.

DON'T MISS

- *The Thinker*
- *The Gates of Hell*
- *The Kiss*
- Claudel sculptures
- Collections

PRACTICALITIES

- Map p406, D4
- 01 44 18 61 10
- www.musee-rodin.fr
- 79 rue de Varenne, 7e
- adult/child €10/free, garden only €4/free
- 10am-5.45pm Tue-Sun
- Varenne or Invalides

PREMIER PHOTO / SHUTTERSTOCK ©

TOP SIGHT
HÔTEL DES INVALIDES

Named after the 4000 *invalides* (disabled war veterans) it was built by Louis XIV to accomodate in the 1670s, this monumental edifice stands sentry over the grandiose, pea-green of Esplanade des Invalides. On 14 July 1789, it was from here that revolutionaries famously pilfered 32,000 rifles before charging to place de la Bastille to storm the city prison.

Église du Dôme

South of the main courtyard is the **Église du Dôme** (Map p406; included in Hôtel des Invalides entry; ⏲10am-7pm Jul & Aug, to 6pm Apr-Jun, Sep & Oct, to 5pm Nov-Mar), which, with its golden dome (1677–1735), is one of the finest religious edifices erected under Louis XIV.

Also south of the main courtyard is the **Église St-Louis des Invalides**, once used by soldiers.

Tombeau de Napoléon 1er

The extremely extravagant tomb of Napoléon comprises six coffins fitting into one another like a Russian nesting doll. Find it in the centre of the Église du Dôme,

Musée de l'Armée

Sobering wartime footage screens at this **army museum** (Army Museum; Map p406; included in Hôtel des Invalides entry; ⏲10am-6pm Apr-Oct, to 5pm Nov-Mar), north of the main courtyard, which also has weaponry, flag and medal displays as well as a multimedia area dedicated to Charles de Gaulle. This is the nation's largest collection on French military history.

Musée des Plans-Reliefs

Within the Hôtel des Invalides itself, the esoteric **Musée des Plans-Reliefs** is full of scale models of towns, fortresses and châteaux across France.

DON'T MISS

- Musée de l'Armée
- Église du Dôme
- Tombeau de Napoléon 1er
- Musée des Plans-Reliefs

PRACTICALITIES

- Map p406, C3
- www.musee-armee.fr
- 129 rue de Grenelle, 7e
- adult/child €12/free
- ⏲10am-6pm
- Ⓜ Varenne, La Tour Maubourg

SIGHTS

Chart-topping sights in this stately neighbourhood include the impressionist-art-filled Musée d'Orsay, massive military complex Hôtel des Invalides (home to Napoléon's tomb) and romantic, sculpture-strewn Musée Rodin. Look out for smaller, lesser-known gems too, such as the Musée National Eugène Delacroix, and some exquisite churches. Allow ample time for ambling in the city's most beautiful park, timeless Jardin du Luxembourg.

St-Germain

JARDIN DU LUXEMBOURG — PARK

See p228.

MONNAIE DE PARIS — MUSEUM

Map p402 (☎01 40 46 56 66; www.monnaiedeparis.fr; 11 quai de Conti, 6e; adult/child €10/free; ⊙11am-7pm Tue & Thu-Sun, to 9pm Wed; Ⓜ Pont Neuf) The 18th-century royal mint, Monnaie de Paris, houses the **Musée du 11 Conti**, an interactive museum exploring the history of French coinage from antiquity onwards, plus edgy contemporary-art exhibitions. The impeccably restored, neoclassical building, with one of the longest façades on the Seine stretching 116m long, squirrels away five sumptuous courtyards, the Hôtel de Conti designed by Jules Hardouin Mansart in 1690, engraving workshops, the original foundry (now the museum boutique), Guy Savoy's flagship restaurant (p237) and the fashionable Frappé by Bloom (p241) cafe.

Coins were minted at the Monnaie de Paris until 1973 when manufacturing was moved to the town of Pessac on the Atlantic Coast. The Ministry of Finance still uses the Paris mint however to produce commemorative medals and coins, many of which are sold in the museum's stylish boutique alongside glass jars of honey from hives on the building's rooftop, medallions featuring the Louvre or Eiffel Tower, and other classy souvenirs.

Skip ticket queues by buying tickets online (€1 cheaper) or from one of the automatic ticket machines, tucked away at the foot of the grandiose, red-carpeted staircase swirling up to Guy Savoy's Michelin-star restaurant.

MUSÉE NATIONAL EUGÈNE DELACROIX — MUSEUM

Map p402 (☎01 44 41 86 50; www.musee-delacroix.fr; 6 rue de Furstenberg, 6e; adult/child €7/free; ⊙9.30am-5pm Wed-Mon, to 9pm 1st Thu of month; Ⓜ Mabillon) In a courtyard off a pretty tree-shaded square, this museum is housed in the romantic artist's home and studio at the time of his death in 1863. It contains a collection of his oil paintings, watercolours, pastels and drawings, including many of his more intimate works, such as *An Unmade Bed* (1828) and his paintings of Morocco.

A ticket from the Musée du Louvre (p108) allows same-day entry here (you can also buy tickets here and skip the Louvre's ticket queues).

ÉGLISE ST-SULPICE — CHURCH

Map p402 (☎01 42 34 59 98; www.pss75.fr/saint-sulpice-paris; place St-Sulpice, 6e; ⊙7.30am-7.30pm; Ⓜ St-Sulpice) FREE In 1646 work started on the twin-towered Church of St Sulpicius, lined inside with 21 side chapels, and it took six architects 150 years to finish. It's famed for its striking Italianate façade with two rows of superimposed columns, its Counter-Reformation-influenced neoclassical decor and its frescoes by Eugène Delacroix – and its setting for a murderous scene in Dan Brown's *The Da Vinci Code*.

You can hear the monumental, 1781-built organ during 10.30am Mass on Sunday or the occasional Sunday-afternoon concert.

The frescoes in the Chapelle des Sts-Anges (Chapel of the Holy Angels), first to the right as you enter the chapel, depict Jacob wrestling with the angel (to the left) and Michael the Archangel doing battle with Satan (to the right), and were painted by Delacroix between 1855 and 1861. Free guided tours of the church (in English) depart on the 1st Sunday of each month at 12.30pm. To delve into the crypt, sign up in advance for a tour (in French) on the 2nd and 4th Sundays of the month at 2pm.

MUSÉE ATELIER ZADKINE — MUSEUM

Map p402 (☎01 55 42 77 20; www.zadkine.paris.fr; 100bis rue d'Assas, 6e; ⊙10am-6pm Tue-Sun; Ⓜ Vavin) FREE Russian cubist sculptor Ossip Zadkine (1890–1967) arrived in Paris in 1908 and lived and worked in this cottage for almost 40 years. Zadkine produced an enormous catalogue of sculptures made from clay, stone, bronze and wood. The museum covers his life and work; one room

TOP SIGHT
ÉGLISE ST-GERMAIN DES PRÉS

The sheer magnificence and magnitude of Paris' cathedral on Île de la Cité makes it hard to believe that this humble 'village' church, built in the 11th century on the site of a 6th-century abbey, was the primary place of worship for Parisians up until 14th century (when Notre Dame was completed). The Romanesque church, officially called Église St-Germain des Prés (St Germanus of the Fields), has undergone numerous facelifts over the centuries.

Part of the original abbey, **Chapelle de St-Symphorien** is believed to be the resting place of St Germanus (496–576), the first bishop of Paris. The Merovingian kings were buried here during the 6th and 7th centuries, but their tombs disappeared during the Revolution.

Over the western entrance, the bell tower has changed little since 990, although the spire dates only from the 19th century.

Until the late 17th century the abbey owned most of the land in the Left Bank west of what's now bd St-Michel, and donated some of its lands along the Seine – the Pré aux Clercs (Fields of the Scholars) – to house the University of Paris (hence the names of the nearby streets, rues du Pré aux Clercs and de l'Université).

DON'T MISS

- Chapelle de St-Symphorien
- Bell tower

PRACTICALITIES

- Map p402, D3
- ☎01 55 42 81 18
- www.eglise-saint germaindespres.fr
- 3 place St-Germain des Prés, 6e
- ⏲9am-7.45pm
- Ⓜ St-Germain des Prés

displays figures he sculpted in contrasting walnut, pear, ebony, acacia, elm and oak. Admission is only free when there is no temporary exhibition; otherwise adult/child admission is €7/free.

LE BATEAU IVRE MONUMENT
Map p402 (4 rue Ferou, 6e; Ⓜ St-Sulpice) Arthur Rimbaud's 1871 poem *Le Bateau Ivre* (The Drunken Boat), depicting a fantastical and frightening sea voyage of a sinking boat from the first-person narration of the boat itself using rich imagery and symbolism, occupies a 300m-long wall spanning an entire block in the heart of St-Germain. Rimbaud wrote the poem at age 16 after being inspired by Jules Verne's recently published novel *Twenty Thousand Leagues Under the Sea*. The 100-line poem was hand painted on the wall in 2012.

BIBLIOTHÈQUE MAZARINE LIBRARY
Map p402 (☎01 44 41 44 06; www.bibliotheque-mazarine.fr; 23 quai de Conti, 6e; ⏲10am-6pm Mon-Fri; Ⓜ Mabillon) FREE Within the **Institut de France** (Map p402; www.institut-de-france.fr; 23 quai de Conti, 6e; Ⓜ Mabillon), the Mazarine Library is France's oldest public library, founded in 1643. You can visit the bust-lined, late-17th-century reading room or consult the library's collection of 500,000 volumes, using an admission pass valid for five consecutive days obtained by providing ID. Schedules for free 1½-hour guided tours in English are posted on its website.

Les Invalides

MUSÉE RODIN MUSEUM, GARDEN
See p230.

MUSÉE D'ORSAY MUSEUM
See p224.

HÔTEL DES INVALIDES MONUMENT, MUSEUM
See p231.

PARC RIVES DE SEINE PARK
Map p406 (btwn Musée d'Orsay & Pont de l'Alma, 7e; ⏲information point noon-7pm Tue-Sun May-Sep, shorter hours Oct-Apr; Ⓜ Solférino, Assemblée Nationale, Invalides) A breath of fresh air, this 2.3km-long expressway-turned-riverside promenade on the Left Bank is a favourite spot in which to run, cycle, skate,

play board games or take part in a packed program of events. Equally it's simply a great place to hang out – in a Zzz shipping-container hut (reserve at the information point just west of the Musée d'Orsay), on the archipelago of floating gardens, or at the burgeoning restaurants and bars (some floating aboard boats and barges).

MUSÉE MAILLOL — MUSEUM

Map p406 (Fondation Dina Vierny; www.museemaillol.com; 61 rue de Grenelle, 7e; adult/child €13/11; ⊙10.30am-6.30pm Sat-Thu, to 9.30pm Fri; Ⓜ Rue du Bac) Located in the stunning 18th-century Hôtel Bouchardon, this splendid little museum focuses on the work of sculptor Aristide Maillol (1861–1944), whose creations primarily occupy several rooms on the 2nd floor, and also includes works by Matisse, Gauguin, Kandinsky, Cézanne and Picasso. All are from the private collection of Odessa-born Dina Vierny (1919–2009), Maillol's principal model for 10 years from the age of 15. Major temporary exhibitions (included in the admission price) regularly take place here.

EATING

The streets of this neighbourhood are lined with everything from quintessential Parisian bistros to chic designer restaurants and flagship establishments with Michelin-starred chefs. Some charming places hide inside Cour du Commerce St-André, a glass-covered passageway built in 1735 to link two *jeu de paume* (old-style tennis) courts. For snacks and fast food to munch on the move, head to rue St-André des Arts, a lively street peppered with tacos, kebab, Lebanese, crêpe and falafel takeaways.

St-Germain

L'AVANT COMPTOIR DE LA TERRE — FRENCH €

Map p402 (www.hotel-paris-relais-saint-germain.com; 3 Carrefour de l'Odéon, 6e; tapas €5-10; ⊙noon-11pm; Ⓜ Odéon) Squeeze in around the zinc bar (there are no seats and it's tiny) and feast on amazing tapas (crab custard tarts with Pernod foam, Iberian ham or salmon tartare croquettes, duck confit hot dogs, blood-sausage macarons, and prosciutto and artichoke waffles), with wines by the glass, in a chaotically sociable atmosphere.

For seafood tapas, head to neighbouring **L'Avant Comptoir de la Mer** (Map p402; ☎01 42 38 47 55; tapas €5-25, oysters per six €17; ⊙noon-11pm); for porcine tapas, nearby **L'Avant Comptoir du Marché** (Map p402; 15 rue Lobineau, 6e; tapas €3.50-20; ⊙noon-11pm; Ⓜ Mabillon). Or for gourmet bistro dining, try for a lunchtime table or evening reservation at **Le Comptoir** (Map p402; ☎01 44 27 07 97; 9 Carrefour de l'Odéon, 6e; lunch mains €14-30, dinner menu €60; ⊙noon-6pm & 8.30-11.30pm Mon-Fri, noon-11pm Sat & Sun; Ⓜ Odéon).

LITTLE BREIZH — CRÊPES €

Map p402 (☎01 43 54 60 74; www.facebook.com/LittleBreizhCreperie; 11 rue Grégoire de Tours, 6e; crêpes €5-15; ⊙noon-2.30pm & 7-10.30pm Tue-Sat; ✎; Ⓜ Odéon) As authentic as you'd find in Brittany, but with some innovative twists (such as Breton sardines, olive oil and sun-dried tomatoes; goat's cheese, stewed apple, hazelnuts, rosemary and honey; smoked salmon, dill cream, pink peppercorns and lemon), the crêpes at this sweet spot are infinitely more enticing than those sold on nearby street corners. Hours can fluctuate; book ahead.

AU PIED DE FOUET — BISTRO €

Map p402 (☎01 42 96 59 10; 3 rue St-Benoît, 6e; mains €9-12.50; ⊙noon-2.30pm & 7-11pm Mon-Sat; Ⓜ St-Germain des Prés) At this tiny, lively, cherry-red bistro, wholly classic dishes such as *entrecôte* (steak), *confit de canard* (duck cooked slowly in its own fat) with creamy potatoes and *foie de volailles sauté* (pan-fried chicken livers) are astonishingly good value. Round off your meal with a *tarte tatin* (upside-down apple tart), wine-soaked prunes, or deliciously rich *fondant au chocolat*.

SIMPLE — FRENCH €

Map p406 (☎01 45 44 79 88; 86 rue du Cherche-Midi, 6e; bowls & mains €15-20; ⊙noon-6.30pm Tue-Fri, to 7pm Sat; 📶; Ⓜ St-Placide) Amid the many eateries on fashionable rue du Cherche-Midi, Simple stands out for its simple salads, soups and detox veggie bowls. Everything, in fact, is super healthy at this fully organic lunch spot. Dozens of fresh flowers in vases decorate wooden tables inside and the pavement terrace is a perfect spot to people-watch over an Omega 3 *assiette* (plate) or gluten-free fish bowl.

OENOSTERIA ITALIAN €

Map p402 (☎01 77 15 94 13; www.restaurant-oenosteria-paris.fr; 40 rue Grégoire de Tours, 6e; mains €12-18; ⏰11am-midnight; Ⓜ Odéon, Mabillon) Vintage tables and chairs only add to the charm of this stylish, industrial-styled eatery – the *cave à manger* (wine-bar-meets-tapas bar) arm of **Casa Bini** (Map p402; ☎01 46 34 05 60; www.casabini.fr; 36 rue Gregoire de Tours, 6e; 2-/3-course lunch menu €25/29, mains €18-29; ⏰12.30-2.30pm & 7.30-11pm; 👪; Ⓜ Odéon) – stocked to the rafters with the finest Italian produce out there. Think fresh creamy burrata, aromatic cured meats from Tuscany, fennel-spiced Sicilian sausage and delicious *piatti* (mains) cooked up by Milanese couple, Sylveria and Enrico.

L'AMARYLLIS DE GÉRARD MULOT PASTRIES €

Map p402 (☎01 43 26 91 03; www.gerard-mulot.com; 12 rue des Quartre Vents, 6e; lunch menu €25, afternoon tea €15; ⏰11am-6.30pm Tue-Sat; Ⓜ Odéon) Pastry maestro Gérard Mulot has a boutique on nearby **rue de Seine** (Map p402; ☎01 43 26 85 77; www.gerard-mulot.com; 76 rue de Seine, 6e; ⏰7am-8pm; Ⓜ Mabillon), but it's at his elegant *salon de thé* (tearoom) that you savour his famous fruit tarts at leisure. Lunch here translates as soup, a slice of savoury tart or quiche, and a decadent cake for dessert. Afternoon tea includes the latter plus dainty sandwiches.

LA CRÈMERIE FRENCH €

Map p402 (☎01 43 54 99 30; 9 rue des Quatre-Vents, 6e; small plates €7-20; ⏰11am-2pm & 6-10pm Tue-Sat, 6-10pm Sun & Mon; Ⓜ Odéon) Beneath an original glass-covered ceiling, this marble-walled *caviste* (wine cellar) is a delicious flashback to 1880s Paris. With a stock of 400-odd wines and an exquisite array of France's finest gourmet goods, it is a delightful spot for an early-evening *apéro* (predinner drink) accompanied by tapas-style dishes (smoked-trout terrine, goat's cheese and olives, black-pudding-topped toast) or a fully-fledged meal.

Reservations essential. If you fail to snag a table, try its big sister nearby, **La Grande Crèmerie** (Map p402; ☎01 43 26 09 09; www.lagrandecremerie.fr; 8 rue Grégoire de Tours, 6e; small plates €6-14; ⏰6pm-midnight; Ⓜ Odéon).

KARAMEL PASTRIES €

Map p406 (☎01 71 93 02 94; https://karamelparis.com; 67 rue St-Dominique, 7e; ⏰8.30am-8.30pm; Ⓜ Invalides, Tour Maubourg) Sweet-toothed gourmets won't do much better than a pit stop at the specialist boutique and *salon de thé* (tearoom) of *chef-pâtissier* Nicolas Haelewy. Exquisite rows of fresh, caramel-spiked cakes jostle for the limelight with caramel-laced chocolate bars, jars of caramel to spread, and chewy bite-sized caramels flavoured with vanilla and *fleur de sel* (rock salt), passion fruit or rose and raspberry perhaps.

★BOUILLON RACINE BRASSERIE €€

Map p402 (☎01 44 32 15 60; www.bouillonracine.com; 3 rue Racine, 6e; 2-course weekday lunch menu €16.90, 3-course menu €35, mains €16-

PARIS' OLDEST RESTAURANT & CAFE

St-Germain claims both the city's oldest restaurant and its oldest cafe:

À la Petite Chaise (Map p402; ☎01 42 22 13 35; www.alapetitechaise.fr; 36 rue de Grenelle, 6e; 2-/3-course lunch menu €25/33, 3-course dinner menu €26, mains €21; ⏰noon-2pm & 7-11pm; Ⓜ Sèvres-Babylone) In 1860 wine merchant Georges Rameau took the innovative move of serving food (to accompany his wares) to customers coming to his shop – and so the oldest restaurant still standing in the capital was born. The kitchen remains firmly grounded in timeless French classics like onion soup and pan-fried calf kidneys.

Le Procope (Map p402; ☎01 40 46 79 00; www.procope.com; 13 rue de l'Ancienne Comédie, 6e; 2-/3-course menu €21.90/28.90; ⏰11.30am-midnight Sun-Wed, to 1am Thu-Sat; Ⓜ Odéon) If you ever wondered what Voltaire, Molière and Balzac dined on in the heady days of 17th-century Paris, reserve a table at this chandelier-posh restaurant where very little has changed since the day it first opened its doors in 1686. Coq au vin or calf's-head casserole in veal stock are tasty blasts from the past.

27.50; ⊙noon-11pm; ; Ⓜ Cluny-La Sorbonne) Inconspicuously situated in a quiet street, this heritage-listed art nouveau 'soup kitchen', with mirrored walls, floral motifs and ceramic tiling, was built in 1906 to feed market workers. Despite the magnificent interior, the food – inspired by age-old recipes – is no afterthought but superbly executed (stuffed, spit-roasted suckling pig, pork shank in Rodenbach red beer, scallops and shrimps with lobster coulis).

Finish off your foray into gastronomic history with an old-fashioned sherbet. Two-course children's menus (€14.50) mean kids don't miss out.

★ANICIA FRENCH €€

Map p406 (☎01 43 35 41 50; http://anicia-bistrot.com; 97 rue du Cherche Midi, 6e; 2-/3-course weekday lunch menu €24/29, 3-/5-course dinner menu €49/58, mains €27-34; ⊙noon-10.30pm Tue-Sat; Ⓜ Duroc, Vaneau) An advance online booking is essential at this glorious 'bistro nature', showcase for the earthy but refined cuisine of chef François Gagnaire who ran a Michelin-starred restaurant in the foodie town of Puy-en-Velay in the Auvergne before uprooting to the French capital. He still sources dozens of regional products – Puy lentils, Velay snails, St-Nectaire cheese – from small-time producers in central France, to stunning effect.

★HUÎTRERIE REGIS SEAFOOD €€

Map p402 (http://huitrerieregis.com; 3 rue de Montfaucon, 6e; dozen oysters from €26; ⊙noon-2.30pm & 6.30-10.30pm Mon-Fri, noon-10.45pm Sat, noon-10pm Sun; Ⓜ Mabillon) Hip, trendy, tiny and white, this is the spot for slurping oysters on crisp winter days – inside or on the tiny pavement terrace sporting sage-green Fermob chairs. Oysters arrive live from the Bassin de Marennes-Oléron and come only by the dozen. Wash them down with a glass of chilled Muscadet. No reservations, so arrive early. A twinset of tables are set on the pavement; otherwise it's all inside.

★CLOVER BISTRO €€

Map p402 (☎01 75 50 00 05; www.clover-paris.com; 5 rue Perronet, 7e; 2-/3-course lunch menu €37/47, 3-/5-course dinner menu €60/73; ⊙12.30-2pm & 7-10pm Tue-Fri, 12.30-2.30pm & 7-10pm Sat; Ⓜ St-Germain des Prés) Dining at hot-shot chef Jean-François Piège's casual bistro is like attending a private party: the galley-style open kitchen adjoining the 20 seats (online reservations open just 15 days in advance) is part of the dining-room decor, putting customers at the front and centre of the culinary action. Light, luscious dishes range from tomato gazpacho with pea sorbet to cabbage leaves with smoked herring *crème* and chestnuts.

★SEMILLA NEOBISTRO €€

Map p402 (☎01 43 54 34 50; www.semillaparis.com; 54 rue de Seine, 6e; 2-/3-course weekday lunch menu €34/40, mains €24-40; ⊙12.30-2.30pm & 7-11pm Mon-Sat, to 10pm Sun, closed early–mid-Aug; Ⓜ Mabillon) Stark concrete floor, beams and an open kitchen (in front of which you can book front-row 'chef seats') set the factory-style scene for edgy, modern, daily changing dishes such as scallops cooked in Vin Jaune wine with crunchy endives or trout with passionfruit and ginger. Desserts are equally creative and irresistible. Be sure to book.

If you haven't made a reservation, head to its adjoining walk-in wine bar, **Freddy's** (Map p402; 54 rue de Seine, 6e; small plates €6-10; ⊙noon-midnight; Ⓜ St-Germain des Prés), serving small tapas-style plates.

★L'ÉTABLE HUGO DESNOYER FRENCH €€

Map p402 (☎01 42 39 89 27; www.hugodesnoyer.com; 15 rue Clément, 6e; lunch menu €24.50, mains €30-40; ⊙noon-2.30pm & 7.30-10.30pm Tue-Sat; Ⓜ Mabillon) Duck beneath the elegant stone arches of **Marché St-Germain** (Map p402; http://marchesaintgermain.com; 4-6 rue Lobineau, 6e; ⊙8am-8pm Tue-Sat, to 1.30pm Sun; Ⓜ Mabillon) to uncover the stylish steakhouse of Paris' superstar butcher Hugo Desnoyer. Vegetarians be warned, there are some delicious veggie dishes too, but some of the walls in the sharp design interior are clad in ginger-and-cream cowhide and the menu is essentially for meat lovers.

★NIÉBÉ FUSION €€

Map p402 (☎01 43 29 43 31; www.restaurantniebe.com; 16 rue del a Grande Chaumière, 6e; 2-/3-course weekday lunch menu €17/22, mains €19-22; ⊙noon-3pm & 7.30pm-midnight Tue-Sat; Ⓜ Vavin) Inviting sunflower-yellow walls set the tone at this new Left Bank hot spot for soul food. Ex-chef at the Brazilian Embassy, Rosilène Vitorino oversees a menu that fuses Brazilian, Creole and African cuisine.

Best up, there are two menus: classic (starring Creole blood sausage with sweet potato and kumquat purée) and vegan (with dishes like sautéed tofu with black rice in a coconut coulis).

CHEZ DUMONET BISTRO €€

Map p406 (Joséphine; ☎01 45 48 52 40; 117 rue du Cherche Midi, 6e; mains €24-40; ⊙noon-2.30pm & 7.30-9.30pm Mon-Fri; MDuroc) Fondly known by its former name, Joséphine, this lace-curtained, mosaic-tiled place with white-cloth tables inside and out is the Parisian bistro of many people's dreams, serving timeless standards such as confit of duck and grilled châteaubriand steak with Béarnaise sauce. Order its enormous signature Grand Marnier soufflé at the start of your meal. Mains, unusually, come in full or half-portion size.

During truffle season (November to March), look out for its truffle menus.

POLIDOR FRENCH €€

Map p402 (☎01 43 26 95 34; www.polidor.com; 41 rue Monsieur le Prince, 6e; menus €22 & €35, mains €13-20; ⊙noon-2.30pm & 7pm-12.30am Mon-Sat, to 11pm Sun; MOdéon) A meal at this quintessentially Parisian place is like a trip to Victor Hugo's Paris: the restaurant and its decor date from 1845. *Menus* of family-style French cuisine ensure a stream of diners eager to sample *blanquette de veau à l'ancienne* (veal in white sauce) and Polidor's famous *tarte tatin* (upside down apple tart). No credit cards or reservations (expect to wait).

Midnight in Paris fans might recognise it as the place where Owen Wilson's character meets Hemingway (who dined here in his day). More than 20,000 bottles are stocked in its wine cellar.

LE TIMBRE BISTRO €€

Map p402 (☎01 45 49 10 40; www.facebook.com/restaurantletimbre; 3 rue Ste-Beuve, 6e; 2-/3-course lunch menu €23/28, 3-/4-course dinner menu €36/45; ⊙7.30-11pm Tue, noon-3pm & 7.30-11pm Wed-Sat; MVavin) As tiny as the postage stamp for which it's named, Le Timbre is run by husband-and-wife team Charles Danet (in the kitchen) and Agnès Peyre (front of house) and has a local following for its daily changing menu of original dishes with a sharp contemporary twist (caramelised endives with Parmesan *crème* and brioche; turbot and clams with marinated cabbage and potato terrine).

STARS OF THE FUTURE

Founded in 1920, **Restaurants d'Application de Ferrandi** (Map p406; www.ferrandi-paris.fr; 28 rue de l'Abbé Grégoire, 6e; Le Premier lunch/dinner menu €28/45, Le 28 lunch/dinner menu €35/45; ⊙by online reservation, closed school holidays; MSt-Placide) is arguably France's most prestigious culinary school, turning out a who's who of industry professionals. You can taste these future Michelin-starred chefs' creations at bargain prices at the school's two training restaurants, **Le Premier** (focusing on classical French cookery) and **Le 28** (high-level gastronomy), overseen by Ferrandi's esteemed professors. Hours vary; online bookings are obligatory.

UN DIMANCHE À PARIS FUSION €€

Map p402 (☎01 56 81 18 18; www.un-dimanche-a-paris.com; 4-8 Cour du Commerce St-André, 6e; menus lunch/dinner/brunch from €29.50/32/38; ⊙restaurant 7-10pm Tue, noon-2pm & 7-10pm Wed-Sat, 11am-7pm Sun; MOdéon) Inside covered passageway Cour du Commerce St-André, this glamorous 'chocolate concept store' incorporates a boutique (where you can buy cakes, chocolates and absolutely divine chocolate-coated herbs and spices), patisserie and chocolate classes (€50 to €80), a tearoom serving decadently rich hot chocolate (open 3pm to 6pm) and a restaurant cooking up chocoholic dishes like ricotta-filled pasta in hazelnut and white-chocolate broth or prawns with cocoa and candied pineapple. Hours can vary.

RESTAURANT GUY SAVOY GASTRONOMY €€€

Map p402 (☎01 43 80 40 61; www.guysavoy.com; 11 quai de Conti, 6e, Monnaie de Paris; lunch menu via online booking €130, tasting menu €415; ⊙noon-2pm & 7-10.30pm Tue-Fri, 7-10.30pm Sat; MPont Neuf) If you're considering visiting a three-Michelin-star temple of gastronomy, this should certainly be on your list. The world-famous chef needs no introduction (he trained Gordon Ramsay, among others) but his flagship, entered via a red-carpeted staircase, is ensconced in the gorgeously refurbished neoclassical Monnaie de Paris (p232). Monumental cuisine to match includes Savoy icons like artichoke and black-truffle soup with layered brioche.

LOCAL KNOWLEDGE

RUE CLER

Pick up fresh bread, sandwich fillings, pastries and wine for a picnic along the typically Parisian commercial street rue Cler, 7e, which buzzes with local shoppers, especially on weekends.

Interspersed between the *boulangeries* (bakeries), *fromageries* (cheese shops), grocers, butchers, delis and other food shops (many with pavement stalls), lively cafe terraces overflow with locals, too.

AUX PRÉS BISTRO €€€

Map p402 (☎01 45 48 29 68; www.restaurantauxpres.com; 27 rue du Dragon, 6e; 2-/3-course menu €38/49; ⏰noon-2.30pm & 7-11pm; Ⓜ St-Sulpice) This cult 1950s bistro with original bar, leather banquette seating and floral wallpaper sizzles with contemporary glamour thanks to celebrity French chef Cyril Lignac who lures a gourmet crowd here with his modern bistro cuisine: think veal sweetbreads, *côte de boeuf* (€95 for two) or scallops with celeriac and a peppery coconut cream.

Les Invalides

LE BAC À GLACES ICE CREAM €

Map p406 (www.bacaglaces.com; 109 rue du Bac, 7e; ice cream per 1/2/3 scoops €3.50/5/6.50; ⏰11am-7pm Mon-Fri, to 7.30pm Sat; Ⓜ Sèvres-Babylone) Apricot and thyme, lemon and basil, strawberry and rose, and a triple hit of orange, Grand Marnier and chocolate are among the 60 flavours of all-natural ice creams at this luscious *glacière* (ice-cream maker). A cloud of Chantilly sugar-whipped cream costs an extra €0.50.

★TOMY & CO GASTRONOMY €€

Map p406 (☎01 45 51 46 93; 22 rue Surcouf, 7e; 2-course lunch menu €27, 3-course/tasting dinner menu €47/68, mains wine pairings €45; ⏰noon-2pm & 7.30-9.30pm Mon-Fri; Ⓜ Invalides) Tomy Gousset's restaurant near Mademoiselle Eiffel has been a sensation since day one. The French-Cambodian chef works his magic on inspired seasonal dishes using produce from his organic garden. Winter ushers in aromatic black truffles (themed tasting menu €95), and spectacular desserts – chocolate tart with fresh figs, Cambodian palm sugar and fig ice cream anyone? – are equally seasonal. Reservations essential.

★EPOCA ITALIAN €€

Map p406 (☎01 43 06 88 88; http://epoca.paris; 17 rue Oudinot, 7e; 2-course lunch menu €20, pasta/mains €16/20; ⏰noon-2.30pm & 7.30-10.30pm Mon-Thu, to 11pm Fri & Sat; Ⓜ Sèvres-Babylone) Star of the French TV show *Top Chef,* Italian chef Denny Imbroisi, is the creative talent behind this A-lister-chic Italian bistro with a sharp, black-and-white interior evocative of 1930s art deco. The short, stylish menu features the best of Italian regional cooking: begin with a Roman deep-fried artichoke or Sicilian squid, perhaps, followed by spaghetti with goat's cheese and black pepper or saffron-laced Milanese risotto.

CAFÉ CONSTANT BISTRO €€

Map p406 (☎01 47 53 73 34; www.maisonconstant.com; 139 rue St-Dominique, 7e; 2-/3-course weekday lunch menu €18/26, mains €18-29; ⏰7am-11pm Mon-Sat, 8am-11pm Sun; Ⓜ École Militaire or RER Pont de l'Alma) Run by Michelin-starred chef Christian Constant, whose flagship **Le Violon d'Ingres** (Map p406; ☎01 45 55 15 05; 135 rue St-Dominique, 7e; 2-/3-course weekday lunch menu €49/55, tasting menu €130, mains €45-52; ⏰noon-2.30pm & 7-10.30pm) is on the same street, this traditional neighbourhood cafe with original bar and mosaic floor cooks up some fantastic staples: veal cordon bleu with mashed potato, herb-roasted chicken or beef stew followed by rice pudding. Breakfast is served until 11am, more substantial food continuously from noon until closing time.

No reservations: enjoy a drink at the bar or on the pavement terrace outside while you wait. More upmarket **Les Cocottes** (Map p406; ☎01 45 50 10 28 135 rue St-Dominique, 7e; 2-/3-course weekday lunch €23/28, 4-course menu €35, mains €18-31; ⏰noon-11pm; 📶), a couple of doors down on the same street, is another Constant hit.

LE FONTAINE DE MARS BISTRO €€

Map p406 (☎01 47 05 46 44; www.fontainedemars.com; 129 rue St-Dominique, 7e; seafood platters from €49, mains €17-35; ⏰noon-3pm & 7.30-11pm; Ⓜ École Militaire) For traditional French cooking look no further than this 1930s-styled neighbourhood bistro with signature lace curtains, checked tablecloths and – best of all – a fishmonger in front shucking oysters at his stall beneath the bistro arches. Snails, *boudin* (black pudding), *andouillette* (Lyonnais tripe sausage) and homemade *confit de canard* (preserved duck breast) are among the traditional mainstays, alongside sensational seafood platters.

RESTAURANT DAVID TOUTAIN GASTRONOMY €€€

Map p406 (☎01 45 50 11 10; http://davidtoutain.com; 29 rue Surcouf, 7e; 3-course lunch menu €55, tasting menus €80-140, wine pairings €70-100; ⏲12.30-2pm & 8-10pm Mon, noon-2pm & 8-10pm Tue-Fri; Ⓜ Invalides) Prepare to be wowed: David Toutain pushes the envelope at his eponymous Michelin-starred restaurant with some of the most creative high-end cooking in Paris. Mystery *dégustation* (tasting) courses include unlikely combinations such as smoked eel in green-apple-and-black-sesame mousse, cauliflower, white chocolate and coconut truffles, or candied celery and truffled rice pudding with artichoke praline. Stunning wine pairings are available.

LES CLIMATS FRENCH €€€

Map p406 (☎01 58 62 10 08; http://lesclimats.fr; 41 rue de Lille, 7e; lunch/dinner menu €45/130, mains €52-72; ⏲12.15-2.30pm & 7-10pm Tue-Sat; Ⓜ Solférino) Like the neighbouring Musée d'Orsay, this is a magnificent art-nouveau treasure – a 1905-built former home for female telephone, telegram and postal workers – featuring soaring vaulted ceilings and original stained glass, along with a lunchtime summer garden and glassed-in winter garden. Exquisite Michelin-starred dishes complement its 150-page list of wines, sparkling wines and whiskies purely from the Burgundy region.

PLUME BISTRO €€€

Map p406 (☎01 43 06 79 85; www.restaurantplume.com; 24 rue Pierre Leroux, 7e; 2-/3-course lunch menu €27/37, 3-/5-course dinner menu €45/65, mains €29-32; ⏲noon-2.15pm & 7.30-10.15pm Tue-Sat; Ⓜ Vaneau, Duroc) A minimalist, 1950s ambience cocoons discerning diners at Plume ('Feather'), the stylish neobistro of talented young Tunisian chef Youssef Gastli. His modern French cuisine translates as scallops with celeriac and horseradish perhaps, or fish of the day with wild rice, saffron, wild herbs and *poutargue* (cured fish roe), complemented by a fantastic wine list featuring wholly organic, biodynamic or natural wines.

DRINKING & NIGHTLIFE

St-Germain's Carrefour de l'Odéon has a cluster of lively bars and cafes. Rues de Buci, St-André des Arts and de l'Odéon enjoy a fair slice of night action with arty cafes and busy pubs, while place St-Germain des Prés buzzes with the pavement terraces of fabled literary cafes. Rue Princesse attracts a student crowd with its bevy of pubs, microbreweries and cocktail bars.

Les Invalides is a day- rather than night-time venue, with government ministries and embassies outweighing drinking venues. Particularly in summer, however, look out for bars along Les Berges de Seine (p233).

St-Germain

★LES DEUX MAGOTS CAFE

Map p402 (☎01 45 48 55 25; www.lesdeuxmagots.fr; 170 bd St-Germain, 6e; ⏲7.30am-1am; Ⓜ St-Germain des Prés) If ever there was a cafe that summed up St-Germain des Prés' early-20th-century literary scene, it's this former hang-out of anyone who was anyone. You'll spend substantially more here than elsewhere to sip *un café* (€4.70) in a wicker-woven bistro chair on the pavement terrace shaded by dark-green awnings and geraniums spilling from window boxes, but it's an undeniable piece of Parisian history.

★AU SAUVIGNON WINE BAR

Map p402 (☎01 45 48 49 02; http://ausauvignon.com; 80 rue des Sts-Pères, 7e; ⏲8am-11pm Mon-Sat, 9am-10pm Sun; Ⓜ Sèvres-Babylone) Grab a table in the evening light at this wonderfully authentic wine bar or head to the quintessential bistro interior, with original zinc bar, tightly packed tables and hand-painted ceiling celebrating French viticultural tradition. A plate of *casse-croûtes au pain Poilâne* (toast with ham, pâté, terrine, smoked salmon and foie gras) is the perfect accompaniment.

★COD HOUSE COCKTAIL BAR

Map p402 (☎01 42 49 35 59; www.thecodhouse.fr; 1 rue de Condé, 6e; ⏲noon-3pm & 7.30-2am Mon-Sat; Ⓜ Odéon) 'Oh my cod!' screams the turquoise-neon 'tag' on the wall, and indeed, this achingly cool cocktail bar with a

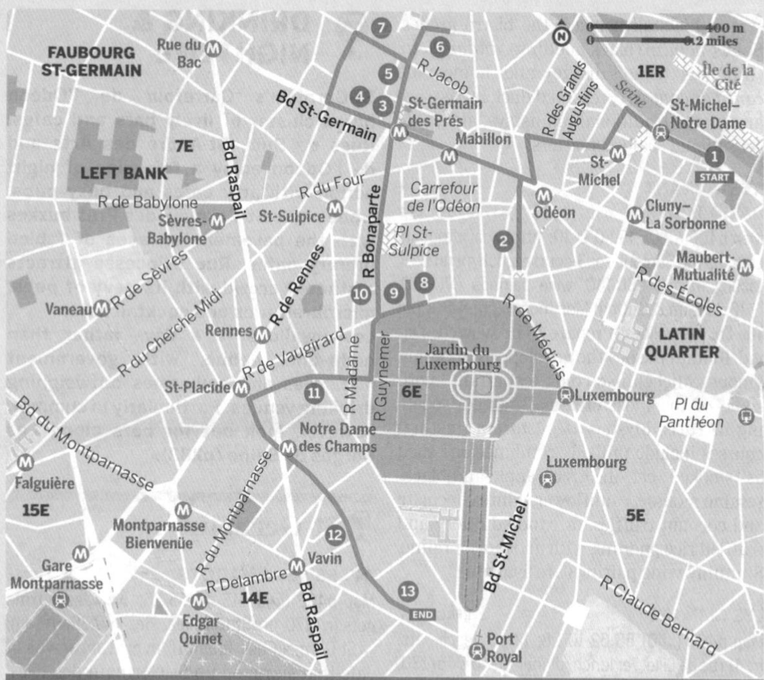

Neighbourhood Walk
Left Bank Literary Loop

START QUAI ST-MICHEL
END 113 RUE NOTRE DAMES DES CHAMPS
LENGTH 5KM; ONE TO TWO HOURS

To retrace the footsteps of literary luminaries, begin with the Seine-side *bouquinistes* (secondhand booksellers, loved by Ernest Hemingway) along quai St-Michel from 1 **Notre Dame** (p195) to place St-Michel.

Continue west then cross the street and duck south along rue Gît-le-Cœur to the 'Beat Hotel', today 2 **Relais Hôtel du Vieux Paris**, where Allen Ginsberg, Jack Kerouac, William S Burroughs and others holed up in the 1950s.

At 3 **12 rue de l'Odéon** stood the original Shakespeare & Company bookshop where owner Sylvia Beach lent books to Hemingway, and edited, retyped and published *Ulysses* for James Joyce in 1922. It was closed during the occupation when Beach refused to sell her last copy of Joyce's *Finnegan's Wake* to a Nazi officer.

Bd St-Germain's 4 **Les Deux Magots** (p239) and 5 **Café de Flore** (p241) were favourite cafes of postwar intellectuals Jean-Paul Sartre and Simone de Beauvoir.

At 6 **36 rue Bonaparte** Henry Miller stayed in a 5th-floor mansard room in 1930, which he later wrote about in *Letters to Emil* (1989). 7 **L'Hôtel** (p291), the former Hôtel d'Alsace, is where Oscar Wilde died in 1900. Hemingway spent his first night in Paris in room 14 of the 8 **Hôtel d'Angleterre** (p291) in 1921.

In 1925 William Faulkner stayed several months at what's now the posh 9 **Hôtel Luxembourg Parc**, and Hemingway's last years in Paris were at 10 **6 rue Férou**. F Scott and Zelda Fitzgerald lived at 11 **58 rue de Vaugirard** in 1928, near 12 **27 rue de Fleurus**, where Gertrude Stein lived and entertained artists and writers including Matisse, Picasso, Braque, Gauguin, Fitzgerald, Hemingway and Ezra Pound.

Pound lived at 13 **70bis rue Notre Dame des Champs** in a flat filled with Japanese paintings, while Hemingway's first apartment in this area was above a sawmill at 14 **113 rue Notre Dames des Champs**.

gold-and-blue, Scandinavian-style interior does excite. Sake-based cocktails play around with matcha-infused cachaça, cinammon-infused pisco and homemade lemongrass syrup; while creative small plates (€5 to €16) titillate tastebuds with shrimp tempura, yellow-tail carpaccio with fresh chilli and a yuzu sauce, deep-fried chicken ravioli.

★LE BAR DES PRÉS — COCKTAIL BAR

Map p402 (☎01 43 25 87 67; www.lebardespres.com; 25 rue du Dragon, 6e; ⊙noon-2.30pm & 7-11pm; Ⓜ St-Sulpice) Sake-based craft cocktails and tantalising shared plates (€18 to €24) by a Japanese chef create buzz at the chic cocktail-bar arm of Cyril Lignac's foodie empire on rue du Dragon – his glam, 1950s-styled bistro (p238) is right next door. The scallops with caramelised miso, avocado and fresh coriander are heavenly, as is the yellow tail sashimi, jellied eel and other sushi.

TIGER — COCKTAIL BAR

Map p402 (www.tiger-paris.com; 13 rue Princesse, 6e; ⊙6.30pm-2am Mon-Sat; Ⓜ Mabillon) Suspended bare-bulb lights and fretted timber make this split-level space a stylish spot for specialist gins (130 varieties). Signature cocktails include a Breakfast Martini (gin, triple sec, orange marmalade and lemon juice) and Oh My Dog (white-pepper-infused gin, lime juice, raspberry and rose cordial and ginger ale). Dedicated G&T aficionados can work their way through a staggering 1040 combinations.

CAFÉ DE FLORE — CAFE

Map p402 (☎01 45 48 55 26; http://cafedeflore.fr; 172 bd St-Germain, 6e; ⊙7.30am-1.30am; Ⓜ St-Germain des Prés) The red upholstered benches, mirrors and marble walls at this art deco landmark haven't changed much since the days when Jean-Paul Sartre and Simone de Beauvoir essentially set up office here, writing in its warmth during the Nazi occupation. Watch for monthly English-language *philocafé* (philosophy discussion) sessions.

CASTOR CLUB — COCKTAIL BAR

Map p402 (☎09 50 64 99 38; 14 rue Hautefeuille, 6e; ⊙7pm-2am Tue & Wed, 7pm-4am Thu-Sat; Ⓜ Odéon) Discreetly signed, this superb underground cocktail bar has an intimate English gentleman's club–style upstairs bar with vintage wall lamps and slinky, red velour stools. But it's downstairs, in the 18th-century stone cellar with hole-in-the-wall booths, that the real cocktail-sipping action happens. Smooth '50s, '60s and '70s tracks only add to the already cool vibe.

LA PALETTE — CAFE

Map p402 (www.cafelapaletteparis.com; 43 rue de Seine, 6e; ⊙8am-2am; 📶; Ⓜ Mabillon) In the heart of gallery land, this timeless *fin de siècle* cafe and erstwhile stomping ground of Paul Cézanne and Georges Braque attracts a grown-up set of fashion-industry professionals and local art dealers. Its summer terrace is beautiful.

FRAPPÉ BY BLOOM — CAFE, BAR

Map p402 (☎07 89 83 79 58; http://frappe.bloom-restaurant.fr; 2 rue Guénégaud, 6e, Monnaie de Paris; ⊙8.30am-7pm Tue & Wed, 8.30am-midnight Thu & Fri, 10.30am-midnight Sat, 10.30am-7pm Sun; Ⓜ Pont Neuf) In keeping with Paris' penchant for stylish museum eateries, its 18th-century mint sports a super-stylish cafe-cum-cocktail bar with designer interior and one of the city's loveliest summertime terraces – in Cour de la Méridienne, one of the Monnaie de Paris' elegant neoclassical courtyards.

PRESCRIPTION COCKTAIL CLUB — COCKTAIL BAR

Map p402 (☎09 50 35 72 87; www.prescriptioncocktailclub.com; 23 rue Mazarine, 6e; ⊙7pm-2am Mon-Thu, 7pm-4am Fri & Sat, 8pm-2am Sun; Ⓜ Odéon) With bowler and flat-top hats as lampshades and a 1930s speakeasy New York air to the place, this cocktail club – run by the same mega-successful team as Experimental Cocktail Club (p128) – is very Parisian-cool. Getting past the doorman can be tough, but, once in, it's friendliness and old-fashioned cocktails all round.

FROG & PRINCESS — MICROBREWERY

Map p402 (☎01 40 51 77 38; www.frogpubs.com; 9 rue Princesse, 6e; ⊙5pm-1am Mon-Wed, to 2am Thu & Fri, noon-2am Sat, noon-1am Sun; 📶; Ⓜ Mabillon) Part of the Frog family that includes several Parisian microbreweries, this good-time pub on one of the Left Bank's liveliest drinking streets is popular for its own-brewed beers, burgers, American barbecue and soul food, and sports screenings. Reserve in advance for weekend brunch (€18).

LA QUINCAVE — WINE BAR

Map p402 (☎09 67 02 80 14; www.facebook.com/quincave; 17 rue Bréa, 6e; ⊙11am-1pm & 5-11.30pm Tue-Thu, 11am-11.30pm Fri & Sat; Ⓜ Vavin) Bar stools at this lively wine bar and shop are fashioned from wine barrels, but on summer evenings most of the action spills onto the tiny street out front. Over 200 varieties of natural wines are available by the bottle, along with tasty charcuterie and cheese platters to soak them up.

Les Invalides

★COUTUME CAFÉ COFFEE

Map p406 (☎01 45 51 50 47; www.coutumecafe.com; 47 rue de Babylone, 7e; ⊙8.30am-5.30pm Mon-Fri, 9am-6pm Sat & Sun; 📶; Ⓜ St-François Xavier) The Parisian coffee revolution is thanks in no small part to Coutume, artisanal roaster of premium beans for scores of establishments around town. Its flagship cafe – a bright, light-filled, postindustrial space – is ground zero for innovative preparation methods including cold extraction and siphon brews. Couple some of Paris' finest coffee with a tasty, seasonal cuisine and the place is always packed out.

THE CLUB COCKTAIL BAR

Map p406 (☎01 45 50 31 54; www.the-club.fr; 24 rue Surcouf, 7e; ⊙4pm-1.30am Mon-Sat; Ⓜ La Tour-Maubourg) At street level The Club has New York–warehouse brickwork and big timber cabinets, but the lounge-like basement, strewn with red and black sofas, is even cooler. Cocktails include the house-speciality Club (lime, fresh ginger and Jack Daniels honey liqueur) and seasonally changing creations, or ask for the bar staff to surprise you with their own concoctions.

ENTERTAINMENT

St-Germain and especially Les Invalides aren't major nightlife destinations – eating, drinking and, above all, shopping are the main entertainments here. For live music, check for events in bars along Les Berges de Seine (p233), or head to the Latin Quarter or the floating nightclubs in the 13e. Cinema-goers are well catered for, with multiplexes concentrated around the Odéon metro station on bd St-Germain.

LE LUCERNAIRE CULTURAL CENTRE

Map p402 (☎01 45 44 57 34; www.lucernaire.fr; 53 rue Notre Dame des Champs, 6e; ⊙bar 9am-9pm Mon, 9am-12.30am Tue-Fri, 10am-12.30am Sat, 11am-9pm Sun; Ⓜ Notre Dame des Champs) Sunday-evening concerts are a fixture on the impressive repertoire of the dynamic Centre National d'Art et d'Essai (National Arts Centre). Whether it's classical guitar, baroque, French *chansons* or East Asian music, these weekly concerts are a real treat. Art and photography exhibitions, cinema, theatre, lectures, debates and guided walks round off the packed cultural agenda.

THÉATRE DU VIEUX COLOMBIER THEATRE

Map p402 (☎01 44 58 15 15; www.comedie-francaise.fr; 21 rue du Vieux Colombier, 6e; ⊙Sep-Jul; Ⓜ St-Sulpice) Founded in 1680, this is one of three Comédie Française venues (p130), along with the Right Bank's main Salle Richelieu and Studio Théâtre. It presents works by classic French playwrights such as Molière.

CHEZ PAPA JAZZ

Map p402 (☎01 42 86 99 63; www.papajazzclub-paris.fr; 3 rue St-Benoît, 6e; ⊙concerts 9pm-1.30am Tue-Sat; Ⓜ St-Germain des Prés) The doors of this snug New York–style jazz club regularly stay open until dawn. Piano duets, blues, sax solos and singers feature on the bill from 9pm. Its restaurant serves traditional French dishes (snails, foie gras, tartare, veal stew).

SHOPPING

The northern wedge of the 6e between Église St-Germain des Prés and the Seine is a dream to mooch around with its bijou art galleries, antique shops, stylish vintage clothes shops, and designer boutiques (Vanessa Bruno, Isabel Marant et al). St-Germain's style continues along the western half of bd St-Germain and rue du Bac with a striking collection of contemporary furniture, kitchen and design shops. Gourmet food and wine shops galore make it a foodie's paradise.

St-Germain

DEYROLLE ANTIQUES, HOMEWARES

Map p402 (☎01 42 22 30 07; www.deyrolle.com; 46 rue du Bac, 7e; ⊙10am-1pm & 2-7pm Mon, 10am-7pm Tue-Sat; Ⓜ Rue du Bac) Overrun with creatures such as lions, tigers, zebras

ART & ANTIQUE STREETS

St-Germain's narrow streets are filled with art and antique shops.

Meander along rue Mazarine, rue Jacques Callot, rue des Beaux Arts and rue de Seine for art galleries.

Edgier galleries include **Galerie Loft** (Map p402; ☎01 46 33 18 90; www.galerieloft.com; 3bis rue des Beaux Arts, 6e; ⊙10am-1pm & 2.30-6pm Tue-Fri, 10.30am-1pm & 2.30-6pm Sat; Ⓜ St-Germain des Prés), with all forms of art (digital video and performance photography included) by contemporary Chinese artists on show at this courtyard gallery.

Art and antique dealers congregate within the **Carré Rive Gauche**. Bounded by quai Voltaire and rues de l'Université, des St-Pères and du Bac, this 'Left Bank Square' is home to more than 120 specialised merchants. Antiques fairs are usually held in spring, while exhibitions take place during the year.

and storks, taxidermist Deyrolle opened in 1831. In addition to stuffed animals, it stocks minerals, shells, corals and crustaceans, stand-mounted ostrich eggs and pedagogical storyboards. There are also rare and unusual seeds (including many old types of tomato), gardening tools and accessories.

CIRE TRUDON GIFTS & SOUVENIRS

Map p402 (☎01 43 26 46 50; https://trudon.com; 78 rue de Seine, 6e; ⊙11am-7pm Mon, 10am-7pm Tue-Sat; Ⓜ Odéon) Claude Trudon began selling candles here in 1643, and the company – which officially supplied Versailles and Napoléon with light – is now the world's oldest candle-maker. A rainbow of candles and candlesticks fill the shelves inside.

AU PLAT D'ÉTAIN TOYS

Map p402 (☎01 43 54 32 06; www.soldats-plomb-au-plat-etain.fr; 16 rue Guisarde, 6e; ⊙10.30am-6.30pm Tue-Sat; Ⓜ Mabillon, St-Sulpice) Tiny tin *(étain)* and lead soldiers, snipers, cavaliers, military drummers and musicians (great for chessboard pieces) cram this fascinating boutique. In business since 1775, the shop itself is practically a collectable.

HERMÈS FASHION & ACCESSORIES

Map p402 (☎01 42 22 80 83; www.hermes.com; 17 rue de Sèvres, 6e; ⊙10.30am-7pm Mon-Sat; Ⓜ Sèvres-Babylone) A stunning art deco swimming pool (originally belonging to neighbouring Hôtel Lutetia, no less) now houses luxury label Hermès' inaugural concept store. Retaining its original mosaic tiles and iron balustrades, the vast, tiered space showcases new directions in home furnishings, including fabrics and wallpaper, along with classic lines such as its signature scarves.

GAB & JO FASHION & ACCESSORIES

Map p402 (www.gabjo.fr; 28 rue Jacob, 6e; ⊙11am-7pm Mon-Sat; Ⓜ St-Germain des Prés) For quality local gifts, browse the shelves of this tiny concept store stocking only made-in-France items. Designers include La Note Parisienne (scented candles for each Parisian *arrondissement*), Marius Fabre (Marseille soaps), Germaine-des-Prés (lingerie) and MILF (sunglasses).

JB GUANTI FASHION & ACCESSORIES

Map p402 (www.jbguanti.com; 59 rue de Rennes, 6e; ⊙10am-7pm Mon-Sat; Ⓜ St-Sulpice) For the ultimate finishing touch, the men's and women's gloves at this boutique, which specialises solely in gloves, are the epitome of both style and comfort, whether unlined, silk lined, cashmere lined, lambskin lined or trimmed with rabbit fur.

LA DERNIÈRE GOUTTE WINE

Map p402 (☎01 43 29 11 62; www.laderniere goutte.net; 6 rue du Bourbon le Château, 6e; ⊙3.30-8pm Mon, 10.30am-1.30pm & 3-8pm Tue-Fri, 10.30am-8pm Sat, 11am-7pm Sun; Ⓜ Mabillon) 'The Last Drop' is the brainchild of Cuban-American sommelier Juan Sánchez, whose tiny wine shop is packed with exciting, mostly organic French *vins de propriétaires* (estate-bottled wines) made by small independent producers. Wine classes lasting two hours regularly take place in English (per person €55); phone for schedules and reservations. Free tastings with winemakers take place most Saturdays.

FERMOB HOMEWARES

Map p402 (☎01 45 44 10 28; www.paris.fermob.com; 17 bd Raspail, 7e; ⊙10am-7pm Tue-Sat; Ⓜ Rue du Bac) Fermob is famed for manufacturing iconic French garden furniture, including the Jardin du Luxembourg's signature sage-green chairs, actually available in a spectacular rainbow of colours. Fermob has another branch (Map p394; 81-83 av Ledru-Rollin, 12e; ⏲10am-7pm Mon-Sat; Ⓜ Ledru-Rollin) across the river near Bastille.

FINGER IN THE NOSE CHILDREN, FASHION

Map p402 (☎09 83 01 76 75; www.fingerinthenose.com; 11 rue de l'Échaudé, 6e; ⏲2.30-7pm Mon, 11am-7.30pm Tue-Sat; Ⓜ Mabillon) This finger-on-the-pulse Parisian children's-wear label thumbs its nose at convention and offers edgy streetwear for kids, such as graphic T-shirts, fleeces and jackets along with sophisticated twists like its line of LBDs ('little black dresses') for teenage girls.

LA MAISON DE POUPÉE ANTIQUES

Map p402 (☎06 09 65 58 68; 40 rue de Vaugirard, 6e; ⏲2.30-7pm Mon-Sat, by appointment Sun; Ⓜ St-Sulpice or RER Luxembourg) Opposite the residence of the French Senate's president, this delightful little shop sells its namesake dolls' houses as well as *poupées anciennes* (antique dolls).

MARCHÉ RASPAIL MARKET

Map p406 (bd Raspail, btwn rue de Rennes & rue du Cherche Midi, 6e; ⏲7am-2.30pm Tue & Fri, organic market 9am-1.30pm Sun; Ⓜ Rennes) A traditional open-air market on Tuesday and Friday, Marché Raspail is especially popular on Sunday, when it's filled with *biologique* (organic) produce.

SABBIA ROSA FASHION & ACCESSORIES

Map p402 (☎01 45 48 88 37; 73 rue des Sts-Pères, 6e; ⏲10am-7pm Mon-Sat; Ⓜ St-Germain des Prés) Only French-sourced fabrics (silk from Lyon, lace from Calais) are used by lingerie designer Sabbia Rosa for her ultra-luxe range. Every piece is unique; items can be custom-made in 48 hours. The list of celebrity clients reads like a who's who including Serge Gainsbourg, Madonna, Naomi Campbell, Claudia Schiffer and George Clooney.

PIERRE HERMÉ FOOD

Map p402 (www.pierreherme.com; 72 rue Bonaparte, 6e; ⏲10am-7pm Sun-Fri, to 8pm Sat; Ⓜ Odéon) Leading *pâtissier* and chocolatier Pierre Hermé has several boutiques in Paris including this one in the heart of St-Germain. The size of a chocolate box, it's a veritable feast of perfectly presented petits fours, cakes, chocolates, nougats, jams and dazzling macarons.

SMALLABLE CONCEPT STORE CHILDREN'S CLOTHING

Map p406 (☎01 40 46 01 15; www.smallable.com; 81 rue du Cherche Midi, 6e; ⏲2-7.30pm Mon, 10.30am-7.30pm Tue-Sat; Ⓜ Vaneau) 'Dream big' is the inviting strapline of this Parisian-chic space, a one-stop shop for accessories, fashion and homewares for babies, children and teens. Brands include Little Eleven Paris, Chloé Kids, Petit Bateau, Pom d'Api and Zadig & Voltaire. It is also one of the few places in Paris to buy exquisite, French-made Maison de Vacances cushions and linens.

MES DEMOISELLES FASHION & ACCESSORIES

Map p402 (☎01 77 10 58 33; www.mesdemoisellesparis.com; 21 rue St-Sulpice, 6e; ⏲10.30am-7.30pm Mon-Sat; Ⓜ Mabillon) Antique cuts of silks, wools and cottons are transformed into floaty bohemian-influenced women's fashion (dresses, knitwear, coats and other separates) by designer Anita Radovanovic, who founded the Mes Demoiselles label here in Paris in 2006. There are five other boutiques in the city.

Les Invalides

★LE BON MARCHÉ DEPARTMENT STORE

Map p406 (☎01 44 39 80 00; http://lebonmarche.com; 24 rue de Sèvres, 7e; ⏲10am-8pm Mon-Wed, Fri & Sat, 10am-8.45pm Thu, 11am-8pm Sun; Ⓜ Sèvres-Babylone) Built by Gustave Eiffel as Paris' first department store in 1852, this is the epitome of style, with a superb concentration of men's and women's fashions, homewares, stationery, books and toys. Break for a coffee, afternoon tea with cake or a light lunch at the tearoom on the 2nd floor.

★LA GRANDE ÉPICERIE DE PARIS FOOD & DRINKS

Map p406 (www.lagrandeepicerie.com; 36 rue de Sèvres, 7e; ⏲8.30am-9pm Mon-Sat, 10am-8pm Sun; Ⓜ Sèvres-Babylone) The magnificent food hall of department store Le Bon Marché sells 30,000 rare and/or luxury gourmet products, including 60 different types of bread baked on site and delicacies such as caviar ravioli. Its fantastical displays of chocolates, pastries, biscuits, cheeses, fresh fruit and vegetables and deli goods are a Parisian sight in themselves. Wine tastings regularly take place in the basement.

LOCAL KNOWLEDGE

SECONDHAND CHIC

When St-Germain's well-heeled residents spring-clean their wardrobes, they take their designer and vintage cast-offs to *dépôt-vente* (secondhand) boutiques, where savvy locals snap up serious bargains. Try your luck at the following addresses:

Catherine B (Map p402; ☎01 43 54 74 18; http://les3marchesdecatherineb.com; 1 rue Guisarde, 6e; ⏲11am-7pm Mon-Sat; Ⓜ Mabillon) Serious fans of Chanel and Hermès should call into this exceptionally curated boutique, which specialises exclusively in items from these two iconic French fashion houses.

Chercheminippes (Map p406; www.chercheminippes.com; 102 rue du Cherche Midi, 6e; ⏲11am-7pm Mon-Sat; Ⓜ Vaneau) Scoop up secondhand designer women's casual wear at this fashion-chic boutique. Sister boutiques scattered along the same street specialise in accessories (No 104), homewares (No 109), kids' fashion (No 110), menswear (No 111) and women's haute couture (No 114).

Le Dépôt-Vente de Buci (Map p402; ☎01 46 34 45 05; 4 rue Bourbon le Château, 6e; ⏲9am-noon & 2-6pm Tue-Sat; Ⓜ Mabillon) The boutique to hit for stylish 1960s vintage.

L'Embellie (Map p406; 2 rue du Regard, 6e; ⏲10am-7pm Mon-Fri, to 6pm Sat; Ⓜ Sèvres-Babylone) Superb selection of vintage fashion.

Ragtime (Map p402; ☎01 56 24 00 36; 23 rue de l'Échaudé, 6e; ⏲2.30-7pm Mon-Sat; Ⓜ Mabillon) Madame Auguet's boutique sells *vêtements anciens* (vintage clothes) from 1870 to 1970.

★MAGASIN SENNELIER — ARTS & CRAFTS

Map p402 (☎01 42 60 72 15; www.magasinsennelier.com; 3 quai Voltaire, 7e; ⏲2-6.30pm Mon, 10am-12.45pm & 2-6.30pm Tue-Sat; Ⓜ St-Germain des Prés) Cézanne and Picasso were among the artists who helped develop products for this venerable 1887-founded art supplier on the banks of the Seine, and it remains an exceptional place to pick up canvases, brushes, watercolours, oils, pastels, charcoals and more. The shop's forest-green façade with gold lettering, exquisite original timber cabinetry and glass display cases also fuel artistic inspiration.

★CANTIN — CHEESE

Map p406 (☎01 45 5043 94; www.cantin.fr; 12 rue du Champs de Mars, 7e; ⏲2-7.30pm Mon, 8.30am-7.30pm Tue-Sat, 8.30am-1pm Sun; Ⓜ École Militaire) Opened in 1950 and still run by the same family today, this exceptional shop stocks cheeses only made in limited quantities on small rural farms. They're then painstakingly ripened in Cantin's own cellars (from two weeks up to two years) before being displayed for sale. Should you want to know how to concoct the perfect cheeseboard, Cantin runs informative tasting workshops.

POILÂNE — FOOD

Map p402 (☎01 45 48 42 59; www.poilane.com; 8 rue du Cherche Midi, 6e; ⏲7am-8.30pm Mon-Sat; Ⓜ Sèvres-Babylone) Pierre Poilâne opened his *boulangerie* (bakery) upon arriving from Normandy in 1932. Today his granddaughter Apollonia runs the company, which still turns out wood-fired, rounded sourdough loaves made with stone-milled flour and Guérande sea salt. A clutch of other outlets include one in the **15e** (Map p414; www.poilane.com; 49 bd de Grenelle, 15e; ⏲7am-8.30pm Tue-Sun; Ⓜ Dupleix).

MAYARO — DESIGN

Map p406 (☎01 80 06 04 41; http://mayaro.fr; 20 rue Amélie, 7e; ⏲10am-6pm Mon-Fri; Ⓜ La Tour-Maubourg) Spanning three floors of a Haussmannian building is this part gallery, part concept store for men, part design showcase and part collaborator. It also variously hosts dinners by celebrated chef Sven Chartier and sommelier Ewen Le Moigne. Inspirational made-in-France products include cabinets, leather shoes, leather-framed eyewear, meteorite cufflinks and digital art.

Montparnasse & Southern Paris

Neighbourhood Top Five

❶ **Les Catacombes** (p248) Prowling the spine-prickling, skull-and-bone-packed subterranean tunnels of Paris' creepy ossuary.

❷ **Station F** (p254) Sharing the buzz, energy and zeal for innovation at the world's largest start-up incubator during a guided tour of this extraordinary piece of architecture.

❸ **Cimetière du Montparnasse** (p250) Visiting the resting places of local luminaries, including Jean-Paul Sartre, Simone de Beauvoir and Serge Gainsbourg.

❹ **Île aux Cygnes** (p249) Traversing the tiny, tree-lined inner-city island from the Statue of Liberty replica towards the Eiffel Tower.

For more detail of this area see Map p412 and p414

Explore Montparnasse & Southern Paris

Here are the cafes, brasseries and backstreets, now swathed by urban grit, where some of the early-20th-century's most seminal artists and writers hung out. The area's tree-filled cemetery is a peaceful spot to escape to – and to visit the graves of many of those same visionaries.

West in the tranquil 15e, take in more great views by strolling Île aux Cygnes (p249) or boarding a balloon 'flight' in the Parc André-Citroën, one of Paris' most innovative open spaces. Other wonderful local parks in this greenified area include Parc Georges Brassens (p251), with rose gardens and even a vineyard, as well as a stretch of the former Petite Ceinture (p253) steam railway line.

To Montparnasse's east, the ever-regenerating 13e is home to the country's national library, Paris' largest Chinatown, some striking street art and even more striking contemporary (and increasingly sustainable) architecture. Don't miss a guided tour of this groundbreaking arrondissement's most recent pride and joy: mind-blowing start-up incubator Station F (p254).

The entire area is strewn with exciting neobistros. No matter where you end up for dinner, head back to the river to dance until dawn on the floating bars and nightclubs moored on the Seine's quays.

Local Life

- **Street life** Join locals shopping for flowers and cheese along traditional commercial rue Daguerre.
- **Spring life** Bring a bottle and fill up on spring water from the Puits Artésien de la Butte aux Cailles (p250).
- **Art life** Delve into the 13e's street art scene starting at Galerie Itinerrance (p250).

Getting There & Away

- **Metro** Montparnasse Bienvenüe is the metro hub for Montparnasse and the 15e. Bibliothèque and Place d'Italie are convenient 13e stops.
- **Bus** Buses fill the gap in areas lacking comprehensive metro coverage. From Gare Montparnasse, bus 91 goes to Bastille. Bus 62 travels from Bibliothèque to Javel via the southern *quartiers*. Bus 21 runs from Glacière to Chatelet. Bus 42 links Balard with Gare du Nord via the western 15e and Eiffel Tower.
- **Bicycle** Handy Vélib' stations include 5-7 rue d'Odessa, 14e; 13 bd Edgar Quinet, 14e; 2 av René Coty, 14e; and two facing place d'Italie, 13e.
- **Boat** The hop-on, hop-off Batobus has docks at Port de Javel Haut, 15e and quai d'Austerlitz, 13e.

Lonely Planet's Top Tip

The metro is tailor-made for cross-town trips, but to whizz around Paris' perimeter, hop on the T3 tram. From the Pont du Garigliano, 15e, it currently skims the city's edge as far as Porte de la Chapelle, 18e. An extension to Porte d'Asnières, 17e, is due for completion by the end of 2018, encircling some three-quarters of the city. Passengers use standard t+ tickets. For updates on Paris' trams, visit www.tramway.paris.fr.

Best Places to Eat

- Ladurée Picnic (p252)
- Le Beurre Noisette (p253)
- Le Cassenoix (p253)
- L'Accolade (p254)
- Le Saut du Crapaud (p252)

For reviews, see p252

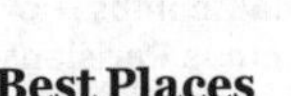

Best Places to Drink

- Simone La Cave (p258)
- L'OisiveThé (p258)
- Café Oz Rooftop (p251)
- Le Batofar (p258)
- Rosebud (p257)

For reviews, see p257 

Best Shopping

- Storie (p259)
- Bièrocratie (p261)
- Adam Montparnasse (p260)
- Marché aux Puces de la Porte de Vanves (p260)

For reviews, see p259 

VIACHESLAV LOPATIN / SHUTTERSTOCK ©

TOP SIGHT
LES CATACOMBES

It is gruesome, ghoulish and downright spooky, but it remains one of Paris' most visited sights. In 1785 subterranean tunnels of an abandoned quarry were upcycled as storage rooms for the exhumed bones of corpses that could not longer fit in the city's overcrowded cemeteries. By 1810 the skull- and bone-lined catacombs – official resting place of millions of anonymous Parisians – had been officially born.

The route through Les Catacombes begins at a small, dark-green belle époque building in the centre of a grassy area of av Colonel Henri Roi-Tanguy, adjacent to place Denfert Rochereau. Walk down 130 spiral steps to reach the ossuary itself, with a mind-boggling amount of bones and skulls of millions of Parisians neatly packed along the walls. Visits cover 1.5km of tunnels in all, at a chilling 14°C.

The exit is via a minimalist all-white 'transition space' with gift shop at 21bis av René Coty, 14e. Bag searches are carried out to prevent visitors 'souveniring' bones.

Bear in mind that this tour is not suitable for young children or the squeamish; under 14s must be accompanied by an adult.

DID YOU KNOW?

During WWII the Resistance held meetings in these tunnels. Today, at night, thrill-seeking cataphiles roam the tunnels illegally.

PRACTICALITIES

- Map p412, F4
- ☎01 43 22 47 63
- www.catacombes.paris.fr
- 1 av Colonel Henri Roi-Tanguy, 14e
- adult/child €13/free, online booking incl audioguide €29/5
- ⏲10am-8.30pm Tue-Sun
- Ⓜ Denfert Rochereau

SIGHTS

This vast swath of southern Paris is a perfect place to explore if you're looking for a local experience away from the tourist crowds. There are also some big-hitting sights here, too, from the creepy skull-and-bone-packed underground tunnels of Les Catacombes to France's national library, Bibliothèque Nationale de France, and the world's largest campus for start-ups.

Montparnasse & 15e

LES CATACOMBES — CEMETERY

See p248.

TOUR MONTPARNASSE — VIEWPOINT

Map p412 (www.tourmontparnasse56.com; 33 av du Maine, 15e; adult/child €17/9.50; 9.30am-11.30pm Apr-Sep, to 10.30pm Oct-Mar; M Montparnasse Bienvenüe) Spectacular views unfold from this 210m-high smoked-glass-and-steel office block, built in 1973. (Bonus: it's about the only spot in the city you can't see this startlingly ugly skyscraper, which dwarfs low-rise Paris.) A speedy elevator whisks visitors up in 38 seconds to the indoor observatory on the 56th floor, with multimedia displays. Finish with a hike up the stairs to the 59th-floor open-air terrace (with a sheltered walkway) and bubbly at the terrace's Champagne bar.

MUSÉE BOURDELLE — MUSEUM

Map p412 (01 49 54 73 73; www.bourdelle.paris.fr; 18 rue Antoine Bourdelle, 15e; 10am-6pm Tue-Sun; M Falguière) FREE Monumental bronzes fill the house and workshop where sculptor Antoine Bourdelle (1861–1929), a pupil of Rodin, lived and worked. The three sculpture gardens are particularly lovely, with a flavour of belle époque and post-WWI Montparnasse. The museum usually has a temporary exhibition (adult/child €8/free) going on alongside its free permanent collection. You can rent an audioguide at reception (€5).

FONDATION CARTIER POUR L'ART CONTEMPORAIN — GALLERY

Map p412 (01 42 18 56 50; http://fondation.cartier.com; 261 bd Raspail, 14e; adult/child €12/8.50; 11am-10pm Tue, to 8pm Wed-Sun; M Raspail) Designed by Jean Nouvel, this stunning glass-and-steel building is a work of art in itself. It hosts temporary exhibits on contemporary art (from the 1980s to today) in a diverse variety of media – from painting and photography to video and fashion, as well as performance art. Artist Lothar Baumgarten created the wonderfully rambling garden.

PARC ANDRÉ CITROËN — PARK

Map p414 (2 rue Cauchy, 15e; 8am-9.30pm Mon-Fri, 9am-9.30pm Sat & Sun May-Aug, shorter hours rest of year; ; M Javel–André Citroën, RER Javel) In 1915 automotive entrepreneur André Citroën built a vast car manufacturing plant here in the 15e. After it closed in the 1970s, the vacated site was eventually turned into this forward-looking 14-hectare urban park. Its central lawn is flanked by greenhouses, dancing fountains, an elevated reflecting pool, and smaller gardens themed around movement and the (six) senses. The helium-filled sightseeing balloon Ballon de Paris is located here. Check seasonal hours signposted at the entrances.

BALLON DE PARIS — VIEWPOINT

Map p414 (01 44 26 20 00; www.ballondeparis.com; 2 rue de la Montagne de la Fage, 15e, Parc André Citroën; adult/child €12/6; 9am-9pm May-Aug, shorter hours Sep-Apr; M Balard, Lourmel) Drift up and up but not away – this helium-filled balloon in Parc André Citroën remains tethered to the ground as it lifts you 150m into the air for spectacular panoramas over Paris. The balloon plays an active environmental role, changing colour depending on the air quality and pollution levels. From September to April, the last 'flight' is 30 minutes before the park closes. Confirm ahead any time of year as the balloon doesn't ascend in windy conditions.

ÎLE AUX CYGNES — ISLAND

Map p414 (Isle of Swans; btwn Pont de Grenelle & Pont de Bir Hakeim, 15e; M Javel–André Citroën, Bir Hakeim) Paris' little-known third island, the artificially created Île aux Cygnes, was formed in 1827 to protect the river port and measures just 850m by 11m. On the western side of the Pont de Grenelle is a soaring one-quarter scale **Statue of Liberty replica** (Map p414), inaugurated in 1889. Walk east along the Allée des Cygnes – the tree-lined walkway that runs the length of the island – for knock-out views of the Eiffel Tower.

Place d'Italie & Chinatown

GALERIE ITINERRANCE GALLERY

(http://itinerrance.fr; 24 bd du Général d'Armée Jean Simon, 13e; ⏲noon-7pm Tue-Sat; MBibliothèque) FREE Testament to the 13e's ongoing creative renaissance, this gallery showcases graffiti and street art, and can advise on self-guided and guided street-art tours of the neighbourhood that take in many landmark works by artists represented by the gallery. Exhibitions and events change regularly.

PUITS ARTÉSIEN DE LA BUTTE AUX CAILLES SPRING

Map p410 (place Paul Verlaine, 13e; ⏲24hr; MCorvisart) FREE You'll often see locals filling containers with the natural 28°C spring water that has bubbled up here from 600m below ground since 1893. It's free, safe to drink, and is said to have health-giving properties thanks to its rich iron fluorine content and low calcium levels (BYO bottle). The four-tap stainless-steel fountain was inaugurated in the year 2000; striking opaque panels describe the history of the *source* (spring).

BIBLIOTHÈQUE NATIONALE DE FRANCE LIBRARY

Map p410 (☎01 53 79 59 59; www.bnf.fr; 11 quai François Mauriac, 13e; €3-9; ⏲10am-7pm Tue-Sat, 1-7pm Sun, closed two weeks in Sep; MBibliothèque) With four glass towers shaped like half-open books, the National Library of France, opened in 1995, was one of President Mitterand's most ambitious and costliest projects. Some 12 million tomes are stored on 420km of shelves and the library can accommodate 2000 readers and 2000 researchers. Excellent temporary exhibitions (entrance E) revolve around 'the word' – from storytelling to bookbinding and French heroes. Exhibition admission includes free same-day access to the reference library.

No expense was spared to carry out the library's grand design, which many

TOP SIGHT
CIMETIÈRE DU MONTPARNASSE

Opened in 1824, Cimetière du Montparnasse, Paris' second-largest cemetery after Père Lachaise, sprawls over 19 hectares shaded by 1200 trees, including maples, ash, limes and conifers. Some of the illustrious 'residents' at Cimetière du Montparnasse include poet **Charles Baudelaire** (No 14, division 6), writer Guy de Maupassant, playwright **Samuel Beckett** (No 66, division 12), painter Chaim Soutine, photographer Man Ray, indsutrialist André Citroën, sculptor Constantin Brancusi, Captain Alfred Dreyfus of the infamous Dreyfus Affair, and philosophers, writers and life partners **Jean-Paul Sartre** and **Simone de Beauvoir** (No 1, division 20), who are buried together right next to the cemetery entrance on blvd Edgar Quinet.

Like Père Lachaise, Cimetière du Montparnasse has its time-honoured tomb traditions. One of the most popular is fans leaving metro tickets atop the grave of crooner **Serge Gainsbourg** (No 60, division 1), in reference to his 1958 song 'Le Poinçonneur des Lilas' (The Ticket Puncher of Lilas), depicting work-a-day monotony through the eyes of a metro ticket-puncher. Gainsbourg enacted the soul-destroying job (since eclipsed by machines) on film when recording the song in the Porte des Lilas station.

DON'T MISS

- Serge Gainsbourg
- Jean-Paul Sartre & Simone de Beauvoir
- Charles Baudelaire
- Samuel Beckett

PRACTICALITIES

- Map p412, E3
- www.paris.fr
- 3 bd Edgar Quinet, 14e
- admission free
- ⏲8am-6pm Mon-Fri, 8.30am-6pm Sat, 9am-6pm Sun
- MEdgar Quinet

claimed defied logic. Books and historical documents are shelved in the sunny, 23-storey and 79m-high towers, while patrons sit in artificially lit basement halls built around a 'forest courtyard' of 140 50-year-old pines, trucked in from the countryside.

GALERIE DES GOBELINS FACTORY, GALLERY

Map p410 (☎08 25 05 44 05; www.mobiliernational.culture.gouv.fr; 42 av des Gobelins, 13e; gallery adult/child €8/6, gallery & tour €15.50/9.50; ⏲gallery 11am-6pm Tue-Sun, factory tours by reservation; Ⓜ Les Gobelins) *Haute lisse* (high relief) tapestries have been woven on specialised looms at the Manufacture des Gobelins since the 18th century along with Beauvais-style *basse lisse* (low relief) tapestries and Savonnerie rugs. Superb examples are showcased in its gallery. Once-weekly guided tours of the factory (1½ hours) lead you through the *ateliers* (workshops) and exhibits of the thousands of carpets and tapestries woven here; tours are strictly by advance reservation through **Cultival** (www.cultival.fr).

LES DOCKS CULTURAL CENTRE

Map p410 (Cité de la Mode et du Design; ☎01 76 77 25 30; www.citemodedesign.fr; 34 quai d'Austerlitz, 13e; ⏲10am-midnight; Ⓜ Gare d'Austerlitz) Framed by a lurid-lime wave-like glass façade, a transformed Seine-side warehouse is home to the French fashion institute, the **Institut Français de la Mode** (hence Les Docks' alternative name, Cité de la Mode et du Design), mounting fashion and design exhibitions and events throughout the year. Other draws include the huge riverside terraces, the odd pop-up shop and hip Australian rooftop bar **Café Oz Rooftop** (Map p410; ☎01 44 24 39 34; www.facebook.com/cafeozrooftop; 34 quai d'Austerlitz, 13e, Les Docks; ⏲3pm-2am Tue & Wed, to 4am Thu-Sat; Ⓜ Gare d'Austerlitz).

PARC MONTSOURIS PARK

Map p410 (http://equipement.paris.fr/parc-montsouris-1810; av Reille, 14e; ⏲8am-9.30pm Mon-Fri, 9am-9.30pm Sat & Sun May-Aug, shorter hours rest of year; Ⓜ Porte d'Orléans or RER Cité-Universitaire) The name of this sprawling lakeside park – planted with horse-chestnut, yew, cedar, weeping beech and buttonwood trees – derives from *moque souris* (mice mockery) because the area was once overrun with the critters. Today it's a delightful picnic spot and has endearing playground areas, such as a concrete 'road system' where littlies can trundle matchbox cars (BYO cars). On Wednesday, Saturday and Sunday from 3pm to 6pm there are marionette shows and pony rides.

PARC GEORGES BRASSENS PARK

Map p414 (http://equipement.paris.fr/parc-georges-brassens-1805; 2 place Jacques Marette, 15e; ⏲8am-9.30pm Mon-Fri, 9am-9.30m Sat & Sun May-Aug, shorter hours rest of year; Ⓜ Convention, 🚊 Georges Brassens) Covering 7.74 hectares, Parc Georges Brassens (named for the French singer-songwriter and poet, who lived nearby) has a large central pond bordered by lawns, and gardens featuring roses and medicinal and aromatic plants. The sloping hill is home to a wine-producing vineyard and an apiary; honey is sold on the first Saturday of each month at the entrance. On Wednesday, Saturday and Sunday kids can ride ponies (€3.50; 3pm to 6pm) and watch a marionette show (€4; 3.30pm and 4.30pm).

Also here is the **Monfort theatre**, with dance, circus and theatre performances, and the weekend book market, **Marché Georges Brassens** (Map p414; www.marchedulivre-paris.fr; 104 rue Brancion, 15e; ⏲9am-6pm Sat & Sun; Ⓜ Porte de Vanves).

A honey and grape-harvest festival takes place on the first weekend in October.

LA CITÉ FLEURIE ART STUDIO

Map p410 (65 bd Arago, 13e; Ⓜ Saint-Jacques) Venture east from Montparnasse along bd Arago, past the eery **La Santé Prison** (the most infamous prison in French history after La Bastille, dating to 1867 and boasting the city's last-standing, dark-green public urinal from 1834 in front), and you come to this romantic cluster of 19th-century artist workshops. The 30-odd half-timbered cottages, laced with quaint cobbled pathways and overgrown gardens, were built in 1878 using building materials from a disassembled pavilion from Paris' Universal Exhibition.

The workshops open their doors to the public once a year, during the **Lézarts de la Bièvre** (www.lezarts-bievre.com) on the 2nd weekend in June, which sees artist workshops all over the 13e and 15e *arrondissement* welcome visitors.

EATING

Since the 1920s bd du Montparnasse has been one of the city's premier avenues for enjoying Parisian pavement life, with legendary brasseries and cafes. The down-to-earth 15e cooks up fabulous bistro fare – along rues de la Convention, de Vaugirard, St-Charles and du Commerce, and south of bd de Grenelle. In Chinatown, try ave de Choisy, ave d'Ivry and rue Baudricourt. Villagey Butte aux Cailles, 13e, is chock-a-block with interesting addresses: rue de la Butte aux Cailles and rue des Cinq Diamants are the main foodie streets. Vibrant food markets fill the nearby bd Auguste Blanqui every Tuesday and Friday morning.

Montparnasse & 15e

★LADURÉE PICNIC PASTRIES, DELI €

Map p414 (☎01 70 22 45 20; www.laduree.fr; 16 rue Linois, 15e, Centre Commercial Beaugrenelle; breakfast/lunch menu €14.50/9.50, sandwiches/salads from €2.40/5.50; ⏲9.30am-8.30pm Mon-Sat, 10am-7pm Sun; ⓂCharles Michels) The first of its kind, Ladurée Picnic specialises in just that – picnics, albeit exceedingly fine, gourmet picnics to take away in the famous patisserie's signature peppermint-green packaging. Luxury salads include lobster or aromatic salmon; there are flavoured waters like ginger and coriander and mint and cucumber; and the rainbow of cakes and macarons are simply out of this world.

★LE SAUT DU CRAPAUD BISTRO €

Map p412 (☎01 85 15 28 35; www.lesautducrapaud.fr; 16 rue des Plantes, 14e; 2-/3-course lunch menu €16/20, dinner menu €35; ⏲7-10.30pm Mon-Fri, noon-2.30pm & 7-10.30pm Sat, 11.30am-3pm Sun; ⓂMouton-Duvernet) Locals pack out this quirky neighbourhood bistro, showcase for the casual Franco-Mexican cuisine of Mexican banker-turned-chef Marco Paz. Cooking pots and guitars adorn the stylish vintage interior and the menu features creative dishes like steak coriander and lime-laced steak tartare, tuna with orange, and baby cuttlefish pan-fried with tequila and black pudding. Sunday brunch (€22.50) is a fabulously vibrant affair, spilling outside in summer.

RAW CAKES VEGAN €

Map p412 (☎09 86 12 73 48; 83 rue Daguerre, 14e; mains €10-15; ⏲10am-8pm Mon, 11am-10pm Tue-Thu, 10am-4pm Fri, noon-7pm Sun; ⓂGaîté) A pretty lavender and fuchsia-pink facade fronts this much-welcomed cafe and cake shop where everything is 100% vegan, gluten-free – and raw. Enticing nut and chickpea burgers, veggie-packed pizzas and meal-sized salads rub shoulders on the menu with fresh juices, smoothies and exquisite uncooked cakes. Sunday brunch (€25) is always a full house.

LE PETIT PAN MODERN FRENCH €

Map p414 (☎01 42 50 04 04; www.lepetitpan.fr; 18 rue Rosenwald, 15e; 2-/3-course lunch menu €16.50/20.50, small plates €2.50-13; ⏲noon-2.30pm & 7-11.30pm Tue-Sat; ⓂPorte de Vanves) Parisians working in the 'hood fill this casual bistro to bursting at lunchtime thanks to a fantastic-value lunchtime menu, but it's after dusk that the gourmet action kicks in with small plates of tapas *à la française* designed for sharing. Think cured ham, duck pâté with pork trotters or duck hearts fried in ginger, washed down with superb wines by the glass.

The lunchtime menu at Le Petit Pan includes gourmet sandwiches, quiches and salads. To sink your teeth into a serious hunk of meat, nip across the street to big sister restaurant **Le Grand Pan** (Map p414; ☎01 42 50 02 50; www.legrandpan.fr; 20 rue Rosenwald, 15e; mains €14-30; ⏲noon-2pm & 7.30-11pm Mon-Fri; ⓂPorte de Vanves).

BOULANGERIE DE LOURMEL BAKERY €

Map p414 (121 av Félix Faure, 15e; items from €1.80; ⏲6.30am-8.30pm Mon-Fri, to 8pm Sat; ⓂLourmel) Situated a short stroll from the gates of Parc André Citroën, this place is a handy pit stop for freshly baked picnic staples: luscious quiches (salmon, leek, tomato and onion, goat's cheese or classic ham-filled Lorraine), baguettes, and sweet treats including éclairs and *clafoutis* (cherry flan).

LE COMPTOIR DU BO BUN VIETNAMESE €

Map p412 (☎09 86 60 94 50; www.lecomptoirdubobun.fr; 22 rue Raymond Losserand, 14e; sandwiches/soups €11-14; ⏲noon-2.30pm & 7.30-10.30pm Mon-Thu, to 11pm Fri & Sat; ⓂGaîté) For a Real McCoy, salmon and ginger *bo bun* (cold rice-noodle salad) or *soupe pho au poulet* (chicken soup) washed down with a Hanoï or Saigon beer or sassy Vietnamese mojito, make a beeline for this colourful Vietnamese eatery strung with decorative lanterns and bird cages. Kudos for the upcycled plastic crates and train carriage.

LA CERISAIE FRENCH €

Map p412 (☎01 43 20 98 98; www.restaurantlacerisaie.com; 70 bd Edgar Quinet, 14e; mains €16-23; ⊙noon-2.30pm & 7-10.30pm Mon-Fri; MEdgar Quinet) Chef Cyril Lalanne shows how inventive southwestern French cuisine can be at this snug 22-seat restaurant behind a cherry-coloured façade. Starters such as snail and chorizo cassoulet are followed by rich, often game-based mains (goose with spiced roast pear, for instance) and desserts like pear and walnut compote with Roquefort (yes, as in the potent blue cheese) ice cream.

L'ATELIER B BURGERS €

Map p412 (☎09 82 41 11 27; www.latelierb.fr; 129 rue du Château, 14e; burger menu without/with dessert €16/18; ⊙noon-2.30pm & 7.30pm-10.30pm Tue-Sat; MPernety) Among the top spots in Paris for pairing a glass of wine or cocktail with a burger and side of sweet-potato fries, regular fries with melted cheese or homemade coleslaw. Seating is inside or out, and fancy burger choices include black Angus with confit onion, rocket and blue cheese, and chunky chicken with aubergine, red onion, pickles and homemade BBQ sauce.

★LE CASSENOIX MODERN FRENCH €€

Map p414 (☎01 45 66 09 01; www.le-cassenoix.fr; 56 rue de la Fédération, 15e; 3-course menu €34; ⊙noon-2.30pm & 7-10.30pm Mon-Fri; MBir Hakeim) The Nutcracker is everything a self-respecting neighbourhood bistro should be. *'Tradition et terroir'* (tradition and provenance) dictate the menu that inspires owner-chef Pierre Olivier Lenormand to deliver feisty dishes such as braised veal chuck with mashed potato and caramelised onions or grilled hake with parsnips and hazelnut-parmesan crumble. Vintage ceiling fans add to the wonderful retro vibe. Book ahead.

★LE BEURRE NOISETTE BISTRO €€

Map p414 (☎01 48 56 82 49; www.restaurantbeurrenoisette.com; 68 rue Vasco de Gama, 15e; 2-/3-course lunch menu €23/32, 3-/5-/7-course dinner menu €36/46/56, mains lunch/dinner €18/21; ⊙noon-2pm & 7-10.30pm Tue-Sat; MLourmel) *Beurre noisette* (brown butter sauce, named for its hazelnut colour) features in dishes such as tender veal loin with homemade fries and caramelised pork belly tender with braised red cabbage and apple, at pedigreed chef Thierry Blanqui's neighbourhood neobistro. Filled with locals, the chocolate-toned dining room is wonderfully convivial – be sure to book. Fantastic value.

PETITE CEINTURE

Long before the tramway or even the metro, the 35km Petite Ceinture (Little Belt) steam railway encircled the city of Paris. Constructed during the reign of Napoléon III between 1852 and 1869 as a way to move troops and goods around the city's fortifications, it became a thriving passenger service until the metro arrived in 1900. Most passenger services ceased in 1934 and goods services in 1993, and the line became an overgrown wilderness. Until recently, access was forbidden (although that didn't stop maverick urban explorers scrambling along its tracks and tunnels). Of the line's original 29 stations, 17 survive (in various states of disrepair).

Plans for regenerating the Petite Ceinture railway corridor have seen the opening of three sections with walkways alongside the tracks. Other areas remain off limits.

In southern Paris, the **Petite Ceinture du 15e** (PC 15; Map p414; www.paris.fr; opp 99 rue Olivier de Serres, 15e; ⊙9am-8.30pm Mon-Fri, 9.30am-8.30pm Sat & Sun May-Aug, shorter hours rest of year; MBalard, Porte de Versailles) FREE stretches for 1.3km, with biodiverse habitats including forest, grassland and prairies supporting 220 species of flora and fauna. In addition to the end points, there are three elevator-enabled access points along its route: 397ter rue de Vaugirard; opposite 82 rue Desnouettes; and place Robert Guillemard.

On the eastern side of Parc Georges Brassens, a *promenade plantée* (planted walkway) travels atop a stretch of the Petite Ceinture's tracks by Porte de Vanves.

LE CLOS Y MODERN FRENCH €€

Map p412 (☎01 45 49 07 35; www.leclosy.com; 27 av du Maine, 15e; 2-/3-course lunch menu €31/36, dinner menu €65; ⏲noon-2pm & 7.30-10pm Tue-Sat; Ⓜ Montparnasse Bienvenüe) One of Paris' rapidly rising star chefs Yoshitaka Ikeda creates utterly original *menus* that change daily but might start with foie gras ice cream and move on to perch sashimi with beetroot, apple and powdered olive oil; green peas in pea jelly with mascarpone; smoked salmon and egg with raspberry foam; and Madeira-marinated beef with butternut squash and carrot purée.

L'ACCOLADE BISTRO €€

Map p414 (☎01 45 57 73 20; www.laccoladeparis.fr; 208 rue de la Croix Nivert, 15e; 2-/3-course lunch menu €19.50/24.50, 4-course dinner menu €35; ⏲noon-2.30pm Mon, noon-2pm & 7-10.30pm Tue-Fri, 7-10.30pm Sat; Ⓜ Convention) Seasonal market products reign supreme at this neighbourhood bistro where rising star Nicolas Tardivel woos a local crowd with his creative, modern French 'bistronomie' – bistro-style gastronomy. The lunchtime *plat du jour* (dish of the day), at €15 including coffee, is an excellent deal. Should you be open to temptation, the vanilla millefeuille, glazed with salted butter caramel, is sublime.

L'ASSIETTE BISTRO €€

Map p412 (☎01 43 22 64 86; http://restaurant-lassiette.paris; 181 rue du Château, 14e; 2-course lunch menu €23, mains €25-45; ⏲noon-2.30pm & 7.30-10.30pm Tue-Fri, 12.30-2.30pm & 7.30-10.30pm Sat & Sun; Ⓜ Pernety, Gaîté) Consist-

PARIS RIVE GAUCHE

Paris' largest urban redevelopment since Haussmann's 19th-century reformation continues apace in the 13e *arrondissement* (city district). Centred on a once-nondescript area south of the Latin Quarter spiralling out from big busy traffic hub place d'Italie, the renaissance of the area known as Paris Rive Gauche was heralded in the 1990s by the controversial Bibliothèque Nationale de France (p250) and the arrival of the high-speed Météor metro line. They were followed, among other additions, by the **MK2** (Map p410; www.mk2.com; 128-162 av de France, 13e; adult/child €11.40/4.90; Ⓜ Bibliothèque) and more recent EP7 (p258) entertainment complexes, the Piscine Joséphine Baker (p261) swimming pool and Off Paris Seine hotel (p292) – both afloat the Seine – and the **Passerelle Simone de Beauvoir** (2006), providing a cycle and pedestrian link to the Right Bank. And work isn't slated to stop for several more years.

Pivotal to this 130-hectare redevelopment zone is the **Paris 7** university campus hosting some 30,000 students. Other institutions to have moved in include the **Institut Français de la Mode** (the French fashion institute) in the stylised former warehouse Les Docks (p251).

The area's mainline train station, Gare d'Austerlitz (p332), is enjoying a €600 million makeover by celebrated French architect Jean Nouvel. The station itself will be overhauled (including €200 million alone on the grand hall's glass roof, beneath which hot air balloons were manufactured during the 1870 siege of Paris), and new shops, cafes and green spaces will open up in the surrounding streets. The renovation is due to wrap up in 2021.

Then there is **Station F** (Map p410; https://stationf.co/fr/campus/; 55 bd Vincent Auriol, 13e; ⏲tours noon Mon, Wed & Fri; Ⓜ Chevaleret, Bibliothèque) FREE, the world's largest start-up campus, in business since mid-2017, where 3000 entrepreneurs from all over the globe dream up ground-breaking new projects and businesses, supported by 30 different incubators and accelerators. Guided tours take visitors on a 45-minute waltz through the gargantuan hangar – a railway depot built in 1927–29 to house trains from Gare de Austerlitz. Spaces open to the public include Station F's **Anticafé** co-working space where hipsters pay €5 per hour to eat, drink and hang out; and **La Felicità**, a restaurant with five different kitchens, terrace, bar and dining in a twinset of original, graffiti-covered train wagons. Both are open 24 hours – another bold Paris first.

Track updates on this innovative area at www.parisrivegauche.com.

ently hailed as one of Paris' best bistros, The Plate is the culinary powerhouse of chef David Rathgebe, from Clermont-Ferrand in the foodie Auvergne. He mixes age-old traditional French dishes like *cassoulet maison* (Toulouse sausage and white bean stew) and *tête de veau* (rolled calf's head) with the occasional unexpected combo (sweetbreads with black truffle risotto) to delicious effect. Reservations essential.

LA CABANE À HUÎTRES — SEAFOOD €€

Map p412 (01 45 49 47 27; 4 rue Antoine Bourdelle, 14e; 12 oysters from €24, 3-course menu €23.90; noon-2.15pm & 7-10.15pm Wed-Sat; M Montparnasse Bienvenüe) Wonderfully rustic, this wooden-styled *cabane* (cabin) with just a handful of tables is the pride and joy of fifth-generation oyster farmer Françis Dubourg, who splits his time between the capital and his oyster farm in Arcachon on the Atlantic Coast. The fixed menu includes a dozen oysters, foie gras, *magret de canard fumé* (smoked duck breast) or smoked salmon.

LA CLOSERIE DES LILAS — BRASSERIE €€

Map p412 (01 40 51 34 50; www.closeriedeslilas.fr; 171 bd du Montparnasse, 6e; 3-course lunch menu €52, mains restaurant €28-52, brasserie €17-27; restaurant noon-2.30pm & 7-11.30pm, brasserie noon-12.30am, piano bar 11am-1.30am; M Vavin or RER Port Royal) Brass plaques tell you exactly where Hemingway (who wrote much of *The Sun Also Rises* here) and luminaries like Picasso, Apollinaire, Man Ray, Jean-Paul Sartre and Samuel Beckett stood, sat or fell at the 'Lilac Enclosure' (opened 1847). It's split into a late-night piano bar, upmarket restaurant and the more lovable (and cheaper) brasserie with a hedged-in pavement terrace.

LA ROTONDE MONTPARNASSE — BRASSERIE €€

Map p412 (01 43 26 48 26; 105 bd du Montparnasse, 6e; 3-course menu €46, mains €16-48, seafood platters €29.50-118.50; 6am-2am, kitchen noon-3pm & 7-11pm; M Vavin) Around since 1911 and as glamorous as the day it opened, elegant La Rotonde stands out from the Les Montparnos 'historic brasserie' crowd for its superior food. Meat comes from Parisian butcher extraordinaire Hugo Desnoyer, salmon and chicken are organic, and brasserie classics are cooked to perfection. Extravagant seafood platters are piled high with prawns, lobsters, crabs and shellfish.

LOCAL KNOWLEDGE

RUE DAGUERRE

Paris' traditional village atmosphere thrives along rue Daguerre, 14e.

Tucked just southwest of the Denfert-Rochereau metro and RER stations, this narrow street – pedestrianised between av du Général-Leclerc and rue Boulard – is lined with florists, *fromageries* (cheese shops), *boulangeries* (bakeries), patisseries, greengrocers, delis (including Greek, Asian and Italian) and classic cafes where you can watch the local goings on.

Shops set up market stalls on the pavement; Sunday mornings are especially lively. It's a great option for lunch before or after visiting Les Catacombes, or packing a picnic to take to one of the area's parks or squares.

LE SÉVÉRO — BISTRO €€

Map p412 (01 45 40 40 91; www.lesevero.fr; 8 rue des Plantes, 14e; mains €16-44; noon-2pm & 7.30-10pm Mon-Fri; M Mouton Duvernet) Steaks served with sensational *frites* (fries) are the mainstay of this upmarket bistro (it's run by ex-butcher William Bernet); other meat specialities include black pudding and pigs trotters. Wash them down with any number of excellent wines, which are chalked on an entire wall. With just 30 seats, reconfirming advance reservations by noon is essential.

LE DÔME — BRASSERIE €€€

Map p412 (01 43 35 25 81; www.restaurantledome.com; 108 bd du Montparnasse, 14e; mains €42-67, seafood platters €85-148; noon-3pm & 7-11pm; M Vavin) A 1930s art deco extravaganza of the formal white-tablecloth and bow-tied waiter variety, monumental Le Dôme is one of the swishest places around for shellfish platters laden with fresh oysters, king prawns, crab claws and much more, followed by traditional creamy homemade millefeuille for dessert, wheeled in on a trolley and cut in front of you.

LOCAL KNOWLEDGE

'LITTLE BRITTANY'

Trains depart from Gare Montparnasse for the windswept region of Brittany, a couple of hours west, but you don't have to leave the capital for authentic Breton crêpes. Due to the Breton population congregating in this area, the station's surrounding streets – especially rue du Montparnasse, 14e, and rue Odessa, 14e, one block west – are lined with dozens of crêperies. Traditional favourites include **Crêperie Josselin** (Map p412; 01 43 20 93 50; 67 rue du Montparnasse, 14e; crêpes €5-10.50; 11am-11.30pm Wed-Sun; ; Edgar Quinet), named after a village in eastern Brittany, and **Crêperie Plougastel** (Map p412; 01 42 79 90 63; www.creperie-plougastel.com; 47 rue du Montparnasse, 14e; crêpes €3.20-11.90; noon-midnight; ; Edgar Quinet), named for the Breton commune near Brest.

Breton crêpes are folded envelope-style at the edges, served flat on a plate and eaten using cutlery – and are best washed down with bowls of brut Breton cider. Savoury *galettes* use *blé noir* – (buckwheat flour; *sarrasin* in Breton), while both *galettes* and sweet crêpes made from white flour use salted Breton butter. Traditional toppings include *andouille* (Breton sausage), and *caramel au beurre salé* (salted caramel sauce; *salidou* in Breton).

Place d'Italie & Chinatown

LA BUTTE AUX PIAFS BISTRO €

Map p410 (09 70 38 55 11; www.labutteauxpiafs-paris.fr; 31 bd Auge Blanqui, 13e; mains €14.10-16.90; noon-midnight Mon-Fri, noon-3.30pm & 6pm-midnight Sat; Place d'Italie) A cinematic cluster of cherry-red chairs flag the pavement terrace of this neighbourhood bistro, *the* spot to lap up the quietly fashionable vibe of La Butte aux Cailles. Inside, flip-down cinema seats mix with an eclectic jumble of vintage seating, while menus featuring burgers, meal-sized salads and creative starters come bound in the sleeve of a vinyl single.

THIENG HENG VIETNAMESE, SANDWICHES €

Map p410 (01 45 82 92 95; 50 av d'Ivry, 13e; sandwiches €2.70-3.50; 8.30am-7pm; Porte d'Ivry, Maison Blanche) You'll know you're in the vicinity of this takeaway joint when you see crowds of locals munching on giant *banh mi* (Vietnamese stuffed baguettes), which have earned Thieng Heng a cult following. Fillings include grilled marinated meats, such as pork or chicken, pickled veggies, fresh herbs and sweet, salty or spicy sauces.

LA TROPICALE ICE CREAM €

Map p410 (01 42 16 87 27; www.latropicaleglacier.com; 180 bd Vincent Auriol, 13e; ice cream per 1/2/3 scoops €3/5/7, lunch menu €8-12; noon-8pm Mon-Fri, 3-8pm Sat & Sun summer, noon-3.30pm Mon, Tue & Thu, noon-7pm Wed & Sat winter; ; Place d'Italie) Pistachio and orange-flower, lemon and absinthe, and mandarin spiced with timut pepper are among the exciting favours at this exceptional ice-creamery near place d'Italie. Ice cream is made on site in the tiny space, and seasonal flavours incorporate gorgeous tropical spices sourced by the creative Cambodian owner and ice-cream maker, Thai-Thanh, on her many travels.

PHO BÀNH CÚON 14 VIETNAMESE €

Map p410 (129 av de Choisy, 13e; mains €7.80-9.50; 9am-11pm; Tolbiac) Factor in a wait at this small, simple restaurant (also known as Pho 14) – it doesn't take bookings and is wildly popular with in-the-know locals for its authentic and astonishingly cheap *pho;* this steaming Vietnamese broth is richly flavoured with cinnamon and incorporates noodles and traditional beef or chicken.

YUMAN HEALTH FOOD €

Map p410 (01 73 74 44 79; www.facebook.com/YumanParis; 70 rue du Chevaleret, 13e; mains €16-17.50; noon-2.30pm & 7.30-10.30pm Tue-Sat; ; Bibliothèque François Mitterand) 'Simple, natural cuisine' is the strapline of this tasty address with scrubbed wood tables and a decent-sized pavement terrace, a short walk away from Station F (p254) and the National Library. Tucked beneath the railway tracks, chef Gilles Tessier cooks up 100% of his dishes using products sourced within a 200km radius of Paris. Several are vegetarian, gluten-free, dairy-free or vegan.

L'ANTHRACITE FRENCH €€

Map p410 (☎01 45 80 63 47; www.lanthracite.fr; 9 Rue Jean Marie Jego, 13e; mains €28-34; ⊙noon-2.30pm & 7.30-10.30pm Tue-Fri, 7.30-10.30pm Sat; Ⓜ Place d'Italie) For refined dining, reserve a table at this elegant 'bistronomique' restaurant with polished parquet, unpretentious wooden tables, the odd decorative bookshelf and exceptional Aubrac beef from France's Massif Central that the bistro matures itself, still on the bone for at least 30 days. The feisty *côte de boeuf* (rib steak; €82/105 for two/three people) with home-made fries and salad is memorable.

SIMONE LE RESTO BISTRO €€

Map p410 (☎01 43 37 82 70; www.simoneparis.com; 33 bd Arago, 13e; 2-/3-course lunch menu €18/22, tasting menu €49; ⊙noon-2.30pm & 7.30-10.30pm Tue-Fri, 7.30-10.30pm Sat; Ⓜ Les Gobelins) A generous smattering of pavement-terrace tables flags this vibrant neobistro with tattooed chef Mathia Di Gino in the kitchen and knowledgeable duo Julian and Charles out front. Daily *menus* created in the open kitchen ooze seasonal products. An exceptional selection of all-natural and biodynamic wines (also available at Simone's nearby wine shop and bar, Simone La Cave, p258 – host to weekly fantastic tastings) pair perfectly with each course.

DRINKING & NIGHTLIFE

The comings and goings of the Gare Montparnasse and its historic brasseries keep things lively. Southwest of place d'Italie, rue de la Butte aux Cailles and the surrounding Butte aux Cailles molehill have a plethora of fabulous options popular with students and locals; places here have a loyal clientele and lack the pretension of more trendsetting neighbourhoods. Especially in summer, you can't beat the floating bars and clubs on the Seine.

Montparnasse & Southern Paris

ARTHUR & JULIETTE CAFE

Map p414 (☎01 48 28 15 55; www.facebook.com/ArthuretJulietteRestaurant; 51 rue des Morillons, 15e; ⊙8am-2am; Ⓜ Porte de Vanves) Sunny Sunday mornings are the best time to lap up the unpretentious Parisian vibe at this staunchly local neighbourhood cafe, named after the owners' two children. Grab a seat on the terrace, across the street from the bulls guarding Parc Georges Brassens, and kick back over a coffee or something stronger. Summer ushers in live rock and pop gigs.

LE PETIT GORILLE CAFE, BAR

Map p414 (☎01 48 28 17 57; 46 rue de Cronstadt, 15e; ⊙9am-2am Tue-Sun; 📶; Ⓜ Convention) A collection of miniature cuddly gorillas is the clue to the kitschy-cool vibe at this fun cafe-bar, one notch up from your regular neighbourhood hang-out with its eye-catching marine-blue façade, stylish pavement seating and neo-retro interior. Great cocktails, beers and wines, plus tasty bistro food (mains €15 to €20) that draws a regular weekend crowd.

LE SELECT CAFE

Map p402 (www.leselectmontparnasse.fr; 99 bd du Montparnasse, 6e; ⊙7am-2am Sun-Thu, to 3am Fri & Sat; 📶; Ⓜ Vavin) Dating from 1923, this Montparnasse brasserie, restaurant and *bar américain* was the first of the area's grand cafes to stay open late into the night, and it still draws everyone from beer-swigging students to whisky-swilling politicians and smartly dressed Parisians who've been coming here for years.

MIX CLUB CLUB

Map p412 (www.mixclub.fr; 24 rue de l'Arrivée, 14e; ⊙midnight-6am Thu, 24hr Fri & Sat; Ⓜ Montparnasse Bienvenüe) Free admission for everyone on Thursdays lures a fun-loving, dance-mad student set to this vast underground club, with 1500 sq m of dance floor and a sound system up there with Ibiza venues. Look for the entrance opposite the main business entrance to the Tour Montparnasse.

ROSEBUD COCKTAIL BAR

Map p412 (☎01 43 35 38 34; 11bis rue Delambre, 14e; ⊙7pm-2am; Ⓜ Vavin) Like the sleigh of that name in *Citizen Kane*, Rosebud harks back to the past. In this case it's to Montparnasse's early-20th-century heyday (the decor has scarcely changed since Sartre drank here). Enjoy a Champagne cocktail amid the quiet elegance of polished wood and aged leather.

Place d'Italie & Chinatown

★LE BATOFAR CLUB

Map p410 (☎01 53 60 37 85; www.batofar.fr; opposite 11 quai François Mauriac, 13e; ⏰6pm-7am Wed-Sat, to midnight Sun-Tue; Ⓜ Quai de la Gare, Bibliothèque) Closed for renovation when we visited, this much-loved, red-metal tugboat promises to be even more fabulous when it reopens. Its rooftop bar is a place to be seen in summer; it has a respected restaurant; and its club provides memorable underwater acoustics for edgy, experimental music and live performances (mostly electro-oriented but hip hop, new wave, rock, punk and jazz, too).

SIMONE LA CAVE WINE BAR

Map p410 (☎01 43 37 82 70; www.simoneparis.com; 48 rue Pascal, 13e; ⏰5-11pm Tue-Sat; Ⓜ Les Gobelins) Tucked away in the 13e, Simone La Cave lures a loyal wine-loving set keen to try its latest, outstanding natural and biodynamic wine selection. *Planches* (chopping boards, €10 to €15) stacked high with cured meats and boutique cheeses, oysters, parsley-marinated anchovies and home-made terrines provide the perfect accompaniment.

L'OISIVETHÉ CAFE

Map p410 (☎01 53 80 31 33; www.facebook.com/LOisiveThe; 8 rue de la Butte aux Cailles, 13e; ⏰noon-6pm Tue-Fri, 11am-6pm Sat & Sun; Ⓜ Place d'Italie) Relax over a cup of tea – there are 70 types to choose from – or try your hand at knitting at this cheery *salon de thé* and yarn shop. Colourful and upbeat in equal measure, it is a hub of local life and a place to slow down (the tearoom's name is a play on the French word *'oisiveté'*, meaning aristocratic idleness).

LA DAME DE CANTON CLUB

Map p410 (www.damedecanton.com; opp 11 quai François Mauriac, 13e; ⏰7pm-midnight Tue-Thu, to 2am Fri, 2pm-5am Sat; Ⓜ Bibliothèque) This floating *boîte* (club) aboard a three-masted Chinese junk with a couple of world voyages under its belt bobs beneath the Bibliothèque Nationale de France. Concerts cover pop and indie to electro, hip hop, reggae and rock; afterwards DJs keep the crowd hyped. There's also a popular bar and restaurant with wood-fired pizzas served on the terrace from May to September.

LE MERLE MOQUEUR BAR

Map p410 (11 rue de la Butte aux Cailles, 13e; ⏰5pm-2am; Ⓜ Corvisart) The tiny, retro Mocking Magpie serves a huge selection of rum punches (more than 20 at last count) and unearths long-forgotten 1980s tracks from the musical vaults.

L'AGE D'OR BAR

Map p410 (☎01 45 85 10 58; www.lagedorparis.com; 26 rue du Docteur Magnan, 13e; ⏰9am-midnight Sun-Wed, 9am-2am Thu-Sat; 📶; Ⓜ Tolbiac) A fully fledged hybrid on the fringe of Chinatown, this lively neighbourhood corner cafe morphs from early-morning breakfast spot to lunchtime fave, to cocktail hot spot and live-music venue throughout the day. Seating is on benches outside or around a rainbow of 1950s-style formica tables in the grungy, dimly lit interior. Tapas staves off munchies.

BATEAU EL ALAMEIN CLUB

Map p410 (www.bateauelalamein.com; opp 11 quai François Mauriac, 13e; ⏰8pm-2am; Ⓜ Bibliothèque) Strung with terracotta pots of flowers, this deep-purple boat has a Seine-side terrace to sit amid tulips and enjoy live bands (flyers are stuck on the lamppost at the front). Less hectic than Paris' other floating clubs moored here, hence the older crowd; concerts starting at 9pm (no reservations) span jazz, world and Piaf-style *chansons*. Hours can vary.

☆ ENTERTAINMENT

Many of the 13e's floating nightclubs have live music. Events regularly take place at Les Docks (p251) and the cutting-edge EP7 with sassy digital art gallery as its façade.

★EP7 ARTS CENTER

Map p410 (☎01 43 45 68 07; https://ep7.paris; 133 av de France, 13e; ⏰7.30am-2am; 📶; Ⓜ Bibliothèque) It is impossible to miss the façade of this brand new cultural cafe and concert venue – the capital's first piece of 'interactive architecture', unveiled in early 2018. Contemporary works of pixel art prance across 12 giant screens covering the facade, creating a dazzling digital gallery. Inside the cultural cafe, named after the vintage vinyl format 'extended play', find art exhibitions and happenings, DJ sets, a trendy bistro

WORTH A DETOUR

CULTURAL ISLAND: ÎLE SEGUIN

A landmark addition to Paris' cultural offerings, **La Seine Musicale** (☎01 74 34 54 00; www.laseinemusicale.com; Île Seguin, Boulogne-Billancourt; Ⓜ Pont de Sèvres) opened on the Seine island of Île Seguin in 2017. Constructed of steel and glass, the egg-shaped auditorium has a capacity of 1150, while the larger, modular concrete hall accommodates 6000. Ballets, musicals and concerts from classical to rock are all staged here, alongside exhibitions.

Outside are amphitheatres, while up above is a panoramic rooftop garden with landscaped lawns. There's an excellent cafe, riverside restaurant and bar on the premises.

It's the first of several arts venues including a contemporary art museum planned as part of the Île Seguin's transformation from a Renault factory to a cultural island.

serving local, fresh, seasonal cuisine (menu €26) and late-night bar with Seine view.

FONDATION JÉRÔME SEYDOUX-PATHÉ CINEMA

Map p410 (☎01 83 79 18 96; www.fondation-jeromeseydoux-pathe.com; 77 ave des Gobelins, 13e; tickets adult/child €6.50/4.50; ⏲1-8pm Tue, 1-7pm Wed-Fri, 11.30am-7pm Sat; Ⓜ Place d'Italie) This striking cinema with a small exhibition (€3) devoted to the history of cinema is a brilliant addition to the Paris flick scene. Where else can you watch silent B&W movies to the sound of a live pianist? The Pathé Foundation is hidden in a former theatre and cinema dating to 1869, but only the façade – sculpted by Rodin – remains. The rest of the building is an unbelievable, five-storey, contemporary 'slug' of a creation by world-class architect Renzo Piano.

Guided architecture tours (adult/child €7.50/4) take place Saturday at noon. The family-friendly *ciné-concerts* (films) at weekends are particularly enchanting.

L'ENTREPÔT CULTURAL CENTRE

Map p412 (☎01 45 40 07 50; www.lentrepot.fr; 7-9 rue Francis de Pressensé, 14e; Ⓜ Pernety) Everything from film screenings to jazz and world music concerts, poetry slams, photography, painting and sculpture exhibitions, art installations and much more take place at this dynamic cultural space. It's a fantastic place to eat, too, with a glassed-in conservatory and dozens of tables beneath the trees in its leafy back garden; Sunday brunch (€24.50) is hugely popular.

CINÉMA LES FAUVETTES CINEMA

Map p410 (Gaumont; www.cinemasgaumont-pathe.com; 58 av des Gobelins, 13e; tickets before/after noon €8.10/12.40; ⏲10.30am-12.30am; Ⓜ Les Gobelins) Classics from the silent era to contemporary films are the focus of this five-screen cinema, which has a dedicated 3D screen and also hosts retrospectives, such as the entire James Bond catalogue or Best Picture Oscar winners. Movies are shown in French and original languages (including English) with subtitles; check the program online.

SHOPPING

The concrete-block shopping mall opposite Gare Montparnasse includes a branch of department store Galeries Lafayette. Savvy fashion shoppers head to the southern 14e to shop for discount designer wear, while the 15e is filled with specialist addresses. In the 13e you'll find Asian grocery stores and supermarkets in Chinatown, and an enormous state-of-the-art shopping mall at place d'Italie.

Montparnasse & Southern Paris

★STORIE HOMEWARES

Map p412 (☎01 83 56 01 98; www.storieshop.com; 20 rue Delambre, 14e; ⏲3-8pm Mon, 11am-2pm & 3-8pm Tue-Sat; Ⓜ Montparnasse) Beautiful objects with *une histoire* (a story) is what this backstreet boutique is all about. Hand-woven Mongolian rugs pile next to silk and cashmere from Afghanistan and Peacebomb jewellery from Laos. Items are artisan, handmade and personally sourced by the well-travelled, British co-owner Fiona Cameron, a former TV journalist. Watch for art exhibitions, story-telling workshops and other occasional events.

ADAM MONTPARNASSE ARTS & CRAFTS

Map p412 (☎01 43 20 68 53; www.adamparis.com; 11 bd Edgar Quinet, 14e; ⏲9.30am-7pm Mon-Sat; ⓂEdgar Quinet) If Paris' art galleries have inspired you, pick up paintbrushes, charcoals, pastels, sketchpads, watercolours, oils, acrylics, canvases and more at this historic shop. Picasso, Brancusi and Giacometti were among Édouard Adam's clients. Another seminal client was Yves Klein, with whom Adam developed the ultramarine 'Klein blue' – the VLB25 'Klein Blue' varnish is sold exclusively here.

BELLEVAIRE CHEESE

Map p412 (☎01 45 42 90 68; www.fromageriebeillevaire.com; 86 rue Raymond Losserand, 14e; ⏲9am-8pm Tue-Sat, 9am-1pm Sun; ⓂPlaisance) For the finest French butter, not to mention a swath of unusual seasonal French cheeses and other top-quality dairy products, make a pit stop at this outstanding place. Cheese can be vacuum-packed to take home.

DES GÂTEAUX ET DU PAIN FOOD

Map p412 (☎06 98 95 33 18; www.desgateauxetdupain.com; 63 bd Pasteur, 15e; ⏲9am-8pm Mon & Wed-Sat, 9am-6pm Sun; ⓂPasteur) Looking more like an exclusive boutique, this ultra-contemporary bakery and patisserie has dramatic black walls that showcase the jewel-like cakes, tarts and artisan breads created by David Granger and Claire Damon – one of France's leading female pastry chefs.

DISCOUNT DESIGNER OUTLETS

Save up to 70% off men's, women's and kids' fashions from previous seasons' collections, surpluses, prototypes and seconds by name-brand designers at the discounted outlet stores along rue d'Alésia, 14e, west of the Alésia metro station (particularly between av de Maine to rue Raymond-Losserand).

Shops pop up regularly and close just as often, so you can never be sure of what you'll find, but look out for two shops stocking designs by **Sonia Rykiel** (Map p412; www.soniarykiel.com; 64 & 110-112 rue d'Alésia, 14e; ⏲11am-6.45pm Tue-Sat; ⓂAlésia). No 64 has lower-priced, more casual clothes, while No 110–112 has Sonia Rykiel's classic lines.

MARCHÉ AUX PUCES DE LA PORTE DE VANVES MARKET

(www.pucesdevanves.fr; av Georges Lafenestre & av Marc Sangnier, 14e; ⏲7am-2pm Sat & Sun; ⓂPorte de Vanves) One of the friendliest in Paris, the Porte de Vanves flea market has over 380 stalls. Av Georges Lafenestre has lots of 'curios' that don't quite qualify as antiques. Av Marc Sangnier is lined with stalls of new clothes, shoes, handbags and household items for sale.

LA CAVE DES PAPILLES WINE

Map p412 (☎01 43 20 05 74; www.lacavedespapilles.com; 35 rue Daguerre, 14e; ⏲3.30-8.30pm Mon, 10am-1.30pm & 3.30-8.30pm Tue-Fri, 10am-8.30pm Sat, 10am-1.30pm Sun; ⓂDenfert Rochereau) All of the 1200-plus varieties of wine at this dazzling rue Daguerre wine shop are organic or additive free. There's also a wonderfully chosen selection of rare whiskies, cognacs and brandies.

LE COMPTOIR CORREZIEN FOOD

Map p414 (☎01 47 83 52 97; www.comptoir-correzien.fr; 8 rue des Volontaires, 15e; ⏲10.30am-1.30pm & 3-7.30pm Tue-Sat; ⓂVolontaires) Caviar, smoked salmon, Corsican honey, wild duck and geese, fresh and dried mushrooms, Berthillon ice cream and truffles in season are among the mouthwatering luxury food products stocked at this head-spinning deli, which supplies some of the city's premier restaurants. If you're staying in a kitchen-equipped apartment, consider picking up pre-made meals (soups, pastas) from here, too.

MARCHÉ EDGAR QUINET FOOD

Map p412 (http://equipement.paris.fr/marche-edgar-quinet-5497; bd Edgar Quinet, 14e; ⏲7am-2.30pm Wed, 7am-3pm Sat; ⓂEdgar Quinet, Montparnasse Bienvenüe) Opposite Tour Montparnasse, this open-air street market teems with neighbourhood shoppers. There's always a great range of cheeses, as well as stalls sizzling up snacks to eat on the run, from crêpes to spicy falafels.

MARCHÉ DE LA CRÉATION MARKET

Map p412 (bd Edgar Quinet, 14e; ⏲10am-7pm Sun; ⓂEdgar Quinet) Stalls overflowing with handmade arts and crafts fill the western end of bd Edgar Quinet on Sunday, drawing a mixed crowd of locals and travellers in transit from nearby Gare Montparnasse.

MARCHÉ BRANCUSI FOOD

Map p412 (http://equipement.paris.fr/marche-biologique-brancusi-4516; place Constantin Brancusi, 14e; 9am-3pm Sat; M Gaîté) Huge selection of *biologique* (organic) produce at this weekly open-air market.

Place d'Italie & Chinatown

BIÉROCRATIE DRINKS

Map p410 (01 53 80 16 10; www.bierocratie.com; 32 rue de l'Espérance, 13e; 11am-8pm Tue & Thu-Sat, 4-8pm Wed; M Corvisart) Craft beers from around the world (such as English Weird Beard, Canadian Dieu du Cieu, Danish Ianø, and Belgian Gulden Draak and Deus Brut des Flandres) but especially France (including Île-de-France-brewed La Baleine, Distrikt and Parisis) fill this bottle-lined specialist shop. It's run by fun-loving young husband-and-wife team Jaclyn and Pierre. Look out for Friday-evening tastings where you can meet the brewers.

LAURENT DUCHÊNE FOOD

Map p410 (01 45 65 00 77; www.laurent-duchene.com; 2 rue Wurtz, 13e; 7.30am-8pm Mon-Sat; M Glacière) Prize-winning croissants made with *beurre Charentes-Poitou* AOC butter are the speciality of this lauded bakery.

TANG FRÈRES FOOD

Map p410 (48 av d'Ivry, 13e; 9am-8pm Tue-Sat, 8am-8pm Sun; M Porte d'Ivry) Chinatown's beating heart centres on this enormous Asian supermarket, where you would be forgiven for thinking you'd been transported to another continent. Spices, sauces, freezers full of frozen dumplings, and kitchen utensils are imported from Asia along with beverages including Chinese beer. Ready-to-eat snacks are sold opposite the entrance.

SPORTS & ACTIVITIES

★PISCINE DE LA BUTTE AUX CAILLES SWIMMING

Map p410 (01 45 89 60 05; http://equipement.paris.fr/piscine-de-la-butte-aux-cailles-2927; 5 place Paul Verlaine, 13e; adult/child €3.50/2, 10 entrances €28/16; hours vary; M Place d'Italie) Built in 1924, this art deco gem of a swimming pool complex – a historical monument to boot – takes advantage of the lovely warm artesian well water nearby. It has a spectacular vaulted indoor pool and, since its 2017 renovation, is the only complex in Paris to have a Nordic pool. In the depths of winter this is where Parisians come to swim 25m laps in a five-lane outdoor pool, heated to a toasty 28°C.

PISCINE JOSÉPHINE BAKER SWIMMING

Map p410 (01 56 61 96 50; www.piscine-baker.fr; quai François Mauriac, 13e; adult/child €6.20/3.10; 7-9am & 10am-11pm Mon-Fri, 10am-8pm Sat & Sun Jun-Sep, shorter hours rest of year; M Quai de la Gare) Floating on the Seine, this striking swimming pool is named after the 1920s American singer. The 25m-by-10m, four-lane pool and large sun deck are especially popular in summer when the roof slides back. Also here is a children's paddling pool. In July and August, plus weekends from late May to September, admission is limited to two hours.

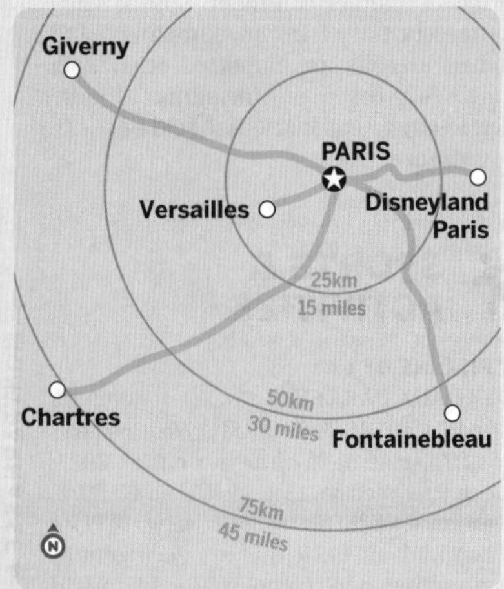

Day Trips from Paris

Disneyland Paris p263

Europe's Disneyland theme park, Disney Village's hotels, shops, restaurants and clubs, and Walt Disney Studios Park bring film, animation and TV production to life.

Château de Versailles p264

When it comes to over-the-top opulence, the colossal Château de Versailles is in a class of its own, even for France.

Fontainebleau p270

A lavish château and rambling forest grace the elegant town of Fontainebleau, and its international business school gives it a vibrant edge.

Chartres p273

Rising from fertile farmland, Chartres' Cathédrale Notre Dame, famed for its beautiful stained glass, dominates the charming medieval town.

Giverny p276

Art and/or garden lovers shouldn't miss Giverny's Maison et Jardins de Claude Monet, the former home and flower-filled gardens of the impressionist master.

TOP SIGHT
DISNEYLAND PARIS

It took almost €4.6 billion to turn the beet fields 32km east of Paris into Europe's first Disney theme park. What started out as Euro-Disney in 1992 today comprises the traditional Disneyland Park theme park, the film-oriented Walt Disney Studios Park, and the hotel-, shop- and restaurant-filled Disney Village. And kids – and kids-at-heart – can't seem to get enough.

Basic one-day admission fees at Disneyland Resort Paris include unlimited access to attractions in either Disneyland Park or Walt Disney Studios Park. A multitude of multi-day passes, special offers and packages are always available.

No picnic hampers or coolers are allowed but you can bring snacks, sandwiches, water bottles (refillable at water fountains) and the like. The resort also has 29 themed restaurants of varying quality and value; reservations are recommended and can be made online up to two months in advance.

Disneyland is easily reached by RER A (€7.60, 40 minutes to one hour, frequent), which runs from central Paris to Marne-la-Vallée/Chessy, Disneyland's RER station.

PRACTICALITIES

- hotel bookings 01 60 30 60 30, restaurant reservations 01 60 30 40 50
- www.disneylandparis.com
- adult/child 1 day single park €63/56, 1 day both parks €83/76, 2 days both parks €150/133
- hours vary

Disneyland Park

Disneyland Park (Disneyland Resort Paris; 10am-11pm May-Sep, to 8pm Oct-Apr, hours can vary) has five themed *pays* (lands): the 1900s-styled **Main Street USA**; **Frontierland**, home of the legendary Big Thunder Mountain ride; **Adventureland**, which evokes exotic lands in rides including the Pirates of the Caribbean and Indiana Jones and the Temple of Peril; **Fantasyland**, crowned by Sleeping Beauty's castle; and the high-tech **Discoveryland**, with massive-queue rides such as Space Mountain: Mission 2 and Buzz Lightyear Laser Blast.

Walt Disney Studios Park

At **Walt Disney Studios Park** (Disneyland Resort Paris; 10am-9pm Jun-Sep, to 8pm Oct-May, hours can vary), a sound stage, production backlot and animation studios provide an up-close insight into the production of films, TV programs and cartoons. There are behind-the-scenes tours, larger-than-life characters and spine-tingling rides like the Twilight Zone Tower of Terror, as well as the outsized Ratatouille ride (based on the winsome 2007 film about a rat who dreams of becoming a top Parisian chef) which offers a multisensory rat's perspective of Paris' rooftops and restaurant kitchens aboard a trackless 'ratmobile'.

Top Disney Tips

- Crowds peak during European school holidays; visit www.schoolholidayseurope.eu to avoid them if possible.
- Pre-plan your day on Disney's website or the excellent www.dlpguide.com, working out which rides and shows you really want to see.
- Buy tickets in advance to avoid the ticket queue.
- The free Disneyland Paris app provides real-time waiting time for attractions but note that free wi-fi is only available in limited areas within the park.
- Once in, reserve your time slot on the busiest rides using FastPass, the park's ride reservation system (limited to one reservation at a time).
- Disney hotel guests are often entitled to two 'Magic Hours' in Disneyland Park (usually from 8am, May to October) before opening to the public, although not all rides run during these hours.

TOP SIGHT
CHÂTEAU DE VERSAILLES

Louis XIV transformed his father's hunting lodge into the monumental Château de Versailles in the mid-17th century, and it remains France's most famous, grandest palace. Situated 22km southwest of Paris, the baroque château was the kingdom's political capital and the seat of the royal court from 1682 until the French Revolution in 1789.

Intending the château to house his court of 6000 people, Louis XIV hired four talented men to take on the gargantuan task: architect Louis Le Vau; Jules Hardouin-Mansart, who took over from Le Vau in the mid-1670s; painter and interior designer Charles Le Brun; and landscape designer André Le Nôtre, under whom entire hills were flattened, marshes drained and forests moved to create the seemingly endless gardens, ponds and fountains for which Versailles is so well known. It has been on Unesco's World Heritage list since 1979.

Sprawling over 900 hectares, the estate is divided into four main sections: the 580m-long palace; the gardens, canals and pools to the west of the palace; two smaller palaces, the Grand Trianon and the Petit Trianon, to the northwest; and the Hameau de la Reine (Queen's Hamlet) north of the Petit Trianon. Tickets include an English-language audioguide; free apps can be downloaded from the website.

Versailles is easy to reach from Paris. The most convenient option is to take RER C5 (return €7.10, 40 minutes, frequent) from Paris' Left Bank RER stations to Versailles-Château–Rive Gauche station. There are also other rail connections, buses and organised tours.

DON'T MISS

- Château de Versailles
- Gardens
- Marie-Antoinette's estate
- Trianon palaces

PRACTICALITIES

- ☎01 30 83 78 00
- www.chateauversailles.fr
- place d'Armes
- adult/child passport ticket incl estate-wide access €20/free, with musical events €27/free, palace €18/free except during musical events
- ⏲9am-6.30pm Tue-Sun Apr-Oct, to 5.30pm Tue-Sun Nov-Mar
- Ⓜ RER Versailles-Château–Rive Gauche

Château de Versailles

Few alterations have been made to the château since its construction, apart from most of the interior furnishings disappearing during the Revolution and many of the rooms being rebuilt by Louis-Philippe (r 1830–48), who opened part of the château to the public in 1837. The current €400-million restoration program is the most ambitious yet and until it's completed in 2020 a part of the palace is likely to be clad in scaffolding when you visit.

To access areas that are otherwise off limits and to learn more about Versailles' history, prebook a 90-minute **guided tour** (☎01 30 83 77 88; tours €10, plus palace entry; ⏰English-language tours 9.30am Tue-Sun) of the Private Apartments of Louis XV and Louis XVI and the Opera House or Royal Chapel. Tours also cover the most famous parts of the palace.

Prams/buggies, metal-frame baby carriers and luggage aren't allowed inside the palace.

Hall of Mirrors

The palace's opulence peaks in its shimmering Galerie des Glaces (Hall of Mirrors). This 75m-long ballroom has 17 sparkling mirrors on one side and an equal number of windows on the other.

King's & Queen's State Apartments

Luxurious, ostentatious appointments – frescoes, marble, gilt and woodcarvings, with themes and symbols drawn from Greek and Roman mythology – adorn every moulding, cornice, ceiling and door in the palace's Grands Appartements du Roi et de la Reine (King's and Queen's State Apartments).

Gardens

Don't miss a stroll through the château's magnificent **gardens** (free except during musical events; ⏰8am-8.30pm Apr-Oct, to 6pm Nov-Mar, park 7am-8.30pm Apr-Oct, 8am-6pm Nov-Mar). The best view over the rectangular pools is from the Hall of Mirrors. Pathways include the Royal Walk's verdant 'green carpet', with smaller paths leading to leafy groves. The gardens' largest fountains are the 17th-century Bassin de Neptune (Neptune's Fountain), a dazzling mirage of 99 spouting fountains 300m north of the palace, and the Bassin d'Apollon (Apollo's Fountain), built in 1668 at the eastern end of the Grand Canal.

Canals

The **Grand Canal**, 1.6km long and 62m wide, is oriented to reflect the setting sun. It's traversed by the 1km-long **Petit Canal**, forming a cross-shaped body of water with a perimeter of more than 5.5km.

PLANNING FOR VERSAILLES

By noon, queues for tickets and entering the château spiral out of control: arrive early morning and avoid Tuesday, Saturday and Sunday, its busiest days. Pre-purchase tickets on the château's website or at Fnac (p61) branches and head straight to Entrance A.

EXPLORING THE ESTATE

The estate is so vast that the only way to see it all is to hire a four-person **electric car** (☎01 39 66 97 66; car hire per hr €34; ⏰10am-6.45pm Apr-Oct, to 5.30pm Feb & Mar, to 5pm Nov & Dec) or hop aboard the **shuttle train** (www.train-versailles.com; adult/child €8/6.10, audioguide €4; ⏰every 20min 11.10am-6.50pm Apr-Oct, to 5.10pm Nov-Mar); you can also rent a **bike** (☎01 39 66 97 66; bike hire per hr/day €8.50/20; ⏰10am-6.45pm Apr-Oct, to 5.30pm mid-Feb–Mar, to 5pm early–mid-Nov) or a **rowboat** (☎01 39 66 97 66; www.versailles-tourisme.com; boat hire per 30 min/hr €13/17; ⏰10am-6.45pm Jul & Aug, shorter hrs Mar-Jun & Sep–mid-Nov).

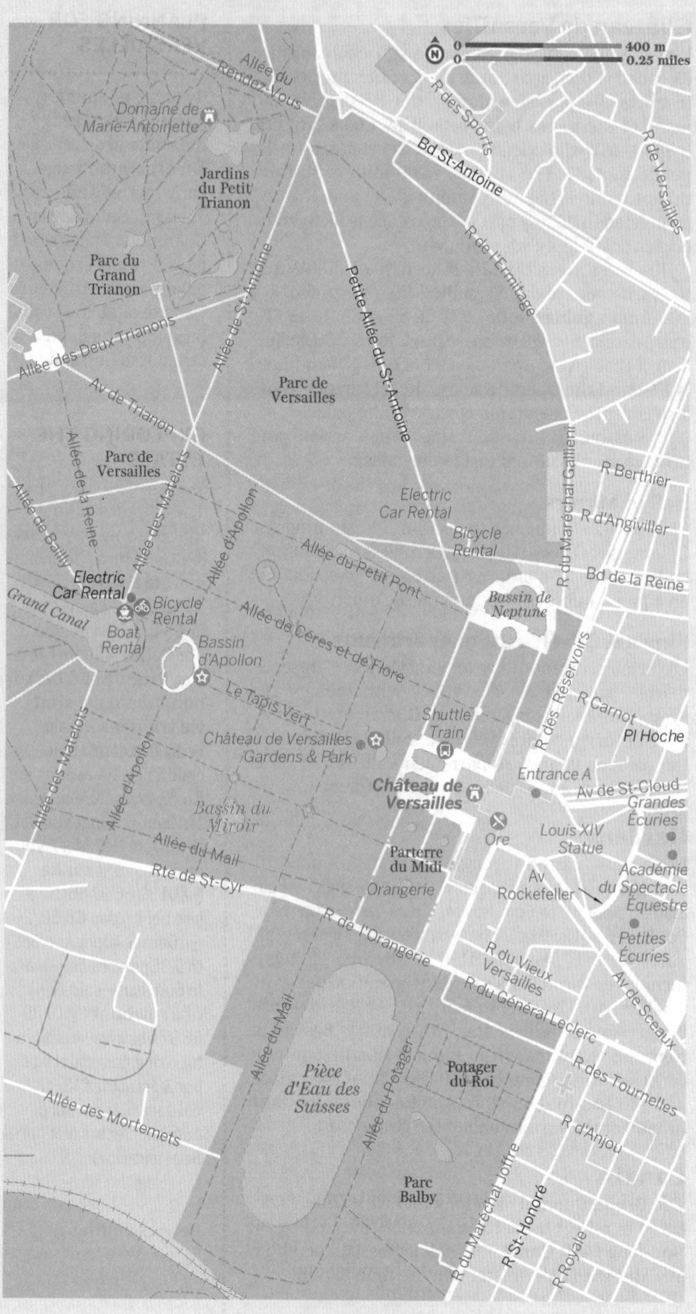

0 400 m
0 0.25 miles
Allée du Rendez-Vous
Domaine de Marie-Antoinette
Jardins du Petit Trianon
Parc du Grand Trianon
R des Sports
Bd St-Antoine
R de Versailles
R de l'Ermitage
Allée de St-Antoine
Petite Allée du St-Antoine
Allée des Deux Trianons
Av de Trianon
Parc de Versailles
Parc de Versailles
Allée de la Reine
Allée des Matelots
Allée d'Apollon
Allée de Bailly
Electric Car Rental
Bicycle Rental
R du Maréchal Gallieni
R Berthier
R d'Angiviller
Bd de la Reine
Allée du Petit Pont
Electric Car Rental
Bicycle Rental
Boat Rental
Grand Canal
Allée de Céres et de Flore
Bassin d'Apollon
Bassin de Neptune
R des Réservoirs
R Carnot
Pl Hoche
Le Tapis Vert
Shuttle Train
Château de Versailles Gardens & Park
Entrance A
Av de St-Cloud
Château de Versailles
Grandes Écuries
Ore
Louis XIV Statue
Allée des Matelots
Allée d'Apollon
Bassin du Miroir
Allée du Mail
Parterre du Midi
Rte de St-Cyr
Orangerie
Av Rockefeller
Académie du Spectacle Équestre
Petites Écuries
R de l'Orangerie
R du Vieux Versailles
R du Général Leclerc
Av de Sceaux
Allée du Mail
Pièce d'Eau des Suisses
Allée du Potager
Potager du Roi
R des Tournelles
R d'Anjou
Allée des Mortemets
Parc Balby
R du Maréchal Joffre
R St-Honoré
R Royale

Grand Trianon

Marie-Antoinette's Estate

Northwest of Versailles' main palace is the **Domaine de Marie-Antoinette** (Marie Antoinette's Estate; www.chateauversailles.fr; Château de Versailles; adult/child €12/free, free with passport ticket; ⏲noon-6.30pm Tue-Sun Apr-Oct, to 5.30pm Tue-Sat Nov-Mar). Admission includes the Grand Trianon and Petit Trianon palaces, and the 1784-completed Hameau de la Reine (Queen's Hamlet), a mock village of thatched cottages where Marie-Antoinette played milkmaid.

Trianon Palaces

The pink-colonnaded Grand Trianon was built in 1687 for Louis XIV and his family to escape the rigid etiquette of the court was and renovated under Napoléon I in the Empire style. The ochre-coloured, 1760s Petit Trianon was redecorated in 1867 by the consort of Napoleon III, Empress Eugénie, who added Louis XVI–style furnishings.

Musical Fountain Shows

Try to time your visit for the **Grandes Eaux Musicales** (www.chateauversailles-spectacles.fr; adult/child €9.50/8; ⏲9am-7pm Tue, Sat & Sun mid-May–late Jun, 9am-7pm Sat & Sun Apr–mid-May & late Jun-Oct) or the after-dark **Grandes Eaux Nocturnes** (www.chateauversailles-spectacles.fr; adult/child €24/20; ⏲8.30-11.30pm Sat mid-Jun–mid-Sep), truly magical 'dancing water' displays – set to Baroque and classical music – throughout the grounds in summer.

DINING AT VERSAILLES

On-site restaurants include Alain Ducasse's **Ore** (☎01 30 84 12 96; www.ducasse-chateauversailles.com; 1st floor, Pavillon Dufour; breakfast menus €12-20, mains €20-36, afternoon-tea platters €35; ⏲9am-6.30pm Tue-Sun Apr-Oct, to 5.30pm Nov-Mar; 📶👪). In the town of Versailles, try delightful cafe **La Cour** (☎01 39 02 33 09; www.versailles-lacour.fr; 7 rue des Deux Portes; 2-course lunch menus €15, Sunday brunch €24; ⏲noon-6pm Wed-Sat, 11am-3pm Sun).

THE STABLES

The **Grandes Écuries** (Big Stables; www.bartabas.fr; av Rockefeller) are the stage for the prestigious **Académie du Spectacle Équestre** (Academy of Equestrian Arts; ☎01 39 02 62 70; http://bartabas.fr; 1 av Rockefeller; training session adult/child €15/10; ⏲by reservation). It presents spectacular Reprises Musicales equestrian shows, for which tickets sell out weeks in advance; book ahead online. In the stables' main courtyard is a *manège* where horses and their riders train. Show tickets and training sessions include a stable visit. The **Petites Écuries** (Little Stables) are today used by Versailles' School of Architecture.

Versailles

A DAY IN COURT

Visiting Versailles – even just the State Apartments – may seem overwhelming at first, but think of it as a house where people ate, drank, worked, slept and conspired and you'll be on the right path.

Some two decades into his long reign, Louis XIV began turning his father's hunting lodge into a palace large enough to house his entire court (to keep closer tabs on the 6000-strong army of courtiers). Sparing no expense, the Sun King employed the greatest artists and craftspeople of the day and by 1682 he'd created the most extravagant dormitory in history.

The royal schedule was as accurate and predictable as a Swiss watch. By following this itinerary of rooms you can recreate the king's day, starting with the **1 King's Bedchamber** and the **2 Queen's Bedchamber**, where the royal couple was roused at about the same time. The royal procession then leads through the **3 Hall of Mirrors** to the **4 Royal Chapel** for morning Mass and returns to the **5 Council Chamber** for late-morning meetings with ministers. After lunch the king might ride or hunt or visit the **6 King's Library**. Later he could join courtesans for an 'apartment evening' starting from the **7 Hercules Drawing Room** or play billiards in the **8 Diana Drawing Room** before supping at 10pm.

VERSAILLES BY NUMBERS

Rooms 700 (11 hectares of roof)

Windows 2153

Staircases 67

Gardens and parks 800 hectares

Trees 200,000

Fountains 50 (with 620 nozzles)

Paintings 6300 (measuring 11km laid end to end)

Statues and sculptures 2100

Objets d'art and furnishings 5000

Visitors 5.3 million per year

Queen's Bedchamber
Chambre de la Reine
The queen's life was on constant public display and even the births of her children were watched by crowds of spectators in her own bedchamber. **DETOUR »** The Guardroom, with a dozen armed men at the ready.

LUNCH BREAK

Contemporary French cuisine at Alain Ducasse's restaurant Ore, or a picnic in the park.

Hercules Drawing Room
Salon d'Hercule
This salon, with its stunning ceiling fresco of the strong man, gave way to the State Apartments, which were open to courtiers three nights a week. **DETOUR»** Apollo Drawing Room, used for formal audiences and as a throne room.

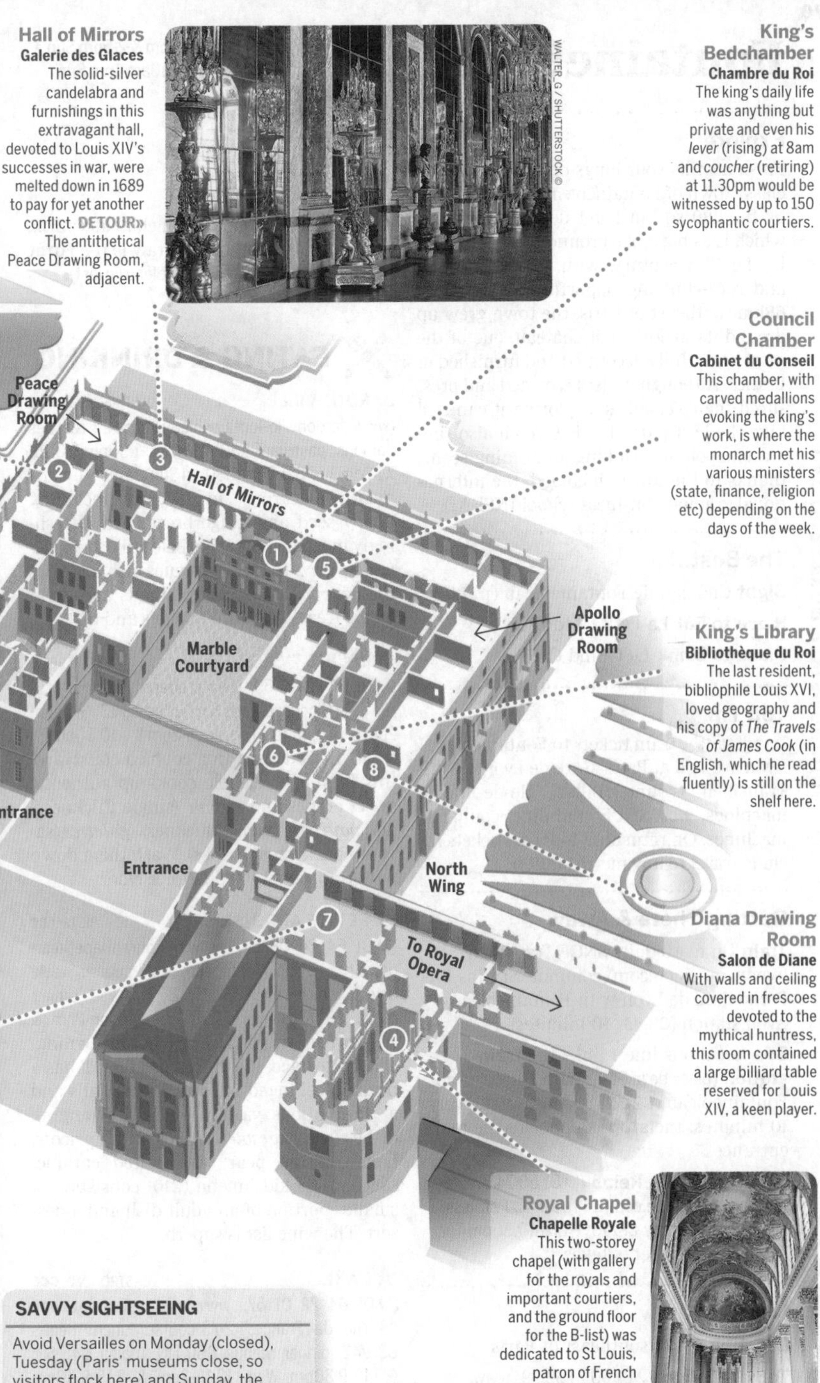

SAVVY SIGHTSEEING

Avoid Versailles on Monday (closed), Tuesday (Paris' museums close, so visitors flock here) and Sunday, the busiest day. Also, book tickets online so you don't have to queue.

Fontainebleau

Explore

Fresh air fills your lungs on arriving in the classy town of Fontainebleau. It's enveloped by the 280 sq km Forêt de Fontainebleau, which is as big a playground today as it was in the 16th century, with superb walking and rock-climbing opportunities. Situated 68km southeast of Paris, the town grew up around its magnificent château, one of the most beautifully decorated and furnished in France. Although it's less crowded and pressured than Versailles, exploring it can still take the best part of a day. You'll also find a cosmopolitan drinking and dining scene, thanks to the town's lifeblood, the international graduate business school INSEAD.

The Best...

Sight Château de Fontainebleau (p272)

Place to Eat La Petite Ardoise

Place to Drink Le Grand Café

Top Tip

Importantly, train tickets to Fontainebleau/Avon are sold at Paris' Gare de Lyon's SNCF Transilien counter/Billet Ile-de-France machines, *not* SNCF mainline counters/machines. On returning to Paris, tickets include travel to any metro station.

Getting There & Away

Train Up to 40 daily SNCF Transilien (www.transilien.com) commuter trains link Paris' Gare de Lyon with Fontainebleau/Avon station (€8.85, 40 minutes).

Bus Local bus line 1 links the **train station** (place de la Gare) with Château de Fontainebleau (€2), 2km southwest, every 10 minutes; the **stop** is opposite the main entrance.

Bike A la Petite Reine (☎01 60 74 57 57; www.alapetitereine.com; 14 rue de la Paroisse; bike hire per hr/day €8/15; ⌚9am-7.30pm Tue-Sat, to 6pm Sun) rents bikes.

Need to Know

Location 69km southeast of Paris

Tourist Office (☎01 60 74 99 99; www.fontainebleau-tourisme.com; 4 rue Royale; ⌚10am-6pm Mon-Sat, 10am-1pm & 2-5pm Sun May-Oct, 10am-6pm Mon-Sat, 10am-1pm Sun Nov-Apr; 📶)

SIGHTS

Aside from its monumental château (p272), Fontainebleau's other big draw is the **Forêt de Fontainebleau** (Fontainebleau Forest).

EATING & DRINKING

DARDONVILLE PASTRIES, BAKERY €

(www.dardonville-fontainebleau.com; 24 rue des Sablons; pastries €1.60-4; ⌚7am-1.30pm & 3.15-7.30pm Tue-Sat, 7am-1.30pm Sun) Melt-in-your-mouth macarons, in flavours including poppy seed and gingerbread, are refreshingly inexpensive at this beloved patisserie-*boulangerie* (bakery). Queues also form out the door for its amazing breads and great picnic treats like mini quiches and tarts.

CRÊPERIE TY KOZ CRÊPES €

(☎01 64 22 00 55; www.creperiety-koz.com; 18 rue de la Cloche; crêpes & galettes €3-13; ⌚noon-2pm & 7-10pm Tue-Thu, noon-2pm & 7-10.30pm Fri & Sat) Tucked away in a cobbled courtyard, this Breton hidey-hole cooks up authentic sweet crêpes and *simple* (single thickness) and *pourleth* (double thickness) *galettes* (savoury buckwheat crêpes). Wash them down with traditional Val de Rance cider.

LA PETITE ARDOISE BISTRO €€

(☎01 64 24 08 66; www.restaurantlapetitear-doise.fr; 16 rue Montebello; 2-/3-course weekday lunch menu €18/20, 2-/3-course dinner menu €32/34, mains €18-20; ⌚noon-2pm & 7-10pm Tue-Sat; 👪) Framed by an awning-shaded terrace, the 'little blackboard' has a beamed-ceilinged interior, stone walls and a scrumptious variety of daily changing dishes (snail *cassolette*, duck with apricots, honey-roasted pear with salted caramel sauce...). Its kids' menu (€10) consists of a smaller portion of an adult dish and a dessert. The wine list is superb.

★L'AXEL GASTRONOMY €€€

(☎01 64 22 01 57; www.laxel-restaurant.com; 43 rue de France; 2-/3-course lunch menus €35/42, dinner menus €60-110, mains €45-58; ⌚7.15-9.30pm Wed, 12.15-2pm & 7.15-9.30pm Thu-Sun) Chef Kunihisa Goto has gained a

Fontainebleau

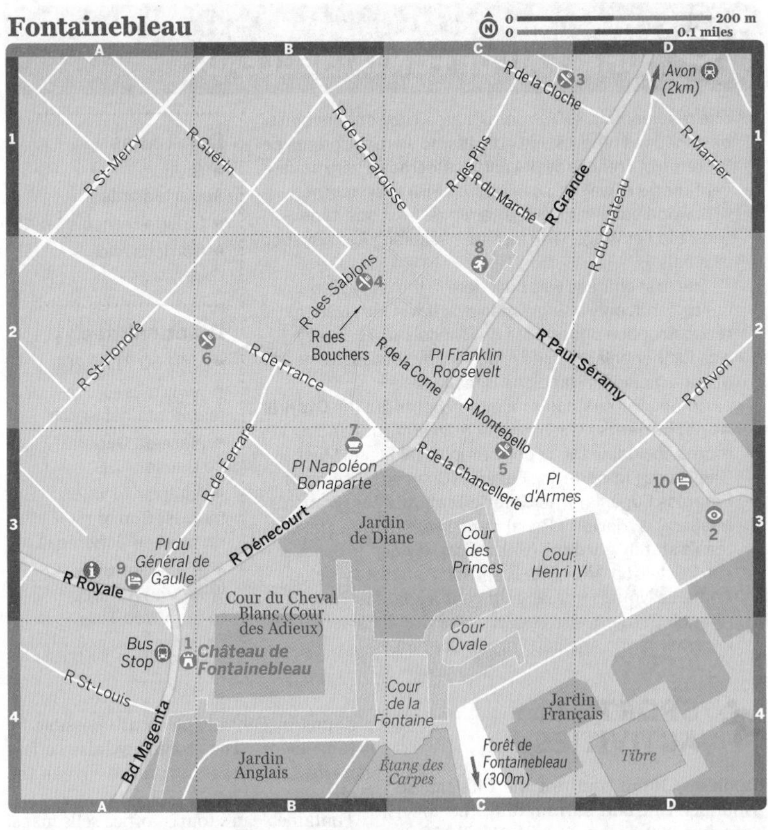

Fontainebleau

Top Sights
1 Château de Fontainebleau A4

Sights
2 Château de Fontainebleau Gardens & Park D3

Eating
3 Crêperie Ty Koz C1
4 Dardonville B2
5 La Petite Ardoise C3
La Table du Parc .... (see 10)
6 L'Axel B2

Drinking & Nightlife
7 Le Grand Café B3

Sports & Activities
8 A la Petite Reine C2

Sleeping
9 Hôtel de Londres A3
10 La Demeure du Parc D3

Michelin star for his inspired flavour combinations: turbot with candied artichoke and yuzu-butter sauce, veal sweetbreads with cinnamon-roasted carrot purée, and mango mousse in a white-chocolate coconut sphere with banana and passion-fruit sorbet. Book several weeks ahead.

LE GRAND CAFÉ CAFE

(www.legrandcafe-fontainebleau.fr; 33 place Napoléon Bonaparte; ⌚8am-1am) In a dress-circle position, this true-to-its-name cafe offers some of Fontainebleau's best people-watching from the huge terrace over a coffee, beer, wine or cocktail.

TOP SIGHT
CHÂTEAU DE FONTAINEBLEAU

The resplendent, 1900-room Château de Fontainebleau once housed tenants and guests who were the crème de la crème of French royalty and aristocracy. Every square centimetre of wall and ceiling space is richly adorned with wood panelling, gilded carvings, frescoes, tapestries and paintings, with furniture including Renaissance originals.

The first château was built here in the early 12th century, but only a single medieval tower survived the reconstruction undertaken by François I (r 1515–47). It was further enlarged and reworked by successive heads of state including Napoléon Bonaparte.

Among the château's many highlights are the **Grands Appartements**, which embrace several outstanding rooms, including the Second Empire salon and Musée Chinois de l'Impératrice Eugénie (Chinese Museum of Empress Eugénie). The **Galerie François 1er** (François I Gallery) is a jewel of Renaissance architecture.The château's stately **gardens** (⏲9am-7pm May-Sep, to 6pm Mar, Apr & Oct, to 5pm Nov-Feb) FREE and courtyards include André Le Nôtre's formal, 17th-century Jardin Français (French Garden), also known as the Grand Parterre, and informal Jardin Anglais (English Garden).

Don't Miss

- Grands Appartements
- Galerie François 1er
- Gardens and courtyards

Practicalities

- ☎01 60 71 50 70
- www.musee-chateau-fontainebleau.fr
- place du Général de Gaulle
- adult/child €12/free, 1st Sun of month Sep-Jun free
- ⏲9.30am-6pm Wed-Mon Apr-Sep, to 5pm Wed-Mon Oct-Mar

SPORTS & ACTIVITIES

Unfolding 500m south of the Château de Fontainebleau and surrounding the town (covering 280 sq km in all), the Forêt de Fontainebleau is one of the Île-de-France's loveliest woods. The many trails here include parts of the **GR1** and **GR11**.

Rock-climbing enthusiasts have long come to the forest's sandstone ridges, rich in cliffs and overhangs, to hone their skills before setting off for the Alps. There are different grades marked by colours, starting with white ones, which are suitable for children, and going up to death-defying black boulders. The website Bleau.info (www.bleau.info) has stacks of information in English on climbing in Fontainebleau. Two gorges worth visiting are the **Gorges d'Apremont**, 7km northwest near Barbizon, and the **Gorges de Franchard**, a few kilometres south of Gorges d'Apremont. Contact **Top Loisirs** (☎01 60 74 08 50; www.toploisirs.fr; guided rock climbing per half-/full day from €40/55, canoe/kayak hire per half-/full day from €25/35; ⏲9am-6pm, hours can vary) about equipment hire and instruction; pick-ups in Fontainebleau are possible by arrangement. The company also offers canoeing and kayaking on the edge of the forest.

Fontainebleau's tourist office sells maps, walking guides and climbing guides.

SLEEPING

★LA DEMEURE DU PARC BOUTIQUE HOTEL €€
(☎01 60 70 20 00; www.ledemeureduparc.fr; 36 rue Paul Séramy; s/d/ste from €132/174/321; ❄📶) A wisteria-draped courtyard garden with chestnut and apple trees is the centrepiece of this charming 27-room hotel. Deluxe-category rooms have their own terraces; ground-floor suites open onto small private gardens. The pick are the suites such as the literary-themed Bibliothèque and travel-themed Voyage (with its own telescope). Its contemporary French restaurant, **La Table du Parc** (5-course vegetarian dinner menu €57, 6-course dinner menu €72, mains €25-44; ⏲12.15-2pm & 7-9.30pm Wed-Sat, 12.15-2pm Sun; 📶), is one of Fontainebleau's finest.

HÔTEL DE LONDRES HOTEL €€
(☎01 64 22 20 21; www.hoteldelondres.com; 1 place du Général de Gaulle; d €138-228; ❄@📶) Classy, cosy and beautifully kept, the 'Hotel London' faces the château. Its 16 rooms are furnished in warm reds and royal blues. Most have air-conditioning and the priciest rooms (such as room 5) have balconies overlooking the palace. Breakfast is €16.

Chartres

Explore

Step off the train in Chartres, 91km southwest of Paris, and the two very different steeples – one Gothic, the other Romanesque – of its glorious 13th-century cathedral loom above. Follow them to check out the cathedral's dazzling blue stained-glass windows and its collection of relics, including the *Sainte Voile* (Holy Veil) said to have been worn by the Virgin Mary when she gave birth to Jesus, which have lured pilgrims since the Middle Ages.

After visiting the town's museums, don't miss a stroll around Chartres' carefully preserved old city. Adjacent to the cathedral, staircases and steep streets lined with half-timbered medieval houses lead downhill to the narrow western channel of the Eure River, romantically spanned by footbridges.

The Best...

Sight Cathédrale Notre Dame

Place to Eat Le Cloître Gourmand (p274)

Place to Drink La Chocolaterie (p274)

Top Tip

Allow 1½ to two hours to walk the signposted *circuit touristique* (tourist circuit), taking in Chartres' key sights. Free town maps from the tourist office also mark the route.

Getting There & Away

Train Frequent SNCF trains link Paris' Gare Montparnasse (€16, 55 to 70 minutes) with Chartres' **train station** (place

TOP SIGHT CATHÉDRALE NOTRE DAME

France's best-preserved medieval cathedral was built in Gothic style during the early 13th century to replace a Romanesque cathedral devastated by fire in 1194. Construction took just 30 years, resulting in a high degree of architectural unity.

Covering 2.6 sq km, the cathedral's 176 stained-glass windows are mostly 13th-century originals. Three over the west entrance, dating from 1150, are renowned for their brilliant 'Chartres blue' tones.

The 105m-high **Clocher Vieux** (Old Bell Tower) is the tallest Romanesque steeple still standing. The 112m-high **Clocher Neuf** (New Bell Tower; adult/child €7.50/free; ⊙9.30am-12.30pm & 2-4.30pm Mon-Sat, 2-4.30pm Sun) justifies the spiralling 350-step climb.

Look out for the **Sainte Voile** (Holy Veil), in Chartres since 876.

Half-hour tours of the 110m-long **crypt** (adult/child €3/2.40; ⊙up to 5 tours daily)– France's largest – are in French with a written English translation. There are also **English-language guided tours** (☎Anne Marie Woods 02 37 21 75 02, Malcolm Miller 02 37 28 15 58; tours €10; ⊙noon & 2.45pm Mon-Sat Apr-Oct, by request Nov-Mar) of the cathedral.

Don't Miss

- Stained glass
- Clocher Neuf
- Sainte Voile
- Crypt

Practicalities

- www.cathedrale-chartres.org
- place de la Cathédrale
- ⊙8.30am-7.30pm daily year-round, also to 10pm Tue, Fri & Sun Jun-Aug

Pierre Semard), some of which stop at Versailles-Chantiers (€13.50, 45 to 60 minutes).

Need to Know

Location 91km southwest of Paris

Tourist Office (☎02 37 18 26 26; www.chartres-tourisme.com; 8-10 rue de la Poissonnerie; ⊙10am-6pm Mon-Sat, to 5.30pm Sun)

SIGHTS

Chartres' beautiful medieval old city is northeast and east of the cathedral. Highlights include the 12th-century **Collégiale St-André** (place St-André), a Romanesque church that's now an exhibition centre; **rue de la Tannerie** and its extension **rue de la Foulerie**, lined with flower gardens, mill-races and the restored remnants of riverside trades: wash houses, tanneries and the like; and **rue des Écuyers**, with many structures dating from around the 16th century.

EATING & DRINKING

LA CHOCOLATERIE PASTRIES €

(www.lachocolaterie-chartres.fr; 2 place du Cygne; dishes €3.80-6.50; ⊙8am-7.30pm Tue-Sat, from 10am Sun & Mon) Soak up local life overlooking the open-air **flower market** (place du Cygne; ⊙8am-7pm Tue, Thu & Sat). This tearoom/patisserie's hot chocolate and macarons (flavoured with orange, apricot, peanut, pineapple and so on) are sublime, as are its sweet home-made crêpes and miniature madeleine cakes.

★LE CLOÎTRE GOURMAND FRENCH €€

(☎02 37 21 49 13; www.lecloitregourmand.fr; 21 Cloître Notre Dame; 2-/3-course menu €27/34; ⊙7.30-9pm Wed-Sat, noon-2pm & 7.30-9pm Sun, closed Jan) Entered from rue du Cardinal Pie, this 17th-century townhouse framed by duck-egg-blue shutters has timber-panelled walls, beamed ceilings and up-close views of the cathedral's north portal. Book at least a week ahead in high season to dine on dishes like smoked pigeon with fir oil, roast salmon with dandelion-root foam and dark-chocolate ganache with hazelnut dust.

LE TRIPOT BISTRO €€

(☎02 37 36 60 11; http://letripot.wixsite.com/chartres; 11 place Jean Moulin; 2-/3-course lunch menus €15/18, 3-course dinner menus €32-44, mains €13-22; ⊙noon-1.45pm & 7.30-9.15pm Wed-Sat, noon-1.45pm Sun) Tucked off the tourist trail and easy to miss even if you do chance down its narrow street, this atmospheric space with low, beamed ceilings is a treat for authentic and adventurous French fare like saddle of rabbit stuffed with snails or grilled turbot in truffled hollandaise sauce. Locals are on to it, so booking ahead is advised.

LE PETIT BISTROT BISTRO €€

(☎02 37 36 44 52; 12 place Billards; mains €16.50-26; ⊙11am-2pm & 7-10pm Tue-Sat) Dishes chalked on the blackboard are all made from the fresh produce at Chartres' iron-canopied market, which the bistro overlooks (terrace seats give you front-row views of the action). Offerings change daily but expect the likes of turbot with black lentils and smoked-garlic aioli or raspberry-marinated veal.

GEORGES GASTRONOMY €€€

(☎02 37 18 15 15; www.bw-grand-monarque.com; 22 place des Épars; 4-/5-/7-course menus €56/78/98; ⊙noon-2pm & 7.30-10pm Tue-Sat) Even if you're not staying at lavish hotel Le Grand Monarque, its refined Georges restaurant is worth seeking out for its Michelin-starred multi-course *menus* and mains such as ginger-marinated salmon with pickled veggies and crustacean bouillon, or blackberry-marinated roast lamb with chestnut purée and green beans. Desserts (confit of grapefruit with Campari gelato, for instance) are inspired.

SLEEPING

LE GRAND MONARQUE HOTEL €€

(☎02 37 18 15 15; www.bw-grand-monarque.com; 22 place des Épars; d/f from €127/157.50; ❄@📶) With teal-blue shutters gracing its 1779 facade, a lovely stained-glass ceiling, and a treasure trove of period furnishings, old B&W photos and knick-knacks, the epicentral Grand Monarque is a historical gem. Some rooms have air-conditioning; staff are charming. A host of hydrotherapy treatments are available at its spa. Its elegant restaurant, Georges, has a Michelin star.

Chartres

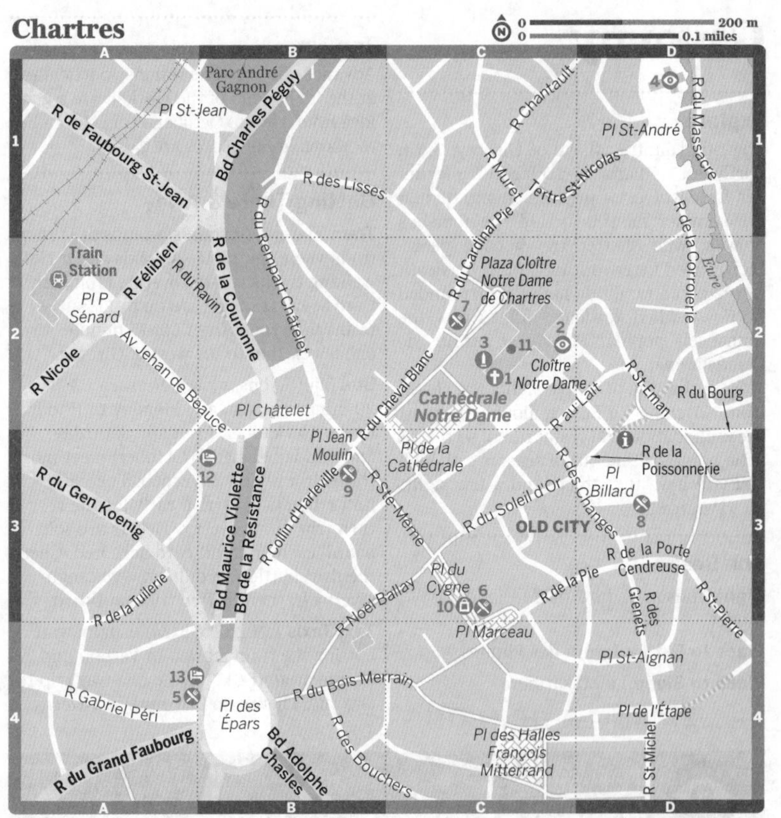

Chartres

Top Sights

1 Cathédrale Notre Dame........................C2

Sights

2 Cathédrale Notre Dame Crypt.............C2
3 Clocher Neuf..C2
4 Collégiale St-André..............................D1

Eating

5 Georges..A4
6 La Chocolaterie.....................................C3
7 Le Cloître Gourmand............................C2
8 Le Petit Bistrot......................................D3
9 Le Tripot..B3

Shopping

10 Flower Market......................................C3

Sports & Activities

11 Cathédrale Notre Dame Tours.............C2

Sleeping

12 Hôtel du Bœuf Couronné.....................B3
13 Le Grand Monarque.............................A4

HÔTEL DU BŒUF COURONNÉ HOTEL €€
(☎02 37 18 06 06; www.leboeufcouronne.com; 15 place Châtelet; d from €92; 🛜) The red-curtained entrance lends a theatrical air to this two-star Logis guesthouse in the centre of everything. Its summertime terrace restaurant has cathedral-view dining and the XV bar mixes great cocktails. Cathedral views also extend from some of its 17 modern rooms.

Giverny

Explore

The tiny country village of Giverny, 74km northwest of Paris, is a place of pilgrimage for devotees of impressionism, though the summer months herald the tour-bus crowds, who shatter the bucolic peace. Monet lived here from 1883 until his death in 1926, in a rambling house – surrounded by flower-filled gardens – that's now the immensely popular Maison et Jardins de Claude Monet.

Note that the principle sights are closed from November to Easter, along with most accommodation and restaurants, so there's little point visiting out of season, although you will have the streets and a few sights all to yourself.

The Best

Sight Maison et Jardins de Claude Monet

Place to Eat Le Jardin des Plumes

Place to Sleep La Musardière

Top Tip

Advance dining reservations, particularly at the higher end of the market, are a good idea from April to October. From November to March, many places are closed.

Getting There & Away

Train The closest train station is at Vernon, from where shuttle buses, taxis and cycle/walking tracks run to Giverny. From Paris' Gare St-Lazare there are up to 15 daily trains to Vernon (from €9, 45 minutes to one hour), 7km to the west of Giverny.

Bus Shuttle buses (single/return €5/10, 20 minutes, four daily Monday to Friday Easter to October, five daily Saturday and Sunday Easter to October) meet most trains from Paris at Vernon. There are limited seats, so arrive early for the return trip from Giverny. Tickets are sold on board, cash or credit card accepted. Check the live shuttle schedule on www.sngo-giverny.fr; there is free wi-fi on board.

Taxi Taxis (☎02 32 51 10 24) usually wait outside the train station in Vernon and charge around €15 for the one-way trip to Giverny. There's no taxi rank in Giverny,

TOP SIGHT
MAISON ET JARDINS DE CLAUDE MONET

Monet's home for the last 43 years of his life is now a delightful house-museum. His pastel-pink house and Water Lily studio stand on the periphery of the **Clos Normand**, with its symmetrically laid-out gardens bursting with flowers. Monet bought the **Jardin d'Eau** (Water Garden) in 1895 and set about creating his trademark lily pond, as well as the famous **Japanese bridge** (since rebuilt).

The charmingly preserved house and beautiful bloom-filled gardens (rather than Monet's works) are the draws here. Draped with purple wisteria, the Japanese bridge blends into the asymmetrical foreground and background, creating the intimate atmosphere for which the 'painter of light' was renowned.

Seasons have an enormous effect on Giverny. From early to late spring, daffodils, tulips, wisteria and irises appear, followed by poppies and lilies. By June, nasturtiums, roses and sweet peas are in flower. Around September, there are dahlias, sunflowers and hollyhocks.

Combined tickets with Paris' Musée Marmottan Monet (p86) cost €20.50/12 per adult/child, and combined adult tickets with Paris' Musée de l'Orangerie (p118) cost €18.50.

Don't Miss

- Clos Normand
- Jardin d'Eau

Practicalities

- ☎02 32 51 28 21
- www.fondation-monet.com
- 84 rue Claude Monet
- adult/child €9.50/5.50, incl Musée des Impressionnismes Giverny €17/9
- ⌚9.30am-6pm Easter-Oct

however, so you'll need to phone for one for the return trip to Vernon. It is preferable to take the shuttle bus back to Vernon.

Bicycle Rent bikes (cash only) at the **Café L'Arrivée de Giverny** (02 32 21 16 01; 1-3 place de la Gare, Vernon; per day €14; 8am-11pm), opposite the Vernon train station; Giverny is 5km from here along a direct (and flat) signposted cycle/walking track.

Need to Know

Location 74km northwest of Paris

Tourist Office (02 32 64 45 01; www.normandie-giverny.fr; 80 rue Claude Monet; 10am-5.45pm Easter-Oct)

SIGHTS

MUSÉE DES IMPRESSIONNISMES GIVERNY — GALLERY

(02 32 51 94 65; www.mdig.fr; 99 rue Claude Monet; adult/child €7.50/5, incl Maison et Jardins de Claude Monet €17/9; 10am-6pm Easter-Oct) About 100m northwest of the Maison et Jardins de Claude Monet is the Giverny Museum of Impressionisms. It was set up in partnership with the Musée d'Orsay, among other institutions, covers all aspects of impressionism and related movements in its permanent collection and temporary exhibitions. Lectures, readings, concerts and documentaries also take place regularly. The audioguide is €4. Admission on the first Sunday of the month is free.

L'ÉGLISE STE-RADEGONDE — CHURCH

Dedicated to St Radegund, this church was originally built in the 11th and 12th centuries, expanded in the 15th century and then greatly restored between 2008 and 2010. It is most noteworthy for being the **resting place of Claude Monet**, whose tomb can be found to your right as you follow the path around the east side of the church, before you reach the graveyard proper.

EATING

LA CAPUCINE GIVERNY — CAFE €

(02 32 51 76 67; 80 rue Claude Monet; mains €5-13; 9.30am-6pm Easter-Oct) This colourful cafe-restaurant at the heart of Giverny is an excellent pit stop for a bite to eat or a beer, either inside or in the garden. The menu runs to reasonably simple fare: sandwiches, quiches, soups and salads, with breakfasts served between 9am and 11am. There's live music between 7pm and 10pm on Saturday from May to September.

★LE JARDIN DES PLUMES — MODERN FRENCH €€€

(02 32 54 26 35; www.jardindesplumes.fr; 1 rue du Milieu; 3-/5-course menus €48/78, tasting menus €98, mains €36-40; 12.15-1.30pm & 7.30-9pm Wed-Sun, hotel closed Mon & Tue Nov-Mar; P) This gorgeous sky-blue-trimmed property's airy white dining room is a handsome stage for chef Eric Guerin's exquisite and inventive Michelin-starred cuisine, which justifies the trip from Paris alone.

There are also four rooms (€195 to €215) and four suites (€295 to €370), combining vintage and contemporary furnishings. It's less than 10 minutes' walk to the Maison et Jardins de Claude Monet.

SLEEPING

LA MUSARDIÈRE — HOTEL €€

(02 32 21 03 18; www.lamusardiere.fr; 123 rue Claude Monet; d €85-99, f €149, 3-course menus €26-36; hotel Feb–mid-Dec, restaurant noon-10pm Apr-Oct; P) This two-star 10-room hotel dating back to 1880 is set amid a lovely garden less than 100m northeast of the Maison et Jardins de Claude Monet. Breakfast costs €11 (or €13 in-room) and savouring a crêpe in the hotel restaurant is a genuine treat. Family rooms sleep up to four people.

LA PLUIE DE ROSES — B&B €€

(02 32 51 10 67; www.givernylapluiederoses.fr; 14 rue Claude Monet; s/d from €120/130; P) You'll be won over by this adorable private home cocooned in a dreamy, peaceful garden. Inside, the three rooms (two of which can accommodate families) are so comfy it can be hard to wake up, but the superb breakfast on a verandah awash with sunlight is always further motivation to cast off the duvet. Payment is by cash only.

LE CLOS FLEURI — B&B €€

(02 32 21 36 51; www.giverny-leclosfleuri.fr; 5 rue de la Dîme; s/d €105/110; Apr-Oct; P) Big rooms with king-size beds and exposed wood beams overlook the hedged gardens of this delightful B&B within strolling distance of the Maison et Jardins de Claude Monet. Cash only.

Sleeping

Paris has plenty of accommodation, spanning all budgets. However, it is often fully booked well in advance, particularly during peak times (April to October, as well as public and school holidays). Reservations are essential at these times, but are also recommended year-round.

While accommodation outside of central Paris might be marginally cheaper, it is invariably a false economy when travel time and costs are considered. Stay in one of Paris' *arrondissements* to immerse yourself in Parisian life.

Hotels

Hotels in Paris are inspected by government authorities and classified into six categories, from no stars to five stars. The vast majority are two- and three-star hotels, which are generally well equipped. All hotels must display their rates, including TVA (*taxe sur la valeur ajoutée;* value-added tax), though you'll often get *much* cheaper prices online, especially on the hotels' own websites, which invariably offer the best deals.

Parisian hotel rooms tend to be small by international standards. Families will probably need connecting rooms, but if children are too young to stay in their own room, it's possible to make do with triples, quads or suites in some places.

Cheaper hotels may not have lifts/elevators and/or air-conditioning. Virtually all accept credit cards.

Breakfast is rarely included in hotel rates; heading to a cafe often works out to be better value (and more atmospheric).

Hostels

Paris is awash with hostels, and standards are consistently improving. A wave of state-of-the-art hostels includes the design-savvy 950-bed 'megahostel' by leading hostel chain Generator near Canal St-Martin, 10e and, close by, two by the switched-on St Christopher's group.

Some of the more traditional (ie institutional) hostels have daytime lock-outs and curfews; some have a maximum three-night stay. Places that have upper age limits tend not to enforce them except at the busiest of times. Only the official *auberges de jeunesse* (youth hostels) require guests to present Hostelling International (HI) cards or their equivalent.

Not all hostels have self-catering kitchens, but rates generally include a basic breakfast.

B&Bs & Homestays

Bed-and-breakfast (B&B) accommodation (*chambres d'hôte* in French) offers an immersive way to experience the city. Paris' tourist office maintains a list of B&Bs; visit https://en.parisinfo.com/where-to-sleep-in-paris.

Apartments

Families – and anyone wanting to self-cater – should consider renting a short-stay apartment. Paris has a number of excellent *résidences de tourisme* (serviced apartments, aka 'aparthotels'), such as the international chain Citadines (www.citadines.com).

In addition to the usual home-sharing websites, rental agencies also list furnished residential apartments for stays of a few days to several months. Apartments often include facilities such as wi-fi and washing machines, and can be good value. Beware of direct-rental scams (above all, never send money via an untraceable money transfer).

Lonely Planet's Top Choices

L'Hôtel (p291) The stuff of romance, Parisian myths and urban legends.

Hôtel Ritz Paris (p282) Synonymous with Parisian style.

Generator Hostel (p283) Hang-outs include roof terrace, cafe-bar, and basement club styled like a Paris metro station.

Hôtel Particulier Montmartre (p285) Montmartre hideaway with an enchanting garden.

Hôtel Providence (p284) Rooms at this luxurious property come with bespoke cocktail bars.

Familia Hôtel (p289) Sepia murals and flower-bedecked balconies in the Latin Quarter.

Edgar (p282) A former convent now contains 13 rooms by different artists and designers.

Best by Budget

€

Hôtel du Dragon (p290) Home-made jam is on the breakfast menu at this heartwarming spot.

Hôtel Diana (p289) Contemporary meets retro in the Latin Quarter.

Cosmos Hôtel (p286) Cheap, brilliant value and footsteps from the nightlife of the 11e's rue JPT.

Hôtel du Nord – Le Pari Vélo (p283) Bric-a-brac charm and bikes on loan.

Mama Shelter (p288) Philippe Starck–designed property with a cool in-house pizzeria.

Hôtel Port Royal (p289) Spotless vintage-furnished hotel with a peaceful courtyard garden.

€€

Hôtel Paris Bastille Boutet (p288) One-time chocolate factory with beautiful art deco tiling and a basement pool.

Hoxton (p282) Paris' outpost of the hot-shot design group occupies an 18th-century residence in the hip Sentier neighbourhood.

€€€

Les Bains (p287) Nineteenth-century thermal baths turned nightclub turned rockstar-hot lifestyle hotel.

Hôtel Crayon (p282) Line drawings, retro furnishings and coloured-glass shower doors.

Hôtel du Jeu de Paume (p289) Romantic haven on the serene Île St-Louis.

Hôtel Molitor (p281) Stunningly restored art deco swimming pool with gallery-style poolside rooms.

Best Design Hotels

Maison Bréguet (p288) Local artists, writers and musicians worked on this 2018-opened hotel inside a former factory.

Hôtel Georgette (p286) Rooms represent 20th-century art movements displayed at the nearby Centre Pompidou.

Hôtel l'Antoine (p288) Dazzling Christian Lacroix designer creation in Bastille.

Le Pigalle (p284) Channels the namesake neighbourhood's spirit with vinyl and vintage turntables in some rooms.

Hôtel Henriette (p292) Bohemian haven in the creative 13e.

Off Paris Seine (p292) Paris' first floating hotel is moored on the Seine.

NEED TO KNOW

Prices

The following price ranges refer to a double room with en-suite bathroom in high season (breakfast not included).

€ less than €130

€€ €130–€250

€€€ more than €250

Taxe de Séjour

The city levies an accommodation *taxe de séjour* (tourist tax) per person per night:

- Palaces (and similar): €4.40
- 5 stars: €3.30
- 4 stars: €2.53
- 3 stars: €1.65
- 2 stars: €0.99
- 1 star & B&Bs: €0.88
- Unrated/unclassified: €0.88
- 3- to 5-star campgrounds: €0.66
- 1- and 2-star campgrounds and marinas: €0.22

Internet Access

Wi-fi (pronounced '*wee-fee*' in French) is virtually always free of charge at hotels and hostels. You may find that in some hotels, especially older ones, the higher the floor, the less reliable the wi-fi connection.

Where to Stay

NEIGHBOURHOOD	FOR	AGAINST
Eiffel Tower & Western Paris	Close to Paris' iconic tower and museums. Upmarket area with quiet residential streets.	Short on budget and midrange accommodation. Limited nightlife.
Champs-Élysées & Grands Boulevards	Luxury hotels, famous boutiques and department stores, gastronomic restaurants, great nightlife.	Some areas extremely pricey. Nightlife hot spots can be noisy.
Louvre & Les Halles	Epicentral location, excellent transport links, major museums, shopping galore.	Not many bargains. Noise can be an issue in some areas.
Montmartre & Northern Paris	Village atmosphere and some lively multicultural areas. Many places have views across Paris.	Hilly streets; further out than some areas; some parts very touristy. The red-light district around Pigalle, although well lit and safe, won't appeal to all travellers.
Le Marais, Ménilmontant & Belleville	Buzzing nightlife, hip shopping, fantastic eating options in all price ranges. Excellent museums. Lively gay and lesbian scene. Busier on Sundays than many areas. Very central.	Can be noisy in areas where bars and clubs are concentrated.
Bastille & Eastern Paris	Few tourists, allowing you to see the 'real' Paris up close. Excellent markets, loads of nightlife.	Some areas slightly out of the way.
The Islands	As geographically central as it gets. Accommodation centred on the peaceful, romantic Île St-Louis.	No metro station on the Île St-Louis. Limited self-catering shops, minimal nightlife.
Latin Quarter	Energetic student area, stacks of eating and drinking options, late-opening bookshops.	Popularity with students and visiting academics makes rooms hardest to find during conferences and seminars from March to June and in October.
St-Germain & Les Invalides	Stylish, central location, superb shopping, sophisticated dining, proximity to the Jardin du Luxembourg.	Budget accommodation is in seriously short supply.
Montparnasse & Southern Paris	Good value, few tourists, excellent links to both major airports.	Some areas out of the way and/or not well served by metro.

Eiffel Tower & Western Paris

HÔTEL DU BOIS HOTEL €€€

Map p366 (01 45 00 31 96; www.hoteldubois.com; 11 rue du Dôme, 16e; d €290-460; ; MCharles de Gaulle–Étoile) In an area with few midrange hotels, this fresh, homey and effortlessly stylish address charms. The pretty reception doubles as a lounge, with an eye-catching collection of terracotta pots. The 39 rooms mix soft hues with Pierre Frey fabrics and well-thought-out touches. Although some of the rooms are quite small, online deals often bring rates as low as €100.

HÔTEL MOLITOR HISTORIC HOTEL €€€

Map p366 (01 56 07 08 50; www.mltr.fr; 13 rue Nungesser et Coli, 16e; d/ste from €300/600; ; MMichel Ange Molitor) Famed as Paris' swishest swimming pool in the 1930s (where the bikini made its first appearance, no less) and a hot spot for graffiti art in the 1990s, the Molitor is one seriously legendary address. The art deco complex, built in 1929 and abandoned from 1989, has been restored to stunning effect.

All 124 hotel rooms are arranged gallery-style in a U shape overlooking the outdoor pool (heated year-round). The rooftop cocktail bar, brasserie, and original changing cabins transformed into contemporary artworks sign off the dramatic ensemble. A smaller indoor 'winter' pool is also on the premises. Prices can drop by half in low season.

Champs-Élysées & Grands Boulevards

HÔTEL CHOPIN HISTORIC HOTEL €

Map p370 (01 47 70 58 10; www.hotelchopin.fr; 46 passage Jouffroy, 9e; d €90-160; ; MGrands Boulevards) Dating from 1846, the 36-room Chopin is inside one of Paris' most delightful 19th-century *passages couverts* (covered shopping arcades). The rooms don't have much in the way of personality (and the cheaper rooms are small and dark), but the belle époque location is beautiful.

HÔTEL JOYCE DESIGN HOTEL €€

Map p370 (01 55 07 00 01; www.astotel.com; 29 rue la Bruyère, 9e; d €200-235; ; MSt-Georges) Located in a lovely residential area between Montmartre and Opéra, this place has all the modern design touches (iPod docks, individually styled rooms, a skylit breakfast room fitted out with old Range Rover seats) and makes some ecofriendly claims – it relies on 50% renewable energy and uses organic products.

★HIDDEN HOTEL BOUTIQUE HOTEL €€€

Map p368 (01 40 55 03 57; www.hidden-hotel.com; 28 rue de l'Arc de Triomphe, 17e; d €419-519; ; MCharles de Gaulle–Étoile) The Hidden is one of the Champs-Élysées' best secrets. It's serene, stylish, reasonably spacious, and it even sports green credentials: the earth-coloured tones are the result of natural pigments (no paint), and all rooms feature handmade wooden furniture, stone basins and linen curtains surrounding the beds. The queen-size 'Emotion' rooms are among the most popular.

★HÔTEL DE CRILLON HISTORIC HOTEL €€€

Map p368 (01 44 71 15 00; www.rosewoodhotels.com; 10 place de la Concorde, 8e; d/ste from €970/1750; ; MConcorde) Built in 1758 by Louis XV–commissioned architect Jacques-Ange Gabriel and transformed into a hotel in 1909, this palatial address at the foot of the Champs-Élysées opposite the Jardin des Tuileries reopened in 2017 after four years of renovations. Its original splendour has been retained throughout its sumptuous rooms and suites, three restaurants and opulent bar.

★HÔTEL EKTA DESIGN HOTEL €€€

Map p368 (01 53 76 09 05; www.hotelekta.com; 52 rue Galilée, 8e; d €325-525; ; MGeorge V) Psychedelic zebra stripes give this 1970s-style fashionista an unusually playful personality, especially in a neighbourhood where sleeping choices tend more towards the classical. Rooms are smallish but modern – smart TVs, Nespresso coffee makers and phone chargers are some of the amenities available. Online rates can drop to €100 in low season, a steal for a room off the Champs-Élysées.

Louvre & Les Halles

HÔTEL TIQUETONNE HOTEL €

Map p376 (01 42 36 94 58; www.hoteltiquetonne.fr; 6 rue Tiquetonne, 2e; d €80, without shower €65; ; MÉtienne Marcel) What heart-warmingly good value this 45-room cheapie is. This serious, well-tended address has been in the hotel biz since the 1900s and is much loved by a loyal clientele of all ages. Rooms range across seven floors, are spick and span, and sport an inoffensive mix of vintage decor – roughly 1930s to 1980s, with brand-new bathrooms and parquet flooring in recently renovated rooms.

Ask for a room in the rooftops with a view of the Sacré-Cœur (701, 702 or 703) or Eiffel Tower (704 and 705)! Shared shower *jetons* (tokens) cost €5; ask at reception.

HÔTEL VIVIENNE HOTEL €

Map p372 (01 42 33 13 26; www.hotel-vivienne.com; 40 rue Vivienne, 2e; d €100-150, tr & q €200; ; M Grands Boulevards) This refurbished two-star hotel is amazingly good value for Paris. While the 45 rooms are not huge, they have all the mod cons; some even boast little balconies. Family rooms accommodate up to two children on a sofa bed. Not all rooms have air-con.

★EDGAR BOUTIQUE HOTEL €€

Map p376 (01 40 41 05 19; www.edgarparis.com; 31 rue d'Alexandrie, 2e; d €235-275; ; M Strasbourg St-Denis) Thirteen playful rooms, each decorated by a different team of artists or designers, await the lucky few who secure a reservation at this former convent/seamstress workshop. 'Milagros' conjures up all the magic of the Far West, while 'Dream' echoes the rich imagination of childhood with surrealist installations. Breakfast is served in the popular downstairs restaurant, and the hidden tree-shaded square is a fabulous location.

★HOXTON DESIGN HOTEL €€

Map p376 (01 85 65 75 00; www.thehoxton.com; 30-32 rue du Sentier, 2e; d €239-549; ; M Bonne Nouvelle) One of the hottest hotel openings of 2017, the Parisian outpost of designer hotel The Hoxton occupies a grand 18th-century former residence. Its 172 striking rooms come in four sizes: Shoebox (from 13 sq metre), Cosy (from 17 sq metre), Roomy (from 21 sq metre) and Biggy (from 32 sq metre). All have intricate cornicing and reclaimed oak floors.

HÔTEL THÉRÈSE HOTEL €€

Map p372 (01 42 96 10 01; www.hoteltherese.com; 5-7 rue Thérèse, 1er; s & d €220-390; ; M Pyramides) From the same people who brought you the Left Bank's lovely Hotel Verneuil, the Thérèse is ideal for those with a fetish for Japanese food – this chic address is steps from rue Ste-Anne and Japantown. Rooms are individually decorated, classical yet eclectic in design.

HÔTEL DES GRANDS BOULEVARDS DESIGN HOTEL €€

Map p376 (01 85 73 33 33; www.grandsboulevardshotel.com; 17 bd Poissonnière, 2e; r from €240; ; M Grands Boulevards) The 50 rooms at this 2018-opened hotel play with the building's Revolution-era roots, and there's a certain aristocracy-repurposes-peasant aesthetic in the design – from rustic curtained headboards to vintage wooden stools and natural organic soaps in the bathroom. Non-guests should drop by Giovanni Passerini's inner courtyard restaurant, or, even better, for cocktails at the rooftop bar.

★HÔTEL CRAYON BOUTIQUE HOTEL €€€

Map p376 (01 42 36 54 19; www.hotelcrayon.com; 25 rue du Bouloi, 1er; s/d €311/347; ; M Les Halles, Louvre-Rivoli) Line drawings by French artist Julie Gauthron bedeck walls and doors at this creative boutique hotel. *Le crayon* (the pencil) is the theme, with 26 rooms sporting a different shade of each floor's chosen colour – we love the coloured-glass shower doors, and the books on the bedside table guests can swap and take home. Online deals often slash rates by up to 50%.

★HÔTEL RITZ PARIS HISTORIC HOTEL €€€

Map p372 (01 43 16 30 30; www.ritzparis.com; 15 place Vendôme, 1er; d from €1000, ste from €1900; ; M Opéra) The Ritz reopened in all its glory in mid-2016 after a four-year, €400-million head-to-toe renovation that painstakingly restored its original features while incorporating 21st-century technology. It's once again Paris' most rarefied address, with a manicured French formal garden and a world-first Chanel spa (Coco Chanel lived here). Also reinvigorated are its prestigious Ritz Escoffier cookery school and legendary Bar Hemingway (p127).

LE PRADEY DESIGN HOTEL €€€

Map p372 (01 42 60 31 70; www.lepradey.com; 5 rue St-Roch, 1er; d €389-429; ; M Tuileries) Enviably secreted behind the Louvre and Jardin des Tuileries on boutique-smart rue St-Honoré, this exclusive address is the last word in luxury hotel design. Guests linger over glossy art books in the understatedly chic mezzanine lounge – if they can drag themselves away from whichever individually themed suite they are staying in.

Exuberant Cabaret evokes the theatrical glamour of the Moulin Rouge with its frilly skirt bedspread, deep red walls and heart-shaped doorframe; Opéra, elegantly dressed in pretty pinks and greys, treats guests to a magical night at the ballet.

LA CLEF LOUVRE APARTMENT €€€

Map p372 (01 55 35 28 00; www.the-ascott.com/france/paris/la-clef-louvre-paris/index; 8 rue de Richelieu, 1er; studio/1-bedroom apt from €740/883; ; M Palais Royal–Musée du Louvre) The contemporary charm of this *residence* (serviced-apartment hotel) extends from the original sculptures and framed artworks in the lobby to the self-contained apartments. All have nifty compact kitchens fitted with fridges, hotplates, fine bone china, Nespresso machines and all-in-one washing machine/dryers; the pick are the corner apartments (ending with '3') with curvilinear windows overlooking the street. Service is outstanding.

Montmartre & Northern Paris

★GENERATOR HOSTEL HOSTEL €

Map p382 (01 70 98 84 00; www.generatorhostels.com; 9-11 place du Colonel Fabien, 10e; dm/d from €33/92; @; M Colonel Fabien) From the 9th-floor rooftop bar overlooking Sacré-Cœur and the stylish ground-floor cafe-restaurant to the vaulted basement bar-club styled like a Paris metro station, and supercool bathrooms with 'I love you' tiling, this ultra-contemporary hostel near Canal St-Martin is sharp. Dorms have USB sockets and free lockers, and the best doubles have fabulous terraces with views. Women-only dorms are available.

HÔTEL DU NORD – LE PARI VÉLO HOTEL €

Map p382 (01 42 01 66 00; www.hoteldunord-leparivelo.com; 47 rue Albert Thomas, 10e; s/d €73/86; ; M Jacques Bonsergent) Offering fantastic value given its prized location near place de la République, this perennial favourite has 23 rooms decorated with flea-market antiques and free bikes for guests to borrow to ride around town. Served in a vaulted stone cellar, breakfast (€8) includes locally baked bread and pastries along with home-made jams.

HÔTEL ELDORADO HOTEL €

Map p385 (01 45 22 35 21; www.eldoradohotel.fr; 18 rue des Dames, 17e; d from €100, with shared bathroom from €65; ; M Place de Clichy) Bohemian Eldorado is a welcoming, reasonably well-run hotel with 33 colourfully decorated rooms above the **Bistro des Dames** (01 45 22 13 42; mains €16-24; noon-2.30pm & 7-11pm), with a private garden. Rooms facing the back can be quite noisy as they look out onto the restaurant terrace, which stays open until 2am – earplugs may be a good idea. Cheaper-category rooms have washbasins only. Breakfast costs €12.

DISTRICT RÉPUBLIQUE HÔTEL DESIGN HOTEL €

Map p382 (01 42 08 20 09; www.hoteldistrictrepublique.com; 4 rue Lucien Sampaix, 10e; s/d from €99/108; ; M Jacques Bonsergent) Superb-value rates and a clean modern design make the District République – on a quiet backstreet behind place de la République – a top spot to stay in the trendsetting 10e. Its 33 rooms are comfortable (two are equipped for wheelchairs) and come with tea- and coffee-making facilities. Triples and superior doubles with fold-out sofa beds make it a good family choice.

ST CHRISTOPHER'S GARE DU NORD HOSTEL €

Map p382 (01 70 08 52 22; www.st-christophers.co.uk/paris-hostels; 5 rue de Dunkerque, 10e; dm/s/d from €29/87/107; @; M Gare du Nord) Steps from Gare du Nord, St Christopher's is a modern backpacker hostel with six light-filled floors and 580 beds. Dorms (including women-only dorms) sleep four to 10 but beds are pricey unless you reserve months in advance. Facilities include a laundry and Belushi's bar and restaurant with live music. No kitchen; breakfast included.

WOODSTOCK HOSTEL HOSTEL €

Map p378 (01 48 78 87 76; www.woodstock.fr; 48 rue Rodier, 9e; dm/tw from €30/70; @; M Anvers) Splashed with bright colours and murals, this well-kept hostel is just downhill from place Pigalle on a quiet street. Both twin rooms and dorms (sleeping three to 10, with women-only dorms available) are kitted out with bunk beds and a washbasin; each floor shares a spotless shower and toilet. Rates include breakfast; there's a kitchen, a bar and a delightful interior courtyard too. There's no curfew, but rooms are closed for cleaning each day between 11am and 3pm.

★HÔTEL PROVIDENCE BOUTIQUE HOTEL €€

Map p382 (☎01 46 34 34 04; www.hotelprovidenceparis.com; 90 rue René Boulanger, 10e; d from €163; ❄@📶; MStrasbourg-St-Denis) This luxurious hideaway, in a 19th-century townhouse in the increasingly trendy 10e, is exquisite. Its 18 rooms (seven with balconies) have rich House of Hackney velvet wallpaper and vintage flea-market finds; the smallest aren't nearly as 'Mini' (by Paris standards) as the name implies. Bespoke cocktail bars in each room come complete with suggested recipes and ingredients.

The downstairs bar-bistro, with a fireplace and delightful summertime pavement terrace, doubles as reception.

★LE PIGALLE DESIGN HOTEL €€

Map p378 (☎01 48 78 37 14; www.lepigalle.paris; 9 rue Frochot, 9e; d €120-280; ❄@📶; MPigalle) This offbeat lifestyle hotel's edgy design reflects the neighbourhood's legendary nightlife, while carefully thought-out details like a postcard taped on the bathroom wall and a key ring jangling with Paris souvenirs add personalised touches to the 40 stylish rooms. Each has an iPad loaded with music, and larger rooms have vintage turntables with an eclectic vinyl collection.

The ground-floor bar and restaurant is a happening space, with DJs spinning several nights a week. A restored jukebox with contemporary tunes is set in the basement music room. Kudos for the good-value 'Pigalle 12' rooms – actually twins with bunk beds (some are connecting, making them ideal for small groups).

HÔTEL JOSÉPHINE BOUTIQUE HOTEL €€

Map p378 (☎01 55 31 90 75; www.hotel-josephine.com; 67 rue Blanche, 9e; s/d from €108/142; ❄📶; MBlanche) Life's a cabaret at this novel, four-star boutique address in Pigalle. Named after 1920s cabaret star Josephine Baker, the hotel has 41 rooms with richly patterned wallpapers broken up by solid colours and 1930s period furniture and light fittings. Black-and-white cabaret photos decorate walls, and downstairs in the sociable library-lounge there's an honesty bar, free coffee and board games.

HÔTEL PARADIS BOUTIQUE HOTEL €€

Map p382 (☎01 45 23 08 22; www.hotelparadisparis.com; 41 rue des Petites Écuries, 10e; s/d €190/210; ❄@📶; MPoissonnière) Soft cream canapés and design books grace the stylish ground-floor lounge at this three-star hotel, and stylishly understated rooms mix warm colours and elegant patterned wallpapers. Breakfast (€12) includes home-made yoghurt and croissants baked on site. It's on a quiet street, with plenty of gourmet bistros nearby.

MÔM'ART BOUTIQUE HOTEL €€

Map p378 (☎01 82 52 26 26; www.hotelmomart.com; 42 rue d'Orsel, 18e; d €180-230, ste €350; ❄📶; MAnvers) Run by the same family since 1971 but stunningly made over (and renamed) in 2018, this four-star Montmartre hotel has just 25 rooms (including one suite), giving it a high level of intimacy. Generously sized rooms come in four different styles, including 'Artistes' rooms with modern-art motifs. There's an interior courtyard, a fitness area, a spa, a destination restaurant and a craft cocktail bar.

R KIPLING HOTEL BOUTIQUE HOTEL €€

Map p378 (☎01 55 31 91 99; www.kipling-hotel.com; 65 rue Blanche, 9e; s/d from €182/199; ❄📶; MBlanche) Themed around Nobel Prize–winning writer Rudyard Kipling, this spellbinding hotel evokes his famous works like *The Jungle Book* in its beautifully wallpapered guest lounge and library, and its 40 rooms done out in pastel blues and greens and whimsical prints such as fluttering butterflies. Several higher-category rooms have balconies overlooking south Pigalle's rooftops.

GRAND AMOUR HÔTEL DESIGN HOTEL €€

Map p382 (☎01 44 16 03 10; www.hotelamourparis.fr; 18 rue de la Fidélité, 10e; s/d from €145/195; 📶; MGare de l'Est) Younger sister to Pigalle's Hôtel Amour, this lifestyle hotel mixes vintage furniture from the flea market with phallic-symbol carpets and the striking B&W nude photography of graffiti artist André Saraiva. The result is an edgy hideaway for lovers in one of Paris' most up-and-coming neighbourhoods. Breakfast is served in the hotel **bistro** (☎01 44 16 03 30; mains €16-30, weekend brunch €21; ⏲8am-12.30am; 📶✍), a trendy drinking and dining address in itself.

JOKE HÔTEL DESIGN HOTEL €€

Map p378 (☎01 40 40 71 71; www.astotel.com/hotel; 69 rue Blanche, 9e; s/d from €136/151; ❄@📶; MBlanche) No joke. This fabulous childhood-themed hotel is a serious contender for Paris' best-value, most fun address, where you can play 'scrabble' or spin the wheel of fortune above your bed each night, hunt for coins stuck in the lobby floor, or check out the toys and board games. Rates include breakfast and all-day complimentary (non-alcoholic) drinks, cakes and fruit.

GRAND HÔTEL PIGALLE DESIGN HOTEL €€

Map p378 (☎01 85 73 12 00; www.grandpigalle.com; 29 rue Victor Massé, 9e; d from €186; ❄@📶; MPigalle) Created by the pioneering Experimental group, which has shaken up Paris' contemporary cocktail scene, this outrageously hip address in south Pigalle (aka 'SoPi') is a sophisticated lifestyle hotel with cocktail 'minibars' in its 37 beautifully crafted rooms, and a fabulous restaurant-wine bar with a menu from lauded Italian chef Giovanni Passerini.

HÔTEL BASSS BOUTIQUE HOTEL €€

Map p378 (☎01 42 51 50 00; www.hotel-basss.com; 57 rue des Abbesses, 18e; s/d from €107/134; ❄@📶; MAbbesses) In the heart of Montmartre on rue Abbesses, an original gold-stone doorway marks the entrance to this contemporary hotel inspired by American graphic designer Saul Bass. Soft greys and blues dress its 36 modern rooms, complete with funky chipboard desks and kettle-clad welcome trays. The complimentary coffee and cakes in the lounge-lobby are a welcome touch. Baby cots are available.

TERRASS HÔTEL HOTEL €€

Map p378 (☎01 46 06 72 85; www.terrass-hotel.com; 12-14 rue Joseph de Maistre,18e; d/ste from €189/285; ❄📶; MBlanche) Enjoy one of the best views of Paris from the rooftop bar of this 1911-built hotel, which received a designer facelift just over a century later. Darkened corridors lead to 92 rooms and suites with striking black and red decor. The vast open-plan lobby has a library-lounge and photo booth; other amenities include a spa and running/cycling cabins.

Honey collected from the beehive on the roof is served at breakfast (€25).

LE CITIZEN HOTEL BOUTIQUE HOTEL €€

Map p382 (☎01 83 62 55 50; www.lecitizenhotel.com; 96 quai de Jemmapes, 10e; d/ste from €150/200; @📶; MGare de l'Est, Jacques Bonsergent) Right on the banks of Canal St-Martin, this 12-room boutique hotel has a warm, minimalist design and a long list of extras including iPads, filtered water and a courtesy tray with a kettle, tea and coffee. Unusually for Paris, rates also include breakfast. The two-bedroom suite (from €280) is a great family choice.

LE ROBINET D'OR BOUTIQUE HOTEL €€

Map p382 (☎01 44 65 14 50; www.lerobinetdor.com; 17 rue Robert Blache, 10e; d/ste from €200/260; ❄@📶; MChâteau Landon) Within a former tap factory (hence the name 'The Golden Tap'), this boutique hotel's parquet floors and tasteful flea-market furnishings mix well with the modern amenities, English Liberty prints and inviting rain showers. Family suites (from €300) are available, and breakfast (hot/cold €15/12) is served in the busy brasserie with a skylit atrium and green vegetal wall.

★HÔTEL PARTICULIER MONTMARTRE BOUTIQUE HOTEL €€€

Map p378 (☎01 53 41 81 40; www.hotel-particulier-montmartre.com; Pavillon D, 23 av Junot, 18e; ste €390-590; ❄📶; MLamarck–Caulaincourt) Hidden down a stone-paved alley behind a high wall, this mansion is one of the city's most magical addresses. Its five sweeping designer suites are decorated with retro flea-market finds, but it's the garden, designed by landscape architect Louis Benech, and fashionable cocktail bar (p148) that really stun. Ring the buzzer outside the unmarked black-gated entrance at No 23.

L'HOTEL DU COLLECTIONNEUR ARC DE TRIOMPHE HOTEL €€€

Map p385 (☎01 58 36 67 00; www.hotelducollectionneur.com; 51-57 rue de Courcelles, 8e; d/ste from €320/600; ❄@📶; MCourcelles) Inspired by the trans-Atlantic ocean liners of the 1930s, this grandly proportioned art-deco property near the Arc de Triomphe has an eye-popping lobby with massive chandeliers and chequerboard marble tiles, which opens onto an 800-sq-metre garden. Lavishly appointed rooms (several with balconies) have marble bathrooms and come with a smartphone with free calls and unlimited wi-fi.

MAISON SOUQUET LUXURY HOTEL €€€

Map p378 (☎01 48 78 55 55; www.maisonsouquet.com; 10 rue de Bruxelles, 9e; d/ste from €375/675; ❄📶🏊; MBlanche) During belle époque, this mansion sheltered a discreet brothel run by Madame Souquet, which provided the inspiration for its 2015 conversion by French interior designer Jacques Garcia to a five-star hotel. Its 20 ravishing rooms, suites and apartments, with richly patterned wallpapers, silks and embroideries, are named for courtesans, while its lounge areas reflect the bordello's former salons.

Along with a glass-roofed winter garden there's a wood-panelled bar and a library, with a small swimming pool and *hammam* in the basement. Look for the art-nouveau red lanterns out front.

Le Marais, Ménilmontant & Belleville

★LES PIAULES HOSTEL €

Map p390 (☎01 43 55 09 97; www.lespiaules.com; 59 bd de Belleville, 11e; dm/d from €35/105; @; MCouronnes, Belleville) Run by hip, witty staff, this brilliant hostel is the Belleville hotspot to mingle with locals over Parisian craft beer at the stunning ground-floor bar, cosy up in front of the wood-burner, or soak up the sun and panoramic views from the roof terrace. Dorms are fitted with custom bunks and ample bedside plugs; rooftop doubles have sleek all-white decor.

COSMOS HÔTEL HOTEL €

Map p390 (☎01 43 57 25 88; www.cosmos-hotel-paris.com; 35 rue Jean-Pierre Timbaud, 11e; s/d from €67/72; ; MParmentier, Goncourt) Cheap, brilliant value and just footsteps from the nightlife of rue JPT, Cosmos is a shining star with retro style on the budget-hotel scene that, unlike most other hotels in the same price bracket, has been treated to a thoroughly modern makeover this century. Breakfast is basic but is also budget priced, costing just €8.

THE LOFT HOSTEL €

Map p390 (☎01 42 02 42 02; www.theloft-paris.com; 70 rue Julien Lacroix, 20e; dm/s/d from €28.50/85/90; @; MPyrénées, Belleville) This bright, private hostel in Belleville has panache. Dorms sleeping four to eight are decorated with patterned wallpaper, bold colours and contemporary furniture; those on the ground floor open onto an idyllic courtyard patio and one dorm upstairs has its own balcony. All rooms have private bathrooms, breakfast is included, and the well-equipped kitchen, open until 2am, doubles as a bar. Rooms close between 9.30am and 3pm for cleaning.

MIJE FOURCY HOSTEL €

Map p386 (☎01 42 74 23 45; www.mije.com; 6 rue de Fourcy, 4e; dm/s/d €35.50/65/85; ; MSt-Paul, Pont Marie) Behind the elegant front door of this *hôtel particulier*, Fourcy welcomes guests with clean rooms and a summer garden to breakfast/hang out in. It's one of three Marais hostels run by the Maison Internationale de la Jeunesse et des Étudiants – the others are **MIJE Le Fauconnier** (Map p386; 11 rue du Fauconnier, 4e; dm/s/d €35.50/65/85; @; MSt-Paul, Pont Marie) and **MIJE Maubuisson** (Map p386; 12 rue des Barres, 4e; dm/s/d €35.50/65/85; @; MHôtel de Ville, Pont Marie). Rates include breakfast; evening meals are available in the vaulted cellar.

Rooms (closed noon to 3pm) have a shower but share toilets in the corridor. No alcohol is permitted; there's a curfew from 1am to 7am.

★HÔTEL GEORGETTE DESIGN HOTEL €€

Map p386 (☎01 44 61 10 10; www.hotelgeorgette.com; 36 rue du Grenier St-Lazare, 3e; d from €240; ; MRambuteau) Taking inspiration from the Centre Pompidou around the corner, this vivacious hotel's 19 rooms reflect major 20th-century artistic movements, including Pop Art, Op Art, Dada, New Realism and Street Art, with lots of bold colours and funky touches like Andy Warhol–inspired Campbell's-soup-can lampshades. Art exhibitions regularly take place in the bright lobby. It's gay-friendly and all-welcoming.

HÔTEL FABRIC DESIGN HOTEL €€

Map p390 (☎01 43 57 27 00; www.hotelfabric.com; 31 rue de la Folie Méricourt, 11e; d/tr from €247/445; @; MSt-Ambroise) Honouring its industrial heritage as a 19th-century textile factory, four-star Hôtel Fabric has steely pillars propping up the red-brick lounge area with dining tables where breakfast (€18) is served, and vintage touches include a Singer sewing machine. Darkly carpeted corridors open to 33 bright rooms with beautiful textiles and cupboards made from upcycled packing crates.

HÔTEL CARON DE BEAUMARCHAIS BOUTIQUE HOTEL €€

Map p386 (☎01 42 72 34 12; www.carondebeaumarchais.com; 12 rue Vieille du Temple, 4e; d from €196; ; MHôtel de Ville, St-Paul) The attention to detail at this antique-filled, 19-room hotel is impressive. From the period card table set as if time stopped halfway through a game, to the harp and well-worn sheet music propped on the music stand, along with chandeliers and silk wallpapers, the decor evokes the life and times of the 18th-century playwright after whom the hotel is named.

HÔTEL EMILE DESIGN HOTEL €€

Map p386 (☎01 42 72 76 17; www.hotelemile.com; 2 rue Malher, 4e; s/d/ste from €139/157/211; ❄📶; Ⓜ St-Paul) Prepare to be dazzled – literally. Retro B&W, geometrically patterned carpets, curtains, wallpapers and drapes dress this chic hotel, wedged between boutiques and restaurants in Le Marais. Pricier 'top floor' doubles look out over Parisian roofs and chimney pots. Breakfast (included in the price) is on bar stools in the lobby; open the cupboard to find the 'kitchen'.

HÔTEL CARON HOTEL €€

Map p386 (☎01 40 29 02 94; www.hotelcaron.com; 3 rue Caron, 4e; d from €209; ❄📶; Ⓜ St-Paul) Footsteps from delightful place du Marché Ste-Catherine, this is a solid mid-range hotel with comfortable (if smallish) minibar-equipped rooms. Soft natural hues give its 18 double rooms instant appeal and the L'Occitane bathroom products are a sweet-smelling touch. Breakfast (€15) in the cream-stone, vaulted cellar is a highlight.

1K PARIS DESIGN HOTEL €€

Map p386 (☎01 42 71 20 00; www.1k-paris.com; 13 bd du Temple, 3e; d/ste/penthouse from €240/440/1040; ❄📶; Ⓜ Filles du Calvaire) Cobalt-blue awnings frame this revamped hotel, whose public areas have a Peruvian theme (Inca motifs, photography and two monitor lizards – Macchu and Pichu – in a glass vivarium). Whitewashed walls give its 50 rooms clean, minimalist lines; for the ultimate indulgence, book into one of the two penthouse suites, each of which comes with a private rooftop terrace and plunge pool.

HÔTEL DU HAUT MARAIS BOUTIQUE HOTEL €€

Map p386 (HDHM; ☎01 79 72 79 76; www.hotelhautmarais.com; 7 rue des Vertus, 3e; s/d from €153/198; ❄@📶; Ⓜ Arts et Métiers) Renovated from top to bottom in 2016, this historic townhouse offers an intimate, independent stay. There's no reception; you receive door codes prior to your arrival, and in-room iPads are provided in place of a concierge. Its 10 rooms are each different in design; most are equipped with kitchenettes. Breakfast can be delivered to your room on request.

HÔTEL JEANNE D'ARC HOTEL €€

Map p386 (☎01 48 87 62 11; www.hoteljeannedarc.com; 3 rue de Jarente, 4e; s/d from €194/204; 📶; Ⓜ St-Paul) About the only thing wrong with this epicentral Marais address is everyone knows about it; book well in advance. Some of the 35 streamlined, modernised rooms retain timber beams or exposed stone walls, while others have feature walls with patterned wallpaper. The pièce de résistance: the 6th-floor attic room (accessible by lift) with a sweeping Paris rooftop view.

HÔTEL DE JOBO BOUTIQUE HOTEL €€€

Map p386 (☎01 48 047 048; www.hoteldejobo.paris; 10 rue d'Ormesson, 4e; s/d/ste from €223/312/490; ❄@📶; Ⓜ St-Paul) If Joséphine Bonaparte was living in today's celebrity limelight, her nickname would surely be JoBo. That's the philosophy behind the fabulously over-the-top decoration of this 2016-opened hideaway, which has 24 rooms adorned with Joséphine's favourite motifs (rose and leopardskin are used in textured wallpapers; roses also adorn the theatrical canopied courtyard garden). Connecting rooms, babysitting and kids' breakfasts are available.

★LES BAINS DESIGN HOTEL €€€

Map p386 (☎01 42 77 07 07; www.lesbains-paris.com; 7 rue du Bourg l'Abbé, 3e; d/ste from €392/715; ❄@📶; Ⓜ Étienne Marcel, Rambuteau) Opened in 1885 as thermal baths (frequented by Marcel Proust among others), in 1978 this iconic address morphed into the Bains-Douches nightclub, made famous by David Bowie, Mick Jagger and a galaxy of celebs. Today it's probably Paris' most fabulous lifestyle hotel, with 39 bespoke rooms – some opening to balconies or terraces – showcasing vintage treasures, luxury fabrics and eclectic design.

★HÔTEL DU PETIT MOULIN BOUTIQUE HOTEL €€€

Map p386 (☎01 42 74 10 10; www.hoteldupetitmoulin.com; 29-31 rue de Poitou, 3e; d €250-395; ❄📶; Ⓜ St-Sébastien–Froissart) A bakery at the time of Henri IV, this scrumptious 17-room hotel was designed from head to toe by Christian Lacroix. Choose from medieval and rococo Marais rooms sporting exposed beams and dressed in toile de Jouy wallpaper, or more modern surrounds with contemporary murals and heart-shaped mirrors just this side of kitsch.

HÔTEL NATIONAL DES ARTS ET MÉTIERS HOTEL €€€

Map p386 (☎01 80 97 22 80; www.hotelnational.paris; 243 rue St-Martin, 3e; d from €280; ; MRéaumur–Sébastopol) Behind a classic cream-coloured Haussmannian facade, this 2017-opened hotel wraps around a central atrium. Some of its 70 soundproofed rooms and suites are interconnecting, and all have state-of-the-art oak floors, geometric bathrooms with terrazzo bench tops and chic grey and blue furnishings. Public spaces include two restaurants (one Italian, one tapas), a serious cocktail bar and a panoramic roof terrace.

HÔTEL ORIGINAL DESIGN HOTEL €€€

Map p386 (☎01 47 00 91 50; www.hoteloriginalparis.com; 8 bd Beaumarchais, 11e; s/d from €237/287; ; MBastille) As its name suggests, this boutique hotel is one of a kind, from its cobalt-blue facade to its vividly coloured public areas and rooms incorporating fairy-tale themes, such as *Alice in Wonderland* motifs. On the top floor of the Hausmannian building, single rooms are tiny at 10 sq metres but have the best views; doubles start at 16 sq metres.

LE PAVILLON DE LA REINE HISTORIC HOTEL €€€

Map p386 (☎01 40 29 19 19; www.pavillon-de-la-reine.com; 28 place des Vosges, 3e; d/ste from €380/920; ; MChemin Vert) Discreetly set off beautiful place des Vosges, this is a sumptuous address loaded with history – the five-star hotel is named after former guest Anne of Austria, queen to Louis XIII from 1615. Its 56 rooms and suites come in either classical or contemporary decor. A leafy courtyard and revitalising spa render it a real country retreat from the urban hubbub. There's an on-site gym; free bikes are available for guests.

Bastille & Eastern Paris

MAMA SHELTER DESIGN HOTEL €

(☎01 43 48 48 48; www.mamashelter.com; 109 rue de Bagnolet, 20e; s/d/tr/q from €119/129/209/289; ; 76, MGambetta, Alexandre Dumas) This former car park was coaxed into its current zany incarnation by designer Philippe Starck. Its 170 cutting-edge rooms feature iMacs, catchy colour schemes, polished-concrete walls and free movies on demand. A rooftop terrace, pizzeria, and huge restaurant with live music and all-you-can-eat Sunday brunch add to its street cred. Book as early as possible to get the best deal.

CITIZENM GARE DE LYON DESIGN HOTEL €

Map p394 (☎01 86 65 07 40; www.citizenm.com; 8 rue Van Gogh, 12e; d from €121; ; MGare de Lyon) This 2017-opened branch of the affordable design hotel chain CitizenM has mural-splashed hallways, hip workspace/lounge areas and a handy location right by Gare de Lyon train station. Icy white rooms hung with art have super-comfy king-size beds, rain showers and 'mood pads' to program ambient lighting; some have sweeping views over the Seine too.

★HÔTEL PARIS BASTILLE BOUTET HOTEL €€

Map p394 (☎01 40 24 65 65; www.sofitel.com; 22-24 rue Faidherbe, 11e; d/ste from €199/279; ; MFaidherbe-Chaligny) A joinery workshop and later a chocolate factory, the Boutet retains its original 1926 mosaic-tiled facade and art-deco canopy, and acknowledges its industrial heritage in its timber-panelled hallways. Ten of its 80 rooms and suites have spectacular terraces. There's a *hammam,* gym and two beauty treatment rooms, but the biggest bonus is the sky-lit swimming pool with a counter current.

★MAISON BRÉGUET BOUTIQUE HOTEL €€€

Map p394 (☎01 58 30 32 31; www.maisonbreguet.com; 8 rue Bréguet, 11e; d/ste from €357/464; ; MBréguet–Sabin) Local creatives were involved in the evolution of this former factory turned five-star property, which opened in 2018: artists' works hang on the walls, writers selected the library's books and films, and musicians put together playlists (performances also often take place here). Some of its 53 art deco influenced rooms and suites have terraces; the two-storey deluxe suite has a private garden.

★HÔTEL L'ANTOINE DESIGN HOTEL €€€

Map p394 (☎01 55 28 30 11; www.hotelantoinebastilleparis.com; 12 rue de Charonne, 11e; d/ste from €184/301; ; MBastille, Ledru-Rollin) A showcase for stunning contemporary decor by Christian Lacroix, the 38-room

Antoine's five floors reflect a different aspect of the Bastille – the 1950s, nightlife at the Balajo ballroom, romance, technology – where the French designer once lived. If you love shocking pink, ask for a 2nd-floor art-gallery-inspired room. Superb amenities include a basement sauna and fitness room, and an honesty bar.

The Islands

HÔTEL DES 2 ÎLES HISTORIC HOTEL €€

Map p396 (01 43 26 13 35; www.deuxiles-paris-hotel.com; 59 rue Saint-Louis en l'Île, 4e; s/d €230/263; ; Pont Marie) A venerable 17th-century building shelters this intimate three-star hotel with 17 classical rooms sporting patterned wallpaper, screen-printed fabrics, original Portuguese *azulejos* (blue-and-white ceramic tiles) in some bathrooms, and ancient wooden beams. Breakfast (€14) is served in the vaulted stone cellar with fireplace (not functioning) and terracotta-tiled floor. Top-floor rooms peep out over Parisian rooftops and chimney pots.

HÔTEL DE LUTÈCE HOTEL €€

(01 43 26 23 52; www.paris-hotel-lutece.com; 65 rue St-Louis en l'Île, 4e; s/d/tr €230/245/310; ; Pont Marie) An elegant lobby-salon, with ancient fireplace, wood panelling, antique furnishings and traditional board games to borrow, welcomes guests at the lovely Lutèce, a country-style three-star hotel with 23 tastefully decorated rooms stacked up on six floors. Those overlooking the village-like street – with *fromagerie* (cheese shop), greengrocer's and chocolate shop – are more atmospheric than those facing the interior courtyard. Breakfast €14.

★HÔTEL DU JEU DE PAUME BOUTIQUE HOTEL €€€

Map p396 (01 43 26 14 18; http://jeudepaumehotel.com; 54 rue St-Louis en l'Île, 4e; s/d €205/305; ; Pont Marie) Romantically set in a courtyard off Île St-Louis' main street, this chic, contemporary four-star hotel occupies a 17th-century royal tennis court. Its 30 rooms are each inspired by a different modern artist. Panton chairs add a design edge to the historic beamed, exposed-stone-walled house, and its leafy patio garden is divine. Facilities include a wellness centre. Breakfast €18.

Latin Quarter

★HÔTEL PORT ROYAL HOTEL €

Map p400 (01 43 31 70 06; www.port-royal-hotel.fr; 8 bd de Port-Royal, 5e; d €95-100, s/d without bathroom €56/58; ; RER Port Royal) This elegant, fourth-generation family hotel, run by great-granddaughter Isabelle and her Uncle Thierry today, wins the prize for the most polished, squeaky-clean budget hotel in Paris (even the cleaners are second generation). Its 46 rooms, stacked across six floors, enjoy impeccably maintained vintage furnishings. The bijou courtyard garden – the spot to breakfast (€8) al fresco on warm days – is a summertime bonus.

★HÔTEL DIANA HOTEL €

Map p398 (01 43 54 92 55; http://hotel-diana-paris.com; 73 rue St-Jacques, 5e; s €78-98, d €105-145, tr €160-195; ; Maubert-Mutualité) Footsteps from the Sorbonne, two-star Diana is budget-traveller gold. Owner extraordinaire, Thérèse Cheval, has been at the helm here since the 1970s and the pride and joy she invests in the hotel is boundless. Spacious rooms sport a stylish contemporary decor with geometric-patterned fabrics, the odd retro furniture piece, and courtesy tray with kettle and white-mug twinset. Breakfast €10.

★FAMILIA HÔTEL HOTEL €€

Map p398 (01 43 54 55 27; www.familiahotel.com; 11 rue des Écoles, 5e; s/d/tr €110/134/152; ; Cardinal Lemoine) Staff at this friendly, third-generation family-run hotel proudly tell you that nothing ever changes at the Familia. Indeed, the sepia murals of Parisian landmarks, flower-bedecked windows, and exposed rafters and stone walls are clearly from a past era. Some of the 32 rooms have weeny balconies; those on the 6th floor peep at Notre Dame. Breakfast €7.

HÔTEL ATMOSPHÈRES DESIGN HOTEL €€

Map p398 (01 43 26 56 02; www.hotelatmospheres.com; 31 rue des Écoles, 5e; d from €132; ; Maubert-Mutualité) Striking images by award-winning French photographer Thierry des Ouches are permanently exhibited at this design hotel where 56 glam rooms evoke different Parisian 'atmospheres' – nature, monuments, Paris by night, the metro-inspired 'urban' and colourful *salon de thé* (tearoom)-style 'macaron'. A small gym, sauna and water massage bed are tucked away in the basement. Express/buffet breakfast €9/16.

HÔTEL LA LANTERNE BOUTIQUE HOTEL €€

Map p398 (☎01 53 19 88 39; www.hotel-la-lanterne.com; 12 rue de la Montagne Ste-Geneviève, 5e; d from €175; ; MMaubert-Mutualité) A stunning swimming pool and *hammam* in a vaulted stone cellar, a topiary-filled courtyard garden, contemporary guest rooms (some with small balconies) with black-and-white photos of Parisian architecture, amenities including Nespresso machines, and an honesty bar make this a jewel of a boutique hotel. Breakfast (€25) lets you choose from hot and cold buffets and includes Mariage Frères teas.

HÔTEL DES GRANDES ÉCOLES HOTEL €€

Map p400 (☎01 43 26 79 23; www.hotel-grandes-ecoles.com; 75 rue du Cardinal Lemoine, 5e; d €135-165; ; MCardinal Lemoine) Spanning three two-storey buildings, this welcoming hotel just north of place de la Contrescarpe has one of the loveliest locations in the Latin Quarter, set around its own private garden courtyard off a medieval street. Rooms are simple but not without charm. Breakfast costs €9; there are 15 on-site car parking spaces costing €30 per night.

HÔTEL ST-JACQUES HOTEL €€

Map p398 (☎01 44 07 45 45; http://hotel-saintjacques.com; 35 rue des Écoles, 5e; s/d/tr/q €188/205/305/456; ; MMaubert-Mutualité) Framed reproductions of famous artworks line the walls of this belle époque–styled hotel. Original 19th-century details include trompe l'œil ceilings evoking cloud-filled skies, an iron staircase and balconies overlooking the Panthéon. In keeping with its old-world spirit, hotel bar Toulouse Lautrec serves absinthe.

HÔTEL RÉSIDENCE HENRI IV HOTEL €€€

Map p398 (☎01 44 41 31 81; www.residencehenri4.com; 50 rue des Bernardins, 5e; d €299; ; MMaubert-Mutualité) This exquisite late-19th-century cul-de-sac hotel has eight generously sized rooms (minimum 17 sq metre) and five two-room apartments (minimum 25 sq metre), done up with regal touches like draped fabrics and four-poster beds in some rooms. All are equipped with kitchenettes (induction cooktops, fridge, microwave and dishes), making them particularly handy for families and market goers.

FIVE HOTEL BOUTIQUE HOTEL €€€

Map p400 (☎01 43 31 74 21; http://thefivehotel.com; 3 rue Flatters, 5e; d from €225; ; MLes Gobelins) Fibre-optic lighting enhances the small rooms at this contemporary romantic sanctum. Rooms become more spacious as you move up the price scale; its One By the Five suite has a phenomenal 'levitating' bed. In-room massages and beauty treatments can be arranged. Rates are often discounted by up to 50% online, making it a better deal than it first appears. Express/buffet breakfast €9/15.

St-Germain & Les Invalides

★HÔTEL DU DRAGON HOTEL €

Map p402 (☎01 45 48 51 05; www.hoteldudragon.com; 36 rue du Dragon, 6e; d €95-150, tr €130-180; ; MSt-Sulpice) It's hard to believe that such a gem of a budget hotel still exists in this ultra-chic part of St-Germain. A family affair for the last five generations, today the ever-charming Roy runs the 28-room Dragon with his children, Sébastien and Marie-Hélène. Spotlessly clean rooms are decidedly large by Paris standards, often with exposed wooden beams and lovely vintage furnishings.

HÔTEL LE CLÉMENT HOTEL €

Map p402 (☎01 43 26 53 60; http://hotelclementparis.com; 6 rue Clément, 6e; s/d from €88/99; ; MSt-Germain des Prés) Excellent value for the style and tranquillity it offers, the Clément has 28 stylish rooms (with beautiful printed wallpapers and fabrics), some overlooking the Marché St-Germain. Rooms on the top floor have sloping ceilings. The proprietors know what they're doing – this place has been in the same family for over a century. Breakfast €14.

★HÔTEL LE COMTESSE BOUTIQUE HOTEL €€

Map p406 (☎01 45 51 29 29; www.comtesse-hotel.com; 29 ave de Tourville, 7e; d from €229; ; MÉcole Militaire) A five-star view of Mademoiselle Eiffel seduces guests in every single room at The Countess, an utterly charming boutique hotel at home in a 19th-century building with alluring wrought-iron balconies. Colour palettes are playful, and the feathered quill pen adorning the desk in each room is one of many cute touches.

Breakfast (€19) is served in the glamorous, boudoir-styled cafe with pavement terrace.

LE BELLECHASSE DESIGN HOTEL €€

Map p406 (☎01 45 50 22 31; www.lebellechasse.com; 8 rue de Bellechasse, 7e; d €149-440; ❄📶; MSolférino) Handily placed near the Seine and Musée d'Orsay, 33-room Le Bellechasse is an enticing, sensorial feast. Entrancing room themes by fashion designer Christian Lacroix – including St-Germain, with brocades, zebra striping and faux-gold leafing; Tuileries, with trompe l'œil and palms; and Jeu de Paume, with giant playing-card motifs – create the impression you've stepped into a larger-than-life oil painting.

HÔTEL PRINCE DE CONTI BOUTIQUE HOTEL €€

Map p402 (☎01 44 07 30 40; www.prince-de-conti.com; 8 rue Guénégaud, 6e; d from €128; @📶; MPont Neuf) Tucked around the corner from the neoclassical Monnaie de Paris, three-star Prince de Conti lives up to its regal name. Toile de Jouy fabrics, impeccably curated vintage furniture and Fragonard bathroom amenities lend rooms a soothing bourgeois elegance; the downstairs salon – with complimentary coffee, honesty bar and books to browse – is a delightful place to lounge. Breakfast €15.

HÔTEL PERREYVE HOTEL €€

Map p402 (☎01 45 48 35 01; www.perreyve-hotel-paris-luxembourg.com; 63 rue Madame, 6e; s/d from €155/172; ❄📶; MRennes) A hop, skip and a jump from the Jardin du Luxembourg, this welcoming 1920s hotel is superb value given its coveted location. Cosy, carpeted rooms have enormous frescoes; on the ground floor, start the day in the pretty breakfast room with herringbone floors and fire-engine-red tables and chairs.

★**L'HÔTEL** BOUTIQUE HOTEL €€€

Map p402 (☎01 44 41 99 00; www.l-hotel.com; 13 rue des Beaux Arts, 6e; d from €323; ❄@📶🏊; MSt-Germain des Prés) In a quiet quayside street, this 20-room establishment is the stuff of romance, Parisian myths and urban legends. Rock- and film-star patrons fight to sleep in the Oscar Wilde Suite, decorated with a peacock motif, where the Irish playwright died in 1900. A stunning, modern swimming pool occupies the ancient cellar.

Guests and nonguests can soak up the atmosphere of the fantastic bar (either for Champagne-fuelled afternoon tea or after dark over live music by up-and-coming new talent) and Michelin-starred restaurant (called, what else, Le Restaurant) under a glass canopy.

HÔTEL D'ANGLETERRE HISTORIC HOTEL €€€

Map p402 (☎01 42 60 34 72; www.hotel-dangleterre.com; 44 rue Jacob, 6e; d from €210; @📶; MSt-Germain des Prés) If the walls could talk... This former garden of the British Embassy is where the Treaty of Paris ending the American Revolution was prepared in 1783. Hemingway lodged here in 1921 (in room 14), as did Charles Lindbergh in 1927 after completing the world's first solo nonstop flight from New York to Paris. Its 27 exquisite rooms are individually decorated. Rates include breakfast.

HÔTEL JULIANA BOUTIQUE HOTEL €€€

Map p406 (☎01 44 05 70 00; http://hoteljuliana.paris; 10 rue Cognacq Jay, 7e; d from €280; ❄📶; MAlma–Marceau, RER Pont de d'Alma) 🍃 Geometric designs and shimmering mosaics give an updated '70s aesthetic to many of the 40 spacious rooms and suites at five-star Juliana; others have art deco or baroque influences. There's a rooftop sun terrace and the health club has a fitness room and steam room. Children get their own range of toiletries.

LE SAINT HOTEL €€€

Map p402 (☎01 42 61 01 51; http://lesainthotelparis.com; 3 rue du Pré aux Clercs, 7e; d from €265; ❄📶; MSt-Germain des Prés) Live the St-Germain des Prés life at this 2016-opened hotel on a peaceful side street strolling distance from the area's churches, markets, literary cafes and the Seine. Some of its 54 rooms and suites have balconies or terraces; all have shimmering fabrics. An open fireplace blazes in the lounge; there's an in-house restaurant, Kult, and bar.

Montparnasse & Southern Paris

3 DUCKS HOSTEL HOSTEL €

Map p414 (☎01 48 42 04 05; http://3ducks.fr; 6 place Étienne Pernet, 15e; dm/d/q from €29.95/99/144; ❄📶; MFélix Faure) A lively bar (open day and night to guests and nonguests), courtyard BBQ and no curfew or lockout give this reinvigorated hostel, a 10-minute walk from the Eiffel Tower, a good-time vibe. Facilities are excellent (self-catering kitchen, small lockers, plus a luggage room and multiple USB outlets and a lamp per bed), there's a women-only dorm and freebies include breakfast.

OOPS HOSTEL €

Map p410 (☎01 47 07 47 00; www.oops-paris.com; 50 av des Gobelins, 13e; dm €33-42, d €90-115; ❄📶; Ⓜ Gobelins) Two gigantic pot plants herald the entrance to this colourful design hostel above a pizza restaurant on busy av des Gobelins. Four- to six-bed dorms and doubles have en suites and are accessible all day. Some peek at the Eiffel Tower. Rates include breakfast, sheets, use of the kitchen and luggage room. No credit cards; no alcohol allowed.

HÔTEL CARLADEZ CAMBRONNE HOTEL €

Map p414 (☎01 47 34 07 12; www.hotelcarladez.com; 3 place du Général Beuret, 15e; d €106-158; 📶; Ⓜ Vaugirard) On a quintessentially Parisian cafe-clad square, this very good-value hotel has comfortable rooms with attractive wallpapers and fabrics. Higher-priced superior rooms come with bathtubs, more space and tend to be quieter. Communal coffee- and tea-making facilities let you make yourself at home. Breakfast €10. Check its website for last-minute deals.

HÔTEL DE LA LOIRE HOTEL €

Map p412 (☎01 45 40 66 88; www.hoteldelaloire-paris.com; 39bis rue du Moulin Vert, 14e; d €110-125, with shared bath €80; 🅿📶; Ⓜ Alésia) Obviously, at these prices don't expect luxury, but do expect a warm welcome and clean, colourful en-suite rooms (18 all-up) at this budget hotel of old. The lovely village-like location on a quiet, quaint lane near Denfert-Rochereau makes it easy to reach both major airports and Gare du Nord, and there's a pretty table-set garden. Breakfast €8.50.

★HÔTEL HENRIETTE DESIGN HOTEL €€

Map p410 (☎01 47 07 26 90; www.hotelhenriette.com; 9 rue des Gobelins, 13e; s €69-209, d €79-309, tr €89-339, q €129-499; ❄📶; Ⓜ Les Gobelins) Interior designer Vanessa Scoffier scoured Paris' flea markets to source Platner chairs, 1950s lighting and other unique vintage pieces for the 32 rooms at bohemian Henriette – one of the Left Bank's most stunning boutique addresses. Guests can mingle in the light-flooded glass atrium and adjoining plant-filled patio with wrought-iron furniture.

OFF PARIS SEINE HOTEL €€

Map p410 (☎01 44 06 62 66; www.offparisseine.com; 85 quai d'Austerlitz, 13e; d from €169; 📶🏊; Ⓜ Gare d'Austerlitz) Should the idea of being gently rocked to sleep take your fancy, check into Paris' first floating hotel by the highly recommended Parisian Elegancia hotel group. The sleek, 80m-long catamaran-design structure moored by Pont Charles de Gaulle sports sun terraces overlooking the Seine, a chic bar with silver beanbags by a 15m-long dipping pool, lounge, and 58 stunningly appointed rooms and suites.

HÔTEL VIC EIFFEL BOUTIQUE HOTEL €€

Map p412 (☎01 53 86 83 83; www.hotelviceiffel.com; 92 bd Garibaldi, 15e; d €169-204; 📶; Ⓜ Sèvres-Lecourbe) A short walk from the Eiffel Tower, with the metro on the doorstep, this pristine hotel has chic orange and oyster-grey rooms. Classic doubles are small but perfectly functional and sport a coffee machine, Kusmi tea and sweet-scented L'Occitane bathroom products. Rates plummet outside high season. Breakfast, served in an atrium-style courtyard, costs €14.

HÔTEL EIFFEL PETIT LOUVRE BOUTIQUE HOTEL €€

Map p414 (☎01 45 78 17 12; https://hotel-paris-petitlouvre.com; 1 rue de Lourmel, 15e; d/tr/q from €109/152/179; ❄@📶; Ⓜ Dupleix) To immerse yourself in the heart of a Parisian's Paris, check into this stylish three-star address, wedged between food shops, and footsteps from bd de Grenelle's bustling fruit and veg market. Reproductions of reclining female nudes and other period art works grace the walls, and 50 contemporary rooms sport regal colour palettes and marble bathrooms. Breakfast €15.

HÔTEL MAX BOUTIQUE HOTEL €€

Map p412 (☎01 43 27 60 80; www.hotel-max.fr; 34 rue d'Alésia, 14e; d from €170; ❄📶; Ⓜ Alésia) Some of the 19 rooms at this contemporary boutique hotel in the heart of the 14e have balconies and all have in-room coffee machines, muted colour palettes, modern art on the walls, timber floors and Italian bathrooms. The stylish lounge and twinset of small gardens beg relaxation. Low season, snag a double for €96. Breakfast €12.

Understand Paris

Paris Today

Paris has bounced back in a big way since the turbulent events of 2015: visitor numbers are at a record high, energetic president Emmanuel Macron is revitalising France's economy, a raft of infrastructure projects are under way, and the capital is gearing up to host 2023 Rugby World Cup fixtures and the 2024 Summer Olympics and Summer Paralympics. The city continues to become greener, with eco-initiatives including more car-free and reduced-traffic areas prioritising pedestrians and cyclists.

Best on Film

Les 400 Coups (400 Blows; 1959) Moving portrayal of the magic and disillusionment of childhood.

La Haine (Hate; 1995) Mathieu Kassovitz' prescient take on social tensions in modern Paris.

Le Fabuleux Destin d'Amélie Poulain (Amélie; 2001) Endearing story of a winsome young Parisian.

La Môme (La Vie en Rose; 2007) Édith Piaf, from street urchin to international superstar.

Midnight in Paris (2011) Time travels back to 1920s Paris and beyond.

Hugo (2011) A tribute to cinema and the legendary Georges Méliès.

Best in Print

Notre Dame de Paris (Victor Hugo, 1831) The classic tale of the hunchback of Notre Dame.

A Moveable Feast (Ernest Hemingway, 1964) Memoirs of the aspiring writer's life in Paris.

Life: A User's Manual (Georges Perec, 1978) About an apartment block's inhabitants between 1833 and 1975.

The Elegance of the Hedgehog (Muriel Barbery, 2008) Bestseller unveiling the world behind a Parisian facade.

The Mistress of Paris (Catherine Hewitt, 2015) True rags-to-riches story of a 19th-century courtesan.

Grand Plans

The gargantuan Grand Paris (Greater Paris) redevelopment project will ultimately connect the outer suburbs beyond the bd Périphérique ring road with the city proper. This is a significant break in the physical and conceptual barrier that the *périphérique* has imposed until now, but, due to the steadily growing suburban population (10.5 million, compared to 2.2 million inside the *périphérique*), a real need to redefine Paris, on both an administrative and an infrastructural scale, has arisen.

The crux of Grand Paris is a massive decentralised metro expansion, with four new metro lines, the extension of several existing lines, and a total of 68 new stations, with a target completion date of 2030. The principal goal is to connect the suburbs with one another, instead of relying on a central inner-city hub from which all lines radiate outwards. Ultimately, the surrounding suburbs – Vincennes, Neuilly, Issy, St-Denis etc – will lose their autonomy and become part of a much larger Grand Paris governed by the Hôtel de Ville.

Other major transport developments include a high-speed train link between Charles de Gaulle Airport and central Paris by 2024. Orly Airport will be served by metro from 2024 and high-speed train by 2025.

Evolving Architecture

Architectural change doesn't come easy in Paris, given the need to balance the city's heritage with demands on space. But new projects continue to gather steam. At Porte de Versailles, 2019's Tour Triangle, a glittering triangular glass tower designed by Jacques Herzog and Pierre de Meuron, will be the first skyscraper in Paris since 1973's Tour Montparnasse (itself set to get a new reflective facade and green rooftop). Other high-rise projects include Duo, two Jean Nouvel–designed towers (180m and 122m) in the 13e, slated for completion in 2020.

Nouvel is also among the architects working on the 74-hectare Île Seguin-Rives de Seine development of the former Renault plant on a Seine island in Boulogne-Billancourt, which is becoming a Grand Paris cultural hub; concert venue La Seine Musicale was the first to arrive, in 2017. Another Nouvel project is Gare d'Austerlitz' multimillion-euro renovation, with hotels and a 20,000-sq-metre shopping area, wrapping up in 2021.

Greener Living

Mayor of Paris Anne Hidalgo is focused on greening the city and reducing car traffic and pollution. Since taking office in 2014, Hidalgo has pedestrianised 3.3km of Right Bank expressway between the Tuileries and Bastille, closed the av des Champs-Élysées on the first Sunday of each month, and established an annual car-free day. In 2017 the city introduced the Crit'Air Vignette (compulsory anti-pollution sticker) for vehicles registered after 1997 between 8am and 8pm Monday to Friday (older vehicles are banned during these hours). Ongoing projects include investing €150 million in cycling infrastructure (including an av des Champs-Élysées cycling lane), reducing parking spaces by 55,000 per year, instigating a city-wide maximum speed limit of 30km/h (except along major arteries) by 2020 to minimise noise pollution, and banning diesel cars by 2024 and petrol cars by 2030.

Transport aside, green initiatives include a goal of 100 hectares of green roofs, facades and vertical walls, a third of which will be devoted to urban agriculture. Green walkways and gardens will connect two of Paris' busiest mainline stations – Gare du Nord and Gare de l'Est – from 2019. A 'pedestrian peninsula' linking place de la Bastille with the Port de l'Arsenal marina is also scheduled to open the same year.

Economic Advancements

In order to compete with other key European cities to attract tourism and investment, Paris has established ZTIs (international tourist zones) that allow late-night and Sunday trading for shops. There are a dozen such zones to date.

Forward steps also include the 2017 opening of the world's biggest start-up campus, Station F, in the 13e, home to some 3000 entrepreneurs. It was inaugurated by President Macron, who is seeking to bring more businesses to the city and country. Unemployment is now at its lowest level since 2009, with a series of labour reforms expected to reduce it even further. The City of Light's future is bright.

population per sq km

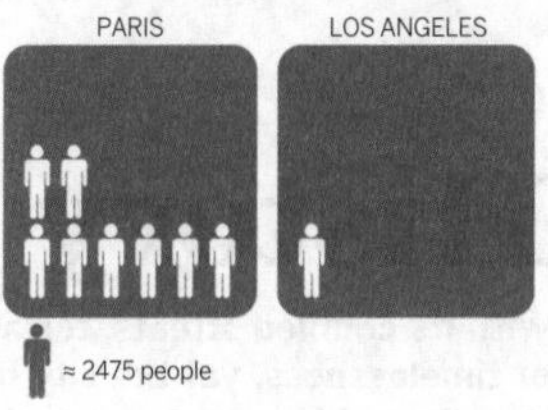

living in Paris

(% of population by area)

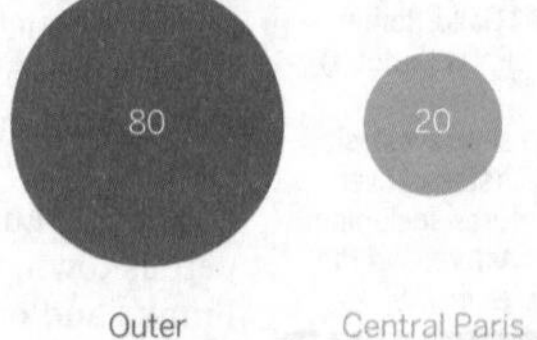

if Paris were 100 people

86 would be French
14 would be Foreign

History

With its cobbled streets, terraced cafes and iconic landmarks, Paris evokes a sense of timelessness, yet the city has changed and evolved dramatically over the centuries. Paris' history is a saga of battles, bloodshed, grand-scale excesses, revolution, reformation, resistance, renaissance and constant reinvention. This epic is not just consigned to museums and archives: reminders of the capital's and the country's history are evident all over the city.

Early Settlers: The Celts & Romans

The early history of Paris is murky, but the consensus is that a Celtic tribe known as the Parisii established a fishing village in the area in the 3rd century BC. Years of conflict between the Gauls and Romans ended in 52 BC, when the latter took control of the territory after a decisive victory during Julius Caesar's eight-year Gallic Wars campaign. The Romans promptly established a new town – Lutetia (Lutèce in French) – with the main public buildings (forum, bathhouse, theatre and amphitheatre) all located on the Left Bank, near today's Panthéon. Remnants of both the bathhouse and amphitheatre are still visible.

Gallo-Roman Paris (Lutetia) features in several classic Asterix adventures, including *Asterix and the Golden Sickle*.

Though Lutetia was not the capital of its province, it was a prosperous town, with a population of around 8000. However, raids by the Franks and other Germanic tribes during the 3rd century AD left the settlement on the Left Bank scorched and pillaged, and its inhabitants fled to the Île de la Cité, subsequently fortified with stone walls. Christianity was introduced by St Denis – decapitated on Montmartre in AD 250 for his efforts – and the first church was built on the western part of the island.

The Roman town held out until the late 5th century – mythically saved from Attila the Hun by the piety of Geneviève, who became the city's patron saint – only to fall when a second wave of Franks overran the area for good.

TIMELINE

3rd century BC

Celtic Gauls called Parisii arrive in the Paris area and set up wattle-and-daub huts on the Seine, possibly in the Nanterre area.

52 BC

Roman legions under Titus Labienus crush a Celtic revolt on Mons Lutetius (site of today's Panthéon) and establish the town of Lutetia (Lutèce in French).

AD 250

St Denis, who brought Christianity to Lutetia, is executed on Montmartre. According to legend, he then carries his head 10km north, to the site of the future royal necropolis of St-Denis.

The Middle Ages: Paris as Capital

One of the key figures in early Parisian history was the Frankish king Clovis I (c 466–511). Clovis was the first ruler to unite what would later become France, to convert to Christianity and to declare Paris the capital. Under the Frankish kings the city once again began to expand, and important edifices such as the abbey of St-Germain des Prés and the abbey at St-Denis were erected.

However, the militaristic rulers of the succeeding Carolingian dynasty, beginning with Charles 'the Hammer' Martel (688–741), were almost permanently away fighting wars in the east, and Paris languished, controlled mostly by its counts. When Charles Martel's grandson, Charlemagne (768–814), moved his capital to Aix-la-Chapelle (today's Aachen in Germany), Paris' fate was sealed. Basically a group of separate villages with its centre on the Ile de la Cité, Paris was badly defended throughout the second half of the 9th century and was raided incessantly by Vikings, who eventually established control over northern and northwestern France.

In the early Middle Ages, most of today's Paris was either a carpet of fields and vineyards or a boggy, waterlogged marsh.

The Paris counts, whose powers had grown as the Carolingians feuded among themselves, elected one of their own, Hugh Capet, as king at Senlis in 987. He made Paris the royal seat and lived in the renovated palace of the Roman governor on the Île de la Cité (site of the present Palais de Justice). Under the 800 years of Capetian rule that followed, Paris prospered as a centre of politics, commerce, trade, religion and culture.

The city's strategic riverside position ensured its importance throughout the Middle Ages. The first guilds were created in the 11th century, and in the mid-12th century the ship merchants' guild bought the principal river port, by today's Hôtel de Ville (City Hall), from the crown. Frenetic building marked the 12th and 13th centuries. The Basilique de St-Denis was commissioned in 1136 and less than three decades later work started on Notre Dame. During the reign of Philippe-Auguste (r 1180–1223), the city wall was expanded and fortified with 25 gates and hundreds of protective towers.

The swampy Marais was drained for agricultural use and settlement, prompting the eventual need for the food markets at Les Halles in 1183 and the Louvre as a riverside fortress in the 13th century. In a bid to resolve ghastly traffic congestion and stinking excrement (by 1200 the city had a population of 200,000), Philippe-Auguste paved four of Paris' main streets with metre-square sandstone blocks. Meanwhile, the Left Bank – particularly in the Latin Quarter – developed as a centre of European learning and erudition. Ill-fated lovers Pierre Abélard and Héloïse penned the finest poetry of the age and treatises on philosophy, Thomas Aquinas taught at the new university, and the Sorbonne opened its scholarly doors.

451

Attila the Hun unexpectedly turns away from Paris to march south; credit is given to the prayers of Geneviève, who later becomes the city's patron saint.

509

Clovis I becomes the first king of the Franks and the first Frankish ruler to convert to Christianity. He declares Paris the seat of his new kingdom.

845–86

Paris is repeatedly raided by Vikings for over four decades, including the siege of 885–86 by Siegfried the Saxon, which lasts 10 months but ends in victory for the French.

987

Five centuries of Merovingian and Carolingian rule ends with the crowning of Hugh Capet; the Capetian dynasty will rule for the next eight centuries.

STAR-CROSSED LOVERS

He was a brilliant 39-year-old philosopher and logician with a reputation for controversial ideas. She was the beautiful niece of a canon at Notre Dame. And like Bogart and Bergman in *Casablanca* and Romeo and Juliet in Verona, they had to fall in love – in medieval Paris, of all damned times and places.

In 1118 the wandering scholar Pierre Abélard (1079–1142) found his way to Paris, having clashed with yet another theologian in the provinces. There he was employed by Canon Fulbert of Notre Dame to tutor his niece Héloïse (1101–64). One thing led to another and a son, Astrolabe, was born. Abélard married his sweetheart in secret and when Fulbert found out he was outraged. He had Abélard castrated and sent Héloïse off to a convent, where she eventually became abbess. Abélard took monastic vows at the abbey in St-Denis and continued his studies and controversial writings.

Yet, all the while, the star-crossed lovers corresponded, he sending tender advice on how to run the convent and she writing passionate, poetic letters to her lost lover. The two were reunited only in death: in 1817 their remains were disinterred and brought to Père Lachaise cemetery in the 20e, where they lie together beneath a neo-Gothic tombstone in division 7.

Dark Times: War & Death

Political tension and open insurrection were brought to Paris by the Hundred Years' War (1337–1453); the Black Death (1348–49), which killed over a third of Paris' population; and the development of free, independent cities elsewhere in Europe. In 1420 the dukes of Burgundy, allied with the English, occupied the capital and two years later John Plantagenet, duke of Bedford, was installed as regent of France for the English king, Henry VI, then an infant. Henry was crowned king of France at Notre Dame less than 10 years later, but Paris was almost continuously under siege from the French.

Around that time a 17-year-old peasant girl known to history as Jeanne d'Arc (Joan of Arc) persuaded the French pretender to the throne that she'd received a divine mission from God to expel the English from France and bring about his coronation as Charles VII. She rallied French troops and defeated the English north of Orléans, and Charles was crowned at Reims. But Joan of Arc failed to take Paris. In 1430 she was captured, convicted of witchcraft and heresy by a tribunal of French ecclesiastics and burned at the stake. Charles VII returned to Paris in 1436, ending over 16 years of occupation, but the English were not entirely driven from French territory for another 17 years.

1066

The so-called Norman Conquest of England ignites almost 300 years of conflict between the Normans in western and northern France and the Capetians in Paris.

1163

Two centuries of nonstop building reaches its zenith with the commencement of Notre Dame Cathedral under the bishop of Paris; construction will continue for over a century-and-a-half.

1358

The Hundred Years' War (1337–1453) between France and England and the devastation and poverty caused by the plague lead to the ill-fated peasants' revolt led by Étienne Marcel.

1572

Some 3000 Huguenots who are in Paris to celebrate the wedding of the Protestant Henri of Navarre (the future Henri IV) are slaughtered on 23–24 August.

The Rise of the Royal Court

Under Louis XI (r 1461–83) the city's first printing press was installed at the Sorbonne and churches were built around the city in the Flamboyant Gothic style. But it was during the reign of François I in the early 16th century that Renaissance ideas of scientific and geographic scholarship and discovery really assumed a new importance, as did the value of secular matters over religious life. Writers such as Rabelais, Marot and Ronsard of La Pléiade were influential, as were artist and architect disciples of Michelangelo and Raphael who worked towards a new architectural style designed to reflect the splendour of the monarchy (which was fast moving towards absolutism) and of Paris as the capital of a powerful centralised state. At François I's chateau, superb artisans, many brought over from Italy, blended Italian and French styles to create what is known as the First School of Fontainebleau.

In 1292 the medieval city of Paris counted 352 streets, 10 squares and 11 crossroads.

But all this grandeur and show of strength was not enough to stem the tide of Protestant Reformation sweeping Europe in the 1530s, strengthened in France by the ideas of John Calvin. Following the Edict of January 1562, which afforded the Protestants certain rights, the Wars of Religion, which lasted three dozen years, broke out between the Huguenots (French Protestants who received help from the English), the Catholic League (led by the House of Guise) and the Catholic monarchy. On 7 May 1588, on the 'Day of the Barricades', Henri III, who had granted many concessions to the Huguenots, was forced to flee from the Louvre when the Catholic League rose against him. He was assassinated the following year.

Henri IV, founder of the Bourbon dynasty, issued the controversial Edict of Nantes in 1598, guaranteeing the Huguenots many civil and political rights, notably freedom of conscience. Ultra-Catholic Paris refused to allow the new Protestant king to enter the city, and a siege of the capital continued for almost five years. Only when Henri IV embraced Catholicism at the cathedral in St-Denis – *'Paris vaut bien un messe'* (Paris is well worth a Mass), he is reputed to have said during Communion – did the capital submit to him. Henri's rule ended abruptly in 1610 when he was assassinated by a Catholic fanatic when his coach became stuck in traffic along rue de la Ferronnerie, south of Les Halles.

Paintings by Jules Hardouin-Mansart in the Chapelle Royal at Versailles evoke the idea that the French king was chosen by God and is thus his lieutenant on earth – a divinity the 'Sun King' believed in devoutly.

Arguably France's best-known king of this or any other century, Louis XIV (r 1643–1715), aka 'Le Roi Soleil' (the Sun King), ascended the throne at the tender age of five. He involved the kingdom in a series of costly, almost continuous wars with Holland, Austria and England, which gained France territory but nearly bankrupted the treasury.

1589

Henry IV, the first Bourbon king, ascends the throne after renouncing Protestantism.

1643

'Sun King' Louis XIV ascends the throne aged five but only assumes absolute power in 1661.

1756–63

The Seven Years' War sees France lose flourishing colonies in Canada, the West Indies and India.

14 July 1789

The French Revolution begins when a mob arms itself with weapons taken from the Hôtel des Invalides and storms the prison at Bastille, freeing a total of just seven prisoners.

State taxation, imposed to refill the coffers, caused widespread poverty and vagrancy, especially in cities. In Versailles, Louis XIV built an extravagant palace and made his courtiers compete with each other for royal favour, thereby quashing the ambitious, feuding aristocracy and creating the first centralised French state. In 1685 he revoked the Edict of Nantes.

From Revolution to Republic

During the so-called Age of Enlightenment, the royal court moved back to Paris from Versailles and the city effectively became the centre of Europe. Yet as the 18th century progressed, new economic and social circumstances rendered the *ancien régime* dangerously out of step with the needs of the country.

During Louis XIII's reign (1610–43) two uninhabited islets in the Seine – Île Notre Dame and Île aux Vaches – were joined to form the Île de St-Louis.

By the late 1780s the indecisive Louis XVI and his domineering Vienna-born queen, Marie Antoinette, had alienated virtually every segment of society. When they tried to neutralise the power of more reform-minded delegates at a meeting of the États-Généraux (States-General) in Versailles from May to June 1789, the masses – spurred by the oratory and inflammatory tracts circulating at places like the Café de Foy at Palais Royal – took to the streets of Paris. On 14 July a mob raided the armoury at the Hôtel des Invalides for rifles, seized 32,000 muskets and stormed the prison at Bastille. Enter the French Revolution.

At first the Revolution was in the hands of moderate republicans, the Girondins. France was declared a constitutional monarchy and reforms were introduced, including the adoption of the Déclaration des Droits de l'Homme and du Citoyen (Declaration of the Rights of Man and of the Citizen). But as the masses armed themselves against the external threat to the new government – posed by Austria, Prussia and the exiled French nobles – patriotism and nationalism mixed with extreme fervour and then popularised and radicalised the Revolution. It was not long before the Girondins lost out to the extremist Jacobins, who abolished the monarchy and declared the First Republic. The Assemblée Nationale was replaced by an elected Revolutionary Convention.

The population of Paris at the start of François' reign in 1515 was 170,000 – still almost 20% less than it had been some three centuries before, when the Black Death had decimated the city population.

Louis XVI was convicted of 'conspiring against the liberty of the nation' in January 1793 and guillotined at place de la Révolution, today's place de la Concorde. Two months later the Jacobins set up the notorious Committee of Public Safety to deal with national defence and try 'traitors'. The subsequent Reign of Terror (September 1793 to July 1794) saw religious freedoms revoked, churches closed and desecrated, cathe-

1793
Louis XVI is tried and convicted as citizen 'Louis Capet' (as all kings since Hugh Capet were declared to have ruled illegally) and executed.

1799
Napoléon Bonaparte overthrows the Directory and seizes control of the government in a coup d'état, opening the doors to 16 years of despotic rule, victory and then defeat.

1815
British and Prussian forces under the Duke of Wellington defeat Napoléon at Waterloo; he is sent into exile for the second time, this time to a remote island in the South Atlantic.

1830
During the July Revolution, revolutionaries seize the Hôtel de Ville and overthrow Charles X (r 1824–30). Place de la Bastille's Colonne de Juillet honours those killed.

drals turned into 'Temples of Reason' and thousands incarcerated in dungeons in La Conciergerie before being beheaded.

After the Reign of Terror faded, a five-man delegation of moderate republicans set itself up to rule the republic as the Directory.

Napoléon & Empire

The post-Revolutionary government was far from stable and when Napoléon returned to Paris in 1799, he found a chaotic republic in which few citizens had any faith. In November, when it appeared that the Jacobins were again on the ascendancy in the legislature, Napoléon tricked the delegates into leaving Paris for St-Cloud to the southwest ('for their own protection'), overthrew the discredited Directory and assumed power.

At first, Napoléon took the post of First Consul. In a referendum three years later he was named 'Consul for Life' and his birthday became a national holiday. By December 1804, when he crowned himself 'Emperor of the French' in the presence of Pope Pius VII at Notre Dame, the scope and nature of Napoléon's ambitions were obvious to all. But to consolidate and legitimise his authority, Napoléon needed more victories on the battlefield. So began a seemingly endless series of wars and victories by which France would come to control most of Europe.

In 1812 Napoléon invaded Russia and captured Moscow, only for his army to be quickly wiped out by the brutal Russian winter. Two years later Allied armies entered Paris, exiled Napoléon to Elba and restored the House of Bourbon to the French throne at the Congress of Vienna (1814–15).

But in early 1815 Napoléon escaped the Mediterranean island, landed in southern France and gathered a large army as he marched towards Paris. On 1 June he reclaimed the throne at celebrations held at the Champs de Mars. But his reign came to an end just three weeks later when his forces were defeated at Waterloo in Belgium. Napoléon was exiled again, this time to St Helena in the South Atlantic, where he died in 1821. In 1840 his remains were moved to Paris' Église du Dôme.

The Second Republic was established and elections in 1848 brought in Napoléon's inept nephew, the German-reared (and -accented) Louis Napoléon Bonaparte, as president. In 1851 he staged a coup d'état and proclaimed himself Emperor Napoléon III of the Second Empire, which lasted until 1870.

France enjoyed significant economic growth at this time, and Paris was transformed by town planner Baron Haussmann (1809–91) into the modern city it is today. Huge swaths of the city were completely

In 1774 a 30m section of the rue d'Enfer (today's av Denfert-Rochereau) disappeared into a sinkhole, revealing an inconceivably precarious network of mining tunnels upon which southern Paris had been built.

Haussmann revolutionised Paris' water-supply and sewerage systems, and created some of the city's loveliest parks. The city's first department stores were built, as were several of Paris' delightful shop-strewn *passages couverts* (covered passages).

1848

After more than three decades of monarchy, King Louis-Philippe is ousted and the short-lived Second Republic is established with Napoléon's incompetent nephew at the helm.

1852–70

Paris enjoys significant economic growth during the Second Empire of Napoléon III and much of the city is redesigned or rebuilt by Baron Haussmann as the Paris we know today.

1871

Harsh terms inflicted on France by victor Prussia in the Franco-Prussian War lead to open revolt and anarchy during the Paris Commune.

1880s

The Third Republic ushers in the bloody-then-beautiful belle époque, a madly creative era that conceives bohemian Paris, with its decadent nightclubs and artistic cafes.

rebuilt (demolishing much of medieval Paris in the process), its chaotic narrow streets replaced with the handsome, arrow-straight and wide thoroughfares for which the city is now celebrated.

The Belle Époque

From 1784 to 1836 the duke of Chartres turned the now-dignified Palais Royal into one of Europe's foremost pleasure gardens – 'the capital of Paris' – home to theatres, casinos, shops, cafes and an estimated 2000 prostitutes.

Though it would usher in the glittering belle époque (beautiful age), there was nothing particularly attractive about the start of the Third Republic. Born as a provisional government of national defence in September 1870, it was quickly attacked by the Prussians, who laid siege to Paris and demanded National Assembly elections be held. Unfortunately, the first move made by the resultant monarchist-controlled assembly was to ratify the Treaty of Frankfurt, the harsh terms of which – a huge war indemnity and surrender of the provinces of Alsace and Lorraine – helped instigate a civil war between radical Parisians (known as Communards) and the national government. The Communards took control of the city, establishing the Paris Commune, but the French Army eventually regained the capital several months later. It was a chaotic period, with mass executions on both sides, exiles and rampant destruction (both the Palais des Tuileries and the Hôtel de Ville were burnt down). The Wall of the Federalists in Cimetière du Père Lachaise is a sombre reminder of the bloodshed.

The belle époque launched art nouveau architecture, a whole field of artistic 'isms' from impressionism onwards, and advances in science and engineering, including the construction of the first metro line (1900). World Fairs were held in the capital in 1889 (showcasing the Eiffel Tower) and 1901 (in the purpose-built Petit Palais). The Paris of nightclubs and artistic cafes made its first appearance around this time, and Montmartre became a magnet for artists, writers, pimps and prostitutes.

But all was not well in the republic. France was consumed with a desire for revenge after its defeat by Germany, and was looking for scapegoats. The so-called Dreyfus Affair began in 1894 when a Jewish army captain named Alfred Dreyfus was accused of betraying military secrets to Germany; he was then court-martialled and sentenced to life imprisonment on Devil's Island in French Guiana. Liberal politicians and writers succeeded in having the case reopened despite bitter opposition from the army command, right-wing politicians and many Catholic groups – and Dreyfus was vindicated in 1900. This resulted in more rigorous civilian control of the military and, in 1905, the legal separation of the church and the state. When he died in 1935 Dreyfus was laid to rest in the Cimetière de Montparnasse.

Historical Reads

- *Seven Ages of Paris (Alistair Horne, 2002)*
- *Suite Française (Irène Némirovsky, 2006)*
- *The Paris Wife (Paula McLain, 2011)*

1889

The Eiffel Tower is completed in time for the opening of the Exposition Universelle (World Fair) but is vilified in the press and on the street as the 'metal asparagus' – or worse.

1914

Germany and Austria-Hungary declare war on Russia and France. German troops reach the River Marne 15km east of Paris and the government moves to Bordeaux.

1918

An armistice ending WWI, signed 82km northeast of Paris, returns Alsace and Lorraine; of the eight million French called to arms, 1.3 million die and another million are crippled.

1920s

Paris sparkles as centre of the avant-garde with its newfound liberalism, cutting-edge nightlife and painters pushing into new fields of art like cubism and surrealism.

WWII & Occupation

Two days after the German invasion of Poland on 1 September 1939, Britain and France declared war on Germany. For the first nine months Parisians joked about *le drôle de guerre* – what Britons called 'the phoney war' – in which nothing happened. But the battle for France began in earnest in May 1940 and by 14 June France had capitulated. Paris was occupied, and almost half the population fled the city by car or bicycle or on foot.

The British expeditionary force sent to help the French barely managed to avoid capture by retreating to Dunkirk, described so vividly in Ian McEwan's *Atonement* (2001), and crossing the English Channel in small boats. The Maginot Line, a supposedly impregnable wall of fortifications along the Franco-German border, had proved useless – the German armoured divisions simply outflanked it by going through Belgium.

The Germans divided France into two: a zone under direct German rule (along the western coast and the north, including Paris); and a puppet state based in the spa town of Vichy and led by General Philippe Pétain, the ageing WWI hero of the Battle of Verdun. Pétain's collaborationist government and French police forces in German-occupied areas (including Paris) helped the Nazis round up 160,000 French Jews and others for deportation to concentration and extermination camps in Germany and Poland.

After the fall of Paris, General Charles de Gaulle, France's undersecretary of war, fled to London. He set up a French government-in-exile and established the Forces Françaises Libres (Free French Forces), a military force dedicated to fighting the Germans alongside the Allies.

The liberation of France started with the Allied landings in Normandy on D-Day (Jour-J in French): 6 June 1944. On 15 August that same year, Allied forces also landed in southern France. After a brief insurrection by the Resistance and general strikes by the metro and police, Paris was liberated on 25 August by an Allied force spearheaded by Free French units – these units were sent in ahead of the Americans so that the French would have the honour of liberating the capital the following day.

Hitler, who visited Paris in June 1940 and loved it, demanded that the city be burnt towards the end of the war. It was an order that, thankfully, was not obeyed.

Essential Historical Encounters

Arènes de Lutèce (Latin Quarter)

Notre Dame (The Islands)

Hôtel des Invalides (St-Germain & Les Invalides)

Les Catacombes (Montparnasse & Southern Paris)

The Extraordinary Adventures of Adèle Blanc-Sec features the swashbuckling adventures of Adèle in early-20th-century Paris. Originally a graphic-novel series created by Jacques Tardi, it was released as a film in 2010.

1940

After over 10 months of *le drôle de guerre* (phoney war), Germany launches the battle for France, and the four-year occupation of Paris under direct German rule begins.

25 August 1944

Spearheaded by Free French units, Allied forces liberate Paris and the city escapes destruction, despite Hitler's orders that it be torched; the war in Europe will end nine months later.

1949

Simone de Beauvoir publishes her groundbreaking and very influential study *Le Deuxième Sexe* (The Second Sex) just four years after French women win the right to vote.

1958

Charles de Gaulle returns to power after more than a dozen years in opposition, to form the Fifth Republic.

Postwar Instability

After Paris fell to German WWII forces on 14 June 1940, the French Resistance cut the Eiffel Tower's lift cables to prevent Hitler from riding to the top. Faced with the prospect of climbing the stairs, he opted out of visiting altogether.

De Gaulle returned to Paris and established a provisional government. But in January 1946 he resigned as president, wrongly believing the move would provoke a popular outcry for his return. A few months later a new constitution was approved by referendum. De Gaulle formed his own party (Rassemblement du Peuple Français) and spent the next 13 years in opposition.

The Fourth Republic saw a series of unstable coalition cabinets following one after another with bewildering speed (on average, one every six months), and economic recovery, helped immeasurably by massive American aid. France's disastrous defeat in Vietnam in 1954 ended its colonial supremacy in Southeast Asia. France also tried to suppress an uprising by Arab nationalists in Algeria, where more than a million French settlers lived.

The Fourth Republic came to an end in 1958, when extreme right-wingers, furious at what they saw as defeatism instead of tough action in dealing with the uprising in Algeria, began conspiring in an effort to overthrow the government. De Gaulle was brought back to power to prevent a military coup and possible civil war. He drafted a new constitution that handed considerable powers to the president, at the expense of the National Assembly.

Charles de Gaulle & the Fifth Republic

Historians debate the overall military effectiveness of the Resistance. But it served as an enormous boost to French morale and continues to inspire French literature and cinema.

The Fifth Republic was rocked in 1961 by an attempted coup staged in Algiers by a group of right-wing military officers. When it failed, the Organisation de l'Armée Secrète (OAS) – a group of French *colons* (colonists) and sympathisers opposed to Algerian independence – turned to terrorism, trying several times to assassinate de Gaulle and nearly succeeding in August 1962 in the town of Clamart just southwest of Paris.

In 1962, after more than 12,000 had died as a result of this 'civil war', de Gaulle negotiated an end to the war in Algeria. Some 750,000 *pieds noirs* (black feet), as Algerian-born French people are known in France, came to France and the capital. Meanwhile, almost all of the other French colonies and protectorates in Africa had demanded and achieved independence. Shrewdly, the French government began a program of economic and military aid to its former colonies to bolster France's waning importance internationally and to create a bloc of French-speaking nations – *la francophonie* – in the developing world.

Paris retained its position as a creative and intellectual centre, particularly in philosophy and film-making, and the 1960s saw large parts of the Marais beautifully restored.

1962

War in Algeria is brought to an end after claiming the lives of more than 12,000 people; three-quarters of a million Algerian-born French citizens arrive in France.

1968

Paris is rocked by student-led riots that bring the nation and the city to the brink of civil war; as a result de Gaulle is forced to resign the following year.

1977

Jacques Chirac, the first Paris mayor to be elected with real power, assumes office.

1978

The Centre Pompidou, the first of a string of *grands projets* – huge public edifices through which French leaders seek to immortalise themselves – opens to great controversy.

A Pivotal Year: 1968

The year 1968 was a watershed. In March a large demonstration in Paris against the war in Vietnam gave impetus to the student movement, and protests by students of the University of Paris peppered the capital for most of spring. In May police broke up yet another demonstration, prompting angry students to occupy the Sorbonne and erect barricades in the Latin Quarter. Workers joined in very quickly, with six million people across France participating in a general strike that virtually paralysed the country. It was a period of creativity and new ideas with slogans like *'L'Imagination au Pouvoir'* (Put Imagination in Power) and *'Sous les Pavés, la Plage'* (Under the Cobblestones, the Beach) – a reference to Parisians' favoured material for building barricades and what they could expect to find beneath them – popping up everywhere.

But such an alliance between workers and students couldn't last long. While the former wanted to reap greater benefits from the consumer market, the latter supposedly wanted to destroy it. De Gaulle took advantage of this division and appealed to people's fear of anarchy. And just as Paris and the rest of France seemed on the verge of revolution, a mighty 100,000-strong crowd of Gaullists came out on the streets of Paris to show their support for the government, quashing any such possibility. Stability was restored.

In 1923 French women obtained the right to – wait for it – open their own mail. The right to vote didn't come until 1945, and a woman still needed her husband's permission to open a bank account or get a passport until 1964.

Modern Society

Once stability was restored the government immediately decentralised the higher-education system and implemented a series of reforms (including lowering the voting age to 18 and enacting an abortion law) throughout the 1970s to create the modern society France is today.

President Charles de Gaulle resigned in 1969 and was succeeded by the Gaullist leader Georges Pompidou and later Valéry Giscard d'Estaing. Socialist François Mitterrand became president in 1981 and immediately nationalised privately owned banks, large industrial groups and other parts of the economy. A more moderate economic policy in the mid-1980s ensured a second term in office for the then 69-year-old Mitterrand.

Jacques Chirac, mayor of Paris since 1977, took over the presidential baton in 1995 and received high marks in his first few months for his direct words and actions in EU matters and the war in Bosnia. But his decision to resume nuclear testing on the French Polynesian island of Mururoa and a nearby atoll was met with outrage in France and abroad, and when, in 1997, Chirac gambled with an early parliamentary election for June, the move backfired. Chirac remained president, but

On 15 October 1959, then senator and future president François Mitterrand was involved in a staged assassination attempt on his own life, now known as the infamous Observatory Affair.

1989

President Mitterrand's *grand projet*, the Opéra de Paris Bastille, opens to mark the bicentennial of the French Revolution; IM Pei's Grande Pyramide is unveiled at the Louvre.

1998

France beats Brazil to win the World Cup at the spanking-new Stade de France (Stadium of France) in St-Denis, north of central Paris.

2001

Socialist Bertrand Delanoë becomes the first openly gay mayor of Paris (and of any European capital); he is wounded in a knife attack by a homophobic assailant the following year.

2002

The French franc is thrown onto the scrap heap of history as the country adopts the euro as its official currency, along with 14 other EU member states.

his party, the Rassemblement Pour la République (RPR; Rally for the Republic), lost support, and a coalition of Socialists, Communists and Greens came to power – under which France's infamous 35-hour working week was introduced.

The book (1971) and film (1973) *The Day of the Jackal* portray a fictional account of the attempts by the OAS (a renegade paramilitary group who fought against Algerian independence) to take de Gaulle's life.

Chirac's second term, starting in 2002, was marred by some of the worst violence seen in Paris since WWII. In autumn 2005, following the death of two teenage boys of North African origin hiding in an electrical substation while on the run from the police, riots broke out in Paris' *cités,* the enormous housing estates encircling the capital where a dispossessed population lives. The violence quickly spread to other cities in France and the government declared a state of emergency. Only 9000 burnt cars and buildings later was peace in Paris restored.

The Presidential Pendulum

Presidential elections in 2007 ushered old-school Jacques Chirac out and the dynamic, ambitious and media-savvy Nicolas Sarkozy in. Contrary to the rigorous economic-reform platform on which he'd been elected and against the backdrop of the global recession, however, Sarkozy struggled to keep the French economy buoyant. Attempts to introduce reforms – eg the scaling back of the extremely generous French pension system – provoked widespread horror and a series of national strikes and protests. Sarkozy's popularity plummeted, paving the way for socialist François Hollande's victory in the 2012 presidential elections.

With France still struggling to restart the economy, Hollande pledged to end austerity measures and reduce unemployment. His failure to deliver on campaign promises saw his popularity plunge even faster and further than Sarkozy's and resulted in a near-total wipeout for French socialists in the 2014 municipal elections. The 2014 election of socialist Anne Hidalgo, Paris' first female mayor, meant the capital was one of the few cities to remain on the political left.

Bertrand Delanoë, a socialist backed by the Green Party, became the first openly gay mayor of Paris (and any European capital) in 2001. He was re-elected in 2008.

Turbulent Times

The year 2015 was a harrowing one for the French capital. On 7 January the offices of magazine *Charlie Hebdo* were attacked in response to satirical images it published of the prophet Muhammad. Eleven staff and one police officer were killed and a further 22 people were injured. The hashtag #jesuischarlie (I am Charlie) became a slogan of support around the globe.

2004

France bans the wearing of crucifixes, the Islamic headscarf and other overtly religious symbols in state schools.

2005

The French electorate overwhelmingly rejects the EU Constitution; the suburbs surrounding Paris are wracked by rioting youths.

2010

Countrywide strikes and protests briefly paralyse the country after the government announces plans to raise the retirement age from 60 to 62 years.

2011

The controversial French parliamentary ban on burkas in public comes into effect in April; Muslim women wearing the Islamic face-covering veil risk a fine.

But worse was to come. On the night of 13 November 2015 a series of coordinated terrorist attacks occurred in Paris and St-Denis – the deadliest on French soil since WWII. Three explosions shook the Stade de France stadium during a football friendly match between Germany and France. A series of neighbourhood restaurants and their outdoor terraces in the 10e and 11e were attacked by suicide bombers and gunmen. Three gunmen fired into the audience of Le Bataclan, where American band Eagles of Death Metal were performing. Over the course of the evening's terror 130 people lost their lives (89 in Le Bataclan alone) and 368 were injured, 99 seriously. Paris went into lockdown, the army was mobilised and a state of emergency was declared.

Parisians responded to the trauma by establishing memorials at the fatality sites and place de la République, which became the focal point for the city's outpouring of grief, and by taking to cafe terraces and other public spaces. The hashtag #jesuisenterrasse (I am on the terrace) represented Parisians' refusal to live in fear.

The city of Paris also refused to allow daily life to be disrupted. The long-planned United Nations Climate Change Conference (COP21) went ahead from 30 November to 12 December 2015. During the conference leaders from around the world reached an agreement to limit global warming to less than 2°C by the end of the century.

The French receive free education and health care, state-subsidised child care, travel concessions for families, ample leisure time and a 35-hour working week.

New President, New Directions

France's most recent presidential elections took place in 2017. The traditional parties were eliminated in the first round, with Emmanuel Macron, who launched centrist, pro-EU movement En Marche! in 2016 – now the party La République en Marche – defeating far-right Front National candidate Marine Le Pen 66.1% to 33.9% in the second-round run-off. At age 39, Macron became France's youngest-ever president. La République en Marche went on to field candidates in 2017's legislative elections and secure an absolute majority (308 seats) in the Assemblée Nationale, allowing Macron to forge ahead with economic reforms.

Late 2017 saw Paris awarded the hosting rights of the 2024 Summer Olympics and Summer Paralympics, which will also see numerous infrastructure projects completed by the opening of the games. Shortly afterwards, France was also awarded the 2023 Rugby World Cup.

The Latin motto *'fluctuat nec mergitur'* ('tossed but not sunk') was adopted by Paris around 1358. Officialised by Baron Haussmann in 1853, it still appears on the city's coat of arms. It became emblematic of the city's spirit following the 2015 terrorist attacks, when Paris' resilience came to the fore.

2014

Spanish-born Anne Hidalgo becomes the first female mayor of Paris after defeating Sarkozy protégé Nathalie Kosciusko-Morizet.

2015

The year is bookended by deadly terrorist attacks, at the offices of magazine *Charlie Hebdo* on 7 January, and at multiple locations including concert hall Le Bataclan on 13 November.

2015

Paris successfully hosts the United Nations Climate Change Conference (COP21), during which world leaders agree on measures to reduce global warming.

2018

Hundreds of thousands of supporters line the Champs-Élysées to welcome home France's football team, following their World Cup victory in Russia.

Fashion

Yves Saint Laurent once declared that fashion is a way of life, and most Parisians would agree. Dressing well is part of the Parisian DNA, the world's eyes are on the city during the biannual fashion weeks, and new labels spring up in the French capital every year. But less well known is that Parisian *haute couture* (literally 'high sewing') as it exists today was created by an Englishman.

Revolution & Drama

Nicknamed 'the Napoléon of costumers', 20-year-old Englishman Charles Frederick Worth (1825–95) arrived in Paris and revolutionised fashion by banishing the crinoline (stiffened petticoat), lifting hemlines to ankle length and presenting his creations on live models. The House of Worth stayed in the family for four generations until the 1950s.

In the 1990s highly creative, rebel-yell British designers such as Alexander McQueen (1969–2010) and John Galliano (b 1960) dominated Paris' fashion scene. One of the industry's biggest influencers, Gibraltar-born and London-raised Galliano moved to Paris in 1991 and became chief designer at Givenchy in 1995. A year later he moved to Dior, the legendary French fashion house responsible for re-establishing Paris as world fashion capital after WWII. Galliano's first women's collection for Dior was spectacular – models waltzed down a catwalk framed by 500 gold chairs and 4000 roses arranged to recreate the postwar glamour of Christian Dior's 1946 showroom on av Montaigne, 8e, in Paris' legendary Triangle d'Or (Golden Triangle).

The downfall of fashion's talented *enfant terrible* was dramatic. In 2011 Galliano was caught on camera casting public insults at punters at his neighbourhood cafe-bar La Perle in Le Marais. He was dismissed by the House of Dior and later found guilty in court of anti-Semitic abuse.

Fashion Museums & Exhibitions

Musée Yves Saint Laurent Paris, 16e

Musée de la Mode de la Ville de Paris, 16e

Cité de la Mode et du Design (Les Docks), 13e

Contemporary Fashion

Outlandish designs by rising stars such as Serkan Cura (who crafts work-of-art dresses from feathers and Swarovski crystals) or world-famous couturiers like 'wild child' Jean-Paul Gaultier (known for putting men in punky skirts and Madonna in her signature conical bra) might strut down the Paris catwalk during fashion week. But you encounter few Cura- or Gaultier-clad women in the metro: Parisian style is generally too conservative for that.

London-inspired street wear jumps off the shelves in trendy shops around rue Étienne Marcel in the Louvre & Les Halles neighbourhood, and Le Marais. The Haut Marais, 3e, is known for its young designer boutiques. Streetwise menswear brand Pigalle is based in the neighbourhood of the same name; it was established by designer and basketball player Stephane Ashpool, who grew up here.

Other names to watch and wear include Antonin Tron, Pierre Kaczmarek (look for his label After Homework), Marine Serre (winner of the LVMH prize in 2017), Valentine Gauthier, Sakina M'sa, and Anne Elisabeth, a well-travelled Parisian designer with boutiques in the 1er and

6e. Christelle Kocher's Koché is based in edgy Ménilmontant. Parisian handbag designers include Nat & Nin, Kasia Dietz and Jamin Puech.

BCBG & Intello

In upper-crust circles, the BCBG *(bon chic bon genre)* woman shops at department store Le Bon Marché or Chanel and rarely ventures outside her preferred districts: the 7e, 8e and 16e. Fast-growing brands like Kooples, Maje, Sandro, Comptoir des Cotonniers and Zadig & Voltaire are huge among BCBG.

The chic Left Bank *intello* (intellectual) shops for trendy but highly wearable fashion at upmarket high-street boutiques such as Agnès b (created in Paris in 1975 by Versailles designer Agnès Troublé – the 'b' gives a nod to her husband) and APC (Atelier de Production et de Création).

Bobo

Bastille, Le Marais and the 10e around Canal St-Martin are stomping grounds of the *bobo* (bourgeois bohemian) – modern bohemians with wealthy bourgeois backgrounds, whose style roots itself in nostalgia for that last voyage to India, Tibet or Senegal and that avowed commitment to free trade and beads. The wildest *bobos* wear Kate Mack and dress their kids in romantic rockesque designs by Liza Korn, at home in 10e.

Younger professional *bobos* frequent concept store Merci or smaller concept stores with carefully curated collections like L'Éclaireur and the Broken Arm in Le Marais. Isabel Marant – with boutiques in Le Marais, Bastille and St-Germain des Prés – enjoys cult worship among Parisian *bobos* thanks to her chic but easy style that teams wearable-year-round floral dresses or denim mini skirts with loose knits and lush scarves. Another favourite is Vanessa Bruno, a Parisian brand again known for its wearable, if slightly edgy, fashion, such as crocheted bra tops, and cotton skirts with metallic thread to maintain shape. On the jewellery front, designs by Marion Vidal are bold, funky and heavily architecture-influenced.

Paris' Brooklyn-styled hipster is similar to a *bobo* but often without the money. Parisian hipsters reject big-name or known fashion labels for a 'purist', often vintage, look.

Paris coined the expression *lèche-vitrine* (literally 'window-licker') for window shopping. 'Tasting' without buying is an art like any other, so don't be shy. The fancy couture houses on av Montaigne may seem daunting but, in most, no appointment is necessary and you can simply walk in.

Ready to Wear

Céline, prized for its stylish and clever minimalism since 1945, is a luxury label so popular it's practically mainstream in its ready-to-wear, 'fashion for everyone' approach. Chloé is the other big ready-to-wear house, created in 1952 and the first *haute couture* label to introduce (in 1956) a designer ready-to-wear collection. Paris' prêt-à-porter (ready-to-wear) industry was born.

Nostalgia & Recycling

Parisians' appreciation of quality means that the desire in less-uber-trendy circles to have an original Hermès scarf or Chanel black dress never tires.

Vintage

Parisian women play safe with classic designs and monotones, jazzed up by a scarf (those by Hermès, founded by a saddle-maker in 1837, are the most famous) or other simple accessory, hence the fervent nostalgia for the practical designs and modern simplicity of interwar designer

THE SHOW OF SHOWS

The Paris fashion *haute-couture* shows fall in late January for the spring/summer collections and early July for autumn/winter ones. But most established couturiers present a more affordable prêt-à-porter line, and many have abandoned *haute couture* altogether. Prêt-à-porter shows (aka Paris Fashion Week) are in late February/early March and late September/early October. Shows are exclusive affairs not open to the general public.

For alternative catwalk action, reserve a spot at the Friday-afternoon fashion show (March to June and September to December) at department store Galeries Lafayette, 9e.

Coco Chanel (1883–1971), celebrated creator of the 1920s' 'little black dress'. Equal enthusiasm for pieces by Givenchy, Féraud and other designers from the 1950s heyday of Paris fashion contribute to the overwhelming demand today for vintage clothing.

Twice a year Parisian auction house Hôtel Drouot hosts *haute couture* auctions. Collector Didier Ludot has sold the city's finest couture creations of yesteryear in his exclusive boutique at Palais Royal since 1975. In St-Germain, Catherine B specialises in vintage fashion and accessories from fashion houses Chanel and Hermès only, with a collection at any one time of some 1500 pieces.

Post-Vintage

Post-vintage fashion is about recycling. Art and fashion studio Andrea Crews, originally based in Pigalle and now at home in Le Marais, was among the first to reinvent grandpa's discarded shirts and daughter's has-beens into new hip garments.

Two films about fashion icon Yves Saint Laurent were released in 2014: the more innocous 'official' film, *Yves Saint Laurent*, directed by Jalil Lespert (using original costumes), and the edgier but much longer unauthorised film, *Saint Laurent*, directed by Bertrand Bonello.

Trends of Tomorrow

Whereas once young designers were snapped up by the big fashion houses, industry prizes and government grants have smoothed the way for a new wave of independent labels.

Each year the city of Paris' Grand Prix Création de la Ville de Paris is awarded to the 'Best New Designer' (working in the trade for under three years) and 'Best Confirmed Designer' (at least three years in the fashion biz). The list of prize laureates is tantamount to a who's who of tomorrow's fashion scene.

Clothing labels to watch include Each X Other (enlisting artists to help design unique fabrics, prints and cuts), Vetements (recycled oversized off-kilter but elegant designs), Jacquemus (deconstructed surrealist asymmetrical concepts), Etudes Studio (chunky genderless contemporary clothing with lots of solid colours), MiniMe Paris (*Alice in Wonderland* meets pop art) and Y/Project (unusual shapes that blur gender lines). Accessories-wise, look out for perforated leather and animal-print shoes (ankle boots, mules, high heels and sandals) by Aleph Mendel, and customisable handbags with interchangeable zip-on leather strips by Amalgam.

Architecture

It took disease, clogged streets, an antiquated sewerage system and Baron Georges-Eugène Haussmann to drag architectural Paris out of the Middle Ages and into the modern world. Yet ever since Haussmann's radical transformation of the city in the 19th century, which saw entire sections razed and thousands of people displaced, Paris has never looked back. Today its skyline shimmers with the whole gamut of architectural styles, from Roman arenas and Gothic cathedrals to postmodernist cubes and futuristic skyscrapers.

Gallo-Roman

Traces of Roman Paris can be seen in the residential foundations in the Crypte Archéologique in front of Notre Dame; in the Arènes de Lutèce; and in the *frigidarium* (cooling room) and other remains of Roman baths dating from around AD 200 at the Musée National du Moyen Âge.

The latter museum also contains the *Pillier des Nautes* (Boatsmen's Pillar), one of the most valuable legacies of the Gallo-Roman period. It is a 2.5m-high monument dedicated to Jupiter and was erected by the boatmen's guild during the reign of Tiberius (AD 14–37) on the Île de la Cité. The boat has become the symbol of Paris, and the city's Latin motto is '*Fluctuat Nec Mergitur*' (Tossed by Waves but Does Not Sink).

Iconic Buildings

- *Eiffel Tower (Eiffel Tower & Western Paris)*
- *Louvre pyramid (Louvre & Les Halles)*
- *Centre Pompidou (Louvre & Les Halles)*

Merovingian & Carolingian

Although quite a few churches were built in Paris during the Merovingian and Carolingian periods (6th to 10th centuries), very little of them remains.

When the Merovingian ruler Clovis I made Paris his seat in the early 6th century, he established an abbey on the south bank of the Seine. All that remains is the Tour Clovis, a heavily restored Romanesque tower within the grounds of the prestigious Lycée Henri IV just east of the Panthéon.

Archaeological excavations in the crypt of the 12th-century Basilique de St-Denis have uncovered extensive tombs from the Merovingian and Carolingian periods; the oldest dates from around AD 570.

Romanesque

A religious revival in the 11th century led to the construction of many *roman* (Romanesque) churches, typically with round arches, heavy walls, few (and small) windows and a lack of ornamentation that bordered on the austere.

No remaining building in Paris is entirely Romanesque, but several have important representative elements. Église St-Germain des Prés, built in the 11th century on the site of the Merovingian ruler Childeric's 6th-century abbey, has been altered many times over the centuries, but the Romanesque bell tower above the west entrance has changed little since AD 1000. The choir, apse and truncated bell tower of Église St-Nicolas des Champs, now part of the Musée des Arts et Métiers, are Romanesque.

Architectural Museums

Cité de l'Architecture et du Patrimoine (Eiffel Tower & Western Paris)

Musée des Plans-Reliefs (St-Germain & Les Invalides)

Pavillon de l'Arsenal (Le Marais, Ménilmontant & Belleville)

Gothic

The world's first Gothic building was Basilique de St-Denis, which combined various late-Romanesque elements to create a new kind of structural support in which each arch counteracted and complemented the next. The basilica served as a model for many 12th-century French cathedrals, including Notre Dame de Paris and Chartres.

In the 14th century the Rayonnant – or Radiant – Gothic style, named after the radiating tracery of the rose windows, developed. Interiors became even lighter thanks to broader windows and more translucent stained glass. One of the most influential Rayonnant buildings was Sainte-Chapelle, whose stained glass forms a curtain of glazing on the 1st floor. The two transept façades of Cathédrale de Notre Dame de Paris and the vaulted Salle des Gens d'Armes (Cavalrymen's Hall) in the Conciergerie, the largest surviving medieval hall in Europe, are other fine examples of Rayonnant Gothic style.

By the 15th century decorative extravagance led to Flamboyant Gothic, so named because the wavy stone carving made the towers appear to be blazing or flaming *(flamboyant)*. Beautifully lacy examples of Flamboyant architecture include the Clocher Neuf (New Bell Tower) at Chartres' cathedral; Église St-Séverin; and Tour St-Jacques, a 52m tower that is all that remains of an early-16th-century church. Inside Église St-Eustache there's some outstanding Flamboyant Gothic arch work holding up the ceiling of the chancel. Several *hôtels particuliers* (private mansions) were also built in this style, including Hôtel de Cluny, now the Musée National du Moyen Âge.

Renaissance

The Renaissance set out to realise a 'rebirth' of classical Greek and Roman culture and first affected France at the end of the 15th century, when Charles VIII began a series of invasions of Italy, returning with some new ideas.

The Early Renaissance style, in which a variety of classical components and decorative motifs (columns, tunnel vaults, round arches, domes etc) were blended with the rich decoration of Flamboyant Gothic, is best exemplified in Paris by Église St-Eustache on the Right Bank and Église St-Étienne du Mont on the Left Bank.

Mannerism was introduced by Italian architects and artists brought to France around 1530 by François I. In 1546 Pierre Lescot designed the richly decorated southwestern corner of the Cour Carrée at the Musée du Louvre.

The Right Bank district of Le Marais remains the best area for Renaissance reminders in Paris proper, with some fine *hôtels particuliers*, such as Hôtel Carnavalet, housing part of the Musée Carnavalet.

The iconic apartment buildings that line the boulevards of central Paris, with their cream-coloured stone and curvy wrought-iron balconies, are the work of Baron Haussmann (1809–91), prefect of the Seine *département* between 1853 and 1870.

Baroque

During the baroque period (tail end of the 16th to late 18th centuries), painting, sculpture and classical architecture were integrated to create structures and interiors of great subtlety, refinement and elegance. With the advent of the baroque, architecture became more pictorial, with painted church ceilings illustrating the Passion of Christ to the faithful, and palaces invoking the power and order of the state.

Salomon de Brosse, who designed the Palais du Luxembourg in the Jardin du Luxembourg in 1615, set the stage for two of France's most prominent early-baroque architects: François Mansart, designer of Église Notre Dame du Val-de-Grâce, and his young rival Louis Le Vau, architect of Château de Vaux-le-Vicomte, which served as a model for Louis XIV's palace at Versailles.

Other fine French-baroque examples include Église St-Louis en l'Île, Chapelle de la Sorbonne, Palais Royal and Hôtel de Sully, with its inner courtyard decorated with allegorical figures.

Interesting and frightening were Le Corbusier's plans for Paris that never left the drawing board. Plan Voisin (Neighbour Project; 1925) envisaged wide boulevards linking the Gare Montparnasse with the Seine and lined with skyscrapers. The project would have required bulldozing much of the Latin Quarter.

Neoclassicism

Neoclassical architecture emerged about 1740 and had its roots in the renewed interest in classical forms – a search for order, reason and serenity through the adoption of forms and conventions of Graeco-Roman antiquity: columns, geometric forms and traditional ornamentation.

Among the earliest examples of this style are the Italianate façade of Église St-Sulpice, and the Petit Trianon at Versailles, designed by Jacques-Ange Gabriel for Louis XV in 1761. The domed building in Paris housing the Institut de France is a masterpiece of early French neoclassical architecture, but France's greatest neoclassical architect of the 18th century was Jacques-Germain Soufflot, creator of the Panthéon in the Latin Quarter.

Neoclassicism came into its own under Napoléon, who used it extensively for monumental architecture intended to embody the grandeur of imperial France and its capital: the Arc de Triomphe, the Arc de Triomphe du Carrousel, Église de Ste-Marie Madeleine, the Bourse de Commerce, and the Assemblée Nationale in the Palais Bourbon. The peak of this great 19th-century movement was Palais Garnier, the city's opera house designed by Charles Garnier.

Art Nouveau

Art nouveau, which emerged in Europe and the USA in the second half of the 19th century under various names (Jugendstil, Sezessionstil, Stile Liberty, Modernisme), caught on quickly in Paris, and its influence lasted until WWI. It was characterised by sinuous curves and flowing, asymmetrical forms reminiscent of creeping vines, water lilies, the patterns on insect wings and the flowering boughs of trees. Influenced by the arrival of exotic objets d'art from Japan, art nouveau's French name came from a Paris gallery that featured works in the 'new art' style.

A lush and photogenic architectural style, art nouveau is expressed to perfection in Paris by Hector Guimard's graceful metro entrances and Le Marais synagogue, the former train station housing the Musée d'Orsay, and department stores including Le Bon Marché, Galeries Lafayette and La Samaritaine.

Designer Rooftops

Cathédrale Notre Dame de Paris (The Islands)

Galeries Lafayette (Champs-Élysées & Grands Boulevards)

Fondation Louis Vuitton (Eiffel Tower & Western Paris)

20th Century

France's best-known 20th-century architect, Charles-Édouard Jeanneret (aka Le Corbusier), was born in Switzerland but settled in Paris in 1917 at the age of 30. A radical modernist, he tried to adapt buildings to their functions in industrialised society without ignoring the human element. Most of Le Corbusier's work was done outside Paris, though he did design several private residences and the Pavillon Suisse, a dormitory for Swiss students at the Cité Internationale Universitaire in the 14e.

ART DECO RENAISSANCE

Recent years have seen a renaissance of some of Paris' loveliest art deco buildings. Neo-Egyptian cinema Le Louxor reopened in 2013. The following year, the luxury McGallery arm of the Accor hotel group opened a five-star hotel and spa in the celebrated Molitor swimming-pool complex in western Paris, where the bikini made its first appearance in the 1930s. In Le Marais, thermal-baths-turned-1980s-nightclub Les Bain Douches – another legendary address – opened as luxury hotel Les Bains after years of being abandoned.

Art deco swimming complex Piscine de la Butte aux Cailles in the 13e reopened in 2017 after renovations that included the installation of the city's first Nordic pool. Another art deco beauty of a swimming pool, Piscine des Amiraux, also reopened in 2017. Built in 1930 by La Samaritaine architect Henri Sauvage, its pool is ringed by two levels of changing cabins.

Founded in 1870 by Ernest Cognacq and Louise Jaÿ, La Samaritaine was, up until its closure in 2005, one of Paris' four big department stores. Bought by the LVMH group at the turn of the millennium and the subject of a bitter preservationist battle in the years that followed, it is finally reopening in 2019 with a luxury hotel, social housing and office space as well as a new department store. The project, awarded to the Pritzker Prize–winning Japanese firm Sanaa, will preserve an estimated 75% of the original art nouveau and art deco exterior.

But until 1968 French architects were still being trained almost exclusively at the conformist École des Beaux-Arts, reflected in most of the early impersonal and forgettable 'lipstick tubes' and 'upended shoebox' structures erected in the skyscraper district of La Défense, the Unesco building (1958) in the 7e, and the 210m-tall Tour Montparnasse (1973).

A signature architectural feature of Paris is the vertical garden, or *mur végétal* (vegetation wall). Seeming to defy gravity, these gardens cover walls in chic boutique interiors, outside museums, within spas and elsewhere. The Seine-facing garden at the Musée du Quai Branly, by Patrick Blanc, is Paris' most famous.

For centuries France's leaders have sought to immortalise themselves by erecting huge public edifices *('grands projets')* in Paris. Georges Pompidou commissioned the once reviled, now much-loved Centre Pompidou. His successor, Valéry Giscard d'Estaing, was instrumental in transforming the derelict Gare d'Orsay train station into the glorious Musée d'Orsay (1986).

François Mitterrand surpassed all of the postwar presidents with monumental projects costing taxpayers €4.6 billion: Jean Nouvel's Institut du Monde Arabe (1987), built during this time, mixes modern Arab and Western elements and is arguably one of the city's most beautiful late-20th-century buildings. Mitterrand also oversaw the city's second opera house, tile-clad Opéra de Paris Bastille, designed by Uruguayan architect Carlos Ott in 1989; the monumental Grande Arche de la Défense by Danish architect Johan-Otto von Sprekelsen (1989); IM Pei's glass-pyramid entrance at the hitherto sacrosanct and untouchable Musée du Louvre (1989); and the four open-book-shaped glass towers of the €2-billion Bibliothèque Nationale de France (Dominique Perrault, 1995).

Jacques Chirac orchestrated the magnificent Musée du Quai Branly, a glass, wood and sod structure with 3-hectare experimental garden, also by Jean Nouvel.

Contemporary

IM Pei's Louvre pyramid paved the way for Mario Bellini and Rudy Ricciotti's magnificent 'flying carpet' roof atop the museum's Cour Visconti in 2012.

Drawing on the city's longstanding tradition of metalwork and glass in its architecture, Canadian architect Frank Gehry used 12 enormous glass 'sails' to design the Fondation Louis Vuitton, which opened in the Bois de Boulogne in late 2014.

Jean Nouvel's Philharmonie de Paris, a state-of-the-art creation with a dazzling metallic facade that took three years to build and that cost €381 million, opened in 2015.

Glass is a big feature of the 1970s-eyesore-turned-contemporary-stunner Forum des Halles shopping centre in the 1er – a curvaceous, curvilinear and glass-topped construction by architects Patrick Berger and Jacques Anziutti, completed in 2016. Another eyesore undergoing renewal is 1970s skyscraper, the Tour Montparnasse.

Clad in a pixelated matrix of glass embedded with LED lights, the new headquarters of national media group Le Monde, designed by Norwegian architectural firm Snøhetta, will be unveiled in 2019.

Jean Nouvel is heading the massive Gare d'Austerlitz renovation expected to finish in 2021. One-third of the budget was allocated to repairing the glass roof.

Porte Maillot will be transformed by Mille Arbres (Thousand Trees), a spectacular tree-topped glass structure by Japanese architect Sou Fujimoto and French architect Manal Rachdi. It will provide a pivotal link between central Paris and Grand Paris (Greater Paris) when it opens in 2022.

A zany structure if ever there was one is auction house Hôtel Drouat. After a late-1970s surrealist facelift by architects Jean-Jacques Fernier and André Biro, the 19th-century Haussmann building was instantly hailed as a modern architectural gem.

Literary Paris

Whether attending a reading at fabled Latin Quarter bookshop Shakespeare & Company, browsing bookshelves in a wine bar in Le Marais or poring over the latest *bande dessinée* (comic strip) in shops dedicated to the genre, Parisians have a deep appreciation of the written word, and literature remains essential to their sense of identity. Couple this with the mass of modern literature inspired by the City of Light and Paris will never leave you short of a good read.

Medieval

Paris does not figure largely in early-medieval French literature, although the misadventures of Pierre Abélard and Héloïse took place in the capital, as did their mutual correspondence, which ended only with Abélard's death.

François Villon, the finest poet of the Middle Ages, received the equivalent of a Master of Arts degree from the Sorbonne before he turned 20. Involved in a series of brawls, robberies and illicit escapades, 'Master Villon' (as he became known) was sentenced to be hanged in 1462, supposedly for stabbing a lawyer. However, the sentence was commuted to banishment from Paris for 10 years, and he disappeared forever. Villon left behind a body of poems charged with a highly personal lyricism, among them *Ballade des Pendus* (Ballad of the Hanged Men), in which he writes his own epitaph, and *Ballade des Dames du Temps Jadis,* translated by the English poet and painter Dante Gabriel Rossetti as the 'Ballad of Dead Ladies'.

Literary Sights

Maison de Victor Hugo (Le Marais, Ménilmontant & Belleville)

Maison de Balzac (Eiffel Tower & Western Paris)

Musée de la Vie Romantique (Montmartre & Northern Paris)

Renaissance

The great landmarks of French Renaissance literature are the works of François Rabelais, Pierre de Ronsard (and other poets of the Renaissance group of poets known as La Pléiade) and Michel de Montaigne. The exuberant narratives of erstwhile monk Rabelais blend coarse humour with erudition in a vast oeuvre that seems to include every kind of person, occupation and jargon to be found in the France of the early 16th century. Rabelais' publisher, Étienne Dolet, was convicted of heresy and blasphemy in 1546, hanged and burned on place Maubert, 5e.

17th & 18th Centuries

During the 17th century François de Malherbe, court poet under Henri IV, brought a new rigour to rhythm in literature. One of his better-known works is his sycophantic *Ode* (1600) to Marie de Médici. Transported by the perfection of Malherbe's verses, Jean de la Fontaine went on to write his charming *Fables* (1668) in the manner of Aesop – though he fell afoul of the Académie Française (French Academy) in the process. A mood of classical tragedy permeates *La Princesse de Clèves* (1678), by Marie de la Fayette, widely regarded as the precursor to the modern character novel.

The literature of the 18th century is dominated by philosophers, among them Voltaire (François-Marie Arouet) and Jean-Jacques Rousseau. Voltaire's political writings, arguing that society is fundamentally opposed to nature, had a profound and lasting influence on the century, and he is buried in the Panthéon. Rousseau's sensitivity to landscape and its moods anticipated romanticism, and the insistence on his own singularity in *Les Confessions* (1782) made it the first modern autobiography. He, too, lies in the Panthéon.

French Romanticism

The 19th century produced poet and novelist Victor Hugo, who lived on place des Vosges before fleeing to the Channel Islands during the Second Empire. *Les Misérables* (1862) describes life among the poor of Paris in the early 19th century. *Notre Dame de Paris* (The Hunchback of Notre Dame; 1831), a medieval romance and tragedy revolving around the life of the celebrated cathedral, made Hugo the key figure of French romanticism.

Other influential 19th-century novelists include Stendhal (Marie-Henri Beyle), Honoré de Balzac, Amandine Aurore Lucile Dupin (aka George Sand) and, of course, Alexandre Dumas, who wrote the swashbuckling adventures *Le Comte de Monte Cristo* (The Count of Monte Cristo; 1844) and *Les Trois Mousquetaires* (The Three Musketeers; 1844).

In 1857 two landmarks of French literature were published: *Madame Bovary,* by Gustave Flaubert, and *Les Fleurs du Mal,* by Charles Baudelaire. Both writers were tried for the supposed immorality of their works. Flaubert won his case, and his novel was distributed without censorship. Baudelaire, who moonlighted as a translator in Paris, was obliged to cut half a dozen poems from his work and fined 300 francs.

The aim of Émile Zola, who came to Paris with his close friend, the artist Paul Cézanne, in 1858, was to transform novel-writing from an art to a science by the application of experimentation. His theory may now seem naive, but his work influenced most significant French writers of the late 19th century and is reflected in much 20th-century fiction as well. His novel *Nana* (1880) tells the decadent tale of a young woman who resorts to prostitution to survive the Paris of the Second Empire.

In France the *bande dessinée* (comic strip) has a cult following. The genre was originally for children, but comic strips for adults gained popularity in 1959 with René Goscinny and Albert Uderzo's now-iconic *Astérix* series.

Symbolism & Surrealism

Paul Verlaine and Stéphane Mallarmé created the symbolist movement, which strove to express states of mind rather than simply detail daily reality. Arthur Rimbaud, in addition to crowding an extraordinary amount of exotic travel into his 37 years and having a tempestuous sexual relationship with Verlaine, produced two enduring pieces of work: *Une Saison en Enfer* (A Season in Hell; 1873) and *Illuminations* (1874). Verlaine died at 39 rue Descartes, 5e, in 1896.

Marcel Proust dominated the early 20th century with his seven-volume novel *À la Recherche du Temps Perdu* (In Search of Lost Time; 1913–27), which explores the true meaning of past experience recovered from the unconscious by 'involuntary memory'. In 1907 Proust moved from the family home near the av des Champs-Élysées to an apartment on bd Haussmann famous for its cork-lined bedroom (now in the Musée Carnavalet). André Gide found his voice in the celebration of gay sensuality and, later, left-wing politics. *Les Faux-Monnayeurs* (The Counterfeiters; 1925) exposes the hypocrisy to which people resort in order to fit in with others or deceive themselves.

FOREIGN LITERATURE: INTERWAR HEYDAY

Foreigners have found inspiration in Paris since Charles Dickens used the city alongside London as the backdrop to *A Tale of Two Cities* in 1859. The heyday of Paris as a literary setting, however, was the interwar period.

Ernest Hemingway's *The Sun Also Rises* (1926) and the posthumous *A Moveable Feast* (1964) portray bohemian life in Paris between the wars. So many vignettes in the latter – dissing Ford Madox Ford in a cafe, 'sizing up' F Scott Fitzgerald in a toilet in the Latin Quarter, and overhearing Gertrude Stein and her lover, Alice B Toklas, bitchin' at one another from the sitting room of their salon near the Jardin du Luxembourg – are classic and *très parisien*.

Gertrude Stein let her hair down by assuming her lover's identity in *The Autobiography of Alice B Toklas*, a fascinating account of the author's many years in Paris, her salon on rue de Fleurus, 6e, and her friendships with Matisse, Picasso, Braque, Hemingway and others.

Down and Out in Paris and London (1933) is George Orwell's account of the time he spent working as a *plongeur* (dishwasher) in Paris and living with tramps in the city in the 1930s. Henry Miller's *Tropic of Cancer* (1934) and *Quiet Days in Clichy* (1956) are steamy novels set partly in the French capital. Then there's Anaïs Nin's voluminous diaries and fiction; her published correspondence with Miller is particularly evocative of 1930s Paris.

André Breton wrote French surrealism's three manifestos, although the first use of the word 'surrealist' is attributed to the poet Guillaume Apollinaire, a fellow traveller of surrealism killed in action in WWI. Colette (Sidonie-Gabrielle Colette) enjoyed tweaking the nose of conventionally moral readers. Her best-known work is *Gigi* (1945), but far more interesting is *Paris de Ma Fenêtre* (Paris from My Window; 1944), dealing with the German occupation of Paris. Her view was from 9 rue de Beaujolais in the 1er, overlooking Jardin du Palais Royal.

Existentialism

After WWII, existentialism developed as a significant literary movement around Jean-Paul Sartre, Simone de Beauvoir and Albert Camus, who worked and conversed in the cafes of bd St-Germain in St-German des Prés. All three stressed the importance of the writer's political engagement. De Beauvoir, author of *Le Deuxième Sexe* (The Second Sex; 1949), had a profound influence on feminist thinking. Camus' novel *L'Étranger* (The Stranger; 1942) reveals that the absurd is the condition of modern man, who feels himself an outsider in his world.

Literary Cafes

- *Café de Flore (St-Germain & Les Invalides)*
- *Les Deux Magots (St-Germain & Les Invalides)*
- *La Belle Hortense (Le Marais, Ménilmontant & Belleville)*

Modern Literature

In the late 1950s certain novelists began to look for new ways of organising narrative. The so-called *nouveau roman* (new novel) refers to the works of Nathalie Sarraute, Alain Robbe-Grillet, Boris Vian, Julien Gracq, Michel Butor and others. But these writers never formed a close-knit group, and their experiments took them in divergent directions.

In 1980 Marguerite Yourcenar, best known for her memorable historical novels including *Mémoires d'Hadrien* (Hadrian's Memoirs; 1951), became the first woman elected to the Académie Française. Marguerite Duras came to the notice of a larger public in 1984 when she won the Prix Goncourt for *L'Amant* (The Lover).

Philippe Sollers, an editor at *Tel Quel*, a highbrow, left-wing, Paris-based review, was very influential in the 1960s and early '70s. His 1960s novels were highly experimental, but with *Femmes* (Women; 1983) he returned to a conventional narrative style. Another *Tel Quel* editor, Julia Kristeva, became known for her theoretical writings on literature and psychoanalysis but subsequently turned her hand to fiction: *Les Samuraï* (The Samurai; 1990), a fictionalised account of the heady days of *Tel Quel,* is an interesting document on Paris intelligentsia life.

Roland Barthes and Michel Foucault are other notable 1960s and '70s authors and philosophers. In the 1990s French writing focused in a nihilistic way on what France had lost as a nation (identity, international prestige etc), and never more so than in the work of controversial writer Michel Houellebecq, who rose to national prominence in 1998 with his *Les Particules Élémentaires* (Atomised). Houellebecq's most recent work is *Soumission* (Submission; 2015), a contentious political satire featuring some of France's real-life politicians in a fictionalised near-future setting.

L'Âge de Raison (The Age of Reason; 1945), the first volume of Jean-Paul Sartre's trilogy *Les Chemins de la Liberté* (The Roads to Freedom), is a superb Parisian novel. His subsequent volumes recall Paris immediately before and during WWII.

Contemporary Literature

Some of the best-known contemporary French writers include Jean Echenoz, Erik Orsenna, Marc Levy, Christine Angot – dubbed *'la reine de l'autofiction'* (the queen of autobiography) – and comedian-dramatist Nelly Alard. Alard was acclaimed for the novel *Moment d'un couple* (Moment of a Couple; 2013), which was translated into English as *Couple Mechanics* in 2016. Author Yasmina Khadra is actually a man – a former colonel in the Algerian army who adopted his wife's name as a nom de plume to prevent military censorship.

Delving into the mood and politics of the capital's notable ethnic population is Faïza Guène, a French literary sensation who writes in an 'urban slang' style. A suburban Paris housing estate where thousands of immigrants live like sardines in five-storey blocks stretching for 1.5km is the setting for *Kiffe Kiffe Demain* and for Guène's second (semi-autobiographical) novel, *Du Rêve pour les Oufs* (2006), published in English as *Dreams from the Endz* (2008). Her third novel, *Les Gens du Balto* (2008), published in English as *Bar Balto* (2011), is a series of colloquial first-person monologues by various characters who live on a street in a Parisian suburb. Guène's next work, *Un Homme, ça ne pleure pas* (2014), shifted to Nice in southern France.

Ex-French border guard turned author Romain Puértolas had an instant best-selling hit with his surreal, partly Paris-set 2013 novel *L'Extraordinaire Voyage du Fakir Qui Était Resté Coincé Dans une Armoire Ikea* (The Extraordinary Journey of the Fakir Who Got Trapped in an Ikea Wardrobe), which won the Grand Prix Jules Verne in 2014. It was followed in 2015 by *La Petite Fille Qui Avait Avalé un Nuage Grand Comme la Tour Eiffel* (The Little Girl Who Swallowed a Cloud as Big as the Eiffel Tower) and the zany farce *Re-vive l'Empereur* (Re-live the Emperor), imagining the contemporary return of Napoléon Bonaparte. In 2017 he published *Tout un Été Sans Facebook* (A Summer Without Facebook), centred on a reading club.

One of France's top-selling writers is Parisian Marc Levy. His first novel was filmed as 2005's *Just Like Heaven*. His latest, *La Dernière des Stanfield* (Stanfield's Last; 2017), is a multigenerational mystery.

French journalist, screenwriter and novelist Tatiana de Rosnay has a prolific output that includes the best-selling *Sarah's Key* (2007), her first work written in English, and *A Paris Affair* (2015).

Painting & Visual Arts

While art in Paris today means anything and everything – bold installations in the metro, digital art projections both inside and outside exhibition spaces, mechanical sculptures, monumental wall frescoes, tiled Space Invader tags and other gregarious street art, including in dedicated street-art museums – the city's rich art heritage has its roots firmly embedded in the traditional genres of painting and sculpture.

Baroque to Neoclassicism

According to philosopher Voltaire, French painting proper began with baroque painter Nicolas Poussin (1594–1665), the greatest representative of 17th-century classicism, who frequently set scenes from ancient Rome, classical mythology and the Bible in ordered landscapes bathed in golden light.

In the field of sculpture, extravagant and monumental tombs had been commissioned by the nobility from the 14th century, and in Renaissance Paris Pierre Bontemps (c 1507–68) decorated the beautiful tomb of François I at Basilique de St-Denis, and Jean Goujon (c 1510–67) created the Fontaine des Innocents near the Forum des Halles. No sculpture better evokes baroque than the magnificent *Horses of Marly* by Guillaume Coustou (1677–1746), at the entrance to the av des Champs-Élysées.

Modern still life pops up with Jean-Baptiste Chardin (1699–1779), who brought the humbler domesticity of the Dutch masters to French art. In 1785 neoclassical artist Jacques-Louis David (1748–1825) wooed the public with his vast portraits with clear republican messages. A virtual dictator in matters of art, he advocated a precise, severe classicism.

Painting Meccas

Musée du Louvre (Louvre & Les Halles)

Musée d'Orsay (St-Germain & Les Invalides)

Centre Pompidou (Louvre & Les Halles)

Musée Picasso (Le Marais, Ménilmontant & Belleville)

Jean-Auguste-Dominique Ingres (1780–1867), David's most gifted pupil in Paris, continued the neoclassical tradition. His historical pictures (eg *Oedipus and the Sphinx*, the 1808 version of which is in the Louvre) are now regarded as inferior to his portraits.

Romanticism

One of the Louvre's most gripping paintings, *The Raft of the Medusa* by Théodore Géricault (1791–1824), hovers on the threshold of romanticism; if Géricault had not died early (aged 33), he probably would have become a leader of the movement, along with his friend Eugène Delacroix (1798–1863; find him in the Cimetière du Père Lachaise), best known for his masterpiece commemorating the July Revolution of 1830, *Liberty Leading the People*.

While romantics revamped the subject picture, the Barbizon School effected a parallel transformation of landscape painting. The school derived its name from a village near the Forêt de Fontainebleau where Jean-Baptiste Camille Corot (1796–1875) and Jean-François Millet (1814–75) painted in the open air. The son of a Norman peasant farmer, Millet took many of his subjects from peasant life; his *L'Angélus* (The

Angelus; 1857) is one of the best-known French paintings from this period. View it in the Musée d'Orsay.

In sculpture, the work of Paris-born Auguste Rodin (1840–1917) overcame the conflict between neoclassicism and romanticism. One of Rodin's most gifted pupils was his lover Camille Claudel (1864–1943), whose work can be seen with Rodin's in the Musée Rodin.

Realism

The realists were all about social commentary: Millet anticipated the realist program of Gustave Courbet (1819–77), a prominent member of the Paris Commune whose paintings depicted the drudgery and dignity of working-class lives. In 1850 he broke new ground with *A Burial at Ornans* (in the Musée d'Orsay), painted on a canvas of monumental size reserved until then exclusively for historical paintings.

Édouard Manet (1832–83) used realism to depict the Parisian middle classes, yet he included in his pictures numerous references to the Old Masters. His *Déjeuner sur l'Herbe* and *Olympia* were both scandalous, largely because they broke with the traditional treatment of their subject matter. He was a pivotal figure in the transition from realism to impressionism.

One of the best sculptors of this period was François Rude (1784–1855), creator of the relief on the Arc de Triomphe and several pieces in the Musée d'Orsay. By the mid-19th century, memorial statues in public places had replaced sculpted tombs, making such statues all the rage.

Sculptor Jean-Baptiste Carpeaux (1827–75) began as a romantic, but his work in Paris – such as *The Dance* on the Palais Garnier and his fountain in the Jardin du Luxembourg – recalls the gaiety and flamboyance of the baroque era.

Impressionism

Paris' Musée d'Orsay is the crown jewel of impressionism. Initially a term of derision, 'impressionism' was taken from the title of an 1874 experimental painting, *Impression: Soleil Levant* (Impression: Sunrise) by Claude Monet (1840–1926). Monet was the leading figure of the school, and a visit to the Musée d'Orsay unveils a host of other members, among them Alfred Sisley (1839–99), Camille Pissarro (1830–1903), Pierre-Auguste Renoir (1841–1919) and Berthe Morisot (1841–95). The impressionists' main aim was to capture the effects of fleeting light, painting almost universally in the open air – and light came to dominate the content of their painting.

Edgar Degas (1834–1917), buried in the Cimetière de Montmartre, was a fellow traveller of the impressionists, but he preferred painting cafe life *(Absinthe)* and in ballet studios *(The Dance Class)* over the great outdoors – several beautiful examples hang in the Musée d'Orsay.

Henri de Toulouse-Lautrec (1864–1901) was a great admirer of Degas but chose subjects one or two notches less salubrious: people in the bistros, brothels and music halls of Montmartre (eg *Au Moulin Rouge*). He is best known for his posters and lithographs, in which the distortion of the figures is both satirical and decorative.

Paul Cézanne (1839–1906) is celebrated for his still lifes and landscapes depicting southern France, though he spent many years in Paris after breaking with the impressionists. The name of Paul Gauguin (1848–1903) immediately conjures up studies of Tahitian and Breton women. Both Cézanne and Gauguin were postimpressionists, a catch-all term for the diverse styles that flowed from impressionism.

Sculpture Studios

Musée Rodin (St-Germain & Les Invalides)

Musée Atelier Zadkine (St-Germain & Les Invalides)

Atelier Brancusi (Louvre & Les Halles)

Musée Bourdelle (Montparnasse & Southern Paris)

César Baldaccini (1921–98), known simply as César, used iron and scrap metal to create imaginary insects and animals, later graduating to pliable plastics. Among his best-known works are the Centaur statue in the 6e and the statuette handed to actors at the Césars (French cinema's equivalent of the Oscars).

Both Georges Braque and Picasso experimented with sculpture and, in the spirit of Dada, Marcel Duchamp exhibited 'found objects', one of which was a urinal, which he mounted, signed and dubbed *Fountain* in 1917.

Pointillism & Symbolism

Pointillism was a technique developed by Georges Seurat (1859–91), who applied paint in small dots or uniform brush strokes of unmixed colour to produce fine 'mosaics' of warm and cool tones. His tableaux *Une Baignade, Asnières* (Bathers at Asnières) is a perfect example.

Henri Rousseau (1844–1910) was a contemporary of the postimpressionists, but his 'naive' art was unaffected by them. His dreamlike pictures of the Paris suburbs and of jungle and desert scenes (eg *The Snake Charmer*) – in the Musée d'Orsay – have influenced art right up to this century. The eerie treatment of mythological subjects by Gustave Moreau (1826–98) can be seen in the artist's studio, now within the Musée Gustave-Moreau in the 9e.

20th-Century Art

Twentieth-century French painting is characterised by a bewildering diversity of styles, including fauvism, named after the slur of a critic who compared the exhibitors at the 1905 Salon d'Automne (Autumn

METRO ART

Art adorns many of the stations of the city's world-famous Métropolitain. Art themes often relate to the *quartier* (neighbourhood) or the name of the station. Montparnasse Bienvenüe, for example, evokes the creation of the metro – it was an engineer named Fulgence Bienvenüe (1852–1936) who oversaw the building of the first 91km from 1886; while Carrefour Pleyel, named in honour of the 18th-century composer and piano-maker Ignace Joseph Pleyel (1757–1831), focuses on classical music.

The following is just a sample of the most interesting stations from an artistic perspective.

Abbesses (line 12 metro entrance) The noodle-like pale-green metalwork and glass canopy of the station entrance is one of the finest examples of the work of Hector Guimard (1867–1942), the celebrated French art nouveau architect whose signature style once graced most metro stations. For a complete list of the metro stations that retain *édicules* (shrine-like entranceways) designed by Guimard, see www.parisinconnu.com.

Assemblée Nationale (line 12 platform) Gigantic posters of silhouettes in red, white and blue by artist Jean-Charles Blais (b 1956) represent the MPs currently sitting in parliament.

Bastille (line 5 platform) A 180-sq-metre ceramic fresco features scenes taken from newspaper engravings published during the Revolution, with illustrations of the destruction of the infamous prison.

Chaussée d'Antin-Lafayette (line 7 platform) Large allegorical painting on the vaulted ceiling recalls the Marquis de Lafayette (1757–1834) and his role as general in the American Revolution.

Cluny–La Sorbonne (line 10 platform) A large ceramic mosaic replicates the signatures of intellectuals, artists and scientists from the Latin Quarter through history, including Molière (1622–73), Rabelais (c 1483–1553) and Robespierre (1758–96).

Concorde (line 12 platform) What looks like children's building blocks in white-and-blue ceramic on the walls of the station are 45,000 tiles that spell out the text of the *Déclaration des Droits de l'Homme et du Citoyen* (Declaration of the Rights of Man and of the Citizen), the document setting forth the principles of the French Revolution.

Palais Royal–Musée du Louvre (line 1 metro entrance) The zany entrance on place du Palais by Jean-Michel Othoniel (b 1964) is composed of two crown-shaped cupolas (one representing the day, the other night) consisting of 800 red, blue, amber and violet glass balls threaded on an aluminium structure. Sublime.

Salon) in Paris with *fauves* (wild animals) because of their wild brushstrokes and radical use of intensely bright colours. Among these 'beastly' painters was Henri Matisse (1869–1954).

Cubism was launched in 1907 with *Les Demoiselles d'Avignon* by Spanish prodigy Pablo Picasso (1881–1973). Cubism, as developed by Picasso, Georges Braque (1882–1963) and Juan Gris (1887–1927), deconstructed the subject into a system of intersecting planes and presented various aspects simultaneously.

In the 1920s and '30s the École de Paris (School of Paris) was formed by a group of expressionists, mostly foreign born.

Capturing the rebellious, iconoclastic spirit of Dadaism – a Swiss-born literary and artistic movement of revolt – is *Mona Lisa,* by Marcel Duchamp (1887–1968), complete with moustache and goatee. In 1922 German Dadaist Max Ernst (1891–1976) moved to Paris and worked on surrealism, a Dada offshoot that flourished between the wars. Drawing on the theories of Sigmund Freud, surrealism attempted to reunite the conscious and unconscious realms, to permeate everyday life with fantasies and dreams. The most influential of this style in Paris was Spanish-born artist Salvador Dalí (1904–89), who arrived in the French capital in 1929 and painted some of his most seminal works while residing here. To see his work, visit the Dalí Espace Montmartre.

One of the most influential pre-WWII sculptors to emerge in Paris was Romanian-born Constantin Brancusi (1876–1957); view his work at the Atelier Brancusi. Two other Paris-busy sculptors each have a museum devoted to their work: Ossip Zadkine (1890–1967) and Antoine Bourdelle (1861–1929).

WWII ended Paris' role as the world's artistic capital. Many artists left during the occupation, and though some returned after the war, the city never regained its old magnetism.

But art endured. Conceptual artist Daniel Buren (b 1938) reduced his painting to a signature series of vertical 8.7cm-wide stripes that he applies to every surface imaginable – white-marble columns in the courtyard of Paris' Palais Royal included. Partner-in-crime Michel Parmentier (1938–2000) insisted on monochrome painting – blue in 1966, grey in 1967 and red in 1968.

A bill in 1936 provided for 'the creation of monumental decorations in public buildings' by allotting 1% of building costs to art. The concept mushroomed half a century later (with Daniel Buren) and now there's artwork everywhere: in the Jardin des Tuileries, La Défense, Parc de la Villette, the metro...

Contemporary Art

From the turn of the 21st century, artists increasingly turned to the minutiae of daily urban life to express social and political angst, using new mediums to let rip.

Paris-born conceptual artist Sophie Calle (b 1953) brazenly exposes her private life in public with eye-catching installations, such as 107 women reading and commenting on an email she received from her French lover, dumping her.

Street art took off in Paris thanks to Blek le Rat (Xavier Prou; b 1951), whose pioneering stencilled black rats across the city inspired artists such as Banksy, as well as French artist Levalet (Charles Leval; b 1988), who pastes lifelike, site-specific images in India ink on craft paper onto walls. Today, street art remains huge; in addition to tiled Space Invader tags and vast murals covering entire high-rise buildings, graffitied streets like Belleville's rue Dénoyez and art-collective canvases like rue Oberkampf's Le MUR, there are now two street-art museums in the city and companies running dedicated guided tours.

Digital art is also gaining ground: arts centre EP7 screens projections onto its facade, and the new L'Atelier des Lumières is Paris' first digital-art museum; both opened in 2018.

Keep abreast of current exhibitions, events and happenings with Paris' contemporary art and design magazine *Slash* (https://slash-paris.com), also on Twitter and Facebook.

Film

Paris is one of the world's most cinematic cities. The French capital has produced a bevy of blockbuster film-makers and stars and is the filming location of countless box-office hits by both home-grown and foreign directors. Fabulous experiences for film buffs range from exploring behind the scenes at an art deco cinema to catching a classic retrospective in the Latin Quarter's many cinemas, or following in the footsteps of iconic screen heroine Amélie Poulain through the streets of Montmartre.

Movie-Makers & Stars

French cinema hasn't looked back since 2012, when *The Artist* (2011), a silent B&W romantic comedy set in 1920s Hollywood, won seven BAFTAs and five Oscars to become the most awarded film in French cinema history. Best Director went to Parisian Michel Hazanavicius (b 1967) and Best Original Score went to French composer-pianist Ludovic Bource (b 1970). Best Actor was awarded to charismatic Jean Dujardin (b 1972), who started with one-man shows in Paris bars and cabarets, and made his name with roles as varied as surfer Brice waiting for his wave in *Brice de Nice* (2005), James Bond in *OSS 117: Le Caire, Nid d'Espions* (OSS 117: Cairo Nest of Spies; 2006), the sexiest cowboy around in *Lucky Luke* (2009) and a WWII French soldier in George Clooney's *The Monuments Men* (2014).

Cinematic Trips

Forum des Images (Louvre & Les Halles)

Cinémathèque Française (Bastille & Eastern Paris)

Le Grand Rex (Champs-Élysées & Grands Boulevards)

Another French blockbuster packed with Parisian talent is Anne Fontaine's *Coco Avant Chanel* (Coco Before Chanel; 2009). The movie tells the compelling life story of orphan-turned-fashion-designer Coco Chanel, played by Audrey Tautou (b 1976), the waifish French actress who conquered stardom with her role as Montmartre cafe waitress Amélie in Jean-Pierre Jeunet's *Le Fabuleux Destin d'Amélie Poulain* (Amélie; 2001), an earlier Paris classic.

One of the most successful French-language films ever is *Intouchables* (Untouchable; 2011). Directed by Parisian Éric Toledano and Olivier Nakache, the comic drama is about a billionaire quadriplegic and his live-in Senegalese carer in Paris. The film scooped Best Foreign Film at both the Golden Globes and the BAFTA Awards in 2013.

French-produced *Taken 2* (2012) was directed by Olivier Megaton (b 1965), a graffiti artist from the Parisian suburbs before turning his creative hand to film-making – with great success.

France's leading lady is Parisian Marion Cotillard (b 1975), the first French woman since 1959 to win an Oscar, for her role as Édith Piaf in Olivier Dahan's *La Môme* (La Vie en Rose; 2007). The versatile actress went on to play an amputee in art film *De Rouille et d'Os* (Rust and Bone; 2012) by Parisian director Jacques Audiard (b 1952). In *Deux Jours, Une Nuit* (Two Days, One Night; 2014), Cotillard plays an employee in a solar-panel factory who learns she will lose her job if her co-workers don't each sacrifice €1000 bonuses offered to them. Her latest roles are in 2017's *Rock'n Roll*, as the partner of Guillaume Canet (her real-life partner), who plays an actor told by his young co-star that he's no longer 'rock 'n' roll' enough to sell films any more; and in *Les Fantômes d'Ismaël* (Ismael's Ghosts) as a wife who returns from a 20-year disappearance.

Animated films have also enjoyed huge success; 2015's *Avril et de Monde Truque* (April and the Extraordinary World) depicts a fictitious world in 1941 Paris under the rule of Napoléon V in the steam age. Marion Cotillard provides the voice of Avril, who, with her talking cat, searches for her missing scientist parents.

Female film-makers include Alice Winocour (b 1976), director of *Augustine* (2012), following a French neurologist and his love interest/patient, and Pascale Ferrari (b 1960), whose film *Bird People* (2014) takes place in and around a hotel at Paris' Charles de Gaulle airport. Look out, too, for Julia Ducournau (b 1983), director of *Raw* (2016), about a vegetarian veterinary student who develops a taste for flesh.

On Location

Paris is the perfect cinematic setting and a natural movie star: look no further than timeless French classics *Hôtel du Nord* (1938), set along the Canal St-Martin, and *Les Enfants du Paradis* (1946), set in 1840s Paris, both directed by Parisian film-maker Marcel Carné (1906–96).

New Wave film director Jean-Luc Godard followed his B&W celebration of Paris in *À Bout de Souffle* (Breathless; 1959) with *Bande à Parte* (Band of Outsiders; 1964), an entertaining gangster film with marvellous scenes in the Louvre.

For decades 'Most Watched French Film' kudos went to *La Grand Vadrouille* (The Great Ramble; 1966), a French comedy in which five British airmen are shot down over German-occupied France in 1942. One is catapulted into Paris' Bois de Vincennes zoo, another into the orchestra pit of Paris' opera house, and so the comic tale unfurls.

In the 1990s Juliette Binoche (b 1964) leapt to fame after diving into the shimmering, bright-turquoise water of Paris' art-deco swimming pool the Piscine de Pontoise in the 5e, in *Bleu* (Blue; 1993), the first in Krzysztof Kieślowski's *Trois Couleurs* (Three Colours) trilogy. A decade later Binoche wooed cinema-goers with her role as a grieving mother in *Paris, je t'aime* (Paris, I Love You; 2006), a staggering work comprising 18 short films – each set in a different Parisian *arrondissement*.

Honoured with the Palme d'Or at Cannes in 2008, Laurent Cantet's *Entre Les Murs* (The Class; 2008) portrays a year in the school life of pupils and teachers in a Parisian suburb. Based on the autobiographical novel of teacher François Begaudeau, the documentary-drama is a brilliant reflection of contemporary multi-ethnic society.

FRENCH CINEMA

1895

The world's first paying-public film screening is held in Paris' Grand Café on bd des Capucines, 9e, in December 1895 by the Lumière brothers, inventors of 'moving pictures'.

1902

Paris magician-turned-film-maker Georges Méliès (1861–1938) creates the first science-fiction film with the silent *Le Voyage dans la Lune* (The Trip to the Moon; 1902).

1920s

French film flourishes. Sound ushers in René Clair's (1898–1981) world of fantasy and satirical surrealism. Watch Abel Gance's antiwar blockbuster *J'Accuse!* (I Accuse!; 1919), which was filmed on actual WWI battlefields.

1930s

WWI inspires a new realism: portraits of ordinary lives dominate film. Watch *La Grande Illusion* (The Great Illusion; 1937), based on the trench-warfare experience of director Jean Renoir.

1940s

Surrealists eschew realism. Watch Jean Cocteau's *La Belle et la Bête* (Beauty and the Beast; 1946) and *Orphée* (Orpheus; 1950). WWII saps the film industry of both talent and money.

1950s

Nouvelle Vague (New Wave): small budgets, no stars and real-life subject matter produce uniquely personal films. Watch Jean-Luc Godard's carefree, B&W celebration of Paris *À Bout de Souffle* (Breathless; 1959).

1960s

France – land of romance: take in Claude Lelouch's *Un Homme et une Femme* (A Man and a Woman; 1966) and Jacques Demy's *Les Parapluies de Cherbourg* (The Umbrellas of Cherbourg; 1964).

1980s

Big-name stars, slick production values and nostalgia: generous state subsidies see film-makers switch to costume dramas and comedies in the face of growing competition from the USA.

1990s

Box-office hits starring France's best-known, biggest-nosed actor, Gérard Depardieu, win over huge audiences in France and abroad. See *Cyrano de Bergerac* (1990) and *Astérix et Obélix: Mission Cléopâtre* (2002).

2000s

Renaissance: Parisian *philanthrope* Amélie is the subject of Jean-Pierre Jeunet's *Le Fabuleux Destin d'Amélie Poulain* (Amelie; 2001), the first of a string of French-made films to succeed globally.

The city has always been popular with foreign film directors, whatever their genre: Bernardo Bertolucci's *Last Tango in Paris* (1972) stars Marlon Brando as a grief-stricken American. Roman Polanski's *Frantic* (1988) is a stylish thriller set in and around the city's seedier quarters that sees Harrison Ford enlist the help of a feisty Emmanuelle Seigner to help him track down his kidnapped wife. Doug Liman's fast-moving action flick *The Bourne Identity* (2002) features Matt Damon as an amnesiac government-agent-turned-target in a gripping story that twists and turns against a fabulous backdrop of Paris. Woody Allen's *Everybody Says I love You* (1996) unfolded on the Left Bank's quai de la Tournelle, while *Midnight in Paris* (2011) evoked the city, along with Hemingway's 'Lost Generation', in the 1920s. Martin Scorsese's Oscar-winning children's film *Hugo* (2011) paid tribute to cinema and Parisian film pioneer Georges Méliès through the remarkable adventure of an orphan boy in the 1930s who tends the clocks at a Paris train station. The crazed antics of Gargamel et al in American movie *Smurfs 2* (2013) were shot on location in Paris at Cathédrale de Notre Dame. Female film-maker Pascale Ferran (b 1960) makes her mark with *Bird People* (2014), set in and around a hotel at Paris' Charles de Gaulle airport.

Music

From organ recitals amid Gothic architectural splendour to a legendary jazz scene, stirring *chansons*, ground-breaking electronica, award-winning world music and some of the world's best rap, music is embedded deep in the Parisian soul.

Jazz & French Chansons

Jazz hit Paris in the 1920s with the banana-clad form of Josephine Baker, an African American cabaret dancer. In 1934 a chance meeting between Parisian jazz violinist Stéphane Grappelli (1908–97) and three-fingered Roma guitarist Django Reinhardt (1910–53) in a Montparnasse nightclub led to the formation of the Hot Club of France quintet. Claude Luter and his Dixieland band were hip in the 1950s.

The *chanson française,* a tradition dating from troubadours in the Middle Ages, was eclipsed by the music halls of the early 20th century but was revived in the 1930s by Édith Piaf (1915–63) and Charles Trenet (1913–2001), followed by 'France's Frank Sinatra', Charles Aznavour (b 1924). In the 1950s Left Bank cabarets nurtured singers like Léo Ferré (1916–63), Georges Brassens (1921–81), Claude Nougaro (1929–2004), Jacques Brel (1929–78), Barbara (1930–97) and the very sexy, very Parisian Serge Gainsbourg (1928–91). The genre was revived in the new millennium as *la nouvelle chanson française* by performers like Vincent Delerm (b 1976), Bénabar (b 1969), Jeanne Cherhal (b 1978), Camille (b 1978) and Zaz (Isabelle Geffroy; b 1980), who mix jazz, soul, acoustic and traditional *chansons.*

Musical Pilgrimages

Cimetière du Montparnasse (Montparnasse & Southern Paris)

Cimetière du Père Lachaise (Le Marais, Ménilmontant & Belleville)

Musée de Édith Piaf (Le Marais, Ménilmontant & Belleville)

Rock & Pop

French pop has come a long way since the yéyé (imitative rock) days of the 1960s as sung by Johnny Hallyday. The distinctive M is the son of singer Louis Chédid; Arthur H is the progeny of pop-rock musician Jacques Higelin; and Thomas Dutronc is the offspring of 1960s idols Jacques and Françoise Hardy. Serge Gainsbourg's daughter with Jane Birkin, songwriter-singer and actress Charlotte (b 1971), made her musical debut in 1984 with the single 'Lemon Incest' and – several albums later – released a cover version of the song 'Hey Joe' as soundtrack to the film *Nymphomaniac* (2013), in which she also starred.

Noir Désir was *the* sound of French rock until its lead vocalist, Bertrand Cantat (b 1964), was imprisoned in 2003 for the murder of his girlfriend. Following his early release from prison in 2007, the controversial singer later formed the band Détroit with instrumentalist Pascal Humbert. Détroit's top-selling first album *Horizons* (2013) was followed by the 2014 album *La Cigale.*

Indie rock band Phoenix, from Versailles, headlines festivals in the US and UK. Lead singer Thomas Mars (b 1976), his schoolmate Chris Mazzalai (guitar), his brother Laurent Brancowitz (guitar and keyboards) and Deck d'Arcy (keyboards and brass) have six hugely successful albums under their belt, including 2017's *Ti Amo.*

Award-winning French psych-punk rock band La Femme debuted with album *Psycho Tropical Berlin;* their latest offering is *Mystère* (2016).

Nosfell is one of France's most creative and intense musicians, who sings in his own invented language called *'le klokobetz'*. His third album, *Massif Armour* (2014), opens and closes in *'le klokobetz'* but otherwise woos listeners with powerful French love lyrics.

In 2011 Sylvie Hoarau and Aurélie Saada formed the indie folk duo Brigitte; their debut album *Et vous, tu m'aimes?* went platinum in France. Their 2014 album *A bouche que veux-tu* also achieved widespread success, as did 2017's *Nues*.

Internationally successful modern pop stars include Christine and the Queens (aka Héloïse Letissier; b 1988), who released her first album, *Chaleur Humaine,* in 2014, and Jain (Jeanne Galice; b 1992), whose debut album, *Zanaka*, was released in 2015.

Electronica

Paris does dance music very well, computer-enhanced Chicago blues and Detroit techno often being mixed with 1960s lounge music and vintage tracks from the likes of Gainsbourg and Brassens to create a distinctly urban and highly portable sound.

Globally successful bands such as Daft Punk and Justice head up the scene. Daft Punk, originally from Versailles, adapts first-wave acid house and techno to its younger roots in pop and indie rock. Its debut album, *Homework* (1997), fused disco, house funk and techno, while *Random Access Memories* (2013) boldly ditched computer-generated sound for a strong disco beat played by session musicians.

Electronica band Justice, raved about for their rock and indie influences, burst onto the dance scene in 2007 with a debut album that used the band's signature crucifix as its title. Justice's more recent works include live album *Access All Arenas* (2013) and *Woman* (2016). Electronica duo from Versailles AIR (an acronym for 'Amour, Imagination, Rêve', meaning 'Love, Imagination, Dream') is also internationally renowned.

David Guetta, Laurent Garnier, Martin Solveig and Bob Sinclair (aka Christophe Le Friant) are top Parisian electronica producers and DJs who travel the international circuit.

Breakbot (Thibaut Berland; b 1981) released his first album in 2012 and gained a rapid following for his remixes. His 2016-released album *Still Waters* includes the track 'Star Tripper', included in Disney's Star Wars–themed music album *Star Wars Headspace*.

Top Five Albums

- *Paris, Zaz*
- *Moon Safari, AIR*
- *Dante, Abd al Malik*
- *Bankrupt, Phoenix*
- *Paris by Night, Bob Sinclair*

World

Paris' world beat is strong, encompassing Algerian raï (artists include Cheb Khaled, Natacha Atlas, Jamel, Cheb Mami), Senegalese *mbalax* (Youssou N'Dour) and West Indian zouk (Kassav', Zouk Machine). In the late 1980s bands Mano Negra and Les Négresses Vertes combined many of these elements with brilliant results, as did Manu Chao (b 1961; formerly frontman for Mano Negra), the Paris-born son of Spanish parents.

Magic System from Côte d'Ivoire popularised *zouglou* (a kind of West African rap and dance music) with the album *Premier Gaou,* and Congolese Koffi Olomide (b 1956) still packs the halls. Also try to catch Franco-Algerian DJ-turned-singer Rachid Taha, whose music mixes Arab and Western musical styles with lyrics in English, Berber and French.

Paris-born Franco-Congolese rapper, slam poet and three-time Victoire de la Musique award winner Abd al Malik has helped cement France's reputation in world music. His albums *Gibraltar* (2006), *Dante* (2008) and *Château Rouge* (2010) are classics; look out for his popular 2015 album, *Scarifications*.

Survival Guide

Transport

ARRIVING IN PARIS

Few roads *don't* lead to Paris, one of the most visited destinations on earth. Practically every major airline flies through one of its three airports, and most European train and bus routes cross it.

On public transport, children under four years travel free and those aged four to nine years (inclusive) pay half price; exceptions are noted.

Flights, tours and rail tickets can be booked online at www.lonelyplanet.com.

Air

Charles de Gaulle Airport

Most international airlines fly to **Aéroport de Charles de Gaulle** (CDG; ☎01 70 36 39 50; www.parisaeroport.fr), 28km northeast of central Paris. In French the airport is commonly called 'Roissy' after the suburb in which it is located. A high-speed train link between Charles de Gaulle and Gare de l'Est in central Paris is planned, but no track will be laid until 2019. When complete in 2024, the CDG Express will cut the current 50-minute journey to 20 minutes. Inter-terminal shuttle services are free. A fourth terminal is due to open by 2025.

TRAIN

CDG is served by the RER B line (€11.40, child four to nine €7.90, approximately 50 minutes, every 10 to 20 minutes), which connects with central Paris stations including Gare du Nord, Châtelet–Les Halles and St-Michel–Notre Dame. Trains run from 4.50am to 11.50pm (from Gare du Nord 4.53am to 12.15am) every six to 15 minutes.

TAXI

➡ A taxi to the city centre takes 40 minutes. Since 2016, fares have been standardised to a flat rate: €50 to the Right Bank and €55 to the Left Bank. The fare increases by 15% between 7pm and 7am and on Sundays.

➡ Only take taxis at a clearly marked rank. Never follow anyone who approaches you at the airport and claims to be a driver.

BUS

There are six main bus lines.

Le Bus Direct line 2 (www.lebusdirect.com; 16-20 av de Suffren, 15e; Ⓜ Bir-Hakeim or RER Champ de Mars–Tour Eiffel) Links the airport with the Arc de Triomphe via the Eiffel Tower and Trocadéro; €17, one hour, every 30 minutes from 5.45am to 11pm.

Le Bus Direct line 4 (www.lebusdirect.com) Links the airport with **Gare Montparnasse** (Map p412; rue du Commandant René Mouchotte, 14e; 80 minutes) in southern Paris via **Gare de Lyon** (Map p394; www.lebusdirect.com; 20bis bd Diderot, 12e; 50 minutes) in eastern Paris; €17, every 30 minutes from 6am to 10.30pm from the airport, 5.30am to 10.30pm from Montparnasse.

Noctilien buses 140 and 143 (€8 or four metro tickets) Part of the RATP night service, Noctilien has two buses that link CDG with **Gare de l'Est** (Map p382; rue du 8 Mai 1945, 10e) in northern Paris via nearby **Gare du Nord** (Map p382; 170 rue La Fayette, 10e): bus 140 (1am to 4am; from Gare de l'Est 1am to 3.40am), taking 80 minutes, and bus 143 (12.32am to 4.32am; from Gare de l'Est 12.55am to 5.08am), taking 55 minutes.

RATP bus 350 (€6 or three metro tickets, 70 minutes, every 30 minutes from 5.30am to 11pm) Links the airport with **Gare de l'Est** (Map p382; www.ratp.fr; bd de Strasbourg, 10e, Gare de l'Est; €5.70, direct from driver €6).

RATP bus 351 (€6 or three metro tickets, 70 minutes, every 30 minutes from 5.30am to 11pm) Links the airport with **place de la Nation** (2 av du Trône, 12e; Ⓜ Nation) in eastern Paris.

Roissybus (€12.50, one hour, from CDG every 15 to 20 minutes from 6am to 12.30am; from Paris every 15 minutes from 5.15am to 12.30am) Links the airport with **Opéra** (Map p370; 11 rue Scribe, 9e).

Orly Airport

Aéroport d'Orly (ORY; ☎01 70 36 39 50; www.parisaeroport.fr) is 19km south of central Paris, but, despite being closer than CDG, it is not as frequently used by international airlines, and public-transport options aren't quite as straightforward. That will change by 2024, when metro line 14 will be extended to the airport. A TGV station is due to arrive here in 2025.

Orly's south and west terminals are currently being unified into one large terminal suitable for bigger planes such as A380s; completion is due in 2019.

TRAIN

There is currently no direct train to/from Orly; you'll need to change halfway. Note that while it is possible to take a shuttle to the RER C line, this service is quite long and not recommended.

RER B (€13.25, children four to nine €6.60, 35 minutes, every four to 12 minutes) This line connects Orly with the St-Michel–Notre Dame, Châtelet–Les Halles and Gare du Nord stations in the city centre. In order to get from Orly to the RER station (Antony), you must first take the Orlyval automatic train. The service runs from 6am to 11.35pm. You only need one ticket to take the two trains.

TAXI

A taxi to the city centre takes roughly 30 minutes. Standardised flat-rate fares since 2016 mean a taxi costs €30 to the Left Bank and €35 to the Right Bank. The fare increases by 15% between 7pm and 7am and on Sunday.

TRAM

Tramway T7 (€1.90, 40 minutes, every six minutes from 5.30am to 12.30am) This tramway links Orly with Villejuif–Louis Aragon metro station in southern Paris; buy tickets from the machine at the tram stop as no tickets are sold on board.

BUS

Two bus lines serve Orly:

Le Bus Direct line 1 (€12, one hour, every 20 minutes from 5.50am to 11.30pm from Orly, 4.50am to 10.30pm from the Arc de Triomphe) Runs to/from the Arc de Triomphe (one hour) via **Gare Montparnasse** (Map p412; www.lebusdirect.com; rue du Commandant René Mouchotte, 14e; 40 minutes), **La Motte-Picquet** (Map p414; www.lebusdirect.com; 88 av de Suffren, 15e; Ⓜ La Motte-Picquet–Grenelle) and Trocadéro.

Orlybus (€8.70, 30 minutes, every 15 to 20 minutes from 6am to 12.30am from Orly, 5.35am to midnight from Paris) Runs to/from **place Denfert-Rochereau** (Map p412; 3 place Denfert-Rochereau, 14e; Ⓜ Denfert-Rochereau) in southern Paris.

Beauvais Airport

Aéroport de Beauvais (BVA; ☎08 92 68 20 66; www.aeroportbeauvais.com) is 75km north of Paris and is served by a few low-cost flights. Before you snap up that bargain, though, consider whether the post-arrival journey is worth it.

SHUTTLE

The Beauvais *navette* (shuttle bus; €17, 1¼ hours) links the airport with **Parking Pershing** (16-24 bd Pershing, 17e; Ⓜ Porte Maillot) on central Paris' western edge; services are coordinated with flight times. See the airport website for details and tickets.

TAXI

A taxi to central Paris during the day/night costs around €170/210 (probably more than the cost of your flight!).

Train

Paris is the central point in the French rail network, Société Nationale des Chemins de Fer Français (SNCF), with six train stations that handle passenger traffic to different parts of France and Europe. Each is well connected to the Paris public-transport system, the Régie Autonome des Transports Parisiens (RATP). To buy onward tickets from Paris, visit a station or go to Oui.SNCF (www.oui.sncf). Most trains – and all

CLIMATE CHANGE & TRAVEL

Every form of transport that relies on carbon-based fuel generates CO_2, the main cause of human-induced climate change. Modern travel is dependent on aeroplanes, which might use less fuel per kilometre per person than most cars but travel much greater distances. The altitude at which aircraft emit gases (including CO_2) and particles also contributes to their climate change impact. Many websites offer 'carbon calculators' that allow people to estimate the carbon emissions generated by their journey and, for those who wish to do so, to offset the impact of the greenhouse gases emitted with contributions to portfolios of climate-friendly initiatives throughout the world. Lonely Planet offsets the carbon footprint of all staff and author travel.

high-speed Trains à Grande Vitesse (TGV) – require advance reservations. The earlier you book, the better your chances of securing a discounted fare. Mainline stations in Paris have left-luggage offices and/or *consignes* (lockers) for a maximum of 72 hours.

Gare d'Austerlitz

Gare d'Austerlitz (bd de l'Hôpital, 13e) is the terminus for a handful of trains from the south, including services from Orléans, Limoges and Toulouse. High-speed trains to/from Barcelona and Madrid also use Austerlitz. Current renovations will continue until 2021. Located in southeastern Paris.

Gare de l'Est

Gare de l'Est (www.gares-sncf.com; place du 11 Novembre 1918, 10e) is the terminus for trains from Luxembourg, southern Germany (Frankfurt, Munich, Stuttgart) and points further east (including a weekly Moscow service); there are regular and TGV Est trains to areas of France east of Paris (Champagne, Alsace and Lorraine). Located in northern Paris.

Gare de Lyon

Gare de Lyon (bd Diderot, 12e) is the terminus for trains from Lyon, Provence, the Côte d'Azur, the French Alps, Italy, Spain and Switzerland. Located in eastern Paris.

Gare du Nord

Gare du Nord (www.gares-sncf.com; rue de Dunkerque, 10e) is the terminus for northbound domestic trains as well as several international services. Located in northern Paris.

Eurostar (www.eurostar.com) The London–Paris line runs from St Pancras International to Gare du Nord. Voyages take 2¼ hours.

Thalys (www.thalys.com) Trains pull into Paris' Gare du Nord from Brussels, Amsterdam and Cologne.

Gare Montparnasse

Gare Montparnasse (av du Maine & bd de Vaugirard, 15e) is the terminus for trains from the southwest and west, including services from Brittany, the Loire Valley, Bordeaux, Toulouse, and Spain and Portugal. Some of these services will move to Gare d'Austerlitz (by 2021, once refurbishment is complete). Located in southern Paris.

Gare St-Lazare

Gare St-Lazare (www.gares-sncf.com; rue Intérieure, 8e) is the terminus for trains from Normandy. Located in Clichy, northwestern Paris.

Bus

Eurolines (Map p398; ☎08 92 89 90 91; www.eurolines.fr; 55 rue St-Jacques, 5e; ⏰9.30am-6.30pm Mon-Fri, 10am-1pm & 2-5pm Sat; Ⓜ Cluny-La Sorbonne) connects all major European capitals to Paris' international bus terminal, **Gare Routière Internationale de Paris-Galliéni** (28 av du Général de Gaulle, Bagnolet; Ⓜ Galliéni). The terminal is in the eastern suburb of Bagnolet; it's about a 15-minute metro ride to the more central République station.

Major European bus company Flixbus (www.flixbus.com) uses western **Parking Pershing** (16-24 bd Pershing, 17e; Ⓜ Porte Maillot).

GETTING AROUND PARIS

Train

Paris' underground network is run by RATP and consists of two separate but linked systems: the metro and the Réseau Express Régional (RER) suburban train line. The metro has 14 numbered lines; the RER has five main lines (but you'll probably only need to use A, B and C). When buying tickets consider how many zones your journey will cover; there are five concentric transport zones rippling out from Paris (zone 5 being the furthest); if you travel from Charles de Gaulle airport to Paris, for instance, you will have to buy a ticket for zones 1 to 5.

For information on the metro, RER and bus systems, visit www.ratp.fr. Metro maps of various sizes and degrees of detail are available for free at metro ticket windows; several can also be downloaded for free from the RATP website.

Metro

➡ Metro lines are identified by both their number (eg *ligne* 1 – line 1) and their colour, listed on official metro signs and maps.

➡ Signs in metro and RER stations indicate the way to the correct platform for your line. The *direction* signs on each platform indicate the terminus. On lines that split into several branches (such as lines 7 and 13), the terminus of each train is indicated on the cars and on signs on each platform giving the number of minutes until the next and subsequent train.

➡ Signs marked *correspondance* (transfer) show how to reach connecting trains. At stations with many intersecting lines, like Châtelet and Montparnasse Bienvenüe, walking from one platform to the next can take a very long time.

➡ Different station exits are indicated by white-on-blue *sortie* (exit) signs. You can get your bearings by checking the *plan du quartier* (neighbourhood maps) posted at exits.

➡ Each line has its own schedule, but trains usually start at around 5.30am, with the last train beginning its run between

12.35am and 1.15am (2.15am on Friday and Saturday).

RER

➡ The RER is faster than the metro, but the stops are much further apart. Some attractions, particularly those on the Left Bank (eg the Musée d'Orsay, Eiffel Tower and Panthéon), can be reached far more conveniently by the RER than by the metro.

➡ If you're going out to the suburbs (eg Versailles, Disneyland), ask for help on the platform – finding the right train can be confusing. Also make sure your ticket is for the correct zone.

Tickets & Fares

➡ Tickets are sold at all metro stations. Some automated machines take notes and coins, though not all. Ticket windows accept most credit cards; however, machines do not accept credit cards without embedded chips (and not all foreign chip-embedded cards are accepted).

➡ The same RATP tickets are valid on the metro, the RER (for travel within the city limits), buses, trams and the Montmartre funicular.

➡ A ticket – white in colour and called *Le Ticket t+* – costs €1.90 (half price for children aged four to nine years) if bought individually; a *carnet* (book) of 10 costs €14.90 for adults.

➡ One ticket lets you travel between any two metro stations (no return journeys) for a period of 1½ hours, no matter how many transfers are required. You can also use it on the RER for travel within zone 1, which encompasses all of central Paris.

➡ Transfers from the metro to buses or vice versa are not possible.

➡ Always keep your ticket until you exit from your station; if you are stopped by a ticket inspector, you will have to pay a fine if you don't have a valid ticket.

TOURIST PASSES

The Mobilis and Paris Visite passes are valid on the metro, the RER, SNCF's suburban lines, buses, night buses, trams and the Montmartre funicular railway. No photo is needed, but write your full name and date of use on the ticket. Passes are sold at larger metro and RER stations, SNCF offices in Paris, and airports. Passes operate by date (rather than 24-hour periods), so activate them early in the day for the best value.

Mobilis Allows unlimited travel for one day and costs €7.50 (for two zones) to €17.80 (five zones). Buy it at any metro, RER or SNCF station in the Paris region. Depending on how many times you plan to hop on/off the metro in a day, a *carnet* (book of 10 tickets) might work out cheaper.

Paris Visite Allows unlimited travel as well as discounted entry to certain museums, and other discounts and bonuses. The 'Paris+Suburbs+Airports' pass includes transport to/from the airports and costs €25.25/38.35/53.75/65.80 for one/two/three/five days. The cheaper 'Paris Centre' pass, valid for zones 1 to 3, costs €12/19.50/26.65/38.35 for one/two/three/five days.

NAVIGO PASS

If you're staying in Paris for longer than a few days, the cheapest and easiest way to use public transport is to get a combined travel pass that allows unlimited travel on the metro, the RER and buses for a week, a month or a year. Passes cover all of the Île-de-France (that is, all zones).

Navigo (www.navigo.fr), like London's Oyster card or Hong Kong's Octopus card, is a system that provides you with a refillable weekly, monthly or yearly unlimited pass that you can recharge at machines in most metro stations. To pass through the station barrier, swipe the card across the electronic panel as you go through the turnstiles. Standard Navigo passes, available to anyone with an address in Île-de-France, are free but take up to three weeks to be issued; ask at the ticket counter for a form or order online via the Navigo website. Otherwise, pay €5 for a Navigo Découverte (Navigo Discovery) card, which is issued on the spot but (unlike the standard Navigo pass) is not replaceable if lost or stolen. Both passes require a passport photo and can be recharged for periods of one week or more.

A weekly pass costs €22.80 and is valid Monday to Sunday. It can be purchased from the previous Friday until Thursday; from the next day weekly tickets are available for the following week only. Even if you're in Paris for three or four days, it may work out cheaper than buying *carnets* (books of tickets) and will certainly cost less than buying a daily Mobilis or Paris Visite pass. The monthly pass (€75.20) begins on the first day of each calendar month; you can buy one from the 20th of the preceding month. Both are sold in metro and RER stations from 6.30am to 10pm and at some bus terminals.

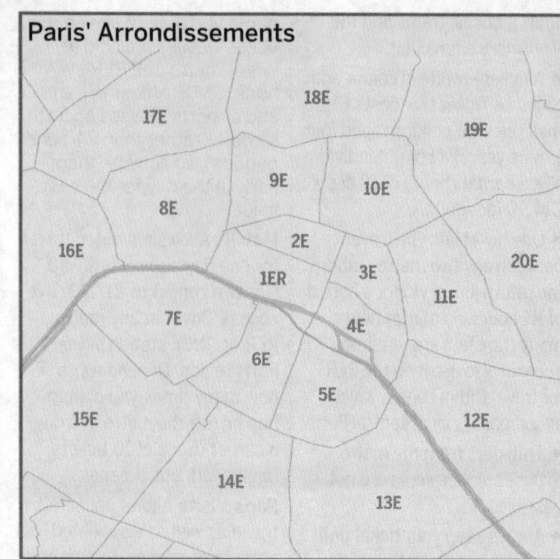

Children aged four to 11 years pay half price.

Bicycle

Paris is increasingly bike-friendly, with more cycling lanes and efforts from the city of Paris to reduce the number of cars on the roads.

Vélib'

The **Vélib'** (☎01 76 49 12 34; www.velib-metropole.fr; day/week subscription for up to 5 people €5/15, standard bike hire up to 30/60min free/€1, electric bike €1/2) bike-share scheme changed operators in 2018; check the website for the latest information. When the handover is complete, it will put tens of thousands of bikes (30% of which will be electric) at the disposal of Parisians and visitors at some 1400 stations throughout Paris, accessible around the clock.

➡ To get a bike, you first need to purchase a one- or seven-day subscription either at the docking stations or online.

➡ The terminals require a credit card with an embedded smart chip (which precludes many North American cards), and, even then, not all foreign chip-embedded cards will work. Alternatively, you can purchase a subscription online before you leave your hotel.

➡ After you authorise a deposit (€300) to pay for the bike should it go missing, you'll receive an ID number and PIN code and you're ready to go.

➡ Bikes are rented in 30-minute intervals. If you return a bike before a half-hour is up and then take a new one, you will not be charged for a standard bicycle (electric bikes incur charges).

➡ Standard bikes are suitable for cyclists aged 14 and over, and are fitted with gears, an antitheft lock with key, reflective strips and front/rear lights. Bring your own helmet (they are not required by law).

➡ Electric bikes are also for those aged over 14. They have a top speed of 25km/h and a range of 50km.

Rentals

Most rental places will require a deposit (usually €150 for a standard bike, €300 for electric bikes). Take ID and your bank or credit card.

Freescoot (☎01 44 07 06 72; www.freescoot.com; 63 quai de la Tournelle, 5e; 50/125cc scooters per 24hr from €65/75, bicycle/tandem/electric-bike rental per 24hr from €25/40/50; ⏰9am-1pm & 2-7pm mid-Apr–mid-Sep, closed Sun & Wed mid-Sep–mid-Apr; Ⓜ Maubert-Mutualité)

Gepetto et Vélos (☎01 43 54 19 95; www.gepetto-velos.com; 28 rue des Fossées St-Bernard, 5e; bike rental per hour/day/weekend €4/16/20, tandem €8/30/45; ⏰9am-7pm Tue-Sat; Ⓜ Cardinal Lemoine)

Paris à Vélo, C'est Sympa (☎01 48 87 60 01; www.parisvelosympa.fr; 22 rue Alphonse Baudin, 11e; half-day/full day/24hr bike from €12/15/20, electric bike €20/30/40; ⏰9.30am-1pm & 2-6pm Mon-Fri, 9am-7pm Sat & Sun Apr-Oct, shorter hours Nov-Mar; Ⓜ Richard Lenoir)

Bus

Buses can be a scenic way to get around – and there are no stairs to climb, meaning they are more widely accessible – but they're slower and less intuitive to figure out than the metro.

Local Buses

Paris' bus system, operated by the RATP, runs from approximately 5am to 1am Monday to Saturday; services are drastically reduced on Sunday and public holidays. Hours vary substantially depending on the line.

Night Buses

The RATP runs night-bus lines known as Noctilien (www.vianavigo.com); buses depart hourly from 11.45pm to 6am. The services pass through the main *gares* (train stations) and cross the major axes of the city before leading out to the suburbs. Look for navy-blue N or Noctilien signs at bus stops. There are two circular lines within

Paris (the N01 and N02) that link four mainline train stations – St-Lazare, Gare de l'Est, Gare de Lyon and Gare Montparnasse – as well as popular nightlife areas (Bastille, Champs-Elysées, Pigalle, St-Germain).

Noctilien services are included on your Mobilis or Paris Visite pass for the zones in which you are travelling. Otherwise you pay a certain number of standard €1.90 metro/bus tickets, depending on the length of your journey.

Tickets & Fares

➡ Normal bus rides embracing one or two bus zones cost one metro ticket; longer rides require two or even three tickets.

➡ Transfers to other buses – but not the metro – are allowed on the same ticket as long as the change takes place 1½ hours between the first and last validation. This does not apply to Noctilien services.

➡ Whatever kind of single-journey ticket you have, you must validate it in the ticket machine near the driver. If you don't have a ticket, the driver can sell you one for €2 (correct change required).

➡ If you have a Mobilis or Paris Visite pass, flash it at the driver when you board.

Boat

Batobus (www.batobus.com; adult/child 1-day pass €17/8, 2-day pass €19/10; ⏲10am-9.30pm late Apr-Aug, shorter hours Sep-late Apr) runs glassed-in trimarans that dock every 20 to 25 minutes at nine small piers along the Seine: Beaugrenelle, Eiffel Tower, Musée d'Orsay, St-Germain des Prés, Notre Dame, Jardin des Plantes/Cité de la Mode et du Design, Hôtel de Ville, Musée du Louvre and Champs-Élysées.

Buy tickets online, at ferry stops or at tourist offices. Two-day passes must be used on consecutive days. You can also buy a Pass+ that includes **L'Open Tour** (☎01 42 66 56 56; www.paris.opentour.com; 1-day pass adult/child €33/17, night tour €27/17) buses, to be used on consecutive days. A two-day pass per adult/child costs €46/21; a three day-pass is €50/21.

Taxi

➡ The *prise en charge* (flagfall) is €4. Within the city limits, it costs €1.07 per kilometre for travel between 10am and 5pm Monday to Saturday (*Tarif A;* white light on taxi roof and meter).

➡ At night (5pm to 10am), on Sunday from 7am to midnight, and in the inner suburbs the rate is €1.29 per kilometre (*Tarif B;* orange light).

➡ Travel in the city limits and inner suburbs on Sunday night (midnight to 7am Monday) and in the outer suburbs is at *Tarif C,* €1.56 per kilometre (blue light).

➡ The minimum taxi fare for a short trip is €7.10.

➡ There are flat-fee fares to/from the major airports (Charles de Gualle from €50, Orly from €30).

➡ A fifth passenger incurs a €4 surcharge.

➡ There's no additional charge for luggage.

➡ Flagging down a taxi in Paris can be difficult; it's best to find an official taxi stand.

➡ To order a taxi, call or reserve online with **Taxis G7** (☎3607, 01 41 27 66 99; www.g7.fr) or **Alpha Taxis** (☎01 45 85 85 85; www.alpha-taxis-paris.fr).

➡ An alternative is private driver system Uber taxi (www.uber.com/fr/cities/paris); you order and pay via your phone. However, official taxis continue to protest about the service and there have been instances of Uber drivers and passengers being harassed.

Car & Motorcycle

Driving in Paris is defined by the triple hassle of navigation, heavy traffic and limited parking. Petrol stations are also difficult to locate and access. A car is unnecessary to get around, but if you're heading out of the city on an excursion, then one can certainly be useful. A Crit'Air Vignette (compulsory anti-pollution sticker) is also required in most instances. If you plan on hiring a car, it's best to do so online and in advance.

Crit'Air Vignette

To enter the city within the bd Périphérique (ring road) between 8am and 8pm Monday to Friday, a Crit'Air Vignette (compulsory anti-pollution sticker) is needed for all cars, motorcycles and trucks registered after 1997, including foreign-registered vehicles. Older vehicles are banned during these hours. The sticker is not necessary for the ring road itself.

There are six colour-coded stickers, ranked according to emissions levels, from Crit'Air 1 to the highest-polluting Crit'Air 6. In instances of elevated pollution levels, vehicles with stickers denoting higher emissions are banned from entering the city. Fines for not displaying a valid sticker start at €68.

For full details and to order stickers online, visit www.crit-air.fr, available in multiple languages including English. You'll need to upload a copy of your vehicle's registration certificate. Allow time for it to be mailed to your home. Prices for a Crit'Air Vignette start at €3.11.

Parking

➡ Parking meters in Paris do not accept coins; they require a European-compatible chip-enabled credit card. The machine will issue you a ticket for the allotted time, which should be placed on the dashboard behind the windscreen.

➡ Municipal public car parks, of which there are more than 200 in Paris, charge between €2 and €6 per hour or €20 to €36 per 24 hours (cash and compatible credit cards accepted). Most are open 24 hours.

Scooters

Cityscoot (www.cityscoot.eu; per 1/100min €0.28/25; ⏲7am-11pm) Electric mopeds with a top speed of 45km/h are available to rent as part of Paris' scooter-sharing scheme, with all bookings via smartphones. No subscriptions are necessary. Any driver's licence (including a foreign-issued licence) is valid for those born before 1 January 1988; anyone born after that date requires a current EU driver's licence.

Freescoot (☎01 44 07 06 72; www.freescoot.com; 63 quai de la Tournelle, 5e; 50/125cc scooters per 24hr from €65/75, bicycle/tandem/electric-bike rental per 24hr from €25/40/50; ⏲9am-1pm & 2-7pm mid-Apr–mid-Sep, closed Sun & Wed mid-Sep–mid-Apr; Ⓜ Maubert-Mutualité) Rents 50/125cc scooters in various intervals. Prices include third-party insurance as well as helmets, locks, rain gear and gloves. A motorcycle licence is required for 125cc scooters but not for 50cc scooters, though you must be at least 23 years old and leave a credit-card deposit of €1000.

Left Bank Scooters (☎06 78 12 04 24; www.leftbankscooters.com; 50/125cc scooters per 24hr €70/80) Rents Vespa XLV scooters including insurance, helmet and wet-weather gear; scooters can be delivered to and collected from anywhere in Paris. You must be at least 20 years old and have a car or motorcycle licence. Credit-card deposit is €1000.

Tours

As one of the world's most visited cities, Paris is well set up for visitors, offering a host of guided tours, from bike, boat, bus, scooter and walking tours (including some wonderful local-led options in off-the-beaten-track areas) to themed options including photography tours and treasure hunts.

Bicycle

Bike About Tours (Map p386; ☎06 18 80 84 92; www.bikeabouttours.com; Le Peloton Café, 17 rue du Pont Louis-Philippe, 4e; Ⓜ Hôtel de Ville) This expat-run outfit offers daytime city tours (adult/child €35/30; 3½ hours), trips to Versailles (€100), e-bike tours to Champagne (€150; minimum four people) and private family tours.

Fat Tire Bike Tours (☎01 82 88 80 96; www.fattiretours.com; tours from €34) Day and night bike tours of the city, both in central Paris and further afield to Versailles and Monet's garden in Giverny.

Paris à Vélo, C'est Sympa! (Map p386; ☎01 48 87 60 01; www.parisvelosympa.com; 22 rue Alphonse Baudin, 11e; Ⓜ Richard Lenoir) Runs three guided bike tours (adult/child €35/29; three hours): Heart of Paris, Unusual Paris (taking in artist studios and mansions) and Contrast, combining nature and modern architecture. Tours depart from its bike-rental shop.

Boat

A boat cruise down the Seine is the most relaxing way to view the city's main monuments as you watch Paris glide by. An alternative to a regular tour is the hop-on, hop-off **Batobus** (www.batobus.com; adult/child 1-day pass €17/8, 2-day pass €19/10; ⏲10am-9.30pm late Apr-Aug, shorter hours Sep-late Apr).

Bateaux Parisiens (Map p366; ☎08 25 01 01 01; www.bateauxparisiens.com; Port de la Bourdonnais, 7e; adult/child €15/7; Ⓜ Bir Hakeim or RER Pont de l'Alma) This vast operation runs hour-long river circuits with audioguides in 14 languages (every 30 minutes 10am to 11pm April to September, hourly 10.30am to 10pm October to March), and a host of themed lunch and dinner cruises. It has two locations: one by the Eiffel Tower, the other south of Notre Dame.

Bateaux-Mouches (Map p368; ☎01 42 25 96 10; www.bateaux-mouches.fr; Port de la Conférence, 8e; adult/child €13.50/6; Ⓜ Alma Marceau) The largest river-cruise company in Paris is a favourite with tour groups. Departing just east of the Pont de l'Alma on the Right Bank, cruises (70 minutes) run regularly from 10am to 10.30pm April to September and every 40 minutes from 11am to 9.20pm the rest of the year. Commentary is in French and English.

Vedettes de Paris (Map p366; ☎01 44 18 19 50; www.vedettesdeparis.fr; Port de Suffren, 7e; adult/child €15/7; ⏲11.30am-7.30pm May-Sep, 11.30am-5.30pm Oct-Apr; Ⓜ Bir Hakeim or RER Pont de l'Alma) These one-hour sightseeing cruises on smaller boats are a more intimate experience than those offered by the major companies. It runs themed cruises, too, including imaginative 'Mysteries of Paris' tours for kids (adult/child €15/9).

Vedettes du Pont Neuf (Map p396; ☎01 46 33 98 38; www.vedettesdupontneuf.com; square du Vert Galant, 1er; adult/child €14/7; ⏲10.30am-9pm; Ⓜ Pont Neuf) One-hour cruises depart year-round from Vedettes' centrally located dock at the western tip of Île de la Cité; commentary is in French and English. Tickets are cheaper

SPECIALISED TOURS

Meeting the French (☎01 42 51 19 80; www.meetingthefrench.com; tours & courses from €15) Make-up workshops, backstage cabaret tours, fashion-designer showroom visits, French table decoration, art embroidery classes, market tours, baking with a Parisian baker: the repertoire of cultural and gourmet tours and behind-the-scenes experiences offered by Meeting the French is truly outstanding. All courses and tours are in English.

THATMuse (www.thatmuse.com; per person excl museum admission Louvre/Musée d'Orsay €25/35) Organises treasure hunts in English and French in the Louvre and Musée d'Orsay. Participants (up to five people, playing alone or against another team) have to photograph themselves in front of 20 to 30 works of art ('treasure'). Hunts typically last 1½ to two hours.

Left Bank Scooters (☎06 78 12 04 24; www.leftbankscooters.com; 3hr tours per 1st/2nd passenger from €200/50) Runs a variety of scooter tours around Paris, both day and evening, as well as trips out to Versailles and sidecar tours. Car or motorcycle licence required.

Paris Photography Tours (☎06 17 08 54 45; www.parisphotographytours.com; 3hr day/night tours for 1-4 people €180) Offers customised tours by professional photographers that take into account your level of experience as well as what you most want to capture, such as nature, architecture or street life. Tours can incorporate lessons on how to improve your photographic skills.

Set in Paris (Map p398; ☎09 84 42 35 79; http://setinparis.com; 3 rue Maître Albert, 5e; 2hr tours €25; ⏲tours 10am & 3pm; Ⓜ Maubert-Mutualité) From a cinema-style 'box office' HQ in the Latin Quarter, it offers two-hour walking tours that take you to locations throughout the city where movies including *The Devil Wears Prada, The Bourne Identity, The Three Musketeers, The Hunchback of Notre Dame, Ratatouille, Before Sunset*, several James Bond instalments and many others were filmed. Reservations are recommended.

Street Art Paris (☎09 50 75 19 92; http://streetartparis.fr; 2½hr tour €20) Learn about the history of graffiti on fascinating tours taking in Paris' vibrant street art. Tours take place in Belleville and Montmartre and on the Left Bank. If you're inspired to try it yourself, book into a 2½-hour mural workshop (€35).

if you buy in advance online (adult/child €10/5). Check the website for details of its one-hour lunch cruises (€41/35), two-hour dinner (€71/35) and Champagne cruises (€104/35).

Bus

Big Bus Paris (☎01 53 95 39 53; www.bigbustours.com; 1-day pass adult/child €35/17, night tour €23/12) These hop-on, hop-off bus tours operate two different routes around the city, with a total of 13 stops. Commentary is in 11 languages; download free apps for iPhone or Android.

L'Open Tour (☎01 42 66 56 56; www.paris.opentour.com; 1-day pass adult/child €33/17, night tour €27/17) Hop-on, hop-off bus tours aboard open-deck buses with three different circuits and 50 stops. Audioguides come in 10 languages.

Walking

Ça Se Visite (☎01 43 57 59 50; www.ca-se-visite.fr; adult/child on foot from €12/10, on kick-scooter from €15/13) Meet local artists and craftspeople on resident-led 'urban discovery tours' of the northeast (Belleville, Ménilmontant, Canal St-Martin, Canal de l'Ourcq, Oberkampf, La Villette) – on foot or by *trottinette* (scooter).

Eye Prefer Paris (☎06 31 12 86 20; www.eyepreferparistours.com; 3-person 3hr tour €225) New Yorker–turned-Parisian Richard Nahem leads offbeat tours of the city. Full-day tours also available.

Localers (☎01 83 64 92 01; www.localers.com; tours from €49) Classic walking tours and behind-the-scenes urban discoveries with local Paris experts: *pétanque*, photo shoots, market tours, cooking classes and more.

Parisien d'un Jour – Paris Greeters (https://greeters.paris; by donation) See Paris through local eyes with these two- to three-hour city tours. Volunteers – mainly knowledgeable Parisians passionate about their city – lead groups (maximum six people) to their favourite spots. Minimum two weeks' notice needed.

Paris Walks (☎01 48 09 21 40; www.paris-walks.com; 2hr tours adult/child €15/10) Long established and well respected, Paris Walks offers two-hour thematic walking tours (art, fashion, the French Revolution etc).

Directory A–Z

Accessible Travel

Paris is an ancient city and therefore not particularly well equipped for *visiteurs handicapés* (disabled visitors): kerb ramps are few and far between, older public facilities and budget hotels usually lack lifts, and the metro, dating back more than a century, is mostly inaccessible for those in a wheelchair *(fauteuil roulant)*.

But efforts are being made to improve things. The tourist office continues its excellent 'Tourisme & Handicap' initiative, under which museums, cultural attractions, hotels and restaurants that provide access, special assistance or facilities for those with physical, cognitive, visual and/or hearing disabilities display a special logo at their entrances. Online, its FACIL'iti service allows you to create your own profile to personalise the web content of parisinfo.com according to your particular motor, sensory and/or cognitive needs.

The Paris Convention and Visitors Bureau's **main office** (Paris Office de Tourisme; Map p386; ☎01 49 52 42 63; www.parisinfo.com; 29 rue de Rivoli, 4e; ⏰9am-7pm; 📶; Ⓜ Hôtel de Ville) is equipped with a service called ACCEO, which makes it possible for people who are deaf or hearing impaired to ask for information. With the help of a French sign-language operator, users can communicate via a webcam, microphone and speakers. Instant speech transcription is available, too.

Resources

➡ Visit www.parisinfo.com/accessibility for a wealth of useful information organised by theme – getting there and around, attractions, accommodation and cafes/bars/restaurants – as well as practical information such as where to rent medical equipment or locate automatic public toilets. You can download the up-to-date 27-page Accessible Paris guide, which is also available in hard copy from tourist-information centres in the city.

➡ For information about which cultural venues in Paris are accessible to people with disabilities, visit Accès Culture (http://accesculture.org).

➡ J'Accède (www.jaccede.com) maintains a searchable database of accessible venues sourced from the local disabled community and has thousands of entries in Paris alone. It is also available as a smartphone app.

➡ Handycairn (www.handycairn.com/en) is a user-friendly, extensive, searchable database of tourist and leisure activities filterable by type of disability, region, type of activity and type of accommodation/restaurant/service with detailed access information under each entry.

➡ **Mobile en Ville** (Map p412; ☎09 52 29 60 51; www.mobileenville.org; 8 rue des Mariniers, 14e) works hard to make independent travel within the city easier for people in wheelchairs. Among other things it organises wheelchair *randonnées* (walks) in and around Paris; those in wheelchairs are pushed by 'walkers' on roller skates; contact the association well ahead of your visit to take part.

➡ Download Lonely Planet's free *Accessible Travel Online Resources* from http://lptravel.to/AccessibleTravel for heaps more useful websites, including travel agents and tour operators.

Transport

The SNCF has made many of its train carriages more accessible to people with disabilities. For information and advice on planning your journey from station to station, contact the SNCF service **Accès Plus** (☎08 90 64 06 50; www.accessibilite.sncf.com). The SNCF also has an 88-page *Reduced Mobility Guide*, available to view interactively or to download in French; go to www.accessibilite.sncf.com/documents-a-telecharger/guide-des-voyageurs-a-mobilite.

Info Mobi (☎09 70 81 93 95; www.vianavigo.com/accessibilite) has detailed information about public transport in the Île-de-France region, surrounding Paris, filterable by disability type.

Taxis G7 (☎3607, 01 41 27 66 99; www.g7.fr) has hundreds of low-base cars and 120 cars equipped with ramps, and drivers trained in helping passengers with disabilities. Guide dogs are accepted in its entire fleet.

PRACTICALITIES

Classifieds Check FUSAC (France USA Contacts; www.fusac.fr) for classified ads about housing, babysitting, French lessons, part-time jobs and so forth.

Newspapers & magazines Newspapers include the centre-left *Le Monde* (www.lemonde.fr), right-leaning *Le Figaro* (www.lefigaro.fr) and left-leaning *Libération* (www.liberation.fr). *Le Parisien* (www.leparisien.fr) is the city-news read.

Smoking It's illegal to smoke in indoor public spaces, including hotel rooms, restaurants and bars (hence the crowds of smokers in doorways and on pavement terraces outside).

Weights & Measures France uses the metric system.

Customs Regulations

Residents of non-EU countries must adhere to the following limits:

Alcohol 16L of beer, 4L of wine and 1L of spirits

Perfume up to a value of €430 (arriving by air or sea); up to €300 (arriving by land)

Tobacco 200 cigarettes, 50 cigars or 250g of loose tobacco

For visitors from EU countries, limits only apply for excessive amounts; see www.douane.gouv.fr.

Discount Cards

Almost all museums and monuments in Paris have discounted tickets *(tarif réduit)* for students and seniors (generally over 60 years), provided they have valid ID. Children often get in for free; the cut-off age for 'child' is anywhere between six and 18 years. EU citizens under 26 years get in for free at national monuments and museums.

Paris Museum Pass (http://en.parismuseumpass.com; two/four/six days €48/62/74) Gets you into 50-plus venues in and around Paris; a huge advantage is that pass holders usually enter larger sights at a different entrance, meaning you bypass (or substantially reduce) ridiculously long ticket queues.

Paris Passlib' (www.parisinfo.com; two/three/five days €109/129/155) Sold at the **Paris Convention & Visitors Bureau** (Paris Office de Tourisme; Map p386; ☎01 49 52 42 63; www.parisinfo.com; 29 rue de Rivoli, 4e; ⊙9am-7pm; 📶; Ⓜ Hôtel de Ville) and on its website, this handy city pass covers unlimited public transport in zones 1 to 3, admission to some 50 museums in the Paris region (aka a Paris Museum Pass), temporary exhibitions at most municipal museums, a one-hour **Bateaux Parisiens** (Map p366; ☎08 25 01 01 01; www.bateauxparisiens.com; Port de la Bourdonnais, 7e; adult/child €15/7; Ⓜ Bir Hakeim or RER Pont de l'Alma) boat cruise along the Seine, and a one-day hop-on, hop-off open-top bus sightseeing service around central Paris' key sights with **L'Open Tour** (☎01 42 66 56 56; www.paris.opentour.com; 1-day pass adult/child €33/17, night tour €27/17). There's an optional €20 supplement for a skip-the-line ticket to levels one and two of the Eiffel Tower.

Electricity

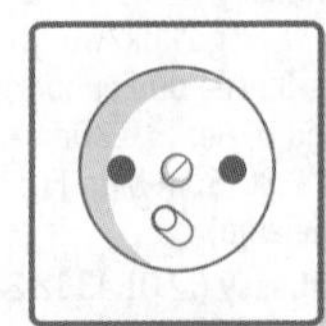

Type E
230V/50Hz

Embassies & Consulates

The following is a list of selected embassies in Paris.

Australian Embassy (☎01 40 59 33 00; http://france.embassy.gov.au; 4 rue Jean Rey, 15e; Ⓜ Bir Hakeim)

Canadian Embassy (☎01 44 43 29 00; www.amb-canada.fr;

35 av Montaigne, 8e; ⓂFranklin D Roosevelt)

Chinese Embassy (Service Consulaire de l'Ambassade de Chine; ☎01 53 75 88 31; www.amb-chine.fr; 18-20 rue Washington, 8e; ⌚9.30am-noon & 2.30-5pm Mon-Fri; ⓂGeorge V)

Dutch Embassy (☎01 40 62 33 00; www.paysbasmondial.nl/pays/france; 7-9 rue Eblé, 7e; ⓂSt-François Xavier)

German Embassy (☎01 53 83 45 00; www.allemagne.diplo.de; 24 rue Marbeau, 16e; ⌚8.30am-4.45pm Mon-Thu, to 2pm Fri; ⓂPorte Maillot)

Irish Embassy (☎01 44 17 67 00; www.embassyofireland.fr; 12 av Foch, 16e; ⌚9.30am-noon Mon-Fri; ⓂCharles de Gaulle–Étoile)

Japanese Embassy (☎01 48 88 62 00; www.fr.emb-japan.go.jp; 7 av Hoche, 8e; ⌚9.30am-1pm & 2.30-5pm Mon-Fri; ⓂCourcelles)

New Zealand Embassy (☎01 45 01 43 43; www.nzembassy.com/france; 103 rue de Grenelle, 7e; ⓂVarenne)

UK Embassy (☎01 44 51 31 00; www.gov.uk/world/france; 35 rue du Faubourg St-Honoré, 8e; ⌚9.30am-1pm & 2.30-5pm Mon-Fri; ⓂMadeleine)

US Embassy (☎01 43 12 22 22; https://fr.usembassy.gov; 2 av Gabriel, 8e; ⌚by appointment; ⓂConcorde)

Emergency

Ambulance (SAMU)	☎15
Fire	☎18
Police	☎17
EU-wide emergency	☎112
France's country code	☎33

Internet Access

➡ Wi-fi (pronounced '*wee*-fee' in France) is available in most Paris hotels, usually at no extra cost, and in some museums.

➡ Many cafes and bars have free wi-fi for customers; you may need to ask for the code.

➡ Free wi-fi is available in hundreds of public places, including parks, libraries and municipal buildings; look for a purple 'Zone Wi-Fi' sign. To connect, select the 'PARIS_WI-FI_' network. Sessions are limited to two hours (renewable). For complete details and a map of hot spots, see www.paris.fr/wifi.

➡ Expect to pay around €4 to €5 per hour for access in internet cafes such as **Milk** (www.milklub.com; 31 bd de Sébastopol, 1er; 1hr €3.90; ⌚24hr; ⓂLes Halles or RER Châtelet–Les Halles).

➡ Co-working cafes have sprung up across Paris; you typically pay for a set amount of time, with wi-fi, drinks and snacks included.

Legal Matters

If the police stop you for any reason, be polite and remain calm. They have wide powers of search and seizure and can, without any particular reason, decide to examine your passport, visa and so on. (You are expected to have photo ID on you at *all* times.) Do *not* challenge them.

French police are strict about security. Do not leave baggage unattended; they are quite serious when they say that suspicious objects will be summarily blown up.

Medical Services

➡ For minor health concerns and to fill prescriptions, see a local *pharmacie* (chemist).

➡ For more serious problems, go to *urgences* (emergencies) wards at Paris' *hôpitaux* (hospitals).

Hospitals

Paris has some 50 hospitals, including the following:

L'Institut Hospitalier Franco-Britannique (IHFB; ☎01 47 59 59 59; www.ihfb.org; 4 rue Kléber, Levallois-Perret; ⓂAnatole France) Private, English-speaking option.

Hôpital Hôtel Dieu (☎01 42 34 88 19; www.aphp.fr; 1 Parvis Notre Dame – place Jean-Paul-II, 4e; ⓂCité) One of the city's main government-run public hospitals; after 8pm use the emergency entrance on rue de la Cité.

Pharmacies

Pharmacies (chemists) are marked by a large illuminated green cross outside. At least one in each neighbourhood is open for extended hours; find a complete night-owl listing on the Paris Convention & Visitors Bureau website (www.parisinfo.com).

Pharmacie Bader (☎01 43 26 92 66; www.pharmaciebader.com; 10-12 bd St-Michel, 6e; ⌚8.30am-9pm; ⓂSt-Michel)

Pharmacie de la Mairie (☎01 42 78 53 58; www.pharmacie-mairie-paris.com; 9 rue des Archives, 4e; ⌚9am-8pm; ⓂHôtel de Ville)

Pharmacie Les Champs (☎01 45 62 02 41; Galerie des Champs-Élysées, 84 av des Champs-Élysées, 8e; ⌚24hr; ⓂGeorge V)

Money

France uses the euro (€), which is divided into 100 centimes. Denominations are €5, €10, €20, €50, €100, €200 and €500 notes, and €0.01, €0.02, €0.05, €0.10, €0.20, €0.50, €1 and €2 coins.

French vendors rarely accept bills larger than €50.

Check the latest exchange rates on websites such as www.xe.com.

ATMs

ATMs (*distributeur automatique de billets* in French) are widespread. Unless you have particularly high transaction fees, ATMs are usually the best and easiest way to deal with currency exchange. French banks don't generally charge fees to use their ATMs, but check with your own bank before you travel to know if/how much they charge for international cash withdrawals.

Changing Money

- Cash is not a good way to carry money; it can be stolen and in France you often won't get the best exchange rates.
- In Paris, *bureaux de change* are usually more efficient, are open longer hours and give better rates than banks – many banks don't even offer exchange services.

Credit Cards

Visa/Carte Bleue is the most widely accepted credit card in Paris, followed by MasterCard (Eurocard). Amex cards are only accepted at more upmarket establishments.

Note that France uses a smartcard with an embedded microchip and PIN – few places accept swipe-and-signature. Some foreign chip-and-PIN-enabled cards require a signature – ask your bank before you leave. Chipless cards (and even some chip-embedded foreign cards) can't be used at automated machines (such as at a metro station or museum).

Opening Hours

The following list covers *approximate* standard opening hours. Many businesses close in August for summer holidays.

Banks 9am to 1pm and 2 to 5pm Monday to Friday; some open on Saturday morning

Bars & Cafes 7am to 2am

Museums 10am to 6pm; closed Monday or Tuesday

Post Offices 8am to 7pm Monday to Friday, and until noon Saturday

Restaurants noon to 2pm and 7.30 to 10.30pm

Shops 10am to 7pm Monday to Saturday; they occasionally close in the early afternoon for lunch and sometimes all day Monday. Hours are longer for shops located in defined ZTIs (international tourist zones).

Post

- Most post offices *(bureaux de poste)* are open Monday to Saturday.
- *Tabacs* (tobacconists) usually sell postage stamps.
- The main **post office** (Map p376; www.laposte.fr; 52 rue du Louvre, 1er; ⏲24hr; Ⓜ Sentier, Les Halles, or RER Châtelet–Les Halles), five blocks north of the eastern end of the Musée du Louvre, is open round the clock, but only for basic services such as sending letters. Other services, including currency exchange, are available only during regular opening hours. Be prepared for long queues.
- Each *arrondissement* has its own five-digit postcode, formed by prefixing the number of the *arrondissement* with '750' or '7500' (eg 75001 for the 1er *arrondissement*, 75019 for the 19e). The only exception is the 16e, which has two postcodes: 75016 and 75116. All mail to addresses in France must include the postcode.

Public Holidays

In France a *jour férié* (public holiday) is celebrated strictly on the day on which it falls. Thus if May Day falls on a Saturday or Sunday, no provision is made for an extra day off.

The following holidays are observed in Paris:

New Year's Day (Jour de l'An) 1 January

Easter Sunday & Monday (Pâques & Lundi de Pâques) Late March/April

May Day (Fête du Travail) 1 May

Victory in Europe Day (Victoire 1945) 8 May

Ascension Thursday (L'Ascension) May (celebrated on the 40th day after Easter)

Whit Monday (Lundi de Pentecôte) Mid-May to mid-June (seventh Monday after Easter)

Bastille Day/National Day (Fête Nationale) 14 July

Assumption Day (L'Assomption) 15 August

All Saints' Day (La Toussaint) 1 November

Armistice Day/Remembrance Day (Le Onze Novembre) 11 November

Christmas (Noël) 25 December

Safe Travel

Overall, Paris is well lit and safe, and random street assaults are rare.

- Stay alert for pickpockets and take precautions: don't carry more cash than you need, and keep credit cards and passports in a concealed pouch.
- Beware of scams such as fake petitions.
- Metro stations best avoided late at night include Châtelet–Les Halles, Château Rouge, Gare du Nord, Strasbourg St-Denis, Réaumur Sébastopol, Stalingrad and Montparnasse

Bienvenüe. Marx Dormoy, Porte de la Chapelle and Marcadet–Poissonniers can be sketchy day and night.

➡ *Bornes d'alarme* (alarm boxes) are located in the centre of metro/RER platforms and some station corridors.

Pickpockets & Common Scams

Nonviolent crimes, such as pickpocketing and theft from handbags and packs, are a problem wherever there are crowds, especially of tourists. Places to be particularly careful include Montmartre (especially around Sacré Cœur); Pigalle; the areas around Forum des Halles and the Centre Pompidou; the Latin Quarter (especially the rectangle bounded by rue St-Jacques, bd St-Germain, bd St-Michel and quai St-Michel); beneath the Eiffel Tower; and on the metro during rush hour (particularly on line 4 and the western part of line 1).

On cafe and restaurant terraces, avoid leaving your jacket containing your wallet or handbag over the back of your chair, and don't leave your phone unattended on the table.

Common 'distraction' scams employed by pickpockets include the following:

Fake petitions After approaching you to sign a 'petition', scammers will use the document to cover your belongings while they swipe them.

Gold ring Scammers pretend to 'find' a gold ring (after subtly dropping it on the ground) and offer it to you as a diversionary tactic while they surreptitiously reach into your pockets or bags (variations include offering to sell you the ring for an outrageous price, or having the ring's 'owner' arrive and demand compensation).

Dropped items Often occurs on the metro. Someone will drop something or spill a bag; your reaction might be to bend down and help them, while their accomplices rifle through your belongings.

Friendship bracelets
Scammers approach you and tie a 'friendship bracelet' onto your wrist, not only insisting that you pay for it but taking the opportunity to fleece you of your valuables.

Taxes & Refunds

France's value-added tax (VAT) is known as TVA *(taxe sur la valeur ajoutée)* and is 20% on most goods with a few exceptions: for food products and books it's 5.5%, and for medicines it's 2.1%. Prices that include TVA are often marked TTC (*toutes taxes comprises;* literally 'all taxes included').

If you're not an EU resident, you can get a TVA refund provided that:

➡ you're aged over 16

➡ you'll be spending less than six months in France

➡ you purchase goods worth at least €175.01 at a single shop on the same day (not more than 15 of the same item)

➡ the goods fit into your luggage

➡ you are taking the goods out of France within three months of purchase

➡ the shop offers *vente en détaxe* (duty-free sales)

Present a passport at the time of purchase and ask for a *bordereau de vente à l'exportation* (export sales invoice) to be signed by the retailer and yourself. Most shops will refund less than the full amount (about 14%) to which you are entitled, in order to cover the time and expense involved in the refund procedure.

Some larger shops offer the refund on the spot (always ask). Alternatively, as you leave France or another EU country, have all three pages of the *bordereau* validated by the country's customs officials at the airport or at the border. Customs officials will take one sheet and hand you two. You must post one copy (the pink one) back to the shop and retain the other (green) sheet for your records in case there is any dispute. Once the shop where you made your purchase receives its stamped copy, it will send you a *virement* (fund transfer) in the form you have requested. Be prepared for a wait of up to three months.

If you're flying out of Orly or Charles de Gaulle, certain shops can arrange for you to receive your refund as you're leaving the country, though you must complete the steps outlined above. You must make such arrangements at the time of purchase.

For more information contact the **customs information centre** (☎08 11 20 44 44; www.douane.minefi.gouv.fr; ⏲phone service 8.30am-6pm Mon-Fri).

Telephone

➡ There are no area codes in France – you always dial the 10-digit number.

➡ Telephone numbers in Paris always start with 01, unless the number is provided by an internet service provider (ISP), in which case it begins with 09.

➡ Mobile-phone numbers throughout France commence with either 06 or 07.

➡ France's country code is 33.

➡ To call abroad from Paris, dial France's international access code (00), the country code, the area code (drop the initial '0', if there is one) and the local number.

➡ Note that while numbers beginning with 08 00, 08 04, 08 05 and 08 09 are toll free in

France, other numbers beginning with 08 are not.

➡ Customer-service numbers are generally more expensive than local rates.

➡ Most four-digit numbers starting with 10, 30 or 31 are free of charge.

➡ If you can read basic French, directory enquiries are best done via the *Yellow Pages* (www.pagesjaunes.fr; click on Pages Blanches for the *White Pages*), which will provide more information, including maps, for free.

Mobile Phones

Phone compatibility You can use your mobile/cell phone *(portable)* in France provided it is compatible and allows roaming. Ask your service provider about using it in France, but beware of roaming costs, especially for data.

Networks Rather than staying on your home network, it is usually more convenient to buy a local SIM card from a French provider, such as Orange (www.orange.fr), SFR (www.sfr.fr), Bouygues (www.bouyguestelecom.fr) or Free Mobile (http://mobile.free.fr), which will give you a local phone number. Ensure your phone is unlocked to use another service provider.

Call credit Count on paying between €1.90 and €5 for the initial SIM card (with a few minutes of calls included), then purchase a prepaid Mobicarte for phone credit. *Tabacs* (tobacconists), mobile-phone outlets, supermarkets etc sell Mobicartes.

Time

➡ France uses the 24-hour clock in most cases, with the hours usually separated from the minutes by a lower-case 'h'. Thus, 15h30 is 3.30pm, 00h30 is 12.30am and so on.

➡ France is on Central European Time (like Berlin and Rome), which is one hour ahead of GMT/UTC.

➡ Daylight-saving time runs from the last Sunday in March, when the clocks move forward one hour, to the last Sunday in October.

Toilets

➡ Public toilets in Paris are signposted *toilettes* or *WC*. On main roads, *sanisettes* (self-cleaning cylindrical toilets) are open 24 hours and are free of charge. Look for the words *libre* ('available'; green-coloured) or *occupé* ('occupied'; red-coloured).

➡ Cafe owners do not appreciate your using their facilities if you are not a paying customer (a coffee can be a good investment); however, if you have young children they may make an exception (ask first!). Other good bets are big hotels and major department stores (the latter may incur a charge).

➡ There are free public toilets in front of Notre Dame cathedral, near the Arc de Triomphe, down the steps at Sacré-Cœur (to the east and west) and at the north-western entrance to the Jardins des Tuileries.

Tourist Information

Paris' main tourist office, the **Paris Convention & Visitors Bureau** (Paris Office de Tourisme; Map p386; ☎01 49 52 42 63; www.parisinfo.com; 29 rue de Rivoli, 4e; ⏰9am-7pm; 📶; Ⓜ Hôtel de Ville), is located at the Hôtel de Ville. It sells tickets for tours and several attractions, plus museum and transport passes.

Information desks are located at Charles de Gaulle and Orly airports. For tourist information around Paris, see Paris Region (www.visitparisregion.com).

Gare du Nord Welcome Desk (Map p382; www.parisinfo.com; 18 rue de Dunkerque, 10e; ⏰8.30am-6.30pm; Ⓜ Gare du Nord) Inside Gare du Nord station, under the glass roof of the Île-de-France departure and arrival area (eastern end of station).

Réception du Carrousel du Louvre (Map p372; ☎01 43 16 47 10; www.carrouseldulouvre.com; 99 rue de Rivoli, 1er; ⏰10am-8pm; Ⓜ Palais Royal-Musée du Louvre) Inside the Carrousel du Louvre shopping complex, this partner of Paris' tourist office has tourist information including maps, and can book taxis and accommodation, though it doesn't sell tickets/passes.

Syndicate d'Initiative de Montmartre (Map p378; ☎01 42 62 21 21; www.montmartre-guide.com; 21 place du Tertre, 18e; ⏰10am-5pm Mon-Fri, 10am-1pm & 2-5pm Sat & Sun; Ⓜ Abbesses) Locally run tourist office and shop on Montmartre's most picturesque square. It sells maps of Montmartre and organises guided tours.

Visas

There are no entry requirements for nationals of EU countries and a handful of other European countries (including Switzerland). Citizens of Australia, the USA, Canada and New Zealand do not need visas to visit France for up to 90 days.

Everyone else, including citizens of South Africa, needs a Schengen Visa, named after the Schengen Agreement that has abolished passport controls among 26 EU countries and that has also been ratified by the non-EU governments of Iceland, Norway and Switzerland. A visa for any of these countries should be valid throughout the Schengen area, but it pays to double-check with the embassy or consulate of each country you intend to visit. Note that the UK and Ireland are not Schengen countries.

Check www.diplomatie.gouv.fr for the latest visa regulations and the closest French embassy to your current residence.

Titre de Séjour

If you are issued a long-stay visa valid for six months or longer, you may need to apply for a *titre de séjour* (residence permit; also called a *carte de séjour*) after your arrival in France. If you are only staying for up to 12 months you may not need it, but you will need to register with the French Office of Immigration and Integration (www.ofii.fr). Check the website of the Préfecture de Police (www.prefecturedepolice.interieur.gouv.fr) or call ☎01 53 71 53 71 first for instructions.

EU passport holders seeking to take up residence in France don't need to acquire a *titre de séjour;* a passport or national ID card is sufficient. Check the Préfecture de Police website to see which countries are included.

Foreigners with non-European passports should check the website of the Préfecture de Police or call ☎01 53 71 53 71.

Visa Extensions

Tourist visas *cannot* be extended except in emergencies (such as medical problems). If you have an urgent problem, contact the Service Étranger (Foreigner Service) at the Préfecture de Police for guidance. If you entered France on the 90-day visa-waiver program (eg you are Australian, Canadian or American) and you have stayed for 90 days, you must leave the Schengen area for an additional 90 days before you can re-enter.

Work & Student Visas

If you would like to work, study or stay in France for longer than three months, apply to the French embassy or consulate nearest to you for the appropriate *long séjour* (long-stay) visa. Au pairs are granted student visas: they must be arranged before you leave home (unless you're an EU resident); the same goes for the year-long working-holiday visa *(permis vacances travail)*.

Unless you hold an EU passport or are married to a French national, it's extremely difficult to get a visa that will allow you to work in France. For any sort of long-stay visa, begin the paperwork in your home country several months before you plan to leave. Applications usually cannot be made in a third country, nor can tourist visas be turned into student visas after you arrive in France. People with student visas can apply for permission to work part time; enquire at your place of study.

Language

The sounds used in spoken French can almost all be found in English. If you read our pronunciation guides as if they were English, you'll be understood just fine. There are a couple of sounds to take note of: nasal vowels (represented in our guides by o or u followed by an almost inaudible nasal consonant sound m, n or ng), the 'funny' *u* (ew in our guides) and the deep-in-the-throat *r*. Syllables in French words are, for the most part, equally stressed. As English speakers tend to stress the first syllable, try adding a light stress on the final syllable of French words to compensate.

BASICS

Hello.	*Bonjour.*	bon·zhoor
Goodbye.	*Au revoir.*	o·rer·vwa
Excuse me.	*Excusez-moi.*	ek·skew·zay·mwa
Sorry.	*Pardon.*	par·don
Yes./No.	*Oui./Non.*	wee/non
Please.	*S'il vous plaît.*	seel voo play
Thank you.	*Merci.*	mair·see
You're welcome.	*De rien.*	der ree·en

How are you?
Comment allez-vous? ko·mon ta·lay·voo

Fine, and you?
Bien, merci. Et vous? byun mair·see ay voo

What's your name?
Comment vous appelez-vous? ko·mon voo·za·play voo

WANT MORE?

For in-depth language information and handy phrases, check out Lonely Planet's *French* phrasebook. You'll find it at **shop.lonelyplanet.com**, or you can buy Lonely Planet's iPhone phrasebooks at the Apple App Store.

My name is ...
Je m'appelle ... zher ma·pel ...

Do you speak English?
Parlez-vous anglais? par·lay·voo ong·glay

I don't understand.
Je ne comprends pas. zher ner kom·pron pa

ACCOMMODATION

Do you have any rooms available?
Est-ce que vous avez des chambres libres? es·ker voo za·vay day shom·brer lee·brer

How much is it per night/person?
Quel est le prix par nuit/personne? kel ay ler pree par nwee/per·son

Is breakfast included?
Est-ce que le petit déjeuner est inclus? es·ker ler per·tee day·zher·nay ayt en·klew

dorm	*dortoir*	dor·twar
guesthouse	*pension*	pon·syon
hotel	*hôtel*	o·tel
youth hostel	*auberge de jeunesse*	o·berzh der zher·nes

a ... room	*une chambre ...*	ewn shom·brer ...
single	*à un lit*	a un lee
double	*avec un grand lit*	a·vek un gron lee

with (a) ...	*avec ...*	a·vek ...
air-con	*climatiseur*	klee·ma·tee·zer
bathroom	*une salle de bains*	ewn sal der bun
window	*fenêtre*	fer·nay·trer

DIRECTIONS

Where's ...?	*Où est ...?*	oo ay ...
What's the address?	*Quelle est l'adresse?*	kel ay la·dres

SIGNS

Entrée	Entrance
Femmes	Women
Fermé	Closed
Hommes	Men
Interdit	Prohibited
Ouvert	Open
Renseignements	Information
Sortie	Exit
Toilettes/WC	Toilets

Can you write down the address, please?
Est-ce que vous pourriez écrire l'adresse, s'il vous plaît? — es·ker voo poo·ryay ay·kreer la·dres seel voo play

Can you show me (on the map)?
Pouvez-vous m'indiquer (sur la carte)? — poo·vay·voo mun·dee·kay (sewr la kart)

at the corner	*au coin*	o kwun
at the traffic lights	*aux feux*	o fer
behind	*derrière*	dair·ryair
in front of	*devant*	der·von
far (from ...)	*loin (de ...)*	lwun (der ...)
left	*gauche*	gosh
near (to ...)	*près (de ...)*	pray (der ...)
next to ...	*à côté de ...*	a ko·tay der ...
opposite ...	*en face de ...*	on fas der ...
right	*droite*	drwat
straight ahead	*tout droit*	too drwa

EATING & DRINKING

What would you recommend?
Qu'est-ce que vous conseillez? — kes·ker voo kon·say·yay

What's in that dish?
Quels sont les ingrédients? — kel son lay zun·gray·dyon

I'm a vegetarian.
Je suis végétarien/ végétarienne. — zher swee vay·zhay·ta·ryun/ vay·zhay·ta·ryen (m/f)

I don't eat ...
Je ne mange pas ... — zher ner monzh pa ...

Cheers!
Santé! — son·tay

That was delicious.
C'était délicieux! — say·tay day·lee·syer

Please bring the bill.
Apportez-moi l'addition, s'il vous plaît. — a·por·tay·mwa la·dee·syon seel voo play

I'd like to reserve a table for ...	*Je voudrais réserver une table pour ...*	zher voo·dray ray·zair·vay ewn ta·bler poor ...
(eight) o'clock	*(vingt) heures*	(vungt) er
(two) people	*(deux) personnes*	(der) pair·son

Key Words

appetiser	*entrée*	on·tray
bottle	*bouteille*	boo·tay
breakfast	*petit déjeuner*	per·tee day·zher·nay
cold	*froid*	frwa
delicatessen	*traiteur*	tray·ter
dinner	*dîner*	dee·nay
fork	*fourchette*	foor·shet
glass	*verre*	vair
grocery store	*épicerie*	ay·pees·ree
hot	*chaud*	sho
knife	*couteau*	koo·to
lunch	*déjeuner*	day·zher·nay
market	*marché*	mar·shay
menu	*carte*	kart
plate	*assiette*	a·syet
spoon	*cuillère*	kwee·yair
wine list	*carte des vins*	kart day vun
with/without	*avec/sans*	a·vek/son

Meat & Fish

beef	*bœuf*	berf
chicken	*poulet*	poo·lay
crab	*crabe*	krab
lamb	*agneau*	a·nyo
oyster	*huître*	wee·trer
pork	*porc*	por
snail	*escargot*	es·kar·go
squid	*calmar*	kal·mar
turkey	*dinde*	dund
veal	*veau*	vo

Fruit & Vegetables

apple	*pomme*	pom
apricot	*abricot*	ab·ree·ko
asparagus	*asperge*	a·spairzh
beans	*haricots*	a·ree·ko
beetroot	*betterave*	be·trav

cabbage	*chou*	shoo
celery	*céleri*	sel·ree
cherry	*cerise*	ser·reez
corn	*maïs*	ma·ees
cucumber	*concombre*	kong·kom·brer
gherkin (pickle)	*cornichon*	kor·nee·shon
grape	*raisin*	ray·zun
leek	*poireau*	pwa·ro
lemon	*citron*	see·tron
lettuce	*laitue*	lay·tew
mushroom	*champignon*	shom·pee·nyon
peach	*pêche*	pesh
peas	*petit pois*	per·tee pwa
(red/green) pepper	*poivron (rouge/vert)*	pwa·vron (roozh/vair)
pineapple	*ananas*	a·na·nas
plum	*prune*	prewn
potato	*pomme de terre*	pom der tair
prune	*pruneau*	prew·no
pumpkin	*citrouille*	see·troo·yer
shallot	*échalote*	eh·sha·lot
spinach	*épinards*	eh·pee·nar
strawberry	*fraise*	frez
tomato	*tomate*	to·mat
turnip	*navet*	na·vay
vegetable	*légume*	lay·gewm

Other

bread	*pain*	pun
butter	*beurre*	ber
cheese	*fromage*	fro·mazh
egg	*œuf*	erf
honey	*miel*	myel
jam	*confiture*	kon·fee·tewr
oil	*huile*	weel
pepper	*poivre*	pwa·vrer
rice	*riz*	ree
salt	*sel*	sel
sugar	*sucre*	sew·krer
vinegar	*vinaigre*	vee·nay·grer

Drinks

beer	*bière*	bee·yair
coffee	*café*	ka·fay
(orange) juice	*jus (d'orange)*	zhew (do·ronzh)
milk	*lait*	lay
red wine	*vin rouge*	vun roozh
tea	*thé*	tay
(mineral) water	*eau (minérale)*	o (mee·nay·ral)
white wine	*vin blanc*	vun blong

EMERGENCIES

Help!
Au secours! — o skoor

Leave me alone!
Fichez-moi la paix! — fee·shay·mwa la pay

I'm lost.
Je suis perdu/perdue. — zhe swee·pair·dew (m/f)

Call a doctor.
Appelez un médecin. — a·play un mayd·sun

Call the police.
Appelez la police. — a·play la po·lees

I'm ill.
Je suis malade. — zher swee ma·lad

It hurts here.
J'ai une douleur ici. — zhay ewn doo·ler ee·see

I'm allergic (to ...).
Je suis allergique (à ...). — zher swee za·lair·zheek (a ...)

SHOPPING & SERVICES

I'd like to buy ...
Je voudrais acheter ... — zher voo·dray ash·tay ...

Can I look at it?
Est-ce que je peux le voir? — es·ker zher per ler vwar

I'm just looking.
Je regarde. — zher rer·gard

I don't like it.
Cela ne me plaît pas. — ser·la ner mer play pa

How much is it?
C'est combien? — say kom·byun

It's too expensive.
C'est trop cher. — say tro shair

There's a mistake in the bill.
Il y a une erreur dans la note. — eel ya ewn ay·rer don la not

bank	*banque*	bonk
internet cafe	*cybercafé*	see·bair·ka·fay
tourist office	*office de tourisme*	o·fees der too·rees·mer

QUESTION WORDS

What?	*Quoi?*	kwa
When?	*Quand?*	kon
Where?	*Où?*	oo
Who?	*Qui?*	kee
Why?	*Pourquoi?*	poor·kwa

TIME & DATES

What time is it?
Quelle heure est-il? kel er ay til

It's (eight) o'clock.
Il est (huit) heures. il ay (weet) er

Half past (10).
(Dix) heures et demie. (deez) er ay day·mee

morning	*matin*	ma·tun
afternoon	*après-midi*	a·pray·mee·dee
evening	*soir*	swar
yesterday	*hier*	yair
today	*aujourd'hui*	o·zhoor·dwee
tomorrow	*demain*	der·mun

Monday	*lundi*	lun·dee
Tuesday	*mardi*	mar·dee
Wednesday	*mercredi*	mair·krer·dee
Thursday	*jeudi*	zher·dee
Friday	*vendredi*	von·drer·dee
Saturday	*samedi*	sam·dee
Sunday	*dimanche*	dee·monsh

TRANSPORT

I want to go to ...
Je voudrais aller à ... zher voo·dray a·lay a ...

NUMBERS

1	*un*	un
2	*deux*	der
3	*trois*	trwa
4	*quatre*	ka·trer
5	*cinq*	sungk
6	*six*	sees
7	*sept*	set
8	*huit*	weet
9	*neuf*	nerf
10	*dix*	dees
20	*vingt*	vung
30	*trente*	tront
40	*quarante*	ka·ront
50	*cinquante*	sung·kont
60	*soixante*	swa·sont
70	*soixante-dix*	swa·son·dees
80	*quatre-vingts*	ka·trer·vung
90	*quatre-vingt-dix*	ka·trer·vung·dees
100	*cent*	son
1000	*mille*	meel

Does it stop at ...?
Est-ce qu'il s'arrête à ...? es·kil sa·ret a ...

At what time does it leave/arrive?
À quelle heure est-ce qu'il part/arrive? a kel er es kil par/a·reev

I want to get off here.
Je veux descendre ici. zher ver day·son·drer ee·see

a ... ticket	*un billet ...*	un bee·yay ...
1st-class	*de première classe*	der prem·yair klas
2nd-class	*de deuxième classe*	der der·zyem klas
one-way	*simple*	sum·pler
return	*aller et retour*	a·lay ay rer·toor

aisle seat	*côté couloir*	ko·tay kool·war
boat	*bateau*	ba·to
bus	*bus*	bews
cancelled	*annulé*	a·new·lay
delayed	*en retard*	on rer·tar
first	*premier*	prer·myay
last	*dernier*	dair·nyay
plane	*avion*	a·vyon
platform	*quai*	kay
ticket office	*guichet*	gee·shay
timetable	*horaire*	o·rair
train	*train*	trun
window seat	*côté fenêtre*	ko·tay fe·ne·trer

I'd like to hire a ...	*Je voudrais louer ...*	zher voo·dray loo·way ...
car	*une voiture*	ewn vwa·tewr
bicycle	*un vélo*	un vay·lo
motorcycle	*une moto*	ewn mo·to

child seat	*siège-enfant*	syezh·on·fon
helmet	*casque*	kask
mechanic	*mécanicien*	may·ka·nee·syun
petrol/gas	*essence*	ay·sons
service station	*station-service*	sta·syon·ser·vees

Can I park here?
Est-ce que je peux stationner ici? es·ker zher per sta·syo·nay ee·see

I have a flat tyre.
Mon pneu est à plat. mom pner ay ta pla

I've run out of petrol.
Je suis en panne d'essence. zher swee zon pan day·sons

GLOSSARY

(m) indicates masculine gender, (f) feminine gender, (pl) plural and (adj) adjective

ancien régime (m) – 'old order'; France under the monarchy before the Revolution

apéritif (m) – a drink taken before dinner

arrondissement (m) – one of 20 administrative divisions in Paris; abbreviated on street signs as 1er (1st arrondissement), 2e or 2ème (2nd) etc

auberge (de jeunesse) (f) – (youth) hostel

avenue (f) – avenue (abbreviated av)

baguette tradition (f) – traditional-style baguette

banlieues (f pl) – suburbs

belle époque (f) – 'beautiful age'; era of elegance and gaiety characterising fashionable Parisian life roughly from 1870 to 1914

bière artisanale (f) – craft beer

billet (m) – ticket

billeterie (f) – ticket office or window

biologique or **bio** (adj) – organic

boucherie (f) – butcher

boulangerie (f) – bakery

boules (f pl) – a game played with heavy metal balls on a sandy pitch; also called *pétanque*

brasserie (f) – 'brewery'; a restaurant that usually serves food all day long

brioche (f) – small roll or cake, sometimes made with nuts, currants or candied fruit

bureau de change (m) – currency exchange bureau

café (m) – espresso

carnet (m) – a book of (usually) 10 bus, tram, metro or other tickets sold at a reduced rate

carrefour (m) – crossroads, intersection

carte (f) – card; menu; map

carte de séjour (f) – residence permit

cave (f) – (wine) cellar

chambre (f) – room

chanson française (f) – 'French song'; traditional musical genre where lyrics are paramount

chansonnier (m) – cabaret singer

charcuterie (f) – a variety of meat products that are cured, smoked or processed, including sausages, hams, pâtés and rillettes; shop selling these products

cimetière (m) – cemetery

consigne (f) – left-luggage office

correspondance (f) – linking tunnel or walkway, eg in the metro; rail or bus connection

cour (f) – courtyard

couvert (m) – covered shopping arcade (also called *galerie*)

dégustation (f) – tasting, sampling

demi (m) – half; 330mL glass of beer

département (m) – administrative division of France

dessert (m) – dessert

digicode (m) – entrycode

eau (f) – water

église (f) – church

entrée (f) – entrance; first course or starter

épicerie (f) – small grocery store

espace (f) – space; outlet

Exposition Universelle (f) – World's Fair

fête (f) – festival; holiday

ficelle (f) – string; a thinner, crustier 200g version of the baguette not unlike a very thick breadstick

fin de siècle (adj) – 'end of the century'; characteristic of the last years of the 19th century and generally used to indicate decadence

forêt (f) – forest

formule (f) – similar to a *menu* but allows choice of whichever two of three courses you want (eg starter and main course or main course and dessert)

fromagerie (f) – cheese shop

galerie (f) – gallery; covered shopping arcade (also called passage)

galette (f) – a pancake or flat pastry, with a variety of (usually savoury) fillings

gare (f) – railway station

gare routière (f) – bus station

goûter – afternoon snack

Grand Paris – greater Paris

grand projet (m) – huge, public edifice erected by a government or politician generally in a bid to immortalise themselves

Grands Boulevards (m pl) – 'Great Boulevards'; the eight contiguous broad thoroughfares that stretch from place de la Madeleine eastwards to the place de la République

halles (f pl) – covered food market

hameau (m) – hamlet

hammam (m) – steam room, Turkish bath

haute couture (f) – literally 'high sewing'; the creations of leading designers

haute cuisine (f) – 'high cuisine'; classic French cooking style typified by elaborately prepared multicourse meals

hôtel de ville (m) – city or town hall

hôtel particulier (m) – private mansion

jardin (m) – garden

kir (m) – white wine sweetened with a blackcurrant (or other) liqueur
lycée (m) – secondary school
marché (m) – market
marché aux puces (m) – flea market
matériel de cuisine (m) – kitchenware
menu (m) – fixed-price meal with two or more courses; see *formule*
musée (m) – museum
musette (f) – accordion music
nocturne (f) – late night opening at a museum, department store etc
orangerie (f) – conservatory for growing citrus fruit
pain au chocolat (m) – chocolate croissant
palais de justice (m) – law courts
parc (m) – park
parvis (m) – square in front of a church or public building passage
pastis (m) – an aniseed-flavoured aperitif mixed with water
pâté (m) – potted meat; a thickish paste, often of pork, cooked in a ceramic dish and served cold (similar to terrine)
pâtisserie (f) – cakes and pastries; shop selling these products
pavés (m) – flattened rectangular loaves of bread
pétanque (f) – see *boules*
place (f) – square or plaza
plan (m) – city map
plan du quartier (m) – map of nearby streets (hung on the wall near metro exits)
plat du jour (m) – daily special in a restaurant
pont (m) – bridge
port (m) – harbour, port
porte (f) – door; gate in a city wall
poste (f) – post office
préfecture (f) – prefecture; capital city of a département
quai (m) – quay
quartier (m) – quarter, district, neighbourhood
raï – a type of Algerian popular music
RATP – Régie Autonome des Transports Parisiens; Paris' public transport system
RER – Réseau Express Régional; Paris' suburban train network
résidence (f) – residence; serviced-apartment hotel
rillettes (f pl) – shredded potted meat or fish
rive (f) – bank of a river
rond point (m) – roundabout
rue (f) – street or road
rue végétale – green-focused, low-traffic street
salle (f) – hall; room
salon de thé (m) – tearoom
SNCF – Société Nationale de Chemins de Fer; France's national railway organisation
soldes (m pl) – sale, the sales
sortie (f) – exit
spectacle (m) – performance, play or theatrical show
square (m) – public garden
tabac (m) – tobacconist (which also sells bus tickets, phonecards etc)
tarif réduit (m) – reduced price (for students, seniors, children etc)
tartine (f) – a slice of bread with any topping or garnish
taxe de séjour (f) – municipal tourist tax
TGV – train à grande vitesse; high-speed train
tour (f) – tower
traiteur (m) – caterer, delicatessen
TVA – taxe sur la valeur ajoutée; value-added tax
Vélib' (m) – communal bicycle rental scheme in Paris
vélo (m) – bicycle
version française (m) – literally 'French version': a film dubbed in French
version originale – literally 'original version': a nondubbed film in its original language with French subtitles
viennoiseries (f) – sweet pastries

Behind the Scenes

SEND US YOUR FEEDBACK

We love to hear from travellers – your comments keep us on our toes and help make our books better. Our well-travelled team reads every word on what you loved or loathed about this book. Although we cannot reply individually to your submissions, we always guarantee that your feedback goes straight to the appropriate authors, in time for the next edition. Each person who sends us information is thanked in the next edition – the most useful submissions are rewarded with a selection of digital PDF chapters.

Visit **lonelyplanet.com/contact** to submit your updates and suggestions or to ask for help. Our award-winning website also features inspirational travel stories, news and discussions.

Note: We may edit, reproduce and incorporate your comments in Lonely Planet products such as guidebooks, websites and digital products, so let us know if you don't want your comments reproduced or your name acknowledged. For a copy of our privacy policy visit lonelyplanet.com/privacy.

WRITER THANKS

Catherine Le Nevez

Merci mille fois first and foremost to Julian and to the innumerable Parisians who provided insights, inspiration and great times. Huge thanks too to my Paris co-writers Chris and Nicola, Destination Editor Daniel Fahey and everyone at Lonely Planet. As ever, a heartfelt *merci encore* to my parents, brother, *belle-soeur, neveu* and *nièce* for sustaining my lifelong love of Paris and France.

Christopher Pitts

Special thanks to my two great co-writers for their advice and input and to all the crew at Lonely Planet who have put so much hard work into making this book what it is. Also thanks to Neil Fazakerley for providing company and conversation for a day. *Bises* as always to the Pavillard clan, and my dearest partners in crime: Perrine, Elliot and Céleste.

Nicola Williams

Heartfelt *bisous* to the many friends and professionals who aided and abetted me in tracking down the best of Paris, including the more-Parisian-than-Parisian and hugely knowledgeable Elodie Berta; savvy local in the 13e, Mary Winston-Nicklin; New Yorker in Le Marais, Kasia Dietz; Rachel Vanier at Station F; Chinatown queen, Stéphanie Ruch; and Maria and Bartolomeo at La Bête Noire. Love and thanks too to my formidable, trilingual *'Paris en famille'* research team, Matthias, Niko, Mischa and Kaya Luefkens.

ACKNOWLEDGEMENTS

Cover photograph: Montmartre, Massimo Ripani/4Corners ©.

Climate map data adapted from Peel C, Finlayson BL & McMahon TA (2007) 'Updated World Map of the Köppen-Geiger Climate Classification', *Hydrology and Earth System Sciences*, 11, 1633–44.

Illustrations pp114–15, pp158–9, pp198–9 and pp268–9 by Javier Zarracina.

THIS BOOK

This 12th edition of Lonely Planet's *Paris* guidebook was researched and written by Catherine Le Nevez, Christopher Pitts and Nicola Williams. They also wrote the previous two editions. This guidebook was produced by the following:

Destination Editor Daniel Fahey
Senior Product Editor Genna Patterson
Product Editor Kate Mathews
Senior Cartographer Mark Griffiths
Book Designer Meri Blazevski
Assisting Editors Sarah Bailey, Judith Bamber, Katie Connolly, Lucy Cowie, Andrea Dobbin, Victoria Harrison, Kristin Odijk, Sarah Stewart, Fionnuala Twomey
Cover Researcher Naomi Parker
Thanks to Nancy Attoh, Jennifer Carey, Elizabeth Jones, Yuki Lo, Angela Tinson, Saralinda Turner

See also separate subindexes for:

- DRINKING & NIGHTLIFE P359
- EATING P357
- ENTERTAINMENT P360
- SHOPPING P361
- SLEEPING P362
- SPORTS & ACTIVITIES P362

Index

Sights 000
Map Pages **000**
Photo Pages **000**

Sights 000
Map Pages **000**
Photo Pages **000**

EATING

Sights 000
Map Pages **000**
Photo Pages **000**

DRINKING & NIGHTLIFE

Sights 000
Map Pages **000**
Photo Pages **000**

ENTERTAINMENT

SHOPPING

SPORTS & ACTIVITIES

Sights 000
Map Pages **000**
Photo Pages **000**

SLEEPING

Paris Maps

Sights
- Beach
- Bird Sanctuary
- Buddhist
- Castle/Palace
- Christian
- Confucian
- Hindu
- Islamic
- Jain
- Jewish
- Monument
- Museum/Gallery/Historic Building
- Ruin
- Shinto
- Sikh
- Taoist
- Winery/Vineyard
- Zoo/Wildlife Sanctuary
- Other Sight

Activities, Courses & Tours
- Bodysurfing
- Diving
- Canoeing/Kayaking
- Course/Tour
- Sento Hot Baths/Onsen
- Skiing
- Snorkelling
- Surfing
- Swimming/Pool
- Walking
- Windsurfing
- Other Activity

Sleeping
- Sleeping
- Camping
- Hut/Shelter

Eating
- Eating

Drinking & Nightlife
- Drinking & Nightlife
- Cafe

Entertainment
- Entertainment

Shopping
- Shopping

Information
- Bank
- Embassy/Consulate
- Hospital/Medical
- Internet
- Police
- Post Office
- Telephone
- Toilet
- Tourist Information
- Other Information

Geographic
- Beach
- Gate
- Hut/Shelter
- Lighthouse
- Lookout
- Mountain/Volcano
- Oasis
- Park
- Pass
- Picnic Area
- Waterfall

Population
- Capital (National)
- Capital (State/Province)
- City/Large Town
- Town/Village

Transport
- Airport
- Border crossing
- Bus
- Cable car/Funicular
- Cycling
- Ferry
- Metro station
- Monorail
- Parking
- Petrol station
- S-Bahn/Subway station
- Taxi
- T-bane/Tunnelbana station
- Train station/Railway
- Tram
- Tube station
- U-Bahn/Underground station
- Other Transport

Routes
- Tollway
- Freeway
- Primary
- Secondary
- Tertiary
- Lane
- Unsealed road
- Road under construction
- Plaza/Mall
- Steps
- Tunnel
- Pedestrian overpass
- Walking Tour
- Walking Tour detour
- Path/Walking Trail

Boundaries
- International
- State/Province
- Disputed
- Regional/Suburb
- Marine Park
- Cliff
- Wall

Hydrography
- River, Creek
- Intermittent River
- Canal
- Water
- Dry/Salt/Intermittent Lake
- Reef

Areas
- Airport/Runway
- Beach/Desert
- Cemetery (Christian)
- Cemetery (Other)
- Glacier
- Mudflat
- Park/Forest
- Sight (Building)
- Sportsground
- Swamp/Mangrove

Note: Not all symbols displayed above appear on the maps in this book

MAP INDEX

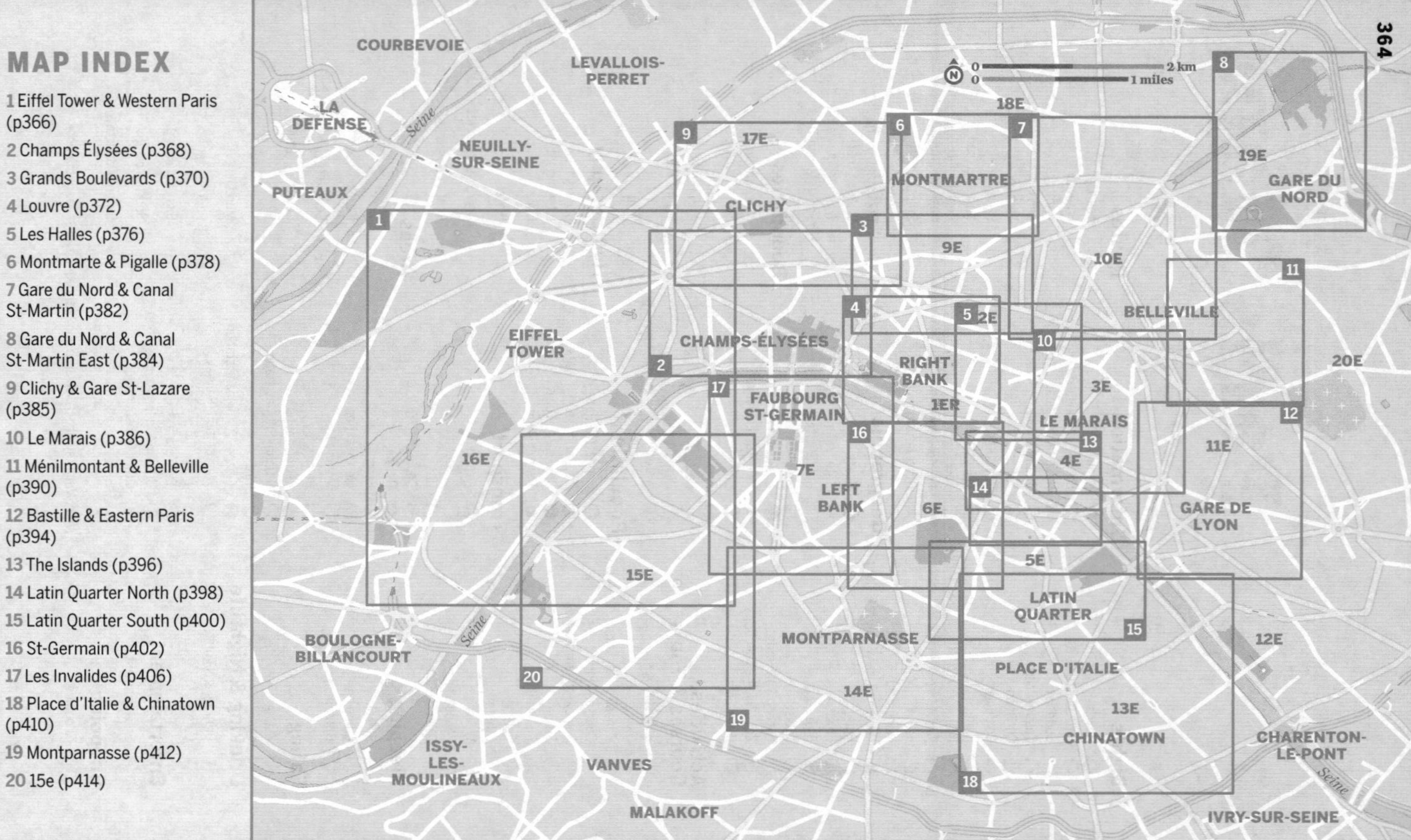

COURBEVOIE
LEVALLOIS-PERRET
LA DÉFENSE
Seine
NEUILLY-SUR-SEINE
PUTEAUX
0 2 km
0 1 miles
18E
17E
19E
MONTMARTRE
GARE DU NORD
CLICHY
9E
10E
EIFFEL TOWER
CHAMPS-ÉLYSÉES
BELLEVILLE
2E
RIGHT BANK
20E
FAUBOURG ST-GERMAIN
1ER
3E
LE MARAIS
16E
7E
11E
4E
LEFT BANK
6E
GARE DE LYON
15E
5E
LATIN QUARTER
BOULOGNE-BILLANCOURT
MONTPARNASSE
12E
PLACE D'ITALIE
14E
13E
CHINATOWN
ISSY-LES-MOULINEAUX
VANVES
CHARENTON-LE-PONT
MALAKOFF
IVRY-SUR-SEINE

EIFFEL TOWER & WESTERN PARIS *Map on p366*

Top Sights (p82)
1 Cité de l'Architecture et du Patrimoine ... E4
2 Eiffel Tower ... F5
3 Musée du Quai Branly ... G4
4 Musée Guimet des Arts Asiatiques ... F4
5 Musée Marmottan Monet ... C5

Sights (p85)
6 Aquarium de Paris Cinéaqua ... F4
7 Bois de Boulogne ... A4
8 Flame of Liberty Memorial ... G4
9 Fondation Louis Vuitton ... B1
10 Galerie-Musée Baccarat ... F3
11 Hôtel d'Heidelbach ... F3
12 Jardin d'Acclimatation ... C1
13 Jardin des Serres d'Auteuil ... A7
14 Maison de Balzac ... D5
15 Musée d'Art Moderne de la Ville de Paris ... G4
16 Musée de la Marine ... E4
17 Musée de l'Homme ... E4
18 Musée du Vin ... E5
19 Musée Yves Saint Laurent Paris ... G4
20 Palais de Chaillot ... E4
21 Palais de Tokyo ... F4
22 Palais Galliera ... F3
23 Parc de Bagatelle ... A2
24 Parc du Champ de Mars ... G5
25 Pré Catelan ... A4
26 Stade Roland Garros-Musée de la Fédération Française de Tennis ... A7
27 Wall for Peace Memorial ... G6

Eating (p88)
58 Tour Eiffel ... (see 2)
28 Arnaud Nicolas ... G5
29 Atelier Vivanda ... F2
30 Bustronome ... F2
31 Firmin Le Barbier ... G5
32 L'Astrance ... E5
Le Jules Verne ... (see 2)
33 Le Petit Rétro ... E3
Les Grands Verres ... (see 21)
Les Ombres ... (see 3)
34 Malitourne ... G3
35 Marché Président Wilson ... F4
Monsieur Bleu ... (see 21)
36 Waknine ... F3

Drinking & Nightlife (p90)
37 Bô Zinc Café ... C6
Café Branly ... (see 3)
38 Frog XVI ... E4
39 St James Paris ... D3
40 Upper Crèmerie ... F2
Yoyo ... (see 21)

Entertainment (p91)
41 Les Marionnettes du Champ de Mars ... G5
42 Maison de la Radio ... D6
Théâtre National de Chaillot ... (see 1)

Shopping (p91)
43 Arlettie ... E4
44 La Grande Épicerie Rive Droite ... D5
45 Lorette & Jasmin ... C6

Sports & Activities (p336)
46 Bateaux Parisiens ... F5
47 Lac Inférieur Boat Hire ... C3
48 Vedettes de Paris ... F5

Sleeping (p281)
49 Hôtel du Bois ... F2
50 Hôtel Molitor ... A7

EIFFEL TOWER & WESTERN PARIS

Key on p365

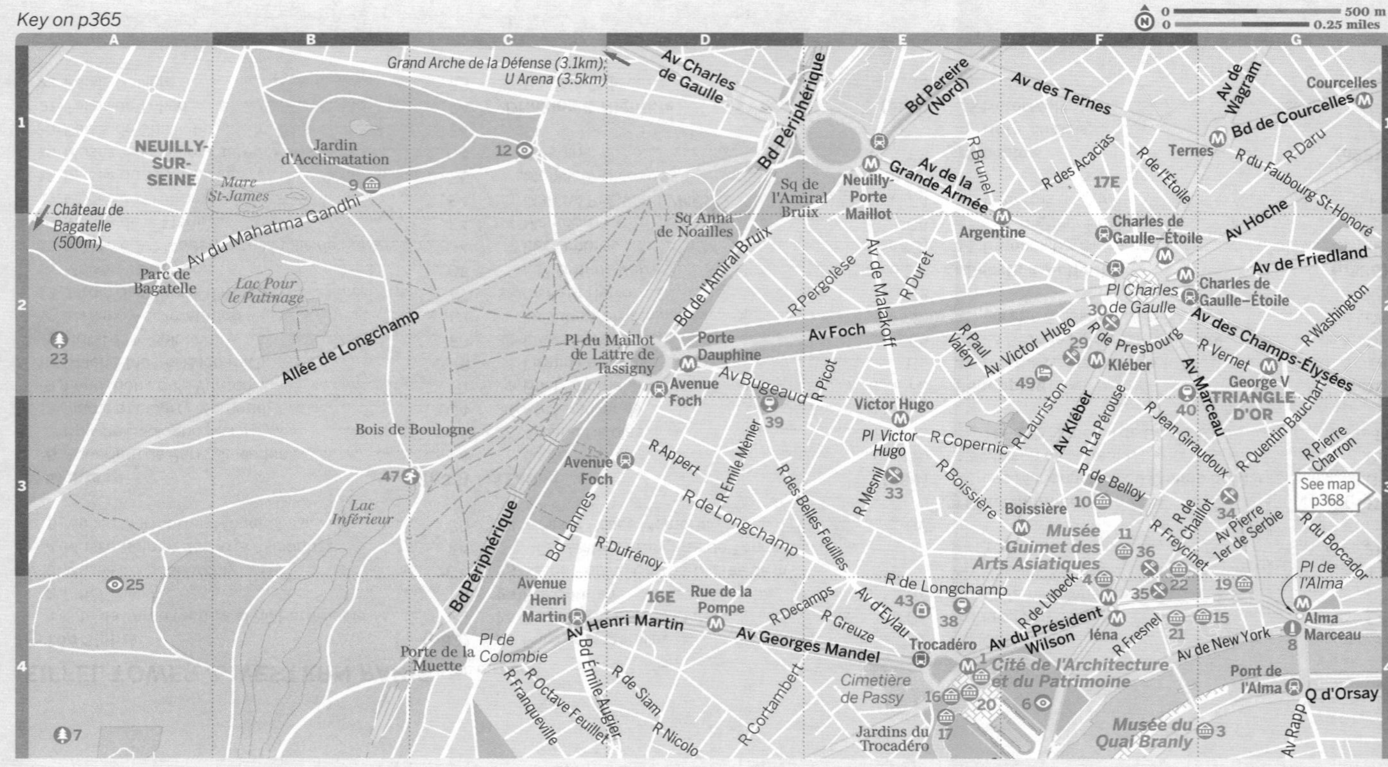

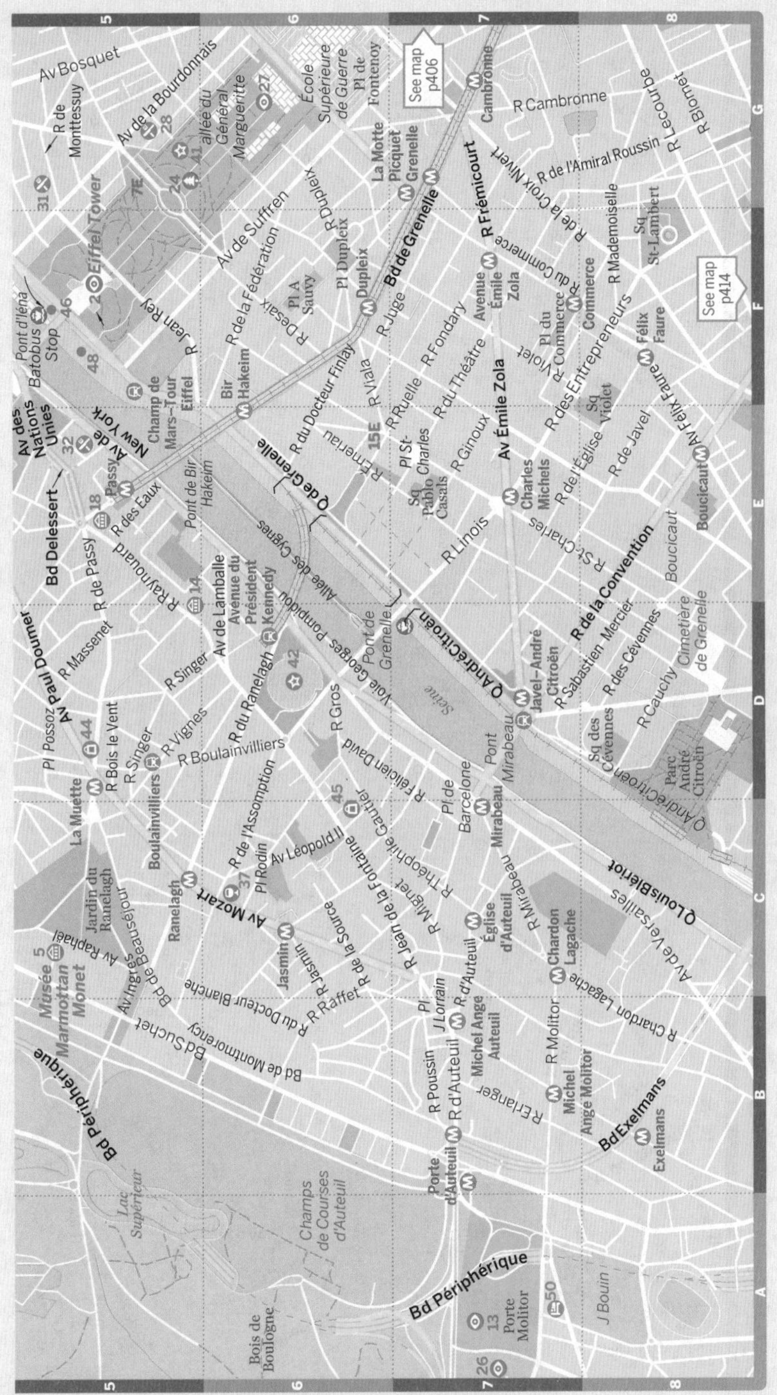

EIFFEL TOWER & WESTERN PARIS
See map p406
See map p414
Av Bosquet
R de Monttessuy
Av de la Bourdonnais
allée du Général Margueritte
École Supérieure de Guerre
Pl de Fontenoy
Eiffel Tower
7E
Av de Suffren
R Dupleix
Pl Dupleix
La Motte Picquet Grenelle
Cambronne
R Cambronne
R de l'Amiral Roussin
R Lecourbe
R Blomet
R de la Croix Nivert
R Mademoiselle
Sq St-Lambert
R Frémicourt
R du Commerce
Commerce
Bd de Grenelle
Dupleix
R Juge
Pl A Sauvy
R Desaix
R de la Fédération
R Jean Rey
Pont d'Iéna
Batobus Stop
Champ de Mars–Tour Eiffel
Bir Hakeim
Av des Nations Unies
Av de New York
Passy
Bd Delessert
R des Eaux
Pont de Bir Hakeim
R du Docteur Finlay
R Viala
R Fondary
Avenue Émile Zola
Pl du Commerce
R Violet
R des Entrepreneurs
Sq Violet
Félix Faure
Av Félix Faure
R Ruelle
R du Théâtre
R Ginoux
Av Émile Zola
15E
R Emeriau
Pl St-Charles
Sq Pablo Casals
Charles Michels
R de l'Église
R de Javel
Boucicaut
Q de Grenelle
Allée des Cygnes
R Linois
R St-Charles
R de la Convention
Bd Paul Doumer
R de Passy
R Raynouard
Av de Lamballe
Avenue du Président Kennedy
R Massenet
R Singer
Voie Georges Pompidou
Pont de Grenelle
Q André Citroën
Seine
Javel–André Citroën
R Sabastien Mercier
R des Cévennes
Cimetière de Grenelle
R Cauchy
Sq des Cévennes
Parc André Citroën
Q André Citroën
Pl Possoz
R Bois le Vent
R Vignes
R du Ranelagh
R Boulainvilliers
R Gros
R Félicien David
Pont Mirabeau
Mirabeau
Pl de Barcelone
La Muette
Boulainvilliers
R de l'Assomption
Av Léopold II
R Théophile Gautier
R Mignet
Q Louis Blériot
Av de Versailles
Jardin du Ranelagh
Ranelagh
Av Mozart
Pl Rodin
Jasmin
R Jasmin
R de la Source
R Jean de la Fontaine
Église d'Auteuil
R Mirabeau
Chardon Lagache
R Chardon Lagache
Musée Marmottan Monet
Av Raphaël
Av Ingres
Bd de Beauséjour
Bd du Docteur Blanche
R Raffet
Pl J Lorrain
R d'Auteuil
Michel Ange Auteuil
R Molitor
Michel Ange Molitor
Bd Suchet
Bd de Montmorency
R Poussin
R Erlanger
Bd Exelmans
Exelmans
Bd Périphérique
Porte d'Auteuil
Lac Supérieur
Champs de Courses d'Auteuil
Bois de Boulogne
Porte Molitor
J Bouin

CHAMPS-ÉLYSÉES

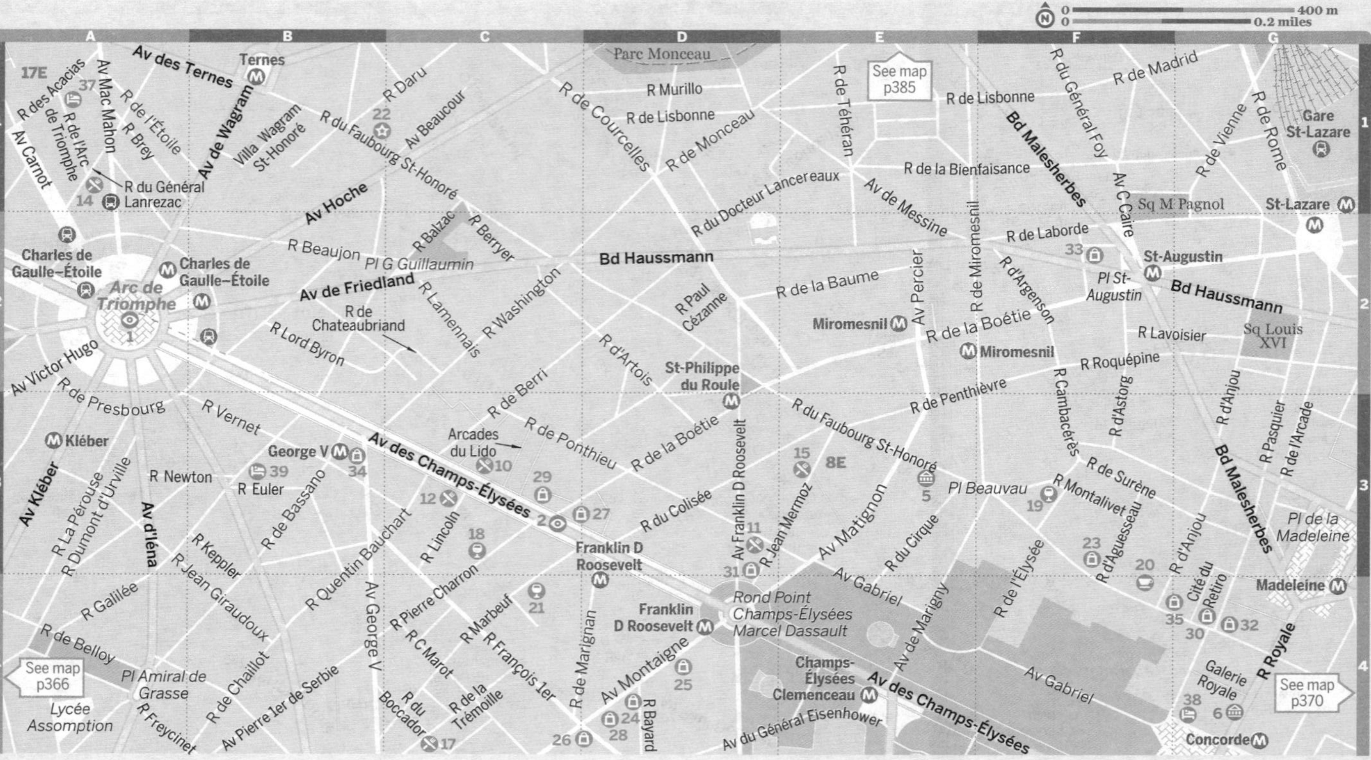

Top Sights **(p94)**
1 Arc de Triomphe ... A2

Sights **(p96)**
2 Avenue des Champs-Élysées ... C3
3 Grand Palais ... E5
4 Jardin de la Nouvelle France ... D5
5 Le Grand Musée du Parfum ... E3
6 Musée Maxim's ... G4
7 Palais de la Découverte ... D5
8 Petit Palais ... E5
9 Place de la Concorde ... G5

Eating **(p98)**
10 86 Champs ... C3
11 Framboise ... D3
12 Ladurée ... C3
13 Lasserre ... D5
14 Le Hide ... A1
15 Makoto Aoki ... E3
16 Mini Palais ... E5
17 Philippe & Jean-Pierre ... C4

Drinking & Nightlife **(p103)**
18 Blaine ... C3
19 Bugsy's ... F3
20 Honor ... F4
21 Zig Zag Club ... C4

Entertainment **(p103)**
22 Salle Pleyel ... B1

Shopping **(p104)**
23 Barbara Bui ... F3
24 Chanel ... D4
25 Chloé ... D4
26 Dior ... D4
27 Galeries Lafayette – Champs-Élysées ... C3
28 Givenchy ... D4
29 Guerlain ... C3
30 Hermès ... G4
31 Lancel ... D3
32 Lanvin ... G4
33 Les Caves Augé ... F2
34 Louis Vuitton ... B3
35 Saint Laurent ... G4

Sports & Activities **(p336)**
36 Bateaux-Mouches ... C5

Sleeping **(p281)**
37 Hidden Hotel ... A1
38 Hôtel de Crillon ... G4
39 Hôtel Ekta ... B3

GRANDS BOULEVARDS

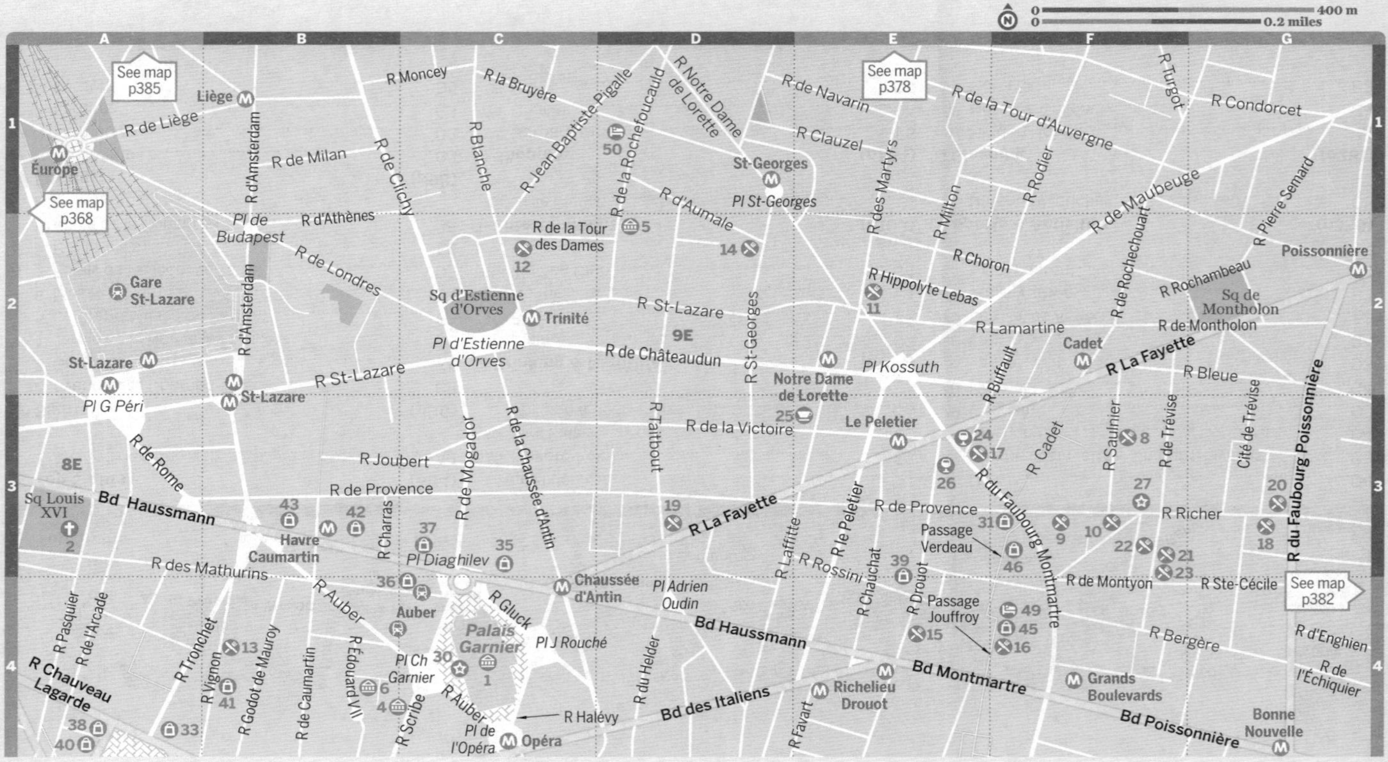

See map p372

Top Sights **(p97)**

1 Palais Garnier ... C4

Sights **(p98)**

2 Chapelle Expiatoire ... A3
3 Église de la Madeleine ... A5
Galerie des Galeries ... (see 35)
4 Musée du Parfum Scribe ... B4
5 Musée National Gustave Moreau ... D2
6 Nouveau Musée du Parfum ... B4
7 Théâtre-Musée des Capucines ... B5

Eating **(p99)**

8 Abri Soba ... F3
9 Bien Élevé ... F3
10 Chéri Charlot ... F3
11 Chez Plume ... E2
12 Détour ... C2
13 Helmut Newcake ... B4
Lafayette Gourmet ... (see 36)
14 Le Bon Georges ... D2
15 Le J'Go ... E4
16 Le Valentin ... F4
17 Les Pâtes Vivantes ... E3
18 L'Office ... G3
19 Mamou ... D3
20 Richer ... G3
21 SuperNature Cantine ... F3
22 SuperNature Restaurant ... F3
23 SuperNature Takeaway ... F3

Drinking & Nightlife **(p103)**

24 Au Général La Fayette ... E3
25 Ibrik ... E3
26 PanPan ... E3

Entertainment **(p103)**

27 Folies-Bergère ... F3
28 Kiosque Théâtre Madeleine ... A5
29 L'Olympia ... B5
Palais Garnier ... (see 1)
30 Palais Garnier Box Office ... C4

Shopping **(p104)**

31 À la Mère de Famille ... F3
32 Boutique Maille ... A5
33 ERES ... A4
34 Fauchon ... A5
35 Galeries Lafayette ... C3
36 Galeries Lafayette – Home & Gourmet ... C4
37 Galeries Lafayette – Men's Store ... C3
Galeries Lafayette Fashion Show ... (see 35)
38 Hédiard ... A4
39 Hôtel Drouot ... E3
40 La Maison de la Truffe ... A4
41 La Maison du Miel ... B4
42 Le Printemps ... B3
43 Le Printemps de l'Homme ... B3
44 Marché aux Fleurs Madeleine ... A5
45 Passage Jouffroy ... F4
46 Passage Verdeau ... F3
47 Patrick Roger ... A5
48 Place de la Madeleine ... A5

Sleeping **(p281)**

49 Hôtel Chopin ... F4
50 Hôtel Joyce ... D1

Key on p374

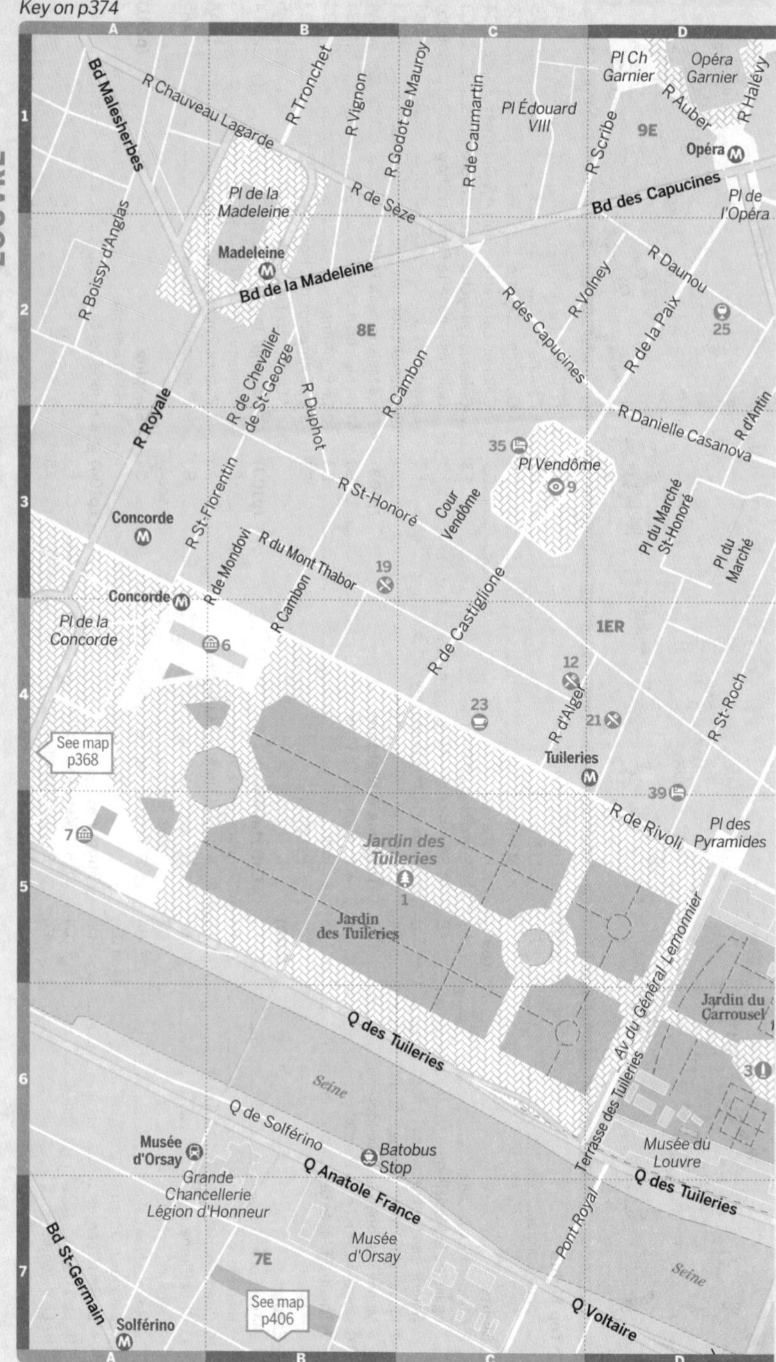

A
B
C
D
1
2
3
4
5
6
7
Bd Malesherbes
R Chauveau Lagarde
R Tronchet
R Vignon
R Godot de Mauroy
R de Caumartin
Pl Édouard VIII
R Scribe
Pl Ch Garnier
Opéra Garnier
R Auber
R Halévy
9E
Opéra
Bd des Capucines
Pl de l'Opéra
Pl de la Madeleine
R de Sèze
Madeleine
Bd de la Madeleine
R Boissy d'Anglas
8E
R Volney
R Daunou
R des Capucines
R de la Paix
25
R Royale
R de Chevalier de St-George
R Duphot
R Cambon
R Danielle Casanova
R d'Antin
35
Pl Vendôme
9
R St-Honoré
Cour Vendôme
Concorde
R St-Florentin
R de Mondovi
R du Mont Thabor
19
Pl du Marché St-Honoré
Pl du Marché
Concorde
R Cambon
Pl de la Concorde
6
R de Castiglione
1ER
12
23
R d'Alger
21
R St-Roch
See map p368
Tuileries
39
R de Rivoli
Pl des Pyramides
7
Jardin des Tuileries
1
Jardin des Tuileries
Av du Général Lemonnier
Jardin du Carrousel
Q des Tuileries
3
Seine
Terrasse des Tuileries
Q de Solférino
Musée d'Orsay
Batobus Stop
Musée du Louvre
Grande Chancellerie Légion d'Honneur
Q Anatole France
Q des Tuileries
Pont Royal
Bd St-Germain
Musée d'Orsay
7E
Seine
See map p406
Q Voltaire
Solférino

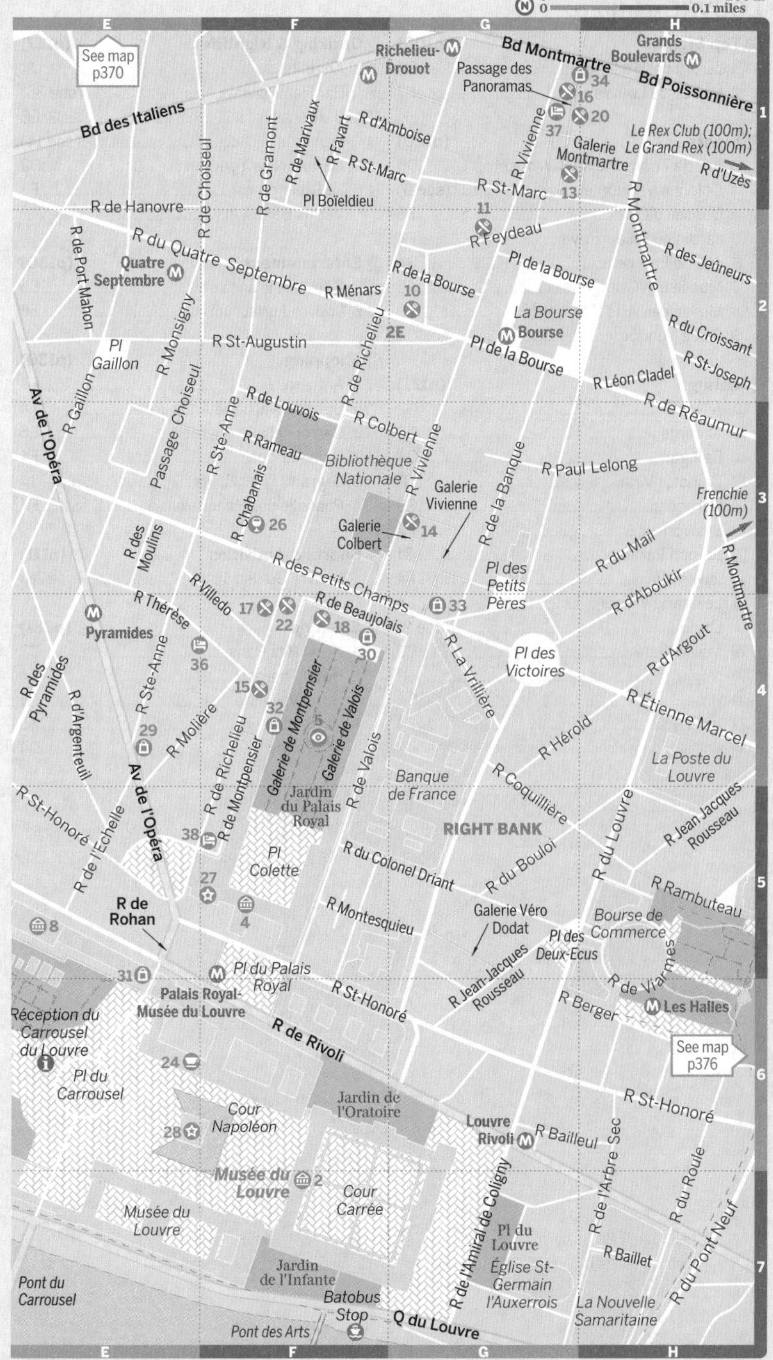

LOUVRE
0 200 m
0 0.1 miles
See map p370
Bd des Italiens
Richelieu-Drouot
Bd Montmartre
Passage des Panoramas
Grands Boulevards
Bd Poissonnière
Le Rex Club (100m); Le Grand Rex (100m)
R d'Uzès
Galerie Montmartre
R d'Amboise
R de Marivaux
R Favart
R St-Marc
R de Gramont
R de Choiseul
R de Hanovre
Pl Boïeldieu
R Vivienne
R Montmartre
R Feydeau
R de Port Mahon
R du Quatre Septembre
Quatre Septembre
R de la Bourse
Pl de la Bourse
R des Jeûneurs
R Ménars
La Bourse
Bourse
R du Croissant
R St-Augustin
R de Richelieu
Pl Gaillon
R Monsigny
R St-Joseph
R Léon Cladel
R de Réaumur
Av de l'Opéra
R Gaillon
R de Louvois
R Colbert
Passage Choiseul
R Ste-Anne
R Rameau
Bibliothèque Nationale
R de la Banque
R Paul Lelong
Galerie Vivienne
R Chabanais
Galerie Colbert
Frenchie (100m)
R des Moulins
R du Mail
R des Petits Champs
Pl des Petits Pères
R d'Aboukir
R Villedo
R Thérèse
R de Beaujolais
Pyramides
R La Vrillière
Pl des Victoires
R d'Argout
R des Pyramides
R d'Argenteuil
Galerie de Montpensier
Galerie de Valois
R Étienne Marcel
R Molière
R de Montpensier
R de Valois
R Hérold
La Poste du Louvre
Jardin du Palais Royal
Banque de France
R Coquillière
R St-Honoré
R de l'Echelle
RIGHT BANK
R Jean Jacques Rousseau
Pl Colette
R du Colonel Driant
R du Bouloi
R du Louvre
R Rambuteau
R de Rohan
R Montesquieu
Galerie Véro Dodat
Bourse de Commerce
Pl des Deux-Ecus
Pl du Palais Royal
R de Viarmes
Palais Royal-Musée du Louvre
R St-Honoré
R Berger
Les Halles
Réception du Carrousel du Louvre
R de Rivoli
See map p376
Pl du Carrousel
Jardin de l'Oratoire
Cour Napoléon
Louvre Rivoli
R Bailleul
R de l'Arbre Sec
Musée du Louvre
Cour Carrée
R de l'Amiral de Coligny
R du Roule
R du Pont Neuf
Pl du Louvre
R Baillet
Église St-Germain l'Auxerrois
Jardin de l'Infante
Pont du Carrousel
Batobus Stop
Q du Louvre
La Nouvelle Samaritaine
Pont des Arts
E
F
G
H
1
2
3
4
5
6
7
2E
2
4
5
8
10
11
13
14
15
16
17
18
20
22
24
26
27
28
29
30
31
32
33
34
36
37
38

LOUVRE *Map on p372*

Map on p372

Top Sights (p108)
1 Jardin des Tuileries ... C5
2 Musée du Louvre ... F7

Sights (p120)
3 Arc de Triomphe du Carrousel ... D6
Colonne Vendôme ... (see 9)
4 Conseil d'État ... F5
5 Jardin du Palais Royal ... F4
6 Jeu de Paume ... B4
7 Musée de l'Orangerie ... A5
8 Musée des Arts Décoratifs ... E5
9 Place Vendôme ... C3

Eating (p121)
10 A Noste ... G2
11 Accents ... G2
12 Balagan ... C4
13 Coinstot Vino ... G1
14 Daroco ... G3
15 Ellsworth ... F4
16 French Paradox ... G1
17 Juveniles ... F4
18 Le Grand Véfour ... F4
Loulou ... (see 8)
19 Maisie Café ... B3
20 Noglu ... G1
21 Uma ... D4
22 Verjus ... F4

Drinking & Nightlife (p127)
23 Angelina ... C4
Bar Hemingway ... (see 35)
24 Café Marly ... E6
Danico ... (see 14)
25 Harry's New York Bar ... D2
26 La Champmeslé ... F3
Verjus Bar à Vins ... (see 22)

Entertainment (p130)
27 Comédie Française ... F5
28 Louvre Auditorium ... E6

Shopping (p130)
29 Antoine ... E4
30 Boîtes à Musique Anna Joliet ... F4
31 Carrousel du Louvre ... E5
32 Didier Ludot ... F4
33 Legrand Filles & Fils ... G4
34 Passage des Panoramas ... H1

Sports & Activities (p111)
Louvre Guided Tours ... (see 28)

Sleeping (p281)
35 Hôtel Ritz Paris ... C3
36 Hôtel Thérèse ... E4
37 Hôtel Vivienne ... G1
38 La Clef Louvre ... F5
39 Le Pradey ... D4

LES HALLES *Map on p376*

Top Sights (p116)
1 Centre Pompidou F7
2 Église St-Eustache C5

Sights (p120)
3 59 Rivoli C7
4 Atelier Brancusi F6
5 Bourse de Commerce B5
6 Forum des Halles D6
7 L'Oasis d'Aboukir D2
8 Musée en Herbe B7
9 Tour Jean sans Peur D5
10 Tour St-Jacques D8

Eating (p121)
11 Au Rocher de Cancale D4
12 Aux Tonneaux des Halles D5
13 Blend C4
14 Boneshaker Doughnuts D2
15 Boutique Yam'Tcha B6
16 Champeaux D6
17 Chez La Vieille B6
18 Clover Grill B6
19 Crêpe Dentelle D3
20 Dame Tartine E7
21 Fou de Pâtisserie D4
22 Frenchie D3
23 Frenchie Bar à Vins D3
24 Frenchie to Go D3
25 La Tour de Montlhéry – Chez Denise C6
26 Le Cochon à l'Oreille C4
27 Le Compas D4
28 Maison Maison B8
29 Salatim C2
30 Stohrer D4
31 Tradi B3
32 Yam'Tcha B6

Drinking & Nightlife (p127)
33 Café La Fusée F6
34 Experimental Cocktail Club D4
35 Hoppy Corner D3
36 La Cordonnerie E4
37 Le Cœur Fou C4
38 Le Garde Robe B6
39 Le Rex Club D1
40 Le Tambour C4
41 L'Ivress D2
42 Ma Cave Fleury E4
43 Mabel D3
44 Marcelle C5
45 Matamata C4
46 Ô Chateau C4

Entertainment (p130)
Forum des Images (see 6)
47 La Place D6
48 Le Baiser Salé D7
49 Le Grand Rex D1
50 Sunset & Sunside D7

Shopping (p130)
51 À La Mère de Famille D4
52 Charles Chocolatier D5
53 E Dehillerin B5
54 Galerie Véro Dodat A5
55 Kiliwatch C4
56 La Fermette D4
57 La Samaritaine B7
58 L'Exception D6
59 Nose C3
60 Nysa D4
61 Room Service C4
62 Sept Cinq D6

Sleeping (p281)
63 Edgar E2
64 Hôtel Crayon B5
65 Hôtel des Grands Boulevards C1
66 Hôtel Tiquetonne E4
67 Hoxton D1

LES HALLES
Key on p375
0 200 m
0 0.1 miles
A
B
C
D
E
F
G
1
2
3
4
R d'Amboise
R Drouot
R St-Marc
R Vivienne
Passage des Panoramas
See map p370
Bd Poissonnière
65
R d'Uzès
Bonne Nouvelle
39
49
R St-Fiacre
R du Sentier
67
R Poissonnière
R de la Ville Neuve
R Thorel
Bd de Bonne Nouvelle
R de Mazagran
10E
R du Faubourg St-Denis
R de Metz
Passage du Prado
Bd de Strasbourg
R du Faubourg St-Martin
R Feydeau
Pl de la Bourse
R de la Bourse
R Montmartre
R des Jeûneurs
R de la Lune
Strasbourg–St-Denis
Strasbourg–St-Denis
Bd St-Denis
R du Quatre Septembre
Bourse
Pl de la Bourse
R de Richelieu
R du Croissant
29
R des Jeûneurs
41
R Beauregard
R Chénier
R Ste-Apolline
R Blondel
R St-Joseph
R de Cléry
R Ste-Foy
R Notre Dame des Victoires
7
14
23
R d'Aboukir
63
R d'Alexandrie
R de Tracy
R de Réaumur
2E
35
R du Nil
Passage du Caire
R St-Denis
R Paul Lelong
R de Cléry
Sentier
24
22
R du Caire
R Vivienne
R de la Banque
43
R Dussoubs
R du Roi François
Réaumur–Sébastopol
R St-Martin
R du Mail
R Léopold Bellan
19
R de Réaumur
R Vaucanson
Pl des Petits Pères
R d'Aboukir
R du Louvre
59
Passage Basfour
Réaumur–Sébastopol
R des Petits Champs
31
R d'Argout
45
R Bachaumont
60
R St-Sauveur
56
34
Pl des Victoires
61
37
R Mandar
R Montorgueil
51
R St-Denis
R La Vrillière
13
11
R Dussoubs
42
36
R de Palestro
R Greneta
Arts et Métiers
R Étienne Marcel
40
30
27
R Greneta
Bd de Sébastopol
R de Valois
R Marie-Stuart
R de Turbigo
R Hérold
55
21
La Poste du Louvre
26
R Tiquetonne
66
46

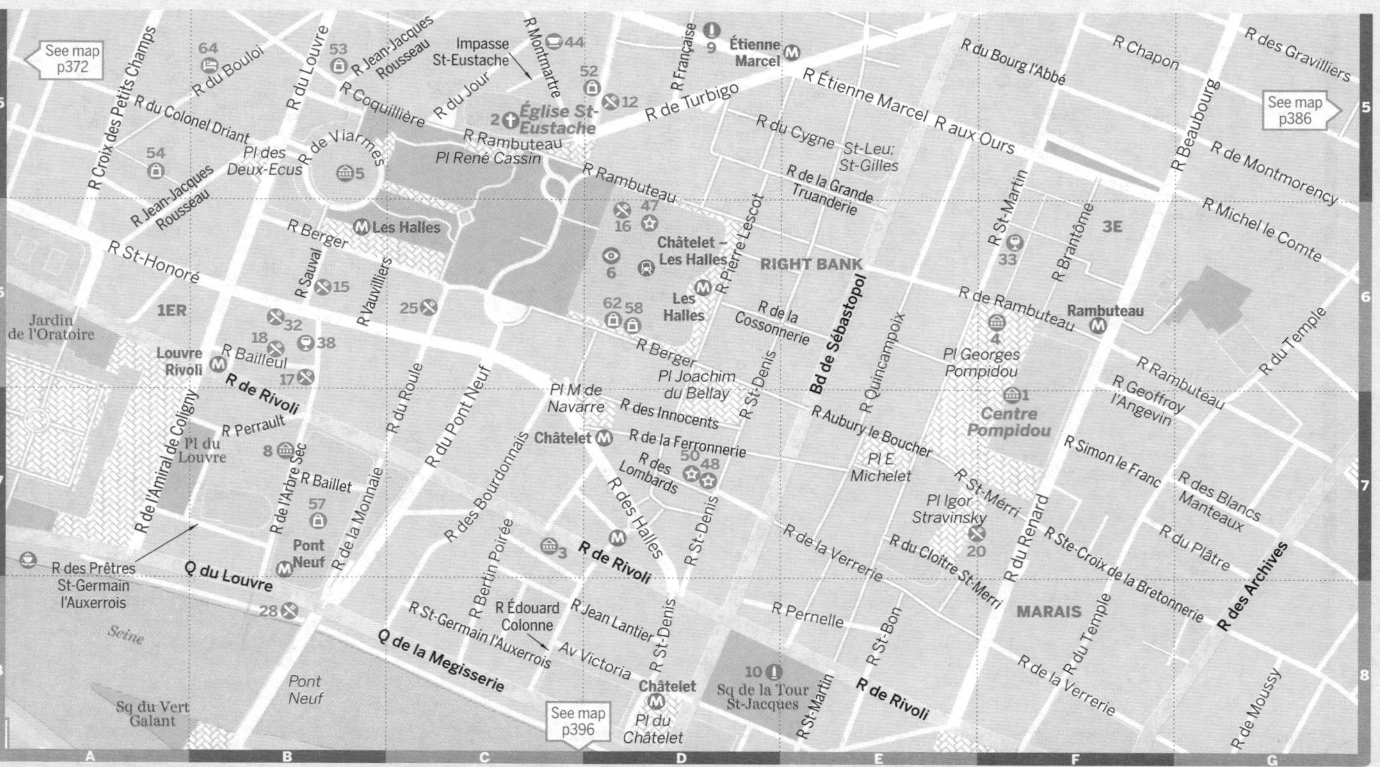
See map p372
See map p386
See map p396
64
R du Bouloi
53
R Jean-Jacques Rousseau
Impasse St-Eustache
R Montmartre
44
52
12
R Française
9
Étienne Marcel
R du Bourg l'Abbé
R Chapon
R des Gravilliers
R Croix des Petits Champs
R du Colonel Driant
R du Louvre
R Coquillière
R du Jour
2
Église St-Eustache
R de Turbigo
R Étienne Marcel
R aux Ours
R Beaubourg
R du Cygne
St-Leu; St-Gilles
R de Montmorency
54
Pl des Deux-Ecus
R de Viarmes
5
R Rambuteau
Pl René Cassin
R de la Grande Truanderie
R Michel le Comte
R Jean-Jacques Rousseau
R Berger
Les Halles
16
47
Châtelet – Les Halles
R Pierre Lescot
RIGHT BANK
R St-Martin
33
R Brantôme
3E
R St-Honoré
R Sauval
15
R Vauvilliers
6
Les Halles
Bd de Sébastopol
R Quincampoix
R de Rambuteau
Rambuteau
R du Temple
1ER
Jardin de l'Oratoire
32
25
62
58
R de la Cossonnerie
4
Pl Georges Pompidou
18
38
Louvre Rivoli
R Bailleul
R Berger
Pl Joachim du Bellay
R St-Denis
R Rambuteau
R Geoffroy l'Angevin
17
R de Rivoli
R du Roule
R du Pont Neuf
Pl M de Navarre
R des Innocents
R Aubury le Boucher
1
Centre Pompidou
R Perrault
Pl du Louvre
8
R de l'Arbre Sec
Châtelet
R de la Ferronnerie
R des Lombards
50
48
Pl E Michelet
R Simon le Franc
R des Blancs Manteaux
R Baillet
R des Bourdonnais
R St-Merri
Pl Igor Stravinsky
R de l'Amiral de Coligny
57
R de la Monnaie
R des Halles
R St-Denis
R de la Verrerie
R du Cloître St-Merri
20
R du Renard
R Ste-Croix de la Bretonnerie
R du Plâtre
Pont Neuf
R Bertin Poirée
3
R de Rivoli
R des Archives
R des Prêtres St-Germain l'Auxerrois
Q du Louvre
R Édouard Colonne
R Jean Lantier
R Pernelle
MARAIS
28
R St-Germain l'Auxerrois
Av Victoria
R St-Bon
R du Temple
Seine
Q de la Megisserie
R St-Denis
10
Sq de la Tour St-Jacques
R de la Verrerie
Pont Neuf
Châtelet
R St-Martin
R de Rivoli
R de Moussy
Sq du Vert Galant
Pl du Châtelet
5
6
7
8
A
B
C
D
E
F
G

Key on p380

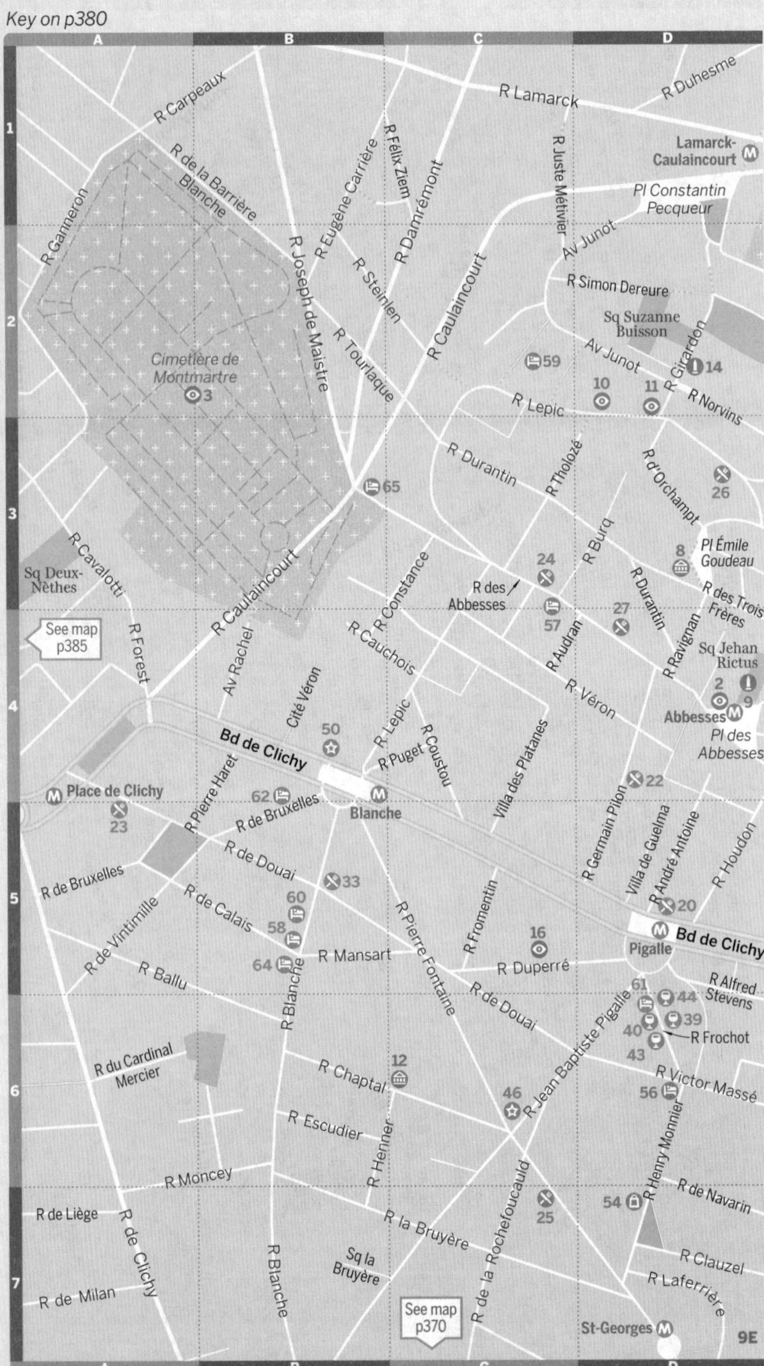

R Carpeaux
R Lamarck
R Duhesme
Lamarck-Caulaincourt
R Félix Ziem
R Juste Métivier
R de la Barrière Blanche
R Eugène Carrière
R Damrémont
Pl Constantin Pecqueur
R Ganneron
Av Junot
R Joseph de Maistre
R Steinlen
R Caulaincourt
R Simon Dereure
Sq Suzanne Buisson
R Girardon
R Tourlaque
Av Junot
Cimetière de Montmartre
3
59
10
11
14
R Norvins
R Lepic
R Durantin
R Tholozé
R d'Orchampt
65
26
R Burq
Pl Émile Goudeau
8
24
R Cavalotti
Sq Deux-Nèthes
R Caulaincourt
R Constance
R des Abbesses
57
27
R Durantin
R des Trois Frères
R Audran
R Ravignan
Sq Jehan Rictus
See map p385
R Forest
Av Rachel
R Cauchois
2
9
R Véron
Abbesses
Pl des Abbesses
Cité Véron
50
R Lepic
R Coustou
Villa des Platanes
Bd de Clichy
R Puget
22
Place de Clichy
62
Blanche
R Pierre Haret
R de Bruxelles
R Germain Pilon
Villa de Guelma
R André Antoine
R Houdon
23
R de Douai
33
R de Bruxelles
R de Calais
60
R Fromentin
20
58
16
Pigalle
Bd de Clichy
R de Vintimille
64
R Mansart
R Duperré
R Pierre Fontaine
R Ballu
61
44
R Alfred Stevens
R Blanche
R de Douai
39
40
R Frochot
43
R Jean Baptiste Pigalle
R du Cardinal Mercier
12
R Chaptal
R Victor Massé
46
56
R Escudier
R Henry Monnier
R Henner
R Moncey
R de Navarin
54
25
R de Liège
R de Clichy
R la Bruyère
R de la Rochefoucauld
R Clauzel
R Blanche
Sq la Bruyère
R Laferrière
R de Milan
See map p370
St-Georges
9E

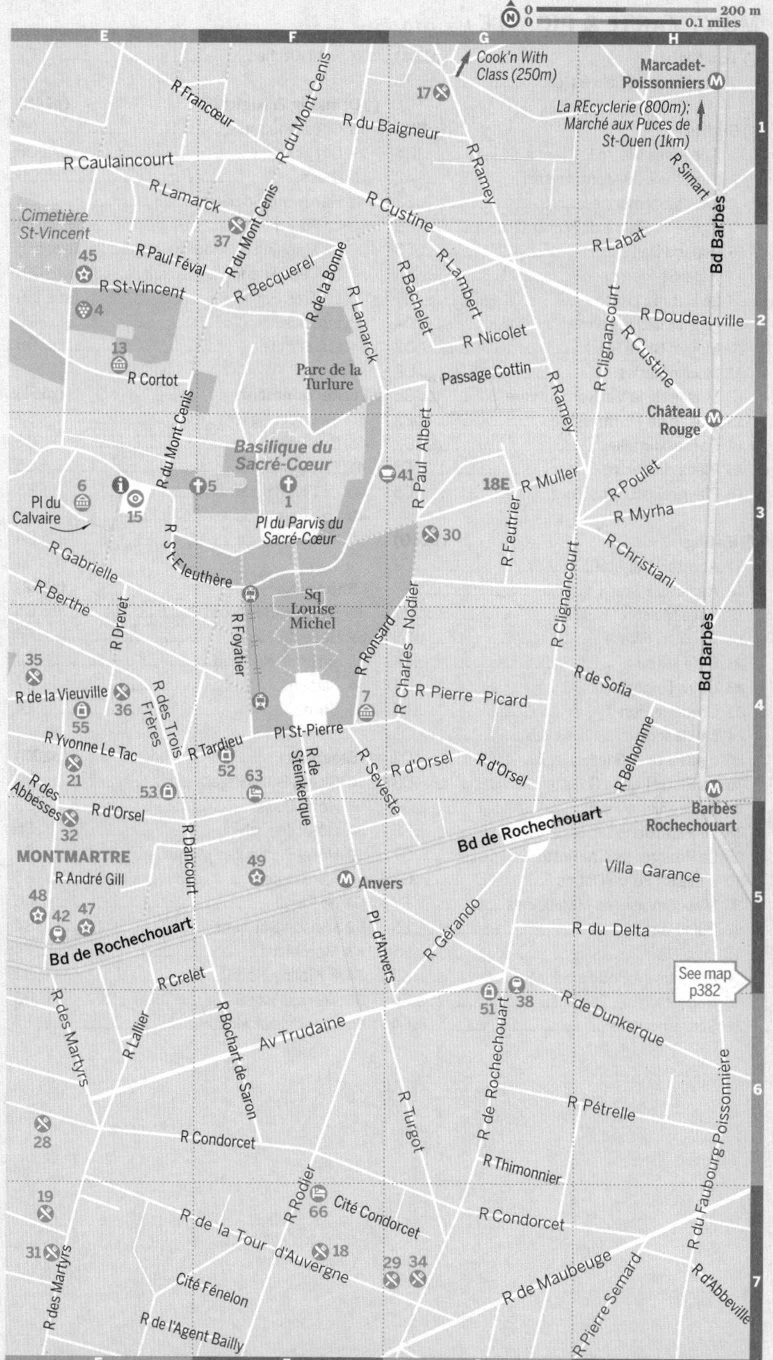
MONTMARTRE & PIGALLE
200 m
0.1 miles
Cook'n With Class (250m)
Marcadet-Poissonniers
La REcyclerie (800m); Marché aux Puces de St-Ouen (1km)
R Francœur
R du Mont Cenis
R du Baigneur
R Ramey
R Simart
R Caulaincourt
R Lamarck
R Custine
Cimetière St-Vincent
R Paul Féval
R Becquerel
R de la Bonne
R Bachelet
R Lambert
R Labat
Bd Barbès
R St-Vincent
R Doudeauville
R Clignancourt
R Nicolet
Parc de la Turlure
Passage Cottin
R Cortot
Château Rouge
Basilique du Sacré-Cœur
R Paul Albert
18E
R Muller
R Poulet
R Myrha
Pl du Calvaire
Pl du Parvis du Sacré-Cœur
R Feutrier
R Christiani
R Gabrielle
R St-Eleuthère
R Berthe
R Drevet
R Foyatier
Sq Louise Michel
R Ronsard
R Charles Nodier
R de Sofia
R de la Vieuville
R des Trois Frères
R Pierre Picard
R Belhomme
R Yvonne Le Tac
R Tardieu
Pl St-Pierre
R de Steinkerque
R Seveste
R d'Orsel
R des Abbesses
Barbès Rochechouart
Bd de Rochechouart
MONTMARTRE
R Dancourt
R André Gill
Anvers
Villa Garance
R Gérando
R du Delta
Pl d'Anvers
See map p382
R Crelet
R de Dunkerque
R des Martyrs
R Lallier
R Bochart de Saron
Av Trudaine
R de Rochechouart
R Turgot
R Pétrelle
R Condorcet
R Thimonnier
R du Faubourg Poissonnière
R Rodier
Cité Condorcet
R de la Tour d'Auvergne
R de Maubeuge
R d'Abbeville
Cité Fénelon
R Pierre Semard
R de l'Agent Bailly

MONTMARTE & PIGALLE *Map on p378*

Top Sights (p134)

1 Basilique du Sacré-Cœur F3

Sights (p137)

2 Abbesses Metro Entrance D4
3 Cimetière de Montmartre A2
4 Clos Montmartre E2
5 Église St-Pierre de Montmartre F3
6 Espace Dalí E3
7 Halle St-Pierre F4
8 Le Bateau Lavoir D3
9 Le Mur des je t'aime D4
10 Moulin Blute Fin D2
11 Moulin Radet D2
12 Musée de la Vie Romantique C6
13 Musée de Montmartre E2
14 Passe-Muraille D2
15 Place du Tertre E3
16 Playground Duperré C5

Eating (p140)

17 Abattoir Végétal G1
18 Aspic F7
19 Belle Maison E7
20 Bouillon Pigalle D5
21 Café Miroir E4
22 Chez Toinette D4
23 Crêperie Pen-Ty A5
24 La Mascotte C3
25 L'affineur Affiné C7
26 Le Bistrot de la Galette D3
27 Le Grenier à Pain D4
28 Le Pantruche E6
29 Le Potager de Charlotte G7
30 L'Été en Pente Douce G3
31 Mesdemoiselles Madeleines E7
32 Pain Pain E5
33 Pojo B5
34 Restaurant Bouillon G7
35 Roberta E4
36 Scaramouche E4
37 Soul Kitchen F2

Drinking & Nightlife (p148)

38 Chez Bouboule G5
39 Dirty Dick D6
40 Glass D6
41 Hardware Société G3
42 La Fourmi E5
La Machine du Moulin Rouge .... (see 50)
Le Petit Trianon .... (see 49)
Le Très Particulier .... (see 59)
43 Lipstick D6
44 Lulu White D6

Entertainment (p151)

45 Au Lapin Agile E2
46 Bus Palladium C6
47 La Cigale E5
48 Le Divan du Monde E5
49 Le Trianon F5
50 Moulin Rouge B4

Shopping (p152)

51 Balades Sonores G5
52 Belle du Jour F4
53 Jeremie Barthod E4
54 Pigalle D7
55 Spree E4

Sleeping (p283)

56 Grand Hôtel Pigalle D6
57 Hôtel Basss C3
58 Hôtel Joséphine B5
59 Hôtel Particulier Montmartre C2
60 Joke Hôtel B5
61 Le Pigalle D6
62 Maison Souquet B4
63 Môm'Art F4
64 R Kipling Hotel B5
65 Terrass Hôtel B3
66 Woodstock Hostel F7

GARE DU NORD & CANAL ST-MARTIN *Map on p382*

Sights **(p137)**
1 Brasserie la Goutte d'Or ... B2
2 Canal St-Martin ... E7
3 Espace Beaurepaire ... E7
4 Institut des Cultures d'Islam-Goutte d'Or ... C1
5 Institut des Cultures d'Islam-Léon ... B2
6 Le 104 ... F1

Eating **(p140)**
7 52 Faubourg St-Denis ... B7
8 Abri ... A5
9 Bob's Juice Bar ... D7
10 Bonhomie ... B7
11 Brasserie Barbès ... A3
12 Du Pain et des Idées ... D7
13 Fric-Frac ... E7
Grand Amour Hôtel ... (see 49)
14 Holybelly 5 ... D7
15 Le Bel Ordinaire ... A6
16 Le Petit Château d'Eau ... D7
17 Le Verre Volé ... D7
18 Marché St-Martin ... C7
19 Marché St-Quentin ... C5
20 Marrow ... C6
21 Matière à. ... E7
22 Pink Flamingo ... E6
23 Sunken Chip ... D7
24 Ten Belles ... E7
25 YAFO ... B5

Drinking & Nightlife **(p148)**
26 Café Lomi ... C1
27 Chez Prune ... E7
28 Gravity Bar ... D7
29 Hôtel du Nord ... E6
30 La Fontaine de Belleville ... F6
31 Le Syndicat ... B7
32 Le Triangle ... F7

Entertainment **(p151)**
Le 104 ... (see 6)
33 Le Louxor ... A3
34 New Morning ... B7
35 Point Éphémère ... F4

Shopping **(p152)**
36 Antoine et Lili ... D6
37 Artazart ... D7
38 Centre Commercial ... D7
39 Centre Commercial Kids ... D7
40 Designers Outlet L'Exception ... F7
41 Frivoli ... E7
42 La Crèmerie ... D7
43 Liza Korn ... D7
44 Medecine Douce ... E7
45 O/HP/E ... C8

Sports & Activities **(p150)**
46 Canauxrama ... F3

Sleeping **(p283)**
47 District République Hôtel ... D7
48 Generator Hostel ... F5
49 Grand Amour Hôtel ... C6
50 Hôtel du Nord – Le Pari Vélo ... D8
51 Hôtel Paradis ... A6
52 Hôtel Providence ... C8
53 Le Citizen Hotel ... E7
54 Le Robinet d'Or ... E5
55 St Christopher's Gare du Nord ... C5

GARE DU NORD & CANAL ST-MARTIN

Key on p381

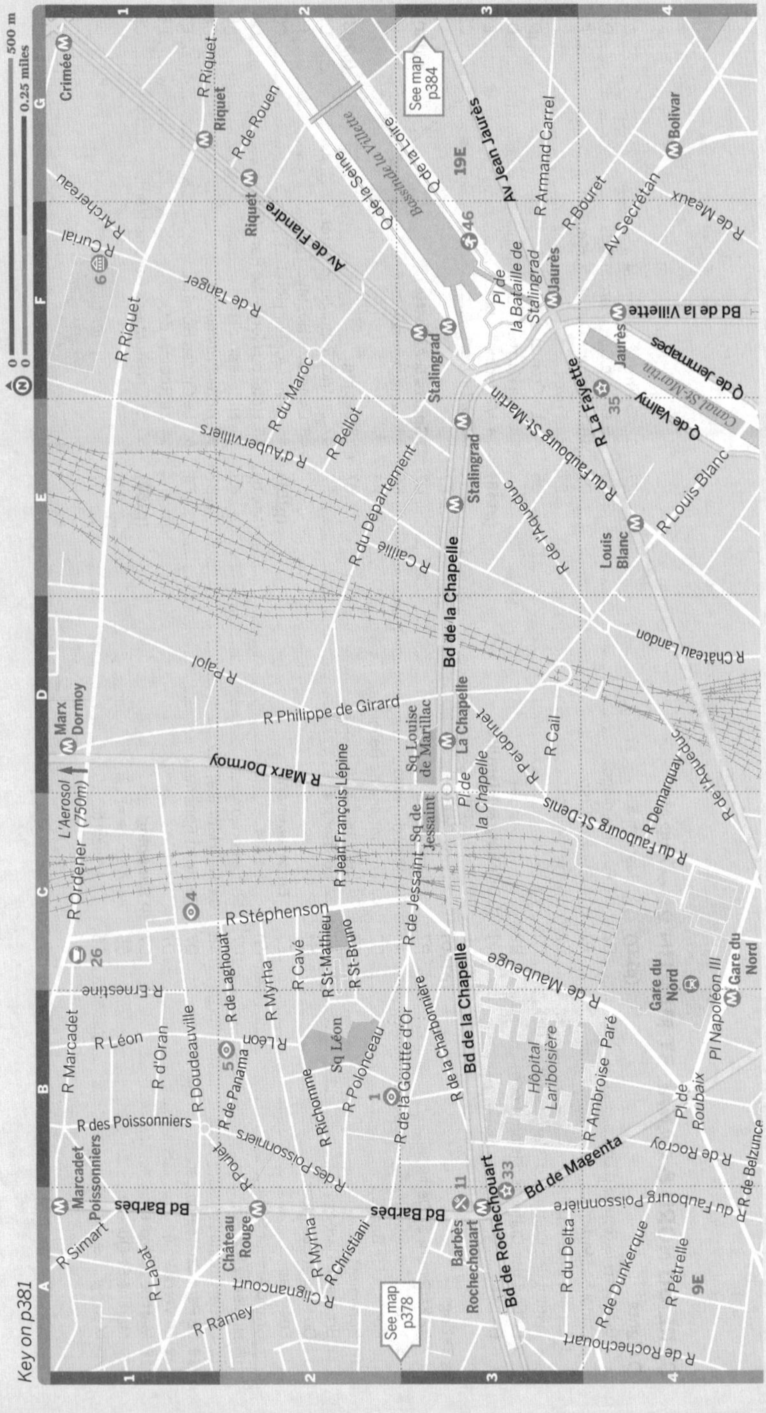

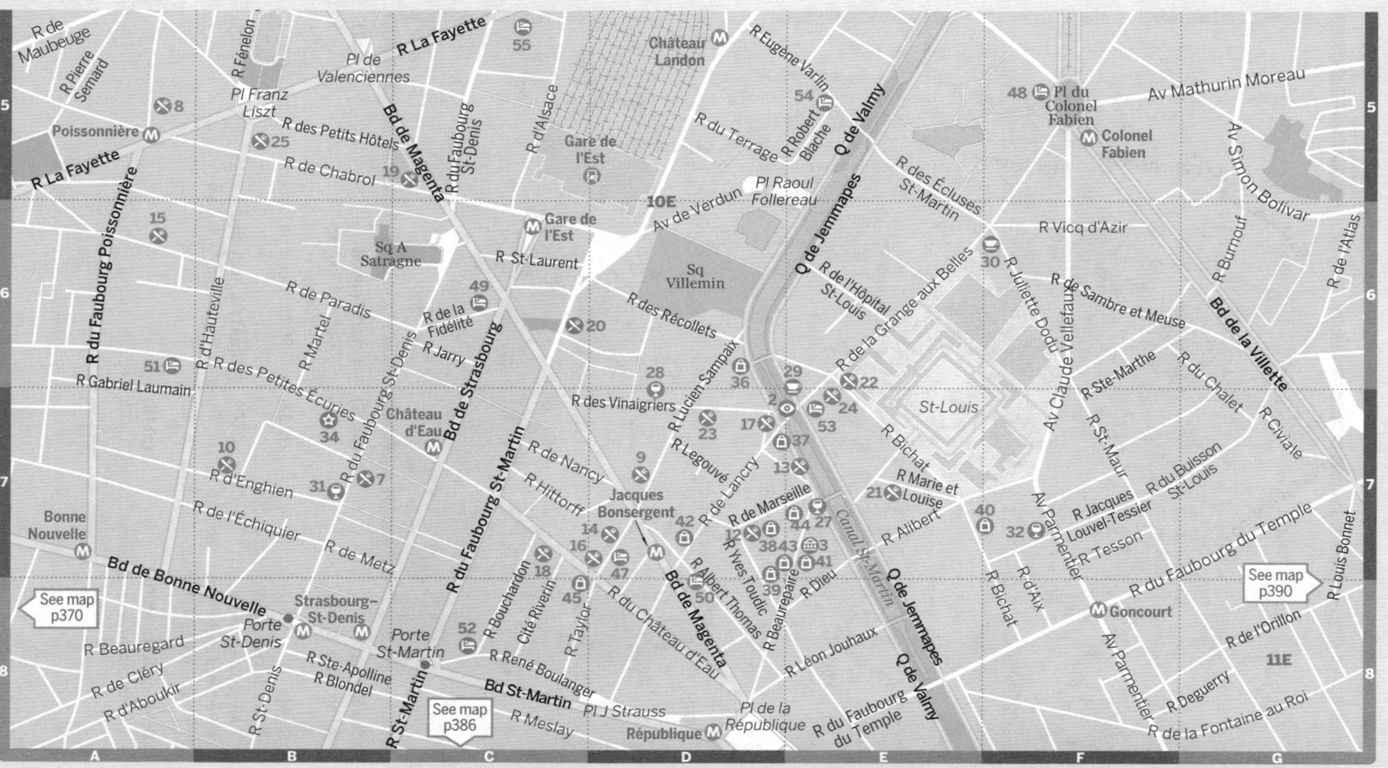

R de Maubeuge
R Pierre Semard
R Fénelon
Pl de Valenciennes
R La Fayette
Pl Franz Liszt
R des Petits Hôtels
Bd de Magenta
R du Faubourg St-Denis
R d'Alsace
Gare de l'Est
Château Landon
R Eugène Varlin
R du Terrage
R Robert Blache
Q de Valmy
Pl du Colonel Fabien
Av Mathurin Moreau
Colonel Fabien
Av Simon Bolivar
Poissonnière
R La Fayette
R de Chabrol
10E
Av de Verdun
Pl Raoul Follereau
Q de Jemmapes
R des Écluses St-Martin
R Vicq d'Azir
R Burnouf
R de l'Atlas
R du Faubourg Poissonnière
Sq A Satragne
R St-Laurent
Sq Villemin
R de l'Hôpital St-Louis
R de la Grange aux Belles
R Juliette Dodu
R de Sambre et Meuse
Bd de la Villette
R de Paradis
R de la Fidélité
R Jarry
Bd de Strasbourg
R des Récollets
R Lucien Sampaix
R Martel
R d'Hauteville
R des Petites Écuries
R Gabriel Laumain
R des Vinaigriers
Av Claude Vellefaux
R Ste-Marthe
R du Chalet
St-Louis
R Civiale
Château d'Eau
R du Faubourg St-Denis
R Legouvé
R de Lancry
R Bichat
R St-Maur
R du Buisson St-Louis
R d'Enghien
R de Nancy
R Hittorff
R du Faubourg St-Martin
Jacques Bonsergent
R Marie et Louise
R Alibert
R Jacques Louvel-Tessier
Av Parmentier
R Tesson
R du Faubourg du Temple
R Louis Bonnet
Bonne Nouvelle
R de l'Échiquier
R de Metz
R de Marseille
Canal St-Martin
R Yves Toudic
R Dieu
R d'Aix
Bd de Bonne Nouvelle
See map p370
Strasbourg–St-Denis
Porte St-Denis
R Bouchardon
Cité Riverin
R Taylor
R du Château d'Eau
Bd de Magenta
R Albert Thomas
R Beaurepaire
Q de Jemmapes
See map p390
Goncourt
R de l'Orillon
11E
R Beauregard
R de Cléry
R d'Aboukir
R St-Denis
R Ste-Apolline
R Blondel
Porte St-Martin
R St-Martin
See map p386
R René Boulanger
Bd St-Martin
Pl J Strauss
R Meslay
République
Pl de la République
R du Faubourg du Temple
Q de Valmy
R Léon Jouhaux
R Deguerry
R de la Fontaine au Roi

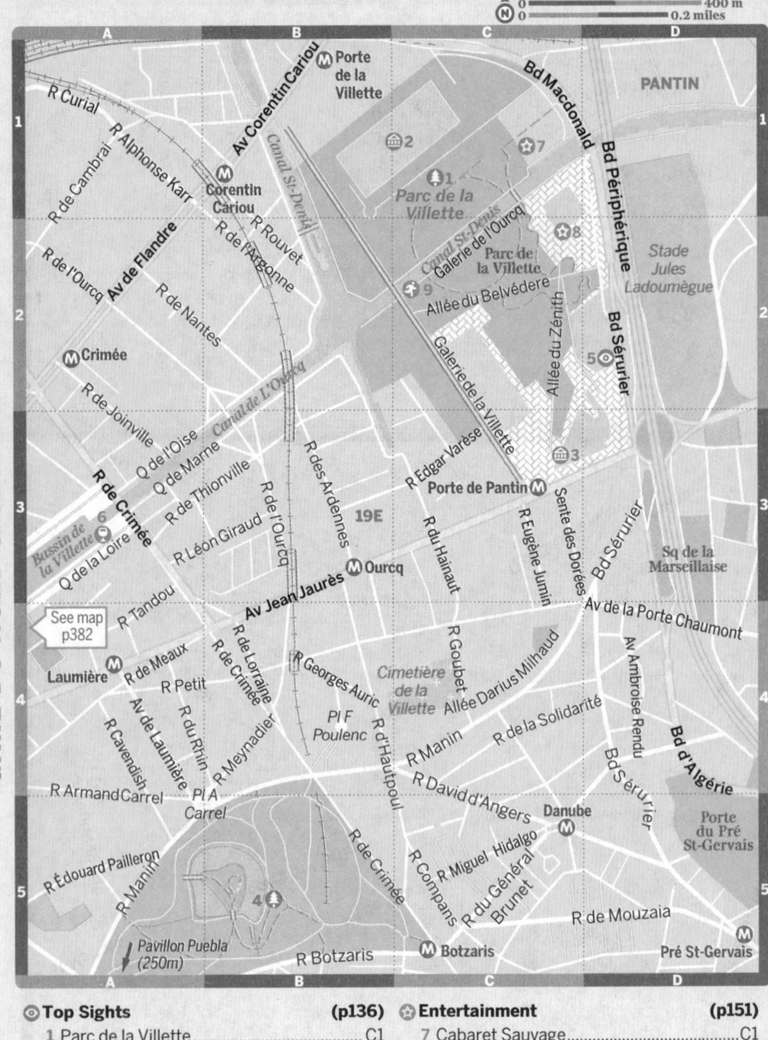

Top Sights (p136)
1 Parc de la Villette........C1

Sights (p137)
2 Cité des Sciences........C1
3 Musée de la Musique........C3
4 Parc des Buttes Chaumont........B5
5 Philharmonie de Paris........D2

Drinking & Nightlife (p148)
6 Paname Brewing Company........A3

Entertainment (p151)
7 Cabaret Sauvage........C1
8 Le Zénith........C2
Philharmonie de Paris........(see 3)

Sports & Activities (p150)
9 Paris Canal Croisières........C2

CLICHY & GARE ST-LAZARE

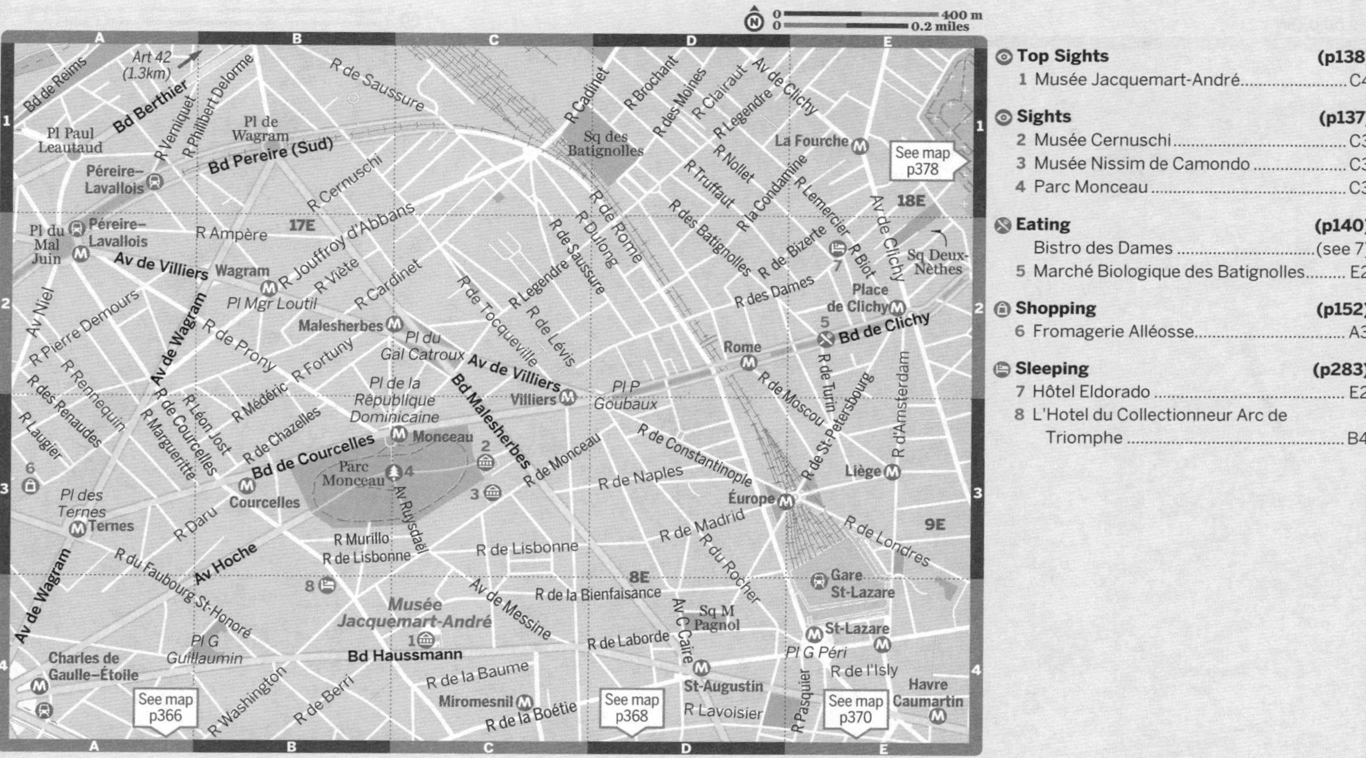

Top Sights (p138)
1 Musée Jacquemart-André C4

Sights (p137)
2 Musée Cernuschi C3
3 Musée Nissim de Camondo C3
4 Parc Monceau C3

Eating (p140)
Bistro des Dames .... (see 7)
5 Marché Biologique des Batignolles E2

Shopping (p152)
6 Fromagerie Alléosse A3

Sleeping (p283)
7 Hôtel Eldorado E2
8 L'Hotel du Collectionneur Arc de Triomphe B4

LE MARAIS

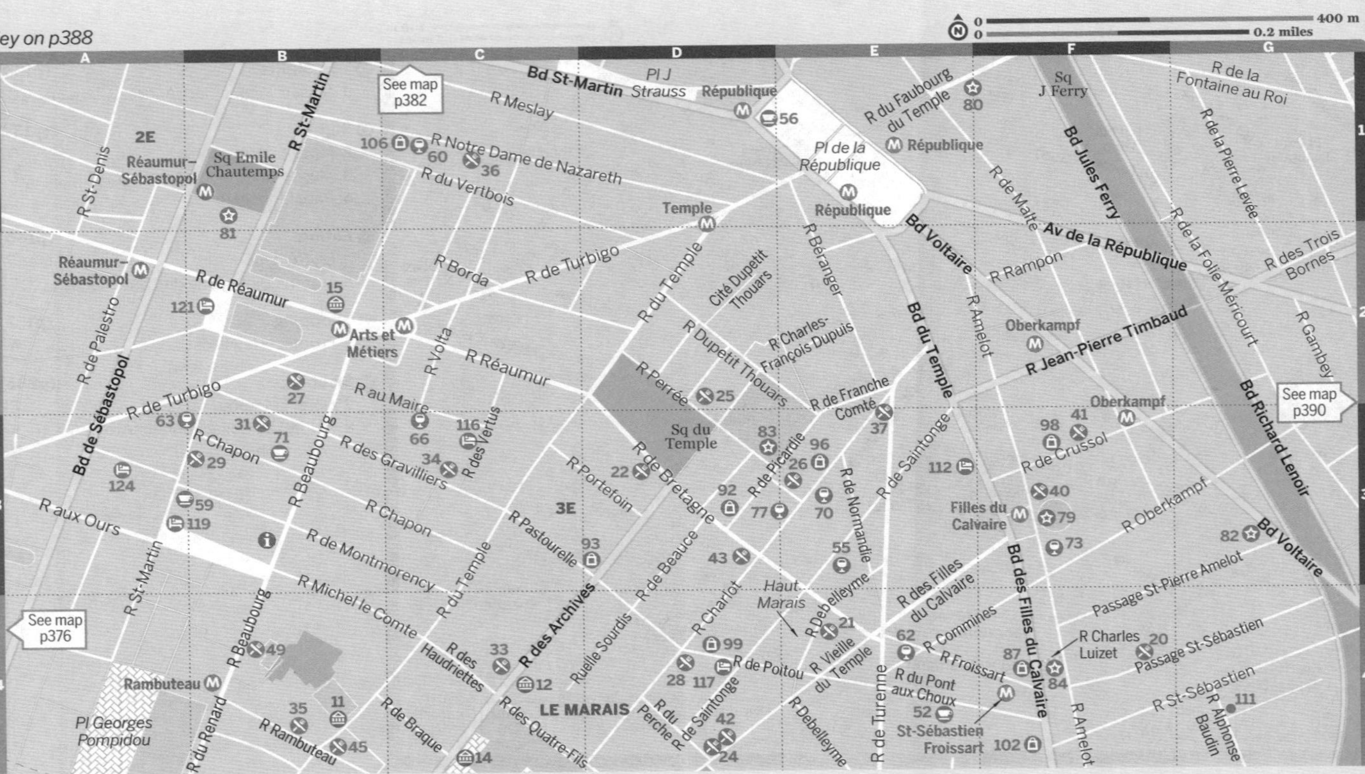

400 m
0.2 miles
Key on p388
See map p382
See map p390
See map p376
Bd St-Martin
Pl J Strauss
République
R Meslay
R St-Martin
R St-Denis
2E
Réaumur–Sébastopol
Sq Emile Chautemps
R Notre Dame de Nazareth
R du Vertbois
Temple
Pl de la République
R du Faubourg du Temple
Sq J Ferry
Bd Jules Ferry
R de la Fontaine au Roi
R de la Pierre Levée
R de Malte
Av de la République
R de la Folie Méricourt
R des Trois Bornes
R Gambey
R Rampon
Bd Voltaire
R Béranger
Cité Dupetit Thouars
R du Temple
R de Turbigo
R Borda
R de Réaumur
Arts et Métiers
R Volta
R Réaumur
R de Palestro
Bd de Sébastopol
R au Maire
R Chapon
R Beaubourg
R des Gravilliers
R des Vertus
R aux Ours
R de Montmorency
R Michel le Comte
R Charles-François Dupuis
R Dupetit Thouars
R Perrée
Sq du Temple
R de Franche Comté
Bd du Temple
R Amelot
Oberkampf
R Jean-Pierre Timbaud
Bd Richard Lenoir
R de Crussol
R de Saintonge
R de Picardie
R de Normandie
R Portefoin
R de Bretagne
3E
R Pastourelle
R de Beauce
Filles du Calvaire
R Oberkampf
Passage St-Pierre Amelot
R des Archives
Ruelle Sourdis
R Charlot
Haut Marais
R Debelleyme
R des Filles du Calvaire
R Commines
Bd des Filles du Calvaire
R Charles Luizet
Passage St-Sébastien
R Froissart
R de Poitou
R Vieille du Temple
R du Pont aux Choux
St-Sébastien Froissart
R St-Sébastien
R Alphonse Baudin
R des Haudriettes
R des Quatre-Fils
LE MARAIS
R du Perche
R de Turenne
Rambuteau
Pl Georges Pompidou
R du Renard
R Rambuteau
R de Braque

LE MARAIS

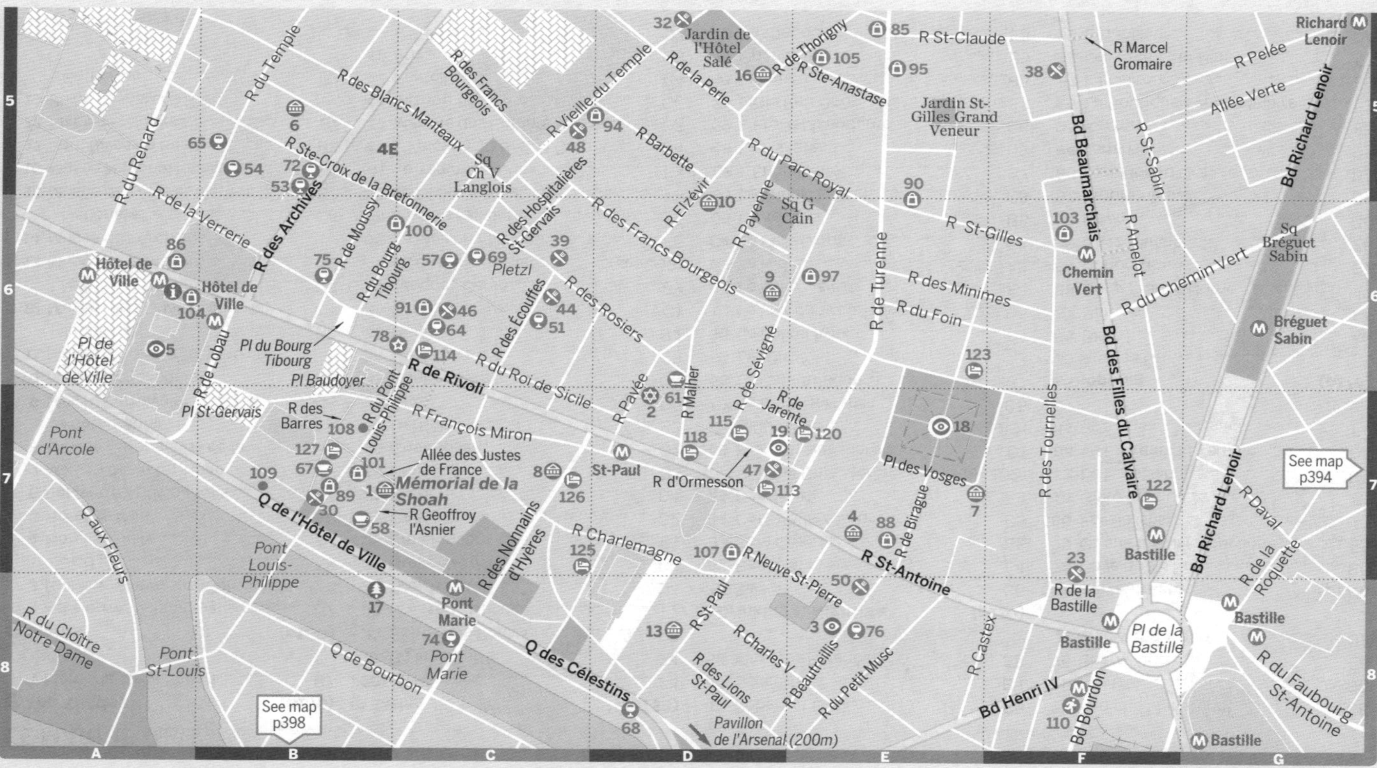
R du Temple
R des Blancs Manteaux
R des Francs Bourgeois
Jardin de l'Hôtel Salé
R de la Perle
R de Thorigny
R Ste-Anastase
R St-Claude
R Marcel Gromaire
R Pelée
Richard Lenoir
Allée Verte
Bd Richard Lenoir
Jardin St-Gilles Grand Veneur
Bd Beaumarchais
R St-Sabin
R du Renard
4E
Sq Ch V Langlois
R Vieille du Temple
R Barbette
R du Parc Royal
R Ste-Croix de la Bretonnerie
R des Archives
R de la Verrerie
R de Moussy
R des Hospitalières St-Gervais
R Elzévir
R Payenne
Sq G Cain
R St-Gilles
R Amelot
Sq Bréguet Sabin
Hôtel de Ville
R du Bourg Tibourg
Pletzl
R des Francs Bourgeois
R de Turenne
R des Minimes
Chemin Vert
R du Chemin Vert
R des Rosiers
R des Écouffes
R du Foin
Bréguet Sabin
Pl de l'Hôtel de Ville
R de Lobau
Pl du Bourg Tibourg
R de Rivoli
R du Roi de Sicile
Pl Baudoyer
R du Pont Louis-Philippe
R Pavée
R Malher
R de Sévigné
R de Jarente
Bd des Filles du Calvaire
Pl St-Gervais
R des Barres
R François Miron
Pont d'Arcole
St-Paul
R d'Ormesson
Pl des Vosges
R des Tournelles
See map p394
Allée des Justes de France
Mémorial de la Shoah
R Geoffroy l'Asnier
Q de l'Hôtel de Ville
Q aux Fleurs
R des Nonnains d'Hyères
R Charlemagne
R Neuve St-Pierre
R St-Antoine
R de Birague
R Daval
Pont Louis-Philippe
Pont Marie
Bastille
R de la Roquette
R de la Bastille
Pl de la Bastille
R du Cloître Notre Dame
Pont St-Louis
Q de Bourbon
Q des Célestins
R St-Paul
R Charles V
R des Lions St-Paul
R Beautreillis
R du Petit Musc
R Castex
Bd Henri IV
Bd Bourdon
R du Faubourg St-Antoine
See map p398
Pavillon de l'Arsenal (200m)

LE MARAIS *Map on p386*

Top Sights (p156)
1 Mémorial de la Shoah ... B7

Sights (p160)
2 Art Nouveau Synagogue ... D7
3 Building Where Jim Morrison Died ... E8
4 Hôtel de Sully ... E7
5 Hôtel de Ville ... A6
6 Lafayette Anticipations ... B5
7 Maison de Victor Hugo ... E7
8 Maison Européenne de la Photographie ... C7
9 Musée Carnavalet ... D6
10 Musée Cognacq-Jay ... D6
11 Musée d'Art et d'Histoire du Judaïsme ... B4
12 Musée de la Chasse et de la Nature ... C4
13 Musée de la Magie ... D8
14 Musée des Archives Nationales ... C4
15 Musée des Arts et Métiers ... B2
16 Musée National Picasso ... D5
17 Parc Rives de Seine ... B8
18 Place des Vosges ... E7
19 Place du Marché Ste-Catherine ... D7

Eating (p163)
20 Au Passage ... F4
21 Biglove Caffè ... E4
22 Bontemps Pâtisserie ... D3
23 Brasserie Bofinger ... F7
24 Breizh Café ... D4
25 Broken Arm ... D2
26 Café Pinson ... E3
27 CAM ... B2
28 Carbón ... D4
29 Causses ... B3
30 Chez Julien ... B7
31 Derrière ... B3
32 Glou ... D5
33 Hankburger ... C4
34 Hankpizza ... C3
35 Huré ... B4
36 Istr ... C1
37 Jacques Genin ... E3
La Cantine de Merci ... (see 102)
38 La Maison Plisson ... F5
39 L'As du Fallafel ... C6
40 Le Clown Bar ... F3
41 Le Tagine ... F3
42 L'Epicerie du Breizh Café ... D4
43 Marché des Enfants Rouges ... D3
44 Miznon ... C6
45 Pastelli ... B4
46 Pozzetto ... C6
47 Rainettes ... D7
48 Robert et Louise ... C5
49 Saucette ... B4
50 Vins Des Pyrénées ... E8

Drinking & Nightlife (p170)
51 3w Kafé ... C6
52 Boot Café ... E4
53 Café Cox ... B5
54 Café Voulez-Vous ... B5
55 Candelaria ... E3
Cinéma Café Merci ... (see 102)
56 Fluctuat Nec Mergitur ... D1
Gibus Club ... (see 80)
57 La Belle Hortense ... C6
58 La Caféothèque ... B7
59 Le 10h10 ... A3
60 Le Ballon Rouge ... C1
61 Le Loir dans La Théière ... D6
62 Le Mary Céleste ... E4
63 Le Nid ... A3
64 Le Pick-Clops ... C6
65 Le Raidd ... B5
66 Le Tango ... C3
67 L'Ebouillanté ... B7
68 Les Nautes ... D8
69 L'Étoile Manquante ... C6
70 Little Red Door ... E3
71 Loustic ... B3
72 Open Café ... B5
73 PasDeLoup ... F3
74 Peniche Marcounet ... C8
75 Quetzal ... B6
76 Sherry Butt ... E8
77 Wild & the Moon ... D3

Entertainment (p175)
78 Cave du 38 Riv' ... C6
79 Cirque d'Hiver Bouglione ... F3
80 Favela Chic ... E1
81 Gaîté Lyrique ... B1
82 Le Bataclan ... G3
83 Le Carreau du Temple ... D3
84 Pop In ... F4

Shopping (p176)
85 Andrea Crews ... E5
86 BHV ... A6
87 Bonton ... F4
88 Bring France Home ... E7
89 Candora ... B7
90 Chez Hélène ... E6
91 Edwart ... C6
92 Empreintes ... D3
93 État Libre d'Orange ... D3
94 Jamin Puech ... D5
95 Kerzon ... E5
96 La Boutique Extraordinaire ... E3
97 L'Éclaireur ... E6
98 Les Petits Bla-Blas ... F3
99 L'Habilleur ... D4

100 Mariage Frères B6
101 Mélodies Graphiques B7
102 Merci F4
103 Odetta Vintage F6
104 Paris Rendez-Vous A6
105 Samuel Coraux E5
106 Superfly Records C1
107 Village St-Paul D7

Sports & Activities **(p179)**

108 Bike About Tours B7
109 La Cuisine Paris B7
110 Nomadeshop F8
111 Paris à Vélo, C'est Sympa! G4

Sleeping **(p286)**

112 1K Paris E3
113 Hôtel Caron D7
114 Hôtel Caron de Beaumarchais C6
115 Hôtel de JoBo D7
116 Hôtel du Haut Marais C3
117 Hôtel du Petit Moulin D4
118 Hôtel Emile D7
119 Hôtel Georgette A3
120 Hôtel Jeanne d'Arc E7
121 Hôtel National Des Arts et Métiers B2
122 Hôtel Original F7
123 Le Pavillon de la Reine E6
124 Les Bains A3
125 MIJE Fauconnier C7
126 MIJE Fourcy C7
127 MIJE Maubuisson B7

MÉNILMONTANT & BELLEVILLE

Key on p392

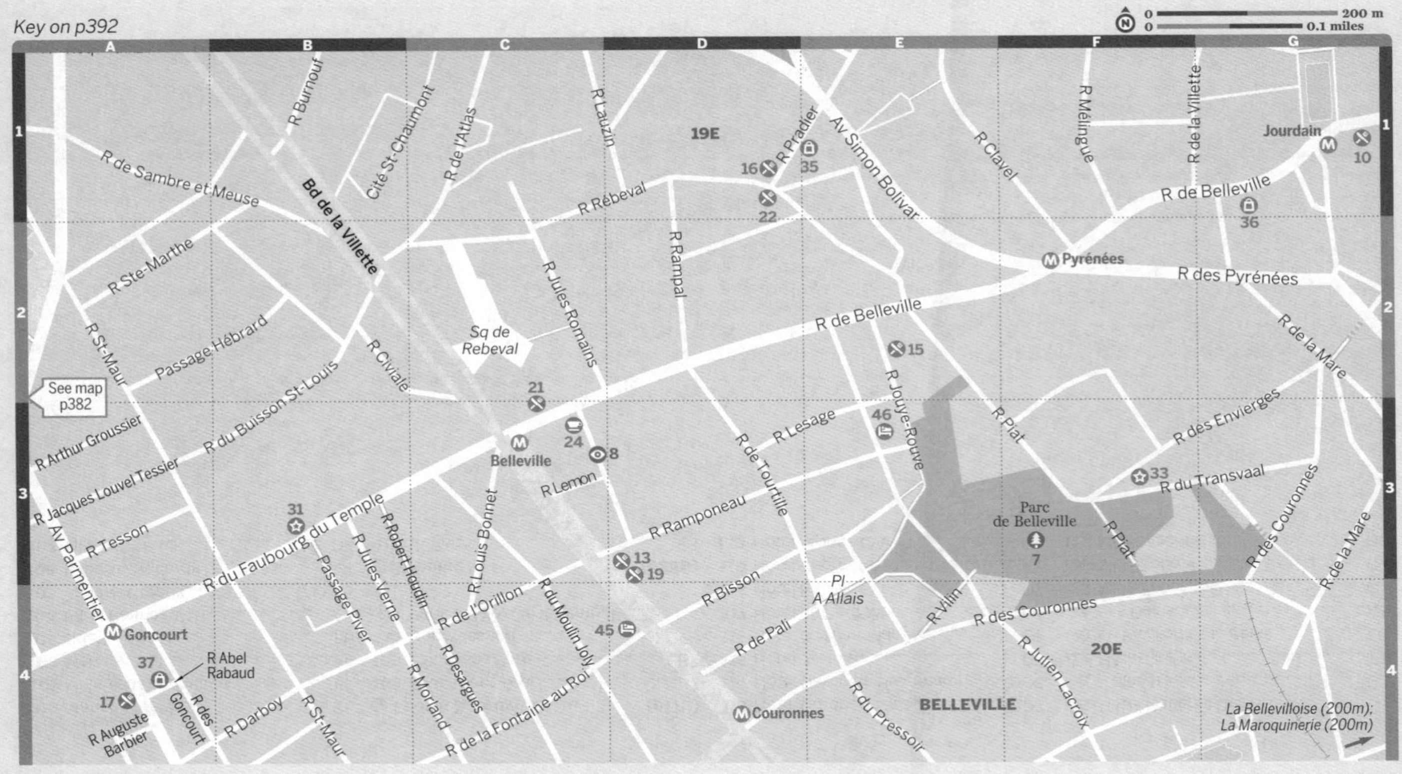

MÉNILMONTANT & BELLEVILLE

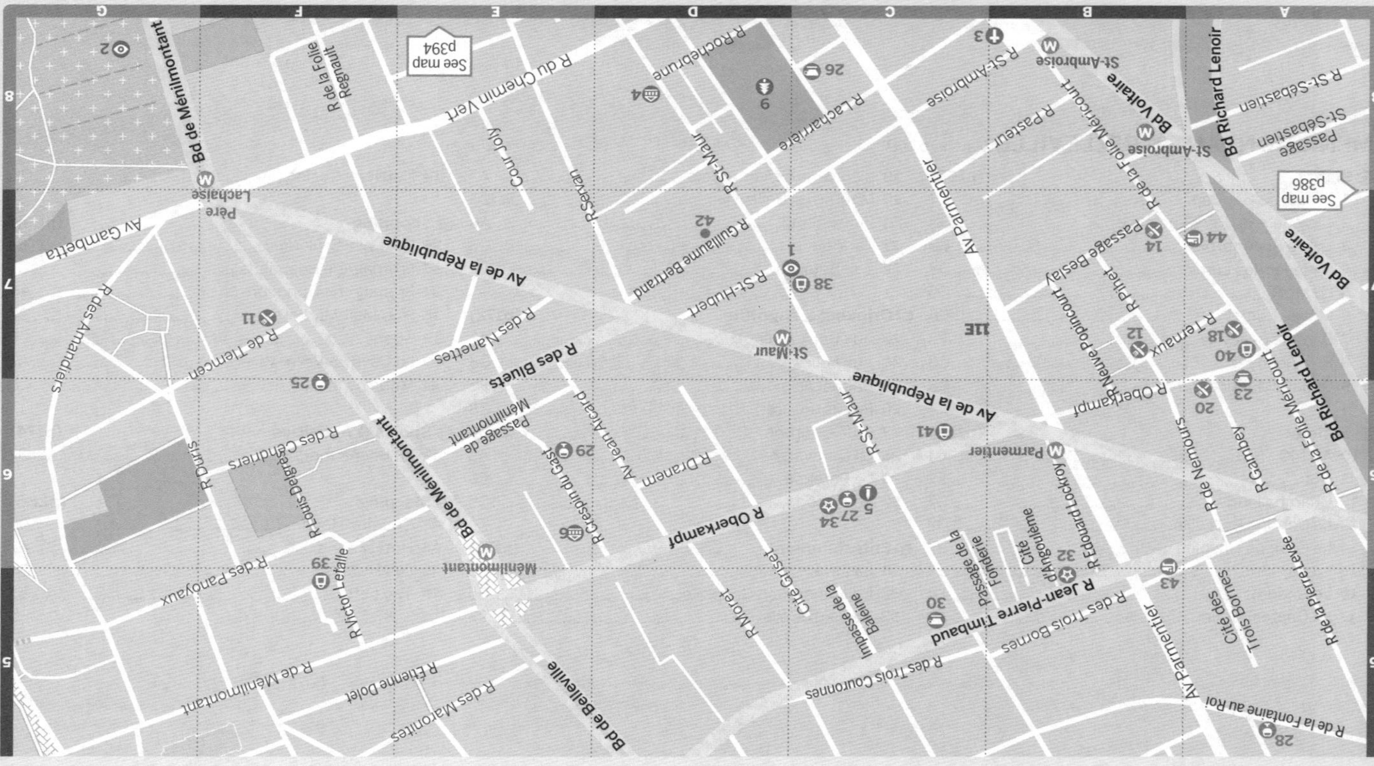

MÉNILMONTANT & BELLEVILLE *Map on p390*

Sights (p163)

1 Brasserie BapBap ... C7
2 Cimetière du Père Lachaise ... G8
3 Église St-Ambroise ... B8
4 L'Atelier des Lumières ... D8
5 Le MUR ... C6
6 Musée Édith Piaf ... E6
7 Parc de Belleville ... F3
8 Rue Dénoyez ... C3
9 Square Maurice Gardette ... D8

Eating (p169)

10 Au 140 ... G1
11 Bøti ... F7
12 Chambelland ... B7
13 La Cantine Belleville ... D3
14 La Cave de l'Insolite ... B7
15 Le Baratin ... E2
16 Le Cadoret ... D1
17 Le Chateaubriand ... A4
18 L'Epicerie Le Verre Volé ... A7
19 Marché de Belleville ... D3
20 Pierre Sang ... A6
21 Tai Yien ... C3
22 Zoé Bouillon ... D1

Drinking & Nightlife (p172)

23 Aux Deux Amis ... A7
24 Aux Folies ... C3
25 Balthazar ... F6
26 Beans on Fire ... C8
27 Café Charbon ... C6
28 La Caravane ... A5
29 Le Perchoir ... E6
30 The Hood ... C5

Entertainment (p175)

31 La Java ... B3
32 L'Alimentation Générale ... B5
33 Le Vieux Belleville ... F3
34 Nouveau Casino ... C6

Shopping (p176)

35 Belleville Brûlerie ... E1
36 Fromagerie Beaufils ... G1
37 Fromagerie Goncourt ... A4
38 Hop Malt Market ... C7
39 Koché ... F5
40 La Cave Le Verre Volé ... A7
41 Made by Moi ... C6

Sports & Activities (p174)

42 La Beer Fabrique ... D7

Sleeping (p286)

43 Cosmos Hôtel ... B6
44 Hôtel Fabric ... A7
45 Les Piaules ... D4
46 The Loft ... E3

BASTILLE & EASTERN PARIS *Map on p394*

Sights (p182)

Colonne de Juillet ... (see 3)
1 Ground Control ... E8
2 Opéra Bastille ... B5
3 Place de la Bastille ... B4
4 Promenade Plantée ... B6
5 Rue Crémieux ... B7

Eating (p184)

6 À la Banane Ivoirienne ... E5
7 À la Biche au Bois ... B6
8 À La Renaissance ... D2
9 Blé Sucré ... D5
10 Buffet ... D5
11 Café Mirabelle ... F2
12 Chalet Savoyard ... D4
13 Chez Paul ... C4
14 CheZaline ... D2
15 Citeaux Sphere ... E5
16 Clamato ... E4
17 Coup d'Œil ... D2
18 Crêperie Bretonne Fleurie de l'Epouse du Marin ... E4
19 Dersou ... C5
20 Gentle Gourmet Café ... A6
21 Jouvence ... E5
22 La Chocolaterie Cyril Lignac ... F4
23 La Pâtisserie ... F4
24 La Robe de la Girafe ... C3
25 Le 6 Paul Bert ... F5
26 Le Bar à Soupes ... C4
Le Bistrot Paul Bert ... (see 52)
27 Le Chardenoux ... F4
28 Le Grand Bréguet ... C2
29 Le Servan ... E1
30 Le Siffleur de Ballons ... E6
31 Le Square Trousseau ... D5
32 Le Temps au Temps ... F5
33 Le Train Bleu ... C8
34 L'Ébauchoir ... E6
35 L'Écailler du Bistrot ... F5
36 L'Encrier ... C6
37 Les Déserteurs ... D4
38 Les Domaines Qui Montent ... E2
39 Les Galopins ... C3
40 Marché Bastille ... B3
41 Marché Beauvau ... D6
42 Marché d'Aligre ... D6
43 Mokonuts ... E5
44 Nanina ... D3
45 Passerini ... C6
46 Septime ... E4
47 Table ... C6

Drinking & Nightlife (p189)

48 Bar des Ferrailleurs ... B4
49 Bluebird ... E5
50 Café des Anges ... C3
51 Concrete ... B8
52 La Cave Paul Bert ... F5
53 La Fée Verte ... D3
54 Le Baron Rouge ... D6
55 Le Bistrot du Peintre ... D4
56 Le Pure Café ... F4
57 Les Sans-Culottes ... C4
58 Louve ... C2
59 Outland ... G3
60 Septime La Cave ... E4
61 Twenty One Sound Bar ... E5

Entertainment (p191)

62 Badaboum ... C4
63 La Chapelle des Lombards ... B4
64 Le Balajo ... B4
65 Le Motel ... D4
66 Le Réservoir ... E5
Opéra Bastille ... (see 2)

Shopping (p192)

67 Chez Teil ... B4
68 Fermob ... C5
69 La Cocotte ... F5
70 La Manufacture de Chocolat ... B4
71 Marché aux Puces d'Aligre ... D6
72 So We Are ... D4
73 Souffle Continu ... F2
Viaduc des Arts ... (see 4)

Sports & Activities (p150)

74 Canauxrama ... A5

Sleeping (p288)

75 CitizenM Gare de Lyon ... B8
76 Hôtel l'Antoine ... C4
77 Hôtel Paris Bastille Boutet ... F5
78 Maison Bréguet ... B3

BASTILLE & EASTERN PARIS

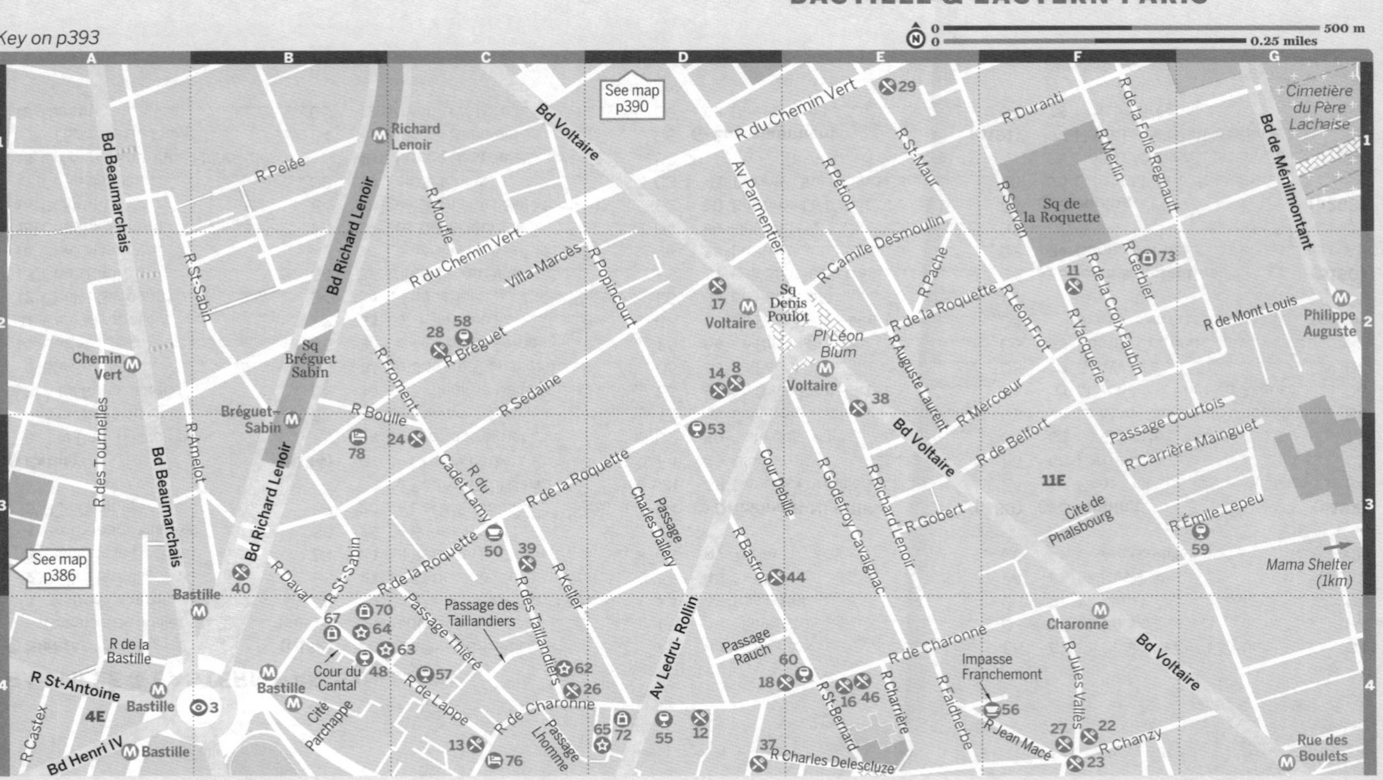

BASTILLE & EASTERN PARIS

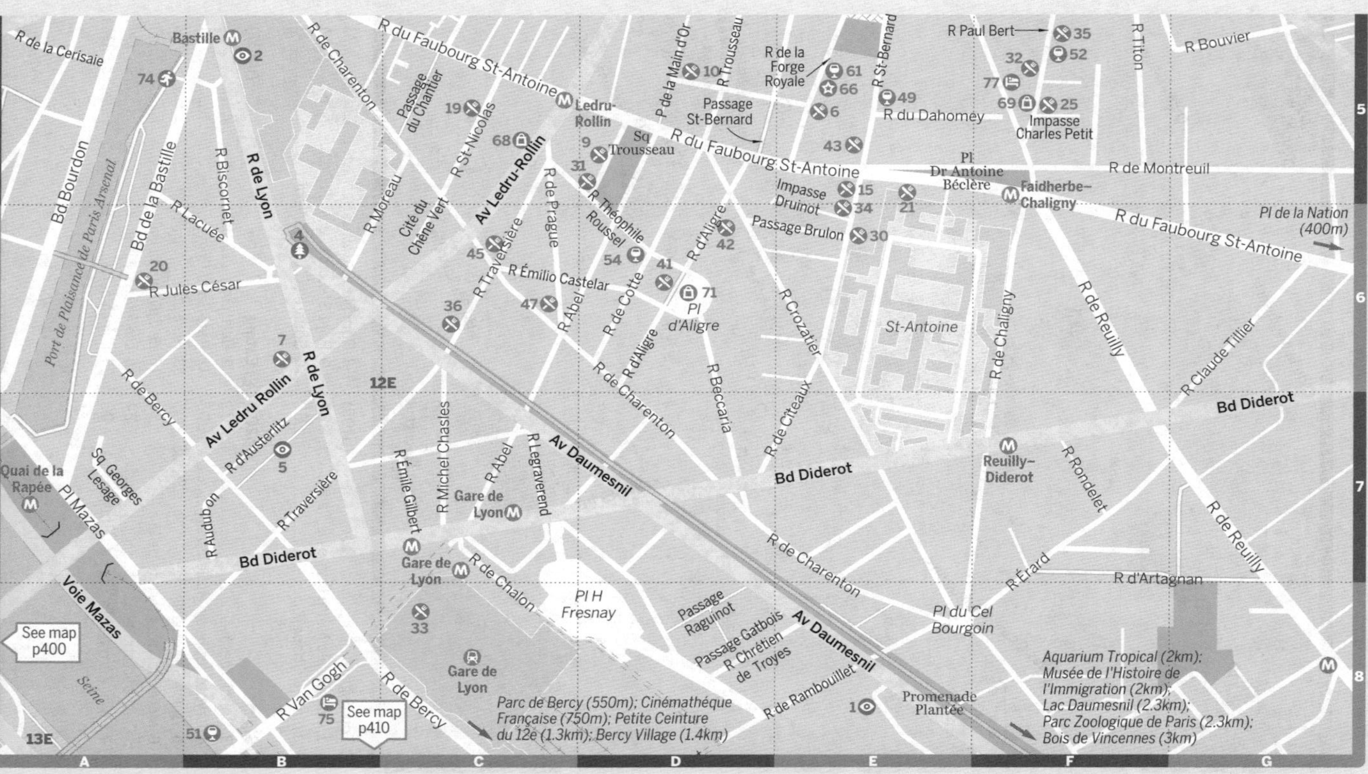

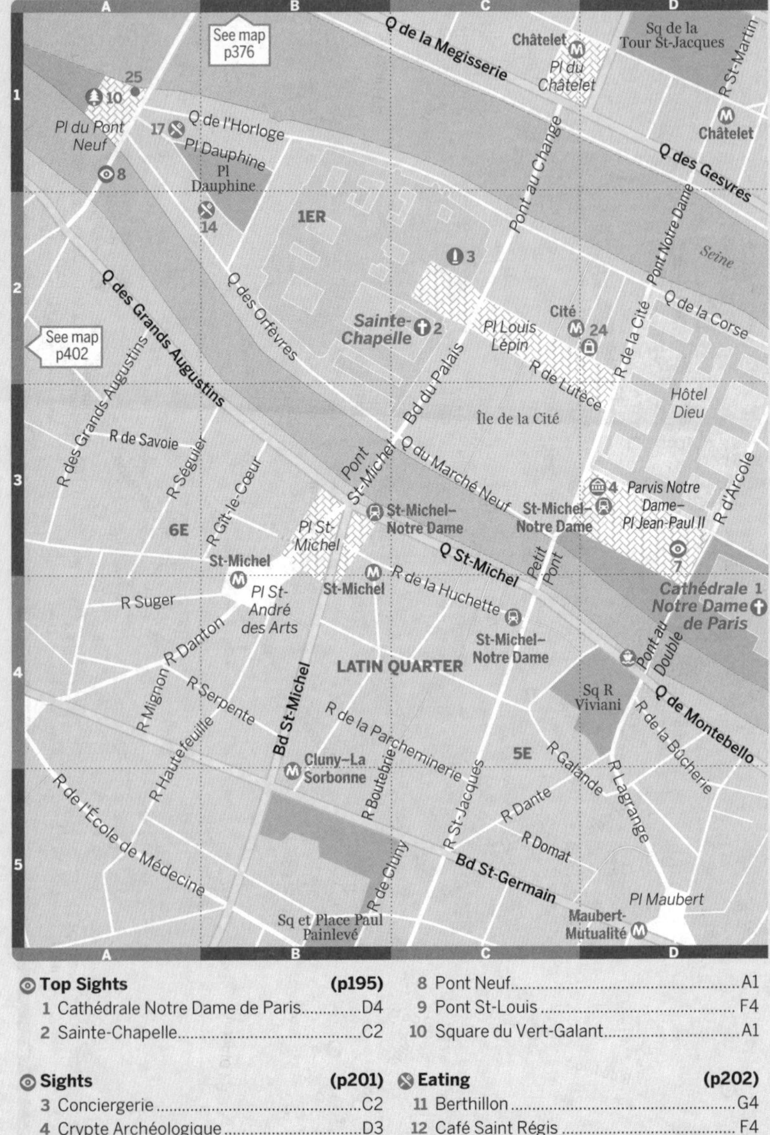

Top Sights (p195)

1 Cathédrale Notre Dame de Paris.......D4
2 Sainte-Chapelle.......C2

8 Pont Neuf.......A1
9 Pont St-Louis.......F4
10 Square du Vert-Galant.......A1

Sights (p201)

3 Conciergerie.......C2
4 Crypte Archéologique.......D3
5 Église St-Louis en l'Île.......G5
6 Mémorial des Martyrs de la Déportation.......E4
7 Point Zéro des Routes de France.......D3

Eating (p202)

11 Berthillon.......G4
12 Café Saint Régis.......F4
13 Huré.......E3
14 Le Caveau du Palais.......B2
15 Les Fous de l'Île.......G4
16 L'Îlot Vache.......G4

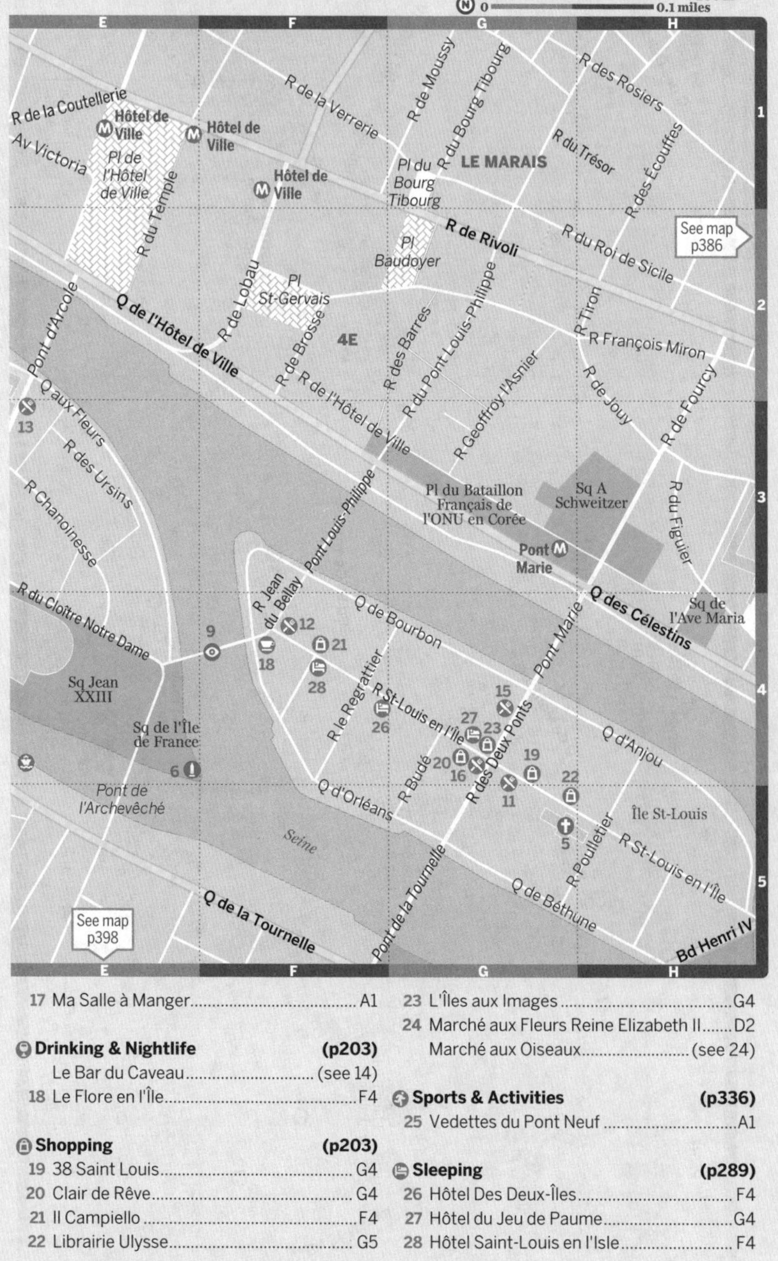

17 Ma Salle à Manger....................................A1

Drinking & Nightlife (p203)

Le Bar du Caveau..............................(see 14)
18 Le Flore en l'Île...F4

Shopping (p203)

19 38 Saint Louis...G4
20 Clair de Rêve...G4
21 Il Campiello...F4
22 Librairie Ulysse..G5

23 L'Îles aux Images.......................................G4
24 Marché aux Fleurs Reine Elizabeth II.......D2
Marché aux Oiseaux.........................(see 24)

Sports & Activities (p336)

25 Vedettes du Pont Neuf...............................A1

Sleeping (p289)

26 Hôtel Des Deux-Îles...................................F4
27 Hôtel du Jeu de Paume...............................G4
28 Hôtel Saint-Louis en l'Isle..........................F4

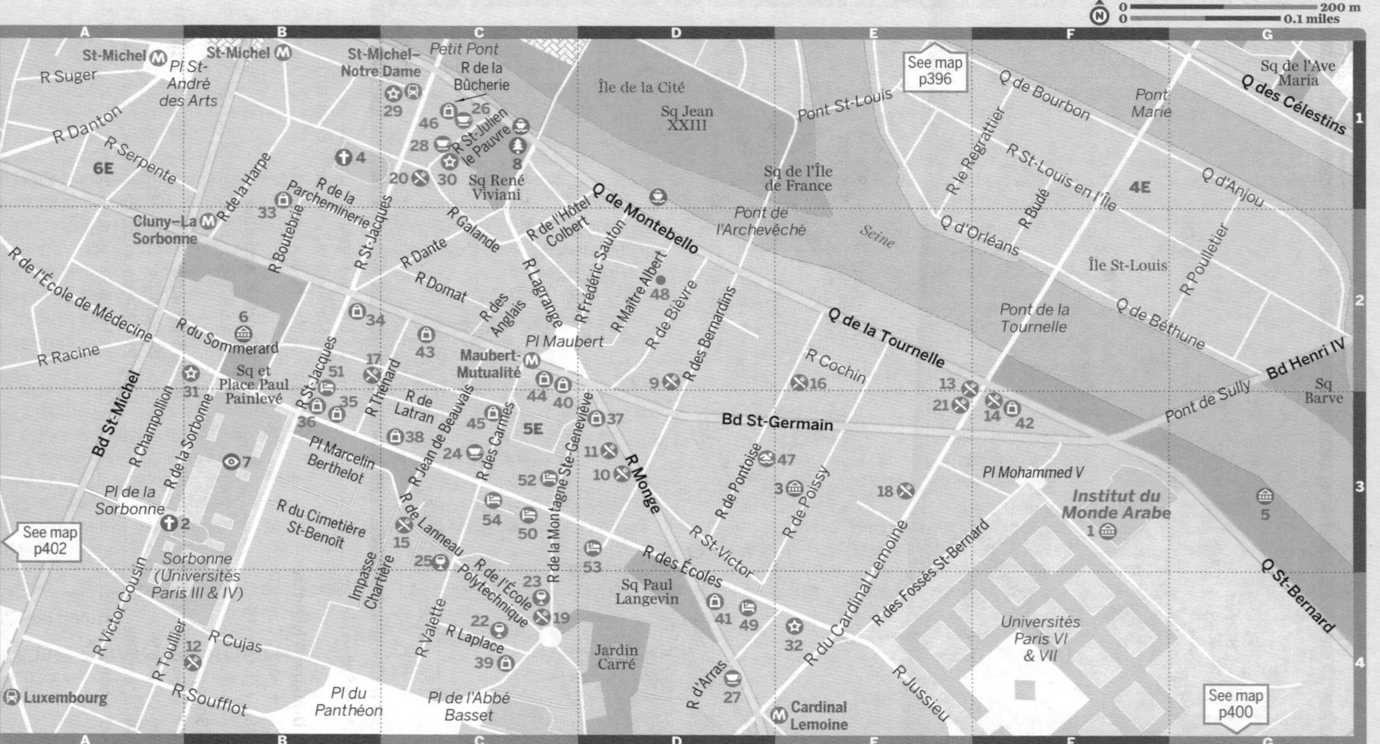
LATIN QUARTER NORTH
0 200 m
0 0.1 miles
St-Michel
Pl St-André des Arts
R Suger
R Danton
R Serpente
6E
St-Michel
St-Michel–Notre Dame
Petit Pont
R de la Bûcherie
R St-Julien le Pauvre
Sq René Viviani
Île de la Cité
Sq Jean XXIII
Pont St-Louis
See map p396
Q de Bourbon
Pont Marie
Sq de l'Ave Maria
Q des Célestins
R le Regrattier
R St-Louis en l'Île
4E
Q d'Anjou
R Budé
Q d'Orléans
Île St-Louis
R Poulletier
Sq de l'Île de France
Pont de l'Archevêché
Seine
R de la Harpe
R de la Parcheminerie
R Boutebrie
Cluny–La Sorbonne
R St-Jacques
R Galande
R de l'Hôtel Colbert
Q de Montebello
R Dante
R Domat
R des Anglais
R Lagrange
R Frédéric Sauton
R Maître Albert
R de Bièvre
R des Bernardins
R de l'École de Médecine
R du Sommerard
R Racine
Sq et Place Paul Painlevé
Pl Maubert
Maubert-Mutualité
Q de la Tournelle
Pont de la Tournelle
Q de Béthune
Bd Henri IV
Sq Barye
Pont de Sully
R Cochin
R Thénard
R de Latran
Bd St-Michel
R Champollion
R de la Sorbonne
R Jean de Beauvais
R des Carmes
5E
R de la Montagne Ste-Geneviève
Bd St-Germain
Pl Marcelin Berthelot
R Monge
R de Pontoise
R de Poissy
Pl Mohammed V
Institut du Monde Arabe
Pl de la Sorbonne
R du Cimetière St-Benoît
R de Lanneau
R St-Victor
R du Cardinal Lemoine
R des Fossés St-Bernard
Q St-Bernard
See map p402
Sorbonne (Universités Paris III & IV)
Impasse Chartière
R de l'École Polytechnique
R des Écoles
Sq Paul Langevin
Universités Paris VI & VII
R Victor Cousin
R Toullier
R Cujas
R Valette
R Laplace
Jardin Carré
R d'Arras
R Jussieu
Luxembourg
R Soufflot
Pl du Panthéon
Pl de l'Abbé Basset
Cardinal Lemoine
See map p400

LATIN QUARTER NORTH

Top Sights (p209)
1 Institut du Monde Arabe ... F3

Sights (p207)
2 Chapelle de la Sorbonne ... A3
3 Collège des Bernardins ... E3
4 Église St-Séverin ... B1
5 Musée de la Sculpture en Plein Air ... G3
6 Musée National du Moyen Âge ... B2
7 Sorbonne ... B3
8 Square René Viviani ... C1

Eating (p210)
9 Anahuacalli ... D2
10 Boulangerie Eric Kayser ... D3
11 Boulangerie Eric Kayser ... D3
12 Croq' Fac ... B4
13 La Rôtisserie d'Argent ... E2
14 La Tour d'Argent ... F3
15 Le Coupe-Chou ... C3
16 Le Petit Pontoise ... E2
17 Le Pré Verre ... B2
18 Le Puits de Légumes ... E3
Le Zyriab by Noura ... (see 1)
19 Les Pipos ... C4
20 Odette ... C1
21 Restaurant AT ... E3

Drinking & Nightlife (p215)
22 Le Piano Vache ... C4
23 Le Violon Dingue ... C4
24 Nuage ... C3
25 Pub St-Hilaire ... C3
26 Shakespeare & Company Café ... C1
27 Strada Café ... D4
28 The Tea Caddy ... C1

Entertainment (p217)
29 Caveau de la Huchette ... C1
30 Église St-Julien le Pauvre ... C1
31 Le Champo ... B2
32 Le Grand Action ... E4

Shopping (p218)
33 Abbey Bookshop ... B1
34 Album ... B2
35 Au Vieux Campeur ... B3
36 Au Vieux Campeur Running ... B3
37 Aux Merveilleux de Fred ... D3
38 Crocodisc ... C3
39 Crocojazz ... C4
40 Fromagerie Laurent Dubois ... C2
41 Le Bonbon au Palais ... D4
42 Le Comptoir ... F3
43 Librairie Eyrolles ... C2
44 Marché Maubert ... C2
45 Mayette la Boutique de la Magie ... C3
46 Shakespeare & Company ... C1

Sports & Activities (p221)
47 Piscine Pontoise ... D3
48 Set in Paris ... D2

Sleeping (p289)
49 Familia Hôtel ... D4
50 Hôtel Atmosphères ... C3
51 Hôtel Diana ... B2
52 Hôtel La Lanterne ... C3
53 Hôtel Résidence Henri IV ... D3
54 Hôtel St-Jacques ... C3

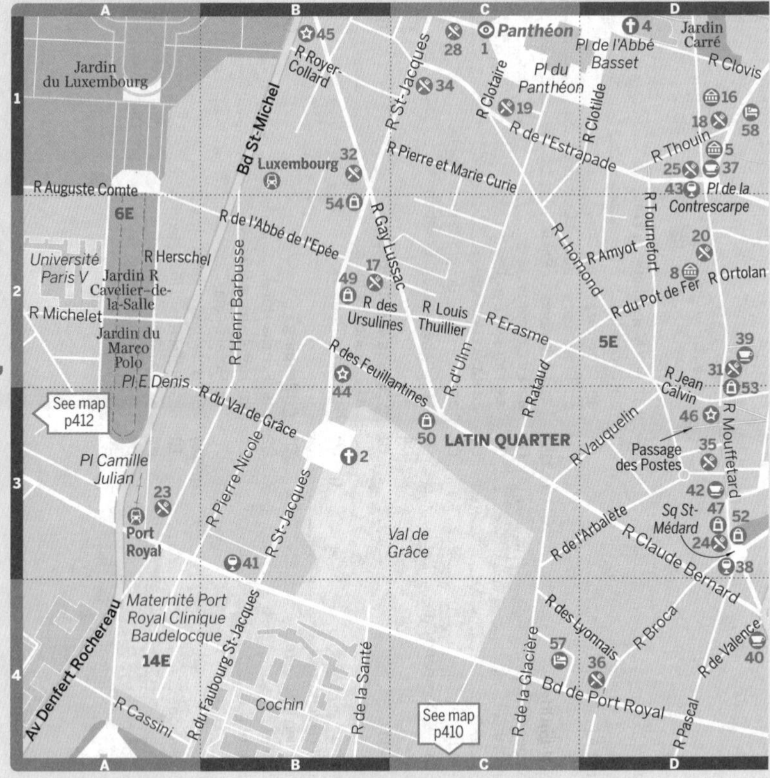

Top Sights **(p207)**

1 Panthéon C1

Sights **(p207)**

2 Abbaye Royale du Val-de-Grâce B3
3 Arènes de Lutèce E1
4 Église St-Étienne du Mont D1
5 Ernest Hemingway's Apartment D1
6 Galerie d'Anatomie Comparée et de Paléontologie H2
7 Galerie de Minéralogie et de Géologie F2
Galerie des Enfants .... (see 9)
8 George Orwell's Boarding House D2
9 Grande Galerie de l'Évolution F2
10 James Joyce's Flat E1
11 Jardin des Plantes H2
12 La Ménagerie F1
13 Les Grandes Serres et Galerie de Botanique F2
14 Mosquée de Paris E2
15 Muséum National d'Histoire Naturelle F2
16 Paul Verlaine's Garret D1

Eating **(p210)**

17 Bistro Le Mauzac B2
18 Bonjour Vietnam D1
19 Café de la Nouvelle Mairie C1
20 Chez Nicos D2
21 Dans Les Landes E4
22 Desvouges F3
23 La Bête Noire A3
24 La Salle à Manger D3
25 La Truffière D1
26 L'Agrume F4
27 Le Buisson Ardent E1
28 Le Comptoir du Panthéon C1
29 Le Jardin des Pâtes E2
30 Le Pot O'Lait E3
31 Les Baux de Paris D2
32 Les Papilles B1

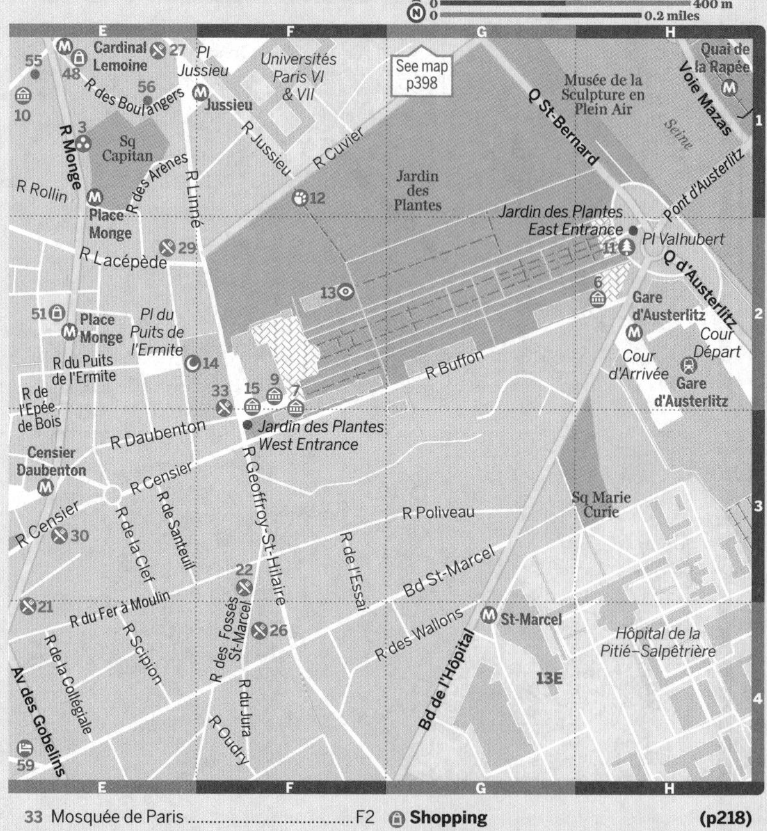

33	Mosquée de Paris	F2
34	OnoPoké	C1
35	Petits Plats de Marc	D3
36	Prosper et Fortunée	D4

Drinking & Nightlife (p215)

37	Café Delmas	D1
38	Cave La Bourgogne	D3
39	Dose	D2
40	La Brûlerie des Gobelins	D4
	La Mosquée	(see 33)
41	L'Académie de la Bière	B3
42	Le Verre à Pied	D3
43	Little Bastards	D1

Entertainment (p217)

44	Café Universel	B2
45	Le Petit Journal St-Michel	B1
46	L'Epée de Bois	D3

Shopping (p218)

47	Androuet	D3
48	Bières Cultes Jussieu	E1
49	Boulangerie Bruno Solques	B2
	Delizius	(see 47)
50	Fromagerie Maury	C3
51	Marché Monge	E2
52	Marché Mouffetard	D3
53	Mococha	D3
54	Nicolaï	B2

Sports & Activities (p221)

	Hammam de la Mosquée de Paris	(see 33)
55	Le Foodist	E1
56	Wine Tasting in Paris	E1

Sleeping (p289)

57	Five Hotel	C4
58	Hôtel des Grandes Écoles	D1
59	Hôtel Port Royal	E4

ST-GERMAIN

Key on p404

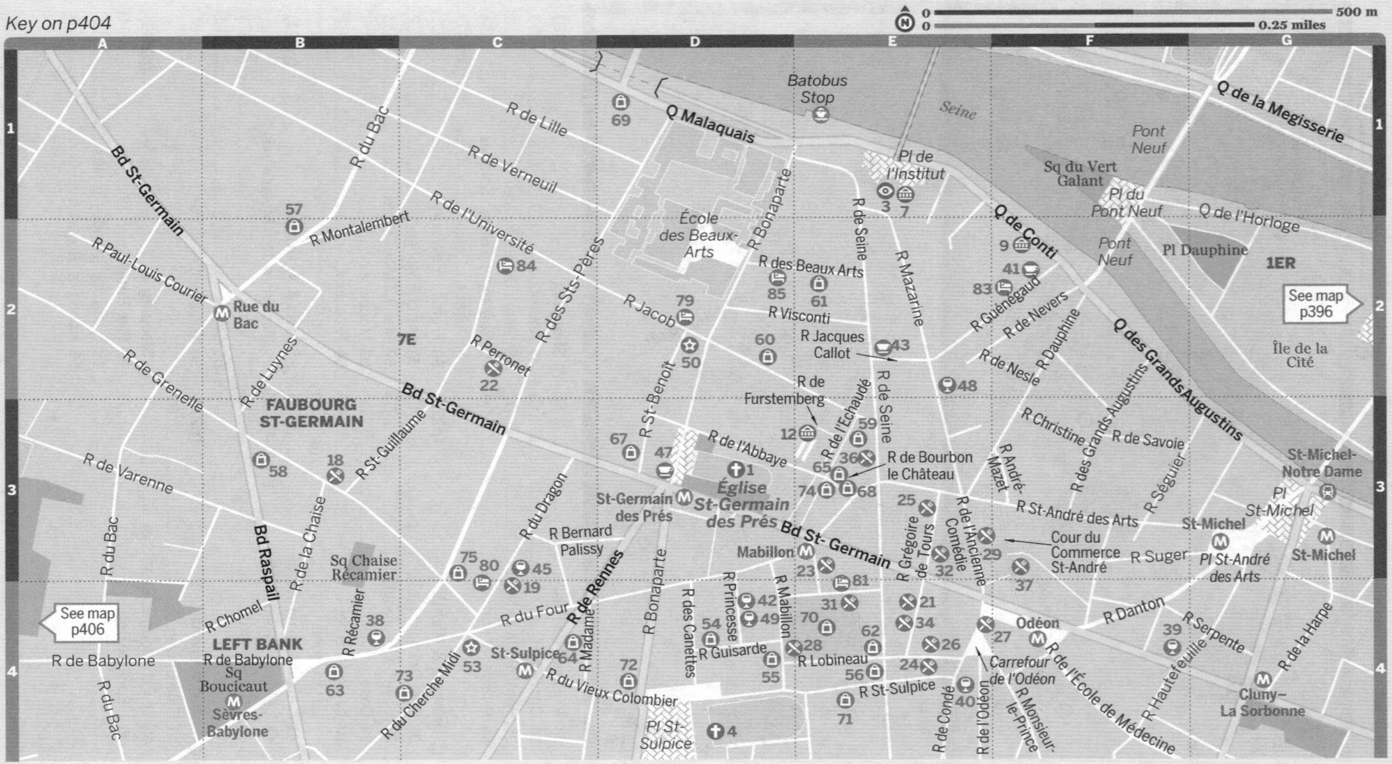

0 500 m
0 0.25 miles

Batobus Stop
Seine
Q Malaquais
Q de la Megisserie
Pont Neuf
Sq du Vert Galant
Pl du Pont Neuf
Q de l'Horloge
Pl Dauphine
1ER
Q de Conti
Pl de l'Institut
École des Beaux-Arts
R de Lille
R de Verneuil
R de l'Université
R du Bac
Bd St-Germain
R Montalembert
R Paul-Louis Courier
Rue du Bac
R de Grenelle
R de Luynes
7E
FAUBOURG ST-GERMAIN
R Perronet
R des Sts-Pères
R Jacob
R Bonaparte
R de Seine
R Mazarine
R des Beaux Arts
R Visconti
R Jacques Callot
R Guénégaud
R de Nevers
R Dauphine
R de Nesle
Q des Grands Augustins
Île de la Cité
See map p396
R de Furstemberg
R de l'Echaudé
R de Bourbon le Château
R de l'Abbaye
R St-Benoît
Église St-Germain des Prés
St-Germain des Prés
R Christine
R des Grands Augustins
R de Savoie
R Séguier
R André-Mazet
R St-André des Arts
St-Michel-Notre Dame
Pl St-Michel
St-Michel
R St-Guillaume
R de Varenne
R de la Chaise
Bd Raspail
R du Dragon
R Bernard Palissy
R de Rennes
Mabillon
R Grégoire de Tours
R de l'Ancienne Comédie
Cour du Commerce St-André
R Suger
Pl St-André des Arts
Sq Chaise Récamier
R Récamier
R Chomel
LEFT BANK
R de Babylone
Sq Boucicaut
Sèvres-Babylone
See map p406
R du Four
R Madame
R des Canettes
R Princesse
R Mabillon
R Guisarde
R Lobineau
R St-Sulpice
St-Sulpice
R du Cherche Midi
R du Vieux Colombier
Pl St-Sulpice
R de Condé
R de l'Odéon
Carrefour de l'Odéon
Odéon
R Monsieur-le-Prince
R de l'École de Médecine
R Danton
R Serpente
R Hautefeuille
R de la Harpe
Cluny–La Sorbonne

1, 3, 4, 7, 9, 12, 18, 19, 21, 22, 23, 24, 25, 26, 27, 28, 29, 31, 32, 34, 36, 37, 38, 39, 40, 41, 42, 43, 45, 47, 48, 49, 50, 53, 54, 55, 56, 57, 58, 59, 60, 61, 62, 63, 64, 65, 67, 68, 69, 70, 71, 72, 73, 74, 75, 79, 80, 81, 83, 84, 85

ST-GERMAIN

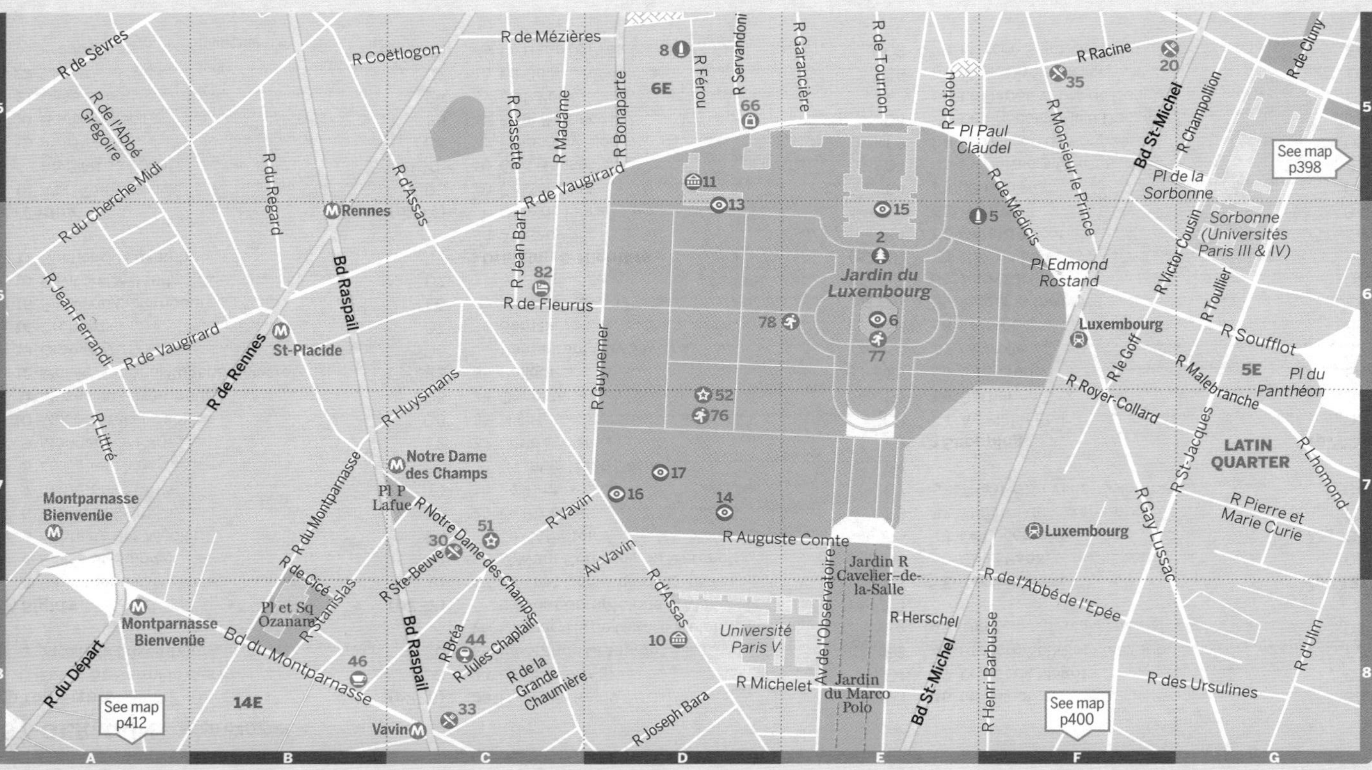

R de Sèvres
R de l'Abbé Grégoire
R du Cherche Midi
R du Regard
Rennes
R d'Assas
R Coëtlogon
R de Mézières
R Cassette
R Madame
R Bonaparte
6E
8
R Férou
R Servandoni
66
R Garancière
R de Tournon
R Rotrou
Pl Paul Claudel
R Racine
35
20
R Monsieur le Prince
Bd St-Michel
R Champollion
R de Cluny
See map p398
Pl de la Sorbonne
Sorbonne (Universités Paris III & IV)
R Victor Cousin
R Toullier
R de Vaugirard
R Jean Bart
82
R de Fleurus
11
13
15
5
2
R de Médicis
Jardin du Luxembourg
Pl Edmond Rostand
78
6
77
Luxembourg
R Soufflot
5E
Pl du Panthéon
R Malebranche
R le Goff
R Royer-Collard
R Jean Ferrandi
R de Rennes
St-Placide
Bd Raspail
R Huysmans
R Guynemer
52
76
R St-Jacques
LATIN QUARTER
R Lhomond
R Littré
Notre Dame des Champs
17
16
14
Montparnasse Bienvenüe
R du Montparnasse
Pl P Lafue
R Notre Dame des Champs
51
30
R Vavin
R Auguste Comte
Luxembourg
R Gay Lussac
R Pierre et Marie Curie
R de Cicé
Pl et Sq Ozanam
R Stanislas
R Ste-Beuve
Av Vavin
Jardin R Cavelier-de-la-Salle
Av de l'Observatoire
R de l'Abbé de l'Epée
R d'Assas
R Herschel
R Henri Barbusse
Montparnasse Bienvenüe
Bd du Montparnasse
R Bréa
44
R Jules Chaplain
10
Université Paris V
R d'Ulm
R du Départ
46
R de la Grande Chaumière
R Michelet
Jardin du Marco Polo
Bd St-Michel
R des Ursulines
See map p412
14E
33
Vavin
R Joseph Bara
See map p400
A
B
C
D
E
F
G
5
6
7
8

ST-GERMAIN *Map on p402*

Top Sights **(p228)**
1 Église St-Germain des Prés ... D3
2 Jardin du Luxembourg ... E6

Sights **(p232)**
3 Bibliothèque Mazarine ... E1
4 Église St-Sulpice ... D4
5 Fontaine des Médici ... E6
6 Grand Bassin ... E6
7 Institut de France ... E1
8 Le Bateau Ivre ... D5
9 Monnaie de Paris ... F2
10 Musée Atelier Zadkine ... D8
11 Musée du Luxembourg ... D5
12 Musée National Eugène Delacroix ... E3
13 Orangery ... D6
14 Orchards ... D7
15 Palais du Luxembourg ... E6
16 Pavillon Davioud ... D7
17 Rucher du Luxembourg ... D7

Eating **(p234)**
18 À la Petite Chaise ... B3
Au Pied de Fouet ... (see 50)
19 Aux Prés ... C4
20 Bouillon Racine ... F5
21 Casa Bini ... E4
22 Clover ... C2
Freddy's ... (see 36)
23 Huîtrerie Regis ... E3
24 La Crèmerie ... E4
25 La Grande Crèmerie ... E3
26 L'Amaryllis de Gérard Mulot ... E4
L'Avant Comptoir de la Mer ... (see 27)
27 L'Avant Comptoir de la Terre ... E4
28 L'Avant Comptoir du Marché ... D4
Le Comptoir ... (see 27)
29 Le Procope ... E3
30 Le Timbre ... C7
31 L'Étable Hugo Desnoyer ... E4
32 Little Breizh ... E3
33 Niébé ... C8
34 Oenosteria ... E4
35 Polidor ... F5
Restaurant Guy Savoy ... (see 9)
36 Semilla ... E3
37 Un Dimanche à Paris ... F3

Drinking & Nightlife **(p239)**
38 Au Sauvignon ... B4
Café de Flore ... (see 67)
39 Castor Club ... F4
40 Cod House ... E4
41 Frappé by Bloom ... F2
42 Frog & Princess ... D4
43 La Palette ... E2
44 La Quincave ... C8
45 Le Bar des Prés ... C3
46 Le Select ... B8
47 Les Deux Magots ... D3
48 Prescription Cocktail Club ... E2
49 Tiger ... D4

Entertainment **(p242)**
50 Chez Papa ... D2
51 Le Lucernaire ... C7
52 Théâtre du Luxembourg ... D7
53 Théâtre du Vieux Colombier ... C4

Shopping **(p242)**
54 Au Plat d'Étain ... D4
55 Catherine B ... D4
56 Cire Trudon ... E4
57 Deyrolle ... B2
58 Fermob ... B3
59 Finger in the Nose ... E3
60 Gab & Jo ... D2
61 Galerie Loft ... E2
62 Gérard Mulot ... E4
63 Hermès ... B4
64 JB Guanti ... C4
65 La Dernière Goutte ... E3
66 La Maison de Poupée ... D5
67 Le Chocolat Alain Ducasse ... D3
68 Le Dépôt-Vente de Buci ... E3
69 Magasin Sennelier ... D1
70 Marché Saint-Germain ... E4

71 Mes Demoiselles E4
72 Pierre Hermé D4
73 Poilâne C4
74 Ragtime E3
75 Sabbia Rosa C3

Sports & Activities **(p228)**
76 Children's Playgrounds D7
77 Grand Bassin Toy Sailboats E6
78 Pony Rides E6

Sleeping **(p290)**
79 Hôtel d'Angleterre D2
80 Hôtel du Dragon C4
81 Hôtel Le Clément E4
82 Hôtel Perreyve C6
83 Hôtel Prince de Conti F2
84 Le Saint C2
85 L'Hôtel D2

LES INVALIDES

Key on p408

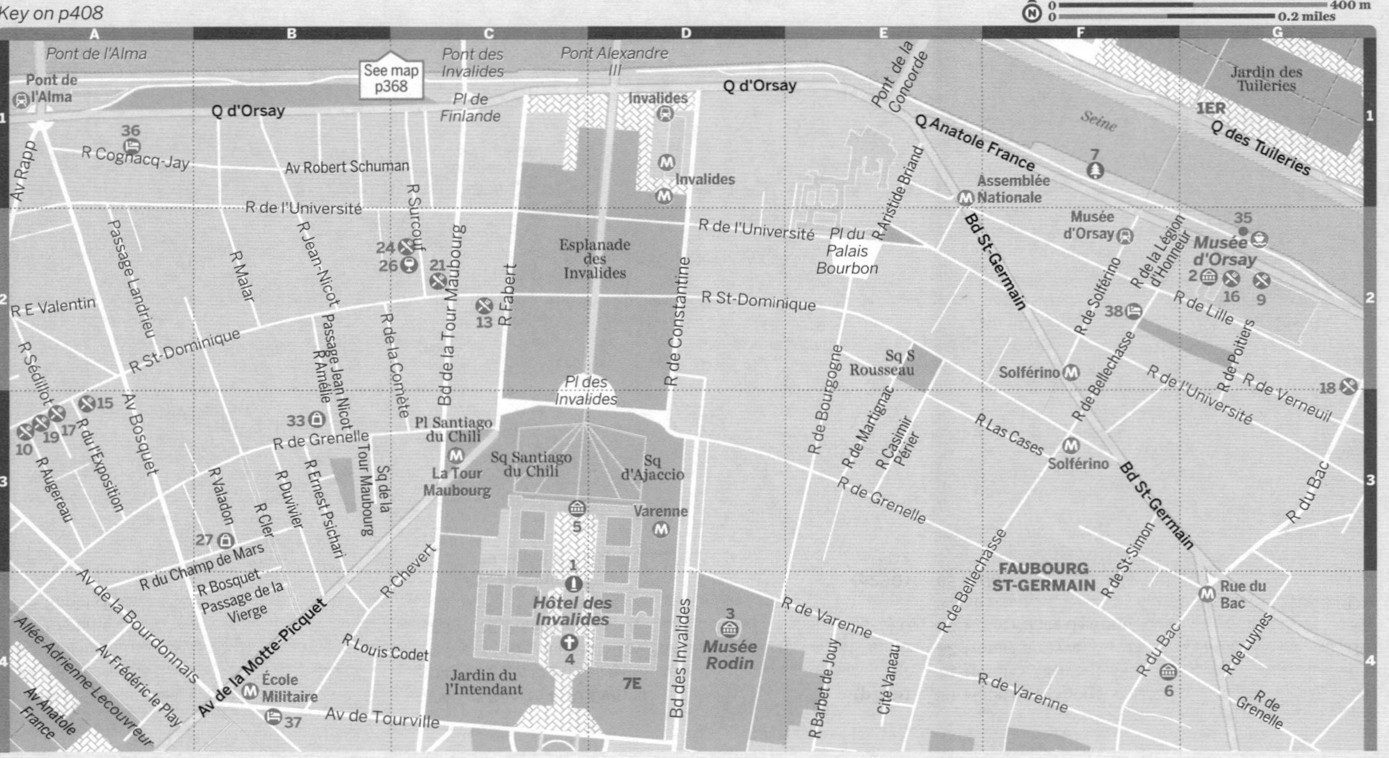

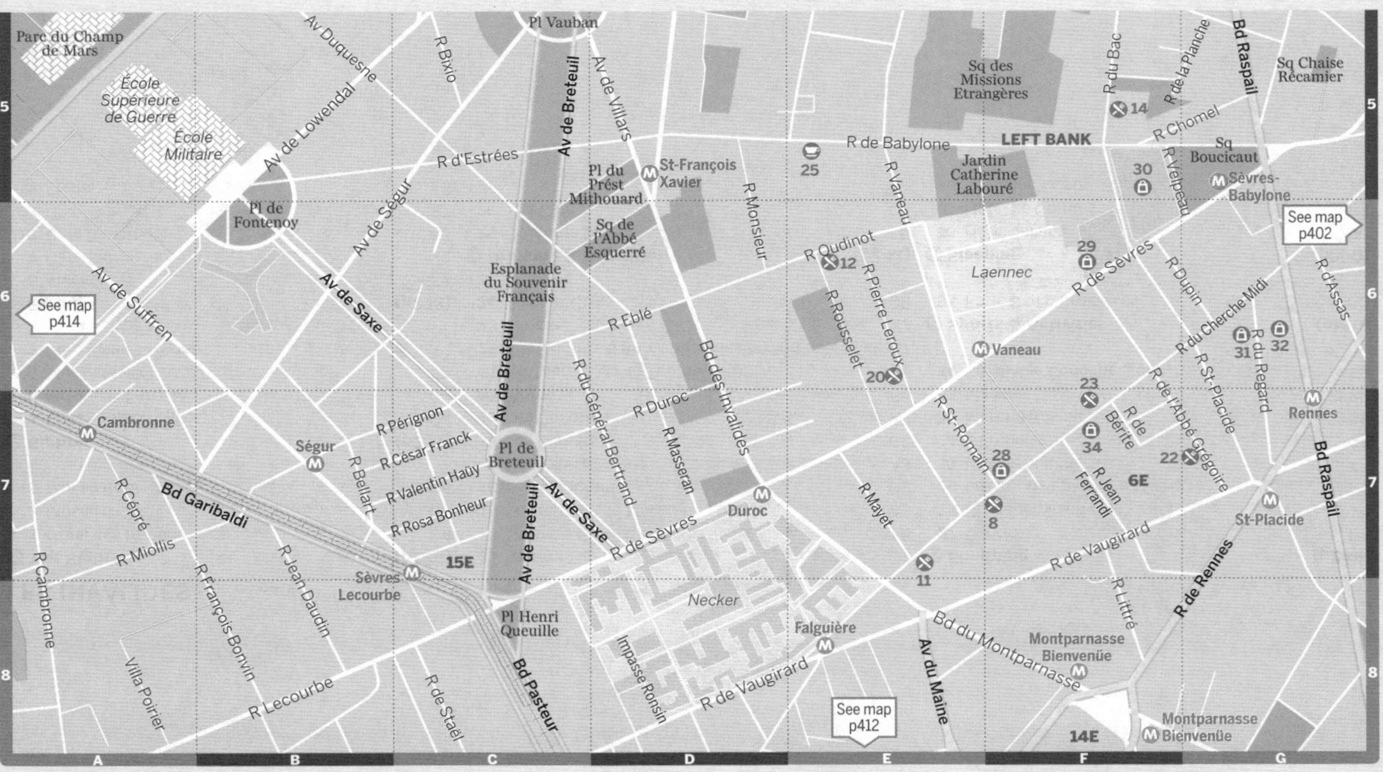

Parc du Champ de Mars
École Supérieure de Guerre
École Militaire
Av Duquesne
Av de Lowendal
R Bixio
Pl Vauban
Av de Breteuil
Av de Villars
Sq des Missions Etrangères
R du Bac
R de la Planche
Bd Raspail
Sq Chaise Récamier
R Chomel
R d'Estrées
R de Babylone
LEFT BANK
Sq Boucicaut
Pl de Fontenoy
Pl du Prést Mithouard
St-François Xavier
Jardin Catherine Labouré
R Velpeau
Sèvres-Babylone
See map p402
Av de Ségur
Sq de l'Abbé Esquerré
R Monsieur
R Vaneau
R Oudinot
Laennec
R de Sèvres
R Dupin
R d'Assas
Av de Suffren
See map p414
Av de Saxe
Esplanade du Souvenir Français
R Eblé
R Rousselet
R Pierre Leroux
Vaneau
R du Cherche Midi
R du Regard
R du Général Bertrand
Bd des Invalides
R St-Placide
R de l'Abbé Grégoire
Rennes
Cambronne
Ségur
R Pérignon
R César Franck
R Bellart
R Valentin Haüy
R Rosa Bonheur
Pl de Breteuil
R Duroc
R Masseran
R St-Romain
R de Bérite
R Jean Ferrandi
6E
St-Placide
R Cépré
Bd Garibaldi
R Miollis
R Cambronne
R François Bonvin
R Jean Daudin
Sèvres Lecourbe
15E
Duroc
R Mayet
R de Vaugirard
R de Rennes
Necker
Pl Henri Queuille
Falguière
Bd du Montparnasse
Av du Maine
R Littré
Montparnasse Bienvenüe
Villa Poirier
R Lecourbe
R de Staël
Bd Pasteur
Impasse Ronsin
See map p412
14E

LES INVALIDES *Map on p406*

Top Sights **(p224)**

1 Hôtel des Invalides ... C4
2 Musée d'Orsay ... G2
3 Musée Rodin ... D4

Sights **(p233)**

4 Église du Dôme ... C4
5 Musée de l'Armée ... C3
6 Musée Maillol ... F4
7 Parc Rives de Seine ... F1

Eating **(p238)**

8 Anicia ... F7
9 Café Campana ... G2
10 Café Constant ... A3
11 Chez Dumonet ... E7
12 Epoca ... E6
13 Karamel ... C2
14 Le Bac à Glaces ... F5
15 Le Fontaine de Mars ... A3
16 Le Restaurant ... G2
17 Le Violon d'Ingres ... A3
18 Les Climats ... G2
19 Les Cocottes ... A3
20 Plume ... E6
21 Restaurant David Toutain ... C2
22 Restaurants d'Application de Ferrandi ... G7
23 Simple ... F7
24 Tomy & Co ... C2

Drinking & Nightlife **(p242)**

25 Coutume Café ... E5
26 The Club ... C2

Shopping **(p244)**

27 Cantin ... B3
28 Chercheminippes ... F7
29 La Grande Épicerie de Paris ... F6
30 Le Bon Marché ... F5
31 L'Embellie ... G6
32 Marché Raspail ... G6
33 Mayaro ... B3
34 Smallable Concept Store ... F7

Sports & Activities **(p150)**

35 Paris Canal Croisières ... G2

Sleeping **(p290)**

36 Hôtel Juliana ... A1
37 Hôtel Le Comtesse ... B4
38 Le Bellechasse ... F2

PLACE D'ITALIE & CHINATOWN *Map on p410*

Sights (p250)

1 Bibliothèque Nationale de France H3
2 Galerie des Gobelins C3
3 La Cité Fleurie A3
4 Les Docks G1
5 Parc Montsouris A6
6 Puits Artésien de la Butte aux Cailles C5
7 Station F G3

Eating (p256)

8 Huré C4
9 La Butte aux Piafs C5
10 La Tropicale D4
11 L'Anthracite C5
12 Pho Bành Cúon 14 .... D6
13 Simone Le Resto B3
Thieng Heng .... (see 28)
14 Yuman G4

Drinking & Nightlife (p258)

15 Bateau El Alamein H3
16 Café Oz Rooftop G1
17 La Dame de Canton H3
18 L'Age d'Or E6
19 Le Batofar H4
20 Le Merle Moqueur C5
21 L'OisiveThé C5
Simone La Cave .... (see 13)

Entertainment (p258)

22 Cinéma Les Fauvettes C4
23 EP7 .... G4
24 Fondation Jérôme Seydoux-Pathé D4
25 MK2 Bibliothèque G4

Shopping (p261)

26 Biérocratie B6
27 Laurent Duchêne B5
28 Tang Frères F7

Sports & Activities (p261)

29 Piscine de la Butte aux Cailles C5
30 Piscine Joséphine Baker H3

Sleeping (p291)

31 Hôtel Henriette C3
32 Off Paris Seine F1
33 Oops C3

Key on p409

PLACE D'ITALIE & CHINATOWN

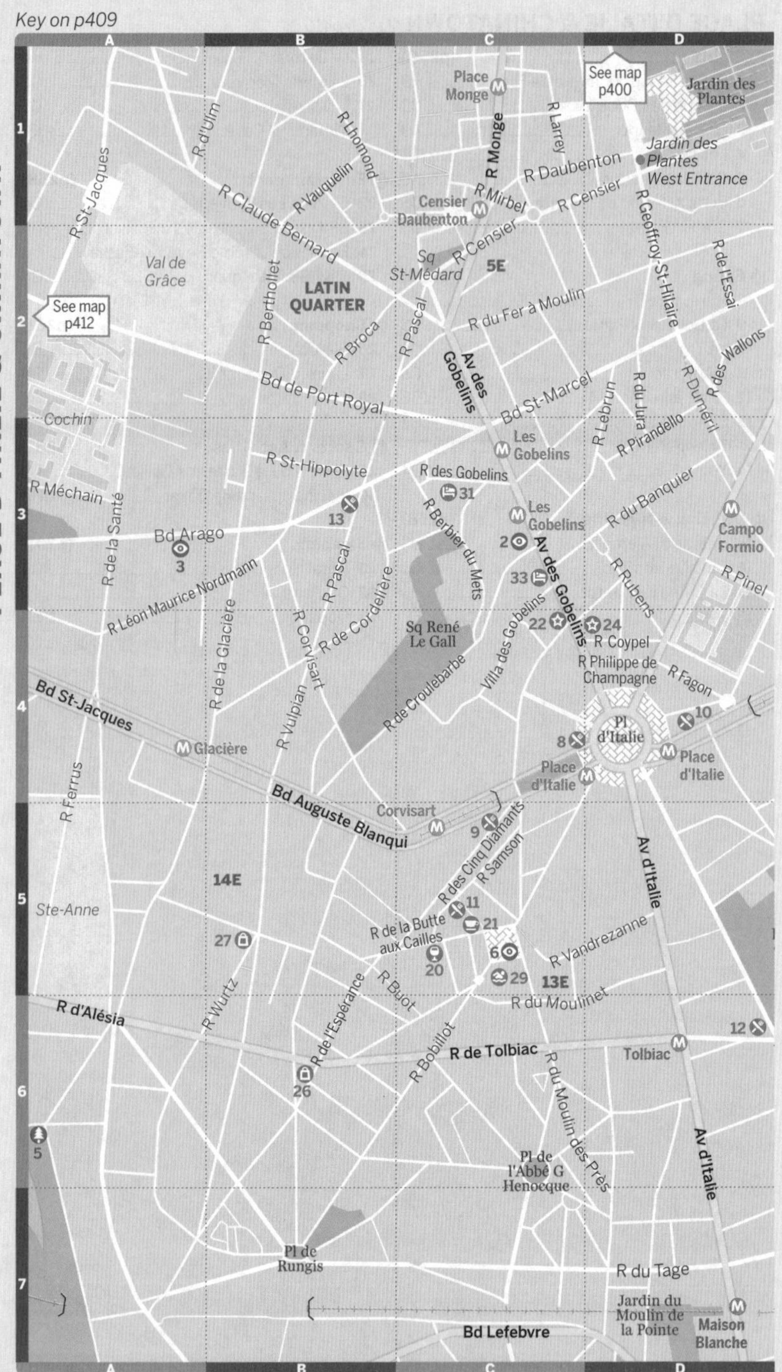

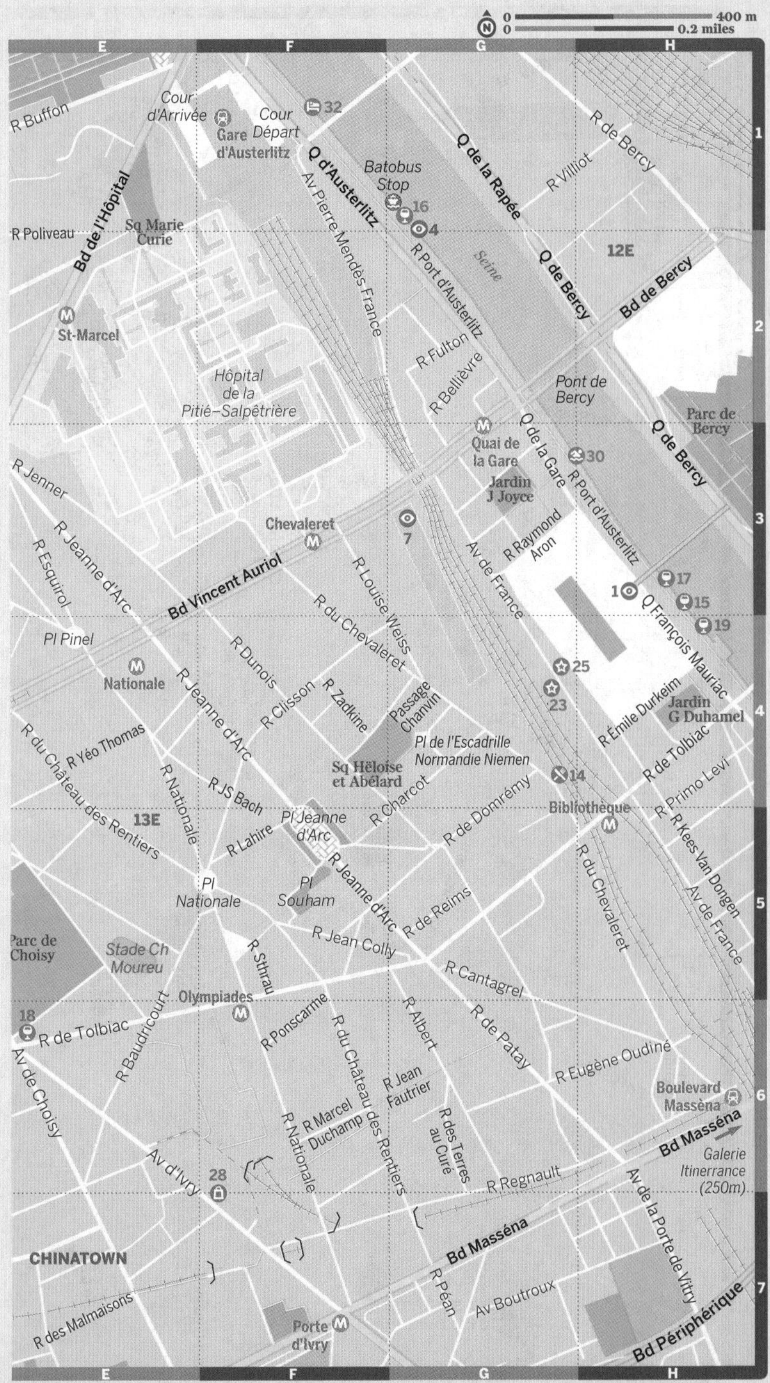

PLACE D'ITALIE & CHINATOWN
0 400 m
0 0.2 miles
R Buffon
Cour d'Arrivée
Gare d'Austerlitz
Cour Départ
32
Q d'Austerlitz
Batobus Stop
16
4
Q de la Rapée
R de Bercy
R Villiot
Bd de l'Hôpital
R Poliveau
Sq Marie Curie
Av Pierre Mendès France
R Port d'Austerlitz
Seine
12E
Q de Bercy
Bd de Bercy
St-Marcel
R Fulton
R Bellièvre
Hôpital de la Pitié–Salpêtrière
Pont de Bercy
Parc de Bercy
Quai de la Gare
Q de la Gare
30
Q de Bercy
Jardin J Joyce
R Jenner
Chevaleret
7
R Raymond Aron
R Port d'Austerlitz
R Jeanne d'Arc
R Esquirol
Bd Vincent Auriol
R Louise Weiss
Av de France
1
17
15
19
Q François Mauriac
R du Chevaleret
Pl Pinel
R Dunois
Nationale
25
23
R Clisson
R Zadkine
Passage Chanvin
R Jeanne d'Arc
R Émile Durkeim
Jardin G Duhamel
R du Château des Rentiers
R Yéo Thomas
Pl de l'Escadrille Normandie Niemen
Sq Héloïse et Abélard
14
R de Tolbiac
R Nationale
R JS Bach
R Charcot
R de Domrémy
R Primo Levi
13E
Pl Jeanne d'Arc
Bibliothèque
R Lahire
R Kees Van Dongen
R du Chevaleret
Pl Nationale
Pl Souham
R Jeanne d'Arc
Av de France
R de Reims
Parc de Choisy
Stade Ch Moureu
R Sthrau
R Jean Colly
R Cantagrel
Olympiades
R Baudricourt
18
R de Tolbiac
R Ponscarme
R du Château des Rentiers
R Albert
R de Patay
R Eugène Oudiné
Av de Choisy
R Marcel Duchamp
R Jean Fautrier
R Nationale
R des Terres au Curé
Boulevard Masséna
Bd Masséna
Galerie Itinerrance (250m)
Av d'Ivry
28
R Regnault
Av de la Porte de Vitry
Bd Masséna
CHINATOWN
R Péan
Av Boutroux
R des Malmaisons
Porte d'Ivry
Bd Périphérique

MONTPARNASSE

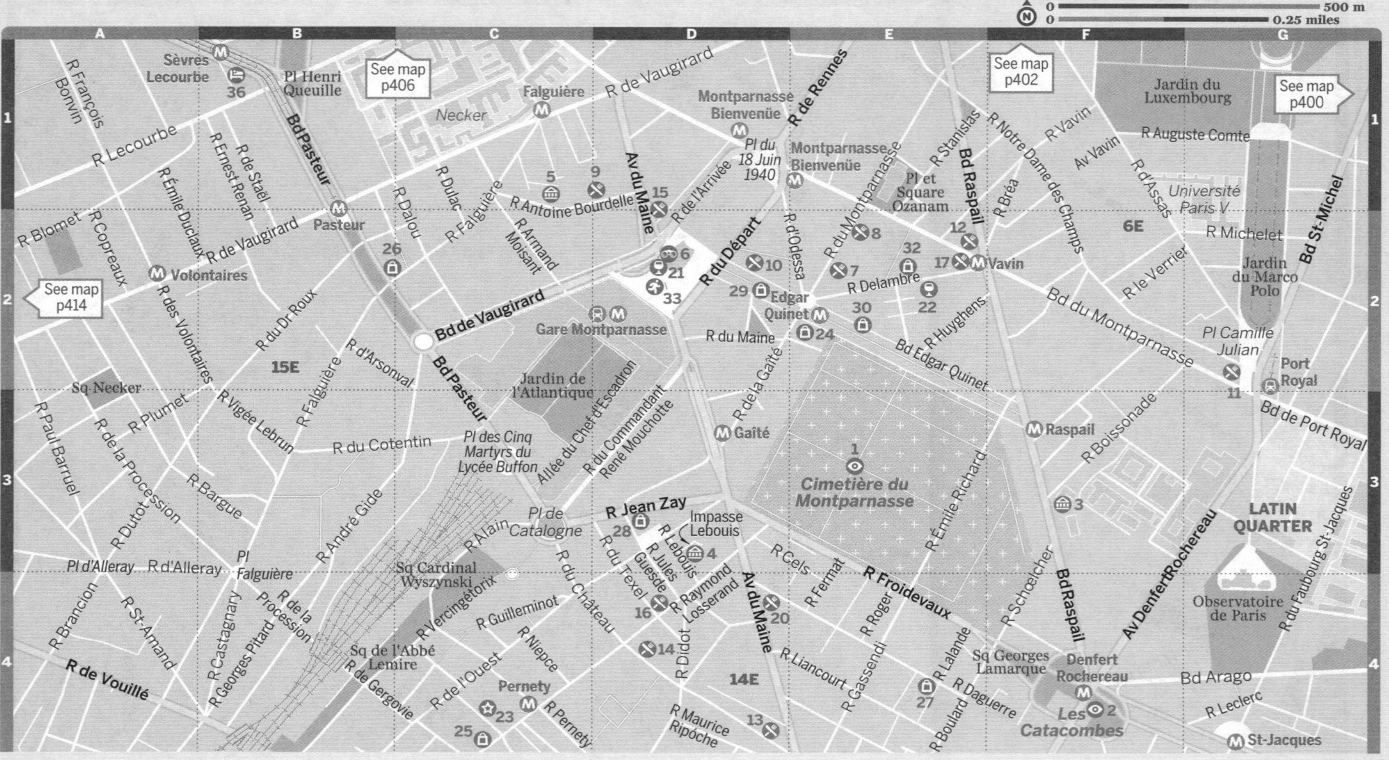

Top Sights (p248)
1 Cimetière du Montparnasse E3
2 Les Catacombes F4

Sights (p249)
3 Fondation Cartier pour l'Art Contemporain F3
4 Fondation Henri Cartier-Bresson. D3
5 Musée Bourdelle C1
6 Tour Montparnasse D2

Eating (p252)
7 Crêperie Josselin E2
8 Crêperie Plougastel E2
9 La Cabane à Huîtres D1
10 La Cerisaie D2
11 La Closerie des Lilas G2
12 La Rotonde Montparnasse E2
13 L'Assiette D4
14 L'Atelier B D4
15 Le Clos Y D1
16 Le Comptoir du Bo Bun D4
17 Le Dôme E2
18 Le Saut du Crapaud D5
19 Le Sévéro D5
20 Raw Cakes D4

Drinking & Nightlife (p257)
21 Mix Club D2
22 Rosebud E2

Entertainment (p258)
23 L'Entrepôt C4

Shopping (p259)
24 Adam Montparnasse E2
25 Bellevaire C4
26 Des Gâteaux et du Pain B2
27 La Cave des Papilles E4
28 Marché Brancusi D3
29 Marché de la Création D2
30 Marché Edgar Quinet E2
31 Stock Sonia Rykiel D6
32 Storie E2

Sports & Activities (p72)
33 Pari Roller D2

Sleeping (p291)
34 Hôtel de la Loire D5
35 Hôtel Max F6
36 Hôtel Vic Eiffel B1

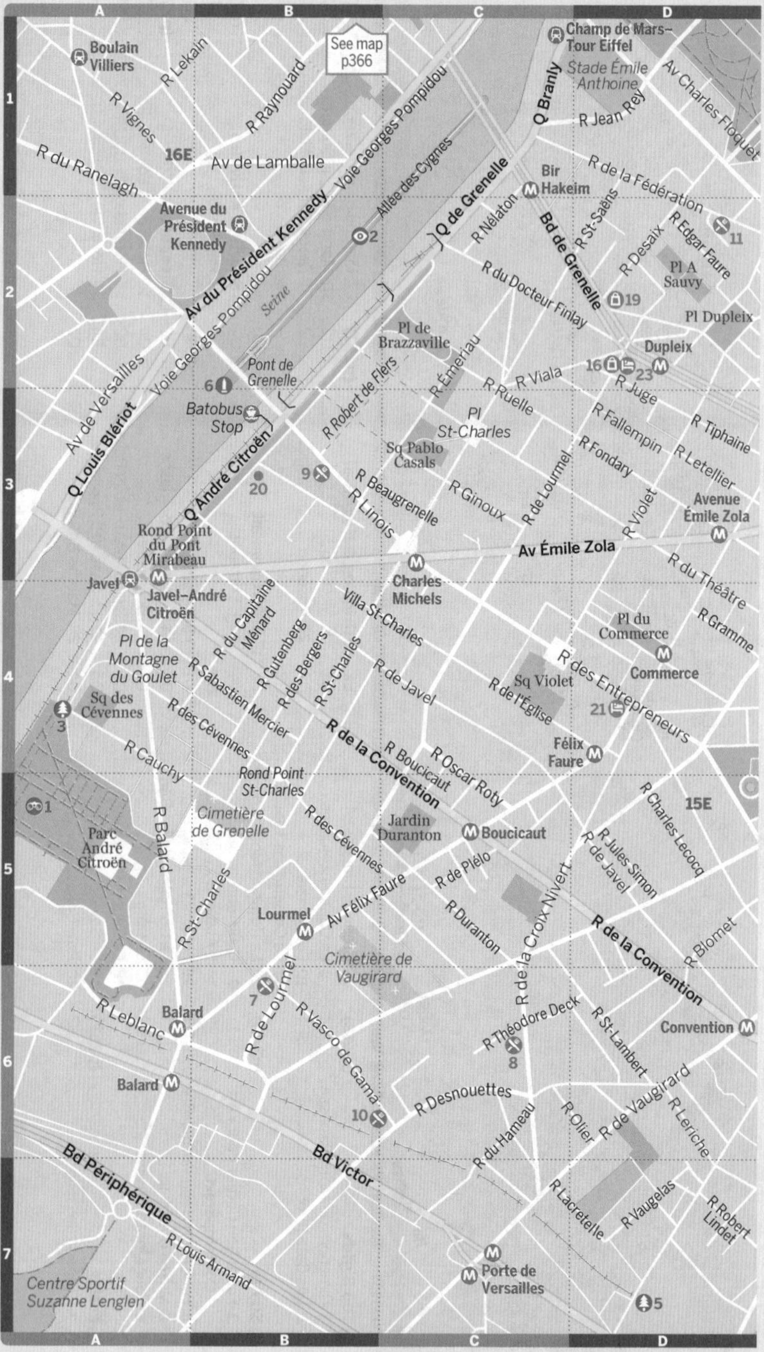

15E

A
B
C
D
1
2
3
4
5
6
7
Boulain Villiers
R Lekain
See map p366
Champ de Mars–Tour Eiffel
Stade Émile Anthoine
R Vignes
R Raynouard
Voie Georges Pompidou
Q Branly
R Jean Rey
Av Charles Floquet
R du Ranelagh
16E
Av de Lamballe
Allée des Cygnes
Q de Grenelle
Bir Hakeim
R de la Fédération
Avenue du Président Kennedy
Av du Président Kennedy
2
R Nélaton
Bd de Grenelle
R St-Saëns
R Desaix
R Edgar Faure
11
Voie Georges Pompidou
Seine
R du Docteur Finlay
Pl A Sauvy
19
Pl Dupleix
Pl de Brazzaville
R Émeriau
Dupleix
Av de Versailles
Pont de Grenelle
R Robert de Flers
R Viala
16
23
6
R Ruelle
R Juge
Q Louis Blériot
Batobus Stop
Q André Citroën
Pl St-Charles
R Fallempin
R Tiphaine
Sq Pablo Casals
R Fondary
R Letellier
9
R Beaugrenelle
20
R Ginoux
R de Lourmel
R Violet
Avenue Émile Zola
R Linois
Rond Point du Pont Mirabeau
Av Émile Zola
Javel
Javel–André Citroën
Charles Michels
R du Théâtre
R du Capitaine Ménard
Villa St-Charles
Pl du Commerce
R Gramme
Pl de la Montagne du Goulet
R Gutenberg
R des Bergers
R St-Charles
Commerce
R Sabastien Mercier
R de Javel
Sq Violet
R des Entrepreneurs
Sq des Cévennes
R de l'Église
21
3
R des Cévennes
R de la Convention
R Boucicaut
Félix Faure
R Oscar Roty
R Cauchy
Rond Point St-Charles
R Charles Lecocq
1
R Balard
Cimetière de Grenelle
R des Cévennes
Jardin Duranton
Boucicaut
15E
Parc André Citroën
R Jules Simon
R de Javel
R de Plélo
R St-Charles
Av Félix Faure
R Duranton
R de la Croix Nivert
Lourmel
R de la Convention
R Blomet
Cimetière de Vaugirard
R de Lourmel
7
R Leblanc
Balard
R Vasco de Gama
R Théodore Deck
R St-Lambert
Convention
8
Balard
R Desnouettes
R de Vaugirard
10
R Olier
R Leriche
R du Hameau
Bd Périphérique
Bd Victor
R Lacretelle
R Vaugelas
R Robert Lindet
R Louis Armand
Porte de Versailles
Centre Sportif Suzanne Lenglen
5

See map p406

See map p412

Sights (p249)

1	Ballon de Paris	A5
2	Île aux Cygnes	B2
3	Parc André Citroën	A4
4	Parc Georges Brassens	E7
5	Petite Ceinture du 15e	D7
6	Statue of Liberty Replica	B2

Eating (p252)

7	Boulangerie de Lourmel	B6
8	L'Accolade	C6
9	Ladurée Picnic	B3
10	Le Beurre Noisette	B6
11	Le Cassenoix	D2
12	Le Grand Pan	F7
13	Le Petit Pan	F7

Drinking & Nightlife (p257)

14	Arthur & Juliette	E7
15	Le Petit Gorille	E7

Shopping (p259)

16	Fromagerie Laurent Dubois	D2
17	Le Comptoir Correzien	F4
18	Marché Georges Brassens	E7
19	Poilâne	D2

Sports & Activities (p51)

20	Le Cordon Bleu	B3

Sleeping (p291)

21	3 Ducks Hostel	D4
22	Hôtel Carladez Cambronne	F5
23	Hôtel Eiffel Petit Louvre	D2

Our Story

A beat-up old car, a few dollars in the pocket and a sense of adventure. In 1972 that's all Tony and Maureen Wheeler needed for the trip of a lifetime – across Europe and Asia overland to Australia. It took several months, and at the end – broke but inspired – they sat at their kitchen table writing and stapling together their first travel guide, *Across Asia on the Cheap*. Within a week they'd sold 1500 copies. Lonely Planet was born.

Today, Lonely Planet has offices in Franklin, London, Melbourne, Oakland, Dublin, Beijing and Delhi, with more than 600 staff and writers. We share Tony's belief that 'a great guidebook should do three things: inform, educate and amuse'.

Our Writers

Catherine Le Nevez

Montmartre & Northern Paris; Le Marais, Ménilmontant & Belleville; Bastille & Eastern Paris Catherine's wanderlust kicked in when she roadtripped across Europe from her Parisian base aged four, and she's been hitting the road at every opportunity since, travelling to around 60 countries and completing her Doctorate of Creative Arts in Writing, Masters in Professional Writing, and postgraduate qualifications in editing and publishing along the way. Over the past dozen-plus years she's written scores of Lonely Planet guides and articles covering Paris, France, Europe and far beyond. Her work has also appeared in numerous online and print publications. Topping Catherine's list of travel tips is to travel without any expectations. Catherine also wrote the Plan Your Trip, Understand Paris and Survival Guide sections.

Christoper Pitts

Eiffel Tower & Western Paris; Champs-Élysées & Grands Boulevards; Louvre & Les Halles Born in the year of the Tiger, Chris' first expedition in life ended in failure when he tried to dig from Pennsylvania to China at the age of six. Hardened by reality but still infinitely curious about the other side of the world, he went on to study Chinese in university, living for several years in Kunming, Taiwan and Shanghai. A chance encounter led to a Paris relocation, where he lived with his wife and two children for more than a decade before the lure of Colorado's sunny skies and outdoor adventure proved too great to resist.

Nicola Williams

The Islands; Latin Quarter; St-Germain & Les Invalides; Montparnasse & Southern Paris Border-hopping is a way of life for British writer, runner, foodie, art aficionado and mum-of three Nicola Williams. Nicola has authored more than 50 guidebooks on Paris, Provence, Rome, Tuscany, France, Italy and Switzerland for Lonely Planet, and covers France as a destination expert for the *Telegraph*. She also writes for the *Independent*, the *Guardian*, lonelyplanet.com, *Lonely Planet Magazine*, *French Magazine*, *Cool Camping France* and others. Catch her on the road on Twitter and Instagram @tripalong.

Contributing Writer

Damian Harper researched and wrote the Giverny content. Damian has been writing for Lonely Planet for more than two decades, covering destinations including China, Vietnam, Thailand, Ireland and London.

Published by Lonely Planet Global Limited
CRN 554153
12th edition – November 2018
ISBN 978 1 78657 282 0

10 9 8 7 6 5 4 3 2 1
Printed in China